CW00531665

Ridgeon

Rides

Again

by George Ridgeon

Copyright © 2021 George Ridgeon

All rights reserved. No part of this publication may be
reproduced, stored in a retrieval system, or transmitted
in any form or by any means without the prior written
permission of the copyright owner.

ISBN 978-1-7399367-0-9

Published by George Ridgeon Publishing, Windy Corner,
3 Chosen Drive, Churchdown, Gloucestershire GL3 2QS

Printed by Clarke Printing,
St James Square, Monmouth NP25 3DN

I dedicate the book to my mother and father, and to the close friends I have lost including, Norman Cobley, Richard Swallow, Richard Browning, Pete Davies, Gordon Bircher, Geoff Fivash and John Meadows, to name but a few.

ACKNOWLEDGMENTS

My thanks to those who have helped and supported me through my darkest and most difficult times, my big brother, Frank Prentice, Chris Witts, Dave Baker and Godfrey Cain. To Stoke Mandeville Spinal Unit, my gratitude for your care and dedication and to the Manx and S100 clubs my thanks for the comradeship. To Chris Brown, Mark Ewing, Barney, The Price family, my morning ladies and others too numerous to mention, thank you for all the help and encouragement. Finally I would like to thank Sue Moore, without whose help and very firm guidance this book would not be finished.

FOREWORD

George I sincerely apologise, I really do. Why? Let me explain.

I agreed to take George on the lap of the TT course on closed roads. No problem I thought, nice and steady, but reading his book you will see that George doesn't take no for an answer and is very, very persistent. On the run up to the Manx Grand Prix he would call me call most every day; I'm ashamed to say that I became annoyed.

At this time I was Suzuki race team manager and had organised a new Suzuki GSX R1100 to do the lap on. The reasons being: it was comfortable, reliable, safe and also maybe a bit of publicity for my employer.

After I had finished my trial I headed up to the TT grandstand where I met George. To my horror waiting near the start line was not my Suzuki but a very well used Norton Commando with cowhorn handlebars. My instant assessment of the situation later proved to be correct, the bike had abysmally poor handling (two up) poor brakes and not a lot going for it. Pissed off, I was! I tried to stay calm and smile, as George was strapped onto the pillion. Just before the off I said, "George, if I'm going too fast just tap me on my shoulder and I'll slow down!"

As we picked up speed, around about the crossroads at the top of Bray Hill an angry man came into my head and said, "okay, if George must ride this bike let's make it memorable" so, down Bray Hill we went flat-out, the bike bucking and weaving with its poor suspension. George's early taps on my shoulder now became painful thumps, to no avail. Looking back, what I did was bad, but maybe not so bad as a couple of years later we did another lap of the TT circuit, albeit a little more leisurely.

Enjoy the book as I have; see that George has been through an extraordinary journey and has come through with flying colours. I'm proud to call him a friend.

Mick Grant; seven times TT winner

I first became 'aware' of George Ridgeon when we both raced at the same Cheltenham Motor Club race meetings at Little Rissington, in the early to mid-sixties. I knew 'of' him back then as that big, noisy bloke with a strange accent, who dwarfed the BSA Bantam on which he manfully toiled around the track! However, I must admit that I never got to 'know' him at that time.

Our racing careers diverged during the latter sixties, as I was lucky enough to join, for a m/c racer with aspirations back then, the fabled Continental Circus, which I continued 'playing in' until I stopped serious racing in 1971. My circumstances at that time led me to start my small, first M/C business in Dunalley Parade, in Cheltenham, during 1972.

It was THEN that I 'really met' George Ridgeon! One morning, myself and Mike Taylor, who was then a mere 14 year old stripling, but who became my stalwart support during the next 25 years of that fledgling business, were startled by the arrival of a BIG, solo BSA Twin in our yard! On which, it happily turned out, was mounted that self-same 'big, noisy bloke' whom I had first encountered at Rissy a few years earlier! Only this time disguised as a big, but still noisily efficient, Glos fireman, complete with that BIG pair of de rigueur, fireman's leather boots!

He noisily stomped in, and introduced himself, I THINK that his NOSE was still its original shape at that time. I came to learn that George was not just big and noisy, but a keen and caring motorcycle racer and a bloke who became the life and soul of my shop every time that he deigned to attend. He often helped us out with rebuilds of British bikes; of which I had little knowledge.

He did once, though, help us out with a couple of Italian models in for some 'tweaking'. Once by tearing a strip off his big pair of fireman's underpants to stuff into the air cleaner of a Garelli moped, after which time it stopped running 'ragged'! (Poetic licence the underpants bit!) And once with a Ducati single which had proved to be a real pig to start, however much I tuned its ignition system!! "ALL it needed," he assured Mike and me, was "a good kicking with my BIG, leather fireman's boots!" Both in-jokes for the three of us involved. But that's it with George, one always seems to end up smiling in his company. There were many times over the years, during which time I came to love and respect George, complete with ALL his exuberances.

Long would that have continued, I must assume, until one morning in 1981, whilst listening to the morning news on Severn Sound radio, an item caught my ears. "Last night a Gloucester fireman was seriously injured during an incident in Gloucester!" My then partner and I looked at each other and we both said in unison, "I BET that's George!" Sixth sense? Dunno. Tragically, we turned out to be correct.

After many months rehabilitation at Stoke Mandeville, George finally made it home. Ending up, seemingly still noisy but now, sadly, half his original height - in a wheel chair - living in his BIG house (It IS George that I am running down, don't forget!) in Churchdown.

From whence, I would estimate, he has subsequently raised hundreds of thousands of pounds for charity, including much for the Manx M/C Club, without asking for anything much in return from his friends! - except from Mark Ewing and Sue Moore, LOL. Two friends who have kept him away from bothering the rest of us, for which I thank them, and providing help well beyond anything any one would dare to ask for; except George that is! Hail to them for services rendered far and away above the call of duty! ALSO, don't forget, HAIL to my dear friend, George.

LONG may he keep on irritating his BIG circle of friends!

Jim Curry; 1968 125cc British Champion

CONTENTS

Chapter 1 to 1959-The fire, am I dreaming?

The alarm sounded, the time 00.30, just half-past midnight, the Tannoy calling for "one pump" followed by a garbled address. I'd only laid my head down at 23:55. At the time we had a loud bell, a Junior Officer would then pick up a direct phone line to Fire Control to get the address.

The radio in the fire pump was turned on, "Control, please confirm fire and address"

"Chimney fire at 92 London Road, Gloucester."
The driver turned right out of the Station, very little traffic on Eastern Avenue, left on Walls Roundabout, so called because of the Walls Ice Cream factory on it, into Barnwood Road then London Road. As we came over a rise, known as Wotton Pitch, we could see flames with smoke all over the road, I grabbed the radio phone.

"Control, we need 2 pumps this is a fire!!!" We pulled up 20 seconds later. I jumped out and before my feet had hit the ground I heard a panicked shout, "There are people trapped inside!" "Control, persons reported, persons reported" I reported in an urgent tone, this triggers ambulance, senior officers, police etc. Little did I know that this was to be my last ever message!

The driver, still in overalls was getting the pump ready, Smith & Flello (2 of my fellow firemen) were slipping on their 50 lbs (25 kg) Breathing Apparatus (BA) sets. I saw flames and smoke engulfing the front room, spreading across the ground floor hallway and rushing up the stairwell. "Run a jet out", I yelled. The lads were doing this when there was another shout from somewhere, "there's someone at the top window."

The window was on the 2nd floor, so over 20 feet up. Dropping the hose, we took the 35' ladder off the pump. We had to do a confined pitch as the pavement was only 7' wide and cars were parked close to the kerb. We jammed the ladder against a car body and the kerb but what are a few scratches when a life is in danger? As the lads had BA on, I went up the ladder to say "don't worry, hang on, another fire engine is coming."

The window was a 4' sash, typical for servants quarters 90 years earlier, so there was only a 2' gap when fully open! My face was 12 inches from this frail-looking man who was choking and dying in front of my eyes, smoke

1

was pouring out of the window. I started coughing, but this poor chap had had it for 10 minutes or more! We'd trained to do carry downs, under safety rules, with the fireman being carried having on an Everest Safety Device, a special 4 mm cord running through a contraption that would lock if the cord went through at more than so many feet per second. Eventually this was deemed too dangerous so instead we trained carrying a dummy, not as good or realistic and even this was in dispute; but in this situation I thought I can, and have to use this method.

I started to pull the man out onto my shoulder but he was struggling, and no wonder, he was choking to death with all the smoke. I had half of him on my shoulder his feet were nearly out of sash window saying to him "relax, don't struggle!" I saw his foot go against the wall, he pushed hard, I thought My God we're going to fall. I remember the many dreams I'd had of falling, it's true, your past life does flash before you..............

"Mummy, mummy, help me" Mum rescued me, so I was told years later, from the small snowdrift by our back gate, "what's all this noise Georgie Porgy." This was at home, 'Janetta', Ash Lane, Down Hatherley just before my 3rd birthday on the 31st March in the bad winter of 1947, the snow didn't finish until the end of

DAD, BIG BROTHER DAVE & A VERY GRUMPY BABY GEORGE

March. I was sent to school that year as Dad was on night shift at Dowty Rotol, making aircraft material and needed sleep, me make a noise? Mum cycled me to school on the back of her old ladies bicycle, as she waved goodbye, I was crying my eyes out! Worms, I'm told, along with snails were part my diet as I loved playing in the garden. At school other children were teasing a spider, picking it up to rescue it, as I went to throw it over into the field it stuck its two fangs into me! It was a garden spider the sort with a big cross on its back. I've respected spiders ever since mum said "If you wish to live and thrive, let the spider run alive." About this time I was taken to the circus, I loved the clowns and when the lions came on in a cage. The man with the lions had a white robe, long hair and beard. I shouted out "Look mum, Jesus" mum went red!

In 1952 when Big Brother Dave was 16, he got a BSA Bantam and tried to teach his eight-year-old brother to ride, which was quite scary! I can't calculate the many thousands of miles I did on the back of a BSA Bantam, the seat was 5" by 8" with 6" deep foam. On any ride of more than 3 or 4 miles my backside got sore very quickly and I started jiggling. Big Brother David didn't mind too much but Dad would shout "sit still", "my backside is sore Dad", "it will be sore when I smack it!" The ride to Senghenydd in South Wales to see his brother and sister was only 60 miles, but took all day, well it seemed like it, it didn't help that Dad stopped in a pub for a 'run out' then had a pint, this was especially true in Chepstow, if it was Sunday as the pubs were shut in Wales, and the last pub in England was 100 yards from the Welsh border. As soon as we got to Uncle Jack's house, I was off down a steep hill to the stream, where I'd spend many hours playing, always getting wet, then smacked for not saying hello to my Uncle Jack and Auntie Jess.

My first recollection of being taken by David to show me the stream was dramatic! On the way back up the steep hill we had to negotiate barbed wire fences keeping animals apart, mainly sheep. I was climbing through the barbed wire fence with Dave holding the wire up when a barb went through his thumb. I remember the blood and seeing the barb completely through his thumb, I had to run to Uncle Jack for help. I spent many happy hours in the stream. Fred, one of my big cousins used to tickle for trout, I watched him with my mouth open in amazement. His job then was driving a horse and trap, delivering milk. On the other side of the stream, as there were no animals, I slid down the hill on a piece of cardboard. At Uncle Jack's funeral I went down to see the stream. Walking along the side, I was able to step over it, but 20 years earlier it seemed a massive roaring river like the Rocky Mountain rivers in the cowboy films or perhaps even the Mississippi, it seemed so massive in the 50s and now so small, I was in floods of tears.

Twigworth Church of England Primary School was an impressive building, built of large stones. It had 3 classrooms as well as small rooms and a toilet for the teachers. A toilet building was built after the war for the pupils at the edge of the playground with girls one end, boys the other. When Horsbere brook flooded it would cut off the girls' toilet. This was remedied by the girls using the boys' toilet at a certain time of day, the boys at another. I enjoyed playtime, throwing a ball at the wall trying to hit specific stones, or marbles and conkers when in season. If naughty, I was put with a girl who was always being naughty, Eileen Sheming. The school desks were doubles, an inkwell on each end and we were supplied with pens that we had a dip in the ink then write on the paper. I am not sure who started it but one of us would throw some ink on the other's paper and vice-versa until both pieces of paper were absolutely useless, smacked legs for us both. Today the paperwork would probably be a work of art!

The inside hallway had many coloured floor tiles. I used to slide along them wearing hobnail boots, the cheapest form of footwear dad could afford, strong and easy repairable as dad had a last. Getting a smacked leg was a regular occurrence.

On 6th February 1952, King George VI died. Dad bought a 12 inch television for £70, all I knew was a jam doughnut was one and a half penny! We watched the Coronation of Queen Elizabeth II, during which, when there was nothing going on they would show a photo of bells ringing. Dowty Rotol had a sports day for the Coronation, I was last or near the back in all the races as usual, but we had a good time with jellies and cakes as rationing was still on. Flags and bunting were everywhere, we didn't have a Union Flag at home but Dad had acquired a Stars & Stripes from somewhere which I enthusiastically tied up with the help of mum! So started the TV era, Noddy and Big Ears, Whirligig with Mr Turnip and Humphrey Lestocq, the Flowerpot Men with Weed, Muffin the Mule and Sooty and Sweep with Harry Corbett, programmes I enjoyed.

Mum was always reminding me of all the things I had done wrong. Even when small I was in trouble, like getting lost on a coach trip to Weston-super-Mare. At the end of the day mum said "where is he?" As panic ensued, it was agreed mum would look on the beach, dad would ask at the police station, but would catch the coach whatever happened as he had to go to work the next day. Mum was running up and down the beach, luckily, as it was going-home time everybody was leaving, Mum shouts "there you are" as I was crawling in and out of the sea, (I was 2 years old), Mum grabbed me "naughty boy what have you been up to", a man shouts "don't worry love I've been watching him, he was enjoying himself".

Mum used to take me for rides on the Bantam, one such trip was to stay with Auntie Win as she was home from Canada on 6 months leave, which she had every 2 years. Auntie Winifred, aged 48 in 1952 emigrated to Canada to become an Anglican Sunday School Missionary. 2 ladies drove a one ton van, which they slept in, visiting all the outlying farms giving out religious material with pictures of Jesus to colour and send off for their

Sunday school lessons. The good thing was I got Canadian stamps when she wrote to mum with a short letter to me. When back from Canada, Aunty Win who was a companion to Miss Raikes (a relation of Robert Raikes who started the Sunday School movement in the 1780s) gave her permission for Mum and me to stop at her home in the village of Llangorse in the Brecon Beacons. The first time was just a weekend with big brother but once Miss Raikes was away for a whole week. Miss Raikes house was very large, more like a mansion well to me, and set in huge grounds next to Llangorse church and a big lake just into Wales. Auntie Win played the organ in the church. As I was there I had to pump it using a long wooden handle whilst she played, when my arm got tired I would stop so the organ would lose power, Auntie Win looked at me with a growling face! I am sure she would have made a good Middle East war correspondent everybody would be scared of her, sorry Auntie Win, my arms didn't half ache, I was only 8. The congregation had gone, well nearly all, just a few including a distinguished man and wife sat in the pews. We had tidied up and were about to leave when Aunty Win said "bow on leaving" so I looked at the man and bowed. She told me "I meant bow towards the altar"!

I would help the gardener pick up grass and try to push a big wooden wheelbarrow. He also bent a pin, tying it to a piece of cotton thread so I could go fishing in Llangorse Lake, but I never caught anything. There was an old vicarage across a field. It was empty so Aunty Win had to open and close the windows every day, as we were there for a week I was given the task. You can imagine a ghostly vicarage, on its own in the middle of a field. One morning I was opening the windows when the door slammed shut, I was out of that building, was the devil after me?

Before Aunty Win went to Canada in 1952 as a missionary, mother and I went with her for a long weekend to the Isle of Wight. Of course the ferry trip and seeing HMS Victory were the highlights for an eight-year-old. Aunty Win was a very religious lady and in "the church army" so stopped in one of their hostels. Mother somehow managed to book a week the next year with me and Dave. This was very exciting as Dave used to take me crabbing. He would smash a mussel from the rocks tie it to a piece of string and dangle it in the rock pools for a crab to grab hold of. He used to build a castle wall with rocks to keep all the crabs in. My big brother was so brave, he would pick up the crab by the shell, as I was only 8 I didn't realise they couldn't nip Dave with their pincers. A mistake Mum and Dave made was that they let me go in a canoe on my own! Although I was getting soaking wet with the water running down the paddle I was

5

enjoying it so much I wouldn't come in (joke: come in number 9, we haven't got a number 9, are you in trouble number 6?).

MUM ON A JAMES, HER 1ST MOTORCYCLE

1949, DAD ON AN AUTO CYCLE

AUNTIE WIN (CENTER BACK) AT EBLEY HOUSE, NATIONAL CHILDRENS HOME, STROUD

DAD WORKING AT DOWTY ROTAL IN 1950'S

Coming home one time mum ran out of petrol, luckily at the top of a hill so she coasted down. We were going quite fast but didn't seem to worry mother! In another of her stories, she was trying to overtake a lorry. The Bantam could only go 45 mph flat-out with the wind behind you, mum said

7

"I put my head down as if racing to try and pass" the lorry driver shouting "come on mother you can do it" Mum always said "he was a cheeky man, but I passed him". Mum was certainly not backwards in coming forwards.

She'd parked the Bantam outside the Bon Marche department store in Gloucester while shopping, when she got back the Bantam wouldn't kick-start. Seeing a chauffeur standing by a posh car, "can you give me a push please", "I'm supposed to stay by this car, madam", "surely you will help a lady in distress" the man was still reluctant, "are you sure it will start madam?" "Of course it will," the bike started straight away. Mum waved and shouted "thank you".

Although we had a television, we played a lot of cards, just the three of us when Dave was working or courting. Mum, dad and me played crib, without explaining the game there is a lot of adding up which they made me do, I had to use my fingers! At the weekend they would buy me a Wagon Wheel, a large round chocolate covered biscuit, but to get the biscuit I had to rewrite the story on the back of the packet about the Wild West, so they did try to get me to do the 3Rs, Reading, Writing and Rithmetic. They did try to get me to write and spell, sadly I was a failure. When Dave was there we played Whist instead.

Dad worked at Rotol during the war which became Dowty Rotol in 1950s. They occupied many large buildings all around Staverton airport which had been a WW2 fighter station. When I was old enough to go to the kids Christmas parties they were held in one of these buildings, the canteen. In the 1950s it was something of a treat having cakes and jellies. A present given to you was great, as well as the food fight which happened when they were trying to organise us to collect presents. There wasn't much food left, so when one of the little horrors, I don't think it could have been me, threw a leftover this started us all off, with a 1000 children, great fun. The entertainment was a man introducing singers who sang songs like 'Put another Nickel in the Nickelodeon,' Mickey Mouse films and a magician. At the 1955 party we started chanting "we want rock 'n' roll, we want rock 'n' roll." One year my present was a flying saucer which was operated by pulling a string cord hard, a plastic ring with blades flew into the sky making a screaming noise. We were showing each other our presents when this lad asked "can I try your flying saucer?" He gave me his six-gun, a colt 45 in a holster to hold. The little B*** ran off. I chased him but he was faster than me so, going back to the party, I asked everyone with a flying saucer "would you like to swap for my six gun" this lad said "yes, I want a six-gun" so we were both happy!

I had to help Dad do the gardening which I hated as he always told me off for not getting the couch grass out. This root he told me, again and again, will not rot down in a compost heap like grass and cabbage leaves, I used to have nightmares about it! I used to think dad didn't like me, making me pick gooseberries. Not only did they grow on a very prickly bush but I then had to help mum top and tail them. Dad would make me laugh "I am now going to sing the well-known song; It's only the hairs on a Gus Gog that stops it from being a grape!" They were like a mini tomato, full of seeds, so I didn't even like eating them. Dad told me "a weed is anything growing where it shouldn't be, so a rose growing in the vegetable patch is a weed"- it's got to be true my dad told me! If dad wasn't looking I used to try to do a runner and go play with a boy up the lane, Graham Taylor. If dad saw me before I got past the high hedge "GEOOOORGE" I stopped and went back, if I made it past the hedge, "sorry dad I didn't hear you" when I was being told off. When he was at work I used play with worms, throwing them, caterpillars and other slugs over to next door's chickens. I used to enjoy seeing them all run around fighting for whatever I had thrown over. Was I being a horrible little sod?

We had an Earth bucket for a toilet. Dad built a small toilet on the end of a shed, it had a shiny wooden surface with a hole in the middle and a bucket underneath. Dad, and sometimes mother had to empty it and dig it into the garden. When old enough, brother and I would also do this chore. Tomato seeds are not compostable as they don't rot down when passing through the body, so tomato plants would be growing all over the garden. For cooking we had a freestanding coal-fired cast-iron grate with an oven on the side, a chimney disappeared up through the roof. In the winter when going to bed mum would take the pieces of metal in the oven and wrap them in newspapers to put in the beds as we couldn't afford a hot water bottle. Mum kept her iron on the top at the back to it keep warm in case she wanted to Iron anything, this would also get wrapped in paper and put in a bed. The fire was burning all day, summer and winter, with a kettle always on the top so the water was always warm. It was brought over the main fire to boil, as dad liked his cup of tea which he used to pour into the saucer then blow on it to drink!

Mum told me she was 32. As I used to go and watch the workmen doing the water and electric trench, they asked "how old is your mum", "32". I think mum told me off. I found out when I was older that she was 41 when I was born. I believe I was a mistake arriving in March 1944, what happened in June 1943?

Luxury started in 1947 when we got mains water and electricity. We had a cold water tap inside, with a washstand underneath it with a bowl. We had a large galvanised bucket in the lean-to outside into which we used to throw waste water from washing and the teapot, dad, if caught short would go to wee in it. This would be thrown on the garden for watering, I think it's called recycling now! Dad kept the drinking water well and hand pump near the kitchen for a few years as he used it to water plants near the kitchen, I was fascinated watching him use the pump. Mum and Dad bought a Creda electric cooker, was this Buckingham Palace? Dad had dug another well up the top of the 25' x 300' garden for watering the plants. He put a corrugated iron sheet over the top for safety but it wasn't very heavy. He'd acquired a cast iron bath which he kept near the well, my job was to fill it. The only way to get water out of the well was to drop a bucket down with a rope on it. There is a knack to doing this, which took me ages to learn. I was up the top of the garden having been asked to fill the bath, I don't know how but I fell down the well. I was lucky as the water only came up to my neck, 4 more inches and you would not be reading this, a good job I didn't fall headfirst. I was in the water, on my toes to stop the water going in my mouth. I did have things to keep me company, snails, dead mice, lots of spiders and nasty things all floating around, a bit like the Raiders of the lost Ark film, perhaps that's why I cringe when I watch these films! Dad had made the well from bricks and there were small gaps so I attempted to climb up but fell back down many times. Dad had made the top smaller, perhaps to stop somebody falling down. With all my shouting I had gone hoarse. Father later told me he came up the garden wondering "where has the little bugger gone now", luckily he heard the splashing, he said his heart stopped beating for a moment. After dad pulled me out I saw Uncle Jack and Auntie Jess who had come down from Wales for the weekend. I was made a fuss of although I had to go to bed as I was very cold. Did I hear them say "well, being hoarse keeps him quiet?"

I used to put elvers in this bath and watch them swim around but they didn't live very long as they needed fresh water. Marvellous really when you think these little elvers swam up the River Severn at high tide coming from the Saragossa Sea! We used to get people pushing an old pram with a tin bath full of elvers, selling them for 6d a half pint, 1/- for a pint. Mother only bought them if alive, as she's used to say "you don't know how long they've been dead." I never liked eating elvers probably due to watching them being cooked alive but as they were cheap I was made to eat them. I think this put me off fish, certainly white fish, but I like smoked haddock and kippers.

Dad was always threatening to lock his top shed because I was always losing his tools but he kept pigeons in it up to 1953. Getting home from school I would usually run to look at the pigeons. One day they were not there "where are the pigeons dad?" "They've flown away son, go and have a look for them" so I went chasing around Ash Lane looking. Of course racing pigeons are trained to fly back to their home. He had either given them away, sold them or maybe even killed them. I found out later that a neighbour's cat had killed one and worried the others. They are very nervous birds, once upset they don't fly very well. I remember seeing dad

crying when a pigeon had a broken leg. The cat belonged to Mr Waite who we normally got on with very well, (he owned the chickens I threw worms to) but this cat kept watching dad's pigeons. Dad had asked Mr Waite to do something about the cat, when he didn't they fell

FROM AN OIL PAINTING BY ANDREW BEER

out. Dad used to say "I'm going to kill that cat one of these days." On coming home from work there was the cat sat there watching the pigeons so it had to go! Arriving home the next night there was a cat watching the pigeons again, the trouble was, dad had not killed Mr Waite's cat, but the lovely old lady, Mrs Marsh, from next doors cat. She used to give me 3d for going to the local shop. She asked mum if she'd seen her pussy cat, "oh no, no we haven't Mrs Marsh." I think mum gave dad a lot of earache about this and he couldn't really go on killing all the cats, so the pigeons had to go. We had an oil painting of "Welsh Amy", a pigeon from the 1920s on the wall. My dad and his brother helped their father race pigeons in Pontypridd, winning many races. Mum didn't like the painting and it went missing after dad had died.

Ash Lane was called "The Field" when the first few bungalows were built, coal merchants, milkmen etc. made a mud track with their horse and carts. The residents brought ash from the power stations laying it down to make a hard surface and so it became "Ash Lane." I used to enjoy going out with mother to the milkman, Mr Hayward. He had big aluminium churns and used special jugs with a long handle to ladle the milk into containers the housewives brought out. Although hard, the ash would go into potholes to add to the ones we made to play marbles! Ash Lane came off Down Hatherley Lane, which was a tarmac road. At the junction, on the left side looking up the Ash Lane was a six-foot hedge, on the right a three foot grass bank. The Lane was only one car's width wide which made passing only for pedal cycles and motorcycles and then carefully. Before I got my own second hand boy's bicycle, I used to ride mums old-fashioned ladies bike falling off it many times while learning to ride. One particular time, I was rushing home for tea and turned left into Ash Lane, without worrying about oncoming cars. I never made the corner, going up the bank and crashing onto Ash Lane banging my head. I pushed the bike back home, worse was to come when mum put Iodine on the cut on my forehead, it stung like hell. One of my many other injuries was when I fell over while making a bonfire for November 5th, larking about doing silly walks, 25 years before Monty Python's Flying Circus. I fell over with a piece of wood which went into my right knee, I still have the scar; again more Iodine! One day I pedalled my tricycle, which had no brakes 3 miles to Longford to play with school friends. When I got home "where have you been, we were worried" another smacked leg!

MUM, DAVE AND ME AGED 3

I started school at age 3, my first teacher was Miss Merit, later becoming Mrs Foster. She taught us everything (I remember trying to spell George with a J!) drawing, plasticine, cutting paper, even sewing a yellow rabbit. 3 of us were being kept in late, me, John Smith and Ronnie Vickers for doing something wrong in a singing lesson, I know that's hard to believe! After-school we were asked to sing The Skye Boat Song, we must have sung it well as we were allowed to go home afterward. On my 10th birthday mother invited John and Ronnie home for some sandwiches and jelly, Mrs Rolf, the head teacher said "Mrs Ridgeon you are brave you have invited the 3 worst children in the school" as mum kept reminding me, and I thought I was lovely.

When older I started walking the 2-½ miles home from Twigworth School with John Smith and Philip Gittins. We'd play marbles and look for things in the hedge-row that had been dropped. I remember we found a 10 shilling note once, John still owes me five shillings!

My last memory of Twigworth School, besides my miserable 11+ exam results, was being told off by Mrs Rolf for being greedy. At dinner times the food was delivered in large metal thermos type containers, some lovely dinner ladies dished it out, We would queue up for our meal, after we had finished eating we were allowed to put our hands up for 2nds, 3rds and on one occasion 4ths, after 5 helpings of rice pudding, a total of 9 meals in the one day. These were very small and I was very big for my age, anyway, Mrs Rolf had me in her classroom, sat at the desk looked over the top of her glasses "why do you eat some much George?" my answer was probably "I am hungry Miss", "doesn't your mother feed you at home?", "Yes, Miss, I get dinner when I get home." Her eyes and mouth opened in disbelief, she sent a letter home to mother. I always think of myself when I watch Oliver Twist "can I have so more please?" nothing stopped me asking for more, the record still stands as school is now closed. The only thing I remember of the 11+ was being asked to write what I would do with five shillings. As mother was always on about saving I answered, I would save most of it, spend 6d on my mum, 6d on sweets and chocolates and 6d on fireworks, which I loved then and still do. I will grow up one-day. As my birthday was March 31st there were cuddles and kisses from the dinner ladies and teachers as we were breaking up for Easter, I was starting at Longlevens SM School after the break.

My big brother was called up to do two years National service (1953 – 55). The first three months he spent training at RAF Melksham and we were invited up to see him "pass out" as a qualified airman. We caught a bus very early in the morning, there were lots of bus changes until Melksham where RAF buses collected the many families As a nine-year-old it was very exciting to be on an RAF Camp with David showing us around his billet, some of the other buildings and some military vehicles. There were lots of little horrors (like me) running around. Then the excitement of the actual "March Past." I asked mum who all the people with yellow on their caps were. Others around us explained it was the Air Vice Marshal and senior officers also the mayor of Melksham. I was shouting "mum there's our

Dave mum, mum". Trying to keep me quiet was virtually impossible as I was so proud of my big brother. I was pleased all the other youngsters were as excited as I was and shouting.

DAVE IN RAF
1953-55

Dave's first post was in Dumfries Scotland. He used to tell a story about how they laughed at a Scottish lad at Melksham who was always asking for salt for his porridge, but in Scotland, when Dave asked where the sugar was, they only had salt   ! He was later stationed to Lincolnshire and used to come home for the weekends, returning to base on Sunday night on his BSA Bantam. I think he came home as often to bring his washing for Mum to do! One Friday night we heard a strange noise as Dave came home, it was a Douglas 350cc Mk5 with crash bars. The Douglas was a horizontally opposed twin with the exhaust pipes coming out forwards and these shiny chrome crash bars going sideways. I was only 9 at the time and shouted "it's got crash bars" but grabbed hold of the exhaust pipe, screaming out as it burnt my hand!

One winter time, he'd broken his leg during exercises and was home for many weeks. In the 1950s breaking a leg was quite serious and you were in plaster for at least six weeks. There was snow on the ground and for some reason we had to walk up to Norton Garage about 1 mile away. Dave was on crutches with his leg in plaster and as we were going along the pavement in the snow he made me laugh saying "I bet these marks in the snow will make people wonder what animal made them" As well as my two small footprints there were two crutch marks on the outside just over an inch in diameter, 1 foot print and a small 2" x 3" mark, the piece of hard rubber cast into the bottom of the plaster so that the ground didn't wear it away. Looking back at these marks made us chuckle!

My first day at Longlevens Secondary Modern School after the Easter break was quite a shock. Twigworth School had 50 pupils, which was a lot to me living in a village, Longlevens had 700 pupils, hundreds of children piled off single and double-decker buses.

All the new children were crowded into a large room. "I am Mr Hemming, deputy head teacher, there are 4 streams A, B, C and D. This is your 1st year so there is a 1 as part of your class group. I will read out 1D, the least academic, then a teacher will take you to your new classroom." He started in alphabet order then I heard "George Ridgeon".

There were 40 pupils in each class of boys and girls with 2 teachers per class. We had Miss Tovey, a pretty lady in her early 20s who wore tight jumpers with a tight skirt worn just below the knee like the 1950s film stars and Mr Porter, a sort of professor looking man with glasses and tweed jacket complete with leather elbow patches.

We were told everything about the school routine: – "a bell will ring for change of class, you finish what you are doing and walk, (he stressed not to run), to your next class or breaks", dinner and day over, when you line-up in your classes in the front playground. Oh my poor head was spinning.

We had Mrs Quarrel for music and country dancing. She made me think of the saying, here's my chest my backside's coming, she wore a tight grey tweed fitted jacket with matching pleated skirt which really showed off these proportions. She appeared to lean forward making it worse, unless it was all her big chest. Country dancing, was held in a wooden hut with a corrugated iron roof. After showing us the steps Mrs Quarrel said "Pick a partner", well never having danced with a girl before I went over to a boy I knew from my old school, Mrs Quarrel's voice boomed out "dance with a girl" so I picked Adela Cleveland, a girl Ugh, I felt very embarrassed as I think Adela did. I remember when I was 5 playing "I'll show you mine if you show me yours" with Adela. One lesson I forgot my daps, so I was dancing in my hob-nail boots and slid on the wooden floor, I had my leg pulled a lot for that one! Mrs. Quarrel caught me talking in lines after the bell had gone the first week and I got 2 strokes on my hand, it stung. But it's never stopped me talking!

Both teachers were easy going, but if naughty we were given 'the dap'. This didn't really hurt so we were often cheeky, it was bend over and 2 light taps on the backside. There was also the plank, a piece of wood 2" x 1" and 3' long, the cane across the backside which could only be given by the headmaster, or the ruler on the hand, each more painful depending on how hard it was applied.

We were told not to bring elastic bands into school, so everybody did! We were in room 7, Mr Porter teaching, I didn't have an elastic band but a burst balloon which I stretched between my fingers after putting a piece of paper around it and gripping the paper with my teeth, *Whoosh,* 4 bits of paper went flying across the room. "You, you, you and you stand up" Mr. Porter shouted before taking us to see the headmaster. I was second in, after hearing "whack, whack" and seeing a boy came out with tears in his eyes I was somewhat nervous as I bent over for two strokes, it didn't half tingle! At end of term mum and dad were reading my report murmuring, good, not very good, dad asked "what's this at the bottom, punishment caning!" In a loud voice he asked "what was that for?" Luckily when I told him about the burst balloon he laughed, perhaps remembering when he was young!

During PE, schoolmaster Mr Hinds went by, we used to call him "Heinz 57 or beans" but not usually to his face, "Hello Sir, how's Sir, how's Beans?" I said, he grabbed hold of my ear dragged me in to his classroom, giving me two hard whacks with a plank. I only had thin football shorts on but deserved it really.

"Sir, there's a mouse in the waste bin" I pointed out, "carry it out and let it go on the field". Walking across the playground, I went to stroke the mouse when it ran up my sleeve. I tried to take off my coat and shirt, the mouse ran away, with pupils in classrooms watching and the boy with me, Jenkins, laughing. Something else that took a long time to live down.

We were doing cricket practice with a cradle which looked like half a barrel with struts. 3 standing each side of the barrel throwing the ball in, which come back out at all angles. A plump lad, Jim Day was at the other end the cradle as the Sports master came round, "keep your eye on the ball boys." The trouble was, it hit Jim in the eye, and he had a corker of a black eye.

I still feel guilty about getting a boy the cane. My big brother brought back some stink bombs from a holiday, the packet saying "the biggest stink since Hitler, only the brave can stand them." One morning I dropped a stink bomb at start of the class, unfortunately a Scottish lad with tussled hair, who was already in trouble, was coming in to be told off by Mr Porter. "Did you let that off boy?", "No sir", then he asked us "Did any of you let it off?" I must admit I was very cowardly saying along with everyone else "No Sir we didn't", he got the cane.

There was a pile of grass turf stored upside down to keep for use at another time, only trouble was we used to have King of the Castle fights on it so the top and sides were worn away. Two of us were given the job of moving it in wheelbarrows to the front of the school, perhaps as a punishment, it was near the end of the day and some classes were already catching their buses home. As we wheeled the last 2 loads to the front of the school we started racing. We were going full tilt as we cranked around the corner with our wheelbarrows full of turf as some schoolchildren were walking to catch their bus. You should have seen them scatter, but we trapped this one lads Macintosh underneath the wheelbarrows just stopping before we ran him over. I can still see his face, white as a sheet.

I was with a group of boys and girls, including Ann who had big boobs and wore tight jumpers, in a classroom, which we shouldn't have been in as it was playtime, when somebody said "What have you got stuffed up there Ann?" another shout "Newspapers", someone else "Let's read the news" We were all trying to pull Ann's jumper up with the other girls hitting us on our heads with their shoes, when a very loud voice said "What are you doing playing around in there, you know you're not allowed?" The teacher told the boys to wait outside his room but not the girls! We were trying to work out what to say, "We were trying to kiss them" someone suggested, I said "that sounds sissy", "you can't say you were trying to get her tits out" was the reply. Going in we were all shaking, "boys if you get caught playing around in class at playtime again, you will be caned", "yes sir" we replied, what a relief. At dinner "spaceman" as we called Bill Owen, the 6' tall science teacher walked past he gave us an "I know what you've been doing" wink.

I dropped my last stink bomb in Mr Frapwell's class, our then form master, luckily the smell didn't happen for a while so I hoped I wouldn't get caught. Later that day Mr Frapwell came up to me "If you do that again Ridgeon you're in trouble", "Ye, Ye Yes Sir". He was a nice gentleman for a teacher, and was also gardening master. I didn't like gardening as dad was always telling me off, but I enjoyed doing the gardening jobs at school. Looking back I think I was better at practical things than academic.

The school was built before the war with additional classrooms put up after the war to deal with the baby boom. These blocks looked like prefab wartime houses, having enough space for a garden between the blocks and the road, where we grew vegetables. One classroom was for Domestic Science. Miss Peachey, who also wore tight jumpers showing off her film star figure, not that I noticed, was in her classroom with another teacher Mr Smart. We were outside having finished some digging, leaning on our spades watching Mr Smart chase Miss Peachey around the classroom. I found out after I left school that she got pregnant and he got dismissed.

The highlight of the day, for me, was dinnertime. Making friends with the dinner ladies was a way to get a bigger dinner. 'Spaceman' said to me "Ridgeon there's two sizes of dinner plate standard size and Ridgeon size". I used to try and eat my nine-year-older brother's dinner at home as it was always bigger than mine, but mum, dad or Dave would clip me around the ear!

There were some good times, one teacher ran a record club at dinnertime. We all did 'the hand jive' to songs like I've got a handful of Songs by Tommy Steele. Many girls had names of popstars on their satchels. I enjoyed metalwork and woodwork which were both practical.

I liked sport, just was no good at it. The only school standard I got was in the shot putt, but 15 seconds for the 100 yards, nowhere near. In the high jump I did 3 feet once and hit the sand so hard I winded myself. Some double sports periods we would have a 2 mile run going through Churchdown and Innsworth. A couple of lads knew a shortcut which saved a mile. I enjoyed cross-country, even going in the school sports day as I didn't finish last. I was 14 when I entered the local youth club cross-

country. I was asked to go in the senior team to make up the numbers but as I was last it scuppered any chance of a team award, in fact, the judge on the final checkpoint ran with me, I was in shorts while he was wearing shoes, long trousers and a Macintosh. I was the youngest runner by four years! As a reward, mum and dad gave me two bob to go to pictures seeing Moby Dick, with the change I got a 3d bag of chips. Once a month in the summer, the school had a coach trip to Cheltenham for swimming, which I enjoyed.

We waited at the big oak tree for the school bus. Once, in the winter a girl appeared to slip in the snow, we horrid boys started throwing snow over her until we realised she'd collapsed, one of the other girls took her home. It was summertime and we hadn't gone very far on the bus when I realised I'd left my satchel at the tree. I got off at the next stop, Twigworth Caravan Park, half a mile away, and ran back to find it. When I got home "What are you doing home?" "Sorry Mum I left my satchel at the big tree so had to come back for it." Luckily my big brother had just come home from work on the railway (steam trains in those days) probably finishing a night shift, "Dave run George to school", talk about a swelled chest, I arrived on the back of his Douglas Mark 5 to calls of "Core George you're lucky".

I was on the back of his Douglas when he waved at another motorcyclist. I shouted over his shoulder "who was that Dave?" Dave turned his head "I don't know," "Why did you wave at them?" "He was on a Douglas!" That was on one of the many trips to the indoor swimming pool in Gloucester. I enjoyed being with Dave when he was not trying to strangle me, perhaps I was a horrible little bugger. He spent hours teaching me to dive in, starting with me sitting on the side of the pool arms outstretched falling forward, then standing on the side crouched arms out then falling in. I was getting braver. One time diving in from a standing position, wearing some home-made swimming trunks, probably a pair of mum's old knickers she had adapted, I hit the water, they came off, well down to my ankles. Dave pulled my leg and I went very red. Gloucester baths had a cartoon sign on the wall saying what you mustn't do! No petting, no bombing no spitting. Next to the sign was a Brylcreem machine, 1d a shot. Dave having wavy hair was always buying some, I calling him "Wavy Davey". On warm summer days he took me to the open-air Lido in Cheltenham. One particular trip I lost him. It was a large open area with hundreds of people, I was standing on the side of the pool shouting "Dave where are you?" Someone pushed me in, I remember turning over and over in the water until 2 girls well young ladies rescued me. Again my horrible big brother pulled my leg about being rescued by girls. It was probably Dave who pushed me. Dave took me to Silverstone 1955 to see Geoff Duke racing. This trip didn't take as long as the ones to Wales. Although both trips were about 60 miles, David on his Douglas, didn't hang about. The trips to Wainlode Hill and swimming in the river were both enjoyable and exciting. It was down a long very twisty lane. I was sat on the back, my arms round his waist hanging on and we would be cranked over going around the corners, it felt very fast. We had a WW2 life preserver we used as a raft, about six-foot long with two pump-up sections, Dave sinking me.

Wainlode Hill was the Weston-super-Mare of Gloucester. On some Bank Holidays, hundreds would get on the grass bank. As there was, and still is, a public house called the Red Lion there, Dad didn't mind going down for the day.

Sadly these trips out finished when Dave started going out with girls, although I only ever remember Susan. I do remember one trip with a group of local lads and lasses from our village, all Dave's age, going for a walk round Ash Lane, mum must have put pressure on Dave to take me along. Heading for the brook over the fields where Dave had taken me many times when I was younger when he was teaching me to climb trees, rabbiting with dad's ferret or picking blackberries. I was happily playing throwing dock leaves into the brook and bombing them with stones as they came under the small bridge, not bothering with what they were doing. I found a big lump of concrete broken off the bridge and threw it in, the only trouble was I didn't let it go and followed it into the water. They had to rescue me which probably broke up their afternoon!

When dad was working or up the Kings Head Pub, mum would take me to whist drives. I had to stand up to deal as I wasn't very good, with all the other players mumbling; it wasn't very encouraging for a 12-year-old. I was playing, following the cards that were laid down when one of the opposition shouted "You finagled" (a posh word for cheated or mistake made). It appears I'd trumped an earlier card, later playing a card of the same suit. Activity in the whole room stopped and I felt 50 pairs of eyes boring into me. After the three players had sorted the cards and said "alright carry on" I heard a sigh of relief from the room and everyone starting playing again, it still haunts me today. Another time there was a big kerfuffle, ladies screaming and standing on chairs with their skirts up around their knees. Although not quite in my teens, I must admit the flash of petticoat got me excited! It turned out there was a mouse. Mother went over, stamped on the mouse killing it and threw it out. "Oh Mrs Ridgeon you are so brave." The number of times I heard this story, mother getting braver every time I heard it. What mum would do to play a game of cards! When Christmas was approaching, we would go to all the whist drives in the area hoping to win a joint or chicken, the top prize at the festive season.

We made many trips to where the steam trains were stored in Horton Road, Gloucester. As well as something to do if there was nothing else, Dave had to find out what shift he was on or changes in his shifts after he'd taken a few days off. On one trip the "Gloucestershire Regiment" was in the yard. This was a very large green frontline steam train perhaps a "Castle Class". Dave said "get into the cab." Well, if you think about it the wheels are 6'6", the rails 6", the sleeper's 9". I was about 10 and although tall for my age, it was "bloody big". "Dave I'm scared", "get up there". I will always remember that trip when I pass The Gloucestershire Regiment Museum as the nameplate of that steam train is on the outside of the museum.

When taking me to Cheltenham, as we crossed Lansdown Railway Bridge Dave would say "stand up and tell me what train is in the station". Holding onto his shoulders, standing up on the foot rests, "it is a very big green train with lots of carriages on" or "trucks carrying coal or Shell petrol, if a freight train" he would reply "oh that's the 3.30 from wherever", I used to think my big brother was very clever. The same thing happened whenever we went on a bridge over a railway, river, or canal, "stand up, tell me what was going on." Dad was taking me to Cheltenham once, as we went across the Lansdown Bridge I stood up "What the bloody hell are you doing?" as the bike started wobbling "I am seeing what train is in the station", "bugger the train, sit down or else".

I think I enjoyed the trips to the pictures with Dave the best, seeing the 1st Norman Wisdom film Trouble in Store, the antics of George Formby, and various war films etc After watching the Dambusters we made a dam at the top of the garden, filling it with water on one side then dropping a penny banger firework in it trying to blow it up. We had a 100 gallon water butt with a tap, which the guttering ran into, so we started dropping penny bangers into this, until it sprung a leak, luckily dad never found out it was us! In the Disney film The Living Desert, the most memorable part was square dancing by the scorpions. They were really fighting but the filmmakers put it to square dance music. When a big spider filled the screen all the kids hid behind the seats, including me, just as I did in Treasure Island when the knife went in the barrel just missing Jim Hawkins.

I was on the back of dad when he got into a lock to lock wobble (either a speed wobble or he may have hit a pothole) coming home from Uncle Jack's in Wales. I hung on for dear life, it was quite scary but exciting, dad pulled over sweating, a car driver pulled up asking "Are you all right mate?" Getting his breath back Dad said "Just about, thanks". He was telling the story that he was only doing 25 miles an hour when the wobble happened "Oh Dad, you were doing at least 40", I used to look over his shoulder to see what speed we were doing. Whether he clouted me then or after I don't remember, but at least I was telling the truth!

Welsh Nan who died in 1956 with 1st grandson Steve

We didn't travel by steam train very often, usually in the winter when we went down to Wales. We got a cheaper fare as Dave worked for British Railways. I would always look out the window, sometimes getting a smut in my eye from the smoke from the steam train. It took ages to get to Wales by train as you had to change trains and stop at every railway station on the way. We made the trip a few times on double-decker buses. Like the trains, you had to keep changing and stopping at all the bus stops. I liked the double-decker as all the kids used to get up on the top deck at the front to see where you were going. With a train you could run around a little more than a bus, but in those days people used to tell you off if you were annoying them. With the BSA Bantam, as well as A and B roads it was stopping at pubs. Whatever transport we used it would take a long time. Although it was only 60 miles to Wales which doesn't seem far today 60 years ago it seemed to take forever.

In 1956 we made the long trip to Cambridge to see dad's cousin, Aunty

COLCHESTER COUSINS

Nellie and Uncle Knox in Newmarket. Their 16 year old daughter had just died, Aunty Nellie said "she studied too hard". I found out later she died of a brain tumour, but no one talked about cancer in those days. The Bantam only did 45 mph flat-out if you were lucky! Now this trip did take forever, especially as it was over 150 miles, my backside was really sore. I was jiggling about asking "dad can you stop, my backside is sore" dad grumpily replying "if you don't shut up and keep still, it will be even sorer when I smack it"! I enjoyed being with Aunty Nellie, she made Victoria sponges and I helped her. We made one for a charity event in the village hall, where the cakes were to be auctioned. Our cake didn't make the auction so we kept it to eat on the trip home!! We also had trips to see cousins in Colchester, who had two sons my age, and relatives in Ipswich who lived near the docks, so we could look at boats through a telescope, whoopee.

I had to laugh when dad got into trouble on the way home from Newmarket. A policeman pulled him over. Dad said "yes officer, can I help you?" The officer in a stern voice asked "did you not see the racehorses?" dad replied in an enquiring voice "yes officer," "why didn't you stop, you must always stop when you see a racehorse, you'll get a ticket next time," "ye, ye, yes, officer we're visitors" dad replied. The police man said "don't you know Newmarket is the home of horseracing?" Dad was sheepish as we rode off "very sorry officer, I won't do it again." When I was feeling brave, I told big brother "Dave, dad nearly got arrested by a policeman."

Christmas is always a special time for children. I remember when I was quite young I had a Bayko set (the Lego of its day) which was for making houses. Seeing it had a damaged corner I pointing this out to Dad or Dave. "Don't forget Santa Claus has a lot of presents to deliver, I expect it got damaged on the journey", "oh yes of course". When I was near the end of my schooldays, 13 or 14 years of age, Dave bought me a crystal set, it's a radio made of only three components, a coil, a variable capacitor and a diode, no batteries. We had a long wire around the house which was used as an aerial.

The next year Dave bought me a short wave set, which had to have a battery. He used it a lot as well as you could get radio stations from all over the world. We were opening the presents on the bed, starting with the stockings but on opening the short wave set some acid was spilled when the battery tipped over. When Mum washed the bedspread, it went into large holes, "how did that happen?" "We don't know Mum". I found out later, that another second-hand present was a suitcase full of an electric train set. It was supposed to be for me but I think my brother enjoyed playing with it more than I did. I remember I had a "Willoughby Cartooner" by Rolf Harris as well as marbles and cowboy guns, sweets were in short supply in the early Fifties! One year, a distant cousin of mums came over from Canada, he brought chocolate, nuts and raisins, I was in heaven.

Dave and I were always fighting. Once, my big brother was pushing me out of bed, he was twice as big as me so I put my foot against the wall which caused a hole as it was only fibreboard. Dad had to use a sort of red tape to repair the wall, a little like the duct tape of today. I believe it was liberated from Dowty Rotol where dad worked.

Plans were made for Dave to get married October 8, 1958 to Susan, they're still married today. That year The Everley Brothers were singing Wake up little Susie so I used to sing it all the time. "David, tell your horrible little brother to go away and stop singing." They moved in to next door where Mrs Marsh used to live

The opportunity for Dave and Sue to buy the house came about when Jim, who was Dave's friend and going out with one of Susan's sisters, found out it was for sale. Jim and his mother, after looking around the bungalow came around for tea with mum and dad. Jim's mother said "I see there's a toilet outside with no running water or flush, how do you get rid of the contents?", father replied "when the bucket's full you carry it up to the top of the garden, throw it in the air but make sure the wind is not blowing towards you" at this

DAVE & SUE'S WEDDING 1958

mother clouts him with the back of her hand "George don't be silly." "I'm sorry about my husband. After you take it up to the top of the garden you dig it into the ground, makes good compost" I was sat there trying not to snigger but Jim's mother didn't look too impressed! As Sue liked the bungalow, mother and father helped them buy it. I helped them cutting the grass and painting, not that I was very good at painting; well I wasn't very good at anything really.

After Dave started going out with girls and got married I had to start fishing on my own. Whether it was me being clumsy or just bad at fishing but I was always getting my line tangled in the trees when trying to cast the hook out into the river.

My last time fishing was at Haw Bridge, a bridge over the River Severn near the village of Tirley, famous for a Grand National motorcycle scramble. It was a good 3 mile cycle ride from home going down the steep Wainlode Hill, then pushing my bike with the fishing gear along the path by the riverside. On a nice sunny day I found a sort of beach after climbing down a 4' bank and spread my gear out. I sat there casting out, munching mum's sandwiches and daydreaming. My daydream was broken by the chugging sound of a barge, one of many going to from Worcester via Gloucester to Avonmouth. In the 1950s much of the cargo such as grain, wood, coal, etc. was carried on the river. I had my keeper's net in the water with a few flounder's in it but I was more interested in watching the boat while sat on my small beach. Following the barge was the wake. At first no problem but, all of a sudden water came up and took my kit into the river including my Macintosh. I was trying to throw all my gear back up the bank when the second wake came taking it all back into the river. Luckily I didn't lose anything important but I had to rescue the Macintosh 3 times, even luckier not to drown, that was the end of my fishing trips.

That blooming Macintosh, I had to take it everywhere otherwise mum wouldn't let me out the house. The last school holiday before leaving, a gang of us went cycling to Newent to pick bluebells. I had the Mac tied somehow on the back of my bike but it came loose, caught in the back wheel and the bike chucked me down the road. I remember John Meadows telling me that I was more worried about my Macintosh than the blood coming from the cut on my knee. Luckily we weren't too far from the finish and the bike, other than straightening the handlebars, was okay. We picked bluebells and enjoyed walking through the wood pretending we were Robin Hood. As we were pushing our bikes out of the wood a man stopped us "you're not allowed to pick bluebells, give them to me." He was bigger than us and even though we were always being called naughty, we were taught to respect our elders. Luckily John had a big saddlebag where he'd put his bluebells, and gave us all a few so we could give them to our mums.

During the last term of school the classes were amalgamated. As a project, we were asked to design a garden area with pathways in the large grassed area outside 2 of the classrooms. The school acquired a supply of 2' sq. paving slabs. Mr Hemming, the deputy headmaster was then our master, his wife, was in charge of the girls. He told us we would be leaving school soon and some of us may be doing work like this. Blowing my own trumpet, my design was chosen and we were all involved in cutting, measuring and laying slabs under the guidance of a teacher, shame we never had a photo.

SCHOOL DAYS NEARLY OVER

We had various talks from different places of work including one from the police. We all enjoyed that one as the policeman showed us pictures of a body with stab marks in it, I know, gruesome little horrors. We had a couple of trips out to factories in Gloucester, one to the foundry which was quite good as they had hot molten metal and lots of machinery. I was fascinated with a big rail that went along the ceiling with big hooks on it carrying various hot pieces of metal from where they had been sand cast. We had to walk between these red-hot pieces of metal, no health and safety in those days. At another engineering firm, Fielding and Platt on the Bristol Road, I asked "how many people work there", "over 700" was the reply. When I told dad of the trips he said "I can get you a job sweeping up at Dowty's" but I didn't fancy it. It was a shame we never had a look around Dowty's.

We had a man from the job centre to advise us, I told him I wanted to be a fireman. "You have to be 18 but you can be a junior fireman at 16, the nearest brigade then was in Bristol, 35 miles away". I wasn't 18 and didn't feel like leaving home yet. Dad told me Mr Hemming said "George is doing well, will you let him stay at school another year?" dad replied "no, George has to get out and do some work". On the 27th March 1959 it was the last bus home from school, the girls were crying, all the boys were cheering and it was four days before my 15th birthday. Buddy Holly had died eight weeks before on 3rd February, his last song going to number one, I guess it doesn't matter anymore, was very appropriate on the day you leave school!

I didn't have a job when I left school but dad had read in the local newspaper that a Butchers boy was wanted at JH Dewhurst. Dad rang up about the interview which was booked for just after my birthday. Mr Burr, a respected member of our village was walking past our bungalow, "hello Mr Ridgeon, George has left school then has he?" "Yes Mr Burr, he's going for an interview at Dewhurst Butchers." "I know Mr Quick who's a boss at JH Dewhurst, ask George to give him my regards". School days were over, a new unknown period in my life was about to start.

CHAPTER 2 1959/61-Work, bikes and girls

I was standing at the big tree on the 1st of April for more than 1 hour waiting for the supposedly hourly service, mum and dad saying "you're a big boy now George, catch the bus and good luck for the interview." They gave me directions how to get to Walter Warner's butchers shop. 4 pm came and went, sweat appeared on my brow, I was going around in every decreasing circle's until I disappeared up my own A***. Luckily somebody who knew me and could see I was looking a bit lost, shouted "do you want to lift to town."

I found the butcher's shop, "Walter Warner" which was shut, and wondered am I at the right shop, how can this be JH Dewhurst Ltd with that name? The shop was opposite the Gloucester swimming baths where big brother used to take me. What a wimp I must've looked, I certainly felt like one-and it was April Fools' Day! I was just a scared 15-year-old walking up and down not knowing what to do.

"Are you George Ridgeon?" a voice made me jump. "Come with me for your interview." As I followed the lady in her 40's, I apologised "I'm sorry for being late, I must have missed the bus, I waited an hour but it's not a very good service." Who said get the violin out? Mrs Hodge, a lovely lady put me at ease saying "don't worry, I was late for my first interview too, long ago now."

I was introduced to Mr Quick, the district manager, who told me this was the head office of JH Dewhurst for Gloucestershire. He was a stern looking gentleman with a receding hairline who seemed to look right through me. I'm not sure what he asked or told me, the only thing I remember saying was "Mr Burr told me to give you his regards" explaining he lived in our village. "Yes a nice gentleman", he told me I looked okay and could start on Monday 6th of April 8am at £3-15/- a week. After telling mum and dad I got the job I walked to the phone box to tell Mr Hemming, my old form master, that I'd got a job.

My first day, just 6 days after my 15th birthday, I had to get up at 7 o'clock, well mum made sure I got up! After a good breakfast, I cycled the 4 miles to my first job, I didn't have a watch but once in Gloucester I saw the time on the clocks on some of the shops said 7.50. I found the shop after going wrong a few times and pushed my bike around the back lane where Mrs Hodge had taken me 5 days before. I saw a group of people stood by the back door "Is this JH Dewhurst?", "yes", "where can I leave my bike please?"

Although most were shorter than me, they appeared much older; I was nervous and showed respect to everyone. I, as a butcher's boy was the lowest of the low.

My first job after putting on a white coat and apron was to clean the big shop window, inside first so they could put a meat display out. I had to mix a substance called "whiting" with water and rub it on to the glass with a muslin cloth from a frozen NZ lamb then polish it off with newspaper. The window was 6ft tall by 10ft wide 'blooming big' my poor arm was already hanging off my shoulder before I got to the outside. Next job was polishing the brass door handles and brass weights used on the scales. In a way I was lucky, this shop was Walter Warner they didn't have the brass 'JH Dewhurst & Co Ltd' on front of the marble underneath the window! I was sent into the fridge looking for "leg of liver" then a "shoulder of lights"! The lights were the lungs, which were sold for cats. No "leg of liver" either. These were some of the many tricks they played on me.

Talk about "health, safety and hygiene." If judged by today's standards all the shops would have been closed down. You had to clean things regularly, knives, meat trays and work surfaces. I would get a bucket of hot water from the sausage factory at the top of the yard, as the shop had no running water. Meat was cut on a wooden table called a Butchers Block which was used to chop, cut and saw. I saw a 200lb quarter of beef dropped onto it. I had to wash the blocks off with muslin when they looked grubby, blood and fat floated about in the bucket of water. In the evening I was shown a type of scrubbing brush with steel bristles and had to brush the block with a sideways action, scraping the rubbish off, my arms were hanging off again.

The Manager, Joe Ward was in his late 50s. There was a boy called Matchwick about 20 and Ron Giles, older than me again, possibly early 20s. There was also a lovely lady, Mrs Roach, in a little office who did all the paperwork. Like a mum, she tried to stop the others being nasty to me. I was told to go to Mrs Roach and ask her for a bill head. I thought this was someone's name but it was a piece of paper with the name of the shop on, I felt an idiot.

Joe Ward moved to another shop and a new manager Ken Finch took over. He was a jolly sort, "George make a cup of tea" he would shout many times a day, saying "wash the bleeding cups this time". I did as he told me, in the bucket of bloody water. I can't remember what he called me but it wasn't very complimentary.

There were five Dewhurst shops in Gloucester, as I had a push bike, if another shop was shorthanded, I was sent. The office upstairs where I had my interview had 3 pretty office girls, I'd never seen pretty girls up close before, all three were older than me. There was also a pretty girl working at a grocery shop up the road which sold Typhoo tea. Christine used to wear high heels which you could hear coming down the street. As she went by the shop, she'd put her head in the door and shout "You who it's Typhoo," a popular TV advert at the time as I was always being sent up there to buy Typhoo tea.

Christine was gorgeous but I could never get up courage to ask for a date, so wrote her a letter. I was horrified to get a letter back "Don't bother me again or I'll call the police." I didn't. Some of the older boys were always chasing the girl's upstairs; being younger I wasn't really involved, just laughed at their antics.

I sometimes helped out in the sausage factory which was interesting. Archie Rodway, the manager, was helped by a Teddy Boy type, like Ron in the shop, both a little scary, using a modern joke, he'd rubbed Viagra in his eyes to make them look hard.

At dinner time, I was eating mums sandwiches after going to the cake shop and fish and chip shop for everyone. The cake shop had a returned school order of sticky buns reduced to 1 ½d each. I bought 8, not many got home! Mr Finch opened his chips to find a fried woodlouse, he sent me back. They gave me a new and bigger bag. When I gave him the chips, he said "I don't fancy them anymore George, you have them." I ate them and my sandwiches.

I started to get fit cycling 4 miles to work and back in all sorts of weather. One night it was pouring with rain, I only had a large yellow cape, they found me a plastic bag for my head. I was wondering why people were pointing and laughing at me until I got home and found that the plastic bag had filled with air and was stood up, mum showed me in the mirror. It did look ridiculous, but it kept my head dry.

Thursday afternoon was half-day and my only time off other than Sunday. If I didn't have to service my pushbike or dad hadn't given me a gardening job, I'd treat myself to the pictures. In those days you could go in and stay there for the rest of the evening, seeing the main and support films twice, although the support film was often rubbish. Gloucester had the Regal, a newly opened ABC cinema, the Hippodrome and the Gaumont all in the town centre and 2 fleapits on the outskirts. One was the Ritz in Barton Street where I saw my 1st X film before I was 16, I was over 5'9". I saw my first Science Fiction film at the Empire near Gloucester Park. There was a long queue at the Regal to see Saturday Night and Sunday Morning, a controversial soap opera, Graham, the assistant manager and brother of Jean from the office, saw me in the queue and found me a seat for free. After the pictures I had a 3d bag of chips which gave me the energy to cycle home, I had a curfew of 10 pm. If it was dark I had to use the dynamo on the back which worked by rubbing on the back tyre, it didn't half slow the bike down!

At Christmas or when there was a special promotion, all Dewhurst shops gave away pencils and balloons. The Dewhurst pencils had the name of the shop and pictures of meat on, I used to take some home to save having to buy any! Mr Finch got me to tie a lot of balloons onto the front shop blind. At going home time on Christmas Eve he told me to push the blind up, "What about the balloons Mr Finch?" he must have been in a silly mood "Let's cut all the balloons free." They floated up the road, cars ran over them making a load "bang," making people look around. As we were cleaning the shop window, we had 1lb of sausage meat left, Ken said "let's all throw some at Mrs Roach," we were all bombing her as she was screaming "No, no, no". That was my first Christmas at work.

Out of my wages I gave £2-10/- , which didn't go up for many years, to mum. I saved most of the £1- 5/- in a post office account, mum told me "look after the pennies and the pounds will look after themselves."

In 1959 big brother, who'd left the railway after he got married in 1958, becoming a car salesman with the Westgate Motor House Group. He took us in a small A35 Austin to Porthcawl, South Wales where dad hired a caravan near his brother's, Uncle Jack, for a week. Uncle Jack's grandsons, Stephen and Wayne were 9 and 11, years younger than me. I enjoyed playing sandcastles with them as my big brother Dave had, years earlier with me. There was a young lad about 18 on the campsite who looked like a film star, all muscles, his cousin was bald at 25. In another caravan was a very pretty 17 year old girl. As we were all roughly the same age we would go to the fairground together but 3 fella's and one girl!! At 15 I felt a bit out of it, but it was my first real holiday. The trip to Porthcawl came to an end and Dave drove us home in a Riley. It was a terrible trip, very bumpy, perhaps the tyres were too hard, and it may have had a cracked exhaust because there was a funny smell in the car making me travel sick. In the middle Cardiff "Dave stop, stop, stop I am going to be sick." Opening the door I nearly hit a lamppost, luckily I was sick on the road not in the car as that would have spoilt the holiday.

Cycling to work I would pass John Meadows house on the Tewkesbury Road. I met John when I was five at Twigworth School. As we both failed the 11+ we both went to Longlevens Secondary Modern School. One particular day he was going to work at the same time as me and I found out that John worked on the cheese counter at the Bon Marche, a large department store in Gloucester so we started meeting in our dinner hour.

One of the jobs at the butcher's shop was to ride a carrier bike delivering orders. Dewhurst had a depot in Russell Street, so if the shop ran out things could be collected from there, we normally had lorry deliveries twice a week. When a load of 1000 frozen lambs came from New Zealand all the butcher's boys were sent round to the depot. A NZ lamb was 32lb, with practice you could carry 2 on your shoulder. I also learned to carry a quarter of beef, all the cycling had started to fill me out.

It's surprising what you could load onto a carrier bike. On one trip I was weaving in and out of the traffic as I approached The Cross, a policeman was directing traffic. I cut in front of this one car when the bike tipped over just as the policeman waved go, I was struggling to pick up all the stuff, by the time I had, the policeman had waved 'go' to the opposite traffic, I got a black look from the driver.

There were lots of butcher shops in those days, not so many supermarkets. I started to think of getting another job to move away from Mr Merritt. I admired him as he served in WW 1, but he shouted and swore at me and everyone else a lot. He also made me work very late on a Saturday night taking his books up to his house.

I went into Harris's Butcher's shop, also in Westgate Street as they wanted a Butcher's boy, and told them that I worked for JH Dewhurst, they gave me the job starting when my notice had run out. I went to see Mr Norman

Davis who had been promoted to district manager as Mr Quick was now area manager. It took me ages to say "sorry but I have to give in my notice, I've got another job". He offered me £4 a week to stay, my pay had gone up to £3-18/- on my 16th birthday. I told him I'd already been offered that so he offered £4-10/-. "There's something else Mr Davies, I don't want to work with Mr Merritt any more, he shouts at me," "okay, start at Bristol Road Monday" I told Harris Butchers I was staying where I was.

I turned up at Bristol Road where Joe Ward was my first manager. It was a quiet shop as those days most people went into the town centre to shop. He'd been managing the shop on his own until I turned up. There was lots of cycling to deliver meat, it helped me learn my way round Gloucester, certainly the Bristol Road area.

A man regularly walked down the street appearing to bowl a cricket ball and shouting very loudly. After watching him a few times, I asked about it and was told that he was in the WW1 and suffered from shellshock. He imagined he was throwing a Mills Bomb, called hand grenades in WW2. The reason it looked like cricket was that he would take a big pace forward and in a bowling action throw the bomb, shouting GRRRR to give extra strength to the throw. Another sad war story was the man who used to sleep rough, lying in the street or on a piece of grass. Some people were unkind, shouting nasty comments. I found out that he'd been in a Japanese prisoner of war camp and couldn't live in a house. War must have been bad.

I was riding home from Bristol Road having left work early because I was being confirmed at Down Hatherley Church by the Bishop of Tewkesbury, when just past the Royal Infirmary in Southgate Street I saw hundreds of people and police on motorcycles coming towards me completely blocking the road. I got off my bike as close to a shop doorway as possible. I saw a lady walking with rags around her feet, camera men taking photos and a film crew with a huge cine camera. It turned out to be Dr Barbara Moore who was walking from John O'Groats to Lands End, the A38 went right through the middle Gloucester. I was stuck there for 5 minutes, good luck to the lady.

Along with many of the local teenagers I'd been taking confirmation classes for some weeks. When I saw the girls in white I said "they look like virgins." To be honest I didn't know what a virgin was I'd just heard the term linked to white.

After I was 16 in 1960 I started thinking about getting a motorcycle. John Meadows mentioned he was getting one, mum, dad and Dave all had motorcycles. The main reason was I needed transport as Down Hatherley was 4 miles from Gloucester, 6 from Cheltenham and 8 from Tewkesbury. The bus service wasn't good and the last bus home was at 10 pm. Dave had seen a 225cc Francis Barnett which he thought would suit me, it had been repossessed by the finance company and was £26 with a full service for £15.

My big brother was a hero to me, especially when I was growing up so I trusted him. We went to see the green Francis Barnett in Bowmaker's car park. Dave told me to sit on it, I did and it fitted well. He arranged for it to be taken to Mr Lyons in lower Westgate Street who did the service, I had my first motorbike. With help from big brother I learned to ride, on went the L plates and another biker takes to the road. My 1st trip was to show John, he had a new 197 Cotton, which was made in Gloucester. So started my motorcycling years, we were going out two or three times a week riding around the County. John and I went to Cranham Woods and were trying to ride through the trees. We'd starting going to watch motorcycle scrambles, the trouble was I couldn't get back up a grass bank. John and I had to push the bike back up, I needed to buy a new back tyre with some tread on.

POSING ON MY FRANCIS BARNETT

My first falling off was in Innsworth Lane, a very tight s-bend going towards home from Longlevens. First a sharp right then left, I was obviously approaching too fast and ended up on the grass verge, no problem, I thought as I started to ride off the verge, not noticing the verge was 12 inches above the road, I fell off in a heap twisting my ankle. When mum asked "Why are you limping George, what have you done?" I told her I'd twisted my ankle on the duck boards in the fridge at work, luckily mum believed me.

Another time I was with John going to Tewkesbury, on a left hand bend on Coombe Hill I hit a lorry that was stopping, probably because I oiled the front brake because it squeaked, I was only 17! I must have been watching

Speedway on the TV, I laid my bike down to avoid hitting the back of the lorry full on, but still hit my right shoulder on the left hand corner of the lorry. It hurt like hell, but I still rode to work, with a large swelling on my shoulder.

Once I had my motorcycle I became even more useful at work. As well as going to the shops in Gloucester I was sent to Cheltenham when they were shorthanded. If I was sent out of Gloucester I was entitled to the bus fare to wherever I was sent. The bus fare to Cheltenham was 5/- return. Petrol was less than 5/- a gallon and a gallon would last me all week, as I lived halfway between Gloucester and Cheltenham I was richer by £1-5/- per week, which I saved as mum had told me to.

One such trip was on a Thursday half day. I was told to go to Dursley. I needed a map, it was more than 10 miles away. By this time I was classed as a Shop Man Cutter, I liked the job and was getting good at it. Serving a lady in the Dursley shop I was asked "can I have a scrag of lamb please Butcher?" You take the bones out of the shoulder of lamb leaving some of the meat on to make a lamb hotpot. The next lady said "Can I have one of those please?" She whispered to me "How do I cook it?" "I'll chop it up for you madam, put it in a stew with onions, potatoes, peas, carrots lots of water and seasoning." I got a smile, my heart fluttered, she was pretty.

March 62, just before John's and my 18th birthdays, we discussed where we could have an illegal drink before we were 18. We decided to go to The Red Lion at Wainlode where we weren't really known! The landlady was called "the Black Widow", her husband had died some years before, and she always wore black, although I've heard tales that she was very jolly and liked chasing men! John and I went in, he ordered a beer and I ordered a cider shandy, dad put me off beer when I was 5 by giving me a taste which I thought was horrible. So, we had our illegal drink, just a week before I was 18!

We used to practice trying to get up the steep Hill at Wainlode, it was 1 in 4. When learning to ride I started at the bottom in first gear and couldn't get up it. I should have started from further back to attack it at about 30 miles an hour changing down the gears as the bike slowed. Well, you have to learn to ride, although I should have been able to get up it in first gear, but I was still learning!

When out one night with John we saw two girls, John got the pretty one Sheila, although Gaynor was jolly. As John lived only a mile from Gloucester centre he probably saw more girls than I did living in a village, well that's my excuse. The first film I went to see paying for a girl was Blue Hawaii with Elvis Presley. The four of us went to the new Regal Cinema in Kings Square. Another film we saw was more of a ghost story, the lady tutor for the children kept seeing this lady ghost crying, by the time she had got to the desk the lady had disappeared but there was a tear still on the desk! John shouted out "A little bitty tear let me down" which was a hit song at the time, everybody laughed but we came out as the girls didn't like the film. I was quite glad, I'm not that good with ghost stories either. I remember we had some good times going to the cinema.

I was then working back at Walter Warner's when Sheila said "my parents are away, shall we have a party?" The girls came down to the shop Saturday morning of the party to collect some sausages, well chipolatas that I had made smaller. They got a discount, as did John for the cheese and ham items. We covering most of the costs of the food and the girls made cakes and sandwiches.

Shelia lived in Longford not that far from John, We used to end up there after a drink in a pub or a coffee bar, all the rage in the early 60s. One night we were playing a game called consequences, which with me living a very sheltered life in a village I'd never heard of. You each had a piece of paper on which you wrote a boy's name, folded it over and then passed it on. Next was a girl's name, what they did on the first date, what was the result etc. With me being brought up exposed to very crude language at Longlevens Secondary Modern I put a very naughty word for what I thought they did. I broke out into a sweat when I heard the first read out "John met Gaynor, they shook hands, and the result was a donkey" It was Gaynor who got my piece of paper, she didn't read the word out, just stuttered "They did it."

The night of the party came and John and I got there early to help set things up. I met John's friends from work at the Bon Marché including Frank Prentice who was even taller than I was at 6' 7", Norman Cobley, Tony Wilson, the Gapper brothers Don and Derek, and many pretty girls one called Wendy. John told me that he had warned them I was a Butcher so very strong and not to chat up my girlfriend which I thought was a load of bull. Music was playing, there was dancing and games, one which was "spin the bottle." On one spin Frank was kissing a short girl, as he had to squat down some rotten so-and-so shouted "don't forget the pull the chain Frank". When Wendy was sat next to me, she kissed me, she certainly liked kissing the boys. After everyone left and the tidying up had been done I asked Gaynor when I'd see her again, "You're not we're finished," so rode I home thinking that was okay except that threesomes, two chaps and one girl didn't work very well.

Sheila cured the problem for me. When I was around at her mum's house the week after the party she'd invited Wendy, who lived 100 yards up the road, in for chat. During the evening I asked Wendy if she'd like to go out for a coffee, "okay my next off shift is Thursday." Wendy was a nurse at Over Isolation Hospital where I spent my 6th birthday with Scarlet Fever. Most of us at Twigworth School had it in 1950 it was very infectious. I was taken to the Hospital with a throat so swollen I couldn't eat. On arrival the nurse gave me a piece of chocolate saying "suck this," it melted in my mouth and easing my sore throat. That was the first food I managed to swallow all day.

Chocolate was in very short supply as it was still on ration. We were all constipated, part of having the fever, and were given suppositories and sat on a potty in our cots. John was in a cot opposite "have you gone yet John?" "No, have you George?" "No."

I got to the hospital early, which was lucky as I realised I didn't have my wallet. I rushed home and grabbed it. I got back to the Hospital and Wendy came walking down less than minute later. We went to Cheltenham for a drink and got lost trying to get out of town ending up on the road to Oxford. When the streetlights ran out I turned around, luckily, I saw a sign to Gloucester. We had a kiss and cuddle at the hospital. Wendy was sat side-saddle on the bike but, just as she was getting passionate the bike fell over, luckily she wasn't hurt, but it killed any sort of passion and I had no contraceptives. I'm not sure how I learned about contraceptives, whether it was from the kids at school, I don't think it was from dad as all I remember him saying was "don't bring any girl home you don't intend to marry!"

We made a date for a few days later. As I was working in Cheltenham, I found a chemist on the Rotunda, I didn't want to go in one near the Butcher's shop where I worked or anywhere else I was known. Even then, I walked up and down outside the chemist for what seemed like an age before getting up the courage to go in a buy a pack of Durex.

The night of the second date came. I'd toured Sandhurst village and the quiet secluded lanes where farmers had barns and haystacks to find somewhere I could take Wendy. I arrived at the Hospital to see Wendy get out of a parked minivan and come over to me "sorry George, I got a new boyfriend. He won't hit you if you don't cause any problems." "Oh, okay that's a shame." I went to the Roma Café, although I was over 18, the Coffee Bar era had started, as the Fonz used to say "it was cool man!" Maybe this was the first time I thought of suicide, *shall I go and jump off Westgate Bridge?* 18 years old and rejected by a girl. The fact that I'm writing this means I didn't.

I was working back in Westgate Street and now I was older, Mr Merritt wasn't quite as nasty. I had my motorcycle and used to drop off a piece of meat to a lady on the way home each Friday night.

I was walking from the shop in my Welly boots, shoes with the meat in an army bag dad had acquired. "Hello George" looking around it was Frank who I'd met not long ago at Sheila's party "coming for a pint in the Fleece hotel?" Frank liked playing snooker and they had a full-size table. We found people were playing pairs so Frank suggested we take them on. I used to play with dad at Dowty Rotol Social Club sometimes, although I wasn't very good. Frank placed 1/- on the table to pay for the electric, challenged the winners and gave me a tip "don't do any hit and hope shots." I still had my Wellington boots on. I'd taken off my motorcycle jacket but didn't want to open my bag to put my shoes back on as I had to go about 8 o'clock to drop the meat off. I didn't do any silly shots but could hear some sniggering when I had to put my one leg onto the table, I'd forgot I had my Wellington boots on!

I'm not sure if it was that night or other time but dropping the meat off at this ladies home in Longford I shut the bike off but it didn't stop, in fact, it started revving up higher and higher, sounding like it was going to blow up. I lent it against a brick wall and hid behind it, luckily it didn't explode, but it revved hard for possibly 10 seconds, until eventually the revs died down. It was explained to me that this sometimes happens when heat builds up in the carbon in the cylinder, not all that uncommon for two strokes with the oil in the petrol of the day, all very concerning to an 18-year-old who knew nothing about anything, luckily, it started and I went home.

About this time John and I were meeting up regularly with Frank Prentice, Norman Cobley and Graham Parsons as we all rode bikes to the coffee bars in Gloucester. The Top Spot opposite the bus station was a regular stop. One night we met up there after I'd had a butchery class at the Technical College to which I had to take a butchery steak knife. When I got home the knife was missing, luckily the butchers didn't ask if I'd brought the knife back and I didn't hear of any stabbings in Gloucester that week.

The Roma was popular and we made friends with a lot of bikers there and heard about a coffee bar in Cheltenham called the Aztec. In the late 60s, after we'd stopped going there, Brian Jones of the Rolling Stones used to get there. I saw in the newspapers that there was also drug dealing going on, which we weren't into.

Frank used to ride a Piatti, a very small Italian scooter, not much bigger than the Corgi that was dropped with the paratroopers in the war. Of course Frank, being 6' 7" had his knees up by his ears so to speak, but we all used to make fun of one another, it was all part of growing up. One night we went back to fix Graham's 150cc Tiger Terrier. All being short of experience and proper tools we ended up cold chiselling the cylinder head to get the nuts off. It cost him £8 to buy another cylinder head.

On the way to the Aztec we saw a motorcyclist broken down so we stopped to help him. He was a riding a two stroke and his plug had fouled up, this had happened to me a few times so I'd started carrying a spare plug and plug spanner. We got him on his way after cleaning his plug.

Dave invited me to ride down to Bude, Cornwall where he was stopping in a large house while on holiday. "Start at 3 am, so you'll get down there for early-morning" he suggested. I asked him to help me map out a route. With his RAF training he made me a roadmap with all the road numbers and towns I would go through and when to change roads.

The Wednesday came but I couldn't wait so I started off at about 2.30 am. Going down the Bristol Road my bike stopped, a dirty plug. I was cursing as I changed a very hot plug in the dark.

Going through Bristol was good as there were street lights, then back onto the A38 with no lights, turning onto the road to Minehead. Turning off before Minehead and going along some twisty roads, I saw a sign for Hump Back Bridge but hit the side of the bridge which curved inwards. My 6V lighting was next to useless so I hadn't seen the curve, I bent my left footrest. It was a good job I'd bought some strong motorcycle boots from Malcolm Davies Motorcycles (a top scrambler and trials rider), called the Mike Hailwood Racing Boot but more like a deep sea diver's boot. My foot still tingled for a few miles!

Around Tiverton the road went round and round to the left, it was narrow and I was going too fast, eventually I dug my right hand footrest into the earth bank and fell in a heap on the road. Both foot rests were now bent backwards but luckily only my pride was hurt. Dawn and dusk were worse than dark to ride in but I enjoyed seeing lots of wildlife.

DAVE, TONY AND I AT BUDE

At about 8.30 I found the house where Dave was staying. I didn't want to wake them all up so I sat down by the front door and fell asleep. The best thing I remember about this trip was going surfing with Dave and his brothers-in-law Chris and Tony.

On one trip John and I were riding to Dursley, we saw a sign saying 4 miles so after another half mile John stopped to look at the sign which said 4 1/2 miles to Dursley. I was also looking at the sign and riding slowly but I hit John's handlebar, we both fell in a heap on the floor.

Saturday nights for most of 1962 and '63 were spent in Cheltenham, the Aztec Coffee Bar, the Snooker Hall for an hour, the pub for a pint and then to the Clifton Ballroom. The dance was held above the Snooker Hall which was above John Collier Tailors, "the window to watch" according to the 60's TV advert, there was also a handy pub over the road. The dances were great, they used to have live bands. I'm not sure if there were ever any big names playing but some were very good. We'd go out for a quick pint then be back at the Ballroom before 11 o'clock. Hearing the Cliff Richard song, I'll be looking for you, we all agreed it must still be the record break, but it was a band. One poor band after being introduced started with Wipeout. They did the laugh at the start, twanged their guitars, all walked forward only to pull their jack plugs out and the music went dead. The 2nd time they were really good.

By this time the twist had come out which saved us really. John had tried to teach me the jive, I felt a bit of a pillock not knowing how to dance. John seemed to be good at everything, living near the town, he was more worldly wise. As it turned out we didn't have to jive, the twist and shake had just started, so we just stood there shaking it all about. The only time the boys danced together was when The Shadows FBI was played, or any good Shadows tune, we all did the Shadows Walk!

At midnight we went back to the Aztec coffee bar. Those that didn't have transport, little Tony Wilson and Stu Gray, would ride pillion. Bringing Stu back one time I started to overtake a lorry and totally misjudged it. I thought I was going to hit the car coming the other way, I slowed up pulling in very close to the lorry to miss the oncoming traffic shouting "sorry Stu" a reply came back "I was a bit concerned George"!

Friday nights would usually be spent in the Tabard pub, just over the road from the Bon Marche where my new friends worked.

One Saturday trip to the Aztec with John, Frank, Norman and Graham, as we went along Down Hatherley Lane we saw a pretty lady with a small motorcycle stopped so we stopped. The bike was a 98 James, the same as my mum told me she'd starting riding on. Big Frank said "hello Alice," it turned out they'd met on the Auto Cycle Union (ACU) training course, 'How to ride a motorcycle'. Alice said "hello Frank, hello George", I wondered who this pretty lady was that knew me.

Alice lived in Ash Lane with her husband Tony who rode motorcycles. He had several including a Triumph Tiger 110, which I used to look at when he went by, he also had a 500 single Norton International. They had two boys Robert 3, Dexter 4 and a daughter Jeanie 7. Believe it or not I was quite a shy person I only knew our next door neighbours, the children I went to school with, a girl called Diane Barnes who I used to walk home from the school bus and Lorraine Stevens who lived further down the Lane. After meeting Alice I now knew someone else up the Lane, we helped clean Alice's plug, got the bike going, then on to the Aztec.

One night at the Aztec I said "nearly half past nine, I'll go and fill up with petrol at the Jet Station" it was 6d per gallon cheaper and closed at 10. Norman, this quiet well brought up young man said "I'll race you." At this time we both had 350cc Royal Enfields. John Meadows dropped his hanky for the starter's flag, in what is now a pedestrianised area in Cheltenham.

41

We shot off up the High Street for 25 yards before turning sharp right into Bath Road, doing 50+ mph in the 30mph area and overtaking someone indicating right, luckily we didn't hit them. I can't remember who won but we filled up with petrol then back to the cafe at a more leisurely pace.

Arriving at the Aztec early one Saturday night, the wife of the owner was struggling to get a pram up the stairs, "we will carry it for you Mrs" she had already taken the baby up. Her hubby gave us 10 free records on the jukebox, we were dancing all night to songs by Little Eva, Dion, the Beatles, The Stones, Cliff and the Shadows etc. We'd get home at 2 o'clock in the morning. I remember dad threatening to chuck me out if I wasn't home by midnight, luckily he never carried out this threat!

On Sunday afternoon riding with John along Down Hatherley Lane, I crashed at the junction with Frogfurlong Lane. A minivan appeared to be parked, I looked behind and moved over as there was only John behind me, I was doing about 40 mph. Little did I realise that the van had been reversing, in those days there weren't reversing lights, his right indicator flashed once before he turned. I braked as hard as I could with 6 inch drum brakes, hitting the side of the van over the back wheel. Not only did I bend my front forks and wheel, but I squashed my finger. The police turned up. I had a letter to attend court as the police were prosecuting the driver for driving without due care and attention. With my brother's help I eventually got £26 compensation after having to go through a solicitor at Whiteman's. Mum told me they were the old family solicitors. There was a pretty lady there called Jenny, secretary to Mr Ring who was dealing with my case, a year older than me, I thought of chatting her up but she just got married.

I was bikeless for some weeks after the accident and was then working in Cheltenham so had a 7 mile ride every morning. Dewhurst had three shops, one of which was underneath the Aztec. This proved useful one night when Frank had his wallet stolen. He'd hung his coat up with the wallet in it at the Aztec, luckily the wallet had no money in it. We noticed it had been thrown out of the toilet window and was on the roof of one of the out buildings at the back of Dewhurst Butchers. There had been a gang of Gloucester Teddy boys, sort of wavy hair-style, long coats and tight trousers there.

The boys were good picking me up all the time, for the Aztec, Clifton Ballroom and the motorcycle scrambles that we'd started to attend. There were also lots of Bon Marché dances and events. One particular event was a treasure hunt ending up at Hartpury Village Hall. Luckily everyone knew where the finish was in case they got lost on the treasure hunt while trying to follow the clues, which was the case with Frank and I. Two, over 6 foot tall guys on a Piatti was a sight to be seen, and we got many rude comments.

We gave up on the treasure hunt when we were totally lost between Tewkesbury and Worcester and went to the Village Hall where there was dancing to Al Kessel and his Orchestra. We kept asking for Bee Bumble and the Stingers singing 'Nut Rocker' on the record break. When 'Come Outside' was playing I kept saying to this girl "come outside", she replied "no get off" as Wendy Richard did in the song.

My brother was by then a good car salesman and he helped me look for bikes. One night we went to see a 125 BSA Bantam. The man had spent £17 on it and was willing to accept this but my brother offered him £15 after asking him if he was the owner and if there was any credit owing on it as he'd learnt from the car trade. I was saying "Dave buy it, Dave buy it" the man didn't accept the £15.

Working in Cheltenham and walking around in the dinner hour I saw a nice shiny 175 cc Francis Barnett for £60. I couldn't wheel and deal in those days and bought it. My brother saw it "nice bike George but the big ends gone, who did you buy it off?" "Stephen's Car Dealers" Dave sort of huffed "I know of them, probably had it in PX for a car." Dave went over to see them. I assume he gave them either a roasting or spoke to them nicely under the old boys act but they fitted a new big end for me. The only trouble was that it was flat as a fart after they'd done it, it wouldn't pull the skin off a rice pudding. I even took the inner silencer out to make it go a little bit better, but it was very noisy. Luckily they didn't seem to mind so much in those days. Our gang was going to a scramble in Lydney, I could only just keep up with them but on the long hill to the scramble I had to get off and push the bike with the engine running in gear, very embarrassing.

With Dave's help we found the ignition timing was retarded, he put it right, but on starting up the bike it went backwards, Dave laughed at me! This isn't uncommon with a two-stroke, luckily after stopping and kick starting it again, it went forward and a lot quicker.

Back with the lads and we attended a motorcycle scramble near Cirencester. John had one of his many girlfriends on the back, Norman took Valerie from the Bon Mache but as Frank and I were girl-less we stopped for a pint in Cirencester and admired the girls. After leaving the pub, I was going flat-out along the Cirencester Road, this was the Roman Road, Ermine Street. Frank now had a 350 BSA B31 which was quicker than my 175 FB even though I had my chin on tank, feet on the back foot rests doing 70 mph.

All of a sudden I went across to the other side of road, the bike shaking like a bucking bronco, I thought I was off, I shut the throttle, I didn't know what was wrong. As the bike got slower so the wobble appeared to get worse but I managed to stay on. The back tyre was flat and I started pushing the bike. Frank came back and we took the back wheel out with the tools we'd started carrying on longer journeys. We took the wheel to a garage in Cirencester, the garages carried everything for car and motorcycle tyre repairs in those days. Frank shone his headlight for me as I put the wheel back in. On the way home it felt very peculiar so I rode home slowly. We'd pumped the tyre up way too hard causing the bike to bump all the way home.

John suggested a camping weekend away to see his sister in Kent. He borrowed a 6' x 3' tent. On the first night we got to Guildford after riding over the Hogs Back which I'd heard about. I was expecting something special but it was just a main road with a sort of a rise, not as big as Horsepools Hill. We got there about 10pm, found a pub, had a pint, and asked if there was anywhere we could put the tent up for the night. The Barman told us to go down the side of the pub, over a bridge to some grass. It was very dark with no streetlamps but we found it, somehow putting the tent up.

The next morning we found we were in the middle of a small housing estate, this was their green or play area with people walking dogs looking at us. A policeman cycled up and asked what we were doing there, we very respectfully replied "We're just leaving, we only stopped for the night officer, and the barman in the pub said we could camp here", "okay, but make sure you don't leave any rubbish," "no officer." Dave had told me not to give any cheek to the police, you'll only end up with a ticket. We were gone in 20 minutes.

I'm not sure why but we didn't get to see John's sister but ended up going to a scramble near Portsmouth after hearing that the Rickman brothers were riding. We had read about them in the motorcycle press, top scramble riders and a business making specialised scrambles bikes. My God could they ride, taking a leap and jumping six-foot or more in the air, we were gobsmacked to use a modern saying. Nearing the end of the day I started to panic, I couldn't find my small ignition key which allows you to start the bike. After walking all around the course we got to the bikes only to find I'd left the key in my bike. John called me a pillock!

Making our way home we stopped in a small wood. We'd started to run out of food and only had a tin of soup and some sausages left, so we boiled the sausages in the soup! On the ride home, it persisted down with rain. I had inherited my brother's Black Prince rubberised motorcycle suit. A common fault with the suit was that they split underneath the arm pits but considering it rained hard all the way home I was only damp under the arms and water had trickled down my scarf inside my jacket, so ended our 1st long distance trip.

Later in 62 John suggested that we go away for a week's camping holiday in Devon and Cornwall. John rode his Cotton and me the 175. The trip started off dry and we went the way my brother had helped us map out. We kept on the A39 coast road going up Porlock Hill, a very steep and scary hill, 1 in 3. My front wheel appeared to go very light going up but we both had our cases on the back of the bikes which didn't help. On the top road it started raining and blowing very hard. There were no villages or shelter so we were crouched behind a stone wall for ages. I was all for going home if it didn't clear up soon, wimp. Luckily it eased and we carried on into Lynmouth, down Countisbury Hill which wasn't as steep as Porlock but a lot longer. I was still learning to ride properly so I was using my brakes instead of being in a low gear. Nearing the end I was going 5 mph, which is fast when you can't stop, very scary. I hit a car with a bump, luckily no damage.

We found a cafe and while having a cuppa and bacon sandwich we saw photos of the Linton and Lynmouth Flood disaster of 1953. I remember seeing it on our new telly, I was only nine at the time. I don't know how many people died but when the ground was too wet to accept any more water there was another heavy rainstorm, the towns were in a gully.

1962 CAMPING WITH JOHN AT WOOLACOMBE

The weather brightened as we made it to Woolacombe. Riding through the small town we ended up camping on the dunes behind the beach. It was blowing hard so it took us ages to put the tent up as it kept blowing back down but were laughing. Next day we found a suitable pub. I watched out while John had a wash and shave in the toilet then John did the same for me, we did buy a pint.

We found a film showing in the local primary school. The chairs were small, hard and uncomfortable, but the film was good, The Sundowners with Robert Mitchum, we all wanted to look like him, some hopes! The morning of the 3rd day someone shook the tent "what are you doing here?" "Camping", "not allowed, if you're not off in two hours I'll call the police." Like Guildford, we were off in 20 minutes. It was cold and damp which probably helped us get going much quicker.

We got to Bude a few hours later as we weren't in a hurry, just enjoying the views. After finding a suitable campsite, we had a lazy couple of days swimming and surfing. The only trouble we had was the paraffin Primus was not working very well. We went to an ironmonger's store, stupidly leaving an egg cooking on a small flame. We told the man the problem, he sold us a jet pricker and a new top with holes in, where the flames come out. When we got back the egg was still not cooked but there was a quarter of an inch of soot on the bottom of the frying pan! It worked really well after we fitted the new bits, the only trouble was it flared up in the tent. We kicked it outside the tent, after the panic was over had another laugh.

On the third day we decided to move on to St Ives but it was so hot we chose to go for a swim before riding off on John's bike dressed in only swimming trunks, crash helmet and shoes, it certainly cooled us down.

St Ives is a beautiful town with very narrow streets. The campsite was better than the last one and luckily we had a very nice couple next door, Don and Greta Lesson from Coventry. They could see we only had a small

46

tent with all our bags and cases and offered to let us put our gear under their flysheet, that made it better but I still woke up with my feet outside! Another couple gave us a wind break, camping people are nice. John suggested we go on a mackerel fishing trip for 10 bob. As we were sailing out the boat bobbed up and down. The only sailing I'd done before was the trip to the Isle of Wight on a much bigger boat. John had gone to Austria on a school trip, dad couldn't afford it so I didn't go. I thought John would be the better sailor. We stopped, just bobbed up and down in one place, all having a fishing line with lots of hooks, and a feather on each hook. John asked me how I felt, "not very good, how are you?" "Not very good either." The man next to John was sick, strangely it was John that was sick next, then me, then the one next to me. In fact everybody sick but the captain, a man and his young son. Other than a slight pull on a line every so often nobody was really interested in fishing.

When the captain told us to bring in the lines there was a huge sigh of relief. He started the engine only to stop again somewhere else. The only ones that wanted to fish were the man and his son. After about 20 minutes we were all sick again. I asked the Captain if we could go home now, everyone agreed except the little boy. I think the captain could see we were all ready to throw him to the fish. He pulled in the lines and took us back. Everyone crashed onto the beach, just lying back groaning. At least the sun was shining.

At Lands End there was a first and last pub, a souvenir shop and a signpost saying John O'Groats 847 miles, London 347 miles, New York 4000 miles, another signpost said Biggleswade 331 miles with a group of people having a photo taken next to it. John and I looked at each other, "where the hell is Biggleswade?" You could pay to have the name of your town put on the signpost.

After a few more days we decided to make our way back, and said goodbye to everybody, especially Don and Greta who I stayed in touch with for many years. We'd mapped a route across Dartmoor. Halfway across the moor my bike started wobbling, pulling up we found the back wheel spokes were all loose with at least one broken. John took as many of the cases and bags as he could carry and left behind the wind break and anything else that we didn't need. It was some relief when we got to the A38 and saw a sign to Newton Abbot but that's when the back wheel completely collapsed. Luckily we were near a farm, after explaining our situation the farmer let us pitch our tent and sold us some milk and eggs.

We had the tent up early enough to get into the Newton Abbot and asked at the railway station the cost of getting the bike home to Gloucester. I replied in a loud voice "six quid!!" We went to the local motorcycle shop "how much to rebuild a wheel?" "£3-10/-" So that was sorted. We explained the situation and asked how long it'd take as we had to get back to work and were told 2 days at most. We went for a pint that night, as there wasn't enough time to get back, take the wheel out and get back before it closed. In the pub we saw an advert for a fair the next night.

Early the next morning we took the wheel to the bike shop then went to the fair, we had a great time. Next day we went to Torquay on John's bike. Looking around the shops we saw a hairdressers, John talked me into having a posh 'TV haircut', two big waves at the front and square cut at back cost, 10/–. It didn't last long wearing a helmet. Once wheel was fitted it was good to go home.

CHAPTER 3   1962/63-The racing bug bites

The swinging 60s, were a bit of daze for me as so much seemed to be happening. In 1962 James Bond 007's first film, Dr No with Sean Connery was released, I've been a fan ever since. The Telstar satellite was launched; Telstar by the Tornadoes was number 1 in UK and America and was produced by Joe Meek who was born in Glos, and Gloucester Cotton Motorcycles launched The Telstar road racer. I was now 18, old enough to drink and everyone had just got over the worrying Cuban missile crisis.

A car salesman by the start of the 60s, David was keen and asked me to test him on car types from Glass's Guide, the traders hand book. I spent hours asking him questions, as I did in the early 50s when he was learning about steam trains! As a reward, he gave me a ride in a TR2 at 100 mph, my stomach was in my mouth, everything was shaking, it was very exciting. It was similar to when he was lent a 500 Matchless twin and treated me to a ride on the back for cleaning it saying, "I'm going to try and do a ton." It vibrated between 50 and 70 mph, I hung on tight to Dave, over 70 mph it smoothed out, we got up to 90 mph!

Dave and Dennis Coombs, after working together for 2 years decided to start their own car business. A group of us helped them do a Tarmac drive. Dave & Dennis treated us to a meal as a thank you. We all crammed into a big car to go to Stroud where a restaurant was doing a promotion. If anyone could eat their special, all meals would be free, I was up for it. However, there was a pea soup fog so thick that after I'd walked in front of the car for a mile Dave suggested we go to the New Inn instead, so Bernie steaks all round.

The 175cc Francis Barnett was going reasonably well but I was worried about the back wheel so I was pleased when Dave found me a 350cc Royal Enfield Bullet. I made a cock up of selling the 175. Someone offered me £37, but I refused it after seeing an advert in MCN "we buy bikes for cash in Swindon and pay your rail fare home." The salesman only offered me £30 "but I have been offered £37," he told me to wait for the manager who offered me £20, I was spitting blood "your salesman offered me £30," he said I should have accepted but that he'd give me the rail fare and the chrome badges off a 350 cc Royal Enfield they had in the showroom. I accepted and hoped that the back wheel would collapse on them; I know, nasty bastard.

The first job on my new bike was to follow Dave to Frome, Somerset where he was trying to sell a black Triumph Herald, it didn't reach the reserve so we stopped at car showrooms on the way home- no sale, but he still gave me 10/- for petrol. The 350cc Bullet was much quicker than the 175cc and I started meeting more bikers in the Roma Café. I always ended up having a race with Jim Davies, he was two up with his wife Marcy but on a 500cc Norton Dominator.

At the 1962 Christmas Eve Bon Marché party I heard, "hello George" It was Ronnie Vickers from primary school days. I ended up taking him home and he suggested going to midnight mass. After mass I went to Frank's for the open invite Christmas Eve party. Mrs P, as we called Frank's mum said "you're late George," "sorry Mrs P I've been to midnight mass". I was in her good books for ever more, just as Frank was with my mum, he always wore a suit as he worked in the offices at Bon Marché. Mum used to ask "why don't you, John and Norman wear a suit like Frank instead of wearing those jeans?" "But mum, Frank drinks" John and Norman agreed in unison, Frank defended himself "don't you believe them Mrs Ridgeon", "I shan't Frank you're lovely." Grrr!

That Christmas was nearly a disaster. Dave & Sue with one-year-old Julie Caroline and a baby on the way (born January 10th Sally Louise) came over for Christmas' dinner, father collapsed unconscious at the dinner table. Dave and I carried him into the bedroom; after coming round he spent the rest of the day very quietly.

He was the same on Boxing Day. I'd arranged to see Ronnie Vickers so dad asked me to give his regards to his family as he'd worked with Ronnie's dad at Dowty Rotol. While talking about the Christmas parties at Dowty Rotol, Ronnie's dad reminded me of the time dad had collapsed in the Trichloroethylene pit, luckily his colleagues had rescued him. On the way home it started to snow, I was following a gritter, well a lorry with two men in the back shovelling out rock salt.

Dad went to work on his Bantam the next day in the snow, Dowty Rotol would stop bank holiday pay if you had the next day off. He collapsed at work and was taken to hospital before being brought home. He was on the sick for months, frustrated with mother fussing round!

I was working in Cheltenham with Stan Dex at a small Eastman's butcher's shop in London Road. I can't remember the number of times I fell off going to or coming home from work. The first few days weren't too bad as the snow was soft but with frosts and more snow it became hard packed; no let up from working in a butcher's shop which was already cold.

The snow didn't stop the gang from wanting to go out. The first Saturday night after Christmas, we all met at Norman's house in Escort Road and decided not to ride to Cheltenham but get a bus. As we waited for the bus the snow was coming down and settling on our hair, someone commented "you look like a monster" we all started singing The Monster Mash, twisting away in the snow while the others in the queue laughed at us. There followed a night in Cheltenham with a train ride home.

Little Tony organised a party in Morton Street which was near Frank's place. The main roads were kept clear but there was a lot of snow on the side roads. I took a bottle of cider as it was a bring-a-bottle party. Things looked good, lots of girls, much twisting and drinking, but I got more tiddly than usual. When someone pushed me I twisted and crashed into a glass panel. I started being sick, they stuck my head under the tap in the kitchen then took me outside until my hair started freezing, it was -10° C. I didn't take much part in the rest of the party, just slumped in a chair being sick every so often, probably somebody spiked my drinks. At the end of the party Frank carried me out and walked me about two miles with me being sick every so often and saying "I want to die."

Frank could see I wasn't fit to ride home so he plonked me on the couch, no blankets so I shivered all night. To make matters worse their dog was shuffling around which made me wonder if someone was coming down the stairs. In the morning Mr Prentice saw me, "what the bloody hell is this doing on the couch?" Mrs P came to my defence and Frank explained that I'd been too ill to ride home. A cup of tea was all I could face, turning down the breakfast offered. When I felt well enough I rode home and went straight to bed, luckily it was Sunday.

It wasn't long before I started wearing two pairs of trousers and numerous vests under a shirt and tie - which you had to wear in the Butcher shop in the 1960's.

It was still two months before my 19th birthday, and on turning up to work one day I found Mr Dex's 13-year-old daughter stood shivering on the doorstep, she told me her dad was very poorly and gave me the keys to the shop. "Okay," I said, "tell dad I'll pop round tonight". Mr Dex had suggested that I go to night school for meat technology classes. It was good learning about the job I was doing. I phoned head office to let them know about Mr Dex. Norman Davies arrived in the afternoon, found the shop all up and running and customers being served. He made a complimentary remark then asked me if I could do the manager's job. In a surprised voice I replied "Yes Mr Davis, I think so." He offered me £12 a week which was £4 a week more than I was getting, with travelling expenses of £1-5/-. I was rolling in money. Although I saved most of it due to mum's frugal teachings, I did part with some of it when I saw a pair a cowboy boots reduced to £5. They were a size too big but I wore two pairs of socks and did I feel like a rocker. As the Fonz would say, "real cool man." I was manager for three weeks as Stan had pneumonia and was quite poorly.

The winter got worse with temperatures as low as -20°C. There were days when there was a slight thaw making the roads much worse because instead of hard packed snow we had frozen slush to ride over. Dad was 'on the sick' for many months, he had angina and was on numerous pills, making him frustrated. He told me tales of how fit he used to be. When he lived in Wales he'd walk home from Cardiff to Pontypridd, 15 miles just to see the star of the day. He worked down the pit and boxed. He made me laugh telling me about coming to Gloucester in 1930 because there wasn't much work around at the time, getting off the train from Wales, he said "your mother was waiting on the platform of the railway station and grabbed me up"; mum would give him a friendly clip! At this point I would like to say thank you to Mike Smith big brother of John Smith who I went to school with. When dad returned to work, Mike detoured from Gloucester to pick him up until he was fully fit to ride his motorcycle.

The only positive thing about dad being on the sick was it released his 150cc Bantam as a spare machine. I was riding it, probably because it was easier to ride than my 350cc Royal Enfield over the frozen slush, it was much lighter making it easier to pick up when I fell off! On one trip I rode at 2 mph with both feet down, I'd even tried riding on the grass verge. I had to keep stopping every few hundred yards as I was sweating despite it being -10°C, it seemed to take ages getting home. The shop was so cold we used to stand in the fridge to drink our tea.

There used to be some pretty ladies that came into the shop, one had big eyes so Stan used to call her "Goo Goo eyes," I was often cheeky when she came in with her little girl. The shop was quiet one day, she leaned forward showing me more of her ample chest and whispered "George do you like me?" in a sultry voice, reminding me of Fenella Fielding the actress who always played the femme-fatal! I immediately went red and taking a big gulp stammered "well, well, well, of course I like you, I like all customers," there was an opportunity missed!

At Christmas a buxom lady customer came in. We had put the decorations up including mistletoe. This lady was in her mid 30's I was still 18, she grabbed hold of me kissing me long and passionately in front of all the other customers, another red face, I was all talk. Stan used to pull my leg something rotten!

We rode our bikes over to the Aztec once the roads were kept clear, well the main ones anyway. On one clear frosty night making our way home, Frank was carrying Stuart who was the only extra passenger, Norman and I started racing from the Rotunda up the short stretch to 'the garage on the roundabout' as we called it. Cranking left my back wheel came around and I slid off just as Norman and his Royal Enfield came sliding past, it must have been black ice. Luckily only our pride was hurt, unlike the night I was going home with John and he fell off in the snow. I helped him up but found out the next day that he'd been rushed into hospital, his spleen ruptured.

We'd started reading MCN, following motorcycle racing, as well as scrambling, trails and grass track which was the only motorcycle sport close to us though enjoyable enough. I'd been to Silverstone on the back of Dave when younger, mum and dad took me to various scrambles, grass tracks and even Speedway once. I remember a funny smell, found out it was Castrol R burning which was to become a drug for me!

Our gang went to watch a scramble at John Draper's Farm, Prestbury. It was very thrilling seeing a row of 30 riders rushing towards a narrow gateway. We attended many local scrambles, as well as watching it on TV on Saturdays. We would be shouting at the TV for the particular rider we had picked. This one race, Jeff Smith, the Rickman brothers, David Bickers and Pat Lampkin were neck and neck with half a lap to go when the BBC commentator said "we are leaving to go horseracing." I was jumping up and down, I even wrote to the BBC, what made it worse was that the horses were only in the parade ring!

We started watching TT clips on TV and listening to radio reports, hearing names like John Surtees, Mike Hailwood and Phil Read, Mike was winning everything at that time. July 1963 we went on 2 bikes to watch the Commonwealth Trophy Meeting at Thruxton Airfield, a round trip of 130 miles. When we arrived we were overwhelmed by the number of parked bikes to look at, British bikes including BSA, Triumph, Royal Enfield, AJS big Twins, as well as BMWs and other exotic bikes, even an MV Agusta.

Sadly Mike Hailwood wasn't there but Phil Read was. The last race of the day was the unlimited final. Phil had a bad push start with 40 machines roaring away and leaving him in the back half riding a Petty-tuned Norton. A big 1000cc Vincent twin took the lead for most of the race with Phil catching up. At the start of the last lap Phil was right behind him as they disappeared from our view on the start and finish line, on the approach to the chequered flag Phil squeezed past the Vincent to take the win. On the way home we stopped at a pub still full of the excitement of the day.

The next week on my half-day I was, as usual, looking in Lundyguard Motorcycles, Gloucester. The shop was long so there were plenty of bikes on display. I was looking through the open workshop double doors, drooling and watching the mechanic working. Geoff Fivash, told me they were building racing Bantams, after I had told him about Thruxton I asked, "can I have a look?" I must have sounded enthusiastic, as he told me to come down to the workshop off Southgate Street.

With John Meadows to hold my hand, I was still a little shy, we found the workshop down a cobbled lane. Geoff introduced us to Dave Hughes and Knocker Coldrick (I never knew his real first name), they were preparing their 125cc BSA Bantams. The design was taken from the German DKW factory, and was called the RT125; after WW2 it was named the BSA Bantam after its makers, the Birmingham Small Arms Co. which had started out making guns for the British Army in 1861. If you were lucky, the road version of the Bantam had a top speed of 45 mph, as mum and dad's one did, and on which I'd been 1000s of miles, oh my sore bum! Geoff told us that George Todd, with help from George Harris, had tuned one to do 100 mph!

John and I were crammed into the small workshop drinking in the atmosphere as there were Bantam bits everywhere. I asked Geoff if he'd help me start building a racing Bantam, "yes, but you have to bring your own hack saw blades." Today they're unbreakable but in 1963 if you looked at them, they broke.

Geoff was very patient and explained some basic tuning principles: "a high compression head, larger carburettor, altering the exhaust port height and making the inlet port larger will make the bike much quicker." I would go and see him to try and learn more about tuning my bike, often taking some meat from the butchers shop with me as bribery after all, he was married with two children!

John showed some interest in buying some Bantam bits but, as he liked girls more I ended up buying his bits adding them to the bike I'd already bought in bits for £2 and another bike bought for £5.

John and I had another holiday in September 1963. We arrived in Blackpool and made camp. John had borrowed a larger tent this time which we slept in and used the small one for our cases, luxury! We rode into town and parked on the Golden Mile. We had a pint and the required bag of chips, just walking up and down drinking in the atmosphere of Golden Mile, 7 miles of lights before bed, we were knackered after the long ride, not many motorways in those days.

A swim in the sea in the morning then a trip around the funfair, it was the biggest we'd ever seen. It cost 5/- to go into the fun house, then everything was free. I think it was supposed to be for small children but there were many other adults, older than us, using the various slides, rides and a spinning platform that people sat on, sliding off in all directions when it started spinning around.

Near Blackpool Tower John noticed a roller skating rink, he could skate and after some persuasion I agreed to have a go. The rink was huge, a type of slate. We strapped on the roller boots and John was out in the middle strutting his stuff whilst I was hanging onto the bar and walking round the outside, every so often I would let go and fall over. A little 10-year-old girl took a shine to me, showing off her roller skating skills and making me feel brave enough to go out into the middle. The inevitable happened, arms and legs in all directions, as the Beano and Dandy comics used to say "crash, bang and wallop," I was lying on the floor groaning. As I got onto my hands and knees I had a cold sensation around my backside, I'd split my white holiday trousers from the front to the back. I crawled off the rink on all fours, making my way to a lady that looked like a mother! "Excuse me have you got a safety pin, I've split my trousers?" In a loud voice she replied "you've split your trousers!!" I whispered "yes, but could you please stop shouting, I'm embarrassed." This cuddly lady who reminded me of Peggy Mount in comedy sketches on TV and films of the 1950s said "there's no need to be embarrassed young man" making me go even redder, but she gave me some pins. Having taken off the boots I walked, well limped, to 'the little boys' room.' As I was attempting to pin my trousers together John came in "what's the matter George?" As I explained he just laughed but said that he could solve the problem and came back with his Belstaff motorcycle over trousers. John persuaded me to go back roller-skating for another 30 minutes before a pint, chips and sleep. Next day looking around the shops, we saw how much it was to go up the Tower, 6/–, much too expensive, the price of a 1½ gallons of petrol! We decided to buy food for a big cook-up. We laid back feeling bloated, enjoying a sunny day listening to the radio. This was long before Radio 1 and 2, we had the pleasure of listening to Victor Sylvester and his orchestra. Then we dozed off for an hour. John later persuaded me to go roller-skating again, I think he was a sadist at heart. This time I was wearing his over trousers at the start which helped protect me a little *as* I was still suffering. We then spent some time looking at the girls as they strolled up and down the prom.

We were only 40 miles from Liverpool so decided to find the Cavern Nightclub where the Beatles had performed. The trip went ok but coming into Liverpool we had never seen so many sets of traffic lights, they had some strange pedestrian crossing lights as well with white, red and amber Xs, luckily no one wanted to cross when we were passing as we weren't sure if we were supposed to go over the X! We parked our bikes near the Town Hall, crash helmets placed underneath the bikes, and walked around, looking in a motorcycle shop, The Bee, which had some nice bikes. We kept asking people "where is the Cavern Nightclub please?" We eventually found it and joined the queue. When we got to the entrance the doorman said "you can't go in" we asked why, trying to be respectful and not to upset anybody as they all looked a bit rough, tough and very big. "You've got dungarees on" was the reply, "these aren't dungarees they're Jeans "we replied, in his broad Liverpool accent the doorman said "they're dungarees up here" we pleaded "we have a shirt and tie on, we've just ridden 40 miles to get here" "Push off, you can't come in, you've got dungarees on". I wish we had the courage to take our Jeans off and go in our underpants but having been embarrassed with split trousers....... We eventually gave up, and went to the pictures. It turned out to be a very good film, Albert Finney in Tom Jones which is a bawdy comedy so we had a really good belly laugh. Getting back late we had a warm cuppa, more biscuits and a short discussion on whether we should go back in trousers another night, deciding no, before head hitting the pillow.

Next day we found a coffee bar where the jukebox was playing The Shadows Wonderful Land, that evening it was to the pictures to see The Longest Day which I still think is one of the best D-Day war films. Next day, John scalded himself making a cup of tea so it was down to the hospital for a tetanus injection and burn dressing before we went back to the fairground ending up in the fun house. John, with his burn kept off the rotating platform. After I'd slid off 2 or 3 times, me with my big mouth suggested "why don't we all hold on to one another?" we did, staying on a little longer, but as the speed went up everyone slid off in one direction with my arm underneath. I had a large friction burn on my wrist, so down to the hospital, tetanus injection and dressing, again.

The time for going home was approaching and looking around the souvenir shops I saw just the thing for dad. It was half a cup, when mum asked "do you want another cuppa?" "Just half a cup" dad would reply. We set off home feeling a little sad the holiday was over. After passing Strensham Services, a bit of a biker's haunt in the 60s, we were on the last bit of the trip. We joined the A38 through Tewkesbury and were racing past the King's Head pub, as we approached the Down Hatherley turning we gave the thumbs up sign to each other, I turned off and John accelerated past.

When I got home mum and dad were as pleased to see me as I was to see them. It's true, absence does make the heart grow fonder! Mum put the kettle on, as she poured me a cup, "do you want a cup dad?" she asked, she called dad, dad as we were both George, "just half a cup" he replied. I enthusiastically shouted "hang on I've got the very thing for you dad" I gave him the half-cup making them both laugh.

In October Frank went to Birmingham to train as a fireman, he'd joined Gloucester City Fire Brigade. He returned each Friday night and we met up at the Tabard Inn. We lost him for any midweek help but at least we didn't get drunk as often!

Frank's Bon Marché leaving party in August 1963 was at the East End Tavern. I ate my usual faggots, mash and peas and apple pie while watching the New Mersey Sound on the TV. I arrived late at the pub, music was playing so a swift cider shandy and two quick twists. I started feeling

57

DANCING WITH DOREEN WHILE HOWARD PLAYS A MEAN GUITAR

a little queasy, not surprising after the big meal I'd eaten earlier. I was standing outside the gents toilet when a young lady came up to me that I'd previously gone out with but who packed me up; perhaps my hands had wandered too far when kissing her goodnight. I was surprised when she asked to go out with me again, just at that moment I felt I was going to be sick, "excuse me I'll be back." After bringing up my dinner I felt much better and went in to join the dancing after saying "okay we'll fix up a date sometime" and had a dance with her before joining the boys. She later came over and said "my friend would like to go out with Norman, can we make up a foursome?" Norman, who by then, had had a few pints asked, "where is she?" She pointed at a group of girls, "oh all right," so we made a date to meet outside the General Post Office on Sunday night.

Norman and I were waiting outside the GPO when a double-decker bus pulled up 50 yards away. I easily saw mine as she was much taller than the other girl who had a timid looking face and mousey hair. Norman said "my god she's got a beard, I'll kill you" I replied "I think I'll kill myself, can we do a runner?" Norman answered "I don't think so, they've seen us." Jane was introduced, "hello, shall we go for a drink in the Fleece Hotel?"

So started a difficult evening, Norman and I kept going to the boys room, he said "she doesn't even speak, just sits and stares at me answering yes or no to any question." I was being rotten, "it's because you are so handsome Norm, I'd fancy you myself if I was a girl," "that's not funny George!" The evening came to an end when we told them we'd got to get home as we'd got work early in the morning. Norman gave me grief for many weeks, I kept apologising adding, "but you did say okay"!

The second break-up with the young lady came after another 'bring a bottle party' when a Bon Marche' employee's parents were away. As usual there was music, dancing, kissing and cuddling; the evening was going well in the large three bed council house. One of the lads said to his girl "do you want to go upstairs?" She enthusiastically replied "okay" so I, with tongue in cheek to my young lady said "shall we go upstairs?" "Yes please." With this reply, if I had been stood up I would have fallen over. We found an empty bedroom, trouble was, after about 20 minutes of lying on the bed fully clothed kissing and cuddling, all was going well when someone knocked on the door, "what are you doing in our bedroom?" resulting in "take me home" from my young lady. As it was 1 o'clock in the morning I went back to the house and kipped on the floor with many other bodies until I was woken up about 3am with "can you run Valerie home?" I was the only one with transport; the only bonus was Valerie gave me a nice kiss goodnight as a thank you.

The next morning the boys went for a swim. A couple of lads had love bites which couldn't be seen when dressed, at least they'd had a good night. When I got home Auntie Win was visiting, back home from Canada on a six-month sabbatical, "George what were you doing last night?" I tried to answer in a matter-of-fact voice "I went to a leaving party Aunty Win", "I hope you didn't drink any alcohol, George", "Aunty Winifred how can you say such a thing" thinking, if she only knew what I was trying to do!

GRAHAM, NORM AND A TIDDLY ME WITH THE BON MARCHE GIRLS

The Bon Marché 'Bring a bottle parties' started in a disused basement in Spa Road near Gloucester Park, they were all the rage at the time as nobody could afford to pay for a party. Although there was just a record player, it was packed with dancers. The plan was to sleep there but as Norman was 17, his sister Bunny turned up to collect him. Norman asked if I wanted to sleep on his couch. I'd just settled down when his dad came in "what's this doing here?" Luckily, as my motorcycle was down at the party, I was left on the couch. Norman took me back in the morning for my bike. It looked like a bomb site, bodies everywhere. We laughed at big Frank sleeping in a pram and someone else in the bathtub!

At another party I was talking to a girl called Brenda. She'd been going out with Frank but earlier Frank had told me that she liked me more, this at least made up for the girl Frank took off me. The party was at another Bon Marché employee's home, Josephine Zecker, very pretty. Brenda lived only 500 yards away from the party so I parked my bike at her house, but when she told me to come in and meet her parents I tried to say no, but she insisted. A joke amongst the boys was that if you met the parents you are half way to getting married. I was as pleasant as I could be but felt very awkward, so suggested we'd better get going as we didn't want to be too late. The party was a little subdued, well it started that way, as Jo's mum was sat in the room with us, just drinking, talking and some dancing, enjoyable enough. Norman was sat down on the couch drinking from one bottle another in his hand, but the booze was running out so somebody asked Norm for his unopened bottle of beer, "I'll swap the beer for a fag", "okay", the chap had taken the beer and began handing his cigarettes to everyone but when he got to Norman the cigarettes were gone "sorry mate none left." Hearing that Norman snatched the cigarette out of his mouth saying "I'll have this one then". Talk about "us and them," it was just like a scene from West Side Story, two gangs facing up to one another. I was saying to myself *hit him Norman* which wasn't normal for me, obviously too many cider shandies! You could have cut the atmosphere with a knife, we were all staring at one another when the mother said, "have one of my fags" which calmed the situation down. At this time Brenda asked me to walk her home, outside in the fresh air I felt better and rode back to the party. Frank told me that when I went out the front door one of the other gang was watching me so he was watching him; we decided to all leave together. Sadly the relationship with Brenda did not last. Although she was very nice, she wouldn't come on the back of my bike, as Frank used to say, "Love me, Love my bike."

Another ruined evening which had started off well was in the Tabard Inn. There were a few us having a pint with Howard, who used to play a mean guitar at the Bon Marché dances. Whilst chatting we noticed a lady in her late 30s with a girl we knew from Bon Marché, Sylvia who was the sister of Sheila, another Bon girl. At a much earlier party Sheila had stopped me helping a girl being sick, for some reason I thought taking her clothes off might help!!!! It turned out it was Sylvia's 21st birthday and one of her neighbours had brought her out for a drink. We joining the ladies and were having a good time. Unfortunately I'd agreed to take Howard home but he didn't mind going to the girl's house for a drink first, so I pushed my bike as we walked with the girls. As we didn't want to drink any more alcohol we had tea and biscuits when somehow I ended up in Sylvia's bedroom. Perhaps she said "I feel tired" and as a gentleman I suggested I tuck her in!

After about 30 minutes she was in her nightdress when Howard started banging on the door shouting "when are you taking me home?" another night of passion ruined, I felt like chucking him in the river!

Friday nights were usually spent at the Tabard catching up with what Frank had done learning to be a fireman, we were amazed at what he had to do and told him about our progress on the Bantam racer. I remember Friday 22nd November 1963, President Kennedy was assassinated, Norman came in with his hand inside his coat, as if to get out a gun from a holster, "I have just flown in from Dallas" he said!

One Friday Frank was in the pub looking sadder than normal. When asked what was up he started his saga. "Well starting with my 350cc BSA, it was stolen in Birmingham, so I had a miserable bus ride home and my girl had packed me in" We gave him lots tea, well beer and sympathy. We talked the usual rubbish, "you'll find another" and helped him drown his sorrows; at least we cheered him up somewhat or was it that we made him forget his sorrows?

Outside, at chucking out time we were still trying to console Frank. Someone gave Frank a cigarette which he dropped trying to light it, he squatted down, but couldn't get back up. This was the first time since I'd met Frank that I'd had seen him so tiddly that he couldn't get up! We helped him onto the back of Norman's bike and told him to make sure he hung on. I followed on my bike, Graham on his. Although we all knew Mrs Prentice, Frank's mum, Graham had gone to school with Frank and knew her best, so we persuaded him to take Frank in. We were chatting outside when 2 lads bumped into us. They took a karate stance "We'll fight you," we replied "why do you want to do that?" we didn't want to have a punch-up, certainly not outside Franks mums! "Just because you're bigger than us were not scared" It took 10 minutes to persuade them we didn't want to have a fight, we were helping our friend. Luckily, they calmed down and we all shook hands. Meanwhile Graham had carried Frank upstairs.

Frank, Norman, John and I were all still searching for the right girl until one night, John met Dorothy. Until then he'd kept coming to the garage even after I'd bought his Bantam bits. The main reason was that Geoff was a great teacher, both of us were learning all about bikes. He gave us so much advice and showed me how to tune an engine. When talking about the bike to Frank's dad he said "I've an electric drill, would you like to borrow it?" Saying yes turned out to be a mistake because when grinding my cast iron barrel I burnt out the drill. Having it repaired cost nearly the same as a new one at £5. I ended up buying one as I still had a lot of work to do. The most expensive job to have done was the welding, it was either 5/- or 10/- a time, I was only earning £6.50 a week.

During November I was working in Ross-on-Wye. One frosty Saturday night I was rushing home looking forward to a Bon Marché dance. After going under a railway bridge, I approached a right-hand bend, shut the throttle, but it had frozen open. I remember crashing through branches, when I stood up I could see nothing, *am I dead?* I thought, then a voice said "are you okay?" I was in 8 foot ditch, it took an hour to get the bike out. I never got to the dance. John took me to collect the bike; luckily the only damage was a missing headlight glass and a sore shoulder.

Frank's 'chucking out do' at Birmingham Central Fire Station was Friday 20th December. I asked to leave Lydney early, where I was then working at Eastman's Butchers, as I was being picked up by Pat Slatter, also from the Tabard days, with John and Dorothy and Norman. We found the fire station and parked up, and finding Frank heading for the bar, as I wasn't driving I ordered a "Vodka Martini with a twist of lemon, shaken not stirred," I'd just seen From Russia with Love, the second Bond movie, it cost me 3/4d.

The 'chucking out do' was in a large function room with a parquet floor that was usually used for lectures. The band was playing some good rock 'n' roll. In one of the breaks Norman and I asked them if they could play a Beatles number, "we'll play it if you sing it" Vroom, Vroom, both of us into reverse gear declining the offer.

On the way home we were somewhat tiddly, it was a good job Patrick was driving, he was a sensible drinker. In his lovely black Austin Cambridge saloon, after going around the centre several times we couldn't find the way out. It was only 20 years since the end of WW2, large towns were still having bomb damage repaired so there were roadworks everywhere. Seeing a policeman, I unsteadily got out and asked the way to Gloucester, he pointed the way and Pat gave him the thumbs up as off we went, he was concerned in case the policeman came over.

Monday was the day before Christmas Eve and it was cold again. I arrived at work at 8am wearing my dad's large army style coat which came below my knees, it was covered in frost. I was cutting whatever was on the block and drinking several cups of tea. Norman Brown said "George, to save you going home tonight I'll pay for you to stop at The White Hart Pub, as you won't get many tips" but he really wanted me to get in earlier next day. I rang our Dave to ask him to tell mum and dad I wouldn't be home that night. The landlady, of German origin, came over "Vhat do you Vont for yor evening meal?" looking at Mr Brown I asked "can I have sirloin steak please?" After the meal, finding there was a bath, I soaked as long as possible, seeing a hot water bottle, I filled it from the hot tap then found one in the bed already, such luxury.

At Breakfast, "do you vant Cornflakes or Veetabix?", "can I have bacon and eggs please, I've got a long day in front of me?" She replied in a schoolmistress type voice "you vill have zee eggs, zee bacon, zee sausage and zee beans after" and after all that it was followed by toast and marmalade. I felt a right fool, not far off 20 and I'd never stopped in a bed and breakfast before. Well set up for a day's work then home before Christmas Eve at Frank's home.

When we left Frank's, Norman couldn't walk so Graham started to carry him with Norm's arm around his shoulder, I pushed my bike and walked with them. After a few hundred yards we passed a Fruit and Veg. shop with dozens of Christmas trees scattered outside, we picked the smallest. There I am, pushing my Royal Enfield with a 2 foot Christmas tree in one hand and my helmet in the other. As we walked down Barton Street passing the Ritz Cinema, Graham bumped into some lads who shouted at us, Graham shouting back at them. A policeman was bearing down on us, "Graham quiet, a policeman is coming." "Excuse me sir what is the number of this motorcycle?" I stuttered "G G GTW 345," "where did you get the Christmas tree?" I was trying to think of something to say other than "we stole it," Graham came to my rescue "I gave it him." The policeman said to Norman "you can go on Sir, while I talk to these 2 gentlemen." Graham lent Norman against a shop window, he gradually slid down until he was slumped on the floor.

Graham started "just because you're working on Christmas Eve…." I whispered "Graham for Christ sake, stop being a pillock." He eventually said "I found it officer," the policeman asked where he'd found it, we persuaded him that the Christmas trees had been all over the road. He took our names and addresses, saying "if we have a Christmas tree reported stolen, I'll be after you" with relief in my voice I replied "thank you officer, good night." I finally got home after dropping off Norman and running Graham home. Next morning I was up, as early as my head would let me, to go with Dave and dad for the traditional Christmas pint up at the Kings Head, Norton then Christmas day this year at Dave and Sue's as dad now had a dickey ticker. I celebrated New Year on Gloucester Cross with hundreds of others welcoming in 1964.

The first test area Geoff found was down a lane to the River Seven only used by farmers, between Haw Bridge and the village of Tirley. Geoff parked his car and trailer and got the bikes off, my Bantam was taxed so I rode there, once there I took off the silencer. It was a little hairy to say the least, as the lane was only wide enough for one vehicle, it was bumpy at 60+ mph, we each took our turn!

There were many WW2 airfields on land which had been returned to farmers, still in good condition, certainly good enough for testing Bantams, if you could find them. I'd been sent to Cirencester for Dewhurst and as I was there for 2 weeks I went for a haircut and asked everyone if there were any old airfields locally. One customer told me to try at Long Newton. On the way home I found the farmer and explained that we were starting Bantam racing and asked if we could use the runway for testing. In those days life was a little easier, "No problem, I like bikes myself" he said. There was plenty of area to test flat out, also a small turning area to race around. On one trip there I was trying to bump start my Bantam, I missed my footing just as the bike started. I was being dragged along unable to reach the front brake and the throttle wide open unable to shut it off, I had to let the bike go. Didn't the others laugh, I wasn't the only one to do this over the weeks of testing, but I did feel like a fool at the time.

I'd made a modification to the Bantam after reading in MCN that Cotton had made a metal air scoop for the carburettor on the Telstar racer, *so* bashing a bit of corrugated iron flat, I made a similar one. Geoff had found a test area near Pershore, only about 20 miles away. Starting out early Sunday morning, I was riding through Tewkesbury when there was a horrible bang. I pulled over and had to strip the bike down in the main street near the war memorial. After taking off the cylinder head and barrel, I saw some bits of metal. It was the remains of the bolt from my go faster air scoop, I hadn't fitted a locking washer. I called myself some nasty names. I became aware of a policeman watching me "where is your tax disc?" I took it out of my pocket and showed him "the bracket's broken" he nodded "okay, where's your Speedo cable?" "That broke, I'm waiting for a replacement," "can I see your licence?" Luckily I carried it with me after my £2 speeding fine 2 years before.

The bolt holding my special air scoop had fallen down the carburettor and been chopped in half, one half stuck very firmly in the piston, the other bit was sitting on the transfer port. I removed it and seeing no more problems reassembled the engine. When I'd finished and as I was putting my bag of tools on my back the policeman asked "you don't expect it to go do you?" "As I'm putting the bike into gear ready to push I hope so officer." I heard a lovely pop, pop, pop sound, and off I went waving to him as he stood and watched with his mouth open. We had another good test day although later I had to scrap the piston with the piece of metal stuck in it, just in case!

As I was working in Cheltenham and my 1st race was 4 weeks away, Geoff asked me to collect some racing leathers from a friend of his, Tim Miles in Winchcombe Street, not far from Williams Motorcycles. He'd fixed up for me to borrow a set off Ron Hamlin who had a lovely G45 Matchless, unusually, though he only had one eye!

Four of us had entered the first meeting of the season with the Bantam Racing Club (BRC) at Snetterton in Norfolk on 27th of March costing £2/10 with insurance. I had to get a parent to sign as I was under 21, I asked mum, as I was too scared to ask dad and it was easier to get around mum. Our first race was on Good Friday it was now mid-February. Geoff asked how I was going to get to the meeting, I looked blankly at him "I don't know, can I come with you?" "I'm taking Dave and Knocker, it's only a 3 bike trailer. Why not get a motorcycle combination and put a flat board on it, many others do?"

Lundyguard didn't have any combinations so I went to Mead and Tomkinson in London Road by the railway bridge. The salesman took me on a route march across the road, they used the arches under the railway bridge for storage and there were dozens of bikes all gathering dust. He showed me a pre-war Big Four Norton 600cc single side valve with girder forks. I thought *this doesn't have much street cred even for scruffy old me!* I reported back to Geoff and the gang at the next workshop meeting. Geoff told me he knew of a 650cc BSA twin for about £30 everything in good order, I asked him to get it for me.

On my next visit to Southgate Street, there, parked in the cobbled road was a 1954 plunger BSA 650 with a child/adult sidecar, BEJ 504, Geoff had got it for £25. I started it sitting astride and immediately rode it into the pavement on the left and was unable to get it back onto the road. I did this a few more times before Geoff said "I'll ride it to Ash Lane in the morning, you give me a lift to work."

Sunday came, I looked pensively at the big BSA twin with sidecar, it seemed to sit there majestically at the front of our wooden bungalow "Janetta". Plucking up my courage on this nice crisp March morning I kick-started it and slowly rode it down Ash Lane, which was full of pot holes. As the front wheel went in the potholes I was zigzagging down the lane, I even clipped the telegraph pole with the sidecar wheel. After what seemed like a lifetime riding just 200 yards I reached Down Hatherley Lane, thank goodness I thought as I sat there knackered. Once rested, I gingerly rode towards the large oak tree which, when young, I imagined was the oak tree where King Charles hid from the Roundheads! I indicated to pull in on the left rotating my right arm clockwise in a circular motion signal. Checking behind, I turned around and rode to Jones's farm, where I'd had the crash 2 years earlier. I turned around and rode back the half mile to the big tree, I did this maybe 20 more times.

Riding towards the big tree I was thinking, okay I've cracked it, but on shutting off the throttle, I immediately went across to the right. I was now on the other side of the road, luckily nothing was coming the other way. In somewhat of a panic I braked hard only to go further to the right with the front wheel hitting the 12 inch earth bank, otherwise I'd have been in the ditch. With sweat pouring off me I thought that perhaps I didn't know how to ride this combination. This incident reminded me of the tale Dave had told me of him riding across the middle of the roundabout on a combination.

After some deep breaths and another 20 or more times up and down I found out that when you shut the throttle you have to turn the handlebars to the left, when opening up you pulled them to the right, I also now realised why in sidecar racing photos, the passenger was hanging out. I thought, *am I really going to ride this combination with a flat board and Bantam 168 miles across the country and back?*

Although the Royal Enfield was still taxed I rode the BSA 650 twin to the Tabard and said to the gang "who wants a joyride up and down the road?"

DAD ON THE LEFT. TAKEN IN THE GYM IN PONTYPRIDD WHERE TOMMY FARR TRAINED IN THE 1920's

Norman and Frank were game so it was, head them up and move them out (from Rawhide, a TV show). Frank jumped on the back as he was very tall, Norman was in the sidecar. We went up Hare Lane and back down Pitt Street in Gloucester. When I pulled up, Norman couldn't get out the sidecar quick enough, he looked as if he'd seen the devil "my God that was scary, felt like I was trapped in the coffin, don't let me do that again". The race meeting was now less than 3 weeks away, I had to make a flat board for the outfit. I bought four 6' x 9" planks from the local timber merchant and with help from dad and some coach bolts the board was fitted to the bike, using the fourth plank to join the 3 together. Once the platform was finished we drilled holes to match the back adjustable hinges and had the board up in the air, using a short piece of timber, to check the front 2 bolts holes. I must have knocked the wood as the board fell down hitting dad on the head who fell to the ground very dazed. I was worried so asked if he was OK, "the last time I saw stars like that was when I was boxing in 1922 and my opponent hit me." I took him into the house and made him a cup of tea, luckily he felt better, but I finished it off on my own!

I asked Frank if he was up to a test run with the Bantam on the flat board, to the small lane in Tirley, he said he was up for a laugh. Frank was trying to show me how to tie the Bantam onto the board, showing me knots he'd learnt as a fireman. After testing the Bantam, I offered Frank a ride on it but he asked to try the sidecar, only to do what David and I had done, on shutting off he went to the right, the bike ended up rocking on a tree stump. I wish I'd had a camera, it looked like something out of the Keystone Cops!

Just before I got the combination in February I was sent to work at the Monmouth butcher's shop, the furthest one away from me. Thursday afternoon my Royal Enfield started leaking oil from the barrel. After spending all that afternoon working on it I found a thread had stripped, rather than doing a botched job, no comments please, I decided to go on the Bantam. It was taxed but had no lights so I left for work as soon as it was light. I explained to the manager that I'd have to stop the night and leave early Saturday. I left work at 4 pm Saturday and was okay until I got the outskirts of Gloucester, it was now dark so drivers were flashing me, I could do nothing. The Bantam was in racing trim but with a silencer and a Speedo cable. I was doing 70 mph, flat on the tank, every driver flashing now. Luckily I got home safely and wasn't stopped by the police.

I spent the Sunday putting the Royal Enfield back together with some Red Hermatite and silver fag paper from dad's 1 ounce of roll up tobacco, forcing it in where the thread was stripped. This was after I'd dropped a gudgeon pin circlip down into the engine. While I was crying on Geoff Fivash's shoulder he said "George, buy a small magnet and attach it to a stiff piece of wire" luckily God was on my side and the circlip attached itself to the magnet.

The Bantam was basically finished, I just had to panel beat some corrugated iron for number plates, paint them white with black numbers while dad looked over my shoulder "tutting". I'd sold the Royal Enfield 350 bullet which I did like as it had some good scratches on it, a term for racing on the road!

I was pleased I was getting better at riding the BSA combination and asked a friend who had one of those little guns that typed letters onto plastic tape if he'd make me a label "George's combo." We were ready for the big day!

CHAPTER 4   1964/65-First race no sleep

Norman agreed to come with me to my first race meeting on the 27th March 1964 at Snetterton, 20 miles from Norwich. Luckily it was Good Friday so there was no need to take a day off work. Thursday was half-day, so in the afternoon I was busy mixing fuel at 20-1 with Castrol XXL, loading the bike and tools onto the flat board while trying to remember the knots Frank had shown me. Mum got the food ready and lectured me not to break the thermos flask as it was expensive. All before collecting Norman and leaving Gloucester at 7pm.

Dave Hughes, a lorry driver, had planned a route for me. We'd worked out it was 168 miles, somewhat daunting. The oncoming headlights were blinding both of us, we struggled as far as Aylesbury before the real problems started, and that's not counting the many times we had to stop to re-tie the Bantam!

The clutch started slipping on the BSA so we were glad when Geoff caught us up. He checked the clutch adjustment but it still kept slipping, so he took Norman in the car taking 150 pounds weight off the clutch. It was a heck of a journey with not many dual carriageways. We went under the bridge where the great train robbery had been the year before and limped through Bedford, Cambridge and Newmarket before stopping at a transport Cafe in Red Lodge village or the Red Hot Dog Café as I called it, renowned by lorry drivers throughout the country. When I hear Candy Man by the Tremolos, it takes me back to when we were huddled around drinking tea and eating a bacon sandwich with bikers as well as those of us going racing, lorry and car drivers, military personnel, even a couple wearing evening dress. I've never seen such a cross-section of people in one place before!

At 2am Geoff again took Norman in the car to save my clutch, but not before we went into a basic urinal. Seeing 'Kilroy was here' written on the wall along with other names I asked Norman if we were going to leave our names, "we sure are George." I told him to write it as people couldn't read my writing. As he was doing it a very tall Black US airman said a in load voice "People who write on shit house walls, Roll the shit in little balls, People who read these words of wit, Eat those little balls of shit!" We were bemused, relieved he didn't hit us, and laughed about it later.

I was making slow progress, feeling 'oh lonesome me,' what a good name for a song! In Thetford, seeing a phone box, I rang the police to ask if any accidents had been reported, explaining that I thought my friends were going to wait for me. The Officer told me that none had and that Snetterton Circuit was 10 miles on the right, which on 6V lights and at 15 mph seemed to take forever. Seeing a sign for Snetterton left and with my brain gone by this time I saw a red phone box. I crouched on the floor, closed my eyes hoping to get some sleep, at least I felt warmer. The rest worked and I was now feeling wide-awake. It was 6am and my brain was now working. Getting back on the main road towards Norwich I found I'd made the right decision, what a surprise. I saw a small circuit sign near a petrol station that I'd never have seen last night. It was just a dirt track and would have been a nightmare in the middle of the night!

What a relief it was to see Norman's smiling face and Geoff's maroon Vauxhall Wyvern. I got the Bantam off the sidecar, fuelled it up and started it. Geoff had raced some years before and explained what we had to do and some of the wheezes. First job was to take the bikes to Scrutineering. They were checking to see if the bike was safe to race while I held the bike steady. I was very nervous watching him as he pulled and pushed everything, it was now 8am.

Next was signing on in a brick building next to Scrutineering. Things perked up as the entries secretary was a pretty lady called Valerie. I saw a plaque dedicated to Archie Scott Brown, the first one armed man to go car racing!

After Scrutineering and sign-on we had to wait for our practice session. A message came over the tannoy system "We need more marshals, no marshals no racing," then a few minutes later, "Bantams for the first novices practice." There was a slight drizzle as we pushed the bike into the assembly area. I could hear a funny noise, it was my nerves rattling. There was a pretty girl wearing black stretch trousers, motorcycle jacket and bowler hat holding a sign that said 'oil at the Esses.' That didn't do my nerves any good.

The marshal waved us off in small groups, once into second gear my nerves went as I had other things to worry about, going round corners and missing bikes. I went as fast as I felt safe around the first bends, Riches then Sears. I did notice that the Bantam in front's back wheel was wobbling and thought, *my God, is mine doing that?*

The Norwich Straight was nearly 1 mile long on the full 2.17 mile circuit, Snetterton had been a bomber airfield in WW2. There was no gearing to change in the early days the only thing we'd done was to acquire a Snell first gear, making it a close ratio gear box. We sounded like a load of bumblebees, it seemed to take forever just holding the throttle wide open.

Getting into a huddle after we'd come in, we were all pleased with our performance and had another practice in 40 minutes. There was a 250cc Greeves rider called Gordon Daniels next to us in the paddock who asked if we had something he could make a paper gasket with. He took a page from our programme, I thought after, *why didn't he use his own programme?* He won the British 250 race with our programme!

Dinner time, sarnies and cold tea with my hero Geoff fixing the clutch on the BSA. The screws holding the springs had all slackened off, after a short test everything appeared okay!

We had a quick look round the paddock and although it was a Bantam Racing Club meeting, there were lots of other bikes including production machines. Many of the Bantams had adaptations to make them go faster. I'd bought some tuning bits for the next race meeting which cost a fortune, well £1-10/- for the crankcase stuffer, plus some other bits, including a Todd high compression cylinder head. For the first race meeting I used an ordinary BSA Bantam head, which I turned the other way round, goodness knows why, if it was raining the plug would get wet. There were strict rules for Bantam racing, cylinder, barrel and crankcase had to be retained as did the three speed gearbox. The mainframe had to be retained but you could add a swinging arm of your own design and you could use any front forks and wheels. Geoff had Yamaha 125cc front forks and brake, but due to shortage of money, lack of time, resources and mechanical experience I was using the Bantam forks and brake which was next to useless as it was half an inch wide and only 5 inches diameter!

The Novice race was called and my nerves were rattling again. Norman started the Bantam, and carried a few tools, spare plug and spanner to the assembly area. I was using a Lodge RL 49 as recommended by George Todd, who lived in Thornbury, Glos.

My trance was interrupted as the bikes came in from the previous race and the 40 starters were ushered onto the start line. The number of starters is decided by the width of the track multiplied by its length. We drew lots from 1 to 40 for starting grid position. I felt the same as when I was about to take my motorcycle test! They held up a sign to stop engines, then the 1 minute board. Petrol on, in gear, my goggles, which had started to steam up, down over my eyes, then the starter waved his flag in the middle of the track and walked to his rostrum raising the Union Jack. It felt like a lifetime until it dropped. I'd read a book on how to start racing, one tip from the author, was that if you were at the back of the grid, start pushing early as the starter was only looking at the first two rows!

I pushed and bumped the bike, hearing pop, pop, pop, I threw my leg over, revved up, slipped the clutch and was away. Quite scary with 39 other motorcycles around you, at least in practice you were let out in small groups. We all got to Riches, I was taking it steady as I was in the middle of about 10 riders again watching the back wheel of the bike in front wobbling, *concentrate!* I told myself. I was passed and I actually passed someone else. 6 laps on a Bantam on a 2.71 mile circuit seemed to take forever, but unlike practice you didn't have quite so much time to ponder. The chequered flag came down, I'd finished my first race.

I was over the moon and Norman shook my hand. We all discussed our performance. Geoff was certainly best of the gang, but we were all happy. Norman and I checked everything, or so we thought, had another sandwich and another look around the paddock taking note of the modifications made to other Bantams.

The call went out for the second race for Bantam novices. Panic again while waiting on the start line but another good start. One good thing I found with racing, especially when there was a big grid was that there was always somebody to race with even if you were at the back. I was in a group enjoying myself when the bike died, another rider just missing me, what could have happened? After the race I was picked up in the breakdown van. It was very embarrassing to find I'd run out of petrol, we hadn't topped up with fuel after practice and the first race, *idiots*. The day's racing was over and Norm tried to comfort me by reminding me he'd forgotten as well. Geoff and the others had finishes. Norman decided we should get going early. We were pleased with the day and felt part of a new fraternity.

ME, MARTIN AND KNOCKER
LOADED READY TO LEAVE

We didn't see Geoff on the way home but many cars and vans tooted as they passed making us feel good. We got to Cambridge in daylight and were making steady progress, stopping for the odd run out in farm gateways. Norman tried to go to sleep only to be woken up when the sidecar wheel hit the kerb because I'd also gone to sleep! The bike had slowed turning to the left and hitting the pavement waking us both up, I only just kept control. This was the start of the worst trip of my life. We started singing, trying to keep awake. I started hallucinating, lampposts would turn into a lorry grille so I'd swerve; overhanging trees looked like monsters and the white line was waving up and down! Coming through Whitney, Norman shouted "stop." I slammed on the brakes "what's the matter Norm?" "Nothing George, but there's an ice-cold milk machine." The freezing cold milk woke us up for a while and the clutch didn't play up, so that was one less problem. We got into Cheltenham so there were streetlights. As we approached the traffic lights by Holy Apostles Church a lamppost changed into a man and jumped into the middle of the road. I braked hard, "Norman did you see that man?" "I did George, where's he gone?" We'd both seen the same hallucination! Only 10 miles to go but Norman was worried, "do you have a bicycle I could borrow to ride home from your house?" "Don't worry I can do the extra 4 miles." I dropped off Norm at 2am.

How I got up at 7 am for work the next day I don't know, I was yawning all the way through. After work I was out with the lads at the Aztec coffee bar. There was no snooker that night and everyone was asking how the trip went. Norm and I told the story with enthusiasm, not forgetting the slipping clutch, running out of petrol and hallucinations. We went on to the Clifton Ballroom. I was twisting away when I noticed Norman asleep under one of the speakers, we gave him some stick about that when we went back to the Aztec before going home. The Clifton Ballroom used to attract some big names. I remember going to see Screaming Lord Sutch on his 'I failed to be an MP for the Monster Raving Loony Party' show. Talk about an energetic show, the police came and told us to get off the tables. I decided Bantam racing would cost a lot and I'd better not go out as much but was pleased when the gang came around asking where the hell I'd been. I got back into the routine of working on the Bantam at Geoff's garage, there was no room in the sheds dad had made before the war. I returned the leathers I'd borrowed as I'd found a tatty set that were okay. Geoff made an expansion chamber. He had welding and panel beating experience which Twigworth garage didn't have, although Mr Teal, the owner, told me tales of helping Ivor Bueb, a top car racer of the 50's. With Norman's help, I made a swinging arm. Sir George Dowty sponsored us with the phosphor bronze bushes Norman made during his dinner time. Geoff had suggested we use some wishbones off a car and we were quite chuffed when finished. Tony Price sacrificed one of his petrol tanks with a flip-top screw-up petrol cap, we got some sheet metal bent and welded and made a special tank spending hours painting a fighting bantam on it.

The next race meeting was in April and it arrived quickly. It was at Cadwell Park in Lincolnshire, also 160+ miles away. Mother again signed the parental guardian form. I was pleased mum and dad were impressed at my first attempt. The meeting was on Saturday, so I had to do a deal with JH Dewhurst, offering them two Thursday afternoons for the Saturday. When Mr Davies, the district manager said no I told him that I would have to leave for another job that would give me the time off. He relented and the deal was done.

Several things about the trip stuck in my mind: an extremely twisty road from Evesham to Stratford, going past the Royal Shakespeare Theatre and going through Warwick right past the Castle. Coventry was all roundabouts and roadworks after WW2 and Leicester was quite scary as it was so large it took ages to get through, but it did have streetlights. We went past the very impressive Cathedral at Lincoln. After Lincoln we rode to Horncastle, then a twisty road towards Louth. I asked "Norman, what are those red

GEOFF, ME, NORMAN AND DAVE

lights in the sky?" "I don't know." The lights were first on one side of the road, then the other side, then back again, they just sort of hung there. I must admit we were a little unnerved, I wouldn't say scared but, what with all the UFO sightings, who can say!! We found the circuit at 1am, it took some time to find the paddock. Like Snetterton, it was all dirt tracks that ended up going to various viewing areas. Eventually we followed some other riders into the paddock and pitched the 6' x 3' tent I still had. We'd hoped to get some rest, but with other riders coming in and a loud bang every 30 minutes like a gunshot, no chance! We found out the next day that this was pea growing season; the bangs were from a bird scarer.

In the morning we found Geoff, who said "we heard your bike going up and down, up and down," they were all laughing. After scrutineering and signing on with the lovely Valerie, the first novice practice was called. Cadwell is a very hilly circuit, even the paddock had several levels. We were using the short circuit. The full circuit went past the assembly gate and we rode backwards down this part of the track to the short circuit waiting area on the centre kart track.

It was well organised, one group of riders waited on the kart circuit area in the middle of the short circuit until the riders from the previous group had come off the track. They then rode down to the start line as riders from the assembly area rode onto the kart track. The safety van came round flashing its lights indicating all was safe then carried on to the paddock with any bikes that had broken down.

There was a red flag at the hairpin in the practice before ours so the riders had to return to the paddock. We made our way down to the start line as other riders came down from the assembly area to wait on the hill for their practice. It reminded me of seeing early films of cars being made on an assembly line. Around came the van flashing its lights, our turn now. The starter waved us off, a short 100 yard dash to a very sharp right-hand hairpin then up a steep hill, revving in first gear, the Bantam wouldn't pull second. I did try once and nearly stalled the bike! Charlies, a sweeping right adverse camber leads onto the back straight which had a dip in the middle, then Park Corner, a sharp right-hand bend followed by Chris Curve, an even longer sweeping bend, a twisty section before Mansfield, a downhill drop, sharp left-hand bend and back to the start and finish line. We had a second practice session before dinner and this time I made sure I had a full tank of petrol. Geoff advised me to put on a one tooth smaller gearbox sprocket, there were 14, 15 and 16 tooth available. I was still learning and taking advice from Geoff.

As we were using the short circuit there were only 28 starters in the races. I started well in both of my races, being a tall lanky git helped but my 13/14 stone didn't. On the little 125cc Bantams some riders were 10 stone or less. We started making friends and recognising faces, Pete Styles is a name that sticks in my mind and Fred Wyatt from Wotton Under Edge. At the end of the day was the long trip home. At least we found out what the UFO was; two tall radio masts, but instead of one red light at the top, there were several running from top to bottom. With better sleep we weren't so tired going home and were back by 1am. Being Sunday next day I could have a lie-in.

The Cheltenham Motor Club (CMC) had held a race meeting in March at Little Rissington, there was to be another one in May, so I went to watch. I enjoyed it so I decided I would join the Club and enter the next meeting in August. I also learnt that the Club had a clubhouse and that Wednesday night was motorcycle night.

Back to Snetterton before another trip to Cadwell on July 4th. It was suggested that John take his car, fitted with a roof rack for the bike (costing 10/- hire charge), with the rest of us and the spares piled in somehow. We

tied the Bantam, minus oil and petrol, onto the roof rack supervised by fireman Frank only to get to Tewkesbury, 10 miles from home, when we heard horrible noises from the roof. Luckily we were by the Gusphill Manor pub car park. The roof rack had broken,

THE BOMB HOLE SNETTERTON

nothing to do with Frank's knots. We took the Bantam off and secured the roof rack. John took me back for my sidecar while Frank and Norman guarded the bike. We left the broken roof rack at my house, and tied the bike on the sidecar. Off we went with Norman and Frank spelling each other to give me someone to talk to. John later got his 10 bob back.

Just over half way on the journey Geoff and the gang caught us up. We carried on, Geoff in the lead, me and Frank in the middle, Norman with John following up. Suddenly, there was a loud bang and sparks which narrowly missed me. A scooter rider had fallen off, luckily missing me by inches but hitting John's car damaging his front wing. The rider had a damaged hand. We talked to him for a few minutes until the ambulance came. Geoff and gang had disappeared before the police arrived, Norm reckoned that Geoff had been overtaking and clipped the rider coming the other way, although Geoff always denied it. After talking with the Police we loaded all the gear onto the sidecar. As Norman and Frank had no motorcycle gear if the weather turned bad, they stayed with John and the damaged car.

20 miles from Cadwell the bike slowed, when I opened it up the bike would cut out. Now I knew the way, I limped to the circuit and slept on the ground for a few hours. Geoff sorted out the bike problem, it was a blocked main jet. Racing, considering the trip up, went ok then we were on our way home with Geoff taking some of the unwanted kit to save weight!

Halfway between Newark on Trent and Leicester I wondered what the bumping and bad handling was, I had a flat sidecar tyre. Luckily garages carried puncture repair kits. Approaching Coventry I was starting to nod off and thought, *I'm not going to do what we did on the first trip.* There was no one with me to keep me awake and no work next day being a Sunday, but every pub I stopped at said "sorry, no room," even in the B&B district in Coventry, was it because I was a biker? I felt like Joseph and Mary, I'd have been happy to sleep in a stable.

After the last refusal I asked for directions to the police station. Frank had told me that the police will always put you up in a cell. After I told him that I hadn't killed anybody, the policeman on the desk made a phone call. The Stoneleigh Agricultural Show was on but he found a B&B that served an evening meal. To add to the luxury, I had a bath then to bed. Next time I saw the lads I found out that Frank and Norman had met two girls in the Wimpy Coffee Bar, Tina and Iris, a trip to remember for all of us.

As well as knowing Frank, Norman and John it helped that I'd made friends with Jim Davies, Garnet Phillips and Big Mick Mitchell at the Roma Cafe in Westgate Street, an 'in' place for bikers with nice frothy coffee. Garnet was called on to help with the next trip to Snetterton in late May, as Norman had a girlfriend. Geoff took my bike as Knocker couldn't go. We rode up on Garnett's 600cc Norton Dominator, starting early and stopping for a run out at a convenient pub to change drivers.

Nearing Cambridge we noticed the dynamo wasn't charging, after checking connections and finding nothing we had to ride on side lights. It was my turn on the front, if a car passed I followed and hung on to them until they turned off. We had some luck when a Triumph Herald passed us. The considerate driver, seeing our problem, gave us thumbs up. All was okay until an Austin Mini went by at 50 mph, at that time Herald and Mini drivers did not like being passed by each other! The Herald went up to 50, as did I, then 60 to get by the Mini, eventually we all were doing 80. When it got to 85 mph I slammed on the brakes and stopped with sweat dripping off me. Garnet asked why I'd stopped, he was enjoying it, but 85 mph in the dark, on side lights, on a strange road!!!

During the day Geoff checked the dynamo on the Dominator but it needed a service. Just after the start of the first race, a Bantam with no rider, overtook me, he must have missed his footing as I did when testing. The bike hit my front wheel leaving me in a pile, damaging my front mudguard so I couldn't continue. The other rider got back on and rode off with me shaking my fist at him. I finished in the second race, with no earth shattering results. By this time Geoff had gone up to the intermediate class, his expansion chamber was working well and a lot of people were taking note of it. We didn't hang around after the meeting and no stopping at a pub as we didn't have a headlight.

Frank had bought an E Type, not the Jaguar, but a 1936 Austin Series E with wire wheels. As it was a convertible Frank said "how about laying the Bantam across the back seat, at least it won't break like John's roof rack" it made me laugh! This trip was to Cadwell Park. We put the tools, oil and fuel on the back seat with the bike across the back. It was a good trouble-free drive for a 30 year old car. I had my helmet and goggles, Frank took his in case it rained.

We arrived in good time, after stopping for a swift half. Sadly it was 'no way Jose' for sleeping in the seats as being a 2 door model, they had a stiff metal back and only leaned forward, so that any rear passengers could get in and out. One of us in the front and one in the back didn't work either so we slept on the bare ground again. It was a good days racing and nice to see the lovely Valerie again, certainly better than the last Cadwell trip on the BSA.

1936 MORRIS, FRANK, NORMAN & GRAHAM

Big Mick Mitchell helped out on the next trip to Snetterton. On one of his many fag breaks near Cambridge he saw a lorry with 'Cyril Ridgeon Builder's Merchant' on the side. Mick with his dry sense of humour said "do you have rich relations that we can get some sponsorship from?" We called in to see Uncle Knox and Auntie Nellie, who told us the building company owners were related and quite rich, but too distant. My first season's racing was drawing to a close. Our regular workshop nights by this time had moved to just off Barton Street which had a high percentage of Afro-Caribbean people living there. We would hear My Boy Lollipop by Millie turned up loud and sing along.

The last trip to Snetterton was with Jim Davies and Garnet Phillips in his A40 van. I asked Garnet why big Mick called him Fish. Garnet or Phil as he preferred to be called told me that he was at school with Mick, he and the other pupils thought Garnet was a fish, he still does!! The Bantam just squeezed into the small A40 van with me in the back with the bike, spares and food. We made good time until hunger raised its head and we pulled over for sandwiches and from somewhere, a delicious cup of onion soup.

About 30 minutes later this strange aroma appeared, regrettably it was from me, and as I was stuck in the back I suffered more than Jim and Garnet. I wonder why they slept outside once we were at the circuit.

The race on Saturday went ok and we saw Geoff and the gang. In the evening we went to see Jim's mother who ran a turkey farm 5 miles away from the circuit. Jim had fixed up for us to stay there; he also had a pretty younger sister to make things even better. At breakfast I mentioned the sausages were very tasty, turned out they were made by a local butcher to a special recipe. As a butcher, I ended up carving the turkey for dinner and offered to wash up, I know, creeping. We said our goodbyes to Mrs Brighton, who told us, "if anyone would like to stop a few days, we can find you plenty of work for board and lodging." Now that is the way to go racing.

I had a few days holiday due to me and contacted Mrs Brighton, Jim's mother, to ask if I could accept her offer. As the saying goes, a change is good as a rest. I was mucking out the milking parlour, loading bales and feeding turkeys. Luckily the weather was good so I enjoyed the few days.

I'd been transferred to an Eastman's branch in Ross-on-Wye. I'd worked at the shop a few times before but the manager had now retired and I was asked to manage it for a few weeks. I was helped by Len King who had a new Triumph Tiger Cub he wanted to run in, so we left my bike at the Dewhurst meat depot and I went on the back of him. Although the A40 is a main road, it's very twisty to Ross. It must have been Len's first trip to Ross, he approached a sharp right-hand bend too fast hitting the brick wall, no major damage but he dented his headlamp rim and broke the glass!

We got the bike into the back cutting room in the dinner hour, and fixed it after buying some new bits from Lucas Motorcycles. Len was transferred somewhere else and Jack Davis came to help for the last two months of the year. He was the brother of the district manager Norman, but nowhere near as keen on promotion, he just liked being a Butcher, was jolly and worked hard.

In November the Motorcycle Show was on in London at Earl's Court. John and I agreed to go up on Sunday. We looked at all the bikes and drooled when we saw a few racers. We asked about army life, they had a very good stand with motorcycles on but as I'd just started racing the thought of joining the Army, didn't stay in my head very long.

We were approaching Oxford with Petula Clark on the radio singing Downtown. As we'd just been downtown ourselves we were singing along and not concentrating, which is why we'd missed the right-hand turning at the roundabout and found ourselves lost in the middle of Oxford. We had to ask some lads the way out and gave one a lift to the ring road. We got home by 2am. It was a good day and I still like the song Downtown.

Christmas was approaching, there were frosts and foggy weather. I'd made friends with the husband and wife at the grocery shop next door and fixed up to stop with them for a few nights in exchange for some meat. This came about because on one of the rides home in freezing fog, I only got half a mile and had to raise my goggles as they were frozen over, then my eyelashes were freezing together. I was stopping every hundred yards to defrost my eyes! I was pleased when after another half a mile the fog cleared and it was just frost and -10°C, I thought *what a pleasure to ride in this!*

At least staying in Ross allowed me to chat up the cuddly girl in the cake shop. We went to the pictures to see Ben Hur, although we didn't see much of the film sat in the back row. After the film she took me down a dark lane for some more cuddling before I walked her home. There were two girls from the local Co-op who used to come in and tease me. At least I got a Christmas kiss, but when the married one kissed me "wow," but like on my Bantam, I was still a novice with girls.

The day before Christmas Eve Jack didn't turn up and it was too late to get help. My God, did I work my bollocks off, dressing the window, trying to serve customers as I was dressing turkeys and chickens. I had to ask customers to wait while I made a cuppa which I drank whilst serving. Jack came in on Christmas Eve with his arm black and blue from the wrist to the shoulder. His arm had saved his face when the stepladder slipped while he was trying to hang a turkey up the day before. Home, then around to Mrs Prentice for their Christmas Eve party. Christmas day was spent at Dave and Sue's, the girls were nearly 1 and 3 and we played with their toys.

January was cold and the Bantam Racing Club Dinner Dance was in London so big Mick Mitchell suggested we stop at his Aunties in Twickenham, Garnet seconded the idea. The trip in Garnet's Austin A40 was luxury to me but the vacuum windscreen wipers kept clogging up with snow and the washers were frozen. We got to big Mick's aunty's and told her we'd be back late. We had over 3 hours to see London but it was so cold that in Soho big Mick suggested we go to see a strip show. It was in a fleapit cinema like those in Gloucester. The place was packed. It was a nonstop review, and as people left we moved forward until we were up at the front. In one act a lady with long legs and fish net stockings performed to 'The Night they invented Champagne' she offered me a drink while wiggling her leg, I didn't touch it. It was the first strip club I'd ever been to and still the best!

At the Dinner Dance and presentation I talked to other riders and some officials. Eventually I had a dance with the lovely Valerie but she already had a boyfriend, so jumping off Westgate Bridge started to look good again! The trip back home was cold but there was no snow. Well done Garnet on driving and big Mick for leading me astray.

Reading MCN I saw that Dave Browning was selling his 250cc Greeves Silverstone for £280. Dave was from Cheltenham, the son of Jack, a car dealer. I'd got to know Jack when I joined the CMC to race at RAF Little Rissington. Dave was always in the local papers for winning races, also for punch-ups and speeding but racing had settled him down. I saw the Greeves in Jack's showroom and was offered a test ride. I jumped at the chance but said it'd have to be a Sunday. After helping Dave unload the Greeves he showed me how it all worked. Starting was easy but trying to rev it to 7000 to pull away, I stalled it twice. On the next attempt I really revved it thinking, it was going to go bang, but it took off like a scolded cat, *my God where has my stomach gone, it's certainly quicker than the Bantam!* I was very enthusiastic; Jack suggested we take a trip to Silverstone to clinch the deal.

I was getting used to the acceleration and starting to like it when I slide off at Woodcote Corner, no damage to me or to the bike just a few scrapes on the fairing. I was pleased it wasn't my fault, the primary chain had broken due to lack of oil which was a weak point in the early bikes. Jack fitted new bits supplied by the local Greeves main dealer, Malcolm Davis Motorcycles. Malcolm was a Greeves works trials and scrambles champion, his brother Tony was no slouch either. I was pleased with the bike and decided to do the deal and collect the bike after my birthday. I had £230 in my post office account and Jack offered me £50 for the

Matchless 500cc sidecar that had been fixed up by Tony Price; I'd had to buy it when the BSA needed a service.

Before the deal was done brother Dave had been to Cotton Motorcycles, he knew Pat Onions who with Monty Denley started Cotton Motorcycles in 1954. Dave tried to get me a new Telstar but couldn't better the £280 for the Greeves which at the time was 28 weeks wages!

I enjoyed the butchery classes at the Cheltenham Tech. which had started when I was working with Stan Dex. I left school at 15 with little education and struggled with many of the Latin words and on many occasions couldn't read my own writing! In one lesson a Scottish Vet with a broad accent was reading from a book on meat inspection, including diseases of animals and parasites and the sex life of some parasitic worms. I was trying to understand and write notes, when he said, "the male worm copulates with the female" I shouted out "what's copulate mean?" There were a few sniggers from the other students, the lecturer said "Mate!" "Why didn't you say that in the first place, it's shorter and easier to write down?" I replied. There were a few more sniggers. I also had to look up the word "equine." Mother was right, If you read more you learn more "can you hear me mother?"

In our group was Mrs Holpin with her sons Fred and Dave. She asked me how much a week I was paid, "£11 a week, Mrs Holpin." She offered me £13 plus petrol money and meat allowance. After discussing it with mum and dad I accepted the offer and started working for her in February 1965. The only problem was the 20 miles ride to Berkeley every morning; her eldest son, Fred, was always moaning that I was late even though I'd started out before 7am.

Fred Holpin senior ran a farm. The Butcher's shop in Berkeley had owed him a lot of money for cattle, so before the creditors closed the business he bought it using some of the money owing to him for his cattle! Mrs Holpin helped in the shop, mainly to keep Fred and David in check, although David did more work on the farm which he enjoyed. The third sibling, Gillian, helped out in the shop when it was short-staffed but mainly drove to Gloucester to pick up meat from the British Beef Slaughterhouse or Weddle's Cold Store and made deliveries to outlying businesses. Gilbert was the van driver for delivering to customers locally. He would sound the horn and people came out to buy meat from the back of the van. Mr Ernie

Idles was past retirement age and just served in the shop so, blowing my own trumpet, they needed a good butcher!

Dave and his partner Dennis Coombs now had their own car showroom on the forecourt of an area owned by Dick Sheppard the stunt driver, known as "The man of a 1000 crashes." His garage was called the White Post Garage, as there was a tall white telegraph pole in front of the property. Dave and Dennis named their business White Post Autos. Dave had my fairing for the Greeves sprayed up using one of the garage repairers that was also on the site owned by Dick. Once, I had a rear puncture on the BSA coming home from butchering at Berkeley, luckily it was by White Post. Dick Shepherd lived above the garage and came to help change my tyre even though they were closed. I was a useless mechanic, some say I still am, but I learnt a lot watching Dick.

As both John Meadows and I were 21 at the end of March, we decided to use Norton Village Hall for the usual 60's style party with sandwiches and savouries. With the help of our parents, well, mothers, we fixed up the hall. John still had friends on the cheese counter of Bon Marche although he'd left to join ICI fibres at £20 a week with three, eight-hour shifts. I was working a 5½ day week at £13 per week and supplied the cooked meats! Frank's brother-in-law Tony Newland owned a cake shop and supplied a cake with 'John and George' written on it, along with a motorcycle made from icing!

Frank and Norman brought along Iris and Tina. Mum called them the Painted Ladies as both wore glitter, false eyelashes, lots of makeup and very short skirts. The Tabard and Bon Marche gang, biker friends from the Roma Cafe plus John's friends from work and some from school days all came. Tony and Alice Price brought mother, leaving their three children at home. Sadly David and Sue were away and dad never made it, he felt too poorly.

We had dancing and a few games I'd learnt at the CMC dances. "First gentleman with a pair of ladies stockings over his arm," was called. In response, you lift the lady up and carry her to the stage, but Marcy took her stockings off, flashing her suspender belt! Jim said that when a pair of green knickers was asked for he was glad she was wearing another colour! The correct answer was two £1 notes, they were green and the slang name was "a nicker"! Little Tony, the so-and-so, put on a record of rugby songs. I heard, "If I was the marrying kind, which thank the Lord I'm not Sir." We sang this, and similar songs at parties, but not to your maiden Aunt, certainly not my Aunty. I took it off as some ladies had red faces!

During the cutting of the cake, John's brother-in-law made a good speech. The bit I remember is, "we may not have Paul and Ringo but we do have John and George." I tried dancing with Mum, she attempted to teach me the waltz but like a crab I kept going sideways, I was starting with the same foot! I danced the rest of the night with Mary who'd come down with the Holpin clan from the Butcher's shop and was a friend of Gillian's. As Mrs Holpin wanted to leave early, I offered to run Mary home. This turned out to be the last trip on the 500 Matchless with sidecar before it went in PX for the Greeves. After the 20 mile ride I asked Mary if I could see her again, "sorry, I'm going out with Gordon." Gordon wasn't all bad, he was a biker as well as a Butcher. He and Mary were married 2 years later.

At the Wednesday CMC bike night, Jack complained that the big end was going on the Matchless, I didn't offer any money back, perhaps I was getting better at wheeling and dealing having learnt from my brother David but I did say "Do you want the Greeves back?" No more was said.

Not having raced since last year I needed some practice on the Greeves. Big Mick suggested going to a practice day at Brands Hatch, so off we went with the Greeves on the BSA. It was lucky Tony Price gave the Greeves a once over, just as we were about to leave he noticed the air screw was missing out of the carburettor, I assumed Dave had nicked it for some reason. Saving the day, Tony broke a twig from the hedge and filled the hole! We rode through the middle of London. Approaching Piccadilly we stopped to ask a pedestrian with a bowler hat, walking stick and briefcase, the way to Brands Hatch. "A20, take the third exit" he said, pointing with his walking stick at Eros. When we moved forward he made a face. "Is anything wrong?" I asked, "Yes, you've just ridden over my foot with your sidecar wheel." I apologised, he grunted as we rode off.

After a briefing, we were let out in groups of 20. I was pleased with the way the bike was going, but in one session the group started racing and I ended up sliding off at Clearways. Sadly the new fairing was looking sorry for itself, the foot rest was broken and the gear lever bent so that was it for the day. I was lucky, the leather racing trousers were very thin and worn through but as it was cold I had my jeans on underneath. I wore away my Christmas present of a leather wallet, but better that than a hole in my backside. Dave cursed me for damaging the fairing.

85

My first meeting in 65 was at Cadwell Park with Big Mick helping. I'd borrowed a small trailer from a local villager to put the Bantam in giving him 10 shillings. Tony Price fixed up a tow bar on the back of the sidecar board. Going past Warwick Castle on an uphill section, we were stopped in a queue and Mick pointing out that there was a police car behind me, "don't roll backwards!!" The trip went well although it was very long with Mick's fag breaks. The weather on race day was good. Dave brought mum, dad, Tony and Alice to watch my first big race on the Greeves.

DAVE, MUM, ME, TONY, ALICE, BIG MICK AND DAD

Practice went okay. The Greeves used R40 mixed at 16-1, the Bantam just straight mineral oil at 20-1. The first race on the Bantam was at least some extra practice. When I heard the tannoy announce "First British 250cc race" all my butterflies took off crashing into one another! I'd practised the Greeves at Brands Hatch and Silverstone, falling off at both, but this was the first race. The flag was up, would it start? *Come on drop the B* flag,* I thought. The bike started as my 14 stone hit the seat, I revved it to 7000 slipping the clutch and was away. After two laps I was lying third I thought, *this is it,* the only trouble was, my 14 stone and heavy-handed clutch slipping caused the clutch to burn out going up the hill, so ended my first race on the Greeves. We didn't get the clutch working as the steel plates had buckled and we had no spares, in fact I burnt my fingers trying to pull the clutch apart despite having waited for the breakdown van and spending another 10 minutes stripping off the fairing and primary chain case. I had another ride on the Bantam before loading and leaving. A wasted journey for my brother, I felt I'd let everyone down!

The clutch was another weak spot on the early Greeves, joining the primary chain case known for leaking oil. I had a steady run home with Mick and found out many years later that brother had stopped for a pint. Alice Price told me "your dad got a singsong going with Dave sat quietly in a corner wearing a look that said "they're nothing to do with me." Dad lived in Wales during his formative years and was always singing. I remember on coach trips we would always get "She'll be coming round the mountain when she comes." Is that why I'm the pain in the backside everybody says I am?

My first win came at Cadwell Park October 1965, it was a British Formula Race Club meeting whose rules were similar to the BRC. The first race started in drizzle, as the flag dropped the skies opened up. I just rode around, many riders pulled off, but I had a finish in the top half. In the second race I was wearing wet leathers that weighed a ton and felt more like a deep sea diver. The track was mainly dry, but water was running across it in places. The Union flag was down, I overtook the leader just before the hairpin and tried to be careful with the clutch on the steep hill and around Charlie's, a right-hand blind adverse camber bend. I was wondering why no one had passed me. As I approached Park Corner, a sharp right, I glanced behind but could see no other riders, for some reason this made me go faster. Two laps later and still no one had overtaken me, *had they stopped the race?* The Greeves only had a 6" back brake but I was locking it causing the bike to snake. The last lap on the last corner, a sharp left called Mansfield and there were still no riders in sight. They waved a blue flag as they'd forgotten the chequered flag but I'd won! The rider I'd passed had fallen off at the hairpin causing chaos, holding everyone up but as top racer Jim Curry said "first under the flag wins."

THE START OF MY 1ST RACE WIN
CADWELL PARK 1965

Butchery in Berkeley was very different, going back to the house every day for dinner I put on a lot of weight. Mondays were sausage 'n' mash, Tuesday, offal of some sort, Wednesday, roast, Thursday, half-day, Friday, tenderloin or chops. Always with home-made apple pie or home-made rice pudding made from real milk. Saturday we had a salad with roast pork, ham, pressed beef and tongue, all cooked at the shop.

Mrs Holpin's daughter, Gill, who wore tight jeans, not that I noticed, was friends with Mary who I met when she called into the shop to see Gill. She told stories about being chased around the fridge when picking up the meat in Gloucester, she didn't seem to complain, God help Gloucester when they went on their girls' nights out! Fred and Dave were always arguing and fighting, once, they were rolling around in the street in their white coats and aprons. I felt embarrassed and was I ashamed of working for somebody like that.

Fred was always running some fiddle or other. He and Dave were only paid £5, but they did live at home for nothing and could borrow the car which was always filled up with petrol. One fiddle was buying ox heads at 2/6 each. When boned out they produced 7lbs of meat which was mixed with rusk and water and sold for dog meat at 1/- per lb. If there was nothing to do on the bike I stayed Thursday afternoons boning out the heads for 1/–, sometimes in the firm's time so Fred could make more money! Fred got the money from the sales but the firm paid for the heads most of the time if Peggy, a pleasant lady secretary upstairs, didn't pick it up, Mrs Holpin turned a blind eye.

Fred also had a nasty temper, it seemed he was always arguing with somebody and moaning I was late, which was fair enough but it was over 20 miles. One Thursday half-day just after 8am Fred, in his usual insulting way, told me I had to work an extra hour or else I was sacked. Not wanting to lose the job at the time I did it but thought, he could have been a little more pleasant about it, instead of being a nasty bastard.

On the way to work a few days later on the main A38 just before the turning for Berkeley, I saw Dave in the middle of the road with cattle everywhere. I stopped to help him round them up and put them back into the field making me even later than usual. Fred in his friendly way asked "why the F* are you late this time?" I told him the tale, which shot him down in flames and saw Gilbert and Ernie smiling behind his back.

Mr Holpin always dressed in scruffy clothes, he made me look tidy, if that's possible. Gordon Bircher told me a tale of when he went to see them for the first time, well Gillian really. When he arrived at the house Fred senior was leaning on the gate, Gordon being polite said "Hello, do the Holpin's live here?" "Oh yes sir" he said touching his cap. "Do you work for them?" "Oh Arh, I do sir, but they don't pay very much, can you lend me two bob to go for a pint tonight?" Gordon gave it to him, was his face red when he came in the house and found out he was the owner, and he never got the 2/- back!

"David, how can a son of mine leave a bloody farm gate open?" Mr Holpin used every swear word in the in the book, "You F*ing idiot to leave the gate open, leaving the bloody gate open, I can't comprehend you'd be so stupid." He'd stop, then start again "You dim-witted bar steward, how could you leave the gate open?" We couldn't laugh as Mr. Holpin was in the room. Luckily he went into kitchen which was down a short passage and couldn't see us before he started again. The only person he could see was Gilbert, the rest of us were killing ourselves laughing, even Mrs Holpin, who was trying to calm her husband down, poor old Gilbert was choking on his meal trying not to laugh.

Once, Fred reared up on me, it was partly deserved. It concerned another fiddle Fred had. He bought sheepskins from a tannery yard in Cheltenham at £3-10/- and sold them for £5 so I started selling them in my own area. A salesman for Hillier's Sausage Company came twice a week for orders, he was a very pleasant man and always chatted to me. When he mentioned that he may buy a sheepskin from Fred I offered to sell him one for £4. I don't know how, but Fred found out and went completely over the top. He was swearing at the salesman in a shop full of customers, telling him to stick his business up his backside and not to come back. He called me some names, I tried to apologise but it didn't help. I rang Hillier's and apologised to the salesman, he replied "not your fault, George, to be honest, I don't like serving him, but I have a job to do." I went to Mrs Holpin and said "I feel I have to leave, I'm not going to be treated like that." Mrs Holpin who could calm the strongest sea, made Fred apologise to us both.

I started to learn to drive while in Berkeley as they had two Bedford Dormobile vans. Gill did all the industrial deliveries including Berkeley and Thornbury nuclear power stations and collected meat from Gloucester. Gilbert drove the adapted van to sell meat, tins, crisps etc. to customers in the Berkeley Vale area. Having a motorcycle licence acted as a provisional car licence in those days, so, with Gilbert, I was driving the van to the house for dinner twice a week. I knew it usually took 3 months for a driving test to come through and I applied for Thursday afternoons only, the test date came back for 1 months' time.

Although I was using every opportunity to drive, I decided to have some lessons with a driving instructor from Berkeley. He gave me a special price as he knew the Holpin family and I made it 2 hour sessions as I had to drive to Gloucester for the test. He was very pleasant and put me at ease but he did tell me off at least twice for doing things wrong. We met at the test station and in the hour drive before the test I asked if I could do an emergency stop. Surprised, he replied "Don't you think you can do one George?" "I don't know I've never done one, it's a bit difficult with a van full of meat." We arrived back at the test centre in Denmark Road. I didn't have much time to worry or revise any Highway Code questions as an Examiner shouted "Mr Ridgeon" as soon as we got there.

I walked round and got in, checked the mirror and adjusted the seat. "Please start the car and turn right at the first junction." I was instructed. With what felt like beads of sweat on my forehead, off we went. I tried to make an extra effort to look in the mirror every 7 seconds. I'd settled down somewhat and felt that all was going well but, coming around the back of the Moreland's Match factory I stalled the car at the junction, *don't panic* I told myself, before Dad's Army made it popular! Handbrake on, out of gear, check the mirrors, start the engine, foot on the clutch, back into gear, handbrake off, looked in the mirror, signalled, turned my head to the right and left to check for any blind-spots before I pulled off. When we arrived back the Examiner asked several Highway Code questions then said "okay Mr Ridgeon you have passed." Wow!

While at Berkeley I started making enquiries about any old sheds as I had nowhere to work on my bike. Gill put me onto a farmer she used to go out with and I bought a large egg hatchery shed for £20, which was nearly 2 weeks wages. He delivered it and with Frank, Norm and a few others helping we put it up. It was quite heavy as it was insulated being designed to hatch eggs. I could now get cracking working on bikes, sorry about that!

Big brother and Sue had moved to Tewkesbury. Mr and Mrs Cheeseman had moved next door with their two sons Dave and Alan. I had been at Longlevens School with Alan and Dave was there as well but was two years older. He worked in Gloucester and as I went past his factory on my way to Berkeley he gave me a gallon of petrol for taking him to work. On one winter trip to Berkeley, snow was already on the ground when, after brushing the snow from the seat which was rock hard and blooming cold as I set off from home with Dave on the back. After I dropped him off, it started snowing harder but I carried on until all the traffic came to a standstill by the Stonehouse turning where the queue disappeared into the distance. After 15 minutes and no movement I used a phone box to phone work and explain why I was late. Another 10 minutes wait and as there was no traffic coming on the other side of the road I thought, *bugger it,* and rode up the wrong side of the road until I got to the problem, the road was completely blocked by a huge snowdrift with many cars stuck.

The snow had drifted blocking the new road. The old road went round the new one in a loop which was now used as a lay by, usually with a hotdog van in it! The old road was quite clear of traffic and the snow hadn't drifted as bad, only about 6 inches. As there was nothing to lose, I started to go around, avoiding the odd stranded car. Every time I got stuck I got off and managed to bump the bike around the obstacle and get going again. When the back wheel was losing traction I started bumping up and down in the seat as I'd seen on the Hill Climbs on the TV. I don't know how long it took, but I wasn't cold by the time I got through this 200 yard piece of road. It was a shame the hotdog van wasn't there, it would have made a fortune. I got to work at about 11am, having started from home at 7am!

It was impractical to go home that night so I was pleased when Mrs Holpin fixed it up for me to stop at a farm 2 miles away. I was quite lucky in a number of ways, I had a nice meal, no 20 mile ride home in the snow and back in the morning, I had a bath, which we didn't have at home, only a tin bath. I was soaking in the bath having put on the record player in the bathroom. When the LP record ended waking me up, I just lay there thinking, luxury. I stood up to change the record and can still feel the electric shock which luckily threw my hand off the record player, I was lucky it did, electricity and water do not mix.

The two years at Berkeley were quite illuminating. At the back of the shop was a slaughterhouse where Mr Holpin had his cattle killed. "George go up and get a pigs pluck," this is the offal from an animal. Entering the slaughterhouse there was a loud bang from the humane killer and from the cubicle where the cattle were stunned, out rolled a 10 hundredweight heifer lying on the floor ready to have its throat cut and hung up so could be bled and gutted. However on this occasion the animal got up and was not a happy heifer, he saw me and charged towards me. After the heifer was subdued I went back to work.

Three of us were working on the block at the same time. I was cutting up half a pig so had it sideways which made life difficult. I was cutting the leg off when the shoulder and middle started to fall on the floor. I put the 10" steak knife I was holding onto the pig to steady it but the pig was still falling so I put my other arm on as well, I'd put my arm on my steak knife. Holding it up I asked "Ernie is it very bad?" "No it looks alright George," but when I bent my arm I heard "bloody hell it's a big gash." Off to the hospital, four stitches, more pain and I'd left the pig to be picked up.

I enjoyed going round with Gilbert, one lady used to give us tea and home-made cake which didn't help my weight. We went to Sharpness, shortly after Dr Beeching had put the axe on many railway lines and these huge steam engines, which were once part of making Britain Great, were now on the scrap heap as electric and diesel were taking over. Thank goodness for the groups that started steam railway preservation societies around the country.

Our gang didn't frequent the Aztec or Clifton very often now, preferring to go for a Bernie steak every so often. I once tasted the wine, after sniffing, swirling it around and saying to the waiter "that will be all right." The rest of the gang laughed, peasants!! One time we decided to try an Indian curry, I never finished it, too hot and I've never had one since!

Christmas came and David picked up mum and dad while I rode my bike over to Tewkesbury for dinner. By this time the girls were now 3 and 4 and one of their toys was a small xylophone with numbers on the keys. It had a music sheet giving you the numbers for a selection of Christmas tunes, we kept getting it wrong but we did laugh.

CHAPTER 5   1966/67-Racing, shall I retire?

Little Tony got married to Doreen, on his stag night we all met at The Lemon and Parkers pub. When I arrived everyone was already there, I ordered my Cider Shandy and put my crash helmet onto Tony's head. He shook his head and the helmet fell off breaking a tray full of glasses, we were asked to leave. We sang as we left "we've been thrown out of better joints than this." We moved on to the New Inn, a 16th century Coaching Inn, and after a few pints we were sat on the stage coach in their yard, singing ""Oh the Deadwood Stage is a-rollin' on over the plains, whip crack away." Later, we carried Tony as he was legless, on our shoulders as if in a coffin while humming the Death March as we crashed into the Tabard. The landlord Fred Titmus asked "what's going on, boys?" "Tony's stag night Fred." "Okay, just keep the noise down." I'm not sure who took who home. Tony was the first of the gang to get married.

My old school friend, John, married Dorothy on October 22nd 1966. On John's stag night I left my bike at his place as we were being picked up. At the Tabard we all chucked £2 in the kitty. I asked where Norman was, Frank replied "he's taken Tina to Aberfan." The slag heap slide, which had crushed a school and houses killing 116 schoolchildren and 28 adults, had been on the news all day. Tina had Welsh relations and my own relations lived 5 miles away in Senghenydd. We had a moment's silence then, toasting John, we started drinking again.

We got a very drunk John to his home but, after helping lift him out of the car, the other bar stewards disappeared, not only leaving me to struggle to the house with him but face whatever retribution there may be. Luckily his sister Ann came to the door. I pushed my bike down the road before starting it to avoid wakening Mrs Meadows. The wedding was in the afternoon, with Frank and me as ushers. Somehow I managed to get up early and called in to see John on the way to have a haircut. On seeing a white faced John I asked him how he was feeling, "just about okay George, where are you off to?" "To get a haircut to look smart for your wedding." The wedding went well. At the reception, like our 21st party, most of the dances were waltz, foxtrot or quickstep but when 'Reach Out I'll be There' by the Four Tops came on it got everybody dancing, John and Dorothy liked this record. They'd bought a bungalow where a few of us had written 'just married' on toilet paper and decorated it ready for their return. We couldn't do this for Tony and Doreen as they were in a first-floor flat! At the Clifton Ballroom the twist still ruled, but after John's wedding I thought, *I must try and get some dancing lessons!*

I sold my Bantam racer for £15 to 3 RAF lads. In reality it was uncompetitive with my 14 stone on it and I was struggling to maintain one bike let alone two. £15 was 60+ gallons of petrol! Having joined the CMC I started meeting like-minded people including a group from Brize Norton: Keith and Tony Smith, their girlfriends Val and Maureen, John Pounder and Mervin Hoare and Merv's girlfriend Linda (to become Lula Bell). Keith offered to take me racing in his van.

Big Mick suggested we go on his new BSA to see Keith and Tony, he wanting to show me how well it went. We were scraping the ground going under Andoversford Railway Bridge S-bend. The farmhouse was a large building with a massive driveway. It was about 8.30 pm when we knocked, a man in his 50's opened an upstairs window wearing pyjamas and asked what we wanted. In a sheepish voice I replied "we've come to see Keith and Tony Smith," "they're out with Mrs Smith, they'll be back 10 pm."

Keith confirmed his offer to give me a lift to race meetings. This was luxury, as once the bike was out of the van, it was large enough to sleep everyone, but in the morning it looked like World War 3. One outing was a double meeting: Cadwell on Saturday and Snetterton on Sunday. Saturday evening I was working in the back of the van trying to change the gearing as Keith drove the van. We were all hungry and broke out Mrs Smith's Victoria sponge, already cut into slices. Keith held his slice in one hand, as he took a bite it fell in half. We panicked when he let go of the steering wheel shouting "where's me cake?" I wanted to fit a 46 rear sprocket, as Cadwell club circuit was 1.5 miles and Snetterton 2.71 miles with a long straight, but couldn't undo one of the studs. As Keith filled up with fuel he explained the problem to the mechanic and asked if he had a hacksaw and vice. The mechanic opened up a workshop full of bikes and tools. It was the Chatterton Racing Team garage at Sibsey, Lincoln, a top racing team always in the MCN, the mechanic wished us good luck.

Practice went well and I was thinking that it didn't take as long to do the back straight as it did on the Bantam. The gearing was correct and I made sure there was enough fuel in it after I'd run out in my first race at Snetterton! I was in the top 10, braking hard and changing down for the left-right sweep, the Esses, when part of my bike overtook me at the same time as the engine stopped. I later found out that leaving the self-puller

94

on the Greeves could put the balance factor out on the Steffa rotor causing the timing side of the crankshaft to fracture through the fixed cam, racing was over for the day. Yet another problem was the self-pulling tool had no locking washer so could work loose allowing the woodruff key to cut through the coil. This not only stopped the spark so I lost a race but had to spend £4 -10/- buying a new coil.

**KEITH SCOWLING WITH HANDS IN POCKETS
ME SMILING MIDDLE RIDER**

Another problem I had due lack of mechanical knowledge was when I was in the first 14 in a heat at Mallory Park with a lap to go when the bike stopped. A hole in the piston had been caused by the timing side oil seal failing, I didn't realise I had to change oil seals and piston rings regularly. On that trip Keith and Tony had started racing but were at a different meeting, so there wasn't even any of Mrs Smith's Victoria sponge. For this meeting I'd hired a 1950 J2 Austin cheaply from a local garage as the sidecar was being repaired, Mike Chandler, another CMC member accompanied me. As we went round a bumpy bend bypassing Barwell near Mallory the van was weaving all over the road, Mike made a dry comment, "I didn't know I'd joined the Royal Navy." The front shock absorbers were useless. Although MOT tests started in 1960 they were sometimes a bit like Arthur Daley from Minder, a bit dodgy!

Mike, although a year older was as big a kid as me. On the way back from Cadwell Park on the twisty section to Evesham we were doing 40 mph on the BSA when an MG sports car overtook us, Mike shouted "catch him up."

I dropped into third gear and accelerated hard catching them up, with the twisty bends we were leaning left and right to stop the sidecar wheel coming off the ground as if we were racing. As Mike was slim he was able to hang over the Greeves as well! I don't think the car liked my old BSA keeping up with them but we enjoyed it.

Mike was the opposite of Big Mick who wanted to stop for a fag break every 20 miles, he didn't want to stop on a trip until we were half way there. Cadwell was 160 miles so we didn't stop until Leicester when Mike pointing out that we were half way. This paid off on one trip to Cadwell. The BSA was not going well and we stopped at the usual garage in Leicester. Having a cuppa I asked "what are we going to do Mike?" "We're halfway George, we are here to go racing, and you're in the RAC so we carry on." I thought he would have made a good general in WW2. We arrived at Cadwell, the bike was going slower and the right hand exhaust pipe was glowing red, I knew this indicated the exhaust valve was starting to fail. I had a good days racing with a top 10 finish and asked Mike if he wanted to try the Greeves. Mike, just as I did, kept stalling the bike, "Mike you have to rev it to 7000." I still remember his face as his bobble hat flew off his head, his mouth dropped opened when the power band came in and after the ride he said "my God George, where has my stomach gone?" despite riding a 650 on the road!!

Mike adjusted the exhaust valve tappet clearance as I strapped the Greeves on the sidecar and we set off. As the miles to home reduced the pipe started to glow bright red. Then as we were going through Evesham, 25 miles from home, a foot long flame shot out of the exhaust pipe, we joked that people might give up drink for a while after seeing the devil breathing smoke and flames. We struggled up the 1 in 7 hill. Although the piston was going up and down there was little power coming from one cylinder so instead of a 650cc we had a 325cc carrying 40 stone. Downhill

I built up to 40 even 50 mph easing the throttle back in 4th gear but, if a lorry slowed us it took forever to get to 30 mph. Geoff Fivash did the cylinder head as I had no valve grinding kit.

30th July 66 at Cadwell Park, Big Mick Mitchell was holding my hand, a good job as I fell off. It was World Cup day, something to do with football I believe! My race was waiting on the start line when they turned the tannoy on and announced "England have scored a goal." Being the idiot I am, I shouted "achtung British schweinhund" all the riders and officials looked at me with a scowl. Perhaps that was why on the approach to Park Corner, as I cranked into the corner, I asked myself, *George, are you laying on the floor? Yes, you are laying on the floor, better get the bike off your foot quick!* I pushed the seat hard with my left foot and luckily the bike just cleared my right foot before it hit the grass spiralling over. I just slid along on the grass with no injury but the bike looked poorly. I was lucky, it was only the fairing, exhaust pipe, foot rest and the seat bracket to repair with no frame, fork or wheel damage. I wrote to Alf Ramsey as he got £2000 for winning the World Cup asking if he'd help me with £10 towards a new fairing. I don't know why but I didn't get a reply.

BIG MICK WITH A RATHER POORLY LOOKING GREEVES

A trip was fixed up with Keith in his Atlas Van in 1966, the gang were all racing at Snetterton with the British Motorcycle Racing Club (BMCRC or 'Bemsee') on the Sunday. Mike Hailwood was riding the Honda 6 at the meeting on bank holiday Monday. Keith was best rider of the bunch of us, a rude joke at the time had the punch line "come on train," we were shouting "come on Keith." After our racing had finished we stayed in the paddock which saved us paying to get in on the Monday but we moved out of the way and had a big cook-up as we watched the incoming racers arrive pulling plush caravans. No motorcycle combinations or small vans and small tents for them, their tents were much larger, like those Arab Sheiks lived in.

Monday morning we walked around the paddock to see who else was racing besides Mike the Bike. We admired the bikes and saw Bill Ivy working on a Tom Kirby Matchless removing the rear wheel. Bill was not only wearing a smart jacket but even had cufflinks. I commented "my mother moans at me, if I don't have my sleeves rolled up." Bill giving me a black look. Keith, Tony and Mervin's girlfriends, Val, Maureen and Lou, went to the ladies. We stayed admiring machines before moving towards the toilet block but we noticed that as the girls went in they were followed in by Fritz Scheidegger who was a top Swiss sidecar racer. We expected him to come straight back out but he didn't, we waited. When he did come out and saw us staring at him he said, "Ach, I vent into zee ladies." All that day and at other race meetings this greeting was used. Sadly Fritz died at Mallory Park March 1967. Practice started with a roar of machines. When Mike started the Honda 6 it sounded like the cry of a banshee howling, with 6 open megaphones and revving to over 18,000 rpm, it could be heard above all the other machines. Like Dracula, it seemed to suck everything out of you, but what a beautiful sound.

Saturday January 7th 1967 was a dark and dismal trip home from Berkeley. The A38 was known as the 'Killer Road' due to the many deaths on it in the 60s. Before the M5 was built it carried all traffic going to and from the West Country. To make it worse the highways department had put an overtaking lane in the middle, in one accident involving a VW camper van, 8 died.

As I approached the left hand sweep through the village of Cam I was more cautious than normal, my front brake was sticking. I always treated this bend with respect as there was a turning to Dursley on the apex and a bus stop on either side, often with a bus pulling out. I noticed a car in the opposite bus stop and a woman crossing the road, unfortunately she stopped on my side of the road when she saw me. The sidecar's known as the safest vehicle on the road as you can change direction quickly, I pulled the handlebars hard to the right as I shut the throttle and leaned to the right trying to keep the machine stable but I felt a sickening thud which nearly made me lose my grip of the handlebars. I was out of control on the wrong side of road on the killer A38! God was on my and the lady's side that night as no vehicles came along for the next 30 seconds, enough time for the bike to come to a stop one foot from a brick wall.

Leaping from my bike, I ran to the lady lying in the road as people stood around, shouting "some of you slow the traffic down." I rushed to the phone box and shouted "get off the phone, I want to dial 999", "I'm already doing that" was the reply. I ran back to the woman putting my gauntlets under her head and asked her how she was, "I am sorry it was my fault" she said. I breathed a sigh of relief, told her not to worry about it now and that the ambulance was on the way. I looked around and asked if someone could get a blanket and glass of water. The lady kept apologising, it was a shame the policeman arrived after the ambulance. He checked the markings and said "if it had been a car or lorry she would be in the mortuary." I'd hit the lady's leg with the sidecar mudguard but it was safe enough to ride home after the police had taken my details.

Although I'd been advised never to go to see anyone in hospital after an accident, I'd hit another human being and it dwelled on my mind as I rode home. I found the lady in A&E, her hair combed and cleaned up, she gave me a smile saying "sorry, it was my fault." I told her I was pleased she was looking better. Paying my insurance 3 months later, it had rocketed up to £4-10/-, the insurance company had paid the lady £800. I complained, "The lady said it was her fault and the police didn't prosecute." They replied that it wasn't worth going to court over and it was too late now.

Our butchery-course group stayed together after passing the second stage of meat hygiene. We somehow passed business organisation, scientific principles, meat inspection and accounting, probably due to the lady tutor offering extra tuition on Sundays to four of us.

It was suggested our class now take the Meat Inspectors' course. After the first few weeks I felt like I was training to be a doctor of dead animals, making sure the animals were fit for human consumption. I was struggling as the names of diseases were in Latin. The course was 5 hours a week, 2½ hours theory and attending the abattoir for practical. Ray Ulla, a meat inspector, took us for the practical and some of the theory. The other tutor, Reg Pitt, owned his own Butcher's shop and managed his mother's two shops. He offered me a job with the Excelsior Meat Co. at Gloucester indoor market at £16 a week. I'd had good times at Berkeley, but many bad, including the accident a week before, so I accepted, saving 2 hours travelling a day and getting £2 a week more. I was nervous giving in my notice and would miss Peggy, Mrs Holpin's cooking, Gilbert, Gill's tight jeans, nearly everybody, bar Fred who made a nasty remark!

The new job was quite restrictive as I was working on a stall. There was a cool counter to display meat in the front, a shelf behind for the till, a small cool room and small cutting block. Apart from this it was all open with the main fridge for each butcher and fishmonger 30+ yards away. The Market Hall was a massive Victorian building with cast-iron beams and pillars. The Excelsior Meat Co. managed by Mike Lee, with Aunty Lillian (Mrs Pitt's sister), was one of 4 butchers, there was the same number of fishmongers. Our stall was opposite Rigby's fish stall run by 3 brothers. I got on with Edwin as he made me laugh telling me tales of his Army days including the D-Day landings. His two brothers did their bit as did their uncle who I called 'Arthur Askey' as he was 5' tall and looked like the 1940/50's comedian. He had a twitch which I asked Edwin about. "He was captured at Dunkirk, a prisoner of war until 1945 and Unk (as they called him), used to give the guards grief, so they hit him with their rifle butts" he explained. It's a good job I wasn't there with my big mouth.

A group of the CMC bike section decided to do the February 1967 Dragon Rally in Snowdonia. John Hammond agreed to come on the back of my combination and we met the rest at the viaduct in Kidderminster, Keith Smith and Val on a 600cc Norton, Brian Chapman on a Honda 90 and Mervin and Lou on a 500cc BSA. On the trip to the rally the faster bikes stopped every 20 miles in a lay-by for us to catch up.

The Saturday was overcast but it seemed to get brighter as we got closer to North Wales or was it seeing more motorcycles which brightens up any dark day for a biker? The last 10 miles of the trip was a long crocodile of various makes of motorcycle, a fantastic sight. We were all talking bikes while crowded around a large bonfire with a beer tent and hotdog van. We didn't take tents, just sleeping bags as they advertised a large community tent, trouble was, the large tent had been pitched on a slight gradient so we kept rolling over into the next person. The journey home was better with the sun shining on Snowdon.

CASTLE COOMBE 1966

I had problems with the Greeves at one of my last races on it at Castle Combe. The first was when warming it up. I kept it running too long and as I pulled away the bike stopped. Big Mick broke the 100 yards dash getting another plug and spanner as the plug in the bike was wet from a build-up of fuel in the crankcases. In the 250cc heat I was lying 6th when the machine stopped, it was the self-puller again. Big Mick told me that I was in front of Rod Scivyer on the works Cotton Telstar. Watching the 250cc final I was stood next to Geoff Duke who was then running a race team for Royal Enfield GP5 250s. In the early 60's there was an explosion of two-stroke racing engines as they were cheaper to produce, many used a Villiers Starmaker engine or as Royal Enfield and Greeves did, an Alpha bottom end with different designs of barrels, so there were more manufactures names on the start line.

We left early as my racing was over. As we went through Stroud we stopped at Halfords in Gloucester Street on the steep hill, when we came out we did a U-turn. While waiting at the junction by the police station, we noticed a policeman walking towards us "Mick, what have we done wrong?" "Nothing that I know of George." The policeman put his hand on the throttle and squeezed the front brake. "Excuse me Sir, do you know Stroud very well?" "I've worked for Dewhurst butchers a few times, but not that well officer." In a friendly but sarcastic voice the policeman said "that's quite obvious Sir, you are waiting to come out of one-way street the wrong way." "Oh dear officer, I am a silly Billy. Do you know Stuart Hughes, he works at Cheltenham police HQ maintaining vehicles?" I was trying to namedrop. Luckily, he let me off. Stuart had been racing a Royal Enfield GP5 at Castle Combe. I was saddened to hear that he'd been killed racing at Mallory Park the next day.

Mum decided to stop riding her 125cc Bantam at the age of 60 and Dave acquired a BMW bubble car which she could drive on her motorcycle licence. It looked like an aircraft cockpit, had a reverse gear, 2 wheels at the front and used a 300cc BMW single cylinder engine. It was quite powerful for what it was but very noisy and designed to take 2 or 3 at a push. I asked Mum if I could use it but didn't tell her I'd asked a young lady who worked on the Peacocks stall in the market, out for a drink. This romance didn't last long. The next date was tenpin bowling in Bristol and the 75 mile round trip next to a noisy engine killed any conversation, another romance bites the dust.

Sat in a Cheltenham pub on a Saturday night in September 1967 I saw an advert for ballroom dancing lessons at Listers School of dancing in Pittville Lawn, I called in on the way home for details. The lady told me that beginners started tonight but it was nearly over and I should come back next week, the cost was 10/-.

The next week, the same pretty girl called Heather made me welcome. I bought a drink at a small bar, it was mainly couples with a few single people and I made friends with a chap about my age. Mrs Lister was a stern looking lady in her late 40s. I saw a certificate on the wall "Janet Lister, winner 1947 West of England dance championship." Her main assistant was Sheila, late 30's and a jolly lady, helped by Heather, 5' 2", eyes of blue and in her early 20's. Mrs Lister took off the record that a few couples were dancing to, "Good evening everybody, the first dance lesson tonight is the quickstep." I'd missed the waltz the week before, and found the quickstep, a little quick, no pun intended. "Will the men take the floor" Mrs Lister boomed out like a sergeant major. With much mumbling we stood facing her, my embarrassment was made worse when she said "please lift your arms in the air like Sheila, then copy the steps she'll do." Sheila lifted her arms, I was thinking *have I got to do that? I must look a complete prat!* I was concentrating on Sheila's figure more than the steps she was taking especially as raising her arms lifted her dress slightly above her knee. Mrs Lister shouting "slow, slow, quick, quick, slow," woke me from my trance. The ladies were laughing at the men going in all directions. Then it was the ladies turn, doing the same moves only backwards. Then we were told to pick a partner. I didn't ask a boy as I did in 1955 but there was a shortage of ladies so I danced with Sheila.

I borrowed the bubble car to work in Stroud, was I getting soft? Coming home I skidded to a stop, it had seized. I put it in neutral and pushed it to the garage that had a WW2 gun turret outside then thumbed a lift 5 miles home. Frank agreed to drive the bubble car while I towed him with my combination. I'd fixed up with Geoff Fivash for him to repair it, he'd moved his workshop near to where Frank lived. Using a short length of rope, Frank, as a fireman, tied the knots. Towing was no trouble but when turning right a cyclist went to ride between the bike and the bubble car before he saw the rope, we all managed to stop in time with no one injured. I can still see the cyclist's white face.

Another time, I ran out of petrol in Bamfurlong Lane near Staverton Airport (yes you are correct, I'm a complete waste of time) and mum agreed to drive the car as it wasn't too far. I towed mum back past Staverton Airport, but when I stopped at the junction, she sounded the horn and got out in tears. "George, you've scared me to death, you were going much too fast." "Sorry mum, am I in the doghouse again?" I was pleased this comment brought a smile to mum's face and got me a slap across the arm.

Brother Dave was always suggesting I buy a car. He'd brought home a Bedford Dormobile workers truck only £15 but 'no sale.' With hindsight it would have been good for taking girls out as well as for the bike. I had to laugh when Geoff Fivash said "tell your Dave I will give him 7 and a half for that van he is selling." I confirmed with him, "okay, Geoff £750 for the van" Geoff choked "No, no, no, £7-10/-!"

So started the dancing years on Saturday nights. I saw the lads in the week and on special occasions. Dancing was keeping me fit. I bought a book to help me learn ballroom dances and put bits of paper on the floor at home for the steps shown in the book so I could practice. I drew the curtains as I felt like a pillock doing it on my own, but I was keen to learn!

The market job was going well, I got a pay rise after I had passed the second butchery exam; I was now on £17 a week. At 06.30 on Saturday 30th September 1967 BBC started Radio 1 and Radio 2 to challenge all the commercial radio stations like Radio Caroline who transmitted from outside the 12-mile limit. All the market traders tuned their radios to the new station to hear "This is Tony Blackburn, welcome to Radio 1." When I hear Flowers in the Rain by the Move, my mind goes back to that day. The song was associated with 'Flower Power' a movement that started in the USA, for peace and love and against the war in Vietnam, not that I was getting any free love!!!

The Meat Inspectors' course was quite intensive. During the second year, Ray Ulla had kept back a heifer carcass for us to see, explaining that as it

103

was a heifer the farmer got a subsidy as it hadn't given birth and the cervix wasn't broken, but after the animal had been killed and cut open the placenta had a calf inside. We were stood around when Ray Ulla cut it open, gallons of fluid ran over the floor and there was a perfectly formed dead calf, it certainly made me wrench. I did ask "when an animal had TB why is whole carcass destroyed?" "Do you think the public would like to know they were eating animal that had TB?" was the reply.

A nice surprise in the market was when I met Uncle Sid, my mother's brother, who had married a German lady. Mum introduced us. David had told me that he'd gone round to see Uncle Sid when he got his first motorcycle. After tea and cakes Uncle Sid gave him 10/- and thanked him for coming but not come again as it upsets his wife! He and his wife came shopping quite often and always talked to me.

Mervin Trinder, who'd married Joan, one of the office girls, in 1959, and managed the Dewhurst branch in Eastgate Street asked me to come back to Dewhurst for £17 a week. "I'm already earning that," I told him. With a disbelieving look he offered me £17.10/-, I told him I'd think about it. I'd worked at Eastgate Street in the 60's with the then manager Harry Green. Harry had been in his 40's and was always worried about his teenage daughter. He told me about when he was in the desert with Monty, up to his neck in muck and bullets, or was it sand and bullets and not a care in the world, but now, with a growing daughter he had more worries than he wanted, he didn't tell me about the people shooting at him. I wonder if my mum and dad thought that way about me.

Early in 1967, after blow-ups due to lack of mechanical knowledge and work problems at Berkeley, I'd thought I'd retire from motorcycle racing and sold the Greeves in the spring. This didn't really work as I started building an A7 BSA 500cc twin. I'd acquired a rolling chassis and spares and was hoping to build a cheap and more reliable racer. I saw an advert for BSA twin spares and contacted Mike Taylor, a London grass track racer who had moved to Churchdown. Mike, as well as riding a 350cc JAP solo machine, raced a 650cc Beezer grass track sidecar, very powerful and similar to the engine I wanted to build. I was hoping to learn from him.

I'd made friends with an 18 year old lad who worked on another butcher's stall who had a biker friend. Both of them had new Triumph Tiger Cubs. I suggested that we support Mike Taylor at the 3 Counties Showground grass track race and went on the back of one of the new bikes. We found

Mike and his wife Maureen, who used to call my A10 BSA the Torrey Canyon as it leaked oil on their drive. The three-day show in June was mainly for farm equipment and animal shows but always ended with various special events including a grass track race. After about an hour the lads wanted to move on, but as a racer I wanted to stay and help so Mike agreed to run me home. It was a good job I stayed, in Mike's second race a rider fell off in front of him, he hit the bike breaking his forks off. Luckily, he only had a few bruises but needed help to load up and to unload at his place, Maureen drove me home after.

I was around Mike's house learning to make my bike go faster when he asked "George, will you passenger me next weekend, my regular passenger is away?" Me and my mouth, it was bloody scary, 60 mph on grass and I had bruises for a month but it was a very enjoyable day, once it was over. During the day Mike said "do you want a cuppa, I'm making some track brew but this isn't race track brew." He explained that he volunteered for the SAS and when working in the jungle for Special Forces he'd learnt how to make it, and went on to say, "but if you tell anyone I'll have to kill you!"

October time I had an offer from Reg Pitt to manage the Excelsior shop in Stroud at £20 a week and decided to accept. Strangely, months earlier I fancied getting on a cruise ship as a steward or kitchen hand, but had no CV, not that I knew what a CV was. I put in my letters that I was a qualified Butcher and had also passed Ballroom dance exams. Cunard was the only positive reply, suggesting I apply again next summer, P and O Shipping Line gave me a shorter but polite no, but from the banana boat Co. Ffyfes Banana Co., who also carried passengers, I got a curt get knotted letter!

Reg had only said turn up on the Monday! I found the first problem was that Ron Giles would be helping me; Ron had been a shop-man cutter when I started as a butcher's boy in 1959. He'd managed large shops even a butchery supermarket section, but appeared to be on a downhill slide. The first morning Reg brought Ron and we both saw the shop for the first time. The previous manager, Mr Morgan, had opened a shop in Gloucester. Reg explained in a roundabout way that his mother instead of wishing him well in his new venture, had stand-up arguments with him in the shop, further explaining "when I told his assistant I was putting you as manager, he left." I couldn't blame him and found out later that he went to Baxter's, another butcher's chain in the 60's.

While I was putting on a shop window display customers were asking "where is Mr Morgan?" "I'm afraid he's left to open a shop in Gloucester." Many asked "where is his assistant?" Lying through my teeth I replied "I think he may have gone with him, I was working for Mr Pitt in Gloucester and he asked me to come over, knowing Stroud is a nice place." This went on day after day, we were making up all sorts of stories. Another problem was when a policeman came in and asked, "can I have a shilling wrap-up?" I asked what a wrap-up was, "Mr Morgan, gives us a sausage, slice of bacon, slice of black pudding and an egg." I told him I couldn't do all that for 1/- but I'd do the best I could, most left without a wrap-up!! A travelling salesman from Bowyer of Trowbridge, put six packs of sausages on the counter, telling me that Mr Morgan always had six. I looked at Ron "what do you think Ron? Mr Pitt makes sausages." As I had to spend money and they were quite expensive, I decided to buy three packs. This turned out to be another mistake as all the packs sold and three customers were unlucky. Adding to the lies about why Mr Morgan left I said "sorry we've had a rush on these sausages but I'll let you have some of Mr Pitt's home-made sausages at a discount for your trouble," most turned them down.

On 25th October 1967 there was an outbreak of foot and mouth disease to add to our misery, with all the restrictions the prices shot up. I talked with Mr Pitt as trade was struggling. Mr Morgan had taken all his best customers with him and trade had fallen from £500 to £300 a week. Reg made a bold move, we offered topside at 5/- a pound when it was normally 8/- and dropped other beef prices as well. It did help a bit but we were still at only just over £350 a week.

We had a horrid problem with damp in the shop so there were cockroaches. I arrived one morning half asleep, putting on my coat and apron I found large black cockroaches, being a wimp I let out a scream and removed my coat and apron as soon as I could to shake them off. In the 60's the pest controller came free, which was just as well as we also had some rats in the cellar!

Christmas trade was going very well, both Ron and I working our cobblers off, goodness knows how Mr Morgan managed £500 every week. The week before Christmas we had another order for a fresh chicken. When I asked Reg his reply was, "defrost a frozen bird, tell him it is fresh." I wasn't going to do that. When I was butcher's boy, a customer bought a cockerel in for us to dress, giving Mr Finch 5/- to do it. When another customer asked for a fresh cockerel and said he would pay the earth for it Ken Finch

106

sold it to him then gave me the job of dressing a small turkey making it look like the cockerel he'd sold!

Possibly my last mistake in this job was asking for payment from the Hotel just down the road to make £500 Christmas week. This upset the manageress and she took her trade somewhere else. I decided I was not a good butcher's manager and what with having to take the books home to work on every Sunday, I was virtually working a 7-day week. It's a good job this was in the winter with no racing bikes to prepare. I got on well with a sweet shop manager and we did a swap, a chicken for 12 large bars of Cadbury's Whole Nut chocolate, Mmmm. I joined the Cadbury Whole Nut Party. There was an advertising campaign on TV against the Cadbury Fruit and Nut Party! Our party rallying song was "nuts, whole hazelnuts, Cadburys take them and they cover them in chocolate," against the other sides "everyone's a fruit and nut case." I wore with pride a pin badge that said "I am a Whole Nut" something all my friends agreed with!

Christmas day I took dad up The Kings Head, Norton, in mum's bubble car. Seeing Dave Cheeseman from next door there, I offering him a ride home as he and dad were certainly over the drink drive limit. I was on my usual cider shandy, but more than the one I normally had. Dad got the usual singsong going in the pub and on the way home. We hadn't finished singing by the time we got back so we carried on the last verse with mum looking at us saying "silly buggers"! Then over to Dave and Sue for Christmas dinner then New Year's Eve at the CMC doing the conga to Little Eva's, The Locomotion.

CHAPTER 6 1968/69-Change of job

Saturday 6th of January at 6.15am I found 3" of snow when I arrived at Horsepools Hill with only one set of wheel tracks in it from the 6am bus going up the hill, and none coming down the other side. I was slipping and sliding up the hill. The beauty of a sidecar, in theory, is that you can't fall off going slow, so I was bouncing up and down to keep traction. Once over the top I stopped for a rest, the journey down was even scarier. I arrived in Stroud wiping the sweat from my brow and wasn't surprised when Ron didn't turn up. I had more customers than usual, all saying that I was one of the few shops open and that they'd had a job to get in, many roads were closed. Reg Pitt arrived with Ron at dinnertime, his jaw dropped seeing the shop full of customers. He asked me how long I'd been open. He was amazed when I told him and said, "well done." This didn't help when, a week later Reg came in and said "Sorry George, I'll have to let you go, I'm putting a friend in as manager." I whimpered and played my violin, but he said, "I'll give you a golden handshake, a week's wages."

The black cloud over my head got blacker. 3 months of misery, hard work, foot and mouth and now sacked. To add insult to injury, after going to college for five years, they changed the syllabus for the meat inspector's exam so I couldn't take it! I called in to Dewhurst Head Office, Norman Davies was still district manager there. I asked him if the job Mervin had offered me was still open. "Why" he asked, "job not working out in Stroud?" "No, not really, it's further to go, crap parking and too much responsibility for the money." Forgive me Lord for more porky pies. He told me to start with Mervin on Monday week.

I contacted the Jobcentre for possible dole money but it was too complicated and, anyway, I was being paid. I bought an employment stamp from the post office to stick on my cards when I picked them up after having to remind them of the promised golden handshake. More snow fell that week so having no work turned out to be a blessing in disguise. It was good job I had an insulated shed to work on the bike.

I asked Dad if he wanted to go for a drink and skittles up the Kings Head on Saturday. He was surprised but agreeable and we used the bubble car, leaving mum watching TV. There was always an open game on Saturday night, after buying drinks we went into the skittle alley. Eventually I plucked up courage. "Dad I've got a problem, I've been sacked. I've got a job already back at Dewhurst, but what are we going to tell mum?" I nibbled some Smith's crisps (cost 6d) after opening the blue packet of salt and shaking it on them while Dad took a sip of his beer. "What do you think you should say George?" "Something like I didn't like it in Stroud, the travelling was too much and Dewhurst wanted me back maybe." Dad agreed to go along with that. Sunday, when mum was dishing up the dinner I told her "I have some news mum, I'm starting back at Dewhurst butchers, I didn't like it at Stroud very much." Mum smiled and said "Oh I am pleased, I always liked Dewhurst." Dad gave me a wink and I explained the week off as holiday pay.

Although I liked the butchery trade, especially the young wives or mothers with young daughters coming in, winking and making eyes at me, hoping I would give them something extra, *stop thinking naughty thoughts*, the job had lost something. With Frank in the Fire Service and having asked about the Fire Service when I was leaving school I started considering it again.

The bike was taking shape. Over the winter, I'd written to BSA for a 500/650 engine tuning sheet, I'd found a fibreglass tank and some go faster chequered tape. I needed a close ratio gearbox, BSA made one for the Goldstar RRT2. I found one in the MCN and rang the dealer. "If I send you £20 will you send it by return of post?" I asked. Six weeks later, having contacted the RAC legal department for help I eventually got the gearbox. It was either collect the spares or get them sent COD.

Coombes and Ridgeon car sales were doing well and when big brother brought home a VW Beetle XJ0 36 he asked if I liked it, and did I want a test drive? He was getting to be a better salesman and convinced me to say yes. As we were driving up Horsepools Hill on the way to Stroud, Dave was pulling out knobs saying which did what. "These are the wipers," he said, the wiper blades started going in and out in opposite directions, with one wiping half the bonnet. Laughing, I had to stop driving! Dave talked me in to buying it so I had to get a tow bar fitted a bit quick. It was my usual bodge job. I bolted it straight onto the bumper nearly pulling it off and had to strengthen it with help from Tony Price who also made a trailer for it. At brother Dave's home in Tewkesbury we admired an Austin Healey 3000. He took me for a spin in it saying, "do you want to drive it?" Luckily we were on a quiet road, when I put my foot down it took off like a scalded cat, then braking hard, it stood on its front wheels! "George what the devil are you doing?" Dave asked, or something similar. I answered with a squeaky voice "Well Dave, that VW beetle you sold me thinks for 10 minutes before moving, and when braking you could do with a parachute to help slow you down" which made him smile. "Wow, what a car!"

THE GREEVES AT LITTLE RISSINGTON

The CMC had lost Little Rissington in 1966. At the last August meeting I'd qualified for the 250cc final. With big Mick helping, I assumed the 250 had been checked after the heat, but in the final, coming over the start/finish line, where mum and dad were watching, the back wheel locked solid. I pulled the clutch in but it did nothing, as the song goes, he flew through the air with the greatest of ease. I came around in the ambulance with mum holding my hand, and thought, *I'd have preferred the pretty nurse!* The reason I'd crashed was the primary chain had broken, the oil trouble again. A Red flag stopped the race as I was lying in the track, I'm told mother ran onto the track shouting "that's my boy." I spent a night in hospital.

The meeting before, again with big Mick helping, the bike was going well until the rotor worked loose damaging the coil. I'd entered Oulton Park the next day as I was considering entering the Manx Grand Prix (MGP) and had applied for a national ACU licence costing 10/– and needed long track experience. When loading up I found a puncture in the sidecar wheel. Tony Price to the rescue, he had a wheel at home. We got the wheel off and then looked at the ignition problem, not getting home until 10pm. We were both feeling tired and not wanting to make any mistakes decided to get an early night but when the alarm went off at 5am next morning we looked at each other and turned over!

The CMC was lucky to find Morton Valence, a disused RAF station on the Bristol Road 5 miles from Gloucester, it was used for the 1967/68 seasons.

I was making inquiries about joining the fire service, but Gloucester City Fire Brigade where Frank was stationed replied that there was no chance, "dead men's shoes only," as there was only one station. Next I tried the Gloucestershire Fire Service. At the Cheltenham HQ, while filling in an application form I found out that they had three full-time stations, Cheltenham, Stroud and Patchway with four day-manning and retained stations. Ken Hill, chairman of the CMC motorcycle section, was in charge of Cheltenham Fire Station and showed me round, I was impressed. I'd written to London Fire Brigade but as there was no offer of help with accommodation, joining the fire service was in limbo!

I entered the Festival of Speed meeting at Lydden Hill, in Kent, on May 18th 1968. It's a very short circuit, just a mile long, but 200 miles away. Garnet towed my trailer with his Austin A40. We stopped for fuel and Garnet asked for a pint of oil, the attendant poured it down the carburettor and we lost 30 minutes cleaning the plugs! It was good day, not only bikes but cars, grass track and even a cycle racing. I know why I liked going to Lydden, a pretty lady called Brenda was in the office. The bike started well but after two laps it started misfiring and I pulled in, the end of magneto had come loose. We were strolling around the paddock and another rider asked if I'd made the final. When I told him I hadn't finished he said "the B final for the also-rans is on next," instant panic to sort the bike out!! I'd found I was much better if I didn't have time to worry about the start and this time there was certainly no time. I was last through the gate onto the track and by the time I stopped the bike the flag had dropped. I was in the top six, I got to 4th on the first lap, swapped places then got 2nd I was really enjoying this race and about to overtake the leader Dickey Allen when Ron Phelps overtook both of us. I overtook Dickey Allen and Ron Phelps was still in sight, the starter indicated last lap so I didn't shut off and went flat out into The Whale Hump ending up in a pile on the track. I picked the bike up wanting to restart despite fuel pouring out of a hole in the tank and no foot rest. Three Marshals dragged me and the bike off the track. When I saw my third finger with no skin on it, and the bones showing when I moved it, my knees went weak.

At Canterbury Hospital the doctor said "we'll have to do a skin graft, count to 10" I don't remember the 10. While waiting for Garnet to arrive I asked a lady what she was in for, "my husband was mowing the grass and tripped breaking his leg," she replied. Life is strange, I fall off at 80 mph and he falls over a stick breaking his leg. Garnet drove back as my arm was in a sling. What made things better was reading the Lydden report in MCN ".......the best race was the B final with Ridgeon and Allen swapping places but Ridgeon crashing out taking Allen with him let Phelps have the glory." Sorry Roger!

FESTIVAL OF SPEED, LYDDEN HILL

I was on the sick. Mother, who'd been a seamstress in the 1920's, cannibalised a shirt using a sleeve to make a glove, covering my hand with the cuff. My bad finger was dressed twice a week in hospital, but after a few days' rest I got used to driving the car so I could get about.

As the TT was on I asked mum and dad if they'd like a few days at the TT and found a B&B in Derby Road for 4 days. The route took us through the Mersey Tunnel which was exhilarating as well as scary! At the other end of the Tunnel a policeman gave me directions. I took the route I thought he told me, but was heading back into the Mersey Tunnel! I did a U-turn in the no U-turn area and went back past the policeman whose jaw dropped. This time I found the correct route and we got to Princes Dock early. I found out when the boat was sailing, where to park for 4 days and where to get a cuppa as dad was gagging for one. I suppose you could call dad a drug addict, he had to have his roll up and a cuppa!

The excitement of seeing the Isle of Man, the beautiful large bay and houses on the Promenade with the mountains in the background is something I'll always remember. It was 6pm, we looked for a cafe as dad was struggling now, and after a light snack to give us the strength we set off uphill to find Derby Road, poor old dad. The landlady was very welcoming, she showed us to our rooms but I could hear bikes, she told me it was evening practice. I was running like a scared rabbit along streets following the noise. I ended up near the bottom of Bray Hill at Ago's Leap and there was the man himself. I saw Agostini with his front wheel in the air at 140+ mph. Regrettably for racing fans, Mike Hailwood had retired from the TT after his epic race with Ago in 1967 and wouldn't return for 11 Years. I saw Renso Pasolini on the Bennelli, lots of Manx Nortons and G50 Matchlesses. After practice I went back to the hotel then for a pint with mum and dad at The Bowling Green Hotel.

Another motorcycle enthusiast was stopping at the B & B, he asked if I'd like to go look at the bikes. I was amazed at the friendliness of the Manx people, he took me to see somebody he knew saying "this is George, he's stopping at our digs," they asked us in for a cuppa and piece of cake. The trip on the electric railway through Laxey to Snaefell Mountain, was a little slow for me but mum and dad loved it. While in Laxey we went to see the Lady Isabella, the largest waterwheel in the world but this was an uphill walk so dad said he'd sit on the bench while mum and I went on up to the wheel. We climbed the 80 feet to the top, mum was 65 acted like a 40 year old, I had a job to keep up with her. The four days passed quickly and having seen some more practice I thought Renso Pasolini on the four-cylinder Benelli, its four lovely up-swept pipes and the MV Augusta 'fire-engines' were the bee's knees, the sounds were fantastic!

We found the car in Liverpool, still with its wheels, joke! On the A-roads heading for Shrewsbury it was very dark and not very enjoyable, especially when the police pulled me over. "Do you know the speed limits sir?" I was very apologetic, "Sorry Officer, just trying to get my parents home, they're very tired and not feeling very well after being on the ferry from the Isle of Man." Shining his light in the back he looked at mum and dad sat there, looking sad, scared and old, then back at me. "Take it steady Sir." Dad called me a cheeky bugger when I said "I've started telling lies like you used to dad," and we all had a laugh.

I missed the May meeting at Morton Valence with my injured hand but did some marshalling. I noticed Dave Browning racing a magnificent Egli

Vincent as well as campaigning a Heron Yamaha, having moved from the Cotton Telstar. He won the British 250cc championship in 1969. He was later involved in a serious head on collision while driving his E-Type which forced his retirement. Dad got excited watching Malcolm Uphill and Selwyn Griffins, both from Wales. DeFazio, a bike dealer from Somerset, rode a special hub steering bike and Dave Simmons was riding a Tohatsu, a high revving 2 stroke which mum said sounded like a bumble bee. Dave Simmons was 125cc world champion in 1969 but sadly died in a caravan fire in 1972. There were many top riders competing including Percy Tate and local lads, John Kidson and Jim Curry.

After two months I'd heard nothing so I went back to Gloucestershire Fire Service HQ. I saw Mr Beckinsale the top civilian who told me that it could be two years before I heard back but that he'd put down on my record that I'd shown interest. While there, I asked what questions they might ask in general knowledge, maths and English were obvious. "Do you know the 2 candidates in the American presidential election" he replied. When I gave the correct answer he said "well done, good luck in the exam."

As I could now ballroom dance I attended various events such as the CMC dances and butchery trade events where I made friends with the Gilder family, farmers near Cheltenham. I'd met the son at Technical College, and his pretty sister at the meat trade dances. Her brother said he wanted me to manage a butcher's shop he was opening soon in Cheltenham, I said I'd think about it.

I was making friends at Listers, two sisters and their husbands had a single pretty friend called Gaynor. I made a date with no particular time to arrive, or so I thought. I ate my usual faggots and peas Saturday night and ended up watching the 1938 Robin Hood film before arriving at Gaynor's house about 8pm. There was some panic, Peter and Angela were there; they'd booked up for a partner dance at The Pheasant Inn at Welland. We just made it, the dance and meal were very enjoyable but with two meals eaten it was a good job there was a lot of dancing!

Our group had several trips out, one was to the Regency Rout held at the Pittville Pump Rooms. Gaynor and I missed the start because she was in The Pirates of Penzance by Gilbert and Sullivan and I went to watch. It was in a boys' school, but the two principal lady characters needed to be women. One line of a song I remember goes "I polished up that handle so carefullee, That now I am the Ruler of the Queen's Navee!" I had a

114

pleasant surprise when the man who had been playing the piano said hello, he was one of the three Burr sons who lived in Ash Lane and used to knockabout with our Dave.

ME   ANGELA   GAYNOR   PETER

Gaynor was dressed in period costume for the play so she had little to do to get ready for the Rout. I hired an outfit but only the red tailed coat and the white knee stockings fitted. I used false hair for long sideburns and wore my white jeans pulled over my knees with the stockings. I made a monocle to hang on a small chain from my lapel and had some silver fag paper on a couple of old buckles to put on my shoes. I thought I must look like a right pillock, but when we got there at midnight, everybody was dressed the same. I felt easier when we found Peter and Angela; another enjoyable night.

Christmas time was spent with Angela, Peter and Gaynor. At The Pheasant, Angela got very tiddly so when we were dancing to All I have to do is Dream, the 1968 version by Glen Campbell and Bobby Gentry, her arms were around my neck and we were ever so close, I was going red. To make things worse going home she said "I want to sit in the back with George." Gaynor sat in the front and Peter was driving. Angela smothered me with kisses, I was getting exceedingly embarrassed as her husband was sat in the front seat, as well as the lady I was supposed to be with. I shouted "Peter, come and rescue me" but Peter and Gaynor just laughed, so I carried on enjoying it!

There were many laughs at dancing lessons. We were all stood there with arms in the air, with my right arm out straight I said "I'm about to turn left," realising my mistake I said "no wonder I didn't pass my driving test." A lady who was quite a laugh and kept getting her steps wrong said, "I think I've got both legs in one knicker hole!" In a practice session for the Tango, Janet Lister took the record off. "That was terrible" she said, then listed everything we'd done wrong, "shoulders slouched, back not straight, not on the ball of the foot, no sharp movements. I'm putting the record on again." No one got up so Mrs Lister shouted "get up" but no one moved. She ordered Peter and Angela to get up. After a few seconds she stopped the record again ordering everyone to pick a partner. Some said Mrs. Lister was a dragon, others, an army training sergeant or a lion tamer with a big whip!

At the end of August Garnet and I agreed to go to Scotland on holiday. Although his Austin A40 was only 800cc it was reliable and I'd not had my 1200cc air cooled VW very long, the little Austin went well. The furthest I had been before this was Oulton Park and Liverpool, we went miles past that taking a break in the Lake District. We pitched the large tent, it needed to be big as Garnet, being a carpenter, had made himself a wooden bed he could put together. He'd sewn some sacking together which slid on the sides to lie on. I'd bought a wire bed that clipped together, unfortunately it was lightweight and I was a heavy lump, if I didn't get it right I ended up on the ground, with Garnet laughing. We had the cases on the top of a roof rack. My dad must've liberated some elastic from Dowty's, it was several yards long and we used it to tie the cases on which came in handy one night. We were chatting and starting to nod off when we heard a ripping sound. In the morning I found Garnet with his feet on one end of the bed, his head on the other end, his bum resting on the ground, all the middle of the sacking had ripped. It was my turn to laugh; the next night we used the elastic to make his bed.

We went to the pictures in Barrow in Furness and Garnet lost his wallet. At his bank we had a palaver trying to prove who he was, eventually Garnet had to ring his branch. The next day we left for Glasgow going over the Kirkstone Pass. I think this is one of the most beautiful sights I've ever seen. We stopped for the night near Dumfries, leaving the next day as it was a bit of an industrial estate and the pub we went into for quiet pint was more like a cattle shed with sawdust on the floor, it was for men who wanted to get drunk.

Fort William, what a beautiful sight, we were camped on the side of a loch and could see Ben Nevis. After making up Garnet's elastic bed, we chatted

116

before going to sleep. He woke me up in the middle of the night and accused me of snoring, "no I wasn't," "Oh yes you were." No, this is not another pantomime. We were just about to get back to sleep, "Zzzzzzzz," the snoring had started again. Despite being woken up we both burst out laughing. The next morning the tent started shaking and a loud Scottish voice said "are ye staying?" "Yes we are" "that's five shillings." We had to give him the 5/- there and then! When we did get outside, the nearest tent was over 50 yards away and that's where the snoring had come from.

We momentarily thought about climbing up Ben Nevis but quickly decided to dismiss the idea. We did however, go and visit Spean Bridge. There is a bronze statue of three commandos, the plinth has "United we Conquer." And the plaque below reads "In memory of the officers and men of the commandos who died in the Second World War 1939–1945. This country was their training ground." I must admit I had a tear in my eye. Sadly the local pub hadn't heard of cider shandy. During the evening someone suggested that as we were so close how about going to John O'Groats. Quite close? The 190 miles on those twisty, narrow Highland roads made it seem as far to John O'Groats as from Gloucester.

We kept commenting on each other's driving. Garnet said "don't tell me how to drive my car," as he was reversing up this narrow road in the middle of the Highlands as a car and caravan was coming the other way, I thought, *he's going into the ditch!* Luckily, the car towing the caravan had a special tow rope. We helped fit it as best we could and pulled Garnett out of the ditch. I think we buggered up the ropes' brackets somehow so we got going quickly. 100's of miles from anywhere, just passing the odd cottage or small township and we arrived at John O' Groats in the early evening. There was just time to visit the souvenir shop where we bumped into an ex-Longlevens School pupil whose surname was Ritchie, who told us he'd found a link to a Scottish clan! After pitching the tent 100 yards from the North Sea we walked to the first and last pub. The 2 lads at the bar were chatting and playing darts, one was a builder, the other a butcher. We had a good night and arranged to pick up some sirloin steaks in the morning. We fell asleep with the fresh air and were up and away early next day to find the Butcher's shop and two sirloin steaks at the right money!

There was more lovely scenery through Glen Coe (said to be the most haunted site in the British Isles) where in 1692 the McDonalds were slaughtered by the British, both Garnet and I were looking behind us wondering if we were going to be attacked with a claymore. We followed the coast through Inverness over the Forth Road Bridge (what a sight the Forth Railway Bridge is) into Edinburgh. The trip was not far off 280 miles. We stopped in the Old Dalkeith Campsite, cooking the steaks on the primus, making gravy from the juices of the steak, with onions, potatoes and peas. As we'd run out of Methylated Spirits for the primus Garnet drove to a chemist to buy some. When he got back he told me they'd asked him how old he was, he told them 24 and asked why they wanted to know. The chemist told him that as some Methylated Spirit is clear, people may drink it so you need to be over 18 to buy it, we both cringed!

We were lucky, the Edinburgh Festival was on. We went to watch the parade and saw a horse and cart with loads of girls on it. A pretty girl gave us a leaflet saying "come and see us tonight," we decided to go. Although they were a religious group, thinking of my aunty Win, I enjoyed it, there was dancing but Garnet was enjoying talking to the girls. We didn't find the type of pubs we were used to, no conversation, just serious drinking, so after a pint we wandered around the city. We decided to call it a day and go home as money was getting short but not before a 2/6d trip around Edinburgh Castle which we found very interesting, we were both war babies and liked castles and battles! The castle was built in the sixth century but was the home of Scottish kings from 1100 when the portcullis was added. With stops on the nearly 400 mile trip for fuel and run-outs it took over 10 hours to get home but we had such good memories of the Lake District, Fort William, Spean bridge, the Highlands, Glen Coe, Forth Bridge and Edinburgh. There were so many beautiful views to remember from our time in Scotland.

As the County Fire Service had said "no new recruits for two years" I applied to be a fireman with the Royal Air Force at Quedgeley after seeing an advert in the Citizen newspaper. It was a civilian fire service at number 7 maintenance unit site [7MU], and even though the pay was only £16-15-

4d I decided to make the break, turning down £20 a week plus a share of the profits by the son of the Gilder family, even though he had a nice sister!

September 3rd 1968 turned out to be a black day. Not because I was due to start a new job but because I heard on radio 4 that motorcyclist Keith Smith from Brize Norton had been killed racing at Crystal Palace. I met Keith in 1965 at the CMC, he took me racing many times, not good news.

I'd somehow passed the entrance exam and reported to the main gate at RAF Quedgeley and was directed to an office where a few others were waiting. We were given a talk by various dept. heads who explained how 7 MU worked. The personnel officer said he was there to help if we had any troubles, I said "Sir, I've just lost a close friend and don't have the funeral details yet." He told me it wasn't a problem and to let him know when I did, which put my mind at rest.

We all went along to our particular jobs, me to the fire station where I saw a smart looking 1950s Bedford fire appliance. I felt surplus but was lent overalls and fire gear that fitted after a fashion, and was now riding the fire appliance. RAF premises couldn't get fire insurance so the fire department was paid for by the government, the City or County Fire services provided backup. At tea break I explained my problem and they let me use the phone. I phoned the local bikers with the sad news, Mervin in Burford suggested a group of racers carry the coffin or at least make the offer to the family.

There were no fire calls that day but I enjoyed doing drill and having instruction on fire pumps. At 1800 hrs, I was starting to learn the 24-hour clock, the appliance went round all eight sites checking the large hangars; they were massive.

Keith's funeral was a sad affair. I'd driven up with Garnet in his beloved A40 and was glad I had someone with me, I was feeling very low. We were following the funeral hearse, an Atlas like Keith had taken me racing in, but black with long glass windows. I told Garnet that at least Keith would be pleased to be going in a race transporter, to be told "don't get morbid George." Me, Keith's brother Tony, Mervin, John Pounder and two others carried Keith's coffin. Although strong I was surprised how heavy it seemed and possibly more awkward than I expected. As we lowered it, I was in floods of tears, in the words of a 60's song Keith was, 'The first of the gang to die.'

119

I got into a routine at RAF Quedgeley and at least I had every Saturday and Sunday off so racing was no problem. The main problem was earning more than £2 a week less and no meat bonus to give to mum. I phoned up Fred Holpin, "Fred, I've got Saturdays off, would you like me to come down and help?" Luckily he said "Yes," so now I had money and meat. I thought afterwards, *why didn't I ask Dewhurst or Gordon Bircher who were both in Gloucester, it would have saved me 20 miles travelling, dimbo!*

After 2 months at the RAF I got a letter from the County Fire service telling me to come and take an entrant's exam, luckily it was on a day off. I was hoping the knowledge I'd gained and having taken the RAF entrants exam would help, I only told the gang.

JOHN POUNDER AND ME

The last meeting that year was at Snetterton. Mervin and Lula Bell were racing their BSA sidecar, Tony rode his Norton, John Pounder, myself and John Hammond were on BSAs as was Bernie Toleman, an up-and-coming young rider from the Cotswolds. I drove my new 1955 VW beetle, taking Jackie, a friend of Mike Chandler's wife, in fact she knew everybody as she was a Sister in Cheltenham General A & E. It was lucky we were driving along a straight road when the head lights went out. I shouted, "what the bloody hell are you doing woman?" Jackie whimpered "sorry, I hit the button with my handbag," we laughed after the initial panic. Arriving at the circuit we pitched the tent by the Brize Norton gang. There was some sombre chat about the 1968 season, this meeting was 6 weeks after we'd lost Keith. Morning came too soon, but the weather was good for October. I blew my 500cc engine up in the first race, Mervin had blown his BSA engine up in practice so I lent him my spare, which the ungrateful bugger broke as well! John Pounder limped in with a finish but we were all pleased Tony had a good ride on his 650cc Norton Dominator.

There'd been a memorable trip to Snetterton with Garnet earlier in the year. Although I had a terrible cold we were sharing the driving of my Beetle and trailer. The Brize Norton gang had caught us up on the road so we had a good excuse to stop at a pub. Someone suggested I have a short to kill my cold, the landlady suggested a port and brandy, "but I don't like port or brandy very much" she replied with a wink, "if you don't like it you can have it free." Hearing the magic word I said "you're on" and starting sipping it. As it wasn't unpleasant, I finished it in one gulp and said "this isn't too bad, I'll have another." In fact I had a third and spent 15/-! I certainly forgot about my cold, the only thing I remember was holding up the ceiling saying "I don't feel my cold anymore." The gang laughed at me, I was 'nissed as a pewt!' Garnet drove the rest of the way so I had a good night's sleep.

I got along well with most of the crew at RAF Quedgley, Roy Creswell, Dennis Sisal, Ted Crowther and Pete Davies. Although the war had been over 20 years, the RAF still had many wartime measures in place. I saw EWS (emergency water supply) tanks everywhere and gun type carriages, with a fire hose round the centre of the wheel shaft with the branch (jet) standpipe and key in a wooden box at the top.

RAF Quedgeley had an annual hose running competition. It was basically a test for the workers on fire drill, a sort of fun day really, they would train for. It was our job to keep the workers on site aware of the risk of fire so there was an annual challenge shield with prizes for winners and runners up from the 8 sites with a slap up buffet! The competition involved a kind of race using a gun carriage to get water onto a target, the fastest of the day winning a shield engraved with their unit. As I raced motorcycles I liked the idea of a competition and suggested to the old boys with me that we have a go. I was pulling hard, Roy shipped the standpipe helped by Ted, I stopped but they hadn't clipped the hose in, laughing, I called them rude names.

On the day of the hose running contest, with the camp Squadron Leader, an Air Vice Marshal to adjudicate, the County Fire Chief, the Mayor, the Sheriff and their ladies were in attendance. We were just the gofers, tidying up after each of the teams and getting ready for the next race. Halfway through the day there was a fire call, well an alarm had sounded. Station Officer Hibbard shouted "to the fire, to the fire." He had a big air force style handlebar moustache, was a short man but the forceful type, he reminded me of Captain Mainwaring from Dad's Army! We went off to the fire, as did the Squadron Leader, the Fire Chief and many of the guests, it was more like a carnival parade! The call was F alarm No. 1 site, as no one knew where F alarm was we were driving around slowly hoping somebody would be waving their arms. These alarms were standard break the glass type, attached to lampposts at each side of the hangars, as well as inside. All the workers were watching the cavalcade drive around, eventually finding F alarm. It had gone off when a lorry backed into the lamppost breaking the glass without anyone realising. Back to finish off the competition. It was no surprise that we had to learn where every alarm was on all 8 sites after this. Every evening the pump, as a fire engine is called, would go around each site checking each large hangar. After the first week we all took one hanger each and after the first few weeks I started going around with only the emergency lighting on, this would help me get used to wearing breathing apparatus (BA) as it's used in the dark, a little scary! On one of the trips around the site I was told they did rifle shooting in one of the buildings. It was the Woodpecker's Rifle Club, run by a retired RAF officer. It turned out to be a sport I liked and got quite good at, probably due to Dave taking me to the fairground in the 1950's where I shot live ammunition with a Winchester style "Cowboy rifle" as well as the air pellets and darts, now it's just .177 air rifles.

Christmas was approaching, I went out with Frank for a pint in my Beetle and we discussed my interview for the County Fire Service next week, we met CB Gorman, a fireman. A bit later we chatted up two pretty girls and were a group of five, when we moved to the next pub we dumped CB. We left the Fox and Elm pub and were driving along Finley Road when we ran out of petrol, sadly not a leafy lane! It was a frosty night, Frank and I were pushing the car with the girls steering, when we heard "help me, please help me." I shouted at the girls to stop the car. It was an old lady locked out of her Council house and smelling of alcohol.

We searched her handbag and pockets but couldn't find key. Seeing a top window open I said "Frank, you're more experienced, you scale the drainpipe." After breaking the downpipe he used the soil pipe which luckily didn't break. After squeezing in through the window and coming out through the front door, we realized the maisonette we'd broken into was the wrong one. When we tried to open the front window on the correct maisonette, it cracked, so after scratching our heads we decided to go through all her pockets again before breaking the front door down. The key had gone through a hole in her pocket and was in the coat lining. We made her a cuppa and the girls put her to bed, which killed any chance of passion and we still had to get fuel! I felt like a pillock, I'd left my coat and hat in the old ladies house. When I called round the next day the old lady asked why her front window was broken, "no idea love, you were lucky we saw you." I grabbed my coat and hat and ran.

There were twelve other applicants at Cheltenham Fire Station. First we were measured and checked; minimum height 5' 7", chest size 36" with 2" expansion, good eye sight without glasses, no criminal record, over 18 and male. Next was a physical strength test; we had to carry a fireman 100 yards in 1 minute or less. Next was a welcome cup of tea. Some of the applicants had dropped out by the time we got to the dictation test; I was hoping they could read my writing. I was disappointed that I struggled with the mathematics test. The last test was general knowledge and there were even fewer of us taking this test. Those left waited for an interview with Assistant Chief Officer Leighton. I saw a very upright person who in a blunt northern accent said "Sit down, you're not very good at Maths and English are you?" I stuttered "well Sir, I've been a butcher for 10 years with little use for either." You had to have a minimum of 40% in each test with an average score over 50% in all three tests, a minimum of total of 150%. "Your maths was 39%, in theory you should have failed, English was 40% but you were good on general knowledge getting 77% which gives you a total of 156%," he said. It was lucky I liked listening to radio 4.

I was told the County had both retained and full-time stations. Cheltenham and Stroud were full-time stations with Cirencester a day-manning station; these were the closest. South of the County, Patchway, on the outskirts of Bristol, was full-time with Kingsway and Severnside day-manning; these were too far away to consider. I was awoken from my trance by him asking why I'd only applied for Cheltenham and not Stroud. "Sir, Stroud is over a steep hill, in snow it can be difficult to travel to" and told him the problems I'd had in the past. Assistant Chief Officer Leighton said "I'm appointing you to Stroud, you will be told your start date by letter." If I'd said "put Stroud where a monkey puts his nuts" I wouldn't have got the job. The letter came, telling me to start at Station 11, Cheltenham on the 13th December 1968 at 0900 hrs. With regret I gave my notice to the RAF. In January I was due to go to RAF Manston for my 3 months training. RAF Manston had been one of the fighter stations in the Battle of Britain in 1940, as a war baby I had been looking forward to this.

On Friday the 13th, which I was hoping was not a bad omen, I reported to Station 11 and was taken to the main admin building. What a pleasant surprise it was to see Roger Hiam who I knew from primary school, I used to be in love with his sister Gillian when I was 10! The day certainly started well, I was given a month's pay, well the remaining two weeks, the princely sum of £28. Sub Officer, Reg Herrington, explained what I had to do. I got my uniform, helmet, axe and boots, a pair of rubber steel toe caps like Wellingtons and a pair of leather 'Cotton Oxford' fire boots. The fire station was separate from the admin buildings with workshops and stores underneath the offices. There was a driveway between the buildings going into a large drill yard enclosed by the fire drill tower, small workshops, appliance room, fire station admin, recreation room and dormitory. After being given a locker I was shown where to stow my fire gear when off duty, there were three long shelves, one for each watch. A fireman was detailed to show me around and let me know what was what. After all that I was detailed to put my fire kit on the water tender. It was the end of the shift and as it was Friday, I was told to report on Monday at 0900 hrs. I was on a five-day week Monday to Friday and part of the watch on duty. The fire service used a 3 watch system, Red, White and Blue similar to the Navy. Blue watch was on the day I started and I was doing fire drill with the crew when a call came in, "Whitbread Brewery fire alarm" I sat in the back all excited but it was a false alarm, a fire alarm had gone off for no apparent reason!

I learnt that a lot of firemen had the odd part-time job, varying from window cleaning to car repairs. I'd started a part-time job already, butchering in Berkeley. A fireman called Whitehouse asked me what my old job was and next shift when I saw him, he told me to go and see Jack Council, a butcher in lower High Street, Cheltenham where I could earn 5/- plucking turkeys. Going to Berkeley was a long drag to earn £2 and a joint of meat a day so I called in on the way home. Jack Council, a short stocky man told me "it's dressing turkeys/chickens plus any other butcher's jobs. When can you start?" I dressed five turkeys, he found me couple of other jobs and gave me 10/- . "You are good, do you want to help me regularly?" The comment made me feel good and we shook hands on the deal. I was nervous phoning Berkeley, "Fred, I'm sorry but I can't help any more, I'm on shift work." It was a sort of white lie, but as expected I got a mouthful of abuse instead of thanks or good luck! I did 2 hours butchering after work unless I was going out and all day Saturday, sometimes Sunday as it was December and he had a lot of work on.

On Christmas day all talk was by me of the Fire Brigade, we played the usual game of cards and there was a New Year party at the Cheltenham Motor Club.

Dave Baker started on Friday 3rd January, three days before Reigate training school, they must have still been short of recruits. I was told to show him around. One thing we both agreed on was the new uniform was crap, the helmet looking more like a WW2 German army helmet, the tunic like a car coat, the axe hung from a strap fixed inside the jacket over the shoulder and flapped about getting in the way. To add insult to injury, we had bright yellow leggings but we liked the Cotton Oxford leather boots.

All the new recruits met at Cheltenham on Monday 6th. We had to be at Reigate by 12 noon. Fireman Bob Jeal volunteered to take us as he knew the shortcuts using old Roman roads.

There were 24 new recruits in total, six of them from Gloucestershire, myself, Dave, Dennis McGill, Jim Godwin, William (Bill) Pratt, and one called Dolby who went ill in the first week and was never seen again. After Dolby left, three Portsmouth lads joined us making a squad of eight, Pete Spargo, Paul Williams and John Debora.

I have to admit I got another wake-up call, the first was starting work as a Butcher, cleaning that large window. We sat in our squads, two at a desk, I was sat with Dave. Commandant Divisional Officer Kent introduced himself, made a welcoming speech and handed us over to Assistant Divisional Officer Spratling, a tall man with a mean looking face. The Assistant Divisional Officer gave a similar talk in a sterner manner before handing us over to Stn Officer Payne. He looking like Quasimodo having a slight stoop and gave us a similar talk, but in a more easy-going way before handing us over to Sub Officer Harry Evans, who was to tell us what we had to do. Harry waited for the last of the senior officers to be clear of the room before saying "right you lot, those gentlemen were officers, I'm not a gentleman but I had a mother and father. You will be sent home if anything goes wrong or you bring this training school or the fire service into disrepute." He introduced three leading firemen, one for each squad. We were squad 3, would be in A hut and had Leading Fireman Nightingale. After the talk we'd be shown our accommodation and how to make beds. Harry, as we called him behind his back, said "my name is Sub Officer Evans, you will either address me as that or Sir, if an Officer is on parade you will say Sir," The list went on, "you will get up at 0600 hrs and make your beds, breakfast is 0700 hrs to 0800 hrs. After breakfast, march from your hut to the front of the appliance room. This is used for storing training vehicles and other equipment, drill is at 0900 hrs. Each week one of you will be squad leader who will salute any Officer, the rest of you, eyes right, all this will come in training." I'm sure he took a breath here, "If you go out in the dinner break you will stay in uniform, if you disgrace that uniform you will be sent home and your career will be over. If you go out at night, do not go out in uniform, do not mention the fire service, if you bring a problem back you will be sent home. Bed by 2300 hrs. You will be checked and any one missing will be sent home!" Dave and I looked at one another, what had we let ourselves in for?

Dinner break was a relief but followed by going to our huts for bed making, military style. We were told in the event of a fire to ring the fire bell, one of our squad was to run to the direct phone to ring the fire service. Sub Officer Evans continued "there is bound to be fire drill, the fire station will know this so won't dispatch fire pumps, but you make the call whenever you hear the bell." There were two fire drills. On the first we phoned the station, assembled outside, did a roll call. One of us was missing, a lad from another group had slept through giving us all a laugh. On the second, a Leading Fireman rang the bell, three of us raced for the phone but it was a prank so when two fire pumps turned up the two Leading Firemen disappeared PDQ.

At 1500 hrs. we had a welcome tea break with much muttering from everyone. Afterwards, the Leading Fireman told us to put on our fire kit and assemble by the appliance room where we learnt basic saluting and marching to an acceptable standard. We were then shown the equipment we would be using during the course, the appliances and two 60' training towers which were basic on all fire stations. I was lucky, I knew Frank who had been a fireman since 1963, I'd had three months experience with the RAF and two weeks at Cheltenham, it all helped. 1700 hrs. could not come soon enough for our evening meal and a discussion on whether we were all going home. A 30 year old from another group kept saying, "bed by 11 o'clock, I have a grown-up family!"

There were table tennis and snooker tables, Dave and I had a lot of fun on these over the next three months. He told me he'd never played table tennis before, then beat the ass off me leading me to think he wasn't telling the truth. We went into town for a quick pint and to see what was there. Having passed my bronze medal, I was pleased to see The Court School of Dancing and said "Dave, I must get there this week, will you come?" but he wasn't really interested. We got back early and were in bed by 2300 hrs, 15 minutes later around came Quasimodo with a torch checking up on us.

Next day at 0600 hrs we spent ages making the beds and folding blankets, checking each other's until we thought they all looked perfect. We went for breakfast in overalls then returned to the dormitory only to find that many beds had been pulled apart, Dave's included but surprisingly not mine! I was playing my transistor radio, everyone moaned as I was listening to Radio 4 so, under pressure I changed it to Radio 1 before we marched to the appliance room for 0900 hrs. We started serious drilling, marching, saluting, attention, stand at ease, about turn. It reminded me of my first ballroom dancing lesson where we were all facing in different directions! The fire engine numbering had been explained to us, one in charge, two the driver, three and four in the back. Our numbers were changed around and after a few cock ups, we got it right. There was more serious drilling to come. Last was a lesson in learning ranks in the Fire Service and the equal ranks in all three Armed Forces, we didn't understand why! There was so much to learn. Most of the other lads were more interested in drinking but we had both changed career and were now earning less money. Our routine after the evening meal was studying until 2100 hrs, stop for a cuppa, play table tennis on the way to and back from the canteen then study until just past 10, sorry 2200 hrs, then bed, our first full day.

The 30 year old from Cornwall kept moaning about having a grown-up family and commented all the time, I thought, for the love of Mike, put a sock in it. Luckily, he stopped after the first week. At 2300 hrs every night an officer came to check we were all there.

Tuesday evening I went to the Court School of Dancing, it was great, lots of girls. Maureen, a dance instructor was gorgeous, but quite short, well compared to me when we were dancing to Albatross by Fleetwood Mac. I did get a date that night, the girl saying she'd meet me by the clock Thursday night. It turned out she'd invited me to a Conservative meeting. I didn't say much as I was brought up staunch Labour and was hoping dad didn't find out!

All hose drills were dry, we weren't using water yet. Friday afternoon was cleaning, polishing, and sweeping as if we were at a Fire Station. Most went home the first weekend, there were just 8 of us left. Harry Evans mentioned on the last parade that Reigate Station had attended a large fire, the firm were grateful and invited any firemen to their dinner dance Saturday night reminding us, "if you cause any problems you will be sent home in disgrace." Saturday daytime was spent studying before getting in the taxi we'd booked, I remember eight of us got into the taxi, it was before seatbelts. We arrived early and had a game of tenpin bowling until the dance started. We all had a good time, I ended up with a Soda Shandy instead of Cider Shandy, probably my Gloucester accent, Oh Arh! We had a late lie-in Sunday morning and started to learn the phonetic alphabet, watched television and enjoyed a pint before bed. We were woken many times during the night by people coming back, all with long faces.

The regime went on week after week, marching to and fro, saluting, then drilling and lectures. I had done some of this at RAF Quedgeley and Cheltenham but not hook ladder drills or live carry downs. This is where you have to trust your equipment. The hook-ladder was 13'3" long, with a 2' bill with serrated teeth and a 6" hook which, when pulled out, hung on the windowsill above you. You climbed up leaning outwards with your arms straight to keep the ladder stable, sliding your leg into the window.

There was worse to come. It certainly wouldn't happen in today's Health & Safety conscious World, but working off the sixth floor of the tower with the hook ladder on the top sill we climbed up from the 5th floor but for some reason didn't slide our leg over the sill but climbed to the top three rungs with a foot either side of the brace that held the hook, with a hand on each of the horns of the ladder, then with one leg on one side of your arm, the other leg round the other arm, letting go the ladder and jumping onto the top of the tower. It was designed to give you confidence in your equipment, if you couldn't do it you would be no good going to a building on fire, well that was the theory!!

Similarly with the carry-downs, the escape ladder on a gun carriage was very stable, pitched to the 3rd floor one man (the body) wearing an Everest safety device was carried down by another in our group. If, when playing the body, you're not on the shoulder correctly you will be most uncomfortable in the groin area. Scarier was when being lowered with a rescue line, a short loop around the shoulders, the long loop around the knees, otherwise you would be hanging upside down! Carry-downs and hook-ladder drills were done weekly. The majority of the course was running out fire hose, changing burst length (pretend) add a length, but without using water at first.

The second weekend I caught a train to London. I found it quite nerve wracking as the last time I was on a train was in 1962, I didn't even know how to open the door. I was going to see Mike and Maureen Taylor who had moved back to London. Mike was the one I was passenger to on his sidecar grass track racer. I stayed Saturday night returning after Sunday dinner to more studying with Dave.

During the third week we had an enjoyable trip to the London Salvage Corps, now amalgamated into the London Fire Brigade. The visit was quite interesting. We learnt how to preserve and save property, in one instance by moving all the property into the middle of the room, putting it on and under a large table and a salvage sheet over the top. This would save it from getting wet from water coming from a fire in the top of the building.

I decided it was time to go home. Other than the short trip to London and the trip to Chepstow in 1962, when I nearly got locked in the carriage, I'd never done a long train journey other than with my parents so I was feeling apprehensive. I was 24, but with several changes I kept asking people if I was on the right platform. On the way back I drove my VW Beetle stopping at Dennis Fire Engines for a 5 minute break and got back around 2200 hrs. There was no check on Saturday or Sunday nights with students returning at all hours.

Being home for the weekend gave me the chance to spend some time in the pub with Frank and Norman, picking their brains about some of the things I was struggling with especially sprinkler systems and air pressure which was either way above my head or I had a crap instructor.

My trips to the Court School of Dancing were saving me from going Doolally. I was always trying to get David to come with me but he didn't fancy it, even after I mentioned the girls. Now I had the car I could run young ladies home. The first I took home lived in Crawley which was a good 20 minute drive, I got a short cuddle before back to bed on my own. Another young lady lived in Reigate so that was better. I took her to see The Thomas Crown Affair starring Steve McQueen and Faye Dunaway with that haunting theme music, Windmills of your Mind. Unfortunately, when we went in the wrong film was showing. I saw the manager, "I thought this was the Thomas Crown Affair." "Next week Sir." He gave us tickets to see it free as the film that was on was crap. One night after taking a lady home I got back just after 2300 hrs, I passed Assistant Divisional Officer Spratling thinking, *cripes*, as Billy Bunter used to say on TV and in the comics. Now I'm the first to admit I'm a pillock, instead of walking back to Assistant Divisional Officer Spratling, apologising and telling him that a lady had missed the bus, I ran into the dormitory. Finding I'd not made my bed, I threw my shoes under it, jumped in and pulled the blanket over my head. The door opened making the sort of creaking you get in the horror movies, the light went on, I heard footsteps coming towards me. I was shaking under the bedding which was ripped off, "Ridgeon, I am sure you'd be far more comfortable in pyjamas." The whole hut burst out laughing. It took a long time to live that down but luckily I didn't get in trouble.

The training was getting harder every week. We were now learning about pumps, gauges and valves and working with water so we started getting wet. We'd learnt how to run a hose in the first few weeks, most fire hose was 50' long and quite weighty, 25 lbs. Changing burst lengths, we started to get fit. It was lucky I had some mechanical knowledge from racing motorcycles as in one exercise I was the pump operator using an old Bedford pump. Four of us were doing a drill. I was supplying the line of hose from the pump to the supposed fire which was run out by two others, the fourth was sorting the hydrant out. I'd started to use the water from the 400 gallon water tank which was half gone when I gave the order to turn the standpipe on. With the water flowing, I slightly opened the water tank refilling valve allowing some to go back in while keeping an eye on the pressure gauge to the fireman on the other end of fire hose who wanted 80 psi. When an order came to replace burst length from the hydrant I had to start using water from the tank again. This got me praise from my colleagues, even a well done from the instructor.

However, I was struggling with the escape ladder. To extend the ladder you had two winding handles, the ladder locking mechanism used a Pawl which will lock on any round when the order "well and lower" is given when the ladder is at the right height. I shouted "extend" then "well and lower," but the Pawl didn't lock onto the round. After missing three times Harry Evans yelled in my ear, "Ridgeon, do you know how this works?" "Yes sir." When the fourth attempt failed, Harry shouted even louder, "Ridgeon, do you know what you're doing?" "No sir." He then showed us how the Pawl worked. I felt bad, but could sense everybody else thinking, thank God that was George and not me! A similar system was used on a Lacon ladder, an aluminium 45' ladder which was gradually replacing the old WW2 and earlier 50' and 60' escape ladders.

We were now used to getting wet and doing more realistic exercises using an area called The Ravine which was near the front of the Fire Station but separated by a large driveway. It was basically a stream with a steep bank on both sides with trees and small bushes. We used lines for lowering pumps down into the ravine and a line from one side to the other for safety. These exercises did teach us a lot about working as a team but we got very wet and muddy learning. There was only one drying room for all 24 students which went down to 23 after one student from Surrey left after three weeks to join the ghost of Dolby from Gloucestershire. It meant a lot of work getting the kit dry and brushed up to an acceptable level for the Officers. When we marched to The Ravine in clean uniforms we'd see another squad coming back in soaking wet gear and covered in mud, but we did have fun, most of us were still in our 20's.

Where did 6 weeks go? We were half way through the course and I decided it was time to go home for the weekend. I took Dave but Dennis McGill and Jim Godwin who lived in Stroud went with Bill Pratt who lived in Bristol. Once home I filled in the parents with what had been happening and found out that there was a St Valentine's dance at the Village Hall Saturday night. I just made it to the Tabard in time for a drink with the lads and told them about the St. Valentine's dance, Frank said he'd come.

We got to the Village Hall at 8pm, the evening got better when I met this gorgeous girl called Babs and danced with her all night. I explained that I was on this course and asked if she'd like to go to the Prince of Wales at Cranham where The Alan King Show Band was playing. This was now our gang's regular Sunday night outing. The Paul Buck Trio played a selection of rock 'n' roll numbers in the break. Babs agreed and told me to meet her by the school on Princess Elizabeth way at 7.30 pm. I arrived early and after waiting for well over half an hour I drove around looking for her. Like a pillock, I'd been waiting at the wrong school. Luckily she was still there and we had a good night. I got Babs address and asked her if she would write to me to keep me sane. I must admit I really looked forward to those letters. I'd never had girls write to me before, except when I was 16 telling me to push off and a girl I met during my second Porthcawl holiday in 1960. In what was to be her last letter to me, she finished with lots of little x's spelling Holland and Swalk. In my letter back I asked her if she was going to Holland and what Swalk was. I never got another letter from her. I found out why after reading in the News the World that Holland means, hoping our love lasts and never dies and Swalk means sealed with a loving kiss, this growing up is hard work!! I realized why soldiers away from home looked forward to receiving letters and read them over and over again, it was exactly what I was doing!

I kept escaping to the Court School of Dancing. The next weekend was a pyjama party and although 24 I was still quite shy so I wore my pyjamas over my cloths. I got warm quickly and kept stripping off until I was down to my swimming costume under my pyjamas. We were doing the Greek, Zorba's Dance, where you link arms around shoulders, take 3 steps sideways, knees bend and 3 steps back, all locked together in a huge circle. Everyone was laughing, until the cord on my pyjama trousers felt loose and I started to feel embarrassed. The dance finished just in time for me to grab the string. I met Lynn that night who was wearing a Shorty Nightie. She lived in Abinger Hammer which was the other side of Dorking so I ran her home. The regime had eased a bit. I didn't get back until 0200 hrs. I found my bed on top of the lockers, the other seven beds were all next to each other like those of the 7 dwarfs! I tipped 3 of them out, one bed hit the window, thank goodness it didn't break and we laughed before getting back to bed!

We crowded round the TV to watch Lulu in a short skirt singing Eurovision songs. Lulu had been in the hit parade with Shout when I started racing in 27th March 1964 five years before.

More training, more studying, more drilling, more of everything, but it was starting to come together. We were volunteered for a joint fire, police and ambulance exercise at Gatwick Airport to be used as bodies from a crashed aircraft. We were loaded onto a bus, with a piece of paper around our necks saying what our injuries were, feeling a bit like evacuees during the war! We were taken to the airport runway and told to start wandering around looking dazed, as if we'd been in an air crash. The joint exercise was in full swing, ambulance, police and fire brigade everywhere. We all looked at what injuries we were supposed to have. John De Bora from our squad, like myself had no injuries but he threw his paper away and told the ambulance man he had a broken leg. The ones not injured were taken to an assembly area, those with injuries to hospital. We got back to A Hut just after midnight and were woken about 4 hours later by the lads who had injuries including John, all moaning they'd been kept hanging around. I must admit the rest of us didn't have much sympathy.

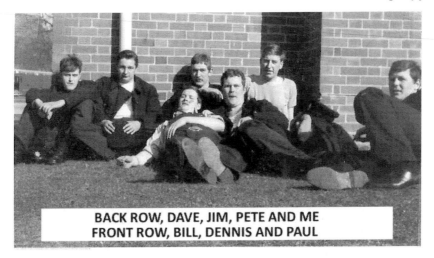

BACK ROW, DAVE, JIM, PETE AND ME
FRONT ROW, BILL, DENNIS AND PAUL

Part of being a fireman was testing things. Our squad went out in overalls carrying a standpipe key and bar with our Leading Fireman to check hydrants around Reigate. This was done for 2 reasons, firstly, it helps you learn the area topography and secondly you learnt where hydrants are. I'm not sure if we did anything wrong but members of the public were stopping and watching us. Were they saying "aren't these firemen good or what are these pillocks doing?"

We were having a pillow fight one night when someone suggested "how about hitting hell out of the other two squads?" This attack was at full swing when a voice boomed out "what the hell is going on here?" It was Stn Officer Payne doing an impromptu inspection. As they couldn't send us all home, we go off with a wigging, Jim Godwin was the only one who stayed in bed; he was married! One Sunday night we must have been feeling even more stupid. We were in our pyjamas ready for bed when Dave Baker challenged me to a race to the top of the tower. Pete Spargo and Paul Williams joined in. I forget who won the race but we had a laugh. On getting back to dormitory Dave said "let's go for a drive in your Beetle George." Grabbing the keys and still in our pyjamas we were driving through the middle of Reigate. We noticed John Debora following us in his van, once out into the country we pulled into a lay-by and jumped out in our pyjamas. John asked, "what the bloody hell (or worse) are you lot doing?"

One Friday afternoon my job was polishing brass and tidying the appliance room. I took my radio and was working away quietly, two Leading Fireman came around making sure everyone was working, grunted and carried on.

10 minutes later Harry Evans came around. "Who said you could have the radio on?" he asked, "the Leading Fireman didn't tell me to turn it off Sir," "well I'm telling you turn it off." "Yes Sir." I carried on without the radio, wishing terrible things would happen to Harry when I heard "Ridgeonnnnnnnnnnnnnn" in a very loud voice from across the other side of the drill yard "on the double." Harry told me to stand to attention then proceeded to bawl me out at the top of his voice accusing me of telling lies, "you told me the Leading Fireman said you could have the Radio on." I said "no Sir, I said they didn't tell me to turn it off." My reply made him angrier, the shouting got louder, I just had to stand and take it. I think we all used to dream about roasting Harry over a fire or lowering him off the tower. He's up in heaven now or perhaps downstairs, so no hard feelings Harry.

The radio came in quite handy in the mornings. We listened to the pop songs and all joined in with certain songs, with Peter Sarstead's Where do you go to my Lovely, when he sang "he bought you a racehorse for Christmas, you kept it just for fun for a laugh" we all went "ha, ha, ha, ha"! With Glen Campbell's Wichita Lineman, we sang "we are firemen for the County." One morning Stn Officer Payne arrived doing another impromptu inspection, "why is McGill still in bed?" "He's been ill all night Sir." "Well get him to the sickbay." We couldn't tell him that he'd came back pissed out of his mind and had been making moaning noises all night, luckily for Dennis, he got away with it!

Most of us kept in with the cooks. One plump girl fancied Dennis and he must have led her on as he told us that she turned up in Stroud one weekend. He had hell of a job getting rid of her before his girlfriend found out! One of the cooks I liked was Italian. I'd taken her out for a friendly drink, but near the end of the course she was taken to hospital for an operation. The same weekend, the Surrey Fire Service was holding their annual quiz. Harry Evans ordered us all to volunteer to be stewards. For some reason I was in an obnoxious mood, perhaps if he'd asked us to volunteer I wouldn't have said anything, but I told him "I can't help as I'm visiting a friend in hospital." I was pleased I went, she did look poorly and said "thank you for coming to see me George, you cheered me up a lot." I was pleased nothing came of me refusing to help at the quiz.

The exams were approaching and we were asked who had a first aid certificate, those who didn't then had to add that to everything else. Dave and I were asking each other questions, practicing the Holger Nielsen resuscitation for those rescued from drowning, and tying each other up with triangular bandages. For the First Aid exam there were six of us in the room all trying to keep an ear on what others were being asked by the St John's Ambulance examiners. The 30 year-old lad from Cornwall was asked to show the human crutch. He fell silent and the examiner asked him again. By this time we'd all stopped what we were doing and were watching. The lad from Cornwall started indicating with both hands his groin region. When the examiner said with a smile, "I said the human crutch not the crotch," we all burst out laughing.

Fire prevention, mathematics, pumps and hydraulic formula, oh my poor head. Then came the actual drills, ladders, carry-downs, pump and running out hose, no one failed, some passing with flying colours, others squeaked through but we were now firemen.

A group of us, not all from my squad, went out for a Chinese meal. I wasn't the sort that experimented with food, not after that curry in the early 60's which was so hot, but I was persuaded to try Chinese and had the beef and bean shoots which I liked as it had a reasonable gravy/sauce. After the meal there was a sweet or pudding as I call it. I chose lychees but it was very bitter and spoilt the meal, but I still like Chinese food.

Friday, 28 March 1969 we were all in full fire gear including Commandant Divisional Officer Kent, Assistant Divisional Officer Spratling, Stn Officer Paine, Sub Officer Evans and the three leading firemen. On the radio that morning it was announced that President Eisenhower had died. He had been the Allied Commander in charge on D-Day, later becoming US President. As one era ended, another was beginning with the closing ceremony and speeches.

The week before the course finished I saw a 650 BSA for sale in the local paper, the bike turned out to be a crashed combination and I offered £10 for the engine as long as the man took it out. I collected it a few days later, it was a shame I couldn't get the rest of the bike home. I'd had engine trouble at the last race and couldn't get home to fix it. We said our goodbyes and with David, the engine and all our kit in car, we left Reigate. On the way home I took a detour to Burford but Mervin had only half finished my 500cc engine so I had to get the bike ready for the first meeting at Staverton Airport on March 30th.

Ridgeon Rides Again

Arriving home after dropping David off and unloading, I said a quick hello to mum and dad then off to the Tabard pub to see the gang and catch up with the news. No lying in bed on Saturday 29th as I had to finish off the engine I'd picked up from Mervin. CMC were lucky to get the use of Staverton Airport, after the loss of Morton Valance Airfield as the new M5, was to go through the middle of it. The Club had been contacted by Councillor John Biscoe, a motorsports fan and on the joint airport committee. He'd put to the committee that as the airport was losing £7000 a year they let CMC put on 3 meetings at £300 a day, we were all hoping it would go well. I was sorry I couldn't help get the circuit ready having only the one day to finish engine off and fit it in the bike for the meeting on Sunday.

I spent half of Saturday trying to put the 500cc engine together, but Mervin had fitted a 500cc barrel with a 650cc crank which had a longer stroke, making it 520cc. As the barrels had spacers underneath the push rods would not fit. It was now late on Saturday so I made a decision to fit the 650cc engine, finishing very late without starting it up. I fitted a 1 1/8" carburettor onto a 1" hole and had no time to check the primary chain, gearing or condition before arriving at the circuit which was less than 2 miles from home. As it was the first meeting it was a learning curve for everyone, but I knew the marshals and officials and they helped me find a place to park on grass! It was very cramped and somewhat overcast with a slight drizzle which didn't help getting the bike going and I had to ask for a push start. As I was taking the bike through Scrutineering I had a sharp intake of breath as I realized I was in the 500cc race on a 650cc bike. With the panic yesterday of fitting the engine it hadn't crossed my mind, but as it was out of a crashed road going sidecar I would only be making up the numbers! I took it steady in practice and it seemed to go okay. My first race was the unlimited heat and I was being blown into the weeds but could hear a metallic noise, a sort of tinkling sound, so I backed off for a finish.

I asked a few senior riders about this metallic noise and was told, "sounds like your valves are bouncing George. As you fitted an old road engine the valve springs are weak and you're over revving the engine for a standard road bike." Even now I still felt guilty about being in the 500cc race as I got into the final. I heard the valves bouncing again, but now I knew what the problem was hoping the bike wouldn't go bang. I finished in the final but at least it was out of the money.

136

It was just two days now before I was to start my new watch with the Fire Service and the job for real. All the returning recruits had 4 days leave before starting whatever shift they were on, mine was the first night shift on Wednesday 2nd April, nearly 10 years to the day since starting at JH Dewhurst! I picked up Babs for the Sunday Alan King Show Band and a pint with the lads, but it was a quiet 25th birthday on Monday 31st as I was still recovering from Reigate and racing on Sunday.

CHAPTER 7   1970-All fired up

I arrived at Cheltenham fire station at 17:30hrs on 2nd April which was probably the first time I'd arrived anywhere early since 6th April 1959 when starting as a butcher's boy! I was assigned to White watch and when I saw Dave Baker who was on Red watch and had finished his first day, I asked him what it was like. I put my fire kit at the back of the appliance room with 30 firemen milling around, it was watch change. I heard "I need a jumper," and thought, *are they cold?* It turned out that if you didn't want to go out on an emergency call, you would ask someone to jump for you, if you had permission from the Officer in Charge.

The 2 minute bell rang; everyone went outside, in bad weather we stayed in the appliance room. Sub Officer Lawson dismissed the day shift and told the night shift to stand at ease. He then detailed the pumps and special appliances; I was number 5 on the water tender ladder, with Eddie Hawkins in charge. We spent 30 minutes doing an inventory including the roof for ladders, and the driver, petrol, oil, water, tyres and fire pump. Although it was done at every change of shift we still found items missing!

At 18:30 the drivers took the water tender ladder and pump escape (the ladder with the big wheels) into the drill yard. The Sub Officer was about to detail a drill as the Fire Bell sounded. With the water tender ladder indicator light on, one pump, the crew including myself mounted the appliance. Eddie came running from the control room shouting "rick fire, Staverton." It was a small rick, 500 yards from the airport I was racing at 3 days before, which we damped down after 30 minutes. Eddie radioed back that the fire was out, we were just tidying up but could leave if another call came in. We heard the radio crackle, the driver ran to the radio while the rest of us hurried our jobs. We were told to "proceed to a car fire Seven Springs Junction. We got back just after 21:30, our evening meal had been put on the hotplate, it was a little dried up but good enough for me. There were no more calls that shift, we did the morning routines, had breakfast then tidied the station until changeover. It was a dream really. When I saw David starting his second day shift he asked if I'd had any shouts, shout being another name for a fire call, the old hands sniggered at us.

White watch was Sub Officer Gordon Lawson, leading fireman Eddie Hawkins, leading fireman Doug Radley, firemen Brian Chambers, Andy Finch, Jim Stephenson, Graham Leighton, Gerry (Percy) Copeland, Mike Compton, Rex Jones, Gordon (Flicker) James, Arnold Pearce, Dick

Browning and Malcolm Nixon, Dick and Malcolm became bike racing friends. When there was a full watch on I would ride No. 5. Although I had done the 3 months training I was on a steep learning curve and usually left to do all the dirty jobs, but that goes with any new job, it was just 10 years earlier that I'd been cleaning that large window!

On day shifts one man was assigned to help the cook, on night shifts one man was cook for those in the mess club. I had joined the job when several changes were happening, the best was the 7-year pay scale being reduced to 4 years. Any new fireman joining who was over 25 would go on to the second level and I was 25 just 2 days before starting my watch. When I joined there was only one mess club for all three watches, but after a union meeting it was agreed that each watch should have its own mess club. I never found out why the change was needed! There was a motion to move to a 56-hour week, an extra 8 hours with a salary increase of £5, which would save one man off every shift. I did argue against this, pointing out that it would do away with nine jobs if you counted Stroud and Patchway. It appeared they weren't worried about the employment situation so some months after returning from Reigate the hours were increased to 56. The positives were an extra £5 a week and easier shifts. I now did 2 days (09:00 to 18:00) 2 nights (18:00 to 09:00) then had 2 days off which gave me one complete weekend every third week which started at 09:00 on Saturday.

I joined the fire brigade union (FBU) when asked as dad had been a strong union man. Not long after Reigate, while still on the 48-hour week, I was starting my shift, leading fireman Hawkins was taking parade but my name wasn't called. "Leading fireman Hawkins, why didn't you call my name?" "It's your shift off George," "it can't be." Eddie was messing me about for a few minutes before assigning me to a pump, it was just a practical joke with everyone smiling. Percy, as we called him, a keen cyclist, told me that this practice had backfired once. As he'd entered the drill yard at Stroud the Officer in Charge shouted "what you doing here Percy, it's your day off?" "Okay" he'd replied, and disappeared back out of the drill yard. The Officer in Charge detailed the crews and the water tender chased after Percy for over a mile to get him back. This was before he moved to Cheltenham.

I was getting to know the other fireman slowly and made friends with Dick Browning who, like me, was a keen motorcyclist, ate a lot, told terrible jokes and was well dressed! I remember when Dick helped prepare

139

Staverton for a race meeting with Malcolm Nixon, Harry and Albert and other CMC members on Saturday. They were hammering in stakes along the runway when a vehicle drove up. The driver said, "the air controller said you must pull the stakes out as aircraft are landing." These were only light aircraft but a twin engine Dakota was expected to land on race day. We initially complained, but he threatened, "if you don't pull them out we will cancel the meeting." We pulled the stakes out. I can't repeat some of the things we said, and later repeated when we got a message, "You can put them back in now."

Eddie Hawkins had volunteered for Korea as WW2 had finished when he was called up for National Service. He looked like Desperate Dan from the Dandy comic, if you annoyed him he would get your arm up your back and bite your ear saying "are you going to behave yourself?" Doug Radley, another likeable leading fireman, was always rolling cigarettes with liquorice fag papers. In one budget the price of tobacco went up so he put less tobacco in his roll up. When he lit up it burnt straight up to his mouth and he had to spit it out, he got his leg pulled about that. Mike Compton from Tewkesbury was as big as me, Brian Chambers was a sort of Teddy Boy with wavy hair and could be a bit of a bully if you didn't stand up to him. One lunch break, not far from me was a sandwich wrapped in cellophane, Brian came and smashed his fist on to the sandwich while glaring at me! "Do that again" I said which he did, along came his friend Andy Finch "Brian what are you doing to my sandwiches?" I was pleased there were no repercussions. Jim Stephenson had transferred from Durham and I could hardly understand his accent, "Whey hey lad" but we got on well!

Ken Hill who I'd got to know through the CMC was a keen biker and Officer in Charge when I went to Reigate. He was known as 'Dofor Hill,' 'it'll do for this and do for that.' When I returned, Ken had been moved to HQ, a new Assistant Divisional Officer, Ernie Taylor with Stn Officer Roger Corbett, nickname Amigo. At Christmas 1971, when Ernie, the fastest milkman in the West by Benny Hill, was No. 1 in the charts, Assistant Divisional Officer Ernie put it on his cards, that was before he started hating us.

The new watch and mess club system was working well enough, but we were having to keep perishable food in the fridge and it'd go missing from time to time, it was brought up at union meetings. One thing I brought up in AOB caused some amusement, "the fire service supplies us with Izal toilet paper, which is like greaseproof paper, no good at all, could we have softer toilet paper?" Even the newspaper I had used when a little boy was better than the Izal toilet roll, but no one seconded the motion, no pun intended, strange, as many brought in their own toilet paper.

There were two classes of mess member: either tea 2/- a week, or £1 for meals and tea. Some firemen not in the mess, boiled water, used a tea bag and powdered milk, and I thought I was a tight bastard!! Dick, myself, Malcolm and Gordon aka "Flicker" as he was always flicking his dog ends everywhere, were a good little team, especially if one of us was kitchen hand. After 21:00 when drill was done we all ended up in the kitchen. Gordon was a good cook and doing liver, onions and bacon which up to then I'd never liked as mother fried the liver in a large lump. Gordon sliced the liver as thin as the bacon and onions. Initially it was fried to seal it, then put into a casserole with potatoes, peas and carrots. In the last 10 minutes he sprinkled stuffing on the top, gorgeous, my mouth is watering as I type this.

At the time, Richard's father had a grocery store so he brought in extra bacon and baked beans, with my part-time butchering I brought in extra sausages and any lamb chops that didn't look good enough to sell. We were having breakfast of lamb chops, bacon, eggs, sausages and black pudding. When we had a meat dish we would usually slop gravy everywhere. I remember one night shift the lads put out a separate table complete with a candle and our names on it! When it was my turn to be mess manager, and liking faggots, I did 2 faggots 4 roast potatoes, mashed potatoes, peas and onion gravy. As not everyone liked faggots, Dick and I ended up with 6 faggots and 8 roast potatoes each. Another night shift I was kitchen hand, in the morning cooking 10 breakfasts. This meant 10 plates on the hotplate, 20 rashers of bacon in one pan, 10 eggs in another with a saucepan of baked beans. It was all cooking when fireman started drifting in early wanting breakfast, I should have told them to "push off" but as I was still a new boy I gave them an egg, 2 rashers of bacon and 2 spoonfuls of beans. They were sat having their meals and I was doing my breakfast, having half a pan of beans left I put them on my plate. You should have heard the roar, so I went around sharing the beans out saying "you should have come at 8 o'clock" stirring it up a bit, "I hope you noticed Sub Officer, they all came up early." It was known as "the great bean fiasco!"

One day-shift I was kitchen assistant to the cook Monica, a nice cuddly lady who I got on with quite well normally. Having been a butcher I knew how to cook meat. I'd learnt at college about cooking times and had helped mum when growing up. Monica had roasted the meat but started to tip all the fat into a dish not keeping any of the goodness to make the gravy, to make matters worse she then drained off all the cabbage water straight down the sink which she should have kept to make the gravy, putting it in the meat tray with the meat juices then thickening with Bisto. She just boiled water and added Bisto gravy. "What are you doing woman?" I asked, as she tipped the fat and water away, she stormed down to the station office. Coming back with the Officer in Charge she said, "get this mad man out of my kitchen." The Officer in Charge asked me why I was upsetting the cook. "She doesn't know how to make gravy" I replied, "she threw all the meat juices and the vegetable water away." I was replaced by another fireman. Monica and I laughed about it many times over the years.

One night shift I bought a pig's head in as one of our gang was in the kitchen. Dick, Malcolm, Flicker and I were sat drinking tea waiting for the food to cook. I'd chopped up the head already at my part-time butchery job, it was boiling away nicely to make some brawn. Those not in the mess club used to come round to see what we were eating, bloody rude really, lifting up each lid. Fireman Rex Jones was doing this, but when he lifted the lid and saw a pig's head with teeth looking at him he screamed and dropped the lid, making us laugh.

During my first year there was an incident in which a fireman had died trying to rescue three children from a mine full of gas. Not long before this happened the union had agreed with management that if any fireman died or was totally disabled in a fire, the family would get £2000, this was two year's pay. However, his Brigade said that as he hadn't died at a fire they wouldn't pay. The FBU's reply was that if £2000 was not paid there would be industrial action. As the Brigade involved took no action the FBU said that after a certain date if there was no fire at an incident, no one would attend.

A senior officer asking firemen on our watch if we agreed with the union, everyone did. When he asked me I replied, "I'd like to Sir but as I am still on my two-year probation, you could sack me." I was an FBU member but the union would accept my position. It was agreed at a union meeting that we would turn out for all emergency calls, but if there was no fire we would return. I was 100% behind the action. As the date got closer the Brigade relented and paid the man's family.

COUPLE FROM WORCESTER, LES SANDERSON, GLYN GILES, DON BROWNING, JOHN HAMMOND AT ACU RALLY CHECKPOINT

In the late 60's, after getting onto the management committee, I got more involved with CMC. There were meetings every Monday, Wednesday MC nights, the odd trial, dances and socials. I also ran a checkpoint for the 1968 ACU rally at the Shell garage at Brockworth. Don Browning was Chairman of the motorcycle section, but asked me to take over as he'd fallen out with another member of the management committee and didn't want to see them at meetings. I took over for Don, keeping him informed of everything relevant to the motorcycle section. The motorcycle racing at Staverton brought in a lot of money for the club, which was then spent by the car and social sections, neither of which made any money, but they did run a lot of events. When we asked for a few pounds to run the checkpoint for the 1969 ACU rally, we had a fight on our hands to get it from the committee. At the 1969 AGM, as the MC Chairman, I was automatically on the CMC committee and 8 MC members put-up for the committee. None of the 8 were voted on, so I was the only one with motorcycle interests on the committee which caused a lot of bad feeling amongst the motorcycle section. I volunteered with Don Browning to do the first shift at the checkpoint at Staverton Airport. After the lack of facilities on our first attempt at running a checkpoint, we had a marquee organized by club member Graham Mudway, electric to boil water to make drinks and food to make sandwiches. We were surprised this year to have a rider start the rally from our checkpoint. At 9am we stamped the riders card to get them on their way. After the rider had left I was chatting to Don who told me that they were forming a new motorcycle club, the North Glos Motorcycle Club (NGMCC). I felt disappointed they hadn't invited me, but they were only asking members who didn't race. I was at the posh function that night but popped into the marquee on my way home. I was surprised to see dozens of bikers, eating, drinking, and sleeping in the marquee so I stayed to help to dish out food and drink. Everyone really enjoyed it. I decided that having so many friends that were going to form a new club I couldn't be motorcycle Chairman, so I organized a motorcycle EGM. Luckily for the CMC, a few of the management committee attended, it came out the current motorcycle committee were not going to run the races at Staverton. New members were found to organize the races but with most of the old ones still coming to the club house on Wednesday nights, there was an air discord for a long time!

Two years had passed since Dave Baker and I had joined the Brigade and we were given notice of our 5 day probationary course to be held at Cirencester, a day-manning station, taken by Stn Officer Nation and Sub Officer Harrington. It was basically going over things we'd learned, or should have in the last two years. One of the lectures was on sewer rescues as after this course we would take our BA (breathing apparatus) course. The lecture was very interesting, explaining different scenarios and how people should be rescued from sewers, drains and rivers. My watch had been on night shift when called out to a sewer rescue where one person was dead, Percy Copeland made the recovery. There was a blockage in the sewer running along the A40, the sewage workers had lifted the manhole cover to find the blockage. One man using rods was swept away, the safety man tried to rescue him but got trapped, the third man called the brigade. The man trapped was overcome by fumes, it was not large enough to go down wearing a BA set, so Percy, who was slim, went down with just the face mask on, the BA set was lowered separately along with an extra line to rescue the man, which Percy tied around his chest. They were there all night, the highways men digging until they found the body, David and I broke into a sweat.

At the start of the course we were told we had to do a 15 minute lecture and had drawn lots for subjects. I had ladders, Dennis McGill, a Reigate 69er, had the hearth kit and David, aircraft crashes. Ladders, the history and evolution, was a good subject. As it was getting late, I used my tape recorder to record my speech and played back in bed. I woke up hearing a click, click, click sound; I'd only fallen asleep through my own lecture!

The day came for our lectures, we were all very nervous and after another draw I was second to go. I didn't think it went too bad considering. All the lectures were reasonable but David, after a nervous start, was good on aircraft and getting onto military aircraft. By this time he was looking out the window, we pulled his leg afterwards asking him if somebody was outside holding up a placard with what he had to say. He continued his lecture, "if you're attending a crash, especially of a military aircraft, you don't go lurping straight in, in case any bombs or other live ammunition are lying about." When he finished, Stn Officer Nation asked, "Baker that was very good, were you in the air cadets?" We are convinced to this day that David replied "F* off." He asked "surely I didn't?" We all said, "surely you did." We all passed the BA course and the class 3 driving test later in the year.

During my first year on white watch the watch organised a Christmas dinner to be held at the Carlton Hotel in Cheltenham. I thought I'd better go, at least there'd be pretty waitresses serving to have a laugh with. I noticed the cutlery had the Hotel's name on and at the end of the evening after kissing her hand, I asked one of the waitresses what she'd think if I kept a spoon. "I don't mind," she said, "I'm leaving this weekend and getting a new job." I slipped a spoon into my pocket. When she came back to tidy up I asked her what job she was going to. "I'm joining the police force" she said with a wink, oops. The next watch's Christmas dinner didn't get off the ground.

At a flooding incident at the public baths, as I was mopping up, I noticed a poster on the wall advertising "melodrama with beer in the auditorium" and asked an attendant about it. She told me, "It's in the old public swimming pool which is a theatre now. It's a bit like an old Time Music Hall where you can shout at the actors and have buxom serving wenches bringing you drinks." I thought it sounded good and mentioned it to Dick, Gordon and Malcolm who all agreed to come.

It was a good evening, although initially we sat quietly with our drinks. In the old days a melodrama was very sad, but this was designed for booing the villain. What started the audience off were those selling programs and ushers, all being dressed in period costume, shouting at the actors, it got everyone in the mood. During a scene change the village idiot came on, said to his girlfriend who was sitting on a log, "close your eyes and catch hold of this" which got a laugh. He gave her a ring to hold. She said "it's round with a hole in the middle." "Yes, that's right," "but I don't know what it is" she said. I shouted "he's offering you his ring piece!"

I'd been going out with Babs for many months, Then, one night when I turned up to take her out she said "sorry George, I'm not going out with you anymore." I asked for a reason but none was forthcoming. Big Frank always said "she was one of a few that was good."

The next trip to dance lessons, I saw Peter and Angela, who said I looked sad. I told her I'd just had a Dear John letter. She dragged me onto the dance floor and started blowing in my ear which got me laughing. Luckily there'd been an influx of new ladies and I met Alison. After dancing with her I asked if she'd like to go out. We went to the pictures and spent Sunday nights at the Royal William. Alison worked for Government Communication Headquarters (GCHQ) in Cheltenham.

I was invited to several GCHQ socials, one of which was a record party. Three times I put a rock 'n' roll record on, when it didn't get played the fourth time I watched and when someone went to take it off I did a John Wayne, "touch that record and you'll wake up dead." As usual I upset Alison, probably something to do with my racing. Shame, as I enjoyed borrowing her younger brother's trials BSA Bantam 175cc.

Having passed my silver medal, my gold exam for ballroom was in January. Christmas had come and gone and the start of the year was very wintry, the exam was on a Sunday. I was on days and had booked an hour's short leave from my overtime. It had snowed heavily on Saturday, by Sunday the snow had started melting and we had a flooding call to Battledown, a posh area of Cheltenham on the side of a hill. The water was coming off the hill and gushing out of an inspection cover, it was close to flooding several properties. One pump was called out with a five-man crew. Eddie gave the order to set the light portable pump to work, it used hard suction to pump water coming from an inspection cover and had two lines of hose to pump to a safe area. At 16:30 hrs we drew lots to see which two of us would stay behind, the Officer in Charge returning to the station. Percy Copeland and I lost out, despite me begging Jim Stephenson who said he was going out himself. Percy used to have a locker full of Playboy magazines, lending them to us to read in stand-down period. He was as daft as a brush, yes, worse than me! I asked the lady of the house we were protecting if I could use her phone and explained why. I told Sheila that I was on a flooding incident and couldn't get there until after 6 at the earliest. She told me to be quick, there were only 10 couples left to dance. At 18:00 hrs we had everything ready to change over so I rang again and was told, "there are only three couples left please get here soon as you can."

At 18:15 hrs the Land Rover arrived with two firemen, we quickly explained the situation before jumping in the Land Rover. I arrived in full fire gear less helmet and axe and told Sheila that I'd be back in half an hour. She grabbing me and said "we want you now George you're on next, the last couple are just finishing" I asked if she minded Percy being there. Percy was kept supplied with ale at the bar while someone lent me a pair of dancing shoes. A jacket appeared from somewhere, I was still wearing my blue shirt and tie. With no time for practice I heard the call "the waltz please." I put my arms around Sheila, my dance instructress, who with a sharp intake of breath said "George where have you had your hands, they're freezing." "Sheila, you don't want to know." The music started. After the waltz, a foxtrot, then a quickstep and lastly the tango. I had one drink in the bar to warm up then we went back to the station before going home, luckily no one said anything about the time.

Our Gold class had started as novices in September 1967 and had some good times. The exam results came some weeks later. The examiner had either, had lumpy porridge for breakfast or got out of bed the wrong side, he certainly wasn't in a good mood. Everybody had been marked down, even the top dancers who usually got a 'highly commended', over 90 marks out of 100, had only got 'commended'. In my other five exams I had got 'commended' i.e. 75%, but this time I got 75% for the quickstep and tango, perhaps as I enjoyed these more but only 73% in the waltz and foxtrot, taking me down to a 'pass'. Even Peter and Angela and her sister Margaret and partner Jack missed out on 'highly commended'. There was one couple who used to bounce when they danced. Mrs. Lister could never get them to stop it, but they always got a good pass mark as long as they did the steps that were in the dance exam curriculum. The couple, in their late 50's, said "oh Mrs. Lister we are disappointed, you told us we had done so well after the exam." Mrs. Lister then made the worst error for any businesswoman, she snapped back "you got everything you deserved, you danced terribly and you let me down." That comment killed our gold class, most stopped going and everyone was mumbling that they didn't want to be insulted like that. It was a shame, we'd had some good times, but a few of us still keep in touch.

One day in 1970 I had a phone call at the Fire Station from Peter, a ballroom dancing colleague, asking if I fancied racing a Mark 8. Before Peter could say the magic word Velocette, I said "yes, where is it?" Peter had been a top scrambler in the 50's/60's. The bike was half a mile from the Fire Station at an impressive house with a large garage, opposite the Boy's College cricket ground. Peter told me to ask for Geoffrey St John. Dick came with me at the end of the shift but there was no answer. Looking through the window of the garage, we saw a gleaming Mark 8 Velo. We both drooled looking at this 1938 350cc overhead camshaft machine. Although it had girder forks it also had a swinging arm, one of the first pre–war machines to do so. This machine was specially built for racing and had won the 1939 350cc Jnr TT giving the legendary Stanley Woods his 10th and final win around the TT course. Stanley finished 4th in the 500cc senior race on a special 500cc Velo but the race was won by Helmut Meyer on a 500cc supercharged BMW for Germany who we were at war with 3 months later. Stanley Woods held the 10 wins record until it was broken by Mike Hailwood!

Going back the next day I met Mr St John, who pronounced it Sin-jin! I said "Peter rang me saying you are looking for a rider." "Yes, he said you were a good rider, would you like to race the Mark 8?" I replied "that was nice of Peter and yes, I would very much like to race the bike." I told him that the CMC had a vintage class and 4 stroke only races at Staverton Airport meetings. The 4 stroke races came about because of the Yamaha 250cc and 350cc dominance, they were so quick. I told him that the next meeting was on 30th March and we agreed I'd enter his bike.

During my early Fire Service years we were still doing hook ladders and live carry downs as we had been taught at training school. I used to have to carry Mike Compton as we were the same size and weight, 14 stone. We'd carry each other down in turn, making sure shoulders were not in privates. The hook ladder drills were the same as at training school, but the FBU stopped hook ladders and live carry downs at the station in the early 70's, we were then reduced to carrying a dummy which was very awkward and not realistic.

I wish I had more courage. At a fire in Pittville which had lots of Regency buildings, there was a lady trapped on a balcony where you couldn't pitch a ladder. I thought about getting the hook ladder to give her some comfort by taking a rescue line but I was still a gofer. I expect I would have got into trouble.

We had a call one night to Leckhampton and were about to call it a false alarm when we heard a shout, it was a fire in a back room. I saw this old man shivering outside the room, and said "come on dad, I'll take you out" giving him a fireman's lift. When I grabbed his hand I felt all his skin come off! I laid him on a salvage sheet, got a neighbour to get a blanket, and tried to calm him down. I found out he'd knocked over the paraffin heater and burnt his hand. Luckily, the ambulance wasn't too long.

Gloucestershire had a lot of retained stations, during summer holidays local firms would close down so many retained firemen would be away on holiday and the County would be short of firemen. On one occasion I went to Northleach with Jim Stephenson as they needed a driver, which Jim was. I would be in the back of the pump unless no Jnr officers turned up, then I would sit in the front with Jim. After checking the appliance, and making sure where everything was, we advised control that we were leaving the station with the bleeper (so we could be contacted) to get some food, as we were allowed to claim up to £1 each when away from our home station. It was a roasting hot day, we'd just finished cooking and sat down to eat when a call came in. I got the message and Jim started the appliance. Two firemen arrived, we waited one more minute to see if anymore turned up, then off to a grass fire. It was close to a small copse so it could have been worse. We radioed back to say we'd put it out and were now available, only to be sent on to a car fire. Once back at the station and washed off, we noticed our food was covered in flies so went down to the Little Chef. Having to make two claims caused a riot with the paperwork, one claim for a meal away from station and the second for a spoilt meal.

A more serious incident at Northleach was a car crash with persons trapped. I was in the back of the appliance with Jim Stephenson for the 10 mile trip to the incident. The Northleach unit had already sprayed foam everywhere by the time we arrived. There was a man in the car. We were struggling to get him out as he was a big chap and thought he was alive as he made a noise every time we moved him. It may have been air in the stomach, the ambulance man in attendance said he was dead. A second person was also dead. I saw Jim Stephenson walking back swinging what I thought was an Indian club, it turned out to be the second man's arm. Jim had worked on a farm, so was quite used to unpleasant things.

Another time I was sent to Newent with Dick Browning. I'm not sure whether it was Dick or I who suggested picking up my Greeves on the way past as we'd taken a J2 15 cwt general-purpose (GP) van. Sub O Lawson gave us lots of work to do, but once the appliance was checked and food sorted, we spent the rest of the day cleaning and checking the bike over in the back drill yard. Luckily, this time there were no calls!

I'm not sure who started it or how I ended up carrying it on but we had a Watch football coupon at two shillings a week each. I collected the money and filled in the coupon. It wasn't that I liked football, motorcycle racing and rifle shooting were my sports but if you wanted to win a fortune you had to do the football pools. One Sunday day shift we were eating a late dinner with the others when someone shouted "How did we do on the football pools George?" "I don't know, I haven't checked them yet, they'll send us the money if we win," I was trying to eat my dinner. They kept on about it, so between mouthfuls I said, "I do the same numbers each week, I'll shout them out, you mark them off." I took another mouthful, "3, 7, 9". By now I'm starting my apple pie and custard, as I shouted each number they answered "draw, away, draw, draw, home, draw, away, draw, draw, away, draw, home." "Well done George" someone shouted, "seven draws and two away matches." Everyone patted me on the back spoiling the end to my dinner. The news spread to the night shift so they added their comments. When I got home I made the mistake of telling mother, she kept on about it all night, me and my big mouth! Next shift I was asked how much money we'd get, "no idea depends how many winners there are."

The alarm bells sounded, Eddie our leading fireman said there was a fire at Sidney Street. Sidney Street was a small backstreet, very narrow and a dead-end. Andy Finch was driving the "Ford Firefly" Dick Browning, Flicker James, and I made up the crew. All stations in the county had a water tender or water tender ladder using a Ford chassis, a specialist company did the bodywork naming it a Firefly. Cheltenham still had a 1950's F1 Dennis PE. Gloucestershire also had a few 1950's Bedford fire pumps kept in reserve for when front-line appliances were being serviced. The crew cab seat was designed to sit facing backwards, probably for safety which nobody ever did. Once dressed in fire kit we were half facing forward looking through the small aperture. We turned into Sydney Street to see a half-naked woman face down on the floor with blood coming from her head. Fire was coming out of the ground floor front window of the terraced house.

I found the hydrant, ran out a line of hose giving it to Andy Finch who was operating the fire pump. Dick and Gordon had run out a line of hose and were attacking the fire, I turned the hydrant on. A water tender carries 400 gallons, a single line of hose used 80 gallons a minute, so that was 5 minutes of water supply, so getting a water supply is urgent when it's a serious fire. I was helping Andy when a little lad about 5 came running around screaming. I caught hold of him and trying to calm him down asked what the matter was, "My baby brother's inside and I started the fire," he told me. I'd hardly finished telling the Sub Officer when larger-than-life Arnold Pearce grabbed hold of me and we both rushed into the fire without BA. The smoke and fire were too bad, we had to come back out. Jim Stephenson and Malcolm Nixon in BA, went in with a hose reel, fireman feeding the hose as they made progress upstairs. Water was being poured onto the fire in the front room through the outside window, a second line was pouring water through the doorway. The sight of Jim putting his head out of the window as the curtains caught fire, shaking his head, telling us the baby was dead, still sticks in my mind today.

Our pump was there for a few hours tidying up when a lady asked, "Is Eddie Hawkins here please, I am his mother?" It turned out she lived nearby. The fire was out, we were just cleaning up making sure everything was safe and keeping an eye on Eddie. We saw his mum patting him on the shoulder and asked him what she wanted "she told me to be careful." We'd pull his leg about that when we felt brave enough. Eddie had been a Royal Marine commando, but that's mothers for you.

Tuesday night shift Dave Baker asked me if it was right that we'd won the pools. I was getting a bit fed up of all the adulation. Wednesday night, after dinner, I was sat having a cuppa with Dick, talking about racing as I was glancing at MCN. "I'll find out how much we've won tomorrow Dick" I said. He looked at me smiling, "you daft bat, we've been having you on." "You bastards" I replied before wandering off sulking.

I had a brainwave, I know, unusual for me. I rang mother from the Assistant Divisional Officer's office, and whispered, "mother we haven't won the pools, they've been having me on." Mother butted in, "Oh that's a shame George." "Yes mother, stop butting in, I want you to ring me at 07:45." Mother butted in again "what time is that?" "7:45 a.m." "Why didn't you say that then?" "Sorry, but whoever answers the phone say, I'm George's mum, there's a letter from the pools company and would George come straight home, then ring off with some excuse like somebody's at the door." My grey-haired mother was then in her late 60's "I don't want to get anyone in trouble," "you won't mother, it's just a bit of fun."

I was cooking the breakfasts when the phone rang, 5 minutes later leading fireman Charlie Hall came up and told me that mum had been on the phone asking for me to go straight home as a letter had come from the pools. I replied "Don't give me all that shit Charlie, I know it's all a practical joke." "No, no it was your mum" Charlie protested in a stern voice, he was from Yorkshire so didn't have much of a sense of humour. "Why didn't you call me then?" "She had to ring off as the water was boiling over." Good old mum. They were all begging me to go home. "I'll lose 2 hours part-time butchering if I do, oh alright, now push off." I told them before going butchering.

Parking up after two days off I heard, "what was in the letter George?" I had a spark of genius, "what letter?" I asked trying to sound casual, "the one from the pools." "Oh that, they asked me to send the copy coupon because there'd been a mistake." A group of my watch crowded round asking if I'd sent it. "Well, I never keep a copy, I do the same numbers every week. Luckily, I found the coupon and put the numbers down that I thought I'd done." Stupid prat, and other such names were floating around from my so-called friends and colleagues so I sarcastically replied, "I don't mind somebody else doing the weekly coupon and collect the money, who's going to do it?" No answer, I was loving every minute, I couldn't believe it was working!

Every shift they asked me if I'd had a reply. I was trying to work out how I was going to materialise a letter from Littlewoods. I had a rulebook I so drafted a rough letter. On a day shift I was told to take something to the workshops which was part of HQ so while there, I nipped upstairs. I went to see Jane, a pretty secretary I'd introduced to Frank at the annual dance, lucky bugger took her out a few times. "Jane, can you help me on the quiet?" I explained about the practical joke and that I'd made up a letter from Littlewoods. "Sounds a good prank, George." I gave her a football coupon and draft letter which said, "Thank you for your assistance, however we must uphold rule 12. A spoiled or altered coupon is looked at by the committee who may or may not accept it." I'd taken that from their rulebook. "I am sorry to say we cannot accept your coupon so cannot award you the 2nd dividend we thought you had won, yours sincerely Cecil C Moore."

I put the letter in my locker, Jane had done a marvellous job. We had a fire call, Sub Officer Lawson told driver Graham Leighton "86 Albion Street, Cheltenham" I was in the back with Dick who was on the curb side as we arrived. He said "Hey George, there's a man waving at me." Jumping out and looking up, I saw a man waving his arms, leaning out of the top window, smoke everywhere shouting for help. "Dick you pillock." I said.

After pitching the 45 foot ladder to the third floor Sub Officer Lawson went up. Two men in BA were sent in with Dick and I was told to take up the hose reel for the BA men. We got to the top floor with the hose and gave it to the BA team, the fire was in the back room of the 3rd floor. I was about to go back down when I saw through the smoke our Sub Officer NOZ (he had a big nose, alright so have I), at the 5' x 3' sash window with the man I'd seen waving his arms, coughing badly. Dick and I went to assist, Dick grabbed the man's legs, I grabbed him under his arms. We carried him down, laid him on a salvage sheet and gave first aid until the ambulance arrived. We were then detailed to clean up, this time we had 3 floors to carry down rubbish. We used a metal dustbin to bring the debris down, it was too far to throw down and too close to the pavement, oh my poor arms.

At home I practiced signing "Cecil C Moore" which was on all Littlewoods football coupons and took the letter in with me on my next shift not knowing quite how to present it. I met Rex Jones coming out with his fire kit, "where you off to Rex?" "Standby at Stroud, they're a man short." In a flash of genius I said "you had better read this then Rex, as you're in the pools syndicate." As he was opening the letter I disappeared into the junior officer's room. I saw Martin Burford, who was also in the syndicate but on another watch. I was explaining to Martin about the hoax when Rex Jones shouted "RIDGEON." I told Martin "they think I've just lost them £700, it's all a joke, don't tell them I am here." I was hiding behind the lockers when Andy walked in, "Martin, have you seen George Ridgeon." "No, Andy, what's up?" "The silly bastard has lost us £700 by doing the football coupon wrong." I felt like James Bond hiding, and said to Martin "I'll stay here until the next bell rings."

The bell rang, I rushed from my hiding place, grabbed my fire kit, dropped it at the back of the appliance room, and went on to the parade ground as Sub O Lawson shouted for us to fall in. I thought there was going to be a riot as all of my watch broke ranks. Sub Officer shouted "get back in line." After parade everybody crowded round calling me all sorts of horrible names, my only defence was "does anyone else want to fill in the pools coupon?" They were moaning at me all morning, so dinner time I told them that it was all a hoax. There were lots of moans but Dick and Malcolm thought it was a good laugh.

After two years of racing BSA twins I moved to a 500cc Triton. I saw an advert in the local paper for a crashed Triton road bike and a Norton wide-line frame was for sale in Hastings. I asked Garnet if he fancied a few days holiday so that we could pick up the Norton frame. It was an enjoyable trip including a swim on the beach where King Harold was shot in his eye with an arrow in 1066.

With Dick's help the Triton was coming together. Although we had the frame, when I saw an advert for a Manx Norton swinging arm in Bristol, I took Alison, the young lady from dancing classes, with me for company to buy it. Once home the swinging arm looked the same as the one I already had, but I thought that as it was out of a Manx Norton it'd make my bike go faster!

Dick had introduced me to the hose repair shop, which was supposed to be used only for repairing fire hose and other fire service jobs but most firemen did carpentry etc in there. I used it during stand down periods, mainly working on engines as there was a good wooden bench and vice. One weekend, when working on the Triton during the tea break the heavens opened so I put the bike in the hose repair shop. A couple of hours later, when I went to get it out I found the petrol had been leaking and had damaged the linoleum floor. This not only got us a telling off but everybody banned from the hose repair shop, Dick and I were not flavour of the month.

The first race on the Mk8 at Staverton turned out to be very exciting as the bike went as well as it looked considering it was 35 years old! I practiced my largest capacity machine, the 500cc Triton first, then managed to squeeze in a practice on the 350cc Mk 8. For the vintage race, Dick was standing by the paddock gate, with a pocket full of spanners and a spark plug. I had a good start and was challenging for 3rd but as I came around paddock bend the bike cut out. I waved to Dick, the only thing we could do was take the oily plug out, put a fresh one in and bump start it. I finished the race, and wasn't even last! As I came in Geoffrey St John was by my van. When we looked at the plug

I'd taken out, it was a Lodge RL54 which is for racing in the Isle of Man not on a short circuit. I jokingly told the owner off, Geoffrey was smiling. I offered to ask the organisers if I could race it in the 350cc open race, but warned it would be outclassed against the modern bikes. He agreed as he wanted to see it being raced. I asked Geoff Garbutt, secretary of the meeting, if I could make up the numbers on the Mk 8 in the 350cc race. He replied "Yes George, just turn up at the start. There's no need to pay as people, including myself, want to see the bike going round." I had another good start, and was in the top half of the 30+ starters when a very quick Yamaha hit my handle bars. I was fighting for control of the Mk 8 and noticed the Yamaha weaving up the track in front of me, both of us were trying to stay on. I finished 11th. We were all pleased as I'd had a finish on the Triton too, a good day.

Just after the Staverton meeting, we took the Triton to Cadwell Park. We borrowed Dick's father's 1000cc Vauxhall van as the VW had damaged steering. This had a couple of benefits, 40+ mpg and the heater worked. I must admit we were broke at the time and Cadwell Park was a 350 mile round trip. One of the jobs at work was topping up fire appliances, officers cars and GP vehicles. When filling in the vehicle logbook you put down how much fuel you'd put in. It had to be in whole gallons so we started putting the excess in a can and by the end of the day we had 4 gallons which at 40 mpg equals 160 miles. You could say we were sponsored one way by the fire service! The bike went okay but it wasn't very competitive.

I returned to Cadwell Park, a month later. I'd started to campaign the Triton for half of 1970 after being overtaken at Staverton in 1969 on my BSA by a Triumph. But the bike had just a Tiger 100 engine from the crashed road bike, no engine tuning, no full fairing and a standard 8" Norton front brake, it was only a modified road bike. However, this particular time at Cadwell I was flat out, chin on tank down the back straight when Mick Broome passed me on a 1938 Iron engine Triumph 500cc in a rigid frame with girder forks, I must admit it pissed me off. I couldn't even pass him on the twisty section. To add insult to injury, he started pulling away on the straight.

Scouring the weekly MCN, I saw a 1967 Greeves Silverstone, ready to race for £175. Luckily I was racing the Triton near to where the bike was for sale so I rang before we left and arranged to call in. There were some notes on tuning and servicing with it. I started the bike up, then offered him £140. He tried to haggle but I didn't move so he asked when I was going to collect it. I told him I'd take it now. He said that he was racing it tomorrow. When I told him I wouldn't come back for it he told me to take it.

I did a deal with fireman Graham Attwood, who was also a biker. He took the Triton and Bedford Dormobile van, that wouldn't go in a straight line and that I'd swapped for my VW, in exchange for a 1965 Austin Cambridge 12 cwt van. This was luxury; radio, heater and 2 reclining seats. You could sleep in the van or cuddle a lady.

The service sheet for the Greeves listed when to change rings and oil seals which was helpful as was the experience of my first Greeves that I'd bought off Dave Browning. I learnt from Dick Sheppard, top international stunt driver, that you should always take a racing engine apart to check is in good condition. So I completely stripped it down, every nut and bolt, checked ring gaps and changed the oil seals. I wasn't so good on the rolling chassis and wheels but as the man I'd bought it from had intended to race the bike the next day, I left the frame, but did ride it up and down the lane to test the engine.

The first race on the Silverstone was New Brighton Promenade in mid July 1970. It was agreed that Dick would drive us in his dad's van saving my energy for the race. When we got there, we chucked the bike out and slept in the back, after devouring some of our sandwiches. Early in the morning, we walked round the track which was a road, well a promenade. It was a sort of dual carriageway with a roundabout every quarter mile. It was just a fun day out to see how competitive the bike was. They waved our practice off, the bike accelerated well, into second gear then third. Coming up to the chicane/roundabout I applied the brakes, the front brake locked solid. He flew through the air with the greatest of ease, as they say.

I was lying on the ground hurting. My goggles had moved over my nose and I could see blood running from somewhere, I was thinking, *oh my God what's happened, will someone run over me?* I heard the bikes going by my head and saw a flash for every noise! I'd run over a rider at the Staverton meeting in May. The incident happened when a rider overtook 5 of us going into a left hand bend. He fell off, I was in the middle of the 5 bikes with nowhere to go, I felt a horrible bump but managed to stay on. Parking the bike against a straw bale I ran back to find I'd hit the fallen rider's head but couldn't recognize him as his face was a mass of blood. The race was stopped, the rider taken to the first aid tent and I rode back to the paddock. I felt worse when I found out it was Cheltenham rider Tim Miles. I first met Tim when Geoff Fivash asked me collect his leather racing suit for our first race in 1964. He gave lots of advice and engineering tips to us novice riders. I felt very bad speaking to his wife at the circuit who said, "don't worry George, that's racing." 3 weeks later I had a message to go and see Tim's wife. I'd been feeling bad since the accident and not getting a great deal of sleep, there was a risk Tim may die. It felt strange arriving at the house, an impressive Regency house on the Evesham Road, not far from William's Motorcycles where I used to look at all the bikes with envy! I nervously knocked on the door and was invited in. Making a cup of tea, Tim's wife explained that no one had been to see her, everyone was keeping away. I explained that I felt that as I was involved in the accident she may not want to see me. She again told me "George, racing is dangerous and it wasn't really your fault." This put me at ease a little and we continued chatting. I had the feeling as we talked that she really needed an adult to talk to, not being able to tell her problems to their three young children. She told me that as Tim was unconscious, his money was paid into his bank account which she couldn't use as it wasn't a joint account. She had been living on child benefit of £3-15/- a week. Luckily, the bank manager had lent her his own money knowing he would get it back. I asked if there was anything I could do and she asked me to move some heavy boxes.

Tim was unconscious for a month. I started calling in on the way home from work. After this incident, when anyone was in trouble I would go and see them to say, "if you want help please let me know."

So I'm lying on the New Brighton Prom wondering if anybody is going to run over me as I had Tim! Luckily they didn't. Practice was stopped and when the ambulance crew came I shouted "don't move me, don't move me" being a wimp of the first order. I arrived at Wallasey Hospital, near the Mersey tunnel and taken to A&E with my arm in a sling and both shoulder and nose hurting. When my turn came the nurse asked for £1-5/-, "what for?" I wanted to know, "road traffic accident," "but I was racing." The nurse rang the police, 15+ minutes later a policeman arrived wanting to see my licence, "not with me officer." "Have you any insurance?" "Only personal accident and third-party, I was racing my motorcycle." A look of horror appeared on the policeman's face and he rang the station. I could hear some of the conversation with the desk sergeant. "I have a very strange thing here" he said explaining what I'd told him "but he's injured." The sergeant replied "book him." I said to the officer "if you nip down to the prom now you can arrest another 200, you'll get promoted." After a few more phone calls they found the Chief Constable who'd given permission for racing on council land, so after 1 hour of hurting I was treated, but I didn't end up paying the 25/-!

Although I'd left the RAF Fire Service, I stayed a member of the Woodpeckers Rifle Club. The target circle was just over an inch wide but when you looked through the rifle sights, at 25 yards, it was very small, like a small black moon. As my scores were in the middle 90's within a year, I was asked to shoot in the Postal Team. I found it surprising how different this was from shooting at the target in practice to improve your score. The card was marked, stamped and signed by two officials before you shot! I was pleased to be considered for the team but very nervous shooting this card, the tension was similar to the start of a motorcycle race except it lasted until you had shot the last of the 10 targets.

There was a nice girl called Maureen who was also a member of the club, at the pub afterwards she had a lot of admirers, including myself. On the odd occasion I used to run her home as I went close where she lived. Sometimes I got a cuppa in her shared house while listening to records, one was Maggie May by Rod Stewart, it was No.1 and we both liked it. At Christmas time 1971, we were in a pub after shooting, I asked again "how about a night out somewhere perhaps the pictures?" She told me she was away for Christmas and the New Year but to ask again in January. In the pub after the first shoot of the year I asked, "Maureen, would you like to go to the pictures?" I nearly fell off the chair when she said yes. Tuesday night I stood for hours outside the cinema, long after the film started, I've been here before I thought. What was that Sandy Shaw song? Girl Don't Come! No Maureen, so I went for cider shandy when out of the Juke box came Rod Stewart's Maggie May, every time I hear this song it makes me think of her.

CHAPTER 8   1971-Racing in God's country

Monday 1st February 1971, I sat with dad as he lit up a roll-up fag. When I was little, dad would ask "do you want to lick my fag paper son?" "Yes please dad" I'd say, holding my tongue out. Dad would run the fag paper up and down it! As soon as he lit it up, he started coughing. I asked why he smoked. "It's the only bit of pleasure I've got left. I can't ride the Bantam with this leg ulcer in case I knock it, even if I could, I can't go up the Kings Head for a pint with this angina and all the pills." Dad explained his frustration and talked about his days living in Wales, when he would walk 15 miles to Cardiff to watch the stars of the day in the 1920's, working down the pit as a miner, boxing and helping his dad race pigeons. "Now look at me" he said. "Sorry I asked dad," "no problem son I had a good life I just don't like being ill."

I enjoyed helping at Jack Council's butcher's shop, cutting meat and serving customers. I got a meat bonus on top of 5/- an hour. I remember when one elderly lady came into Jack's shop, I asked her, "are you next young lady?" "Don't be so impertinent, anyone can see I am not young" she snapped. I apologised and said "I was just trying to be pleasant Madam" which got a "Mmmm" noise from the lady, however, most of the ladies loved it. One cuddly lady asked for a bit of undercut, another name for fillet steak, giving me a wink!

I was working at the butcher's shop after an uneventful night shift when I got a phone call, "Mrs. White here George, your father's just died. Can you come home please?" I told Jack as I ran past him. I drove home with my headlights on, breaking all the speed limits, it's a good job there weren't any speed cameras then. Mum was in tears, "Dr Drake has just gone, he believes dad had a heart attack." I gave her a cuddle. "I had a terrible shock when I woke up. Dad must have got out of bed to have a run out in the pot, he was just lying against the bed." We only had an outside earth bucket toilet so had a chamber pot nicknamed guzunda. "Come on mother, put the kettle on, I'll go and say goodbye to dad." I plucked up the courage to go into the bedroom. Dad was half in the bed as Dr. Drake wasn't strong enough to put him in completely. I think that was the worst job of my life, putting my father in bed knowing he was dead. I crossed his arms as they do in films, pulled the sheet up to his chin leaving his head visible, and brushed his hair. Dave arrived and we all sat there in shock. Dave knew more about what to do than I did, even though I was in my 20's, he rang the Co-op Funeral Parlour. They arrived, and we had a drink of sherry to toast father. After Dad had been taken away, Dave said he'd take mother over to stay with him and Sue in Tewkesbury. We agreed I'd tidy the house up. I rang the fire station and found that I was entitled to four days compassionate leave. I washed dishes, wiped off the table and all surfaces and swept the floors. After taking all the bedding off dad's bed, I made mother's and took the bedding, and other washing to the launderette in Barton Street. I went to see Mrs. Prentice, who could see I was upset and asked me what the matter was. "Dad's died" I said and burst into tears. Mrs. P gave me a cuddle and made a cup of tea. I asked her if I should leave dad's bed bare or make it. She suggested I make the bed to look as if it will be slept in, put some new curtains up and consider decorating the room. After pie and chips, I picked up the washing, went home and made the bed up as Mrs. Prentice had suggested. I could see it was right decision, the room looked as normal as mum would expect to see it. I got all the jobs done inside and out, even emptying the 'earth bucket,' digging it into the garden. I was trying to keep busy, trying not to dwell too much on the fact that my father had just died. Having another cuppa I decided there was no point of sitting here on my own so I rang the station and told them I'd be coming in for my night shift, I thought it best to keep busy.

All the station knew my father had died, most patted my shoulder and said the words we all say, but every time I heard the words, my eyes would well up with tears as I thanked them. A few asked why I'd come to work, but one remark was very cruel.

By the time dad died, I'd started selling ladies tights and knickers. This happened by chance after attending the 1970 annual fire service dance. I took my ballroom dancing partner, inviting her brother and his wife to this posh dance. While having tea and biscuits at her bungalow afterwards, I found out her brother was a schoolteacher who also ran a business retailing ladies underwear. "George, have you ever thought about selling ladies tights?" I gave him a swift reply, "not for a minute, if I was selling anything it will be motorcycle parts." "No, not you personally, ask your friends wives and girlfriends to sell them," he said, and went on to explain, "I sell you a box of 12 Mivista tights for 3/- a pair, you sell them to your friends wives and girlfriends for 3/6d, they sell them for 4/-. On a dozen pairs of tights you both make 6/-, a gallon of petrol. All you have to do is deliver the tights and collect the money. I'll give you a pair to show around." He was a good salesman, I took a dozen pairs plus the free one. I asked Frank's girlfriend, Zandra, John's wife Dorothy and Norman's wife

Tina, within days they all rang up wanting more tights. The third week, I bought 70 dozen and a few boxes of ladies briefs which also sold well.

Some of the firemen's wives started selling them and I suppose this was how the cruel and hurtful remark from one of my watch came about: "George will you be selling your mother a shroud for the funeral?" Luckily for the person who said it I wasn't a violent person, also I didn't want to fight on the day my father died. I mentioned it to Dick who said "he's just a pillock, his brain can't control his mouth," which made me smile. Going into work was the right thing to do, even though I broke down every so often. I was keeping busy and Dick was telling me jokes and winding me up.

Dave had more than one problem. His wife, Susan, was rushed into hospital for an operation, at least mother was kept busy looking after the girls, Julie and Sally. As well as working, Dave was popping in to see Sue in hospital and sorting out the funeral. I was busy with work, part-time butchering, popping over to see mum and doing more work around the house, during which I found dad's false teeth. I contacted Dave to find out what was happening with the funeral and told him I'd found fathers false teeth, "chuck them in the dustbin" was his response. I couldn't do that. I took them to the Co-op Funeral Parlour and asked if they could put them in the coffin. "No problem at all Sir, it's a nice thought," which made me feel a bit better. Dad didn't like wearing them, except for eating. I remember sitting in the King's Head in the 1950's with my lemonade and packet of crisps, when one of dad's friends asked him "where are your teeth tonight, George?" "The wife's with me, she's wearing them." Mother gave him a friendly slap, I sniggered.

When mum came home she liked the way I'd done the bedroom, by then I'd put new curtains up as Mrs. Prentice had suggested. Before dad died, they'd considered a kitchen extension and had an architect draw up some plans which included an inside toilet. When dad was on the sick during the bad winter of 62/63, I was left with the job of emptying the bucket! On this one day it was -20°C, the ground was frozen and covered with snow, and the contents of the bucket were also frozen. I used dad's coal miners pick to get the contents out of the bucket but put it through the bucket, which I left up the top of the garden until March 1963!

Although the plans had been done for the extension, dad used to say "I'm sorry mother, I just don't feel well enough at the moment, perhaps in the summer." I asked Mum if she'd like me to ask Garnet if he could build the extension, she replied, "yes, I think dad would like us to do the extension." Garnet came around, "I'd be pleased to do it for you Mrs Ridgeon. George, if you help labouring it'll bring the price down."

April 1971, Garnet married Lynn Drake, the daughter of the landlady of The Prince of Wales pub, where Garnet had his stag night, Lin had a girl's night out. There were 20 plus crammed in the back bar, I'm not sure if they had an extension or if it was a lock-in but we were certainly drinking after hours with lots of noise and jollification. I and another guest started telling jokes, he told one, then I would reply, then him again. A friend of Garnet's, a big farmer called Dave, told me he designed the first hay baling machine that made round bales. He was the size of a haystack and laughed so much he had to sit down crying. Mum was invited to the wedding so I had to half behave, but it was a lovely day. At the reception the only available lady was the photographer who was quite posh but I made a date or at least got her telephone number. After Garnet and Lin had left, a group of us had intended to do something to their flat but as it was three floors up they got away with it.

On a night out for a drink with the posh photographer, she told me that she'd been invited to take photos at a posh wedding and could bring up to four friends with her, would I like to go? The official invite arrived and on the bottom was printed "Dress, DJ" not knowing what this was I asked at dancing lessons. What a pillock I felt when I was told "Dinner Jacket." I should have realised because I'd recently bought a double-breasted dinner jacket off one of the other dancers who'd treated himself to a new one as he had put on too much weight. I added a pair of dress trousers from The Famous Tailors who were having a sale of smoky clothes after a large fire next door at Tesco's in Cheltenham.

We arrived at this large house and went to the free bar to find it was a champagne reception, or whiskey, gin, vodka, brandy, an array of mostly shorts. When I asked for my usual cider shandy, they looked at me somewhat strange. After a discussion with the barman, I had an orange juice, I even tried a champagne shandy! I was introduced to the lady of the house who was a titled lady, so royal connections maybe! I danced with the wives of the Mayors of Gloucester and Cheltenham, other dignitaries and the photo lady, while the husbands were leaning on the bar talking politics, a good night. I took the photo lady out a few times, but trying to have a cuddle in her mini car, although better than my van, was a bit difficult. Have you heard about the sexually transmitted disease "Crampies?" It's from trying to have sex in a small car!

Life was getting busy, I was a fireman, a part-time butcher, delivering tights, racing the Greeves, ballroom dancing and rifle shooting, and now, labouring on the bungalow extension. Talking with Dick at the station, I told him I was considering entering the Manx Grand Prix and asked what he thought. He told me to go for it. Mother was not very happy. Dick and I decided to go on the MCN day trip to see the senior TT to get the feel of it, it sounded like a good crack! The Thursday night of race week at 19:00, we waited at Gloucester Railway Station. The last carriage on the train had a large sign "MCN TT special" on it and we packed in with fellow enthusiasts. Birmingham was a main collecting area, carriages from all over arrived, hundreds got off and onto the train to Liverpool which was now packed with motorcycle fans. At Liverpool there were 1000's of fans all walking to the Princes Dock to catch the midnight ferry. As the saying goes, we were packed like sardines. Dick and I lay where we could on the deck, heads on our kit bags full of food, chatting and reminiscing until we drifted off, to be woken up at 05:00 as the boat docked.

We walked to the TT grandstand and sat stuffing our faces from our large food store. We saw a sign that said, 'Lap of the TT course 50p', decimalization had come in February 1971. The coach filled up fast. All I remember of the coach trip was going down Bray Hill and around Quarter Bridge. With the warmth and comfort of the coach we slept most of the way, but felt better for it. After a warm cup of tea in a café, we walked to Braddon Bridge as the 125cc race was due to start at 10am. Luckily we found a place under the trees as the sky went dark. We were trying to stay awake by counting the road bikes going around before the roads closed, over 120 a minute, so nearly 10,000 an hour. It started to drizzle as we heard the start of the 125cc race on the tannoy system, the bikes starting at 10 second intervals. Number one was Barry Sheene on a Suzuki but he retired. The sound of open megaphones on the 125cc Honda CR93 4 stroke revving to 14,000 rpm, the expansion chambers of Yamaha, Maico, MZ and Bultaco 2 strokes 10,000+ rpm, all came screaming over the tannoy. The race was won by Chas Mortimer at 83.96 mph in the rain, 2nd Borje Jasson on a Maico, 3rd John Kiddie on a Honda. The rain was now steady, but delving in to our food store, we were happy enough until we heard the dreaded announcement, "there will be a delay" then "sorry the race will be run Saturday!"

Grumpy motorcycle enthusiasts were walking back to Douglas. I suggested to Dick that we should go to the Isle of Man Steam Packet Company (IOMSPC) to find out about sailings for the Manx Grand Prix. In front of us in the queue, a man complained "I paid to see the Senior TT and haven't seen it." The man behind the counter replied that the IOMSPC would honour his ticket until 6pm on Saturday. Dick and I looked at each other hearing this! I booked passage for the Manx then told him we were on a day trip to see the Senior and hadn't been able to. He repeated that they would honour the ticket to Liverpool up to 6pm Saturday.

We wondered if the railway would do the same. At the British Rail office the man informed us that as far as he knew no boats were sailing tonight. On hearing this a lot of bikers went back to the IOMSPC. "British rail said no boats are sailing tonight." "Sir, I can guarantee all boats are sailing, go home tonight or we will honour your ticket up to 6 pm Saturday" was the reply. By now a larger angry group of bikers had descended on the rail office. I explained to the man "the IOMSPC guaranteed that all ferries are sailing. If we stay on will British Rail honour our ticket?" He said yes so I asked him to put it in writing. His face went an ashen colour, and he got on the phone with a very worried look, a lynch mob was looking at him. All of a sudden, "that's it, bugger it George, let's go home" Dick boomed out, making me, and everyone else jump, especially the British Rail man on the phone! "Okay by me Dick" I said and we left the British Rail man to the angry mob! Dick was on leave, it was me that would have had to get Saturday off if we'd stayed!

We needed somewhere warm to dry off and decided on the cinema. It turned out to be a good film, Shirley MacLaine and Clint Eastwood in Two Mules for Sister Sarah, a comedy cowboy film with lots of girls and shooting. We hung our shoes, socks and the rest of our wet clothes over the seats in front, luckily the cinema wasn't too full. We ate our cooked chicken and sausages with various sandwiches, our mothers didn't want their little boys to starve! We stayed in the cinema until chucking out time before getting on the boat which was full of tired, damp motorcyclists.

It was just as well Dick threw a wobbly and we came back early. Firstly, I got to work and didn't have to give up one of my bank holidays, secondly, a boat carrying a highly flammable liquid was leaking in Liverpool Dock so it was closed to all boat traffic. Mick Dunn was on the Island watching the TT. He caught the Saturday night ferry not realising, it had been diverted to Ardrossan in Scotland. When Mick ran out of petrol on his motorcycle,

164

he rang his dad for help! I hate to think what Dick would have done with an out of date ticket for Liverpool to Gloucester. Had we been in Scotland, we could still be in prison for murdering a Scottish Rail official who wouldn't let us on the train!!

MY GOOD FRIEND DICK, WITH MY TRITON AT CADWELL

The extension at "Janetta" was going well, I was enjoying doing the labouring and Garnet had a good bricklayer. I was to find out how good a friend Garnet was. He had to get a small digger up the side of the bungalow to dig a hole for the septic tank, the gap between the bungalow, the digger and the hedge was about 6". With all the noise, mum was in tears, Garnet said "Mrs. Ridgeon, let me take you over to my house, you can keep my wife Lin company so you don't have to listen to the noise."

With a hole dug for the septic tank and the rhubarb moved up the garden, a lorry turned up with 300 concrete blocks. As the gofer, I unloaded the blocks, stacking them in front of my Austin van, then back to helping Garnet. My van was full of ladies tights as some of the ladies from dancing bought them. I got dressed up for dancing, but seeing the blocks and feeling a pillock, I got back into working clothes and moved the blocks behind my van.

I received a letter saying that I'd been accepted for the Lightweight (Ltw) MGP. I hadn't made too many plans but did know that Dick couldn't help. Driving home from work, I passed The Red Apple Garage, and saw Ray Wakefield, who I'd met at CMC. He was married now with a child and worked in Cheshire. I pulled up blocking the road, "what are you doing

August, I've been accepted for the MGP, wannabe my mechanic?" He gave me his address and asked me to keep him informed.

I was racing the Greeves at Thruxton and had a seizure, causing me to slide off. The gudgeon pin had fractured so a little concerned with the Manx only two months away, I sent the piston and gudgeon pin to Greeves. Their reply was very vague, but did say that I was using five-star fuel, which the local top racers said was rubbish, so I made sure I changed the piston and pin every six races as the service sheet suggested, but it was a worry with the Manx coming up.

John Gardner from Stroud fixed me up with digs in Hillary Park, Douglas, with Mrs Doris Jackson. She sent me a letter saying that the front door would be left open. I arrived at 6am, left some rhubarb and apples by the stairs, after seeing a note telling me that my bedroom was third on the left and breakfast was at 8am. At breakfast I saw John and his mechanic Mike (Beefer) Smith, and met Ben Tandy, dad of Geoff.

John explained, "Saturday there's lot to do, we have to sign on and as you're a newcomer you've got the Crossley Tour on Sunday." This was a coach trip started by Dick Crossley, a rider who thought newcomers should have more knowledge of the course. After signing on we got a stern talk on safety at the riders briefing. John told me all the dos and don'ts, impressing on me that I must have a plug bag. It was best to use a small pencil case attached to the bike or fairing, for a plug, plug spanner, wire and screwdriver as its 37.73 miles each lap! I fitted the leather bag with straps on the fairing bracket. John continuing the long list; "when it is not your practice, go watch from somewhere, if it rains go out for practice as it may rain in the race, jet up for first practice, stop after 3 miles to check the plug colour (plug chop) to see if it's running okay" my poor head was spinning!

The coach trip was on Sunday, rider Mike Kelly talking us through each bend, what gear to be in, braking points and lines etc. I wished I'd had paper and pencil to write it all down. There was a welcome break at Ramsay for tea, before back on the bus and up the mountain section. Talking to the rider next to me, we weren't sure if it was helping or scaring us. When we got back I checked the bike over and made the alterations suggested by John. Ray arrived Sunday afternoon, first practice was in the morning at 6:15am.

I didn't sleep well and heard a race bike running at 4am, practice wasn't until 06:15. At 5am I had a cuppa before leaving and queuing up for scrutineering. John had advised me to keep away from Ken Harding, Chief Scrutineer, saying that he's a bit of an ogre. I jumped on hearing a voice boom out, it was Ken ripping someone's bike apart "this is a dangerous course, your bike is terrible, look at it." The poor rider was trembling! He always did this first practice, he thought it would get other riders to make sure their bike was fit to go on the course. Many riders would change to a longer queue just to miss Ken. Somehow my bike passed, *thank you Lord.* I was to have many battles with Ken over the years!!

We were lined up on the start in pairs, a voice came over the tannoy, "this is Jack Woods your controller for this morning. It's still too dark to start so there'll be a 15 minute delay until 6:30 am." With some of the other riders, I went behind the TT scoreboards to a very basic urinal for a quick run-out. I'd started the bike up at Mrs. Jackson's and had the trip around the course the day before, but I was feeling apprehensive, until I heard the first bikes starting. I turned the petrol on, the engine was cold as we weren't allowed to start them until given permission in the morning, unless, like the 4am bike you rode it from your digs. The bike started, the revs creeping up to 6500 down Bray Hill and up to 7000 through Quarter Bridge. After Braddon Bridge and Union Mills there's a long straight, so I pulled up, lent the bike against a white cottage wall and checked the plug. It was a dark colour, so safe to carry on. Just after the plug chop I saw a rise so changed down to 4th, seeing another rise, I changed into 3rd but found the road was still straight for 500 yards before a sweeping right, Glen Vine!

More sweeping bends, but I'd remembered Ballacraine as it had the pub on the corner, leading to more sweeping bends. Past Sarah's Cottage, a bumpy uphill section, the bike was all over the road, but Greeves were designed as scramblers! Cronk y Voddy Straight was even bumpier. I tried to ride the lap as if I was on a road I'd never been on before but knowing that nothing was coming the other way. My head just missed a brick wall at Hanley's. I was trying to concentrate but thinking *can I learn all these bends?* Ramsay, hooray, I remembered this is where we'd stopped for tea. On the rise towards the mountain around the famous Ramsey Hairpin, I was admiring the views when a bike went by me, just missing the wall at Water Works! Across the Mountain Section, I remembered the odd bend from the Crossley Tour; Bungalow, Creg Ny Baa, Hillberry and arrived at Governors Bridge. As this is a very tight hairpin the coach didn't go round this section, we all got out and walked around wondering if we could get

167

around it, but I did get round and arrived back at the start.

I'd been lucky enough to borrow a 5 gallon Greeves tank from a rider in Cardiff and started with a full tank, again, as advised by John, to get used to going down Bray Hill with a full tank. As I started a 2nd lap Ray gave me a wave, still steady down Bray Hill, well everywhere really. I saw where I'd stopped to do my plug chop, and still slowed for the rise but only went down to 4th gear, Glen Vine was steady in 5th. At a corner just before Ballaugh Bridge, Bishop's Court, I kept shutting off, when a fraction later I could see round the corner!! Arriving at Ramsay, *that was quick,* I asked myself if I was enjoying it! What I didn't like about the mountain section, was that the bike sounded as if there was something wrong with it. Talking with John afterwards, the fact that there were no houses or hedges to keep the noise in, made the bikes sound different! The sunlight blinked in my eyes as I was slowing for Governors Bridge, making better job of it than I had on the first lap. I pulled in after the chequered flag and Ray took the bike.

We saw riders heading for a large marquee and followed them to the refreshment tent for a cuppa and biscuit. I fell in love with the MGP tea girls, Maureen, Rita, Liz and another lady who always wore dark stockings, they brightened the morning up no end. Beefer Smith was there waiting for John who'd retired. We'd arranged that if anyone of our team retired, Beefer would pick us up after the 'roads open' car had been through.

After early morning practice, we were at breakfast when a pretty milk lady called Christine came in for a chat with Doris. It was fun, as she was as cheeky to us as we were to her. I was sat next to Geoff Tandy's dad, "tell me Ben have I really done 2 laps?" John chirped up, "my 1st lap, a clip-on broke, you lucky bugger George."

We worked on our bikes in a large double garage which had an up and over door and was off a narrow lane. Jobs included checking the points and taking the head off. John asked if I was pulling the gearing and after a discussion, we lowered it by 2 teeth. We took the primary cover off to check the chain was okay with no cracked rollers, I'd change this after 4 laps. The first dinner time, John showed us a good chippy he'd found last year, after that we took turns getting the chips. Mrs. Jackson shouted "cuppa lads," we went into the kitchen where bread-and-butter would appear, talk about luxury. No Monday evening practice for the

Lightweights, so we watched from Governors Dip as it was close to the grandstand and I was hoping to learn from other riders.

Tuesday evening practice there were two long lines for scrutineering. Ken Harding was doing one line so I joined the other. Unfortunately, Ken moved to my line. Some riders changed to the queue he had been doing which was now longer than the one I was in only for Ken to change back. I couldn't avoid him all week. When he got to do my bike I was trying to keep my mouth shut! Two more laps, I was feeling quicker but still nervous at the two rises into Glen Vine, and still shutting off at Bishop's Court. I found the bottom of Barregarrow quite scary. When coming over the top you can see right through the bend, but after a drop-down, a little like Bray Hill, there's a cottage on the left that turns Barregarrow Bottom into a blind bend, so I eased back.

No Wednesday morning practice for us. Doris's brother, Gordon, a marshal at the Creg, invited us to come and watch. We were sat under the overhang of the pub waiting for the first bikes, Gordon had got the Chief Marshal, who wears a white coat, to give me an arm band. The noise of bikes could be heard, and we could see a speck come around Kate's cottage, uphill from us, ¾ mile away. One rider gave us a scare as he overshot, the flag marshal was quick with a stationary yellow flag. Once he was sorted, a marshal patted him on the shoulder when it was safe to go, another rider pulled in to retire. I was sat watching this seagull fly low over the fields wondering why everyone was running around. It was a rider off, what I thought was a seagull, was a bike with a white fairing that had gone straight on at Kate's Cottage turning over and over. The Chief Marshal shouted "take the stretcher." I volunteered to go, leaving the older ones at the Creg. We started running, but didn't last long as it was all uphill, we arrived knackered. A marshal was with the rider, the others waving yellow flags. Once the rider was on stretcher we carried him down the hill. The rider was unconscious, so we flagged down at least two riders asking them to tell the marshals at the Creg to get an ambulance and inform race control. We had to wait for the end of practice, in those days there was no helicopter for amateurs.

On Ray's advice, I decided to fit a new big end at Neal Kelly Motorcycles, the Greeves agent on the Island. We changed the primary chain after the first four laps, checking it after every practice and shimming the gearbox if it was slack, Greeves method of primary chain adjustment. Thursday was a big day, practice was 2pm to 5pm giving riders a daytime practice, but it rained. I did two steady laps but at least I'd got a wet practice. I was glad I had a body belt, it helped my back as the course was so bumpy. I bought it from a local grass track racer. I had a go on his BSA 250cc before he sold it; it was scary, even going slow.

I don't know why, but I still had nerves waiting and watching as a scrutineer was shaking the bike, testing everything, pulling the brakes. I'd been told that a scrutineer had pulled the front brake lever on one bike so hard the nipple came off, then said, "I expect you're glad I did that, and it didn't happen on the course!!" Friday evening practice, I was quicker again. Around Glen Vine I stayed in top, including the two rises, although I sat up. I was feeling more comfortable everywhere. As I approached Bishops Court, getting closer to the area where I shut the throttle, I kept saying to myself *don't shut off, don't shut off*. My chin was on the tank, but the cautious side of my brain said *I hope I've got the right corner!* I was just about to brake, as the bend opened up, I stayed on it in top gear. Talk about relief, not that you had time to relax when doing 100 mph on a bumpy road with other riders trying to pass you. So that was the first corner I mastered. I started the second lap, Bray Hill in top but not flat out. The sun shone through the trees in both morning and evening practice, but there were "beware of sun" signs, it could blind you.

Early in practice week we were surprised to see a couple watching us work in the garage, with their pretty daughter. They introduced themselves and their daughter, Sheila. We realized we'd seen them taking photos at race meetings. Mr. and Mrs. Edwards were talking to John, I chatted up Sheila. "I'm sure I've met you somewhere Sheila." "You stood next to me at Mallory Park when Cooper and Ago had that race," she replied. I explained that I'd raced at Aintree on the Saturday and decided to call in and watch the epic battle between Giacomo Agostini on the MV and John Cooper on the Trident on the way home. We blagged our way in as the racing bikes were in the back, ending up on the scaffolding viewing area. After practice, Mr and Mrs Edwards declined our invitation so we ended up taking Sheila to a pub.

I bought a book, with a solo and sidecar section, on how to ride fast around the TT course and asked Sheila if she'd like to accompany me around the course, learning the corners. We left early Saturday, first stop was at the bottom of Bray Hill, I showed Sheila the photo in the book and she put an X where I thought the peel off point was. It took nearly 2 hours but we did this all the way round the course, There were crosses everywhere, I thought I was doing the football pools.

For last practice we'd fitted new clutch plates so they'd bed in and we could adjust the clutch over the weekend. The bike was going well but, going faster, I started finding bumps that hadn't been there before, one was at Ginger Hall Pub. Although the clutch had started to play up and the bike wasn't changing gear very well it didn't affect top speed. Left by the pub, which had a high hedge, right, left then right, I was still cranked over trying to lift the bike up for the straight when the front wheel came off the ground, my heart skipped a beat. With the clutch playing up, I struggled round Ramsey Hairpin, the Gooseneck and Governors. Pulling into the pits, I told Ray I'd got a clutch problem. I was only going to do one lap but after adjusting the clutch I started another. It was no better, at Glen Helen section the bike went Whaaaaaaaaaaaaaa and stopped. I thought, *my God, what now?* and swore. I started to take the tank off to check the plug, then it hit me, I was out of fuel, so I pushed it to the Glen Helen Pub. After I reported to the marshal that I'd retired and needed collecting somebody bought me a pint while I waited to be picked up. I'd broken John's rule about going out with a full tank to get used to going down Bray Hill, but I knew I'd enough fuel to do the one lap I intended to do. Yes, serves me right. Once back at the digs I said, "tell me Ben, have I really qualified to start the Manx Grand Prix?" John poked his tongue out, just a bit of fun. Saturday night, after collecting Sheila, we all piled down some pub or other. We knew we had a lot of work to do on the bikes but needed some relaxation, and were pleased with practice week.

Before stripping the Greeves, I rode it to Renold Chains who were stopping at the Douglas Bay Hotel at the end of the promenade on the old Laxey road. A Renold representative would rivet your chain free but you had to buy the chain, unlike at the TT where it was all free. This lad, well gentlemen, if he liked you, gave you a good price. The lad, whose lovely wife helped him, was Vic Doyle and in his 50's. I rode back and adjusted the chain, one of the many jobs on the list! Stripping the primary side, we decided to use two good used clutch plates with one new one. I did several practice starts around Hillary Park, if anyone came out and moaned, they weren't Manx people, Mrs. Jackson called them, "come overs!" As for all the bumps I found on the circuit, this was good news, it meant I was going faster!

171

One interesting trip I had with Sheila was to get a new primary chain from Renold, I took an old chain with me so I didn't get the links wrong. We headed for the Douglas Bay Hotel where I'd been told all the top riders, Hailwood, Surtees, Agostini etc stopped. It had two entrances. As usual, I missed the first, we'd just passed an electric tram on its way to Snaefell. We got to the second entrance and turned left, only trouble was it was for pedestrians and had steps. The electric tram was 200 yards behind me, luckily there was a six-foot wide gravel walkway. I put my foot to the floor, the wheels spun on the gravel. On tick over, creeping very slowly, we just turned left into the entrance as the tram went by. Looking at Sheila I said "that was exciting," I can't remember her answer.

There were 3 races; the Ltw for 250s, Jnr for 350s and Snr for 500s The Ltw and Jnr were on Tuesday, the Snr on Thursday. I checked everything twice, I'd even fitted new tyres towards the end of practice from Ken Inwood who gave me good advice on tyres, gearing and jetting. I ran over Ken's legs at Staverton, we always joked about it. The Lucas electrical dealer on the docks would give you a free plug cap if you were using a Lucas magneto. My Greeves had Steffa ignition so I sent Ray down as could tell lies easier! You were given vouchers for laps done in practice that you exchanged when buying fuel so you didn't pay Manx tax. We took fuel cans to Shell petroleum on the docks, 2 stroke riders taking oil to mix. You told them how much fuel you wanted and they gave you large labels to put your pit number on, this was all done by Monday afternoon. You could ride your bike to Mylchreests Garage for the 'Weigh In' (scrutineering) where lots of people crowded around the gateway. John suggested it would be better to go in his VW van with Beefer driving. The bikes and helmets were scrutineered and kept overnight at the Garage. It was an even tighter inspection than for practice and we were pleased they passed.

The only problem I had practice week, other than learning the course, was the expansion chamber cracking so a lot of welding was needed. I made sure any tension was relieved with better rubber mountings. A small crack also appeared in the rear fairing mounting, bolted between the engine and frame. Harry, Doris's husband, having made an electric welder out of a vacuum cleaner, don't ask me how, welded it up. The spot welding he'd done was successful when I double-checked on Sunday. I was told that after the 'weigh in' it was traditional to watch George Formby in No Limit. The film shown before it was a pirate film, the actor playing Blackbeard looked like John Tickle who had bought the Manx Norton rights. There were various shouts when different actors came on, "what is John Tickle/Neil Kelly/Ken Harding," names we knew, "doing in this film?"

The morning of the race, we had to be at Mylchreests Garage by 8:30am. I asked Mrs Jackson for Manx kippers for breakfast which put John off a little, sorry John! The only fish I ever liked was kippers and smoked haddock, which mum used to buy, I hated whitefish and elvers. After breakfast, wearing leathers, we went to collect our machines and a number for the back of our leathers, I was 77. We lined up on the road outside the garage waiting for the word to go. We had to ride from the garage along the promenade, I found this was quite a spectacle as hundreds if not thousands were lined along the 2 mile route. We then turned up Summerhill which was 1 in 4. John had told me to hold back so I could accelerate up in a low gear, some riders had burnt their clutches out last year. Then it was a sharp tight left-hand bend at Onchan, past another good pub the Manx Arms. This road joined the course at Governors Bridge but we went straight on to the start finally stopping at our pits.

Ray and Beefer had put tools and spares into our respective pits, the 30 minute Claxton sounded then 20 as we pushed our machines to our start line positions on the Glencrutchery Road. When the 10 minute Claxton sounded there was an announcement, "Your race controller here, there is a dog on the course so there will be a 10 minute delay." This was doing my nerves no good at all, another rush behind the scoreboards for a run-out, I forget the number times I tried to go with nothing happening. I was talking to other riders hopping from foot to foot trying to calm my nerves. Ray, sat on the bike said "for God's sake George, calm down." Many riders were already sat on their bikes, I'd wandered off again talking when the first two bikes started so ran back to Ray who was getting a bit agitated. He greeted me with "where the bloody hell have you been?" We restarted the bike to warm it up as we had 5 minutes before my start. When we stopped the engine we fitted a tried and tested spark plug that had been used for one lap in practice, more advice from John as some riders fitted a new plug which didn't work! We arrived at the coned area, Ray had to leave me but was only 5 feet away outside the cones if there was a problem. I don't know who was more nervous, Ray or me. Petrol on, no goggles to get steamed up as after the crash at New Brighton Prom I'd bought a spaceman type helmet with a bubble on the front. This certainly saved my nose at Thruxton earlier in 71 when I fell off, the bubble had a scratch mark on the front, it's now a trophy on the shed wall.

173

I did have to push the helmet back a little so my breath wouldn't steam up the visor even with rubbing liquid soap on the inside, a trick Ray showed me. With bike number 78 I went onto the start line, the flag eventually dropped, that 10 seconds seemed so long. I pushed hard, as I let the clutch go I bounced on the seat, the bike fired, I threw my leg over not bothering to put my feet on the foot rests, just head on the tank, open the throttle, slipping the clutch to get into the power band, now both feet on foot pegs.

Number 78 was on a Yamaha, although I was away first he passed me just after the end of the pit lane with his much superior speed but I was happy with my start. This was nothing like a short circuit race, one lap of the mountain circuit at 37.73 miles was more than a day's short circuit racing, and I had to do 4. Down Bray Hill in top gear I watched the other rider pulling away, as advised I was letting the tyres warm up. At Ago's Leap the front wheel went light, then the dark section with the overhanging trees down to Quarter Bridge. I was getting more confident going along towards Braddon Bridge when another Yamaha came past me. My Greeves was rated at 32 BHP, and that was being generous, a Yamaha was 45 BHP, most 250cc Yamahas would go as fast as a British 350cc and some 500cc machines.

Union Mills, a fast right and left, a straight then approach Glen Vine in top gear for the two rises and right-hand sweep, just sitting up on the first lap. Along this section on the right hand side was a lovely bungalow which had a separate garage with a walkway made from Manx stone, I did like it, then snapped at myself "George, get your mind back on the race." I was now happier as the bike was pulling well. The section from Union Mills to Greeba Castle was 4 miles flat out, brake when seeing the red phone box go down 2 gears then watch out for any sunlight in the trees. Next, Greeba Bridge then a fast twisty section to Ballacraine. Over Ballig Bridge, a jump until the 1960s, the front wheel still went light, left hand sweep of Doran's Bend then a right hand sweep, where in practice I was trying to change down for the next left-hander and getting my foot trapped underneath the gear pedal, so I either had to leave it in the higher gear and change down after or change down earlier, always decisions. I opted for the wimpy one, changing down early. As there are over 200 bends to the left and 200 to the right, trying to remember which bend you're at and which gear to be in was quite difficult. The Glen Helen section I was still learning, first left hand bend there's a garage and a white wall with a stream behind it, this was very tight corner, the Black Dub, the second left hand looked the same but could be taken flat out, I didn't do it with much conviction. The next left was similar to the first with a brick wall, you had to know which bend you were at as all three approaches looked the same. This last bend was The Glen Helen Hotel where I'd pushed to on Saturday night after running out of petrol.

The right-hand sweep at Sarah's Cottage, also called Creg Willey's Hill, I was taking it as two right-hand bends, but during practice I saw riders going round much quicker in one sweep. Now the bumpy Cronk-Y-Voddy straight which was bumpier the faster you went, your back wheel bounced off the ground and the revs momentarily rose before the wheel hit the ground again. I had a lock to lock wobble (tank slapper) on the bumpy Sulby Straight in practice so had done my steering damper up tighter. The damper was basically a sprung steel spider pressed down with a wing nut onto some friction plates, it did help a little.

Now around the right-hand flat out sweep at the end of the straight, and down to a left at the 11th Milestone. I could see some bikes in front, getting excited, was I catching somebody? Handley's Bend, named after Walter "Wal" Handley who had crashed there after becoming the first rider to win two races in one week in 1925, a left then right with a high garden wall that your helmet got very close to. On to the approach to Barregarrow Top and Bottom, I was now finding more bumps and jumps, which was good, it meant I was going faster following advice from John. I sat up at Barregarrow Bottom, the bike shaking its head.

Change down one gear for the 13th Milestone, 3 right hand bends dropping another gear into the left then back to top along the bumpy straight right into Kirk Michael. You were going down the main road of this small town, in my case at 95 to 105 mph, with noise echoing from the close buildings. Coming out I'd been seeing what looked like a hedge all week, but while on my trip around with Sheila I'd found it was a brick wall covered by ivy so I remembered that. There were bends I liked but felt I could go faster, Rhencullen was one. It had two right-handers, it should be one sweep, and faster then, lifting the bike up with all your might for the left just missing a white cottage then trying to lift the bike up before a right hand rise and a drop as the bike went light, going "weeeee," I will grow up one day!

Bishops Court I still respected but was flat in top gear, chin on the tank as I approached. This was a corner I talked myself through, just lifting my head to give myself a little confidence. Still flat out towards Alpine Cottage, change down to 4th back to 5th for the sweeping bends towards Ballaugh

Bridge, this time taking it in 2nd gear, a slight jump, The Raven pub on the right, I was too close for comfort, I'd been told riders have hit the pub. I passed the lady in white, so named by Agostini as she always wore white. She's believed to be the first lady marshal, sadly I'd not found the time to go and give her Roger Corbett's best wishes, perhaps I felt a little shy, unusual for me. More bends as I passed the nature reserve which during the war housed German and Italian internees. Through Quarry Bends, always dark with many overhanging trees leading you on to Sulby Straight. The quicker you got through Quarry Bends the faster you hit the straight, so could pull a higher gear, I was hanging on for dear life. Chest and chin on the tank being bashed about, good job I had the body belt on for these long bumpy roads. Sulby Straight is over a mile long including the right hand sweep past Sulby Hotel, another good pub, now halfway!

Approaching Sulby Bridge, I never found the drain on the left-hand side that Albert Moule, one of the travelling marshals and a retired Manx and TT rider, said he used as his peel off point. I'd seen riders parked on the side of the road broken down so, in theory, I wasn't last but am sure I'd passed someone. Arriving at Ginger Hall and the leap I'd found Saturday night was even scarier as I took it faster! Arriving in Ramsey I braked earlier as the front brake wasn't working as well as it did at the start, perhaps I was trying harder. 2nd gear for the right left of Parliament Square then back in 3rd for May Hill, past Stella Maris and around Ramsey Hairpin. Roger Corbett named his bungalow in Bishops Cleeve, Stella Maris, the only house you passed twice in one lap after the tight left hand Ramsay hairpin and where he broke his leg when he crashed there!

I saw a Yamaha stuffed into the brick wall at Water Works, good job the wall was there because there was a long drop the other side. I found out later that the rider was Ron Rowlands from Cirencester, you can imagine which part of his anatomy was bruised and he was on his honeymoon, all the Glos riders pulled his leg when he was feeling better! Gooseneck next, the sharp right-hand uphill bend with adverse camber, if you had the time to look back the Ramsey Bay is a lovely sight but it's the start of the bumpy climb to Mountain Mile, so no chance today. Not worrying about the noise change from the bike, climbing the Mountain Mile in 5th gear.

The Veranda was another bend I was getting better at, I was in top gear with my head just above the screen to give me a little confidence. A slight drop down to Bungalow, then over the railway lines. Now at the highest part of the course, the 32nd Milestone. Once, in practice, I actually got round it in top gear, God knows how, I'd forgotten to change down but I didn't have the nerve to do it again. The 32nd is three left-hand sweeps. For the first, the line is close to the bank, near the Marshals' hut, middle-of-the-road for the second and close to the bank again for the last one then the drop-down to Windy Corner, named because it was open to the sea. Arriving at Kate's Cottage, I remembered the rider we'd carried on the stretcher. I'd found out that he took a long time to recover so made sure I was in the right place! Now the drop to The Creg, blipping the throttle changing down using the gears to help braking. I was now taking it hard in 2nd but you had to watch you didn't drift out onto the grass bank where people sat, then down the mile long straight with a right-hand sweep before the left-hand bend a short straight approaching Hillberry, Signpost Corner, Bedstead and Governors. My God, I've done a lap in an actual race. I looked at Ray in the pits who gave me the thumbs up.

Down Bray Hill, this time although sitting up a little, I was flat out in top gear. The front wheel came up a little more at Ago's then steady to Quarter Bridge, you could say I respected this section of the course. Even faster around Glen Vine for the second lap, chin on the tank, bike in top gear all the way. I started noticing more bikes on the side of the track. I was beginning to enjoy myself and couldn't believe it as I was slowing for Governors Bridge, *where had the rest of the lap gone?* I had to stop for fuel. When a rider passes Signpost Corner on race day a light comes on above their number on the scoreboard to warn the pit crews that their rider is on the way. Ray was waving a union flag as I was riding a British bike, but I still nearly overshot my pit. Ray said "you're doing well George, how is it going?" "Okay."

We needed 5 gallons. Following advice, we'd put 8 gallons in filler, with my fire service knowledge, I knew the higher the head the more pressure, and another plus, the last 3 gallons could be put in the van, it made it smell nice! Ray checked the fuel level several times before shutting the quick release filler cap, had a quick wipe around and checked the clutch adjustment was okay. The scrutineers also checked the bike over.

You had to restart the bike yourself so into 1st gear, hearing pop, pop, pop, leaping aboard and away. Everything was going well then, I was trying to get to the left on the bumpy drop-down to Governors, braking hard and using the clutch to change into 1st gear, but as I got round the hairpin I had no clutch! The lever came back to the bar. I didn't want to stall the bike, so being very careful using the throttle, I accelerated slowly up the rise.

This was difficult only using 3000 revs, power didn't come into 6000+. I pulled into the pits in 1st gear.

Ray asked me what the matter was. I had to take my helmet off to answer "the clutch has packed up." We put the bike on the main stand so that we could both work on it. We removed the quick release on the fairing, Ray held the side of the fairing out allowing me to adjust the clutch mechanism. We discounted taking the primary cover off to see what the problem was, as that would have been the end of the race. After adjustment the clutch appeared to work. Ray suggested only using the clutch to change down, changing up I would just close the throttle and push the pedal down, a little like double declutching with older vehicles.

Helmet on, push start on my own again, who said motorcycle racing is easy? I changed into 5th gear to go down Bray Hill but carefully having a dodgy clutch. Around Quarter Bridge everything seemed to be going well but on arriving at Ramsey had beads of sweat on my forehead knowing I had to go round the hairpin and Gooseneck! Taking things very steady, I changed down, not abusing the clutch. I went round Ramsey Hairpin changing up without using the clutch, stayed in low gear to Water Works then carefully changed up around the sweeping bends to arrive at The Gooseneck.

I positioned myself early and used the clutch to get into 1st gear, the sweat was running down my face as I negotiated the tight right adverse bend. I was around, into 2nd, 3rd 4th gear, the bike was pulling 7000 rpm so I went into top, leaving it there but dropping back to 6000 rpm, just trying to nurse the bike home.

I started to calm down, it was the last lap and I was thinking, *no more problem corners so no clutch needed!* Through the Bungalow and 32nd, all downhill. I started to break extra early for The Creg, had to be careful here as the brakes were getting warm. I relaxed now, assuming I was home and there were no apparent problems. Approaching Signpost, the lever came back to the bar, I thought *bollocks*, a technical word. I took it steady around Signpost and Bedstead which was very bumpy.

All of a sudden a black cloud descended over me, I had to get around Governors Bridge and the Dip. I started to slow down really early, braking hard and changing down with no clutch, the gearbox did not like this at all. I was in 1st gear well before the corner, the bike was going chunk, chunk, as the speed of the wheel and engine were different, I momentarily put my hand up in the air, hoping the marshals would realize I had a problem. I was so close to the left hand side my knee was rubbing against the grass bank, I was taking a giant right-hand sweep. I may have left the course but came back on and got lined up to go down into the Dip. I was in 1st gear thinking, *déjà vu, I've been here before*.

I eased out of the dip, again 3000 rpm, the marshals waving yellow flags warning of a slow rider. This time I was a little more cunning, closing and opening the throttle, trying to keep the engine running weak in the hope that it would pick up. It appeared to be working, the revs crept up, 3500 rpm, 4000 rpm, and 4500 rpm. By the time it got to 5000 rpm I was halfway along the start and finish straight, and praying *please Lord let it get to 6000 rpm*. As it hit 6000 and the power band I changed to 2nd as I crossed the start and finish line. Had I really finished a Manx Grand Prix?

What was that strange sensation as a warm feeling came over me? I had done the same as Geoff Duke, Mike Hailwood, John Surtees, Ernie Lyons, Stanley Woods and other heroes; I had finished a race on the Isle of Man mountain course. I pulled up at the end of the pit lane and the bike stopped. Ray ran up and hugged me, others were there including Beefer. Ray pushed the bike into the finishers' enclosure for me, where all the bikes that had finished were collected.

179

The 1st three bikes had been displayed and the presentation done by the time I finished. Sat by the bike recovering, I was told that Charlie Williams was 1st, Phil Carpenter 2nd, and 3rd was local hero Danny Shimmin, known as the fastest coalman, and boyfriend to Rita, a MGP tea girl. The first 6 all rode Yamahas, except Danny, who was on a Suzuki. John Gardner retired, he rode a quick Kawasaki which like the early works Yamahas had rotary disc valve carburetion making the engine wide. It had a bulbous fairing which looked really stylish.

We went to the beer tent, beer for Ray and Beefer, cider shandy for me. We were celebrating, and chatting to other riders who had finished, but I was still in a dream. After watching the Jnr race from the pits, which was won by Steve Moynihan on an Aermacchi at 91 mph, we collected John and Sheila for celebrations and commiserations.

GORDON, THE MANX MARSHAL, ME, BEN TANDY AND BEEFER

Myself, Ben, Beefer and Gordon, Doris's brother, decided to go for a game of golf, well a large pitch and putt close to the paddock. We'd asked John to join us, but he came up with some feeble excuse, and Ray was visiting friends. So we were spending Wednesday morning relaxing, laughing at each other's shots, when John drove round in his VW van, and who was sat next to him but Sheila. I thought *the bar steward*, my fault for not inviting her. John had made a date with her for the next night as well. At breakfast next morning I was giving John some stick, "Mrs Jackson what do you think, John stole my girlfriend!" When Christine the milk girl, came in I asked her, "Christine, what do you think of John stealing the young lady I been taking out all week? When we asked him to play golf with us he stabbed me in the back by saying he had something else to do, it was taking my girl out!!" Christine also gave him grief. I asked her if she'd go out with me tonight to cheer me up. When she said "I can't, I'm going out with the boyfriend" I put on a puppy dog face "Can't you tell him a white lie to save me jumping off Douglas Head Cliff with a broken heart?" Christine went away but came back later saying "Okay, I've put him off." I took her out that night and saw her again before we went home, cheered me up no end.

A few days before going home, Ray and I checked all the spares and got ready to pack as we didn't feel like stripping the bike down, I'd do that when I got back as we still had the Thursday Night Presentation; each rider was given 2 tickets. We watched the Snr from the Creg, Nigel Rollason won on a 351cc Yamaha, I believe it was the first time a non-British machine had won the MGP Snr! Ken Huggett, Norton was 6 seconds behind having had gear problems at Governors, I know the feeling well!

In the evening our gang arrived at The Villa Marina and got drinks, then like everybody else going "vroom vroom" and leaning to the left and right reliving our races. Riders who were getting an award were asked to assemble at the left-hand side of the stage, when called go onto the stage, to collect their award and leave on the right-hand side. The MC for the evening was Peter Kneale, he introduced the guests who were giving away the awards for each race. My race, the Ltw was up first, the Mayor of Douglas presenting the awards. They started with the riders finishing in speeds up to 75 mph, when it came to speeds finishing up to 80 mph I heard my name, "41st George Ridgeon." In my excitement to get on the stage, I tripped and nearly fell, heard a few titters, but didn't care one iota. Even with two pits stops and two steady laps, I'd averaged 80 mph, one-hour 53 minutes to do 152 miles. I took the award, then, looking at the audience, raised both hands in the air before going back to the gang and talking about the fortnight. They say that the first time is always the best and this Manx Grand Prix will certainly live in my memory. I got home in the middle of night so went to bed before showing my finishers award to mum, big brother and the gang. I probably bored everybody with my stories. Then back to work, was it all over?

I had to get ready for two meetings, the end of September and early October, before the end of the season. I'd missed the last meeting at Staverton on August Bank Holiday as I was at the MGP. I fixed the Greeves, the ball bearing, part of the clutch release mechanism, had crushed in the gearbox to clutch shaft. Luckily it didn't take that much effort to get it out with Tony Price making a special tool, emery paper wrapped round a steel rod in an electric drill to ease the middle of the gearbox shaft taking off any marks.

1971 was a bit of a charity year for the Brigade. When Red Watch held a bath tub race on Pittville Lake raising money for Guide Dogs for the Blind, our watch, had a discussion with everyone throwing in their two-penn'orth. Dick Browning and Percy Copeland were keen cyclists and suggested borrowing various tandems or making a trike like on The Goodies TV show. By chance someone had seen a newspaper article on the Lions Club riding a 35' long bike raising money for charity.

We found out that the bike was made and owned by Rickman Engineering in Hampshire, two top motorcycle scramblers who ran an engineering business. They were contacted and agreed we could visit. It was decided Stn Officer Corbett, me, Graham Leighton and leading fireman Eddie Hawkins would go. I got talking motorcycling to them, telling them I'd seen them in 1962 hoping it helped our cause. They agreed we could borrow the bike, explaining that it was 35' long, made from a roof truss with Matchless front forks and wheels. It was designed for 12 to pedal, linked with bike chain to a Matchless gearbox, 7 passengers and another person steering. They built it for the Carnival but had to fit a sidecar as they found when testing that just a ½ degree of lean took 16' to straighten out again. We left after Stn Officer Corbett had fixed up that the fire service would arrange collection. Stopping for a meal I saw the cutlery had the name of the Cafe on but when I was parading my acquisition, "how did this spoon get in my top pocket?" the Stn Officer was most indignant I'd pinched a spoon.

Senior officers in the fire service arranged through RAF Innsworth for a low loader that usually carried large aircraft spares and propellers to pick up the bike. We kept it in the appliance room, the bike was as long as our HP so it just went in. All the watch agreed to pedal, although newly promoted Leading Fireman Arnold Pearce had broken his leg, luckily we had a new fireman on the watch, who'd transferred from Cirencester with a Scottish sounding name who we called Mac. Noz Lawson, our Sub Officer, agreed to steer and we borrowed Cliff James, fire control, for the sidecar.

We picked Sunday, 22nd November to do the ride, the only trouble was that Dick Browning was getting married on Saturday the 21st at 3pm. Saturday morning we had an early breakfast at 07:00 hrs, then with 4 pedalling and one steering, we rode the bike, with two fire pumps following, just over a mile, from the Station to Cheltenham Promenade for some publicity. Luckily there were no fire calls. Malcolm and I stayed with the bike which was parked on the promenade. We'd arranged for two firemen to stand in for us, with volunteers from other watches agreeing to help. Dick went straight home, after making the excuse that his father had to go to hospital. Only a few knew he was getting married, only Malcolm, Gordon (Flicker) and I were invited and we were under the penalty of death not to say anything. Although Arnold was on the sick with his leg in plaster, he arrived at the Promenade with the rest of the shift at 09:00. At 12:00, Malcolm, Gordon and I said that we had to go. Arnold and the others asked where, "we've something special on, tell you tomorrow." I'd arranged with a local crane hire service to lift the bike onto the back of the fire service GP lorry at 15:00 hours. I was told the next day that the large mobile crane had blocked the Promenade for 20 minutes loading the bike, it must have been a sight to see. I missed out talking to the newspaper, I must be slipping, but at least the crane firm got a lot of publicity with everyone seeing the commotion.

Dick and Susan's wedding went well and I believe I behaved myself fairly well, but after Dick and Sue left for a night in a hotel, we decorated their new home with the obligatory toilet paper plus banners saying "just married." The next day we all arrived at Brockworth Airfield where the bike had been parked in a hangar.

As we were trying to get in the Guinness Book of Records, there were reporters and cameramen. The Lions Club held the record at 4 hours, was invalid because they rode up and down the airfield runway, stopping and changing the complete crew each time. The Guinness Book of Records rules state: "you can only stop once every hour for five minutes for calls of nature no other reason."

When doing anything for charity I find it easy asking for money but asking for sponsorship for my racing I found it difficult. I went in to Walls Ice Cream, Woolworths and Whitbread's etc, I raised £30 when petrol was 35p a gallon, our watch raised £300, the same as Red Watch on their Bath tub race, equal to £6000 today. The starting time came, Gordon Lawson was steering, wives, daughters and friends, as passengers, 12 peddling and Mike Compton was changing gear. The fire service mobile workshops were in attendance which was a good job as on the first lap the gear pedal fractured, we were stuck in the gear we were in. The perimeter track was more than two miles long, as we approached the pit area we shouted that we needed a spanner. With everyone still pedalling, Mike had to undo the gear pedal. He threw it to the workshop staff who welded it as we pedalled around again. As we passed the pit area again, they threw the repaired

183

pedal back and Mike refitted it. We had to momentarily stop pedalling to change gear. The 5 minute break every hour couldn't come quick enough especially for those who couldn't live without a quick drag on a fag. We ended up doing 3 and 3/4 hours, sadly for whatever reason we didn't get in the Guinness Book of Records.

The long bike

I saw mum in her furry hat as we finished. She was stood by Dick's new wife Sue, his mother, brother Kelvin and his two dogs. Dick shouted "there are my dogs" giving me the opportunity to shout, "Just to let everyone know, Dick got married to Sue yesterday. What about, there's my new wife Dick?" everyone cheered.

At the end of 1971, through Dave Baker, I made friends with Eric Dewhurst who had just finished the Jnr firemen's course with Wally Walton, both of them joined Dave on red watch. The four of us agreed to go for a midday Christmas drink. At closing time the other firemen that had turned up drifted off. We decided to see if Arnold Pearce was at home. He brewed home-made wine and as I gave him rhubarb and apples he was always saying "pop around to try it." On the way, when stopped at traffic lights, a tiddly Wally got out of Dave's car and bent the aerial in half on my Austin van, as Queen Victoria would have said, "we are not amused." We banged on Arnold's door but there was no answer, Dave was feeling stupid, so he pulled up a wallflower and posted through Arnold's letterbox! Arnold was a big man, if he was upset you were in trouble, so we left PDQ for Eric's flat.

At the flat, for some reason, Eric started throwing his furniture out of the window, as he was on the second floor it didn't do it much good. Then, Dave and Eric started wrestling and falling over the couch. I somehow got to work at 18:00 tripping over the hessian mat by the front door. Eddie was in charge that night, after parade he called us to the back of the appliance room. In a very stern voice he said "I wasn't in charge last night, but if it happens tonight, you will be over the road." A couple of firemen had drunk too much at the bar!!

185

CHAPTER 9   1972-Of blackbirds and swallows

Racing in the early 70s was a laugh if Dick was with us, he had taught us a song which we sang on the way home. West Country pop star Adge Cutler and the Wurzels had a hit record with 'The Blackbird Song', but we sang an old country version.

"I know wur there's a blackbird's nest, I know where Ee Be,
Ee be in yonder turnip field and I be arter Ee.
Ee spies I, and I spies Ee, Ee calls me a bugger and a liar,
When I find that blackbirds nest, I'll set the bugger on fire.
Four and 20 years working on a farm, you cannot take the rise out of I,
There ain't no bird on this yer farm that can hide his nest from I.
Oh I wish I wur back 'ome in Gloucester, where the birds they flock and hide,
I clap my hands and laughs like buggery just to see those blackbirds fly".

I was pleased my 250cc Greeves was going well. I'd started checking the points between practice and the race, making a few people laugh as I had a blanket over my head and used a light and battery to show when the points were open. I was getting good reliable finishes.

In April, I had a memorable trip to Cadwell Park with Dick and his brother Kelvin. I was now using my Austin 12 cwt van as it would sleep 3 once the bike was out. While waiting for my 250cc race I saw another Greeves and shouted "hello Greeves." Pushing forward, I found the rider was Richard Swallow. We were both on the front row of the grid and when the flag dropped both Greeves started well. Richard's brothers, Bill and Alec, took a photo, it showed us 20 yards in front of the other bikes, mainly Yamahas, still being pushed. Richard finished 3rd and I was 6th in the open 250cc race. I was introduced to Bill and Alec and became great friends with Richard who ended up more like a little brother as he was 9 years younger than me. On the way home Kelvin, who was in the back of the van passed wind. I use this phrase just in case any ladies are reading this to avoid saying farted! It was very smelly, Dick and I had to open the side windows, Kelvin laughed. 10 minutes later he did it again, it smelled even worse. Dick shouted "open the window, take a breath, hold it and close the window." Kelvin was dying from the smell of his own s **t in the back!

CADWELL PARK. I'M No 77

Reading MCN, I saw a 350cc Greeves engine for sale only 30 miles away in Wyre Piddle. It turned out to be a genuine 350cc Oulton engine and I was buying it from Bertie Goodman's grandson. Bertie raced a Velocette in his youth, later he was Managing Director of the family run business, Velocette Motorcycle Company.

I bought the twin port engine with the original twin exhaust system, and squeezed the larger engine into the 250cc rolling chassis I'd bought off Paul Carver, a quick rider who had retired from racing as he was moving to Australia. Dick and I did much of the work at the fire station, not in the hose repair room from which we got banned, but using the work surfaces in the washroom area which had hard plastic tops. As this was next to the dormitory we couldn't work past 2300 hrs. It was soon ready to test and we took it to Chedworth Airfield, a disused WW2 airfield in a poor state about 10 miles from Cheltenham.

When we got there we couldn't find anyone to ask permission from but we found a 5 bar gate and went in. The bike started well, the engine revving up to 8000 rpm but I couldn't get it into the power band under load which was 6000 to 8000 rpm. It was a bit of a wasted journey, other than solving the problem, a 4 stroke needle in a carburettor fitted to a 2 stroke bike! I rode my BSA through Birmingham to Amal Carburettors. As I was about to leave, the friendly Amal man gave me directions to get home using spaghetti junction which was only 500 yards away. Going up the slip road a sign said "M6 North or South." I thought, *I don't want to go north,* but as I went past Fort Dunlop I realised I was going to London. I made a U-turn at the next junction and got to work just as my watch were told "on your markers, fall in"!

The next time we went to Chedworth, we found the gate chained and padlocked, so we took it off its hinges. A Land Rover drove up with a stern looking man in it wearing a flat cap, tweed jacket and green wellington boots, "why are you on our land?" I explained that we'd been told we could test our bikes if we didn't annoy anybody. He wasn't impressed and told us we shouldn't be there. Luckily I had my uniform on. As I took my motorcycle jacket off I said "sorry, we'll pack up and go. We wanted to test the bike before the first meeting next week as it's a new project." I put my sad face on. The man stuttered a little on seeing the blue shirt and said "well you're here now, carry on but next time ring up first." We thanked him and took his phone number, back on went the Barbour jacket and crash helmet. When the bike came into the power band, the 50' wide rough track, looked very narrow. I just stopped before the wire fence, even though I had an Italian, 8" twin leading shoe brake in place of the 7 " British hub. I told Dick when I got back, "it went like s*** off a shovel," a technical term meaning very fast.

Top rider, Jim Curry had started a repair shop in Dunalley Parade not far from the Fire Station. I'd stopped working at the butcher's shop and was hanging around at Jim's workshop trying to pick up tips. I looked in a box of motorcycle parts and said "A10 BSA, Jim?" "A7 actually, could you rebuild it?" I must have been feeling cocky, "yes, I can do it blindfolded." Jim offered me £10 to rebuild it and get it going. So when I wasn't working at the Fire Station, racing bikes or gardening at home, which I was now in charge of with dad upstairs watching, I was helping Jim. I got the BSA going, and after the customer tested it and paid the bill, Jim asked me if I'd like to come round and help when I wasn't working, he'd pay me 5/– an hour.

So started a period of working on bikes and getting paid for it, getting advice from Jim on racing and making friends with Harry and Ivor who were mechanics working up the road from Jim. Harry was a mate of Jim's and went to many of his races. One tale that got related many times was when Jim was racing in Czechoslovakia just after the 1968 revolution. He fell in love with a girl and brought her back hidden in the van! Harry had said "I want out, if we get caught, we will be shot" and left Jim to travel home with Hannah on his own. I met Hannah at Mallory Park in 1970 when she was pregnant, my goodness, Petra is in her late 40s!

HELPING OUT AT DUNALLEY PARADE

Harry was always wheeling and dealing. He had a Ford Thames which was ideal for racing, you could get 3 people in the front, and you could get 3 bikes in the back. Harry was a bugger, he showed me a MOT form with ticks on, saying "look how good the van is." It was the failure certificate, but he put everything right and both of my Greeves went in easy.

The first meeting with the 350cc was at RAF Wroughton, a 3 mile plus airfield circuit, run by the NGMCC. It was used at the time by the Queen Alexandra Nursing Auxiliary. It poured down for the 350cc race but I finished 7th, and thought *at last, I've made a right decision*. As it was the first meeting at the circuit I went to watch at a corner I couldn't get round very well, a blind bend with a slight rise. When a rider came over the rise, chin on tank, flat out without moving, his front wheel in the air, I thought *my God*. It was Jim Curry, who I was now helping. Jim used to do the Continental Circus, he was the man at Dowty's that Norman was referring to when he said "this racer came in with broken Aermacchi racing bits and I helped him fix it."

The next meeting on the 350cc Greeves was Snetterton. Jim was racing a special 450cc Honda bored out to 500cc, when we should have been working on customer's bikes! 350cc practice was first and the bike was flying until it suddenly stopped. Back in the pits we found a holed piston.

As the 250cc was going well I decided to change the plates to blue for the 350cc race! Cheating I know, but I'd paid for the race, was outclassed and nobody seemed to worry. I wasn't last!

When Geoffrey St John said "George, I like overhead cam engines that don't leak oil, like the Mark 8 Velo you race. Would you like to go half shares on a G50 matchless? I'll service and work on the bike, you just ride it. If you pay half, I hope you'll keep it looking nice and enter it in the 1973 Manx Grand Prix," I agreed.

After many more piston failures on the 350cc I finally traced the root of the problem, it was the matchbox float not supplying enough fuel. I was also using a single fuel pipe which didn't allow enough fuel to pass through for the larger 350cc engine. I found out too late that the original production bikes had the same problem. I fitted 2 float chambers and an extra fuel tap and fuel pipe. This solved the problem but caused another, as the float chambers kept flooding when turned on, my lack of mechanical knowledge! In the two meetings after changing to this setup, I found the engine was running too rich. No I had not won the football pools, there was too much fuel to air ratio, but the bike was going well so I started jetting down, then put the project on hold when the G50 arrived.

Geoffrey had done a deal on a G50 Matchless in Blackpool, I went with Dick to Thornton Cleveleys to collect it from Vin Duckett Motorcycles. Vin had ridden the bike in the TT. The £450 which Geoffrey had paid was the going rate at the time, but today they're worth £25-£30,000! Vin told me there was a special lightweight clutch available nearby, I bought it on the way home.

At the start of the racing season, I was finding the 250cc, with regular maintenance, was getting good results. John Gardner who'd fixed me up with digs at the '71 MGP, suggested I enter the Southern 100 (S100) races at Castletown, Isle of Man in July as there was an award for the fastest British bike which last year had been won by an old man with a white beard! During the first meeting in 1955, which was over 24 laps, so was approximately 100 miles, it rained so bad in the final that the club gave everyone who finished a plaque, this became the tradition. I also entering Scarborough, which was two weeks after the S100 races, John told me that it's like a mini Isle of Man.

I'd fixed up to go to the S100 in John's VW van, the engine was in the back but it had a large side door. As well as John and Beefer Smith they brought a teenager called Dave to help me. I discovered when we got to the dock, Dave and I had to hide in the back of van under a pile of spares, which saved £15. When John drove onto the boat, a group of bikers crowded round to look at the bikes, as we got out the group got bigger. We arrived in Castletown Square, John found out where camping was and we pitched our two tents, then down to the George pub for a pint. On Sunday the pubs were open all day but closed at 10pm.

We had all day Monday to prepare the bikes for first practice at 5am on Tuesday, yes there is such an hour! After breakfast John suggested we go down the pub for a swift half, while there we could have a wash and brush up, you could say "S*, shave and shampoo"! There was good camaraderie in the campsite, but I found out that there were many other riders on British bikes, including Richard Swallow who I'd met at Cadwell Park, a rider on a Royal Enfield GP5 and several other Greeves riders. I got on well with Mick Withers who told me he would have won the trophy last year but he retired on the last lap. Perhaps the other British bike riders had, like me, heard about the old man with a white beard winning!

Signing on was in the Rugby Club at 7 pm, licence checked, forms filled in to say who you were and what you did, then all down to the George Hotel. Good news for me, there was music in the back room, a good rock group and lots of girls. I was in my element as I'm not one for leaning on the bar talking, especially when there are girls about, I could dance now. I noticed this one rather nice lady and ended up dancing with her all night. She had a friend, but luckily another rider, Jimmy Hill was chatting her up. All the bars were heaving with riders, if not dancing, talking bikes. As the evening was nearing the end I asked the nice lady "what time have you got to get home?" "While 11 o'clock" I queried "while 11 o'clock?" It appears she was a Lancashire lass and "while" means by that time! Walking her home I found out she was married with two children but her husband was away for the week working, she invited me for coffee at 11 o'clock the next day.

4am and Scrutineering came too soon. John had taken me around the 4¼ mile circuit a few times, I'm not sure if this helped or scared me more! There were three long straights, several sharp right-hand bends, one exceedingly tight right-hand hairpin and some left, right sweeps, lots of brick walls everywhere, quite challenging. We were in a holding area for first practice, it was a road joining the circuit and I could see the travelling marshals going around. I'd seen these for the first time at last year's MGP, checking the course was clear. My nerves were starting to fray at the edges when they dropped the rope and waved us away. We joined the course three quarters along the home straight. After a few hundred yards, a right/left sweep leading to a right turn, Ballakeighan, then a bumpy straight to Iron Gate, over a railway bridge before the left hand sweep past a farm. The Isle of Man had a Victorian railway and I saw a steam train puffing along during the daytime. The left hand sweep past the farm was called Ballanorris, but Mick called it "Cow Shit Bends" as you could always see where the cows had crossed the road for milking.

A short rush to Ballabeg, to what I believe is, the tightest hairpin I ever had to get around. A short straight past George Short's house, a top rider from the Isle of Man whose wife used to watch from their front door so I always waved. Then a left, right sweep Ballawhetstone. For some reason I always found this one difficult, then 3 left hand bends a short straight into a left, right, left right sweep which had many names as it went through Billown Farm, the official name was, Billown Dip. I called it "The Black Hole," others "The Bomb Hole." I don't know why, but I found that after practice and a few laps of the race, I could go through this flat in top gear, nearly 100 mph, which is surprising as it had a high stone wall on the left with a pavement and a 3' stone wall on the right. It was then a slight downhill bumpy ride to Cross Fourways, basically, a crossroads but at an angle so the right could be classed as a hairpin! A bumpy 300 yards rise to Church Bends, which I liked, but treated with great respect as there were brick walls and pavements. Then came a very long straight with a right-hand sweep, another short straight, fast left-hander into tight right, Castletown Corner, by a concrete bus stop, then into the home straight. I did two more laps before pulling into the paddock for a welcome cup of tea at 6am.

There was an evening practice and another early morning practice on Wednesday before the races starting at 5.30pm. The race programme was sidecar, 250cc, 350cc and Senior which is now up to 750cc. The atmosphere was good in the campsite, if possible even more friendlily than the Manx GP as most riders were camping. One thing I did notice was a lot of young girls walking about chatting to the riders, I remember one called Christine. I'd been warned that they were from the local school, some as young as 13, they certainly didn't look it, thank goodness I was warned.

I'd brought some rhubarb from home to give to Mrs Jackson, the landlady, when we went to Douglas after early-morning practice, wash and brush up, not forgetting my 11 o'clock cup of coffee with the lady I'd met Monday night. As I was leaving the paddock, feeling mischievous, I put a stick of rhubarb up Mick Withers' Greeves exhaust pipe. After seeing Mrs Jackson and getting pie and chips from the Manx chippy, I found when I got back to the paddock my union flag that I'd tied to my tent was missing. I'd rescued the flag from a fire at a church hall in St Pauls, they were going to hold a jumble sale and somehow it caught fire, shame as they were raising money for the church. I found the flag, which was good quality but very faded, and rescued it as it was going to be thrown away. I'd secured the flag to an Isle of Man fence post I'd borrowed from a broken fence and flew it with pride from my tent. I asked around if anyone had seen my union flag, most laughed and pointed towards the old bucket toilet. Mick Withers had tied it to, what was by now, a very smelly toilet that no one was using, we did have a laugh.

The 250cc race came and we were waved off from the assembly area for our warm-up lap. This was my first time on the start line. The 24' wide, A5 road to Port Erin, looked very narrow with 45 riders, plus reserve riders who started at the back, all lined up in 13 rows. Dave, with Ray Wakefield, who had come over for a few of days, were on the start line with me. We fitted a dry spark plug, saw the 1 minute board, petrol on, got the bike in gear and rolled back on compression, the track cleared of everyone but the riders.

Just before the flag dropped, Dick Swallow had a problem, he pushed his bike off the start line and worked on it on the grass verge. I had a momentary thought, *I was at least in with a chance now*. Everybody started pushing, I could hardly see the flag being near the back. I didn't know where I was in the order or if any British bikes were in front of me, I just kept going as fast as I could without colliding with any of the other riders who were weaving in all directions. This was one of the most exciting starts I had ever had! I passed a few on the twisty section with 50 miles ahead of us.

After a few laps I found I had the "black hole" off to a T, flat out in top with chin on tank, if there were no other riders in my way. I was still struggling through Cross 4 Ways and Church Bends. On the long straight after the fast right-hand sweep, I became aware of a marshal standing on the edge of the pavement wearing a white coat, all flag marshals wear white coats. It was very helpful as, if you took the bend too close, you could hit the curb which was shaded by trees, that's why he stood there.

I changed down for a fast left-hander, then through the 1st gear Castletown Corner, before being back on the mile long start/finish straight. I kept trying to squash myself even flatter on the tank behind the fairing; the bike seemed to be going well. I was with a small group of riders and gaining on them in the twisty section where I was pleased I could keep up with the much faster Yamahas but I was losing out on the long straights. "Whoosh," I was lapped by the leaders, Charlie Williams, Ray McCulloch and Tom Heron, possibly 30 mph faster than me in a straight line, as well as being better and lighter riders, but as long as there were no British machines in front on me I was happy. I saw the last lap flag, a few more riders lapped me, Don Pagett, Roger Sutcliffe and RJ Healey making up the top 6. The bike kept going for the last lap, so I had an 11 lap finish. Once back in the paddock first port of call was the tea tent girls, I was dying for a cuppa and snaffled a biscuit on the way.

After watching the other races with Ray, Dave, John and Beefer, we put the bikes away and it was down to the George again to see the results. They were pinned on a board in the snooker room, which was heaving with riders pushing and shoving, trying to see where they'd finished. We eventually got to the 250cc sheet. I'd finished 13th and heard my name being used in vain, Mick Withers was 15th he said "I could see your big fat bum but couldn't catch it." I'd won the Mularney Trophy and there was a bonus. I was classed as one of the fastest 45 and selected for the Southern 100 Championship race, on a 250cc Greeves! I was really pleased, but asked other riders "how come I, on my lowly Greeves, was in the fastest 45?" I was told that many riders had qualified in 2 or 3 races but they could only take up one space on the grid.

After breakfast we checked the points, reset the ignition timing and checked the jetting which was okay. The gearing was okay, we checked the rear chain tension and fitted a new duplex primary chain, cleaning the clutch at the same time. I'd acquired a Griffin clutch which was all metal. I'd written to Castrol, who not only supplied me with some R40 vegetable racing oil but also a very thin oil for the primary chain which looked like water, it was an hydraulic oil. We got it all finished just before the afternoon start, the championship race was first, the sidecar championship race finishing off the meeting.

Déjà vu on the start line, this time with 750cc, 500cc, 350cc and 250cc bikes, all faster than me, or so I thought. I was still contemplating the pride of being in this race when riders around me started pushing. As we rushed over the start line, I knew I was outpaced, I just tried as hard as I could to keep up with some of the slower riders and enjoy the extra ride.

I was surprised and pleased to be with a pack of riders, well 3 or 4, so I wasn't alone and not totally outclassed, it made me try harder. After possibly 8 laps, I was passing through the Iron Gate, over the humpback railway bridge and cranking left for Cow Shit Bends, about six foot away from the stone wall on my right, when Ray McCulloch on his Yamsel went between me and the wall, my heart did start beating again eventually!! Before Ballabeg I was lapped by Charlie Williams, over the next half mile, Don Pagett, Stan Woods, Roger Winterborn lapped me. By the home straight, Tom Heron and Selwyn Griffiths lapped me as well. My dad used to like Selwyn because he came from Wales!

There were no bikes in front of me coming into the Black Hole, I was committed with chin on tank about 100 mph, but after the first blind section I was catching up a rider very quickly, he was dawdling in the middle of the track! A thought flashed through my mind, *that 12' does not look very wide to go through at 100 mph!* To this day I don't know if I closed my eyes, but somehow I passed the rider! I had just passed the start/finish and was cranking right for Ballakeighan when a bike lapping me cut underneath hitting my front wheel with his back, I was sliding down the road. The pavement stopped me and the bike from hitting the wall. As the Fred Astaire song goes, I picked myself up, dusted myself down and started all over again. The bike looked okay, into 1st gear, the marshals were running towards me but I was gone, but not before more bikes lapped me. I saw the chequered flag at the end of that lap.

As I pulled into the assembly area there was some excitement as the Aermacchi ridden by Ian Thompson from Birmingham caught fire, the Fireman on duty in the paddock quickly put it out but I gave my bike to Ray and shouted at Ian "get the tank off," grabbed some tools and helped him. Ian, who worked at Girling had got me some rear suspension units. He asked why we needed to take the tank off. I replied "perhaps it's unlikely, but if the fire did reignite, now there's no fuel to burn."

All of a sudden my shoulder started to hurt so I went to the medical centre, the doctor decided I should go to Nobles Hospital for an x-ray. A lady

195

volunteer took me as I was only walking wounded and the organisers wanted to keep the ambulances for the last race. While driving to Douglas I was chatting to the lady as we approached Fairy Bridge, a tourist attraction where the Manx fairies live, you're supposed to wave or at least acknowledge them. I was wondering what I should do when the lady raised a hand as we went over the bridge, so I said "hello fairies." Nothing was broken, just a bad strain, but I was told to keep the arm in a sling for a few days.

I was walking into town as the gang had already left for the presentation. I was passing the Witch's Mill which looked like a windmill but had no blades. I knocked and asked the strange looking lady who answered if they had a phone I could use, as I'd hurt my arm. She dialled the number for me and I spoke to Tony and Alice Price, telling them all about the races including the crash and asking them not to tell mum I fell off. After the call the father, mother and a young teenage girl who was making eyes at me invited me to stay, but I had a good excuse and said "sorry, I have to collect an award."

When I arrived at the presentation, the lads asked how I was. I told them about the hospital and stopping at the Witch's Mill. Everyone threw their hands up in horror "you never went in there did you?" "Yes, to make a phone call, what's wrong?" "They're real witches", "get away, you're pulling my leg." All the locals confirmed that they were witches. I didn't know whether to believe them or not but I did have a strange sensation while I was there. Lucky I didn't stay or I may not have been able to tell this story!!

With the help of one of the lads, I collected my 250cc finisher's award and The Mularney Trophy, which was donated by Syd Mularney, a top motorcycle engineer of the day. When I got my finishers award for the championship race I was surprised I wasn't last and asking to use the microphone, I thanked all the marshals and officials before adding "if the rider who hit me off will buy me a drink, I'll forgive him." When looking at the results I saw that Ray McCulloch had retired, perhaps from scaring me to death! In the pub later with the gang and a young lady, a fight started. I suppose it was a bit stupid watching with my arm in a sling, I got kicked in the ankle as I couldn't get out of the way quick enough. It was a difficult night, sleeping with my arm in a sling and a sore ankle. Before leaving the Island, I found out that I'd been accepted for the MGP, and agreed to get phone calls from the young lady I'd danced with, at the phone box by the Village Hall.

No work for a week, luckily it was mid-summer, so lying in the sun helped my shoulder. Every Sunday I went to the phone box waiting for the lady to ring at 3pm, I don't know why I was doing it, she was married and living in the Isle of Man, but she was pretty.

The 2 weeks before the Scarborough race meeting passed quickly. Cheltenham racer John Stevens had agreed to take me in his diesel Austin J2 as long as I paid for the fuel. Sadly John crashed the van into a tree breaking the headlights the day before we were due to leave so I had to go in my van. Dick and I set off but had clutch problems. We found a garage and fitted a new set of rubber seals in the master cylinder. It all worked but we lost a valuable hour and had to stop for a sleep near Malton.

It was my first time at this track and I was a little nervous, many top riders were competing, including Mick Grant. First practice I struggled up the steep rise immediately after a hairpin. Talking with Dick and other riders I thought the bike was too weak low down in the carburetion. On checking, I found I'd left the 106 needle jet in which was good for flat-out straights for the S100 but no good for short circuits. I refitted the 109 needle jet. Second practice the acceleration problem was solved, the bike was going well. There were 3 hairpins and some flat-out left and right-hand bends, the track was nearly 2 miles long, the downhill section to the start and finish was unnerving as it was narrow. The racetrack was a public road through the park but as it was owned by the council they could close it without breaking any road traffic or highways laws, like New Brighton promenade. After practice, I found a puncture and bought a new tube from Ken Inwood, so another panic. On finishing the first race I found I'd qualified for the final, but my foot rest hangar on the nearside had cracked. I found someone with a brazing kit, so it was another panic to get to the 250cc final.

Lined up with all these big names I was feeling quite chuffed, but 20 yards after the start, the exhaust pipe fractured right across the expansion chamber. Luckily, I had a full fairing on the bike which stopped it falling on the ground and having me off. The downside was it sounded like World War 3 inside my fairing and I lost top end power. I was passed by a Bultaco single and tried harder on Mere Hairpin, but tried too hard and ended up lying on the floor, it was more of a falling over. Looking at the bike, the

197

footrest that had been brazed was all bent round so I couldn't continue. The 200+ miles trip home, took 10+ hours, but Dick and I felt quite good as we'd been talking with top riders and the bike went well despite the problems.

The G50 was ready, I took it for its first race, along with my Greeves, to a NGMCC meeting at RAF Colerne, my last meeting before the Manx. When fitting the Greeves engine, after sorting all the problems from Scarborough, I dropped it on my right foot, but other than a bruise I thought no more of it. The Greeves went well, the meeting was a good test for the Manx. I was getting used to the G50 Matchless, enjoyable but different!

Ray Wakefield, my mechanic, was meeting me over at the Manx. I was feeling quite perky when we were waved off the Ferry at 6am so decided to drive around the course, I'd had a reasonable night's kip on the boat. Although it was dark I'd been told that if you knew where you were going in the dark it'd help in the daylight! Pulling up the mountain I passed a small motorcycle, the crash helmet had sharks teeth on it so I knew it was Roger Cope from Oxford who I'd met last year, I gave him a toot. I got to Mrs Jackson's at 7am and saw a note saying which room I was in and leaving the apples and rhubarb, I went for an hour's rest before breakfast. Beefer drove John Gardner and me to sign on. I was quite shocked to find out I was number 15, John was quite envious, but at the time I wasn't sure if it was a good thing or bad. I would have so many Yamahas passing me, but as there was nothing I could do about it why worry. We saw the newcomers off on their coach trip before going back to the garage and getting the bikes ready for Bank Holiday Monday practice at 06.15am.

John, now riding a Yamaha, and I both qualified for the race. I had a few problems during practice week. During one early-morning practice the rotor came loose even with a nut and locking washer. My right foot started hurting with all the gear changes, there's over 400 bends. I eventually realised it was from when I dropped the engine on my foot, the doctor gave me some cream. On Wednesday night I had a stud, which held the long aluminium nuts, strip in the crankcase. Luckily we found it when checking the bike over Thursday morning. It caused a panic as I didn't have time to strip the whole engine as practice was 2pm – 5pm. With fairing, head, barrel and exhaust off we found an engineer who fitted a Helicoil thread insert and just got the bike ready in time to do a lap. The sun was very bright and I noticed that the sun flickering through the trees on several parts of the circuit was taking my concentration away, I had to shout at myself!

After chatting to Mike Chandler, who had helped me in the mid 60's, in 1972 I started sending begging letters. Mike had started racing a nice 250cc Ducati, he just wrote to Castrol and they sent him some oil. After my oil came, I painted the bike in Castrol colours and put some large Castrol stickers on it. I sent another begging letter after finding out Motorcraft racing plugs were made by Ford, two boxes arrived. My Ford Thames had two large Castrol stickers on the back doors and Motorcraft stickers on the sides. This however turned out not to be to my advantage, when pulling up in town, an irate lady lambasted me for cutting her up, "I followed you with those horrible stickers" she said.

Mrs Jackson told me that Christine, the milk lady, had got married, disappointing, but we were there to race motorcycles. I had qualified early on, completing the 5 laps, at least one of which was above the qualifying speed. I felt I was going faster in places, finding more bumps and jumps that weren't there last year. Ray fitted a new primary chain every 4 laps, we changed the gearbox oil, fitted a new rear chain and tyres, and cleaned the brakes for the 'weigh in' on Monday night. Regrettably Sheila Edwards, the nice young lady I'd met in 1971 wasn't there, unless she was avoiding me!

Race day came, I was trying to convince myself I'd nothing to worry about starting no 15, 70% of the riders were Yamaha or Suzuki mounted, all faster than me. Every bike that passed me was already at least 10 seconds in front on adjusted time. I remembered a wartime saying "keep calm and carry on."

I pushed the bike forward, number 14 was on the start line on his own, I with number 16, just 10 seconds to wait. I started quicker but was overtaken before Bray Hill. As many riders had told me, it takes a long time to learn the Manx but I was now going flat out through Glen Vine and more aerodynamic, flat on the tank. With help from Tim Miles, who I ran over in 1970, we mounted the seat back a bit. As I was 6' 3" tall, I also had special clip-ons made that were 2" forward so I could get completely flat on the tank. I had to make different fairing brackets to allow for clearance when turning the handlebars.

199

I was pleased the bike was going well. Although bikes were pulling away on the straights, I was keeping pace with them on the more twisty sections. I was still quite nervous in the Glen Helen section, it's twisty with brick walls, picturesque, but there's no time to look around and confusing with many corners all looking the same. I hung on past Sarah's Cottage, as it's very bumpy, as was the Cronk y Voddy straight, where, just before the right-hand sweep I was passed by a Yamaha. After the straight, the course was really all bends and sweeps and the rider held me up. I just didn't have the power to overtake when he slowed up or maybe I wasn't brave enough. I was still learning myself but perhaps he would have learnt something from me if I'd got past him. I was with him to Ramsay, nearly 20 miles, but on the mountain section he disappeared. Although miffed I'd been held up, I did have the satisfaction of keeping up with a Yamaha for a while that cost 10 times what my bike cost!

I started the second lap and was now going down Bray Hill flat-out, chin on tank, feeling really comfortable. It was the same at Glen Vine, and at The Veranda, I was crouched down all the way round the 4 right-hand bends. It cheered me up after the race when Geoff Hands from Chipping Camden, riding a Yamaha, told me that when he caught me up at the Black Hut, he thought he'd overtake me around The Veranda but I left him by 100 yards. It really boosted my morale. Geoff eventually passed me after the Bungalow on the straight rising to the highest part of the course before the 32nd.

Ray was waving the union flag as I pulled into the pits for fuel. Ray and a scrutineer checked the bike over, including after last year, the clutch. The bike was warmer and it took a second longer to start after the pit stop, my heart stopped for a moment but I was in top gear by St Ninian's. I started noticing machines broken down at the side of the course, so at least I wasn't last. We'd geared the bike so that it'd pull 6800 rpm, which mine really didn't want to go over, we'd worked out it was about 105 mph flat-out. All of a sudden I was at Governors dip then giving Ray the thumbs up as I passed through the start and finish to start the last lap. Ray's job was now over, it was up to me to finish. I had 2½ gallons of fuel left and it was getting less all the time, the bike seemed to be flying. I was on the drop-down to The Creg, whether it was due to my confidence or the fact that I couldn't stop the bike, I went round it flat-out in 2nd gear, the fairing touching the grass bank. I saw Harry Turner, John Stephens and others watching, they told me after the race that they'd fallen off the bank as I was so close.

EXITING GOVERNORS DIP

After crossing the line I tried to pull up by the end of the pit lane but overshoot it by a few feet. When I saw Ray we shook hands and said all the usual rubbish, but I was over the moon with a good finish with no particular scares! We were then on holiday, so to speak.

We watched the Jnr race in the afternoon and helped friends get their bikes ready for the Snr on the Thursday. After the 'weigh in' Wednesday night, we went to the Crosby pub, it had lots of photos of the races on the walls, as did most of the pubs on the course. We also made a trip to the George Hotel, Castletown to see the lady I danced with at the S100.

Leaving Nobles Park, where the TT grandstand and paddock were, we noticed three ladies in their 60's looking lost, and asked if we could help. "Yes young man, we're trying to find a bus stop, we need to get to the promenade." "Jump in ladies, we're going that way." We got two in the front and one in the back with Ray. When we dropped them off they offered some money, which we refused and suggested that if they wanted to help they buy some Manx Grand Prix badges. We happened to see them the next day, proudly displaying their badges. I told the story to the TT Special, lady reporter, who put it in with a comical note about 'the good Samaritan', did I get some stick about that!

At the presentation we were the first group, the Mayor of Douglas presenting the prizes and awards. My starters badge now had two rungs to its ladder, 1971 and 1972. I got my finishers award and a sheet of race results and speeds. I was 24th at an average speed of 82 mph, fastest lap 84mph, not too shabby considering I was a private entrant, weighed 14 stone, and was on a British single. I know this was eight years after 1964 when Gordon Keith won at 87 mph, but he was on a works Greeves and 3 stone lighter! Ray said, looking at the results, "this tells us something George," "what's that Ray?" "There were 22 Yamahas and one Crooks Suzuki in front of you, all the rest of the British, European and Japanese were behind you, get a Yamaha." I agreed with Ray, but being British I still liked to race British bikes. When I told Ray about the G50 Matchless, it cheered him up.

We said cheerio to everyone, Richard Swallow invited us up to see the family in Huddersfield.

I was bubbling over with enthusiasm at work telling Dick all about the Manx. Now that I was helping Jim, I decided to stop selling the ladies tights and other regalia I'd started in 1970 as it was taking up too much time! Mother was due to return from a Saga old people's holiday. The weekend after my Manx trip, Jarno Saarinen was racing at Mallory Park Race of the Year, he'd just won the 250 world championship. I was on Saturday and Sunday nights and would have to ride up during the day, but as I'd not seen mother for 3 weeks I would be in the doghouse! As I was on my BSA 650cc, I went straight home from work, "come on mother, we're off to Mallory Park." Blagging our way in for free as I still had my uniform on, we watched the race from the first aid area, Jarno won. I nearly shook his hand, but had to leave straight after the race. Coming out of a 30 mph area, mother saw a large 40 mph sign "George, you aren't going over 40 are you?" "No mother." I'd been doing 60 mph all through the 30 area. I had to leave mother to walk two miles home to get back to work just as they were going on parade! I sold the 350cc Greeves to Bryan Robson. Looking back now, I was short of money, but should have kept the 350cc as I'd sorted the problems, but hindsight is easy after the event.

Jim Curry, had a deal selling new Hondas, he used to get them through Skellerns of Worcester as he used to race for them. Jim showed me an Ambassador 250cc Villiers Twin and said "I have just paid £7.50 for this, give me that and you can have it." Gullible me, after testing it I said "I've got to give your profit, how about £10?" I later found out he only paid £5!

I used it to get to work, it was a nice bike so I rode it to Huddersfield to see Dick Swallow in December. It was so cold, I was following vehicles as closely as I dare! I knew Bill and Alec, and met their mum, dad and another brother Tom. The boys took me to a good disco in the evening where I had another learning experience, even though I was 28. In the bathroom, there was another white bowl next the toilet, I asked Richard what it was. "It's a Bidet" he said, I was none the wiser.

Settling in for winter, I still had my dancing, rifle shooting and helping Jim. I was looking forward to getting the G50 Matchless ready for next year's Golden Jubilee Manx Grand Prix.

CHAPTER 10   1973-Half a sponsor

The first weekend in March I was at Mallory with Dick and Malcolm, it was so cold there was frost on the inside of the windscreen. We were parked opposite Dave Featherstone, RAF motorsports team, who I'd met at the MGP. Dave was selling his TR 2B 250cc Yamaha, the last Yamaha racing bike that used air cooled engines before moving to the water-cooled TZ. Dave asked me to make him an offer, I glibly replied "£500 Dave." He said it was the best offer he'd had, but that he wanted £600. We exchanged phone numbers, as he was based in Cyprus I had to send telegrams. There were no spares, it was Japanese and I raced British bikes, but if you wanted to win!

The question of whether to buy the bike or not was solved when I was helping at Jim's workshop! I heard one of the many lads there ask if anyone wanted to buy his house for £1,500. "Not me" said Jim, as did the others, but I asked if I could have a look. Jim's ears pricked up, "keep me informed George." It was a terrace house in Bloomsbury Street, off Gloucester Road, near the gasworks. It was very grotty but cheap, I told Jim it was worth a look and we agreed to go halves. I told Dave Featherstone "sorry, I bought a house." I'll never know how I would have gone on a Yamaha, but I had a ½ share on a G50.

Life was getting busy, fire service, helping Jim, ballroom dancing, rifle shooting, motorcycle racing and now a house to do up. I'm not sure how we found the time, but we worked on the house for a few hours each day. We got John Stevens, a builder and bike racer to do some of the work we couldn't. Not realising John and Rita were intending to get married, I called in for a cuppa, and said "Rita, would you accompany me on a night out with Frank and Norman?" Rita had a son and daughter, 12 and 13, who whispered "is this about the wedding?" I asked "what wedding?" Rita explained that she and John were getting married soon. "Sorry Rita, doesn't matter, I'll ask someone else." In fact we had a nice night out before the wedding, sort of half a hen night! Norman, Tina, Frank, Zandra myself and Rita went to Ken's Chinese restaurant on the Cattle Market. There was music and dancing, they were playing, Yellow Ribbon or Yellow River, am I getting old?

I was helping Jim when he took a nice 350cc cream and blue Triumph twin in PX, it looked immaculate. I rode it up and down and said to Jim that I'd ride it round to the registry office where John and Rita were getting married. They had a photo taken sat on the bike and were pleased I'd turned up. I mentioned the Triumph to Dick at work, he loved it and I got Jim to do him a deal. I borrowed it to go to the TT as Jim was racing.

Although John was a builder he did a couple of botched jobs on our house, one was laying a concrete floor. The house was finished and sold for the asking price, so we had some profit, until the purchaser's solicitor came back to us as the surveyor had found there was no plastic damp proof membrane under the concrete floor. Either no sale, or we agreed to knock £200 off, so a smaller profit and pissed off but it still helped the finances.

A friend of Geoffrey's wanted a rider for his 350cc Manx Norton. I went to see the gentleman who lived on a farm in the Cotswolds that had many outbuildings full of classic bikes and cars. I tested the 350cc Manx Norton, it didn't go as well as it looked, so I asked if I could try the 7R as it was like my G50. After testing the 7R I told him it went much better. In a matter-of-fact voice he replied "oh that's just an old hack." I said "but it's much quicker than the Norton." He insisted it was the Norton or nothing. I took the bike to Mallory Park, but practising on the Norton was dangerously slow. Luckily, I had the Greeves and the G50 as well, otherwise it would have been a wasted day. When I made him aware of this he asked me to take the bike to a Norton expert he knew, I was pleased the expert had heard of me. The expert found the valve timing was out by half a tooth and looking at the engine numbers said "this machine belonged to Rodney Gould." The late Keith Smith had bought the bike. Getting out my hanky I polished the tank (yes, me polishing) as I looked skyward talking to Keith. Sadly I didn't ride the Norton again.

In one of the outbuildings was a lovely 1000cc Vincent Black Shadow. I jokingly asked if he'd like me to give it a service at the fire station, and give it a test ride to Mallory Park. I was surprised when the owner said "yes okay, it's fair exchange." The club meeting was on Sunday so I collected the bike Saturday afternoon. Some of the designs features were before its time, dual single leading front brakes and twin suspension units under the seat. The last Black Shadow was built in 1955 and had a top speed of 125 mph, the racing version was called Black Lightning. At that time, no other bikes could get near that.

With Dick's help, I checked the bike over. We took the front wheel out, cleaned the brakes, then checked tyre pressure, chain tension, engine and gearbox oil levels and cleaned it, not that it really needed cleaning, it was ready for the morning. I got dad's old army kit bag, loaded with food and tools, on my back, but when I tried kick-starting the bike it was only firing on one cylinder and was making a peculiar sucking noise. Doing the Tony Price routine, I checked for a spark and fuel but there was no compression, the exhaust lifter was open in the one cylinder. The cable disappeared into the timing side cover and was slack so the cover had to come off to fix the problem. As I was leaving I noticed the Speedo wasn't working and realised I'd put the front wheel in the wrong way round. Because it's a dual single leading front wheel it looked the same either way. As it wasn't causing a problem, other than no Speedo, and the brakes were working well, I carried on.

I did the twisty 30 miles to Stratford-upon-Avon in 29 minutes, what a machine. I went through many small towns and villages, good job there were no speed cameras in those days as over 100 mph was no effort at all with the good road holding. Luckily I checked the bike over at Stratford, and noticed that the alloy caps on the top of the engine were working loose. None of spanners I had with me were large enough so I did them up hand tight and checked them every 20 miles!

At Mallory, as usual, I had no passes but managed to blag myself and the Vincent into the paddock with my fire service shirt and tie on. Walking around, I found a Vincent sidecar outfit and borrowed a special spanner to do the caps up. I returned to the station, turned the front wheel back around and suggested he wire lock the alloy tappet caps. What a memory the ride was.

I sent off the Manx Golden Jubilee entry for the G50 mentioning that I'd done the S100 races and had won the Mularney Trophy in 1972.

I was persuaded to take the leading fireman's exam, and found it wasn't about the fire service. It was more like the entrance exam, mathematics, English and general knowledge. It became more like a reunion club with the same old faces turning up each year for another go at passing. Whether it was everything I had going on, or general booze ups, but my general knowledge was not as good as it used to be, there was no improvement in English either, but I did a little better in maths. I remember a couple of questions from the general knowledge exam: who was Edmund Cartwright? Mick Clapton from Cirencester put 'the boss of Bonanza'; what won the Grand National? Many answered, 'a horse and jockey.'

From Headquarter's Station we were sent to do various jobs at retained stations. Cinderford had dances, so I started attending and met a young lady called Joyce who I took out for some time until, again, I messed the relationship up! We had a memorable fire call to a Cinderford factory fire. With Cheltenham attending, there were 6 pumps in total. I was detailed to put dollies (3' lengths of old fire hose filled with sand) across the doorways on the stairwell to divert the water rushing down the 4 story building, the fire was on the top floor. We were there all night.

One night at 23:00 hours we had a call for two pumps to Pegglesworth Farm, we all thought, where the hell is that? Each pump had six small metal filing cabinets, with cards in alphabetic order, for all the roads in the area. I was in the back with Malcolm Nixon trying to find the correct card while being thrown from left to right. We found it wasn't far from Chedworth, where we'd tested the 350cc Greeves, basically in the middle of nowhere, and shouted directions.

We heard the Divisional officer, John Cook, on the radio asking for information on the fire. He was told two pumps had been called to Pegglesworth Farm, we laughed at his reply, "where the hell is that? Please confirm how to get to the address." Control gave him directions after ringing the farm. The farmer had said that there was no fire, so he ordered one pump to return, the other pump to investigate and report back. As our pump was in front, with leading fireman Charlie Hall in charge, we carried on, and found a fire in one of the houses for farm workers, there was smoke everywhere. An outward call could be made from any of the houses, but incoming calls, all went to the main farm. Charlie Hall reported back to control that another pump was needed. I was now qualified to wear BA and went in with Malcolm to find a fire in one of the bedrooms, the fire was burning up through the floor. Once the fire was out, having no electricity, we put our new halogen lights to work and got rid of the burnt material. We found the cause and the seat of the fire; an electrician had put a nail through the main cable to a storage heater they'd fitted the week before. As this was heavy duty cable, the nail became a mini heater, eventually catching fire. The Jnr Officers have to make out the fire report with possible cause; there was no doubt about this one!

I'd passed my Breathing Apparatus course a few weeks before, it was a hard but very interesting course. We started by learning how much air we use when breathing normally, working hard and at rest, it was quite technical. If you were trapped, to conserve air you take off the set placing it beside you and relax, that is, if you can relax when you are trapped with your distress signal unit (DSU)

Reg Weaver, Keith Huxley, Dave Baker, Pat Slatter, A N Other, Me

sounding out at 95db. We learnt how to strip down the apparatus, replacing O-rings and disinfecting face masks. Once proficient in servicing, we practised putting the BA set on as fast as possible. It weighed 50lb, and as there were six of us training, it turned into a race! We visited various stations including, Stroud, to use their training sewer and Severn Side near

Bristol, which, although a Day Manning Station, was near a very large industrial area so had Oxygen or O2 BA which lasted 1 hour. I felt very strange wearing this when pushing a car around the drill yard and I had a sort of pain in the chest. I was told afterwards that it took a long time to learn to wear a 02 BA which was used a lot in WW2. Having learnt the majority about BA, the fun of learning the "smoke dance" came next.

I'd had some practice at the "smoke dance" before I was qualified to wear BA. Leading fireman Eddie Hawkins had given us a drill during a risk visit to Cheltenham Racecourse. A risk visit was learning all about the dangers that could happen at any particular location on our station ground. After a look round various buildings, we were blindfolded in the grandstand to simulate being in a fire, it'd be dark with smoke and heat, so you wouldn't be able to see where you were going. We'd practised at the station, but this was a strange environment, and blindfolded, there was a little tension involved. You had to make sure your weight was on your back foot and, with your other leg, you banged the floor very firmly in front of you. This was to make sure there was some floor there and it hadn't burnt away or collapsed. At the same time swinging your left arm from right to left so that the back of your hand touched any obstacles in front of you that may be hot. Your right hand went up and down to make sure there are no wires or obstacles hanging down that were hot or live electrical cables, again, using the back of the hand, so that if you touched any live electric cables, your arm would be thrown away from you. The same with a door handle, always touch with the back of your hand, if there's a fire on the other side it could be hot. If opening a door outwards, put a foot against it to make sure any blowback wont knock you off your feet! This was before firemen wore protective gloves.

We had a fire call to a building with three floors, the fire was in the basement. One crew wearing BA was fighting the fire, the heat and smoke were going upstairs. I was detailed with Dick to wear BA and search the rest of the building. The heat barrier going up the first set of stairs was as bad as the earlier fire with Arnold Pearce when he pushed me down into the basement, but once past the heat barrier it was more bearable! We searched the next floor room by room, together. When in BA you don't search on your own, however, on the top floor the smoke was very thin so we decided to split up. It didn't warrant doing the "smoke dance" but we did a full search, over, under, in and behind any object or furniture. As I searched one bedroom I got to a wardrobe with nothing on top, or inside, but as it was on an angle I moved it out to search behind it when I saw this head looking at me, it made me gasp. On investigation, the head was for keeping a wig on! I felt a right pillock so I'm keeping this to myself!

I collected Ray on the way up to the ferry for the S100, covering him up for the crossing, but I'm sure the seamen knew! We arrived in Castletown and saw those we'd met the year before, Richard Swallow, Mick Withers plus the gang from the Worcester Auto Club. Although I'd had a some good rides on the G50 it wasn't ready for the S100, Geoffrey was rebuilding it for the MGP, I just had my trusty Greeves for the British 250cc battle, which was having a resurgence of interest with a quarter of the entry on British bikes. Tuesday morning practice was a few steady laps to relearn the circuit and checking it would pull the gearing used last year. I went back to bed for a couple of hours after breakfast, leaving Ray to check the bike then, to Castletown for a s***, shave and shampoo in the George Hotel.

Evening practice went well but there was only time for a quick check over for morning practice before down to The George Hotel and music in the back room. We met the girls from last year, they'd left their fellas at home babysitting so I couldn't walk the Yorkshire Lass home afterwards!

The S100, like the MGP, was like the United Nations, English, Scottish, Irish and Welsh, flags flying, a really good atmosphere. Practice at 5am then get bike ready for the evening races.

The first race was the Karts. I used to call them go-karts but those are toys at fairgrounds. These lads camped away from us so we didn't see or hear much of them, thank goodness, the karts were noisier than our bikes. There was a 197cc class for Villiers and 250cc class all in the same race. My race was next, 45 riders left the collection area as the karts came in. On the start line, the 5 minute klaxon sounded, I stopped the bike, put a fresh plug in, flag up, flag down and away.

I always thought, with 45 riders rushing down it to the first bend, Ballakeighan, where I got hit off last year, the road seemed very narrow for a two-way A road. I was going well, and just went as fast as I could. On the 7th lap, woosh, as I was lapped by the quicker riders, Charlie Williams, Ray McCullough, Steve Machin, John Newbold, Bill Ray, and Tom Heron, all on 250cc Yamahas twins. A few laps later the last lap flag was shown, I prayed to the Lord to keep me going for 1 more lap, an 11 lap race for me.

While watching the other races I shouted for the Worcester Auto Club lads, Chris East was 13th, Jon Parkes, 19th but surprise, Pete Howles on a 500cc Dominator was 11th! We chatted up the refreshment girls before getting the bikes back to the campsite, then went down to see the results. The George Hotel was again heaving with bodies in the snooker room which had been given over to the S100 club for the results. I was 16th out of 45 starters, 3 more bikes in front of me than last year but I was 1st British bike, winning the trophy again, but not invited into the fastest 45 this year.

Thursday was a little flat. We supported the local riders who'd qualified for the championship race, Pete Howles finished 13th, with Chris East and Jon Parkes, both on G50s, 21st and 22nd. At the presentation Thursday evening, I got my finisher's award and the Mularney Trophy then into the bar for some ale, well cider shandy for me, before dancing with the nice young lady. We said our goodbyes in the morning and left for Douglas. I was a little nervous calling into the MGP race office before catching the

boat as I'd changed my class to the Senior race and it was Jubilee year but I'd been accepted.

Back home, I called into the local newspaper to show them the trophy and got my phizzog (face) in the paper. I used to get a lot of stick and comments like, "I see you put your results in George." All I was doing was promoting motorcycling, giving them the results of various meetings and local riders, otherwise it would have been just cricket, football and rugby, no mention of bikes or other minority sports.

Mike (Beefer) Smith was going out with a young lady who had a friend in Cheltenham so we all had a few evenings out together. When Frank said "George, my girlfriend Zandra is organising a coach to the mediaeval banquet in Tewkesbury" Mike was keen. At The Old Mill, Tewkesbury (a flour mill built in the 1800s) I asked the lady taking our tickets why it said "Cow beam", "that's Low beam" she said. With the fancy writing, the letter L looked like a C. Offering us a glass of punch she suggested that as we were last in, we finish it quickly. Our table was long, each person had their own stool. There were no forks, only a spoon, knife and two Prinknash Abbey (a local Abbey that made worldwide renowned pottery) beakers. Picking up one of the beakers I took a drink, but the red wine was too sour for me, the other beaker had mead in it which I drank, a serving wench refilled it, so I drank it, she filled it up again, I slowed up.

We were all asked to stand up as the Lord came in. His speech of welcome including telling us not to make love to our neighbour's wife while food was being eaten and many other risqué statements, like not urinating under the table! He then went round the tables making fun of several guests, when he got to ours, he said "welcome to the Black and White Coach Station rent a crowd," we all cheered. "One of the drivers, Taffy, I am not saying he's got a big mouth but they park the coaches in there at night." After some laughter he continued, "I'm told George Ridgeon will hang himself before the evenings out." As I was now quite tiddly, on hearing my name, I stood on my stool waving my serviette, before crashing to the ground in a heap. On standing up I said, "I jumped, where was the rope?" This was only 30 minutes into the evening, a member of the ladies skittles team, a young girl, was out of it with her head on the table. I found out later, that Dave, Frank's younger brother, had told the Lord he could pull my leg, I wouldn't mind; thanks Dave. Mike's young lady was normally reserved, but not with alcohol. We were having some banter when she started hitting me with a long French bread stick. With a singsong later, it was a really good evening. Before leaving, my leg felt strange, it was blood. I was so inebriated I hadn't felt the pain of hitting the stool as I fell off. Back in Cheltenham we were staggering around holding onto one another, it took a long time to get back to the girls' flat where we all crashed out unable to drive. Although it didn't stop me working, my leg was black and blue with some discomfort. I got a certificate off the Dr and made a claim on my American Accident insurance policy.

Geoffrey St John had completed the rebuild, the G50 was now ready. As it was the Golden Jubilee, mum said she'd like to come so I asked Big Mick, his wife and three-year-old Mandy to look after her, fixing them up in the digs where we stayed in 1968 and within walking distance of Mrs Jackson's, again taking her the now usual rhubarb and apples. John Gardner was now riding a Yamaha 250cc that he'd brought after his retirement in the S100 on his quick, but unreliable 250cc Kawasaki, which was put into retirement. Ray was again supporting me. He was the manager of a treatment works in Prestbury, Cheshire, I used to pop in on the way home when racing at Oulton Park or Aintree.

August bank holiday Monday, 6am was first practice. The bike went well but something wasn't right, it oiled the plug twice on the overrun, luckily nowhere on an uphill section. Going for second lap, I settled in, it was much faster than the Greeves, top speed was good and it was pulling 7000 rpm but the plug oiled up again. I got back on an N5 road plug which I usually only used for starting the bike from cold!

After a general discussion back at the digs, we went round the Paddock Hotel (campsite) discussing the problem but no one had any real ideas. Monday night practice, it again oiled up several times, again I finished the lap on an N5. We checked the ignition and value timing, eventually the engine went bang. Having done the required speed and 5 laps I'd qualified for the race.

I went to see mum every morning, and greeted three-year-old Mandy with "morning" as said by Ed Stewart on Junior Choice. She started saying it to everybody! The G50 engine was apart on the floor when mum came in, "what's the matter with the bike George?", "big end's gone mum", "does that mean the bike won't go very well?" We all smiled, "sadly, no mum!"

QUARTER BRIDGE

This is when I got to know John Goodall and Roger Haddock better. Roger I knew as he was a member of the Worcester Auto Club and raced a 7R AJS at Staverton. John rode a G50 in a Vendetta frame, similar to the Seeley! John, after checking the stripped down engine recommended I buy a new barrel, piston rings and big end, explaining that the reason I was oiling plugs was that Geoffrey had put the oil rings in upside down. I bought the spares from Arthur Keeler who had taken over selling G50 spares.

We went down to the bus station at midnight having being told they had a fly press. I shall always remember John Goodall and Roger Haddock rebuilding my engine in their best suits, I became a gofer, go for chips, go for a packet of fags, and go make a cuppa, they were both supposed to have been going out for a meal. Roger had a tie on which kept floating into the engine, John shouted "for goodness sake Roger, take that flaming tie off." Their wives were patiently watching. This was the spirit of the MGP, a rival would build your engine for you!

213

Ridgeon Rides Again

Saturday was the last night of practice and I needed to run the new barrel and big end in for race. All was going well until after 5 miles, I started to feel uncomfortable, getting to the 11th mile stone I was in agony, and my back was aching. I realised I'd not put my body belt on, proved it certainly did work. I took it steady to protect my back and tried not to lose concentration. As I pulled in to the pits Ray urgently asked "what's wrong now, I thought you were going for two laps?" I told him, the bike was going well but I'd forgotten my body belt and needed a pee. I put the body belt on after I'd relieved myself and started out for one more lap. It was lucky I did, entering Ramsay the front fairing bracket broke, the fairing was rubbing on the front wheel. Pulling into a small housing estate I asked if they had any cable or cord. An old washing line was offered. I didn't need a quick lap, so spent some time with the residents tying up the fairing. Unfortunately, it came up trapping my hands on the clip-ons, I was in some discomfort but I finished the lap.

Sunday started with checking the bike, but there was a proposal to form the Manx Grand Prix Riders Association (MGPRA) and a special meeting was arranged at the Woodbourne Hotel, there was a reasonable turnout of riders. The first committee for the MGPRA was Robin Sherry, George Costain, Bob Dowty, Alan Sheppard and Eddie Crookes.

After the meeting it was back to checking the bike from the back wheel to the front. I'd found someone to braze the fairing bracket making it even stronger and Ray twisted my arm to clean it, ugggh. Tuesday, we watched the Ltw race. I felt some sadness as I was in it last year, but I helped where I could, that's the spirit of the Manx. Dave Arnold won. The Jnr race started at 1pm, Roger Haddock had a fastest lap of 92 mph on a 350cc, in practice my fastest lap was 88 mph and my bike was a 500cc! I was pleased John Gardner on his Yamaha was 21st and John Hammond 28th. The race was won by Phil Haslam at 99 mph.

As it was Golden Jubilee year, the Manx organisers arranged a party, to be held Wednesday evening, after the bikes had been checked through Mylchreests Garage for the 'weigh in'. I was feeling confident as I rode the G50 to Mylchreests, then it was on to the party with John and Beefer. The party was held in the Villiers Pub on the Front as it had a large functions room. Helped by alcohol, I basically acted the goat and played silly games!!

As I waited at Mylchreests Garage the next morning for the parade to start, I was thinking, *why did I stay out to 1am?* 114 riders paraded along the

Promenade. Visor up to let some fresh air in, at least it woke me up. A few riders were brought up in the breakdown truck, which may have been a blessing in disguise as they had 30 minutes to cure the problem which they wouldn't have had if they'd broken down on the first lap.

Finding my pit, I checked the bike and the spares Ray had brought to the pit whilst I was collecting the bike. The Claxton sounded for assembling on the start line, with the four stoke at least the oil stayed warmer longer. I fitted a plug that'd been used in practice, and as Ray tapped me on the shoulder, with bike number 37 on my left I entered the coned area ready for the start. It's a different technique to start a 4 stroke, especially a big single, as they have much more compression. The first part is the same, rolling the bike back on compression; the nerves were showing as I checked the petrol was on for the third time, in gear, pulling the clutch in, running, jump side-saddle onto the seat (bumping), at the same time letting the clutch out. On the two-stroke you start it with a quarter throttle, on my 500cc Matchless, and all big singles, the throttle is closed until the engine is turning over, then gradually open the throttle when the engine picks up, raise the revs while slipping the clutch, and away.

Being a lanky git at 6' 3", I could start the bike well, as long as the ignition timing and carburetion settings were correct. My heart started beating again as I rushed down Bray Hill, number 37 close behind. It was a nice day so I was enjoying the ride but needed to pull my finger out. The G50 recommended maximum revs are 7200, but I was happy if I was pulling 7000 or even 6800. On the long 4 mile rush past the Crosby Hotel and the Highlander they had a speed trap, after the race all riders were eager to see their speeds. It cost 5p and they were always slower than hoped for. Braking hard as soon as I saw the red phone box for Greeba Castle, Greeba Bridge, arriving at Ballacraine, the pub on the corner highlighted in the 1935 George Formby film No Limit when a rider crashed into the bar. It's heavily protected with straw bales now. I couldn't go as fast through Bishop's Court as I did on the Greeves, and sat up. Arriving at the right-hander at Alpine, it also seemed tighter on the G50! I must admit I was disappointed with my practice times of 88 mph. Last year my fastest lap on the Greeves was 84 mph, the G50 was twice the size. The front wheel went very light at Ballaugh Bridge. I waved to Gwen, the lady in white, who I knew now, having stopped by for a cuppa many times. *Start concentrating George,* I thought as I arrived at May Hill and Stella Maris. I always thought of Roger Corbett at this point as he named his bungalow Stella Maris after breaking his leg in his 1st Manx there. At least the brakes on the G50 worked a lot better than those on the Greeves, Ramsey Hairpin, Water Works, Gooseneck and now the Mountain Mile.

ON THE MOUNTAIN

On the long downhill section I was pulling 7000 and now brave enough to keep flat on the tank around the right hand sweep until braking hard for the sharp left at Brandish. Approaching Hillberry, It seemed just like seconds until I was around the dip at Governors Bridge, with five more laps to go.

I felt comfortable and hoped I was lapping quicker. Pulling in on the third lap for fuel, Ray filled the bike up and with a scrutineer checked around it, before I left the pits for the final stint. It must have been going well as the forth lap seem to go so quickly. Rushing down Bray Hill on the fifth lap I didn't even feel tired. Dropping down the mountain everything seemed to be well. I negotiated Governors Bridge Hairpin, then into the dip, but the engine went bang. I coasted round the dip and had to push up the steep side of the rise to keep out of the way of other riders, the marshals had yellow flags out. The engine had seized, our race was over.

Packing up our pit and loading the bike we felt a little down. The race was won by Paddy Read (RAF team) at 96.889 mph. Joe Thornton was 2nd with John Goodall just 15 seconds behind him. There wasn't much chance of me beating John after he built my engine, thank you John, as he average 94 mph. I'd arranged for the lady from Castletown to come to the presentation with me at which, I got somewhat sloshed drowning my sorrows, but that didn't stop me cheering all the winners and riders getting awards. The evening came to an end and I somehow got the lady home. Next day, Ray helped me tidy the garage and load the van. I had just two local meetings left but only on the Greeves.

We had a two pump call to the National Coal Board's research station at Stoke Orchard. I was in BA with Flicker James, using a guideline for first time in anger, as the building was quite large. Guidelines hadn't been in use long, they were brought in after two firemen died in an underground RAF station; they were found only a few feet from the entrance/exit. The BA guideline had 2 small tags every 8 feet, the shorter one being the shortest way out, the longer one going to the fire, so you could find your way out! Flicker and I went through several double fire doors on the enclosed stairwell to the 1st floor, we were tying off the guideline where possible but especially on any change of direction. We also took a hose reel, as it wasn't feasible to take a line of fire hose with a hand controlled branch as we couldn't tell the pump operator to turn the water on and a fully charged line of hose would be unmanageable.

We got to the first floor, there was no evidence of fire at the head of the stairs but we saw smoke. A few yards along the corridor we saw a door burnt away. We used the hose reel, and when the smoke had cleared we could see stars in the sky. We were trying to ask each other how this could be as it was a copper roof and we'd seen no flames on arrival but, talking to one another with our masks on we were hardly audible! It turned out the whole roof section was smouldering above our heads. When we got closer we saw a Radiation Trefoil on the side of the door that had burnt away. The Radiation Trefoil is three yellow triangles in a circle meaning radiation is stored there, I thought I was going to s*** myself. This was not long after I'd grown a moustache, long side boards and a goatee beard. I'd avoided several of these phases for some time but had recently weakened to peer pressure. We were using the old Mk 4 BA set, air on demand type, some smoke was being sucked around my mask, which didn't fit well with my extra facial hair. When I saw the radiation sign I thought, *this facial fuzz is going*. Our whistles started sounding, informing us that we had 10 minutes air left. Leaving the hose reel and guideline bag we got out.

With a sigh of relief once outside, we found there were now 6 pumps and firemen everywhere. When the situation had been explained to the OIC, he ordered another line of hose and more firemen wearing BA. He put me in charge of the BA board, taking over from our driver who could now concentrate on pump operating. As this was going to be a big BA job, a retained fireman was used as a runner. Gordon Flicker James, went for a

217

rest before being sent in with another partner. I gave my runner the BA armband, this is important as it denotes he can't be given an order by anyone while he's taking a message. When sending in a BA crew into a fire you take the name tag carrying the key for the distress signal unit (DSU) asking the person's name to make sure it's the same name as on the yellow tag, which should be filled in at changeover, slot it into the BA board, working out the time and how much air in his cylinder. We had 6 firemen working in 3 pairs in the fire, another 6 sat there wearing their sets, ready to put their face masks on in case of emergencies or to relieve. I'd worked out when their whistles should sound and sent in relief crews, crews coming out informing me what was happening as they collecting their tags. I then sent my runner to update the OIC.

The canteen van arrived (about time too) as we'd been there over three hours and would be for some hours yet. Many fireman used to moan when I was on the BA board as I did everything to the letter, but two fireman had died, possibly due to bad BA procedure. I took their tag while shouting "name." On more than one occasion I'd get the response "you know me," I'd shout again "name," and was surprised to have a senior officer say "well done."

I was on duty one Saturday daytime when the phone rang. The duty man shouted "a young nurse wants a partner for a dance tonight, tickets paid for anybody interested?" Most of the firemen were married or had girlfriends, I asked for more details. She'd been given two tickets plus a coach ticket, to the Park Hall, Wormelow, and someone had let her down. This was a good place for shows with top entertainers, I'd seen Bert Weedon, Victor Sylvester Jnr Orchestra with Don Lang from 65 Special there and 'free' was the magic word. I collected her, parking near the coach station where everyone had to meet. Turned out Frank and Zandra were on the trip as Zandra worked at the coach station, so we joined their table. Although the young lady was pleasant she didn't seem that interested, perhaps she just needed a male escort to save face. We had the odd dance but as she kept wondering off I danced with the ladies at our table, plus the odd lady I fancied. One lady I thought was giving me a wink as we danced. She was married but suggested I fix a date up with her friend who was nice. After being introduced to her friend and having a few dances with her I fixed up to meet her at Cheltenham Town Hall next Saturday 22nd of December.

I got there at 9 pm I wandered round for ages not seeing the lady I was supposed to meet, but I did notice two girls sat together and asked if one of them would like to dance. The taller one, called Dinah said "yes please." After dancing I sat with them, as I'd found from experience, that if you left them someone else may sit down with them. Dinah introduced me to her friend Margaret. An hour later when dancing with Dinah, I saw the lady I was expecting to meet, dancing, she gave me a wink. At the end of the evening when Dinah and Margaret went to get their coats I asked her "where the heck have you been, I was looking for you for an hour?" She gave me her phone number, apologised and said she'd had some problems. I rang arranging for her to come to Mrs P's Christmas Eve party, after which we went back to Ash Lane for an hour before she drove home to Leominster. This cuddle was only possible because mother had gone over to Dave's on Christmas Eve. I contacted Dinah on Sunday arranging for a drink Boxing night in Chipping Camden which went well and took her to the CMC New Year's Eve party, another good evening.

CHAPTER 11   1974-Making decisions

My fuel bill had rocketed. I was either going to Leominster, an 85 mile round trip or to Ebrington, a village just outside Chipping Camden nicknamed Yuperton, 60 miles. I decided Leominster had to go. After seeing Dinah a few times, I fixed up for Dave Baker to take Margaret out. Dinah, Margaret, Dave and I had some good evenings out, one at Bowden Hall with the Morton Fraser Harmonica Gang who were often on the TV in the 50's and 60's.

Frank was marrying Zandra in January, luckily his stag night was the week before the wedding. The large room at the Bristol Hotel was packed. It was an old-fashioned stag night, with a blue comedian who, after his filthy jokes, introduced the stripper. As part of the young ladies act she rubbed oil over her boobs then sprinkled talcum powder over them and headed for a chap in a suit and glasses. He looked quite posh, sat in the front row enjoying the show, especially when she was gyrating close. It was a surprise to him, and everyone else, when she pulled his head into her ample breasts covering him in oily talc including his glasses, we all cheered. Despite having talc and oil all over his suit, he was busy cleaning his glasses so that he could see the rest of the show. One fireman, who was the worse for wear, made an unpleasant remark, the young lady threw his beer over him, and us. We didn't mind, we were all still laughing at the man covered in oily talc. At the end of the evening Frank stood on a chair addressing the throng crowded in front of him. He was quite tiddly (what a surprise) and shouts "are you friends of mine?" "Yes Frank." "Will you do anything for me?" "Yes Frank." "Get ready then," he dives off the chair without warning. Luckily, we caught him, everyone collapsing in a big pile laughing. It was a good end to a good night.

Norman, little Tony, Graham, John and I took Frank home, and although it was midnight, we played cards for an hour while Frank slept it off upstairs. Norman, Graham and John went home, I slept on the floor in a sleeping bag as I wasn't fit to drive, Little Tony and Doreen slept upstairs. Doreen had been out on a hen night with Zandra. I was woken up by a ringing noise, going to the telephone in the hall I picked it up but the ringing kept going, so I opened the door, luckily it was on a safety chain. I was confronted by a drunk Dave Baker, CB Gorman and Phil Spiller. I asked them what they wanted. "We want to throw Frank in the tank" (A water tank at the fire station used for pumping drill) was the reply. I said "I'm on the phone, go away." By this time, Doreen was stood at the top of the stairs in her nightie shouting "don't let them in." After I realised there was no one on the phone I told the lads to push off.

The wedding went well. Before going to the reception, Frank's sister-in-law Ruby came to help me decorate the house with the usual toilet paper and a wooden bird I'd made, which was supposed to look like a stork. I had a short extension ladder in my van and as we were fixing the bird we noticed a small window open, Ruby suggested we go and put rice in the beds. By the time we finished, CB Gorman had run across from the fire station to see who was breaking into Frank's house, luckily nobody noticed us being late for the reception.

Frank's brother, Dave, did a good job as best man. After toasts to the bride, groom and bridesmaids, I asked everybody to toast the parents for without them, we wouldn't be here. The reception was all finished by 5 o'clock, so a few of us decided to go for a meal. I just had time to collect Dinah before we all met up at Ken's Chinese restaurant, a popular eating house on the cattle market in St Oswald's Road. The evening came to an end when a member of staff came and unlocked the fire door by us. "That makes you feel better?" the man asked, Dave Baldwin, in a very dry voice replied "good job there was no fire before you unlocked it." We mentioned it to fire safety! When I next saw Tony and Frank both mentioned the rice in the beds, Tony and Doreen had stopped a second night!

The 74 season started with a bit of a cock-up on my part. Dick Browning agreed he would come round early Sunday, March 2nd for the first Mallory meeting, as we'd agreed to leave at 5am. I'm not good in the morning and decided to go up the evening before. I tried, without success, to contact Dick, I hadn't seen him for three days due to our shift pattern. No mobiles in those days so I left two passes on the door with a note saying "I've gone up last night." As there was a frost, it was cold sleeping in the van so I lit the Calor gas single burner. I woke up coughing, in a terrible smelly fug, and opening the window to clear it, I could have died of carbon monoxide poisoning. The day went well, I had some good rides and the weather warmed up. I saw Les Hart who I'd met a few times and who looked like the TV presenter, Bamber Gascoigne. He talked about going to the Manx Grand Prix so we agreed to share my van and swapped phone numbers. Sadly Dick never made it to Mallory, he told me he'd turned up at the bungalow but decided not to come.

This sadly ended the long distance trips with Dick and Sue, however, they

221

still helped at local meetings. One of the last trips with Dick's wife, Sue, was to Lydden Hill where I'd damaged my finger 18th May 1968. We'd made a weekend of it as it was a Bank Holiday. After the racing we went to the White Cliffs of Dover, an amazing site, we could see France. As we were walking along, Dick said "Can you smell something George?" We laughed, and accused each other of passing wind, but it was getting stronger, then we saw what was causing it! There was a man of the road, he had numerous layers of old clothes on, a big woolly hat and gloves, well socks on his hands. He'd probably never washed, he appeared to be very dirty but had a kindly face, and gave us a smile. Although he didn't ask for anything we felt sorry for him and gave him some of our food, he thanked us. We must have felt really sorry him for Dick and me to give food away! We'd had some good racing at Lydden Hill, I remember helping somebody with a Greeves clutch problem, seeing my first full face helmet when many were still wearing the old pudding basin types and being amazed by the sidecar outfits which had started using Mini, Hillman Imp and Saab three cylinder two-stroke engines instead of motorcycle engines.

There was some excitement when a moneymaking opportunity came up to drive a lorry back from Germany. Holmes Transport of Cheltenham had contacted someone at the fire station, obviously not through the front office! They had a contract to bring in Magirus Deutz lorry cabs, so I left for Germany along with 20 other firemen and Holmes Transport drivers, who I found out after the first trip were army personnel who went missing down the pub, they were hoping firemen would be more reliable. The trip took 3 days, I took a large bag of food. We were picked up at 06:00 for the trip to Heathrow. The first problem for the organisers was that half of the drivers flew to Stuttgart, my half to Munich. While waiting at Munich station to get to Stuttgart, I bought some postcards, only to go into a cold sweat when I went to pay as my wallet containing my passport wasn't in my pocket. After a moment of Cpl Jones, Dad's Army, "Don't panic, don't panic" I found I'd taken my wallet out and put it under my arm, pillock. It felt a bit like the Great Escape film, getting on a train with everybody reading German newspapers. We met up with the other drivers and had a coach trip to Ulm, where we saw the tallest church spire in Europe.

We relaxed at the Magirus Deutz factory, drinking some sort of coffee, munching sandwiches and enjoying the break. Then it was all rush to the lorry cabs, checking oil, water and finding where all the controls were. We had no maps and were just told to follow the man in front. The second problem was that we were driving on the wrong side of the road for us, it was even worse at roundabouts. We were going along carefully when I did something right, which as you know is unusual for me! I was watching ahead and saw our lorries turning off, however, the two in front of me went straight on, I decided to follow the column. As I couldn't communicate with anyone I could do nothing until we eventually pulled into a service station. The two missing drivers, Officer John Cook and Gordon, eventually arrived, John making us laugh telling us he'd been asking people how to get to England. I was pleased when we got to the German/Belgian border. We kipped in the cabs while we waited for the garage to open and filled up with fuel. The boss man had a deal with the garage owner, 1 Pfennig per litre, so 2000 litre was 20 Dm!!

The convoy to Zeebrugge was uneventful and we got there 2 hours early, so we all went to the beach to sun ourselves and swim in our underpants. However, waiting to board the boat, I was burning up and rushed into the toilets to throw water on myself. On the boat there was a sauna, but I used the shower to keep cool. I must admit I was falling asleep on the long trip from Dover to a lorry firm on the M6 near Oulton Park. I slept on the coach trip back and got back just in time for work. I looked like a lobster, sunburnt legs, back and arms, but couldn't go sick so I was uncomfortable all day. I called in on the way home to see Brenda, the NGMCC entries secretary, who luckily had some After Sun.

Over the year there were three other trips delivering cabs. The third trip, which turned into a disaster, was to deliver cabs to a Cheltenham lorry firm. The garage on the German/Belgian border was open, so there was no chance for a rest. I was falling asleep when I hit a 45 gallon oil drum filled with concrete to protect road workers, missing their old-fashioned wooden trailer by a couple of feet and ended up in a ditch on the side of the motorway. The Belgian police accused me of sleeping at the wheel, which I denied, claiming "something ran in front of me." Luckily this was in Belgium, German police are very strict. On the first trip, a Holmes driver hit a German car and was fined 100 marks on the spot. When he argued, he was fined 200 marks! I think Holmes lost the contract after my accident as the damage to the cab was 49,000 Dm about £8000 in 1974!

I had to fill in some strange accident reports. One was after a call to a Winchcombe apple farm. On arrival, we found a small fire, so our pump wasn't needed. As I was trying to reverse, a retained fireman said, "No need to turn around, follow the road down there it'll take you out." After a while we started going through small apple trees which gradually got even smaller. As these were hitting the fire appliance, I stopped and told Eddie I'd have to reverse. He replied "George keep going forward, that's an order." I stopped when we got out of the trees to find the blue light and searchlight were broken off! I think Eddie and I had dreams about doing nasty things to that retained fireman!!

Eddie again got lumbered with me driving, this time onto Cleeve Hill to a grass fire. It was along a narrow earth road with a drop one side and a high bank on the other. It was negotiable in the daylight with care but coming back in the dark, I should have asked for someone to see how close I was to the bank. I scraped the lockers on the bank, so had another accident report to fill in.

We'd been larking around on night shift, upsetting Captain Mainwaring as we called Martin Burford. In the morning, the tannoy boomed out "fireman Ridgeon, duty office." Eddie told me to take 4 BA cylinders to Rank Xerox, Mitcheldean. "But Eddie, you know I'm going racing at Staverton." "Don't argue, get on with it." As I was about to leave Martin said "George, I would double-check with Eddie about going." I told him I'd been given an order. I realised I could pick my helmet up on the way back from Rank Xerox as I'd left it at home. Arriving at Xerox, the guard on the main gate asked "what fire?" When I contacted the station Eddie said "return to station, I'm not amused." I collected my helmet and Martin got a bollocking as he'd lied to Eddie about control asking for 4 BA cylinders. He wanted to get his own back on me for messing him about.

A call out to Balance Bobbins in Andoversford, a wood manufacturing company, was an interesting fire where Dick and I wore breathing apparatus. We saw smoke from miles away, but the panic receded when we saw it was the vent blowing all the smoke out. Dick and I were detailed BA. Crawling in with a charged line and controlled branch was difficult enough, not helping was hearing explosions above us. We eventually found the seat of the fire and were opening the jet, when World War 3 started with bangs, flashes and stars. We knocked the jet off as we dived for cover. On closer inspection, we could see it was a three-phase circular saw on fire and decided to try and find the power switch, only to get a jet of water from the other side of the building, more red, white and blue sparks. As we were cleaning up we realised the explosions we'd heard crawling in, had been caused by the air trapped in the porous sheeting of the concrete asbestos corrugated roof as it burned away!

I entered the Greeves, G50 and the Mark 8 Velo, at the March meeting at Staverton, Dick was helping me as it was local. I was chatting to Tony and Alice Price who had brought mother, "George, we're having trouble with Dexter, he's 16 and wants to start racing and not go to college to do mechanical engineering, any ideas?" Seeing Dexter on his own I offered him a go on my Greeves at the May meeting at Staverton if he went to college. Dexter agreed, much to the relief of Tony and Alice. Geoffrey St John told me, "a friend asked me who could race his 1935 Scott. I suggested you, as I want to check the 1938 Velo over."

It was a good Saturday meeting at Llandow. After helping to build the circuit, I had a good race with Gordon Morse and Enso Ferrari, a quick Ducati rider. We'd left everyone else behind, but coming around paddock bend after a shower the three of us slid off. Gordon remounted, as did Enso, but my bike wouldn't start, as the exhaust pipe was blocked with earth. Dave Smith won, he always admitted he went slower in the wet so he didn't fall off.

A NGMCC meeting at Gaydon, then back at Staverton. I'm not sure how but I ended up offering Harry Turner a ride on the Greeves as he was always helping me with welding. I am not sure which races we all entered but Jeff Garbett, secretary of the meeting, turned a blind eye. Tony and Alice arrived with Dexter and his younger brother Robert. I pushed the 1935 Scott, which was a somewhat different animal as it had a hand change, to scrutineering, Harry and Dexter took the Greeves and G50. I took the G50 out for practice first, telling Dexter to follow me for a lap but going round the first bend I looked behind and saw Dexter with one foot down drifting towards the grass, the same at next corner, was I going too fast? I gave Dexter a wave and cleared off. I'm pleased to say Dexter did not fall off and told everyone that he'd enjoyed it. Harry then went out for his practice.

As I didn't need to practice on the Greeves, only my largest capacity bike, I just squeezed into the last session on the Scott. Never having ridden a hand change bike before, I came to the first gear change with some trepidation. As I pulled the clutch in, I had to let go of the throttle and brake to move the lever through a gate system. Changing down was more hairy, you are trying to brake to slow down, then letting the clutch out with the back wheel slowing the machine more, with a bit of a wobble. I think, the 1920's and 30's riders were heroes!

225

In the dinner break I went to top the Scott up with 5 Star petrol when the owner said "that's too good for it," I replied "okay, you do it," I had the G50 and Greeves to top up and check. The vintage race was called, the flag dropped and I was away, but ran out of petrol on the first lap. The owner hadn't put any in. Other than that we all had a good day with no breakdowns or crashes and I was pleased Dexter was going back to college.

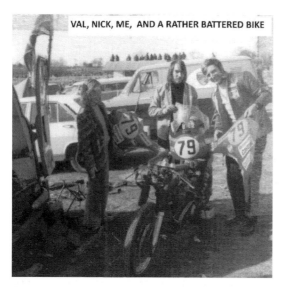

VAL, NICK, ME, AND A RATHER BATTERED BIKE

After Staverton, was a Saturday evening trip to Mallory with Dinah, Nick Thompson and wife to be Valerie, meeting Chris Brown and his girlfriend there, all six of us sleeping in my Ford Thames. Next day practice went well, but in the 500cc race, in the middle of 28 riders, I had a heavy fall on Gerard's bend, knocking myself out. I came around in the first aid centre asking "nurse can I have a kiss?" still lecherous even with a bang on the head! The bike wasn't too bad considering, but the fairing was well broken. I didn't feel too bad but, trying to be sensible after being knocked out, I let Nick drive. He couldn't get on with the column change and was crunching the gears, so I said "okay Nick. I've had enough I'll drive."

Three weeks later I was back at Mallory for a club meeting, using the short circuit which cut out the hairpin and used the paddock road, basically one big oval. I'd fitted a new fairing, a different type as I couldn't get an original G50 one, but in first practice I found it was touching the front wheel. I was hack sawing lumps off it when a rider, with Geoff Cook on his helmet, came up and said "George, my passenger hasn't turned up yet. Will you be my passenger for first practice?" "Not in a month of Sundays" I told him. "But George, if I don't go out I won't qualify. Once qualified, I can use my passenger when he turns up." Me being a sucker for a sob story gave in, "okay, but only if you go slow." Geoff knew my name because he was the son-in-law of Les Judkins, a Bantam racer I knew from 1964.

I quickly familiarised myself with the outfit, where I had to hang on, pushing and jumping on the small platform for practice. Geoff followed everyone out as they cleared off, we were trundling along at the back, with me thinking I'm enjoying this. The next lap the other outfits weren't pulling away, in fact they were getting closer but, as we were still on our own, I was still okay. The third lap, there were 8 of us going around Gerard's with me trying to shout "slowdown, slowdown." Not a great deal of use with a full face helmet on and while leaning over the back of a 650cc BSA Twin revving at 7000 rpm with open megaphones! We were going down Stebbe Straight and I thought, *he's never going to get round this right-hand bend through the paddock,* but I still got over the back wheel. Geoff pulled hard right on the handlebars, as we drifted around the bend I momentarily came up for the centre apex then back over the rear wheel onto the start and finish straight. When I saw the chequered flag for end of practice I shouted "thank God." When we stopped, Geoff asked if I'd like to passenger him in the race, "not bloody likely" at the same time, taking great steps in the opposite direction. Shame really, if he'd gone steadier, I may have gone for a second practice. We've had many laughs about this since. I went very steady in my race to get some confidence as the Southern 100 was only 4 weeks away.

We had gone back to a 48-hour week, and this was my first night shift with a new group of firemen. A call came in halfway through drill, two pumps to Linbar, in Windsor Street. I was in back with Nigel Kirby and Dennis Wright, hoping it wasn't a false alarm, me and my big mouth. The building was well alight, the officer in charge called for two more pumps. The drivers got the pumps ready to deliver water as everyone else was breaking into the delivery lorries to move them away from the burning building. The Stn Officer arrived and radioed control for two more pumps. The retained firemen arrived, and helped to get two jets out, the pumps from Gloucester and Tewkesbury arriving shortly after. Eventually the canteen van arrived, so we had a hot cup of tea, we were there all night. Linbar was a retail food distribution warehouse, a lot, if not all of the stock was ruined. It couldn't be sold, but was safe to eat if you weren't fussy. Jam donuts for example, were smoky on the outside but cellophane wrapped, our mess club was stocked up for ages. Our argument was that it would only be chucked away, remember, I'm a war baby!

I was sent on a primary school inspection to Winchcombe. After making myself known to the headmistress, I walked round checking fire doors and fire extinguishers, all satisfactory. I told the headmistress I was going to do

227

a fire alarm test next. "Do you have to?" she asked. I replied "surely it is better to have the children do it wrong today than during a fire. Would you want a child's death on your conscience?"

I sounded the alarm and was standing in the playground watching when two children carrying the milk crate came up, "what do we have to do please?" I told them "it's very good you're asking me, but ask your teacher as this is a test." After the test I addressed the children, "that was very good, give yourself a round of applause." I pointed out to the headmistress that two children had asked me what to do and suggested they should have fire drills at the beginning and middle of each term, and explain the fire drill to all new children.

At another school inspection I was complained about! I was sent into the wilds, passing a nice pub that Dad used to go in the 1950's, The Hobnails. Alderton primary School had cast iron fires with tall chimneys. The trouble was, it was Christmas time, there were decorations everywhere, and they were drying paintings the children had done on the wire safety guard. I asked for those to be taken off. On the next shift the officer in charge told me he'd received a complaint saying that I'd been officious and asking if I'd withdraw my report. I disputed the officious comment, and said "if you don't want the job done properly, send someone else. They were drying paintings on the top of the fire and had decorations up, what would you've done?" I wonder why I didn't get on in the fire service, could it be because I always seemed to be upsetting people.

Rory Blackwell had taken over as instructor on the class III driving course from Ted Belcher who had retired, Rory had more of a sense of humour. There were three of us on the course, one driving the other two sat in the back, watching through the window. We initially went to Brockworth Airfield to do various manoeuvres, to check we could drive the appliance, before we were let loose on the unsuspecting general public! It certainly gave me confidence. One day driving in Bristol, Rory said "turn left at the next junction." When I did, the road disappeared out of the top of the windscreen, I had to lower my head to look up the road. It was Spring Hill, a 1 in 3 gradient. This was bad enough, but coming out of a side road to turn left back onto the downhill section I was clenching my backside. I don't know which was worse, when I was driving or watching the others do it from the back. I studied the Highway Code again learning about low gear, downhill driving, most vehicles were still on drum brakes which faded if used all the time. On test day, Ted Nurse, transport officer and an

MOT driving test examiner said "George start the test." I turned the lights on and walked round making sure the lights worked and were clean, then checked the tyres. With beads of sweat on my forehead I did the cone test making sure I could see them in the mirror, we all passed.

The usual gang turned up to take the leading fireman's exam. There was a change in the syllabus, maths was about the same but English literature was now included. The invigilator told us "read the prose then answer the questions about it." I must have had my scarecrow head on, I asked "what's prose?" I heard a few giggles and remembered when I'd asked what copulate meant. The article was about Wellington and the Battle of Waterloo. I found this easier, as at least I could read it again. They'd also changed general knowledge, giving you four potential answers, one of which was stupid, so there was a 1 in 3 chance of getting it right. I did the ones I could answer first as the time soon ran out. Mathematics was a little easier this time, perhaps it helped learning about fire pumps and working out water capacities, I'd just passed my class III with pumps and gauges.

The leading fireman's exam results came out and I'd passed, however Ken Watkins who was very confident about what his mark should have been told us that he couldn't understand how he got more marks than was possible for the questions he'd answered. We came to the conclusion that not enough had passed so they'd multiplied the results by a few % with me, Dave and Ken passing!

The usual gang was at the Southern 100, I was obviously hoping for a third win of the Mularney trophy. Richard Swallow again had trouble in practice, Mick Wither's friend had a spare crank and I rebuilt Richard's engine. Richard, 'the bar steward', won the trophy, as he pissed off and left us. I had no time to chat having to get the G50 ready for the senior race which was now up to 750cc.

I was waiting on the start line on the G50, less than one hour after racing my Greeves. I had a good start catching many good riders including Brian Banglestein on his immaculate Petty Manx with double disc brakes, while my Matchless had only a single sided drum brake. For three laps we were side by side, coming in to Castletown corner my drum brake was squealing. Having twice chickened out to Brian, the third time I fended him off, even when coming around Town Corner where I saw Roger Jennings sat on his backside with a stupid grin under that ginger moustache. Roger had dropped his bike, which was also an obstacle on the track; riders were going all over the place to miss him, his bike and the concrete bus stop which was taken away by next year. A big thank you to all marshals.

As nothing seemed to be hanging off the G50, I went down to the pub to confirm the results from the 250cc race and found I'd finished 23rd only doing 10 laps, Richard had finished 15th, winning the 1st British Bike trophy doing 11 laps, he also qualified for the championship race for the fastest 45 riders, as I had in my first year. On the G50 I was pleased with 13th but I only did 11 laps. I tried to console myself as it was my first race on a real road and I did get in the championship race.

The championship race was Thursday afternoon. My nerves were rattling so I told jokes on the start line and thought *come on starter drop the flag*. As I was on a slightly more competitive bike this year I was up with the first 50% of the field at the start. Arriving at Ballakaighan, I was close to Bill Swallow, Richard's brother, on a very quick 500cc Velocette, we both cranked over together with two other riders when Richard dived under the four of us on his 250cc Greeves, remember I did say he was fast. Bill and I kept up with the other two but Richard was 50 yards ahead. A lap went by and we weren't catching Richard, although we didn't have much time to worry about that because the four of us were trying to pass each other, it was very enjoyable. On the third lap, we suddenly started catching Richard, his hand was up to indicate a problem.

Bill and Richard's father was a Velocette agent and had built Bill's blooming quick Velo, Bill was now leading our bunch. I was swapping between third and second. On one of the sections I was quickest on the black hole, proper name Billown Dip, perhaps Bill missed a gear, but I passed him managing to stay there until the end of the race. At the presentation I found out I was 25th but 15 seconds quicker for my 11 laps than in the Senior race. Bill was 28th and Richard was 30th and last to finish, he had a clutch problem. Before returning home I found out I'd been accepted for the 1974 MGP.

I'm not sure who suggested entering the Tewksbury pram race but, along with Percy Copeland, I turned up at the event run by Tewksbury retained firemen to raise money for the Fire Services Benevolent Fund. I dressed in a wig, one of mother's old dresses and an even older pair of knickers that even she didn't wear any more, we never threw anything away, if nothing else we could clean the bikes with them! We borrowed a pram. Many of the teams were dressed up, one pram was decorated as a chessboard and the pushers as Spassky and Fischer who were in the world chess championships. The serious ones wore running shoes and shorts.

It was a long race, from Tewkesbury Abbey up to the War Memorial, a good quarter of a mile then left to the Black Bear, the oldest pub in Gloucestershire. We had to stop at various pubs, supposedly to drink a pint of beer, then turn the glass upside down over your head. Percy was trying to drink it with me shouting "chuck it over your head." Percy protested "but it is free," "we're in a blooming race" I said. I didn't drink beer, so not a problem to me. The wig was the first thing to go into the pram, followed by the knickers as they kept falling down, at least the spectators had a good laugh at me trying to take them off! We each took turns in the pram, "I must be off my trolley" I shouted at Percy as he was laughing. I was pushing Percy the last few hundred yards to the finish back at the Abbey, when a tyre came off again. We were nowhere near the front of the race, so I said "no point in putting it back on Percy," but the pram was all over the road. We nearly hit a police motorcyclist leading traffic though the town, I could see him cringe as this out of control pram was heading for him, luckily we missed, that would have been a strange accident report! When we finished, we paid in our sponsorship money, as the saying goes "never again."

While helping Jim Curry in Dunalley Parade, there were a few funny incidents. Harry and Ivor were car mechanics up at the top of the yard, little Mike, Harry's 15 year old nephew, helped out wherever he was needed on Saturdays and some evenings. I was helping Jim one day, when Mike came down asking for some sugar for Harry and Ivor. I don't know how it happened but basically Jim gave the sugar to Mike with a message something like "buy your own bloody sugar." Moments later Ivor came storming in, threw the bag of sugar on the floor, saying "stick it up your ass." No one had any sugar!

Jim had acquired a 350cc Ducati Sebring and while kick-starting it, the bike kicked back twisted his ankle. He fell on the floor screaming, we all fell about laughing. To add insult to injury, I started the bike and said "that's how to do it Jim." I don't know why, but he gave me a rude answer. I started the bike up every time I helped Jim and he would shout abuse at me. Arriving one morning and starting the Ducati, it kicked straight back, twisting my ankle, with a loud scream I fell over lying in the road, now it was his turn to laugh. I came to conclusion there must be something wrong with the bike. When I could walk on the ankle, well limp, I checked the timing, the auto advance was rusted and fixed on full advance! Jim let me ride the machine about, which helped advertise it was for sale, I even had a day trip to see Manx friend, David Jones near Oswestry. His brother arrived when I was there and as the registration number was DDD, David said "brother, just the registration for you, dim, daft and dozy."

Jim left me to drill some metal but I wasn't getting on very well. When Jim came back he showed me how to use the drill, it was an all singing, all dancing one from Czechoslovakia, it had a reverse setting, which I'd had it on! Jim told me that the exchange rate for iron curtain countries currency wasn't good, so it was best to buy good quality tools with any winnings.

An old moped brought in for repair wasn't running very well. On checking, we found it had some old rag in the air cleaner. As we had no foam, we put some clean rag in, got it going better and said "we are feeling a little ragged." (A joke, Jim and I still share!)

For many months Jim had his racing 450cc Honda Black Bomber in the workshop. It distracted us as we were always fiddling with it, drinking tea looking at it, or discussing how to make it go faster. When it was moved we could get on with some work and earn Jim some money, I was working on an MZ engine casing that had a seized clutch arm. After spraying WD40 everywhere, I had the arm held in a vice whilst I rotated the crankcase and pulled, when bang, I was sat on the floor, nose bleeding. The arm had jumped out of the vice, the casing hitting me in the nose. My sympathetic mates said it couldn't miss as my nose is so big. Oh, I was in pain!

This was days before Nick and Valarie got married. Harry and I were there, luckily at the back of the registry office with other biker friends. When the registrar got to "Nicholas Atwell Thompson, do you take Valerie to be your lawfully wedded wife?" Harry and I sniggered. He continued, "Valerie, do you take Nicholas Atwell Thompson......." Harry and I sniggered again, I had to squeeze my nose to stop laughing, which hurt as it was still painful. The registrar finished "Nicholas Atwell and Valerie, you are now man and wife." The congregation clapped while Harry and I rushed out of the registrar's office laughing our heads off. At the reception, we recovered some sort of composure and apologised for laughing which started everyone else off. As usual I ended up telling stories including the one about "Boras the Bald Bavarian Baron" which I'd learnt from Frank and which had a risqué ending, "I'd rather have my pretty panties parted by the perfectly pointed penis of Percy the Proud Prussian Pecktor, than my buttocks bashed at by the balls of Boras the Bald Bavarian Baron." Nick's grandmother, a jolly lady, said "George, how did you manage to get all that out?" I replied "granny, what a thing to say at a wedding", making her laugh even more!

Arriving at the fire station for a night shift I saw a letter addressed to me. Opening it, the first thing I saw was a pair of hands shaking, I assumed it was to do with the Independent Order of Foresters, a friendly society I'd recently joined, but looking further, it said congratulations on your Littlewoods win. I couldn't get the contents of the envelope out quick enough, it was about our watch weekly pools syndicate. I thought, how much have we won? When I pulled the cheque out I stood there speechless and gave a sly look left and right to see if anybody was close, it was for £300!! There were 14 in the syndicate, so it was nearly a week's wages each! There were a few who were a couple of weeks behind with their 10p, going up to one of them I said "you are two weeks behind with your football, I want my money." He paid me, as did the others, perhaps they guessed something by my tone of voice. At dinner, I told them "I've won us a week's wages each lads."

We had a call out to a trapped cow. It was a heifer in calf that had slipped down a bank into a stream. The animal's legs had got so cold she was unable to stand. Andy Finch, Graham Leighton and I along with the farmer were stuck in the stream for 90 minutes, my shoulder against a cow's, sorry heifer's, backside. We got a hose around the heifers head and neck, then used a fire engine to pull it up the wet slope. Another shift I was detached to help Benson Howell, an old hand who now checked fire hydrants. We ended up helping Nigel Kirby push a concrete mixer up a steep drive to a bungalow he was doing up. I admired Nigel, he had left the army in the early 50's with a wife, baby and mortgage. He did extra work to pay the mortgage, and borrowed money to buy an old cottage next door which he rented out. When the cottage was paid off he bought the property we'd pushed the concrete mixer to.

Although Eddie was very conscientious and by the book, he had a sense of humour. They took our fire axe off us in 1974. On the last day Eddie carried his axe in with his arms outstretched, as if he was carrying a small baby while humming the Death March, we all joined in. At the time, you could buy an axe and belt from stores. A group of us wore our own fire axe on duty as only two small axes were carried on the appliance. Even the wearing of our own axe was stopped eventually, however, we could use one off the appliance! It didn't help to keep telling senior officers that it was too late when you get top of the ladder to decide you needed an axe. We had a call to Cheltenham racecourse for a jump on fire. It turned out to be a rubbish fire. Dave Campbell, a jolly fire control operator, said over the air, "I hope you did not take a fence?" Arriving at the fire station Eddie said "11 to 1 closing home station aunty Charlie", the other operator with no sense of humour said "please repeat message"!

I'd agreed to fix Les Hart up with digs for the Manx and for us to travel over together. When we got to the IOM we did a lap of the course before getting to Mrs Jackson's. Les and I shared a room, on going to bed the first night I saw he had pink pyjamas on, "Les, I don't know whether to call you Bamber Gascoigne or the Pink Panther." He became The Pink Bamber!

Bank Holiday Monday morning practice went well with the 6 speed Shaftleitner gearbox. Having bought it just before coming over, I did have one problem with it, the gear pedal worked backwards to what I was used to, I went into the wrong gear several times. Les also had a good practice. Tuesday practice wasn't so good. I had big end trouble, so went back to the bus station to make friends with Fred who was a keen biker and had just moved to the Isle of Man from London. Fred, as well as helping me at the bus station, started coming around the workshop. The big end problem was a blessing in disguise, taking the engine out we found the bottom frame had started to crack. The repair did not look very pretty but we slapped some black paint on to cover it up. With help from the other G50 lads I was starting to learn about the G50, first under supervision, then on my own. It took two hours just to set the valve timing.

The rest of the practice went well except for some carburettor problems, it was spitting back coming around the gooseneck. I was told that the carburetion was too weak, aka lean, too much air to fuel ratio and to lift the needle or use a richer slide. I was still finding the occasional wrong gear with the new 6 speed gearbox but it was getting less every lap of practice. Thursday afternoon practice, I just did one lap, Les Hart did two perfect laps, stopped, filled up, then did two more. He was happy having done his race distance with no problems, after retiring last year. We readied our bikes over the weekend. Les was racing Tuesday, so Ray and I agreed to help in his pit during the race. We took Les to get his petrol Monday morning, and in the evening to the "weigh in." We then took him for a quiet drink to settle his nerves.

Les made a very good start but retired early, "rider perfectly okay" as Peter Kneale and the other commentators would say. When I collected Les he was fuming, he'd done four perfect laps on Thursday. When we stripped his bike, it had a piston seizure due to a blocked main jet, Manx Gremlins can be cruel. The only bright spot, Les had eight free gallons of petrol for his van!

Following the success of the impromptu 1973 Golden Jubilee rider's party, the MMCC gave each rider two tickets for a function on Tuesday night to be held at The Douglas Head Hotel near Manx Radio. This was better organised than last year and there were prizes for many of the stupid games. I won engine oil and a Double Diamond lamp. Four of us entered 'the boat race.' Each member of the team had to drink a pint of beer then tip the empty glass over their head. I was last and anchor-man, I tipped the full glass of beer over my head without drinking any, so we won. I still have the Double Diamond table lamp.

Wednesday I got the petrol sorted and feeling brave, rode my bike to the "weigh in" where hundreds were watching, after which, with Ray and Les, it was off for a quiet drink.

After the parade along the promenade and up the dreaded Summer Hill, we lined up for the start. After the usual nerves it was a good start, it helps being a lanky git with long legs. At Ramsay I saw bike number 14 leaning against a wall with bent forks and wondered who the rider was. I pulled into the pits at the end of the 3rd lap for fuel. I was enjoying myself, I'd passed a few and some had broken down, Ray shouted "you're doing well." Away again and I settled in quickly. I waved at Ray as I was starting the last lap, arrived at Ramsay with the mountain section to climb one more time! I was thinking as I went through the 32nd and Windy Corner on the last lap, now it's all downhill, some riders had pushed in from here to finish! As I pulled away from Brandish, a tight right left-hander, I felt something happen! Breaking into an immediate sweat I pulled the clutch in and coasted, then started to let the clutch out hoping problem had cured, it hadn't. The engine must have seized. I was trying to find neutral while coasting as I was still going fairly fast down towards Hillberry, at the same time I slowly moved to the right hand pavement, so other riders had a clear run.

I started to push in when I saw Eric Corns go past, he'd been one minute in front of me on the start line. I was at Signpost, but my brain was gone by now and I was thinking *if I can get to the finish within one minute I'll beat Eric*, however I was a mile from the start! From Signpost to Bedstead there were no pavements, so it was a bit dodgy keeping to the side the riders didn't use. No pavement at Governors Bridge either, and very narrow, so yellow flags were being waved. Around the dip then the hard push up the steep side, déjà vu, I'd done this last year. At least as I pushed across the finish line I knew I'd done six laps and got a finish. I jumped aboard the bike as I crossed the finish line and stopped in pit lap knackered! Ray rushed up to help and told me that the leader, then the second man, then some of the top six had dropped out. With the retirements, we worked out that I was lying in 18th place and well within a replica time. Eric Corns got one, he was 27th and finished in 11/10ths of the winner's time, however the Manx Gremlins had struck. If I hadn't ridden to the "weigh in" I may have done another mile, serves me right for being cocky! Number 14 was Jon Parkes from Worcester, luckily he was all right, he was in with a chance of winning the newcomer's award.

I finished 36[th,] not last and I'd been averaging 88 mph, Bernard Murray won. Bernard did the double, winning the Jnr as well, but Eddie Roberts had the fastest lap at 101 mph and won the Ltw race. Again I had the pleasure of going onto the rostrum to collect my finisher's award. As I was coming off a group of young Manx lads asked for my autograph, after my name I drew a union flag, I still had the Union flag I'd rescued from the fire in 72. Friday night was spent at the Crosby Hotel with other riders, who like us, were catching the boat Saturday morning.

We were in the van, waiting to load onto the ferry, Les was hidden in the back. The sea very rough and the vans were backed up. Some clever dick shouted "they're craning the vans on the boat." When he heard this, Les started panicking and wanted to get out. I told him to stay put, they weren't craning the vans on. The boat was going up and down 6 feet with the swell. Each van had to line up with the ramp, when the boat came down, a sailor would bang on your van twice, and you had to go for it, you had 15 seconds before the next wave hit. I could hear Les praying very quietly under the tyres and sleeping bags, when our time came. I went round the boat until I found a lower deck and managed to curl up on a seat, there were bodies lying everywhere. I could hear this banging and crashing, making me think the boat was still in the dock but was told it was the waves crashing onto the boat when it came out of the sea. I was awoken from a sound sleep by some bar steward shouting "fire", or so I thought, or was it a nightmare. I'd never seen the sea that rough, it was a terrible trip and I was seasick a few times on the four hour crossing. I was glad when it was over.

LOCAL PRESS CUTTING

Among local riders who did well in the Manx Grand Prix were (20) George Ridgeon 500cc Matchless (107) Andy Alexander 500cc Triumph (22) Ron Rowland 250cc Yamaha (80) Derek Akerman 250cc Yamaha

I dropped the G50 straight back to Geoffrey St John to fix and took the Greeves to Gaydon airfield for a NGMCC meeting where I met up with some of the lads from the Manx. I was getting to know Mick Dunn and his dad, who ran South Shropshire Motorcycles. Mick raced a nice Beart green

Greeves, Francis Beart was a well-known tuner and sponsor, all his bikes were green. His 250cc Greeves was the Griffon scrambler motor with a 64mm stroke 70mm bore with Honda forks and a disc brake, mine was 66 x 72. He asked about the Manx as he wanted to enter so I suggested he keep in touch, we could go together as Les wasn't going next year. Mick also raced a G50 Seeley.

There was a social dance to raise money for something at work that I mentioned to a few of the old Lister's gang. As Dave Baker was on duty, Dinah brought Margaret over and met us at the station. Dave was working, he initially sat with us for a few minutes before he drifted away saying he'd been given some work to do. After he'd been missing for an hour Dinah and Margaret started asking what was up with him. I knew there was a problem and tried to waffle "he's on duty and got to keep making sure the station's okay." Making an excuse to go to the boy's room I found David and asked "what the bloody hell are you doing David, you are dropping me in the Kaki." He mumbled on about finding another girl who lived in Cinderford. I bollocked him, "what do I tell the girls, why the hell didn't you tell me before the dance?" I told the girls he wasn't feeling well. I don't think they believed me, and although I was dancing with both girls, it took the edge off the evening. Dave finished with Margaret shortly after this, however it didn't spoil my relationship with Dinah. I was pleased Margaret didn't hold it against me, I wouldn't have minded holding it against her!

With Dinah, I attended many dance functions. One was at Cheltenham Motor Club when we dressed up as vampires on Halloween night. I remember one Halloween in the late 1960's when 4 ghostly pole bearers in top hats and capes carried a coffin in. After it was put down, the lid opened, and Rich Barton came out dressed as Dracula! This particular night there were no others dressed up so we just took off our hats and other paraphernalia remaining dressed in black. I had an invite from Dave Jones, a MGP friend from Kinnerley, to their ACU annual motorcycle dinner/dance. It was excellent meal and a nice pudding, sweet to you posh people, so I asked a waitress for an extra one. Another waitress, while clearing up, asked if everything was okay. I told her the sweet was very nice and to my embarrassment, both girls bought me a sweet at the same time. I just managing to eat them, Dinah said "serves you right."

Life was drifting, the old mates were married now except Dave Baker. I somehow found out about a strip club in Dursley run by a retired policeman. Dave and I went along, it was good to have a night out discussing all our problems. The venue was a large Edwardian house with videos in some of the various rooms, every so often a stripper did a turn. Even the plump barmaid took her top off, but it put me off my cider shandy! The bright part of the evening, as far as I was concerned, was a choice of fish & chips or pie & chips included in the £1 entry fee. So another year was over with the New Year's Eve dance at CMC where I did the conga to the Locomotion by Little Eva!

CHAPTER 12   1975-A trip to London

The Fire Service and many council departments were in confusion after the 1974 general election when the Tory government changed County boundaries throughout the UK. In the Fire Service, Gloucestershire gained Gloucester City but lost Kingsway, Severnside and Patchway which became Avon. This did mean there was another whole-time station close, whose firemen could do standbys, manpower permitting. On one such occasion, I was sent to Gloucester, where I knew Eddie Willey, leading fireman in charge. After telling me which pump I was riding, he said "George, we're having a special meal to celebrate the Sub Officer being away, it's 25p extra." I told him I could claim up to £1. He sternly replied "no George, if you want a 75p standard meal we'll do you egg and chips or, you come in with our Lasagne, wine and sweet," which I did, while thinking *you miserable old so-and-so*, but at least he'd told me.

The Staverton meeting was approaching. We now had a spare G50 engine that Geoffrey had acquired and fitted, after our return from the Manx, while he repaired the other engine. He told me it wasn't the fractured big end that stopped the bike but the flywheels flexing in and out caused a main bearing to overheat and seize up. I wonder if I hadn't ridden to the garage would the engine have lasted just that little bit longer. In February I drove to Chipping Camden, staying the night at Dinah's as I was going to the North Glos MCC practice day at Gaydon only to find snow on the ground in the morning. After many phone calls, I didn't go, instead I stayed and had breakfast in this large farmhouse, Dinah's family were farmers. At the next club night I found out a few had turned up for the practice, but it didn't happen.

Jim asked me to ride a Honda 250cc over to tax a bike a customer was picking up later that day. Elmbridge Court had been an MOD admin base in the war and was now used by many government agencies, including motor tax. I was riding carefully as it had left foot gear change! At the counter a pretty lady took my forms and was making light conversation, when she said "there's a birthday party Saturday, I need an escort, would you like to go?" Rather surprised I said "I'm working that night, perhaps we can fix up another night out" and got her phone number. When I tried to start the Honda it was dead as a dodo, no spark. I felt a bit of a fool going back in to use the phone, "Jim the bike won't start there's no spark." Jim suggested I check the handlebar to see if the kill switch is on, some bar steward had turned it to off! I fixed up a trip out with Patricia, the lady who took my forms, to pick bluebells, after a few more dates with Pat, I decided I wasn't going to Chipping Camden again.

I'd sent a letter at the end of 1974 to Loctite with a photo of my bike at the MGP, displaying one of their stickers, asking for some more of their product. The year before I'd written a begging letter, "Dear Sir I do road racing, please give me some Loctite." I received a large tube of nut lock and bearing fit. Early February I received a reply from Loctite saying that they were willing to send me any of their products, was I dreaming? A few days later I got a phone call, "my name is Chris Loft from Loctite, we want you to bring your bike to London. What day can we come and see you and do you know a restaurant where we can talk it over?" I was stationed in Cheltenham and struggled until I remembered a hotel in the High Street.

I nervously waited in the bar, Chris had brought a colleague and during the meal explained that Loctite were holding a press launch in the Europa Hotel. Representatives from JPS F1, British Leyland and other users of Loctite products would be there, but Triumph Motorcycles had union problems, a sit-in, so no bikes were going in or out. Loctite had heard good reports of my racing. We fixed up an interview and photos, Loctite would make me a presentation at the launch in June. Chris and a cameraman arrived at "Janetta." I had to explain why I liked and used Loctite. Chris had me speaking into a tape recorder, I had to do it several times as I wasn't used to being interviewed. As it was springtime, the lambs were bleating, which also put me off. Then they took photos of me pointing to where I used their product on the bike. I was somewhat embarrassed, as my shed was a large chicken hatchery.

I parked my tatty Ford Thames, complete with Loctite and Castrol stickers outside the Europa Hotel, Park Lane, a man in top hat and tail's opened the door. Wearing jeans and a Loctite paddock jacket, I was waiting at reception, stood next to Cyril Fletcher but too nervous to say hello and thinking, *here's where I get the horse laugh when they say George Ridgeon, never heard of you*. I signed in and asked where I could park. The attendant in the basement car park asked me to leave the keys in the van, "but I've a £500 motorcycle in the back." "Sir, that Rolls-Royce is worth £10,000, but the keys are in it!"

Chris Loft came to my room, "George, we've just had the 1909 Renault arrive and have to take it the Savoy would you like to come?" This immaculate car had been brought up by Colin Wilson, the chief mechanic

241

at Beaulieu Motor Museum. I got up early and went with Colin to collect the Renault. What a marvellous car. As we drove past Buckingham Palace, I did a Royal wave, the policeman looked both ways then gave a salute! It was all hands to the pumps getting the various vehicles down the ramps as there was a 2' drop into the function room. I helped with a JPS F1, an Austin, 1909 Renault, Reliant 3 wheeler, a diesel engine, and my G50.

As we were both from the West Country, I sat with Chris at the presentation. There was a large screen and recorded interviews. First up was the JPS, as the person spoke various still photos were shown, the 1909 Renault was last but one, they even showed Chris repairing his 125 Frances Barnett. Finally a recorded voice said, "as well as all of these large businesses, even George Ridgeon uses Loctite," my face was on the screen. I wanted to crawl under a stone, especially when I heard myself speaking

and the lambs bleating. I heard some laughing especially at my Oo Arr accent, which made it worse. After a buffet and drinks I stood by my bike so people could ask questions, several admired my racing motorcycle. There were several beautiful girls in overalls and denim caps posing for a photo with me, then an hour's break before the dealer's demonstration. Again I sat by my new-found friend, we were both a little tiddly, laughing at each other's West Country accent. After we packed up, Chris asked if I was going home, "no Chris, you said I was booked for two nights and I've had some drinks, so I'll stay."

I made the mistake of going for a walk around Soho, a young lady asked if I'd like to go back to her flat for £6. After a moment's thought I said, "yes, okay", "give me £6 and I'll go and get some contraceptives." "I've got some." "I have to get them from my supplier, or else." I never her saw again. I only told Frank, who said that he'd probably have done the same, but I did have a big stock of Loctite products.

The first meeting at Staverton was the weekend the clocks went forward, Dick had said "see you about 7 am." 7am came and went, as did 8am, as

9am was approaching I was in the van about to leave when Dick screeched to a halt in his frog eyed Sprite "sorry, I put the clock backward!" I was practising on the Greeves and following Ken Inwood when he slid off his Norton, I ran over his legs then fell off. Picking myself up, I checked Ken was okay, luckily I was on the Greeves which was over 100 lbs lighter than a G50. Ken had brought his mother to look after his spares van when he was racing. I had to buy a new fairing off Ken, he joked "I wasn't doing much business so thought I'd fetch you off." Every time I saw his Mum she would say "you ran over my little boy." During the break, sat having a sandwich, Mick Dunn came over asking if he could pick my brains about the Manx GP, no comments please. His dad had always been in the motor trade and was a good engineer, despite Mick beating me, I agreed we should go to the Manx together.

Jim Curry asked if I wanted to buy a 750 Triumph for £500. This was the bike he'd sold to Sir Alf, as he called him, but he couldn't keep up the pavements so Jim exchanged it for a cheaper bike. Knowing Jim, he wanted to offload it quickly to make a quick buck. As the Triumph was less than a year old and over £700 new, I did the deal. Riding to Gloucester going through Longford where I got my first speeding ticket 1962, I was pulled over by the police, "do you know what speed you were doing Sir?" With my bottom lip quivering I said "I've just bought the bike officer." As I took my helmet off, I felt the officer, seeing a 31 year old biker, was starting to feel sorry for me so I continued my grovelling "it's a job making it go slow officer." I was pleased when he said "I'll let you off, but make sure you do go slower or else." After showing him my documents and mentioning the fire service, I said "Yes officer, thank very much," grovel.

I met Bob and Sue Moore at the CMC, Bob wanted a lift to race meetings, he was then racing an ex Ginger Blainey/Roger Corbet Norton, Sue seeing the 750cc Triumph asked for a ride, quite nice having a 20-year-old on the back! Bob got a 250cc Greeves two years later, Gordon Morss, Bob and I had many good races in classic and single cylinder classes.

As I had the Triumph and the TT was approaching, I suggested a trip to the Isle of Man to Pat. Pat was divorced and living in Longlevens where we agreed to start from on the Tuesday of race week. Plans were nearly scuppered as it snowed heavily across all of the UK, including the Isle of Man on Monday 2nd of June, luckily it'd melted by Tuesday. Loading up, I put my army kitbag on Pat's back but she nearly fell off backwards so I moved it to around my neck, resting on the tank. Arriving at Princes Dock

Liverpool, bikers were crowding around a transistor tuned to Manx Radio, listening to the TT race which had been postponed from Monday. Jim Curry was having a scratch around as was Roger Corbett and a few others I'd met at the Manx GP who'd transferred to the TT. On the boat back I bumped into Don Morgan, a fire officer stationed at Stroud. He'd taken his father who was in his 70's on the back of the Tiger 110 he'd bought new in 1958. It was lucky we both stopped at the first garage as he noticed my rear light was not working and helped me fix it.

Patricia was coming to bike night at CMC, dances and local race meetings with me but when mum found out I was stopping overnight at this lady's house now and again, she said "George, I cannot go out and face the neighbours because you're living in sin!" Alice and Tony Price, took Mum to Staverton races where, after meeting Pat, she liked her.

Geoffrey St John asked me to go and see him; in his garage was a Seeley rolling chassis. "George I don't think you're keeping the bike as nice as it should be." "I thought I was keeping it tidy, I am racing it." "George, I'm suggesting you have the MK3 Seeley chassis previously owned by Vin Duckett, you have one of the G50 engines, use your 6 speed gearbox and keep the fairing but supply an exhaust system and the bike is yours." I asked what happened if I didn't get on with the new bike, I was used to the G50. "I suppose you'd better go back to the G50." I asked him what his plans were. "I've got a new Matchless rolling chassis and an engine, I'll use the genuine seat and tank off our bike, your good wheel and make a new bike up. What's left over, I'll sell it, it's worth £450."

As it was late June, with the S100 only weeks away, I started building the bike straight away. Gordon Morss helped weld a high-level exhaust system I had acquired, as well as giving me a lot of moral support, by midweek it was looking like a racing bike. I asked Dick if he thought I should I buy the G50 rolling chassis and engine spares, we agreed I should. I must admit to telling Geoffrey St John a porky pie, "mother has lent me some money and I can pay the £450 for the remains of the G50." I was annoyed at his answer "sorry George, I've sold it to a friend." I protested "but you told me I could ride it if I couldn't get on with the Seeley and I wanted to take some spares to the S100." "Sorry George, I changed my mind, and sold it to a friend." I was feeling grumpy, I had no spares, they weren't as easy to get as the Greeves or as cheap. At least the bike was ready with my six speed gearbox now the right way round, 1 up and 5 down.

The trip to the S100 was quite interesting. I took Tony Russell and Les Hart (Pink Bamber), how we got four bikes in my Ford Thames I don't know. We collected Ray from Altrincham on the way to the boat. We were camped in Paulson Park, ¾ mile from the start. There were two public houses on the edge of the park, by the Victorian railway line, The Duck and The Viking, both within walking distance, so we had a choice for morning ablutions. To get into the park with a vehicle, you went under the railway line through a stone arched bridge built for 1860s steam trains, only one vehicle wide and on a tight bend with a stream you could end up in if not concentrating! There were railway gates by the pubs that were only opened for large vehicles to gain access otherwise there was just a pedestrian access gate to the pubs.

LES HART, ME, RAY WAKEFIELD, TONY RUSSEL

We signed on at the rugby club near Town Corner then on to an alehouse, The George, with music and girls. The old landlord Bob Waldron, had moved to The Ship Inn on the harbour, you could fall in coming out the pub tiddly if you weren't careful! Early to bed, early to rise for 5am practice. I was pleased that both bikes went well. After breakfast I checked the bikes over, especially my new Seeley. Evening practice also went well with no problems.

245

After evening practice we went to the pub to discuss how the practice went, after which we all went to a lady's flat, she was a friend of the lady I met in 1972. There was a gang of riders and girls there, Les was the first to leave after too much falling down water, we left 30 minutes later. When we got to the bridge the water was across the roadway, the stream had risen. Entering the camp my lights picked up Les staggering across the park. He told us that when he'd got to the water, he thought it was the stream so turned right, after hitting the brick wall, he had to wade through!

I had a steady morning practice and worked on the bikes all day for the evening race meeting The British bike class in the 250cc race was getting very competitive with Richard, who won last year, Mick, myself, Jon Worthington, and new riders, Marty Ames, Ron Leighton and Mick Dunn, who I was taking to the Manx in 6 weeks, was getting some road racing experience, even George Fogarty was riding a Greeves. The flag dropped, in the usual rush, I could see the rear of Mick Dunn ahead of me. Ray told me that there was at least one British bike in front of me after we came in. The race was won by Neil Tuxworth.

Tony Russell was in the 350cc race, so his bike had been checked and he was just leaving for his race as we were coming in. After getting the Seeley through scrutineering for the Snr race, we watched the 350cc race from the assembly area, it was a heck of a race between two NI riders, Ray McCullough just beating Mervin Robinson with Neil Tuxworth 3rd just missing out on the double. Tony retired but Richard Swallow had a 10th on a 350cc Yamaha, after being picked up by the breakdown van in the 250cc race. I had a good ride, again having a battle with Bill Swallow and Pete Swallow (no relation) and again scared to death when Bill Smith, Les Trotter and Roger Sutcliffe (1st, 2nd and 3rd) lapped me, only 11 laps completed again.

All loaded up, back to the campsite, then down the pub to see the results. The result sheet showed Mick Withers as 1st British bike, but Mick had borrowed Frank Chapman's 250cc Yamaha after Frank was injured in practice. Ron Leighton had won the fastest British bike, Mick Dunn was second, then me, was I putting weight on? Les Hart had a 12th and I was 9th on the Seeley, winning some money, we both qualified for the invitation race in which I later finished 20th. I was chuffed as it was in front of Les on his Yamaha, admittedly only a 250cc but 100 pounds lighter than my bike and only about 5bhp less. Richard Swallow finished 7th on his new Yamaha.

It was another good night at the presentation which opened with the Miss Southern 100 competition. I'd rescued a railway horn from the scrap bin at the fire station, it had been used for warning of oncoming trains when working on railway lines. A few of us blew it to noisily support the winners. After some dancing in the street to a good disco, I even got one of the Worcester, Hewlett twin's (aka the Norton twins) wives on the stage for a jive where the presentation had been. On the way home I found out Mick Dunn and I had both got rides in the Snr MGP.

Hearing about a nurse's party at St Paul's Maternity Hospital, I twisted Dave Baker's and a few other firemen's arms to come with me. Dave and I saw a gorgeous blonde called Maria, only trouble was, she liked Dave. Maria, introduced me to one of her friends who kept me company for the rest of the evening. Dave ended up with a new girlfriend. I was at Stroud Stn a few days later when fireman Cliff Bodenham grabbed hold of my lapels and pushed me up against a wall, "what's Dave Baker like?" "Da, Da Dave's all right, why do you ask?" "He's taking my daughter Maria out." I thought *bloomy heck, glad I'm not taking her out!*

Just one meeting with the NGMCC to make final adjustments before the MGP to the G50. On the Greeves, I had a brilliant ride chasing Dave Smith riding his ex-works Lawton Aermacchi, he kept looking behind to see if I was there, I was riding on a part of the tyre I'd never used before. After the race Dave told me "I looked back and saw you, I thought I could lose you, but you were always there." It cheered me up, we still talk about it.

Although the G50 went reasonably well I decided, after a talk with Geoffrey St John, it needed a complete engine strip down. The only G50 spares I had were jetting and some special tools, I had to buy extra Seeley sprockets for gearing as they're different to the G50 Matchless. I'd been advised to service the oil pump during strip down. I pulled the pump apart and lapped the side parts on a sheet of glass with fine grinding paste to take away any high spots and give more oil pressure, but I was running out of time to get the bike together. I'd managed to work out the rear sprocket size to fit deciding on just two teeth smaller than the S100 circuit, at least the rolling chassis was up together!!

I turned up at South Shropshire Motorcycle Shop, it's difficult to describe Mick's face when he saw my engine in a box of bits, a sort of screwed up disgusted look! Discussing the trip to the Manx over a cuppa I agreed to go in his new Sherpa 1500 van. We loaded his immaculate, also Beart green, Seeley G50, we used to pull Mick's leg, "did some green paint fall off the back of a lorry?" then my chassis and boxes of parts. When we got to the docks, 3 hours early, I heard a West Country voice and saw Geoff Thomas from Bristol, Geoff was riding for his first time in the MGP.

We agreed to go for a meal and found a Bernie restaurant. A pretty waitress was serving us so we pulled her leg, but on the next table there was a grumpy man who moaned about everything. When she brought the bill I asked her if her phone number was on it, which made her laugh! As we left I shouted out "what a marvellous meal, what fantastic service, a lovely restaurant, anybody that moans must be a miserable old so-and-so." Mick and Geoff slunk out but it got a few cheers, smiles and nods from other customers. Back to the dock, although it was Mick's van, I persuaded him to be covered up with tyres and sleeping bags as my name was on the booking form. Mick did ask "is this legal?" "Not at all Mick, but everyone does it!"

At Mrs Jackson's Mick and I shared a room, Nigel from Northern Ireland and a Londoner Steve Bowers with his mechanic friend were there. Arriving early Saturday morning we had all weekend to get ready, but Mick, and Geoff had to go on the newcomers' coach trip, I was busy dropping the engine in. Luckily Roger Haddock from Worcester, who'd helped build my motor in 1973, was stopping in the B&B across the road. I mentioned I'd rebuilt the motor, and he told me that he always pushed the machine around with the plug out to make sure the oil was circulating. What a godsend seeing Roger was, I pushed the bike around Hillary Park a few times, 500 yards each complete circuit, with no oil coming through. 27 small Allen screws hold the outer cam chain case on, after removing the oil pump, we immediately found the problem, me!! I hadn't lubricated the pump, so when the gear drive rotated it was only pumping air. After lubricating it, I pushed the bike around, the oil was circulating; thank you again Roger.

After the boys got back from their coach trip, Roger suggested that the four of us do a slow lap around the course, as Steve had a Ford Escort, we used that. Roger sat in the front, describing road position, peel off point breaking points etc, but even in the 30 mph zone on Bray Hill, Steve was going too fast. Roger said "slowdown, I am trying to help you learn the course." It was the same approaching Quarter Bridge, sadly, Steve kept going too fast, spoiling the trip, well for us, but at least I did get one lap in. I advised Mick, Geoff and Steve, the new London lad, to fit a plug bag for plugs, tools, wire etc. Mick said "I don't need a plug bag, my bike won't go wrong" "Mick it's 37.73 miles around for one lap, if you have a minor problem, you may be able to fix it and finish the lap, speed in the early stages isn't important," it fell on deaf ears.

Bank Holiday Monday morning practice, I had two steady laps with no apparent problems. I eventually found Mick who appeared to be running around like a headless chicken, "my bike stopped, a battery wire broke and I had to borrow tools off a marshal." "Mick, I hate to say I told you so, but I told you so, fit a plug bag." "No, it won't go wrong again." Ray arrived and I met Gerry Jenkins (Jenko) who worked at Mick's dad's shop, we were all crammed in the large garage checking the bikes. I must admit I envied the way Mick enjoyed cleaning his bike. Monday afternoon Mick rang his father, we could all hear, "hello dad, I did a lap but a wire broke, I've sprayed the exhaust system and the bike's all cleaned." After this when Mick was working on his bike, either myself or Gerry would say "hello dad, how do I take the plug out?"

Next practice I did two more laps. With Ray and Gerry I walked over towards Mick, who had a grin on his face "see, I told you, two laps no problem." Then he told us "I saw two lovely girls at Ramsey Hairpin, I gave them a wave and a smile, hi girls!" He demonstrated his Royal wave and broad smile, showing two black teeth, he didn't like the dentist! I was looking his bike over, "Mick, what's all this oil running down your front fork leg?" The oil was brake fluid, coming from the brake line, it'd been rubbing on the front wheel. Mick said "that's strange, it's never happened before." I gave him a dig "there you are Mick, what did I tell you, the unusual happens over here." The big smile had gone, but he was still adamant "it won't go wrong again." After Mick's tale of saying "hi girls," when we greeted one another, we did a Royal wave, had a stupid grin and said "Hi Girls." After explaining this to other riders, it spread around the paddock, again Mick was frowning with a "Huff!"

We didn't really associate with the London lad Steve, too cocky, but his friend Dave was okay.

Wednesday morning practice, I needed one lap to qualify, Mick needed two and Steve Bowers, who'd been having various troubles, three, but there were still five practice sessions left. I just did the one lap then found Ray and Gerry to be told that Mick had broken down at, Union Mills, and needed to be collected. As practice still had 20 minutes to run, we loaded my bike and went to the tea tent until the roads opened. We got to Union Mills but no sign of Mick or his bike, asking around, we were told they'd been picked up 20 minutes ago. Getting back to the garage, we found Mick looking at his bike with a long face. We bollocked him, sorry, we told him off, Mick sort of stuttered "another riders' van arrived and they said they'd drop me off." As Mick looked a little worried we told him we were only joking, and asked what the problem was. "It went bang" he replied. After breakfast he rang his dad, "Dad, help".

My bike, whilst not unduly fast was going reasonably well, so after giving it a quick check I started helping Mick get his engine out, turning the rear wheel we could hear horrible clanking noises. Mick's dad arrived not long before evening practice with a small case for clothes and big one for G50 spares. "Don't worry son" he said.

ME, RABBITING AS USUAL, 83 MICK WITHERS ON VELO, LES HART, FAR RIGHT IN GLASSES

My bike went bang in the evening practice, the garage was full of G50

MICK AND I STUDY THE PROBLEM

engine pieces the next day! Steve Bower's Kawasaki triple had been having minor seizures and he was complaining about his rear suspension, ordering new rear suspension units from a London dealer, cash on delivery. When they arrived, he'd sorted the

problem, so he told the postman to return them, not wanted. We were disgusted, I told him off "what's the dealer going to think about MGP riders? He may not help another rider when they need it". Steve's friend Dave, a chubby likeable chap, was the opposite of Steve. He was a strong chapel man, and on the first Sunday asked us to tell Steve he was going to the chapel for an hour. When we told Steve, his response was "if he's not here, I'll have a lie down." Another time, we found Dave asleep in the garage having worked all night, "tell Steve I'll be back soon." Steve's reply, "if he's not going to make an effort, I'll go down the beach." I can't repeat what I was thinking.

We stripped both bikes down. Mick's problems: both valves were bent, the piston wasn't too damaged and the crank looked okay. The small gear drive on the timing had broken, this stopped driving the oil pump and cam chain which caused the piston to hit the valves. His dad said "don't worry son, just a complete strip down." Mr Dunn could see we'd been pulling Mick's leg, "why is your bottom lip going up and down Mick? You can clean the inside of the piston, while it's apart." My problem was the big end again, back to the bus depot to see Fred again. He invited us up to his home in Peel to meet his wife, Joc who rode a 125cc Honda. Fred uncovered a Triumph, with the well-used saying, "I must get this finished one day."

Under Ray's supervision, after we'd rebuilt the crank we were, well Ray was, trying to true the crank on Harry's lathe, we both missed Thursday afternoon practice. Ray and I decided we didn't have the necessary expertise, so we took the crank to a G50 expert. We were all working in the garage when two lads started chatting to us, John Daly had broken down, as he had the year before, and Fred Pettit, his mechanic ending up helping us. Mick's bike was back together for Friday night practice, he had two steady laps. With Ray, John and Fred we rebuilt my engine, it took two hours just to do the cam timing. Mick was back from practice and kept us supplied with refreshments as he told us about his ride. We finishing at 1

ARTWORK ON THE FAIRING

am, I'm not sure who suggested we go and try the bike out but we all agreed. Unloading half way between Kate's Cottage and the Creg we started it up, Mick followed with the van lights on, oil was coming through and it sounded okay. Saturday night was the last practice, we all qualified. Sunday, I took Mick to the MGP riders Association AGM. Monday was spent working on the bikes, an evening drink at a pub on the course then finishing the lap. Tuesday we watched the Ltw and Jnr from the pit area.

I don't think Mick's dad would let him come drinking and doing silly things so Mick gave us his tickets for the rider's night at the Douglas Head Hotel. Ray, John, Fred and I went, Gerry was consoling Mick. As well as the boat race there was another silly game where four volunteers were made up with lipstick, powder and paint, by four ladies, why did I do it? There were several piles of ladies clothing ranging from underwear to dresses, when the music stopped we had to put on an article from each pile, first underwear, a ladies girdle then knickers, brassieres lastly a dress. When the organiser, Ken Harding, yes the beast of the scrutineers tent, said "First to take all the clothes off is the winner" I stripped down, and shouted "finished" to be told I was still wearing the girdle, but it was so comfortable, better than my body belt!

Wednesday, we took Mick down to sort the petroleum out, leaving the bikes and helmets, in the garage, ready for the "weigh in" then Mick went shopping for an hour leaving us in a garage. With Gerry and Ray, I found a small paintbrush and some black paint, we painted an arm, teeth and 'hi girls' on the fairing, and on the back of Mick's helmet. We were loading the bikes into the van when he saw the painting, he was jumping up and down, but it was too late to do anything. After Mylchreests Garage we went for a quiet drink, John and Fred joining us. While we were chatting, John was strumming his dad's guitar which had been through WW2 including D Day.

Mick was nervously looking forward to the parade, I passed on the advice I'd received to hang back on the ride up Summer Hill. On the parade we did the "hi girls wave" to the 100's watching. Waiting on the start line was Ray with Jenko who was helping Mick.

The flag dropped, the adrenaline flowed and I made a good start. I was in front of the rider I started with and pleased he didn't pass me, some very fast riders went by, but could see I was catching other riders. Before I knew it I was at Ballacraine, just missing the wall of the pub and shouting at myself "start concentrating." I was pleased I didn't wobble as much as previously at Doran's, I'd never passed a rider coming into the Glen Helen section, many had passed me, but I caught and passed a rider on the inside, *my God*, I thought, *the bikes going well*.

The long Cronk y Voddy straight seemed even bumpier than ever, the corners were coming thick and fast. Kirk Michael seemed even narrower this year. I felt I was riding well, and passed another rider through Bishop's Court. I was lining up for Ballaugh Bridge when there was a big bang, don't panic Mr Mannering! I had a slight wobble before I got the clutch in. Once over the bridge I pulled into the left, reporting to the Marshal that I'd retired, to be collected after the race.

The Marshal saw me across the road to The Raven pub where the landlord kindly gave me a meal. I watched the race from the pub carpark seeing Mick circulating as was Steve Bowers. The race was won by Sam McClements. Mick finished 43rd Steve Bowers 48th, John Goodall was 7th, and Jon Parkes from Worcester was 21st and first non-Japanese bike home on his G50 at 90 mph.

Although disappointed I'd broken down, I was in good company, the winner of the Jnr race, Wayne Dinham, Alan Jackson, Roger Cope and local hero Danny Shimmin, all on sponsored bikes also had DNFs. I congratulated Mick and, begrudgingly, Steve Bowers, who had been unpleasant to everybody all week including his own mechanic. At the presentation Thursday night, I chatted to Mick Withers who'd retired on his Velo and Stuart Hicken who'd let me have some spares, on his Vendetta G50, our group of this time failures, commiserated with each other.

When leaving the Palace Lido, where the presentation was that year, to stagger home, we saw Danny Shimmin put his hand down the front of a girls blouse and remover her brassiere. She, larking about, pushed Danny who fell down the steps. We asked each other "how could he remove a ladies bra one-handed?" and helped pick up a rather drunk Danny, not that we were much better! We were hanging onto one another as we staggered along the promenade and seeing a photo booth all crowding in. We were putting Mick on top of a post box, when a policeman with a white helmet and a long black truncheon came over, "do you think it might be a good idea to get him down gentleman?" In a slurred voice someone said "what a good idea Oscifer." As we past the Chippy Mick said "I swant some hips." So ended another Manx Grand Prix.

The first meeting after the Manx was a NGMCC meeting at Gaydon airfield. As I'd been doing well in the 4 stroke class, I was ringing around G50 people trying to scrounge some spares. Jon Parkes suggested that I ring Brian Coleshill. In my best grovelling voice I said "Mr Coleshill, I've just returned from the MGP on my G50, but with a broken connecting rod. I'm doing well in the 4 stroke class and wondered if you could you lend me a spare crank or engine." "I don't lend spares, but I may lend you the bike, how will I know you if I come to the meeting?" "I have a blue Ford Thames with Castrol and Loctite stickers on, and flying a union flag." "I like that, I may see you there."

I was working on the Greeves at Gaydon, when a Jaguar, towing a trailer with an immaculate G50 on it pulled up. A short, stout man in his early 50's hopped out, he had one leg and a crutch. "George, I assume" he said, as he shook my hand. I unloaded the bike, looked it over, and found it fitted when I sat on it, although it'd been built for a smaller rider. I rushed to Scrutineering then to practice on it.

In the break, he asked me about myself, then said "to save you asking, I lost a leg in a railway accident. In the race rev to 7400 in 1st 2nd gears at the start." Querying this, I said "I thought 7200 was maximum revs." "As long as it's not sustained, 7400 is okay, make them pass you, rather than you passing them in the race." I thought, *here speaks a good sponsor who knows what he's doing, no wonder Alan Barnett lapped at 101 mph at the TT on this bike.*

The 250cc single cylinder race was called, I got a reasonable start and was just trying to get used to racing on short circuits again. It was a good ride, I finished 6th. The tannoy boomed "4 stroke only race" I pulled a tag for the second row of the grid. The tension was a little more this time as I was riding someone else's bike with orders what to do. I made a good start, revving it to 7400 in 1ˢᵗ and 2ⁿᵈ gears and was in the top 6. I was trying hard, grinding the exhaust on the floor, thinking *this didn't happen in practice* as I passed two riders. I was so involved in the race that I was surprised to see the chequered flag, where had those 6 laps gone? When I got back to the van Brian was sort of hopping up and down on one leg shaking my hand "4ᵗʰ George, that's the best result I've had for a long time, I've had some right Wally's riding the bike." So, not only was I pleased with the result, but the sponsor was too. I told Brian about grinding the exhaust and maybe the frame, we felt that the problem was that I was heavier than most riders, and the bike could have done with longer suspension units, it appeared to hold the track like it was on rails. Colin Seeley made his name racing sidecars and started building his own frames before making them for solo machines. This frame was a Mk 2, a full frame where the Mk 3 and 4 used the engine as part of the frame and so were lighter, but I felt not as stable as the Mk 2. It was a good ending to the 1975 racing season.

BRIAN COLESHILL'S G50

A call came in for one pump to the M5 near Tewkesbury, there was a car fire with a person trapped. One pump from Tewkesbury, was already there when we arrived, Eddie Hawkins was in charge, I was in the back with Percy. We saw the car on fire, one fireman was trying to get the 5X branch to work. The 5X was a blood based foam making branch. It allows air to mix with the foam and water which expands at 10 to 1. I helped the young retained fireman, to get the foam gun working, having two switches for air and foam it wasn't easy. The appliance was parked at an angle in front of the accident, so other vehicles didn't run into us. The police in attendance, were setting out cones and we started to cut the man out. I must admit it got the adrenaline going, everyone was working as a team.

We had a call out to Beckford on the way to Evesham, a house near a railway bridge. A gas main had fractured and the leaking gas had caught fire. As it was close to the house I was detailed to spray water to stop the house catching fire but not to put the fire out as leaking gas could cause an explosion, the gas board turned the supply off. At another gas incident, some years earlier, we were on the way to Knightsbridge, near Coombe Hill not London, and as we were in front, we couldn't understand the message from the other pump, ambulance required at this incident, how did they know? The Sub Officer had fallen out of the other pump due to a faulty door, he had a broken finger.

It was a bad time with the IRA, and we had many hoax bomb calls. One such incident was near the gasworks, a suspect package had been spotted in a garage. Senior fire and police officers were looking at the package, while we all waited for the bomb squad who, on arrival, took cover behind a wall 200 hundred yards away from the package, looking at it through binoculars. You could see the look of horror on the faces of the police and fire officers who had been walking around the package, when they saw how cautious the bomb squad were, they were ashen white with beads of sweat. As it looked like being a long job, there was a canteen van, I was drinking tea, and munching a sandwich when I heard a loud bang. Nearly dropping my tea, I said "this was the real thing" however, it was the bomb squad exploding the box which turned out to be a hoax.

Ken Watkins, Dave Baker and I, having passed the leading fireman exam, had started studying for the Sub Officer exam. It was good to have somebody else on my watch interested in studying, Dave was on red watch. As the exam got closer, studying increased, when we were on shift, Ken and I would ask each other questions. At least this exam was about the fire service, pumps, fire prevention and taking drill, even when Dave and I were on a night out, we discussed the exam. Next time I was on shift I was allowed to take a 4-man ladder drill. I had given the order slip and pitch the 35' ladder to the third floor. Roger Smith was standing in from Gloucester City, and I noticed he was footing the ladder differently to the other firemen. As the other two were extending the ladder, it made it unstable and looked as if it was going to fall, I shouted "still" (a term meaning stop, danger) Once the other two firemen had stopped extending the ladder, I put my hand on it to try and steady it, but they let the extending line go, trapping my finger. My finger was squashed flat, and I was rushed to the hospital.

It must have looked very dramatic, a fireman in uniform taken into the casualty at Cheltenham General Hospital which was 500 yards away. I was taken straight in to a cubicle, as it had started to hurt, they gave me an injection which stopped the pain. Once things had calmed down a little I realised it was the finger I'd damaged when racing in 1968. It looked bad at first, where it had been trapped, my finger had gone flat but luckily the shape started coming back. There was no major damage but I needed a couple of days off work, not a very good start to my Sub Officer drill taking.

Exam day arrived, Dave, Ken and I, together with the other candidates, assembled in the main lecture area at HQ to hear a talk by Reg Herrington and Eric Nation, the same men who had taken us for our entrance exam 6 years ago, on what would we be doing. Several officers asked me questions about appliances; what kit they had and where, what type of pumps. I was trying to answer, but couldn't concentrate as Dave Baker was taking drill, I knew it was Dave as his voice was so loud it kept interrupting my train of thought. I apologised to the invigilator and explained that the noise outside was putting me off. I found out afterwards, that Dave had been told off, well informed his shouting was too loud and would let the other candidates know what drills he was doing. Afterwards Dave, I and Ken went for a pint, some weeks later we found out we'd passed the Sub Officer exam.

Next was a class 2 driving course as the rescue appliance (RA) was now based in Cheltenham. Derek Blackwell, the driving instructor who we all called Rory, was at the fire station on Monday for the 5 day course. The RA took four, Rory and the three under instruction. After airfield and cone practice we each had two days driving around the County, when Rory was satisfied with our driving, we started learning about all the rescue equipment. The kit was extensive and varied, including two large booms with steel hawser cables on two separate drums. On Wednesday, as we were driving towards Gloucester Station I asked Rory if we could stop so that I could buy a MCN, we parked the 20 ton fire appliance outside a small newsagents! During the tea break I read "For sale, G50 engine and spares, Barry Needle." There was an address, but no telephone number so at dinnertime I wrote, and posted a letter. I was thinking as I drank a cuppa at afternoon tea break, that the engine could be sold straightaway, so I sent a telegram, "Barry will buy engine, collect tonight George Ridgeon." Grovelling to mother to borrow her reliant, as it was economic, quicker and more comfortable, I left just before 7pm. I found the address, near Port Talbot, and over a welcome cup of tea asked Barry about his crash at Glentramman. The bike had suffered a lot of damage to the front end so he'd decided to break it. Barry told me he'd had three telegrams; "interested, ring me," one from Mick Dunn, "I will buy ring me" and mine, Mick never forgave me! Driving back I thought *I should have bought the gearbox as well maybe even the frame, but I'd just spent £500, too late now!*

Next day, as part of the driving course we went to Ashchurch Army Camp which was an MOD transport depot. I used to love going past it in the 1950's, it was filled with guns, tanks and DUWKs (DUWKs were used on the D-Day landings and could go on water or land). After being checked out by a soldier who came with us, we drove through the camp. I saw one of the many large hangers open I asked "what are all those yellow camouflaged Land Rovers for?" I was told that they were for the Shah of Persia but because of the troubles they weren't releasing them to the religious leader, Ayatollah Khomeini! The military had lent us some old heavy vehicles to use, we were pulling and pushing them with the booms and hawser cables. Rory showed us that if we were to lift a heavy vehicle by one side, to save twisting the chassis, we must have the other boom out at the same angle and attach it to an immovable object. Friday was the driving exam, Ted Nurse, transport officer with MOT qualifications, did all the usual things, I remember sweating as I reversed through the cones and was pleased we all passed.

I'd failed a leading fireman's promotion board, miserably, the position was given to Eric Dewhurst who'd been at Cirencester day manning station. Eric started a week before I passed my class 2. On the first day shift I was detailed to ride the specials. I hadn't finished checking all three machines when a call came in for a rescue appliance to Maisemore Bridge, Gloucester, there was a car in the river. After Eric had radioed in that we were preceding, I asked him what he knew about the rescue appliance, "not a thing George" he said, so I told him I'd just passed my course.

The fire appliances from Gloucester were already there when we arrived, and a police diver was putting on a wetsuit. Eric and I saw a car, half submerged, close to the bridge parapet. I pulled up adjacent to the vehicle, put the platforms down, similar to the hydraulic platform to steady the chassis, then swung the one boom out over the bridge in line with the car, extending it clear over the bridge, then I swung the other boom out shouting "put a fire appliance opposite the other boom." Attaching the steel hawser cable to the front of the appliance to take the weight, I took up the slack. I extended the other cable down to near the car. Bernard Allcock, a Gloucester fireman, told everyone including the officer in charge that the Severn bore was due any minute.

As fireman Allcock had warned, the bore came, taking the car away from the bridge to disappear on the other side of the river bank. "Thank you Lord," I said, it prolonged the agony of me making any mistakes!! Eric nodded. We moved the appliances to get traffic moving again, the police divers searched for the car. By the time it was found, I was never more pleased to see Rory Blackwell turn up. Rory was a gentleman, although he was telling me what to do, he maintained the illusion that I was still in charge. Once the police found the car I shouted out the orders as Rory whispered them to me, as if I knew what I was on about! I told the divers to take a line across attached to the hawser cable, which they pulled across as I fed it out, attaching it to the car. Once the car was out and on the bank we made it safe. As there was nobody inside, probably joy riders had dumped it in the river. At 17:00 Eric radioed in that we were returning to the station and available, both of us relieved. Rory did say that the weight of the car was negligible against the strength of the chassis, only very heavy loads needed the extra Boom, and told me I'd done well. Wow. It was a good day, especially when a dinner was sent down from Gloucester fire station.

We had another call with the RA, to a timber yard in Cheltenham, where I felt its potential wasn't used. A forklift had tipped over a bank, trapping a man's leg underneath. The senior officers there didn't know much about the RA, and were putting their faith in the jacking equipment to take the weight off the man's leg. I suggested positioning the RA at right angles, one cable to the top of the forklift truck, the other cable through a shackle to the bottom to take the strain, so it doesn't move, then pulling the top bringing the forklift completely off his legs, but the officers decided to use the old method.

Assistant Divisional Officer Ernie Taylor, finding out that we'd passed the Sub Officer exam, suggested we take the station officer's exam while we were still in the learning mood. Assistant Divisional Officer Taylor, with other officers, had started an IFE (Institute of Fire Engineers) course which would help us with the exam, as it was a lot more technical.

Although Ernie was helping with the exam, up to that time we hadn't got on that well and I'd had a couple of run-ins with him! Once, our watch was on drill, up to dinner time, with me and three other firemen, on pump escape drill for the last hour. We think he thought one of our watch had dropped him in trouble with his wife! In another incident, two pumps had been sent to Andoversford for a shop fire. The phone in a public phone box was ringing, I asked Lfm Hawkins if I should answer it. He told me to explain there was a fire incident and they should ring back later. As I left the phone box, Ernie shouted, "what the hell are you doing?" "Leading fireman Hawkins detailed me to Sir" "that's all right then" and I thought I was so lovable!!

For some reason I used to rub Sub Officer Gordon Lawson (Noz, as he had a big nose) up the wrong way. Not long after I started all the firemen were moaning about something. So in the tea break I mentioned it to our Sub Officer but when nobody backed me up, I got my first black mark. On nights, we were allowed to sleep between 23:00 and 06:45, if there were no calls. Noz would always kick my bed in the morning, so Dick and I swapped beds. Dick asked him why he was kicking his bed. It took a few days for Noz to start kicking my bed, we changed back again after a few weeks! For some reason Dick could do no wrong in our Sub Officer eyes, after morning tea break, Noz left his lunchbox, with one chocolate finger in it, Dick sucked all the chocolate off. At dinner time, Noz shouted "Ridgeon, I will get you for this" nearly sticking the finger with no chocolate up my nose. "Nothing to do with me Sub." I don't think he believed me, but never suspected Dick at all!

The year ended with the NGMCC presentation dinner and the CMC Christmas party at the club house. Worcester Auto Club was invited to the CMC party as they provided a lot of the marshals at CMC meetings. When Rocking all over the World by Status Quo came on, there would be two rows of bodies all head banging, with Harry Turner usually doing a striptease! In my spare time, I was studying for the station officer's exam.

CHAPTER 13   1976-God built my engine

The studying was hard for the Stn Officers exam; as well as firefighting, equipment, and fire prevention, there was legislation and general scientific principles including dreaded electricity. Arnold Pearce, now a senior officer, offered to help as I gave him apples and rhubarb for his winemaking. After two hours of going through previous exam papers, covering licensing and what the fire service did at such premises, most of it was still above my head, but what he showed me did help. He wished me good luck, in a pessimistic voice I replied "I won't pass, I know nothing about electricity." "George, what are virgins and virgins are rare." With an open mouth I said "what are you talking about Arnold?" "George remember these two sayings, What Are Virgins, equals watts, amps and volts in a triangle, watts at the top, amps and volts at the bottom. Take anyone 1 of these 3 away you either divide or multiply. The same with Virgins Are Rare, volts, amps and resistance, again a triangle with volts at the top." "Well that's easy to remember, thanks Arnold, virgin has taken on a new meaning." Back to studying as well as bike preparation, although Brian Coleshill had said that I could borrow the Mark 2 G50 for the first meeting.

Patricia liked going on holidays, she had a week in Florida when I was at the 1975 Manx. She suggested we spend a week in Spain somewhere, I picked Ibiza, Wednesday to Wednesday. Luckily I didn't need any nasty injections to go to Europe. I was still quite nervous about flying, especially when the plane took off. We got a Thomson Holiday bus to the Hotel, which although out of town, was close to the sea and had its own pool. There was a village close by where you could hire cars and scooters.

I'd never been abroad before, other than the driving trips to Germany. The breakfast was continental, no eggs and bacon, but plenty of it. We made friends with another couple, hiring a car each for a drive around the island. We filled up with fuel after two hours driving, as I drove out the garage I asked Pat "why is this fool on my side of the road?" quickly realising I was on the wrong side, pillock.

Pat had Spanish tummy one day, diarrhoea on the toilet and being sick down the bidet, me being horrible made a raspberry noise, then a being sick noise, finishing off with ratatata, luckily, I was okay. The Hotel had a resident band and a good Spanish compère. On the first night there was a Miss EL Greco, the name of the hotel, competition. There were many daughters and two nice girls on their own, being very friendly, but I behaved myself as Pat was with me. Next night was Mr EL Greco which we entered for a laugh, the small village had no nightlife, so we made our own. There was a regular bus to the nearest town, where we saw the police with their three cornered hats, there was a flat bit to the wall where they lent against it! We hired a scooter one day, and had a ride around ending up on a beach drinking Sangria, a fruity drink, and riding back to the hotel feeling a little peculiar. I found out Sangria was alcohol, I thought it was squash as it had a lot of fruit floating around in it!

Saturday was glamorous grandmother night, so some of us went to the weekly mediaeval banquet, like the one in Tewkesbury, plenty of eating and drinking. I was disappointed with the couple we'd made friends with as they refused to sit next to two Sikhs in our group, however, this was soon forgotten when the drinking started. There was a noisy German crowd, even noisier than me. After the Spanish waiters had filled the glasses using a large jug with a long spout, you drank the wine from a distance! The Germans were doing it while counting loudly, I said "I'd better have a go, to wave the flag." Standing up, I started pouring and drinking, when I could swallow no more, I just opened my mouth wide, luckily it all went in as I was leaning backwards, there were four people stopping me falling over, as I leant back to keep my head level. Somewhat sozzled I started a singsong on the coach home, dad's favourite, 'She'll be coming around the mountain when she comes.'

I found a motorcycle scramble on Sunday. We used a hired scooter to go to the scramble, which was up a steep hill, the so-called road full of rocks! A sign said Caballero 10 peseta, Señoritas free, the circuit was like all British courses, hilly. We sat on the grass with lots of people around watching a few races, not knowing anyone just enjoying the noise and spectacle. The next race I saw a rider wearing a union flag helmet, I jumped up shouting "come on Britain" cheering and waving my arms getting excited. Patricia said "George stop making a fool of yourself, people are looking at you." After the race a Spaniard came over with a large sheepskin of wine offering us a drink, the Spanish bikers could see I was an enthusiast, the British lad was working there, he did motocross in UK.

Leaving the circuit, I knocked the exhaust off while riding back on the rocky track and had to ride a very noisy two-stroke scooter, seeing a cafe ahead, I coasted to it, as I could also see a three cornered hatted policeman. A quick coffee to warm-up, then leaving Pat guarding the scooter, I found an open garage. Seeing a man working on an Austin mini, I used my Spanish phrase book and moving my hand appropriately said "Spannero?" Pleased that I got the exhaust back on, and there was no visible damage, I thanked the man. He pointed to the mini which wasn't running. It turned over alright, so there was plenty of life in the battery, I swapped the two middle plug leads over and the car started, the man started kissing and hugging me. "Get off" as Eric Morecambe used to say!

Monday was drag night. I wore Pat's brown dress and my roll neck jumper, with some towels stuffed up it for boobs, going as Old Mother Riley. Arthur Lucan used to wear multi-coloured socks in the 1940 films, I only had long socks to wear with my baseball boots. I used a headscarf, making it look like the old wartime headdress. There were some really good drag costumes, a chap was dressed in a bikini with oranges for boobs, another, in a corset and stockings and one who looked like a Spanish lady, who said when interviewed "my name is old mother Riley." When it was my turn I said "I'm the real Old Mother Riley, not that imposter, here kitty, kitty," Old Mother Riley had a daughter named Kitty! We were put into two groups of five with our arms linked around each other's shoulders, the band struck up the Can-Can. I was next to the chap in the bikini, while high leg kicking, one of the oranges fell out of his bikini top, I put my foot on it squashing it and went down, taking all the others with me. We just lay on the floor laughing, as was everyone else.

The last event was a Hawaiian night, and we were given flower hoops. There were some very nice ladies wearing grass skirts, showing lots of leg, I did suggest that I get my hedge cutters out! I decided to wear my swimming trunks and two small hotel towels, after remembering a cartoon in the Daily Mirror where an African native had a very long loincloth with the caption "he's only boasting." I used them lengthways so they went down to my knees. When it was my turn to be interviewed, I picked up one of the drumsticks not being used, poking it from behind through my legs, so that when the compare was asking me questions the front of the towel went up and down. The women in the front were crying with laughter. This was my first holiday abroad, I really enjoyed it.

I got the Greeves ready for the March meeting at Staverton, and was hoping I would ride Brian's Mk 2 G50. At the end of last season, I'd fitted a cylinder head with a different combustion chamber shape on the Greeves, that Gordon Morss had lent me, to see how it went. Starting the Greeves up in the Ash Lane, it sounding okay. At Staverton I was pleased to see Brian and the G50 arrive while I was pushing the Greeves through scrutineering, I took it straight to scrutineering, and first out for practice.

In the afternoon, I had a good ride on the Greeves. In the heat for the open 250cc race I finished second, the bike was flying. In the 250cc open final I finished 7th, just out of the money. Sadly the CMC didn't have a single cylinder race. In the 4 stroke only heat, I qualified for the final. The main runway was wide enough for one line of 30 riders. Basil James, the starter, moved to the rostrum and dropped the flag, bump, clunk, and the bike stuttered to a halt. I had it in 2nd gear, I put it in first, and it started okay, but everybody else had cleared off, so I rode the six laps to last-place. Sadly, this lost me the use of the G50. When I got back to the paddock, Brian bollocked me asking "why didn't you pull in after first lap, you wasted 5 laps of a race engine." Brian did thank me for getting him enthusiastic again, but said he would be training a young rider up, I thought, *I buggered that up!*

I was pleasantly surprised to have a letter from the lovely lady Caroline from Castletown, Isle of Man saying she was living at her father's boarding house in Blackpool and would I go and see her. My heart skipped a beat wondering what this was all about? I got around mother to borrow the Reliant 3 wheeler. I forget what lies I told her, and the white lies I told Patricia, about why I wanted to go to Blackpool.

The drive on the M5 was atrocious, it was absolutely pouring down, and the Reliant kept cutting out if I went over 40mph, as water was getting on the plug leads. Luckily the weather cleared up after Birmingham. I got to Blackpool and found the house but there was no answer. It was in a long line of terraced houses, most of which were Bed-and-Breakfasts.

I checked the letter again, right street, right number, going around the back I jumped over the locked gate and knocked on the back door, still no answer, when I tried the door it opened. It was a bit cheeky, but I made a cuppa and sat down, after putting the rhubarb inside the front door. After a bit, I heard the front door open and Caroline talking to someone she quickly got rid of, probably on seeing the rhubarb. She gave me a smile and cuddle, saying "how did you get in?" I left the questions as to why she'd asked me to come up, did she want to me to marry her, had she left her husband, until later, when she added "there's a dance on with a good group at the local pub."

I was dressed up in my posh suit, now comes another worldly wise thing I was about to learn, at the age of 30. Although I thought I was smart, she was brushing me down to trying to smarten me up, I know a waste of time. "George, which way do you dress?" I thought for a moment before replying "it changes, sometimes I put me right arm in sometimes my left

264

same with trousers." Okay, stop laughing. She was asking this as she was brushing around my nether regions, it means which way was my private parts hanging, to the left or to the right. This is the trouble with not being well read, like in 1972 at Richard's house when I didn't know what a bidet was!

The dance was going well, and we were chatting when she eventually told me she'd left her husband. I had it half right, but it wasn't me she wanted! She'd met this Australian and was going over there to live, leaving her children. She'd asked to see me to warn me that if I saw her husband and children, I wouldn't ask how she was. Why didn't she just tell me that in the letter?

I was studying for the Stn Officer exam and helping Jim Curry move his shop to Evesham. Dave Parry had taken over Jim's workshop. Dave was a good engineer, he'd done machining work for me when he was at Cotswold Engineering. I used to call into Dave's on the way home from night shift, to find out what was going on in the world of motorcycling, Dave had more of a business head than Jim and ending up running the yard.

I felt happy with the practical side of the fire service but needed to do more work on hydraulics, mainly the mathematical side, especially as we were now working in bars; with nights out with Frank I was more used to leaning on bars! I thought newtons lived in ponds, when I joined the fire service it was all in either pounds or pounds per square inch. I started to read about electricity from the fire service manuals, as you cannot see electricity move, I found it very hard to understand, but a good cure for insomnia, I woke up with my head on the desk more than once.

On the day of the exam, we assembled at Stroud Technical College, which is fairly central for the County. The practical questions were in the first part of the exam, followed by legislation, I didn't struggle as much as I feared I would. The science papers were in the afternoon session, my stomach felt like it used to, when I was about to start a race. The invigilator said "you may turn over your paper." After a couple of minutes, a few asked how soon they could leave, they were told, 30 minutes. I felt like leaving, but as when racing bikes, you don't give up trying until the flag drops.

The first question was on friction of water in the fire hose, I thought *I know all about this,* putting my name at the top of the paper, I started to write, then thought *perhaps I don't* and left it to later. I moved onto the fire protection question but I wasn't too sure! I looked at the two electricity questions, the first question was "you have a device of 3 Amps and 240

Volts what is the resistance?", drawing the 2 triangles "what are virgins" no , "virgins are rare" yes, that's the one, we have volts and amps but resistance is missing. Dividing amps into volts, the answer is 80 ohms. I knew resistance was measured in ohms. The second question was about earthing electrical systems, which I'd read about! Once I'd done the electricity questions I'd settled down, and went back to the friction loss and fire prevention questions. A month later I was amazed to find I'd passed the Stn Officer exam, and me still just a fireman.

Saturday, June 19th, Cheltenham fire station had a charity dance and fundraising evening, with profit from a light buffet being boosted by other events such as outdoor attractions including skittles. I made four comic firemen, like those on Candlewick Green, after seeing something similar at a fete some years earlier where four cats had shoes thrown at them. I also made a spinning wheel, like a roulette wheel, with numbers 1 to 10 on it, went to an off-licence and got some bottles of Pomagne, Champagne cider, for £0.50 a bottle, on sale or return, but the skies opened and it rained and rained and rained.

Most of the outside attractions were cancelled, including my firemen, but I brought my spinning wheel in. The Skittles was run, but modified to bowling from the tower in the dry with the skittles and the sticker getting very wet, even with his fire kit on! I went around asking people to buy a 10p ticket, all 10 sold. I moved the wheel to where people were dancing so they could see it spinning, then gave a bottle to the winner, which helped to sell the next 10 tickets! After about 20 spins, all the bottles of Pomagne were gone, I'd made a profit and was saved from taking any back.

I was racing with the NGMCC at RAF Wroughton near Swindon the next day. The track was very damp during practice but the day got better and we raced in brilliant sunshine. This was the start of the summer of 1976, little did we know it was to last 6 weeks with no rain and temperatures of 35°C. The first few weeks saw our fire calls increase from the usual 3 in 24 hours to 10. Turning up at work one day, we had no Jnr officers, I ended up informing control as it appeared nobody else wanted to. Control told me that a Jnr officer was being sent from Patchway fire station. Stn Officer Corbett detailed a fireman to be in charge of each pump, luckily we had full complement of firemen. Nigel Kirby was in charge of the pump I was on. Within minutes of being detailed, a call came in, one pump to field fire on the A40. As we were passing the turning for Gloucester near the Frog Mill Hotel, we saw a large grass fire and dropped a fireman off with a grass beater, no more than a mile further along the road was another fire, so we dropped another off, Nigel informed control. It was just Nigel, the driver and myself now, when we got to the incident there were two fields on fire, Nigel radioed control for another pump. The two firemen, we'd dropped off, arrived, after thumbing lifts with passing cars. We were there for a few hours before being sent on to another grass fire. With the number of fire calls going up, this meant servicing was being done more often, as the mileage between services was being reached more quickly. We had one pump with no locker door and had to store the rest of the kit were we could. We were given salt tablets on the pumps. Having not been told how to use them, one fireman swallowed a pill whole with a glass of water, he was immediately sick, it should have been dissolved in a jug of water!

We had a call to Gloucester, a fire in a hairdressers. Once the fire was out we were supposed to be tidying up, but were using the hair washers to cool ourselves down, in full fire gear, the temperature about 30°C and the fire, we were hot! I think a barn fire or a large grass fire was worse, in the middle of nowhere you can't get any refreshments. I do remember one farmer bringing out bottles of beer which I didn't like, having been put off it at the age of 5 by my Dad, but on this occasion it tasted like nectar!

Within a week there was a hose pipe ban, the grass turned yellow and even trees started dying. I did see Cheltenham Borough staff watering some flowers on a roundabout, I'm sure I complained, but never heard any comeback! When on nights, we started to sleep outside, one shift we had a very light drizzle, so as the Bible says "take up thy bed and walk", we just moved the mattresses into the appliance room, although what little rain that did fall, did no good. Often, when arriving on a night shift, we would be dispatched to relieve the day crew fighting a fire, sometimes not getting back until past midnight. With grass fires, as it stayed hot all night, we sometimes missed grub altogether so we started carrying sandwiches and squash. With the grass turning brown and trees dying, the countryside started to look completely different. At home, we'd kept the septic tank, although it had become redundant when the mains sewer was installed up the Ash Lane in 1974. There was a fairly high water table in the village, so it always had a few feet of water in it, back to the bucket and rope for watering the garden.

We had a call to Ullenwood Golf Course where a light aircraft had crashed. Ullenwood is a large estate, which also housed The Star Centre for Disabled Youth, near the Air Balloon pub at Birdlip, for those who know Gloucestershire. I'm sure the golfers were tearing their hair out as we drove across the golf course, to this single engine monoplane crash, it was lucky the ground was rock hard from the long hot summer. We were ordered to put foam around the aircraft with the appliances being kept up wind of the incident. There were two bodies in the Piper Comanche aircraft, a doctor pronounced them dead at the scene. The police were on site, and we were ordered to leave everything as it was, the plane was carrying large drums of extra fuel and the Civil Aviation Authority (CAA) needed to see it. The CAA arrived and more police. The blood foam was now beginning to get down the throat a little as the temperature was above 30°C. When the CAA said everything was okay, the OIC asked for volunteers, there were four of us. It was quite difficult handling two large bodies with so many broken bones, we were all covered in foam and what with the smell of fuel, the blood foam and damage to the bodies I must admit I was coughing a little, however we got them out, and laid them by the ambulance.

I decided after three years of unreliability with the G50, to ask John Goodall to build my engine. I took the engine to RAF St Athan, near Porthcawl, where we had our first holiday in the caravan in 1959/60. John was an RAF sergeant on the technical side, he showed me round which I found very interesting. I went back two weeks later to collect the finished engine, hoping to avoid last year's fiasco, it cost me £50 which I felt was quite a good price. I also had Barry's spare engine.

I saw a 500cc Goldstar for sale in the MCN, it was in Cheltenham for £175, which was quite cheap as they were normally £250. I rang the man and asked if I could call in on the way home from work. At first the bike looked okay, the engine was an aluminium cylinder barrel, engine number ZB 32 in a BSA frame. I raced a BSA but the gearbox looked different, however the man showed me a picture in the Goldstar book of the gearbox, then the phone rang. On his return he told me "someone else is coming in 30 minutes, do you want it or not?" I said I'd take it now and paid him the asking price. It turned out it was a plunger engine and gearbox, in a swinging arm frame. Some weeks later I found a plunger frame in Suffolk and did a deal over the phone. I contacted Roger Corbett, who as well as being a top motorcycle racer had started a transport business, delivering specialist equipment. "Roger, I'm going up to Suffolk, can I take anything for you to help pay the petrol?" I'd contacted him the year before, knowing he went up to London I asked him to collect a fairing from Ken Inwood for me, Roger collected it, charging me a gallon of petrol only. After I'd done the trip to Suffolk, Roger asked if I'd like to help him by doing some driving as his business was going well, so all through the hot summer, in shorts and a pair of baseball boots, I went to Wales, Scotland, Midlands and London, earning petrol money for the Manx GP.

The Seeley G50 was ready for the S100, I was using the same settings for the G50 and Greeves as the year before. I took Robert Price, who was now 16 and starting racing, having bought a 1963 Greeves racer, it would be good practice for him, helping me with my Greeves. It had been agreed that I would pick Ray Wakefield up on the way there. On the way, Robert asked "what is that humming noise?" we saw that the temperature gauge was on hot. I pulled over onto the hard shoulder and lifted the central engine cover, no need to get out of the vehicle on the motorway. Luckily I was carrying a gallon of water, and finding a rag before releasing the radiator cap, filled it up, only to have it boil again, at least we were near a services. After filling up with petrol, I rang Ray and asked if we could pick him up at the services nearest to him.

I gave Jackie a kiss on the cheek for bringing Ray to the services, and after loading his kit, we were off again, boiling twice more. I had an old horse type blanket in the back of the van, to cover bikes, we used it to save scalding ourselves, as the van filled with steam each time it boiled, we got this off to a fine art. The van started humming a mile from the docks, but we took a risk, seeing the boat we thought great, but the sailors were waving their hands indicating no. All the ramps were up and secured, we'd missed the boat, so we went to the fire station, a fireman on the day shift said that we could sleep on the floor. We took him out for a pint in the evening, in the morning he kicked us out.

We allowed two hours to get the boat. It was less than 3 miles but we found a hold-up, we didn't panic at first but after a 20 minute wait I asked someone what was going on, to be told it was an Orange Day parade, there's a large population of Irish in Liverpool. As it was still going on, I started doing my Cpl Jones in Dad's Army "Don't panic Mr Mainwaring," it passed eventually, we just made the boat.

The paddock was now in the field opposite the main assembly area, signing on, and scrutineering, the only trouble was it had a built-in alarm clock when the first bikes started up, very early at 4:30 am! I did a lap of 73 mph on the Greeves in the first practice session, pulling the gearing I had, if I wasn't 14 stone, it would have pulled a lower gear for a few more mph. The G50 was also going well, with no apparent problems. The beauty of having an extra pair of hands, was someone else to cook breakfast and two of us checking the bikes before going down the pub for ablutions. Ray was buying Robert beer, even though I'd said he was underage. Although it was very hot in the Isle of Man, there was no water shortage, so we could wash as much as we liked. I didn't win the Mularney Trophy but enjoyed the 250cc race, friend Richard Swallow was 20th, myself 28[th,] note to self, must

lose weight. The senior race went well too, and I got into the invitation race. I'm not sure whether it was celebrating getting into the invitation race on the G50 or drowning my sorrows for not winning the Mularney trophy in the 250cc race. I was 16th in 750cc race. We were quite tiddly when we left the pub, walking, or was it staggering back to the campsite. I was woken up by rain, and saw Robert attempting to urinate, half in and half out of the tent, a grumpy Ray, put his foot against Robert's backside and gave a hefty shove. In the morning Ray complained about his behaviour. I defended Robert saying "well, it's your fault, for getting a 16 year old drunk." I saw Caroline's husband in the bar of the George Hotel, he told me he'd be moving back to Huddersfield with the children. I called into the MGP office as we left the Island, I'd been accepted.

One S100, I took Geoff Garbutt, CMC race secretary to help me. We were woken by the police in the middle of the night, "any of your crew missing? We've got a drunken male who could only say campsite." In the morning, we found a man lying on the grass!!

Arriving for duty at Cheltenham I saw a poster advertising the 1st Tewkesbury Bath-tub race, they'd dropped the pram race which supported the benevolent fund. A Bath-tub race sounded easier and more fun than the pram race so I contacted Tewkesbury to find out how to enter only to be told, "sorry George, it's all full up." "Oh, you want a Tewkesbury team to win." "We only have one bath left and have used all the donated foam up to make them float." I replied "I was going to supply the bath and make it float myself," "okay come and pick this bath up."

I asked the officer in charge if it was OK to keep the bath in the back of the appliance room while we found a way to make it float. I'd talked Jim Mason into being the second in the bath with Brian Bates as team manager. In 1971 Nigel Kirby had been on Red watch when they had a charity bath-tub race so I asked him what was the best way to make the bath float, to which he replied"I used a tractor inner tube." I asked Harry and Ivor where I could get a cheap inner tube from. They recommended Firestone and told me to mention their names. I saw the manager, and explained that Harry and

Ivor had suggested I talk to him, who I was, why we wanted the inner tube and that we'd put their name on the bath. He liked the idea, gave us one for free, and a rude message for Harry. Whitbread's Brewery was next on the list of sponsors as their HQ was in Cheltenham, they not only made a donation, but supplied crates of beer for the entrants and 3 Whitbread T-shirts for us to wear. I went to Dave Parry Motorcycles to tell them what I was doing, Dave said "put my name on the bath and I'll give you £5."

Jim, Brian and I started to work out how to make the inner tube fit. It was a tight fit, so we used some old fire hose attached to the bath, around the tube and back to the bath, so it wouldn't come off. The Boy's College Swimming Baths was next to the fire station. We fixed up with the college authorities to test the bath, and with the okay from the Stn Officer, contacted the Echo for a photo shoot to get some publicity for charity, the fire service and the Boys College. After finishing the night shift, Jim, Brian, Stn Officer Corbett and I went round to the baths, and the bath was lowered into the water. It certainly floated, but it looked high in the water as there was no weight in it yet. Getting in was another matter, it reminded me of the 1950's when Big Brother took me in a rowing boat that rocked from side to side, "Dave, I'm scared"!

Jim got in first then me with Brian steadying the bath, but when he let go it immediately turned over, much to the amusement of everyone there. It was a good job we tested it early. The waterline was too high, there was no stability. Wondering if the tube was too inflated we let some air out. The bath was steadied again, after we posed for the photo it turned over again. The photographer said "don't worry, I got a good photo before you turned over." Back to the drawing board.

On our next shift, the three of us and Nigel discussed the problem and agreed we needed a bracing bar at the back with two empty 5 gallon drums. I had one at home, and we scrounged another from the workshops. We got some 2" by 2" wood, long enough to be able to strap the drums to using more scrap fire hose. Another test and our bath was now unsinkable, don't mention the Titanic! Speaking to the Tewkesbury firemen they said "we've tested our bath tubs, you won't beat us."

We found sitting facing one another, as we'd been told the other teams were doing, wasn't ideal for racing, it was suggested that we both face forward. At first I was in the front kneeling, we swapped and Jim tried, but it was too uncomfortable. We decided to fit a length of hose halfway along the bath, so that whoever was in front, could turn round after the start, sitting with his back against the fire hose. We tried it and it worked well, from somewhere two large canoe paddles appeared.

The race was in early August. After booking in, we lowered the bath into the River Severn by St John's Bridge, near to the oldest pub in Gloucestershire, The Bear. 11 baths were in the water, all but one from Tewkesbury: fire station, Rotary club, rugby and football clubs; we were the only outsiders. Most people were laughing at our bath to which I'd fixed a Union Flag, we had Whitbread on one side, Firestone on the other, and a large piece of cardboard on the back with Dave Parry Motorcycles, HELP another upside down, Titanic and QE3 on it.

We were having some gentle banter with the other bathtubs when we saw a motorboat coming down the river too fast, the lady driver let go of the steering wheel when she saw the baths in her way! All 11 baths were trying to get out of the way, on the crowded riverbank everyone was laughing, it was lucky no one was injured. The motorboat did hit us, and bashed into St John's Bridge, but no damage was done and it was some entertainment before the race even started, it looked like a Keystone Cops silent movie.

The starter called everybody into line, the starting pistol went bang and with a big cheer from the crowd, the other teams went off, we hung back, paddled a little before Jim turned around, we didn't want to draw attention to ourselves by being different from everybody else. Two teams, possibly rugby teams, paddled straight into one another and started attacking each other, both sinking, we overtook two slower baths quite quickly, which left five in front.

We got into a rhythm with me at the back shouting "together, together" although it was for charity, to me it was still a race. We overtook two more, and could see a bridge a few hundred yards ahead which we were convinced was the finish. Brian was running along the bank shouting encouragement, we overtook another, we were now second and closing on the leader with about 50 yards to go. We just squeezed by on some choppy water, we were in the lead and shouted to Brian "is this the finish?" "No, it's another quarter of a mile to the old mill." We both shouted "bloody hell!"

We were trying to find words of encouragement for each other, we'd used our sprint finish too early. Trying to keep the rhythm, every so often I shouted "together, together" but my mouth was so dry. With both of us facing forward, we didn't know how close anyone was. The old mill was getting closer, we could see a small wooden jetty with lots of officials on it, now 20 yards away, it appeared the officials were saying "slow up okay you have won." I smelt a rat and shouted "keep going Jim." When well past the line, we stopped paddling to find Tewkesbury fire team was less than 5' behind us!

We eventually turned the bath upside down which was difficult with the two oil drums on, and broke my flag. As we swam towards the jetty we could hear "boo, hiss, boo, hiss." I thought, *is this a pantomime?* Once out of the water the crowd were shouting abuse and "you cheated"! After a quick discussion with Jim, I told the organisers "you can stick your trophy." This was after we'd donated the money collected and the free beer given

to us by Whitbread for all competitors. We were persuaded to take the prize from the Mayor of Tewkesbury, a post Jim Mason was to hold in the middle 2000's! Stn Officer King had organised the award ceremony, he'd taken over from Clarrie Heath who was somewhat of a character in Tewkesbury folklore and had retired some years before.

Stn Officer King in welcoming the Mayor, said that he was ashamed of people being so unfriendly, especially as it was a charity event, he mentioned the money we'd donated, and that we were competing at our own expense, which we had other than borrowing the van for the actual trip over. I was going to go back to Whitbread's suggesting they make a larger donation and had some extra publicity as they'd sponsored the winning bath. Luckily I hadn't, the next night in The Echo newspaper on one side of the front page was the heading "Cheltenham win first bath race" but on the same page "Cheltenham firemen accused of cheating by Tewkesbury Licensed Victuallers who would not support the benevolent fund again as the Cheltenham fireman had cheated with a special unsinkable rubber ring." We found out that many people had lost money because they were gambling on a Tewkesbury team winning. I felt

273

ashamed, having my name in the newspaper saying that we'd cheated at a charity event, however I cheered up a little when I next saw Dave Parry, instead of £5 he gave £7.50 "George, I was really pleased to see my name leading the race all the way up the river with 1000s watching on the banks." I'm still trying to find a cine film if anyone took any.

The MGP arrived, Mick Dunn was stopping at Mrs Jackson's with his wife Jackie and two children, John Daly stopped with Nanny Dugdale as he called her, he was racing his 500cc Triumph Daytona again and popped around with updates. Ray had come over and was stopping at his usual accommodation and I made contact with Fred. Steve and Barry were stopping with Fred and his wife Joc as everyone called her. We agreed, if there were no problems in practice, which pub we'd go to for a good night and a singsong, always travelling the correct way round the circuit, supposedly a Manx and TT tradition.

John and I were at the Woodbourne, which was within walking distance from our accommodation. The Woodbourne had a very jolly landlady and 100's of photos of motorcycle racing around the walls. Leaving the pub at chucking out time, I bumped into a slightly inebriated, very pretty young lady, and asked her if she'd like to come to my digs for a cuppa. She said yes but when we got to her taxi, her friend said "no way." John worked marvels, looking very hurt he said "Oh don't worry about my feelings, I know I'm ugly but it doesn't matter." The other girl started feeling sorry for him and agreed to come as well. When the taxi driver chipped in "I want my call out fee" we paid it before going back to Mrs Jackson's for a tea and cake. I showing the young lady my bike in the garage, had a kiss and cuddle, then we took the girls back to their tent on a campsite just off Bray Hill, John and I stopped for another hour!

Halfway through the next day, John came around saying "come on George, we have to pick the girls up." I replied grumpily "I have a bike to get ready". Although John was racing he wanted to go, so after he kept nagging, we collected the girls. When they saw how old and knackered we looked without the alcohol haze, the day didn't go well. After a while I said "we have to get back for practice, would you like to come and watch?" but they didn't want to, we didn't see them again.

I was working in the garage when I heard a terrible scream from the house, Emma had gone into Mrs Jackson's mother's room, there were pills all over the floor with Emma sat in the middle, no one knew how many she'd swallowed, if any. As Mick was away getting spares, I was the only one there with a vehicle. Leaving the oldest girl with Mrs Jackson, I grabbed the little girl, and with Jackie, rushed to Nobles Hospital. I was standing in A&E feeling surplus, when I heard a Welsh voice from behind the curtain. A bare backside was looking at me, it was Barry Needle, he'd stabbed his bum getting over an iron fence while watching at Sulby. When a doctor said "I need to do some work on him," I replied "cheerio Barry, keep your end up!" He had to have extra foam on the seat of his TZ Yamaha to stop the pain. As little Emma would be there for some time, Jackie said they'd make their own way back. When I told Mick what had happened, with his dry sense of humour, he said "last time I bring the Mrs and kids." Luckily, Emma hadn't eaten any of the pills and was fine. Mick had moved to a 350cc Yamaha, at breakfast I quizzed him on his gearing so I could work out the approximate speed he was doing, 145mph was the rumour going around the paddock. I should have realised Mick didn't know what his gearing was, but it did cause a buzz.

I was now friends with John Daly, and got to know his sister Ann who I called mud flap Annie, after she showed me a picture of her racing a Yamaha with mud flaps on, in a production race. Ann was married to Rupert Murden and had two children, Janet 10 and John 9. We were still doing the 'high girls' wave when greeting one another, especially when we saw Mick Dunn, until one night drinking in the Crosby. We started making motorcycle noises, Rupert did a very good Manx Norton and G50 single noise by making his throat rattle while saying "rhubarb." We ended up shouting "halt, who goes there?" when seeing one of the gang, the response was "rhubarb, sounding like a Manx Norton." Yes, you're right, completely nuts, but we had some fun.

Practice was nearly over, John was round saying "I'm going flat out through quarry bends in top." This was a dark twisty section, 3rd or 4th gear if you had a 5 speed box, if you were lucky. We checked his bike, he was on Brands Hatch gearing, so from then on, when we saw John we said "jet down, and gear up John."

On race day I did the 'high girls' wave along the prom, Ray was not on his own in my pit, he had Fred to keep him company. Steve and Barry were in John and Mick's pits. All of a sudden it was just 10 seconds to go as the pair in front of me were flagged away. Even though I'd been racing for five years, I was still a bag of nerves while waiting for the start. The bike was going well enough, but felt I wasn't riding as well as I did in 1975. Although in practice I'd broken 91 mph average for a lap, I didn't think I was going that fast but, as good riders have said "the fact you are riding smoothly can mean you are actually going quicker." I came in for fuel on the third lap, and three laps later, having had no major problems or scares, I finished 23rd with a race average of 88 mph. I only just missed a silver replica, as the cut off speed was 89 mph. Les Trotter won the race on a Crooks Suzuki at 98 mph. John Daly finished but Mick had a DNF. Friday was our last night and the gang went to the Crosby for a singalong with John Daly and his father's guitar. Rupert and Ann had to catch the midnight boat, as they left, we all stood up and shouted "halt who goes there?" Rupert did the "rhubarb" noise, other drinkers must have been thinking, *they've escaped from somewhere!!*

Gaydon was being taken over by British Leyland as a test circuit so this was to be the last race meeting there. This was a shame, although only a short circuit, it was very demanding, the paddock was close so you didn't have to walk miles to watch when you weren't racing and it was only 40 miles from home. In the MGP, when you cross the finish line at the end of the race, you have to stop at the end of the pit lane, only a few 100 yards away. Coming round paddock bend on the G50, I saw the chequered flag signalling the end of practice, I sat up and shut off, another rider hit my clip-on so hard it actually moved, luckily not trapping my hand but we both wobbled. Wally, I'd forgotten that I was on a short circuit with the rest of the lap to go before pulling in.

The 125cc twin and 250cc single cylinder race was called, I put my hand into the bag to pull a number out, and it was on the back row of the grid, "damn, and other profanities" I mumbled, with 35 starters that was 8 rows back. I'd read a book when I started racing in 1964 where the author suggested that if you were at the back of the grid, start pushing before the starter drops his flag, as he is only looking at the front few rows. The flag hesitated, I pushed, luckily he carried on dropping the flag and my bike started. I missed all the riders still pushing, and came out third. I was following two riders on twin 125cc Yamahas, managing to pass them before the end of the first lap. As the saying goes 'the red mist descended,' if they want to pass me, let them try. I rode hard and didn't look back. On the last lap, I caught up Robert Price who'd just started racing. I momentarily thought, *shall I not lap Robert, but there maybe somebody up my exhaust pipe,* I was 1st!

The last race of the day, at the last race meeting, was the 4 stroke only race. John Goodall started the race as he'd crashed at the Manx and wasn't fit enough to compete. There had been a 15 minute hold-up as a sidecar in the previous race had spilt fuel around the circuit. John shouted "are you ready?" He walked to the rostrum holding the flag aloft, then down it went! A good start put me in the top 10. I overtook a few riders and noticed a few off, starting the third lap, I was leading the race thinking, *my goodness, can I win two races in one day?* The answer was no, coming into the right-hand bend at the end the start and finish straight, braking hard and changing down two gears, suddenly I was sliding along the track and decimated a straw bale. Luckily I didn't hurt myself or the bike too badly, but had to be picked up after the finish. Back in the paddock we found out that 12 riders had fallen off in the race due to a fuel spillage all around the course caused by a 2-stroke, but I did win the 250cc single cylinder race at the last meeting.

Back to the reality of work but at least the long hot summer was starting to cool. In the Isle of Man, I'd been having baths and showers as often as I wanted. Here, we were still having to save water, we'd put a brick in each of the water closets to save water, turned off the automatic flush on the urinal at night, only flushing the toilet when you went to number 2 and saving bath water to water the garden, as the hosepipe ban was still in force.

I heard, at Dave Parry Motorcycles, that Williams Motorcycles were having a BMW test day. Luckily I had my crash helmet in the van and was wearing my Motor Craft jacket given to me by Ford as I used their plugs for racing. The salesman asked if I'd like to test the RS 1000. I gulped, "that sounds very nice, can I borrow a pair of gloves?" I mentioned that I was a Cheltenham fireman and raced motorcycles, I was pleased when he said "I've heard your name."

I was told to follow a route going through Bishops Cleeve, left at the pub heading for Tewkesbury, turn left at the traffic lights, through Pamington, known as 'seven bends,' and back through Bishops Cleeve. I was also told that I must keep to the route for insurance purposes. I set off very steady, I'd fallen off a racing bike at Staverton in the 70's having slammed the back brake on, thinking it was the gear pedal. I found it difficult in built-up areas to keep to the 30mph once I became confident. After negotiating the very tight left hand corner closely followed by a right in Bishops Cleeve then going through the sweeping left/right hand bends, still in the 30 mph area, I was struggling, *I thought they said this was good at road holding,* until I realised I was doing 80 mph in a 30mph area! I slowed until I got into the de-restricted zone then opening the throttle to over 100 mph, it was so easy. I was now getting used to the flat twin 1000cc monster. Although it was off the route I rode to Dave Parry's, "Dave can you service the bike please?" We had a laugh.

We had a fireman join the watch who'd transferred from London Fire Brigade (LFB) we called him Mexican Pete as he was tall and slim, with a small moustache. I bought his 500cc Triumph Tiger 100 and his wife's motorcycle suit which fitted Pat.

I had some time on my hands after Jim Curry moved to Evesham and our dancing lessons at Listers finished after Mrs Lister upset everybody, so I finished off the year with some part-time work at a taxi firm in Cheltenham.

December was very cold with frosts and snow, most normal sports were cancelled, but it didn't stop trials and scrambles, the TV had to show more of this. There was a thaw just after Christmas so Cheltenham Racecourse was gearing up for their New Year's Day meeting, however, with the thaw a land drain fractured flooding the course, we took one pump on a special duty call, to pump the water off the course and into a small stream. This was standard practice, if there was an emergency call, the pump would leave, luckily for the racecourse, there were no calls. They supplied us with a warm meal and even a gold cup ticket which I let George Rudolf have for £1 as he'd helped me racing and liked horseracing.

CHAPTER 14   1977-Jubilee year, first depression!

I thought, being a royalist, union flag waver and racing British bikes, that 77 would be a good year as it was the Queen's Silver Jubilee year, but it was a sad day at Cheltenham when we lost our 1950's Dennis F1, a real fire engine! We did keep the 60 foot WW2 escape ladder fitted on a Ford Firefly chassis.

Dave Baker decided to marry Maria on St George's Day 23rd April, but as the time got closer he kept asking "am I doing the right thing George?" "Dave, how the heck do I know, I've already buggered up I don't know how many relationships. Maria, living in Stroud, picked the Church on the Hill near Nailsworth, Dave asked me to be best man. I went out and bought a book, How to be a Best Man, and was surprised to find out what you have to do; pay the vicar and the organist, get the wedding party lined up at the reception, get wedding presents sorted, a bit like, stick the broom up my a*** and I'll sweep the floor in the same time!

As well as the wedding happening, the racing season had started. The first race was a club meeting on the 20th March at Mallory Park. The usual gang was there, as well as Gordon Morss, so a good scrap on the Greeves to look forward to, but instead, I came round in an ambulance, drifted off again, then came round in the First Aid centre at Mallory Park before drifting off again. Next time I came round I asked where I was, to be told, "you're in an ambulance on the way to Leicester infirmary." I woke up with doctors around me, complaining that my knee was hurting, I thought I heard "we'll put a drain in" would they screw a big tap into my knee? I finally woke up in bed on a ward. I was told I'd crashed on Gerards, same bend as 1974, flat out in fourth, but I don't remember a thing. I had a disturbed night before an early morning wash then breakfast, immediately being sick all over the bed, the nurse said "don't worry, it's a delayed reaction to being unconscious." Brother David came to collect me, when dressed, I looked in a mirror and saw my nose was flat to my face. The doctor told me as I was leaving that they'd wondered why I complained about my knee with my nose damage, my helmet must have turned when it hit the ground. It was a good job it wasn't an old pudding basin. Gordon Morss sorted out my bike, and found someone to drive my van home.

I was off work for two weeks. I saw a consultant who asked "do you want a quick wrench job on your nose or smacked with a big hammer and black and blue for a long time?" Being a coward I replied "I don't like the sound of that much," "okay quick wrench job it is then." 40 years is too late for regrets! I don't know why, but I started feeling sorry for myself, I'd never done that before, despite all my other crashes, I just got on with it. I was walking around with a flat nose until the operation then a slightly bent nose. I tried to cheer myself up by thinking *you're luckier than the 500 people who died in Tenerife when two Jumbo jets crashed on the runway,* but somehow I couldn't feel for them, just me!

I told my doctor "I don't feel very happy, is life worth living?" He gave me a pick me up. When I took a pill I started feeling tired, lay on the bed, waking up hours later. I threw them all down the toilet, I didn't want to get hooked! Dave Baker came to see me regularly, he was a bag of nerves before I had my accident, now he was climbing up the wall "will you be well enough George?" The accident was only four weeks before the wedding. I said "Dave, I'll get there even if I'm dead" trying to cheer both of us up! He was relieved when I got back to work. We went to Ken's Chinese restaurant for Dave's stag night, with two of his watch, Roger Smith and Stan Skinner, Dave was now stationed at Gloucester. I liberated a sugar bowl as a memento, but it took ages to get rid of all the sugar from my coat pocket!

On the day of the wedding, I drove Pat's Mini to collect Dave from his sister's. His sister decided my tie wasn't straight and starting trying to smarten me up, I ended up standing on the cat's saucer of milk as I backed away from being tidied up, eventually we were both ready. While driving over Horsepools Hill, we talked about the old days. Arriving at the junction of Painswick Road, I asked Dave if it was all clear, "yes," or so I thought he said, we missed a car by inches. "George, what the b***** hell are you doing?" "You said it was okay." "Oh no I didn't" - not another pantomime!

As we passed the bus station in Stroud, I remembered a winter in 1960 with a quarter of an inch of frost on my motorcycle gloves, there were lots of memories as we swapped stories trying to calm nerves until we got to the church. There were a few there that had travelled a long way, Dave talked to them as I was checking with the vicar that everything was okay. Dave and I were wondering where Maria's brother was, as he was bringing special service sheets as well as being an usher. I had to leave Dave as I needed to be on the door ushering until Stan Skinner arrived and I could give him the job.

Maria's brother eventually arrived and passed out the service sheets, he'd been having a new set of tyres fitted to his car, Maria said something unrepeatable to him at the reception I believe!! Being the cheerful sod I am, I said "Dave the Church is full, so no backing out now" Dave calling me some nasty names.

The service was going well until the vicar asked for the ring, I dropped it, it bounced on the floor luckily, not going down one of the many gratings, phew. A few of the lads made an arch of axes over the couple as I paid the vicar and organist, I was nearly late for the photos. I was now getting nervous, the speeches were starting after the meal. I introduced the bride's father who toasted the bride and groom, then David made his speech, with me whispering "no waffling Baker." Dave replied "I'm even getting barracked by the best man" which caused a laugh, then he toasted the bridesmaids, and it was my turn. I had a roll of newspaper, like a scroll "I've just written a few words" then I dropping one end, as it rolled across the table onto the floor, it got another laugh, which relaxed me a little, "I fell asleep listening to my own speech on a tape recorder, I hope the same thing doesn't happen to you." I told tales about Reigate, standing in the cat's saucer and mentioned the parents without whom there would have been no wedding.

I had a list from Dave which included the time they had to catch the train, and kept chasing them around saying, "Dave the time is getting on, keep moving" as Dave and Maria were going round the tables talking to their guests. A group of us put rice and confetti in their case, and put "just married" and a tin can on Pats car, as I was driving them to the train. Back in the reception, I chased Dave again "you have to get changed." I found out after the wedding that every time one particular auntie got to talk to David and Maria I came along, "Move along the bus please" I hope she's forgiven me! I drove Dave and Maria to the station, where we had a 20 minute wait, just as the train was moving off I threw confetti through the open window. When he got back, Dave told me that it went over some young lad, but that he laughed. Back at the car, I couldn't find the key, *my God, I hope I haven't thrown them on the train.* Walking up and down the platform, I saw them 12" from the edge, *thank you Lord!*

As Dick had moved to Stroud fire station, I asked John Wright, on white watch, to come and help me at the May meeting at Staverton Airport as he was a good mechanic. In the 250cc race I had a good dice with a single cylinder Montessa, we nearly collided at paddock corner! In the four strokes only race, I was vying for second place, with Mick Dunn and Dave Pither from Morton in Marsh, "God," I mean John Goodall, having cleared off. Riders wondered how he went so fast, he never seemed to hurry. We started catching John, looking at one another thinking, *are we allowed to overtake John?* He raised his arm to indicate he had a problem, so heads down and we really started trying now, with the chance of being first. In the run down to the hairpin, we were all very close, Mick leading, went onto the grass, we followed. Although we lost time we still held the first three places when we got back onto the track. Mick having a disc brake, braked much later than me and Dave, for paddock bend getting the win, I was 2nd and Dave 3rd.

I was still getting bouts of depression, was it the crash, or not getting married? I tried to put this to one side, and get ready for the Queen's Jubilee, which I was celebrating with my old village, Down Hatherley. We collected scrap iron, to raise money for the party to be held at the cricket club in Wood Lane.

We stored the collected scrap metal around the back of Jim and Josephine's caravan. I decided to give most of my 225cc Francis Barnett which I'd crashed early in 1962 and had been stored in the back garden ever since, the bike had been rusting away for 15 years and it was for a good cause. I kept the back number plate. Like thousands of other Jubilee parties in the country, we all dressed up, had flags and long tables, the jubilee cake was cut by Robert Vallinder as he was born in 1952. We played some silly games and ending up singing the National Anthem, *congratulations Your Majesty.*

The Jubilee party and scrap metal collecting had restricted the time available for working on the bikes for the S100, which was now a few weeks away, with a NGMCC meeting as a last practice.

I saw an advert for a contract butcher. Although I had plenty of work with the bike and working on my auntie Win's house in Barnwood that I'd bought in 1972, I thought I would make enquiries, I'd always fancied trying contract butchering. The job turned out to be the contract side of British Beef. Already having a job, I thought I could help part-time, but was told they didn't take on part-time staff. As I knew Neville Wilkins, now manager of British Beef Slaughterhouse from our college butchery days, I gave him a call. After I explained, he said he'd put a word in for me. I got a call from the contracts manager, "Neville explained the situation, if you don't mind being temporary you've got the job."

Neville was right, it was totally different, and not as enjoyable as working in a Butcher shop. There were, no customers, you were in a room with no windows, and it was a little like working on a conveyor belt. In a Butcher shop you cut the whole fore or hind quarter up yourself, here the top man did it with a chainsaw, which I thought was sacrilege, having learnt by using the hand saw! He would throw various cuts to the various men and lady butchers. You would be boning out the same joint for 2 hours before a tea break and lastly the foul language, even 17-year-old girls were using the F word every other word. At the end of the week the pay, plus a cheap joint made up for it, it only lasted for a few weeks until they found a full time butcher but it was an experience.

Frank told me that Gloucester Fire Station had organised a run to Bath fire station for charity, so I entered. There were 40 of us running 2 miles in pairs, then a rest before another 2 miles, all running the last mile through Bath. As we were assembling at Gloucester, I saw Stn Officer John Gough in an army T-shirt, having been in the Grenadier Guards, his T-shirt said "Join the army, meet interesting people from far-off countries, and kill them!" I ran with Bunny Coles, unfortunately, our 2nd leg was the last 2 mile stretch and, we had to run the last mile with everyone else. Luckily the station had a shower as I started going stiff. Dancing at the evening function, I ended up doing a striptease.

Bath Run, I'm stood behind the man having his pulse taken

I picked Ray up, and we arrived on the IOM a day early for the S100. Although I was trying to get both my bikes ready, I chased round suggesting we had a Queen's Jubilee party. A few showed interest, with Jack Higham, his missus and Mick Withers helping, we decided to hold it Wednesday, after early-morning practice and before the evening races. A few of us started with a radio playing 70's music and playing some silly games, others joining in. We had sleeping bag races, 3 legged and wheelbarrow races, not forgetting the 4 a side tug of war, British bike riders versus Japanese and 4stroke riders vs. 2stroke, that got everybody shouting. I was asking for loose change to give all the children a penny for entering or crashing out, 2p for top three and 5p for winning in the children's races. George Fogerty was enjoying himself, I expect World Champion to be, son Carl, was one of the youngsters. After the 3 legged race, I organised one with 5 people in a team, one behind each other, with opposite legs tied together. I laughed when I saw John Daly being dragged along the ground, luckily no one was injured. We decided to end the party, with everybody on a tug-of-war, using all the ropes we could find joined together. One of the sidecar rider's daughters, had a broken arm, she started it. We were all pulling when the rope broke, and everyone ended up on the floor laughing, a perfect end to the party. Probably because of the party I retired in both the 250cc and 500cc races, but I had been accepted for the Manx.

As I didn't have to rush back, I decided to enter the Jurby races, held on the Saturday, at the end of the S100. I spent all day Friday repairing the bikes. Luckily, the problem on the G50 wasn't serious, on the Greeves, I only had to fit a new woodruff key on the engine sprocket. Ralph Crellin, a Manxman, invited us to sleep on the floor, at his home near Sulby. We took Ralph and his missus to the pub before getting our heads down. I thought I'd been woken by a train but it was Ray snoring, I threw my shoe at him which at least made him move and stop for a while.

We were getting the bike scrutineered, I was behind Brian Banglestien in the queue. Brian was a really nice chap, but you could call him an eccentric, when not in a full-face helmet, he wore a long black wig with dark glasses, he looked a bit like Roy Orbison. The scrutineer asked him to put his helmet on, the rules had recently changed, instead of just inspecting the helmet, it had to be checked when being worn. Brian didn't want to take his wig off in public so he went to his van to change. There were several rumours, one of which was, "Brian was a millionaire or the boss of a big company and he didn't want anyone to know he raced motorcycles!" Jurby was where all the riders went during Manx and TT time to test their bikes. In those days you could just turn up with no supervision, if you fell off hard luck. Jurby was very bumpy, but we all had a good day as the sun shone.

Before I went to the Manx Grand Prix I attended another leading fireman's promotion board. There were two posts available, one at Gloucester and the other as assistant to the BA officer. One question was; "How could you stop the rivalry between Gloucester and Cheltenham?" I can't remember the exact words I used, but I answered "the only way is to transfer everybody from Gloucester to Cheltenham and vice versa, as you'll never stop rivalry." I was asked how I'd respond if I was offered the BA post. Good as that was, I said "thank you sir, but I would decline, I want to stay operational." Graham Nash, city fireman was asked what he wanted, "I prefer Gloucester but am willing to do the BA job" was his reply. I was later called in and offered the job of leading fireman at Gloucester to start 1st of August. I asked if they'd honour my booked holidays, not telling them it was to race in Isle of Man!

Although there'd been many watch changes over the years there was some regret moving from Cheltenham where I'd started in the Brigade.

Gloucester had been a brigade on its own and had a large workshop with a pit for servicing vehicles, which was now just used for storing fire appliances. On evening shifts or at weekends, firemen, with OIC approval, used the workshop to service their cars. There was a grinding and polishing wheel, plug cleaner and good benches with vices, so I was able to work on my engines getting them ready for races. As I was working on an engine, with a cuppa and the radio playing, various firemen would say "nothing better to do George?" It made me smile.

Mrs Jackson had stopped doing B&B, so we started camping in Nobles Park, a.k.a. The Paddock Hotel, along with other riders. It was quite primitive in those days, with a small portaloo flush toilet, sink and small shower and a cold tap for drinking water. The good side, you were yards away from scrutineering and the start line on the Glencrutchery Road. Many traders such as Ken Inwood, Ernie Coates, Dennis Trollope and tyre and carburettor people were also in the Park, handy if any parts were urgently needed. With many riders around, you could pick their brains if you had a problem, it was easier arranging meetings at various pubs, impromptu parties, barbecues and close when attending the Manx GP riders Association AGM in the Hailwood Centre. The negatives: the campsite was grass and everything got muddy if it rained, you could lose your tent in the wind, it was not as comfortable as B&B, and you had to do your own cooking, which meant food shopping.

I now had a spare engine, I'd found a four-speed gearbox, but just had the one Mark 3 frame which had cracked at the top by the engine mounting and had been brazed. Practice went well, other than the usual minor problems during qualifying, although I did have one incident, I suppose I nearly had a crash. Approaching Ballaugh Bridge I caught up a rider, we nearly touched when we went over the bridge together, I just missed The Raven Pub's brick wall. I remembered the number, when I checked, it was Emilio Toone, I apologised and we both had a good laugh. At the "weigh in" you could enter a club team, all three riders have to finish and the team's total time calculated. I entered a team for the CMC, finding anyone who wanted to ride to make the team up. I asked the organisers if Emilio Toone was in a team yet, as the answer was no, I forged his signature, and put a note on his seat saying "Emilio you are in the CMC's club team!"

We attended the MGP Supporters Club dinner organised by Gwen Crellin. Gwen was a lovely lady, who although a widow in her late 50's worked tirelessly for the MGP through the supporters club. The dinner was a sit down affair. There were the usual speeches before Danny Shimmin, a Manx coalman and a bit of a character, did the auction of donated items to raise funds for the rescue helicopter. Danny started; "who wants a sack of coal delivered for £1?" many hands went up, the price rising to £6.

There was no rescue helicopter at the Manx, despite the TT having had one for many years, paid for by the IOM government. In 1970, The Manchester 17 MCC started raising money to provide a rescue helicopter on race days, the first appearance was in 1971, which was my first MGP. They carried on up to 1975, but in 1975 rider Mick Bird crashed badly in practice, when the helicopter didn't operate, so he was left with serious injuries until practice was finished. This fired up Gwen, and the MGP supporters club was formed, raising money to support the helicopter for both practice and race days.

On Monday, I went to watch the "weigh in" for the Jnr and Ltw, then during the races, helped in the pits and encouraged friends who were racing. I was able to have a special word with Richard Swallow who finished less than 5 seconds behind Dave Hickman on a Yamaha who did 99 mph in the Ltw race. After the Tuesday night rider's night at the Douglas Head Hotel, where again, I was being stupid, my poor old suit was soaked in beer, good job we had Wednesday to recover before presenting the bike for the "weigh in" Wednesday evening.

Ralph Crellin with a French Knight!!!

The parade route from Mylchreests changed, it now went towards Quarter Bridge then backwards up the course. I felt it had lost some of its importance with this route, not as many people were watching. I was wearing a red, white and blue tabard mother had made. Looking at the photos afterwards, I looked more like a French Knight going into Battle at Agincourt as it was three stripes rather than a union flag, but I'd made an effort for the Queen. The Claxton sounded to line up, Ray and Ralph gave me the usual tap on the back as I went into the coned area. The bike started well.

The first two laps were going well but, I noticed on opening up after slow bends that the bike cut out, easing the throttle back, it picked up. At the fuel stop, I tried to explain the problem to Ray and Ralph. The bike started after the pit stop, but the cutting out was getting worse if anything. At least it was going well, once the throttle was eased back. I was pleased to see Governors Bridge on the last lap and punched the air as I crossed the line. I braked to stop and pull in, but on opening the throttle the engine died, the magneto had lost its spark!

The race won at 100 mph by Stephen (Snuffy) Davies from North Wales, a really likeable chap and a nutter like me. I was 46[th,] nowhere near silver replica time, in fact only Alec Swallow finished behind me, we were the last two to finish. Gloucester riders Derek Ackerman, Dave Pither and Ron Rowlands retired as did friends Mick Dunn, Richard Swallow and John Daly. Strangely more Yamaha and other 2 strokes retired, than British 4 strokes! We went to the presentation Thursday, then gathered at the Crosby Hotel, John, with his dad's guitar, for our last night and our usual singsong.

I had three hospital visits in 1977 but for good causes. Zandra gave birth to Matthew Prentice, Dorothy to John Wesley Meadows and Tina to James Cobley, all Jubilee babies, but news on the horizon was bad as the pay dispute in the fire service wasn't looking good. After numerous meetings over many months the FBU named November 14th as the date selected to go on strike if there was no settlement.

Chris Witts was in charge of the fire station one night. We had a call to Southgate Street, a fire in the basement of an 1880's 3-storey building. Chris sent in two BA with a high pressure hose reel. A man came out of the front door, Chris asked if there was anybody else in there, "No" was the reply as he coughed with smoke inhalation. Another man came out, again this one said that no one else was in there. I urged Chris to radio in a person's reported message to control, this means people may be trapped, when a third came out, 8 in all came out by the time we'd put the fire out. Pete Davies who was fighting the fire told us, "they were trying to get in the back door, so as well as putting the fire out we were trying to stop them going back in." We didn't know if the same men were going back in or if it was new ones coming out! It appeared to be some sort of communal lodging house. Luckily the fire was contained to the basement, and only smoke throughout the building, Chris and I still laugh about it.

I had a meeting with Divisional officer Joe Nash, who told me bluntly "I didn't want you at Gloucester, I prefer leading fireman Nash," (No relation) which did not do my confidence much good. I soon found out being a leading fireman was not a bed of roses, you had the Sub Officer, Stn Officer and above kicking you and firemen, who weeks before you worked with, were now kicking you too.

Being a bachelor, I had no heavy outlay or responsibilities, other than owning my aunt's house, 59 Barnwood Road, and I'd borrowed £500 from the bank which I was paying back at £20 a month, when I was only taking home £70 a month! I'd started to do the house up. Neal McDonald, a fireman at Gloucester, was living at, and making alterations to number 63 with his wife Jean, so we helped one another and picked each other's brains. I did spend a lot of money keeping the racing bikes going, but not as much as a family man with two children and mortgage!

I voted against a strike, mainly because I didn't want to withdraw my labour from helping people, as well as doing a job I enjoyed. There was some nastiness now with the press, one particular paper had printed something detrimental about firemen and the union, it was barred from the meeting for all Gloucestershire union members, where the majority voted to go on strike if no agreement was reached.

I was searching my soul and thinking of my Father, a strong union man, who would say "you have to stick together to be strong," but I still wasn't happy, and wrote to Aunty Win in Canada, that I'd heard about work drilling for oil in Alaska. She wrote back "that's very hard life!" I also thought about working for nothing, but that wasn't practical, if I had worked, I would have given my wages to the fireman on strike.

At least bike racing kept me cheerful, especially at the NGMCC meeting at RAF Colerne, just off the Stroud to Bath Road. Practice had gone well and I qualified for the 250cc and the 500cc 4 stroke races, when a chance to ride the new Cotton racer came up. The machine had an Austrian Rotax, single cylinder, water-cooled engine. Pat Onions, who together with Monty Denley, took over ownership of the Company in 1954 had retired, to concentrate on the NGMCC. To my surprise, the new boss Terry Wilson, came over "George would you ride the Cotton in the single cylinder race, Dave Tandy decided he couldn't get on with it." I rode it up and down the paddock, readjusted the levers and said "okay, I like it." The bike had Brembo twin disc front brakes and a single rear disc, my Greeves only had a 6" back brake and 7" twin leading shoe front! Being tall, I could start the bike well, and I was lying fourth, but coming into paddock bend I locked the back wheel and slid off. I did get back on and finished the race, Terry Wilson was quite pleased with the result. I apologised for slipping off, and suggested that, as I'd qualified for the 250cc final, I ride the Cotton in that.

289

I must admit, I forgot the rule that you must ride the bike you qualified on. I finished in the top 10, there was nearly a protest for riding the wrong bike, but as I wasn't in the money, it didn't happen. I said to Terry "I've entered a race at Silverstone in October, if I adjusted the machine more to my riding position would you let me ride it?" "Okay George, as you helped us test it." The October race was postponed as Silverstone was being resurfaced, and would be held in November!

It was less than two weeks until the strike was due to start, unless an agreement was reached, we were all popping in to the station to find out what was going on. Everywhere I went, people were asking me "you're not going on strike are you George?" I brushed the question aside by saying that negotiations were still going on, I tried to relax at dancing, but the problem stayed in the back of my mind.

On the deadline date all three watches and fire prevention staff, were at the station before 09:00, the night shift was still working. There was no word yet and Ron Jones, one of the union Reps, was on the phone. Everyone was mumbling to one another, the press there, it was tense just waiting. They were some officers in the FBU but most were in the National Union of Fire Officers (NAFO) so they weren't governed by the vote. No word of a deal came so we were on strike, John Gough gave Frank a half bottle of whisky as he drove off.

NAFO weren't on strike and would get any pay rise on offer, which was p***ing everybody off, it was made worse by Robin Gray being made up from acting Stn Officer to full Stn Officer. He joined NAFO before the strike, causing a stab in the back feeling, he'd deserted his workmates for money. It was initially decided that we would do our watches on picket duty, so in theory working for nothing, however that was quickly changed. After a few days we agreed to work a rota system, with 7 groups of 8, it was just two picket duties a week, one day and one night.

The first week was no hardship for anybody really. I had my bikes to work on, in fact reading in the MCN that a Seeley Mk4 rolling chassis, was for sale in Liverpool, I bought it, also to my surprise, the meeting at Silverstone was still set to go ahead in late November. I went over to the Cotton factory to adjust the back brake, making the bike suit me better.

On the way to Silverstone, going through a wooded area near Stow on the Wold I saw some trees cut down and a pile of large logs, I thought *hope they're still there when we come back, good for the brazier in front of the fire station.* The Works Cotton went well in practice, after which, I checked the bike over with particular attention to the siphon water cooling system. I won the first race, the trip to the factory to adjust the back brake so it wasn't so fierce had paid off. The weather was dry but cold, so when not working on the bike, I went into the café and bought something warm, yes I spent money!! In the second race, the bike started well but I ran over somebody's foot who was still pushing. I was vying for first spot when the temperature gauge started climbing fast! I backed off keeping the revs down, with a two laps left I dropped to 3rd. With one eye on the red line on the rev counter, the other on the temperature gauge, which was above its safety level, I really needed a third eye, to watch where I was going! My left hand was on the clutch lever, just half a lap to go as I approached the corner I'd first fallen off at in 1965 testing my first Greeves, I was hoping the same didn't happen again. I finished 3^{rd,} so ended my riding the works Cotton.

On the way home, the logs were still there, but when I put this huge log into the back of van, it went down even more. Stopping at the fire station on the way home, I threw the log out saying "this should last a bit longer." They cheered and started chopping it straightaway. With members of the public bringing in many and various pieces of wood for the brazier, we had a huge pile of wood.

I was surprised and pleased to have a call from Neville Wilkinson from British Beef, "George, do you want help out the contract Butcher as the chap they had hired was no good and they got rid of him?" I'd thought of ringing him, but didn't want to go grovelling, perhaps Neville knew I might need some money.

The same people were there and the girls still used bad language, but I got great satisfaction when cutting and boning a piece of meat, and I found out more about the common market. To keep the price up for farmers, a certain number of cattle were purchased, British Beef were paid to cut them up, shrink-wrap the meat in plastic, and chill. I found out what a beef mountain was. I didn't really understand it, but it was a different type of subsidy to keep the price up for the farmer. This meant more expensive meat for the consumer, and to add insult to injury, it was usually sold cheap to Russia, instead of some third world country! The job, although part-time, was bringing in money, and I could buy meat cheaper for myself and the lads.

291

A month before the strike started, I was officer in charge on the day a man came onto the station and said "we run a tile delivery business, we're looking for drivers until we get set up." I told him to leave a phone number, gave him mine, and told him I'd find him a rota of drivers. This is what Dave, Frank and I were doing when convenient, when the strike started. We had two spare people who could do it at short notice if necessary.

When driving past a fire station we could stop for a chat. I was driving in London which was quite scary, one-handed with the A-Z in the other. I stopped at a fire station, introduced myself, and was having a chat about the strike, when an elderly lady started laying into the fireman. "My brother was killed in the war, this strike is disgraceful" we were all trying to pacify her. I said "excuse me my dear," before I had time to say anything else the lady replied "don't you my dear me." I did admire the lady, who wasn't scared at all. I again chipped in "excuse me my love" which made it even worse! I then said "I can only apologise madam, I'm from Gloucester, that's the way we speak down there, I certainly didn't want to show you any disrespect." After delivering the tiles, I got lost, and ended up stuck in traffic turning into Harley Street. Thank goodness for the A-Z, I tried to avoid the traffic and ended up going through Regents Park, eventually getting out of London.

The driving job was cash in the hand, but with British Beef tax was taken out at source, so I decided to pop into the tax office. I explaining that as a fireman I was on strike, and asked if there was any chance the money I was earning butchering could have my tax code attached so that I paid less. The very nice young lady said "I could, but it would be a lot of paperwork and complicate it when you return to work, and you would lose out," did I chat her up?

I attended the CMC and NGMCC end of season functions, but as I was on strike, I couldn't really enjoy myself, I was still touchy when anybody made a sarcastic remark about the strike. There was some fun when a NGMCC committee member held up an envelope, "this is free membership for next year, who wants it?" It was strange but nobody made a move, he repeated "come on, don't be shy, who wants it?" I made a move as did somebody else, we ended up charging, nearly knocking the committee member down and ending up in a pile on the floor with everybody laughing, I had the free membership.

Whenever I passed the station, I popped in to ask if there was any news. For a while newspapers were taking pictures and something was on the news every night, but after a big fire at Battersea Power Station there was a news blackout on fires. The Royal Navy were helping to fight fires in Gloucester during the strike. When a Green Goddess, a wartime fire engine, went by, we all waved. Two of our lads, Don Saunders and C B Gorman, were ex- navy, Don on top, CB in submarines, Don had a Red Ensign that he waved as they went by.

The dreaded Christmas was coming, I was now feeling really sorry for myself, crashing, getting depression and now on strike! I used to like Christmas when I was young, but now it was just a lot of hard work. I always tried to be nice to people all the year round, not just two weeks a year. I liked to attend midnight mass to celebrate the birth of Jesus, but with the strike no one was feeling happy.

Negotiations didn't seem to be going very well. Some Christmas lights appeared around our lean-to made of salvage sheets, it looked a bit like a stable where Jesus was born! We had no Christmas tree, so myself and Phil Dyer chopped a down a fir tree at the side of the station, was it George Washington who said "I did it with my axe?"

Christmas dinner on strike! Me, Arthur Williams, Dick Chew, Chris Witts on camera

Our group had drawn picket duty on Christmas day so the eight of us agreed to split the day. Len Griffin, who ran the Chequers Chip Shop, had been supplying us with fish and chips every dinnertime and 21:00 hours. What a surprise, when at dinner time on Christmas Day, Len supplied a full meal. I suggested we have our meal on the forecourt of the station, we were on strike and shouldn't be ashamed, everyone agreed. A trestle table appeared from the station, along with Chris Witts, Richard Chew and Arthur Williams. We had Christmas dinner with passers-by taking photos.

We were relieved at 2pm so I went over to my big brother's. I wasn't really in any sort of mood to celebrate, but enjoyed playing with Julie and Sally's toys.

CHAPTER 15   1978-A classic parade

The New Year came and went, the only good thing about the strike was I forgot about being depressed being so miserable!! The FBU had turned down one offer after six weeks of strike action. One thing had convinced me that we were underpaid, perhaps wrongly, was a fireman with a wife, two children and mortgage repayments claimed benefits, not for himself as he was on strike, and was getting £2 a week less than when he was working, so a person out of work, with the same commitments, would be getting more.

After nine weeks, the same offer was again made to the FBU, but this time it included a guarantee that all future pay rises would be linked to the upper quartile (posh word for quarter) of male manual workers' wage rises. Everyone that had been on strike was in the dining/recreation room when in came the now Assistant Divisional officer John Gough, with another officer and Robin Gray, the atmosphere could have been cut with a knife. Although Robin had been a really likable fireman, the majority felt that he'd stabbed us in the back by leaving the FBU and joining NAFO days before the strike. Everyone was mumbling so the union rep Ron Jones, said that unless he (Robin) left the room, we would cancel the vote, he left. The offer was accepted and we went back to work.

The first duty shift started as if nothing had happened. Off duty firemen stayed on as there was a lot of administration to sort out with everybody's pay and tax. The council were offering an interest free loan of £200, to be paid back by monthly deductions from pay. Being brought up by mother, to save and to look after the pennies so that the pounds looked after themselves, I accepted the loan, and paid it straight into my building society, which was paying 10% interest! There was still tension between some officers and firemen, but basically we returned to doing the job, drills, risk visits and fire calls.

I was collecting something from the Green Shield Stamp shop, opposite the Bon Mache, and was stood there daydreaming, *what's the next job?* A light came on in the brain, and I headed for the doorway with purpose in my step. I went down three steps, holding the banister rail while looking at items displayed on the wall on the left side, when "bang," I was sat on the floor with blood pouring from my nose. The steps lead down, not to what I thought was a glass door, but to a fixed glass window. Staff came to help, taking me to their restroom. After I'd somewhat recovered, I thanked them, but thought I'd probably sue them!! I went to the family solicitor, who'd dealt with my motorcycle accident 1962. Mr Ring had retired so Mr Whiteman himself dealt with it. We walked the half mile to the shop doorway, after looking he said "yes we can do something." He told me that they wanted a report from a consultant which would cost £35, good job I was sat down, it was nearly a week's wages. Luckily the depression had gone and I was back in a fighting mood, I paid it. Some weeks later I was told that they'd made an offer of £50 plus all expenses, I'd asked for £100. I told Mr Whiteman I'd leave it in his hands but to get as much as he could. I settled for £80 compensation, £35 for the consultant report, plus Mr Whiteman got his expenses, but my poor old nose!

I heard about an auction of engineering equipment, near Stroud in early February, I was always looking to buy tools. There was a large hall full of various items. Outside the hall, lot 1 was a large pile of clear plastic machine covers, but there were some black ones, about 5' long, 3' wide, okay to cover a motorcycle. Lot 2 was 3000 flexible tubes, 2" diameter, lot 5 was 5 drums of hydraulic oil. It was slow start for lot 1, I bought them for £34. I bid £5 for the tubes to get things moving and was surprised to win the lot. I bought the 5 gallon drums of hydraulic oil cheap. Inside the hall, I was interested in 10,000 cable ties, numerous electric motors and other electrical equipment, even an old-fashioned type, bacon slicer, which as an ex-butcher, I thought I might be able to shift. I spent £400, mother had a mild wobbly at me for bringing more junk home. I couldn't sleep for tossing and turning, *what would I do with all the stuff I'd bought*? I needed help with the electric motors and contacted Tony Powell, chairman of the local Vintage Club. Tony was an electronics expert; he'd made an electronic ignition for my Greeves in 1976. He was always busy, when I collected him he was willing to come, as long as we stopped off at the Vintage Club first. We got there to find members struggling to remove a tree stump. As it was close to a wall, I used my heavy duty jack that I'd rescued from work. Similar to jacking a car apart when rescuing someone, we used various pieces of wood and the wall to push the stump out. Tony then came home with me, the problem was the electric motors were 110 volts, but they were cheap, I still have a few if you want one!!

I'd told the Vintage Club members that I'd a feeling the airport didn't want us racing there anymore and asked how they felt about putting on a vintage parade at a race meeting, everyone was enthusiastic. When I said to Tony "right we have a month before Staverton March meeting, how many bikes can you get?" a look of horror appeared on his face. "We couldn't do it that quickly George," At the Wednesday bike meeting of the CMC I told everyone "I'm willing to do the work to run a vintage parade at the May meeting to show the council we're nice people."

Patricia found a cheap week in Benidorm. The drive to Luton airport was not good, okay, I got lost, why are women no good at reading maps? Although the weather in Benidorm was overcast, it was much warmer than home in mid-February. The hotel looking very posh outside with its own swimming pool. One reason why holidays were cheaper in Spain, they have no fire regulations, certainly nothing like we had in the UK. There was a stairway leading from reception, to the top floor with no fire doors. There were scooters for hire so, taking refreshments, we mapped a 30 mile round-trip, with a list of attractions to visit. We rode through the mountains and as it was warm, we stopped for a lie down. I must've nodded off, but was woken up by Pat's screaming, there were small lizards, which reminded me of the newts I used to catch in my village, running everywhere, including over Pat!!

The Moorish castle, although closed, was very impressive. It reminded me of the film El Sid with Charlton Heston. It was now 3pm, and we started to make our way home through more mountains, but it was cold out of the sun. Going through a small village, I saw a cafe and with my Spanish phrase book ordered, "Dos coffee." As Pat was cold I also ordered her a "Uno Grande Brandy" the girl serving us looked bemused! By now we were quite hungry, again, I checked my phrase book, "Pan" for bread, "Queso" for cheese. The girl was now looking blankly, so again I said "Pan and Queso" this appeared to make it worse. By this time the old men playing cards, wearing their black berets and looking like something from the Spanish Civil War, were watching the entertainment, one of them shouted in Spanish "they want some bread and cheese you silly girl." She nodded and brought a lump of dry bread and some cheese. Being so hungry, we weren't worried, but I broke out into a cold sweat, when I remembered I'd no Spanish currency, well not enough to pay what was less than £1 in local currency. Like a cowboy drawing at lightning speed, I pulled out my Spanish phrase book, showed her an English pound note, and told her that it equalled the 130 pesetas. Luckily she believed me, accepted the £1, and even gave me 20 peseta change!

On a walk, not far from our hotel, I heard someone trying to start a car and failing, I could see the man just turning the key and pumping the accelerator pedal, so I offered to help. I indicated for him to open the bonnet, pointed to the sparking plugs and said "spannero" while making an undoing movement! I took the plugs out, two were wet, after drying them, the car nearly started. I took them out again, but this time put the wet ones in the dry cylinders and the dry plugs in the wet cylinders, after spinning the engine over to clear out any spare fuel. This time the car burst into life to a huge cheer from a cafe opposite, the man offered me some money. After looking at the phrase book I told him not to mention it. He hugged me, I did the Eric Morecambe "get off"!

Pat and I made friends with a young Spanish married couple and went out with them for a meal. They ordered Paella, a rice dish with lumps of meat in. When I lifted my fork and saw an octopus leg, complete with suckers, I dropped my fork with a scream, the rest of the restaurant turned to look, Pat said "for goodness sake George, stop making an exhibition of yourself," me?

The holiday was over after a final swim in the sea and an evening at a nightclub with Spanish dancing and a man with balls on long strings that he twirled around his head, which looked dangerous if they hit him in the wrong place! Our travel group was called together and informed there was a problem with our aircraft causing a delay. They didn't know how long the delay would be, and we were to wait in the lobby. Although we'd had breakfast, it was hours ago, so we agreed to go to the café over the road in groups. At the airport, many hours later, there was another delay and many were grumbling. I could understand families with young children having a whinge, but not really the elderly, they were leaving a warm country, and the temperature in the UK was -5°C with snow on the ground. I found two comfy seats and we soaked up the sun. We got back to the UK late and went through customs with a very large donkey, a present for Pat's granddaughter Clarissa.

I went to the NGMCC practice day but while riding the G50 I ended up in a large pothole. To be honest I wasn't concentrating, the wartime tarmac had lifted and there was a 4" deep hole, the size of a car. When I got the bike back to the van, I found a large dent in the aluminium rim, I hadn't checked the tyre pressure, it was less than 10 psi, no wonder the bike wasn't steering very well. Luckily I only had to buy a new rim as the front tyre wasn't damaged. I went to Frank Jones, now 70, he'd been a wheel builder for Cotton Motorcycles, and did a good job for a racer. The wheel was finished in time for the March meeting at Staverton where I'd entered the Greeves, the G50 and the Mark 8 Velo.

A 4 stroke only movement was gathering pace nationally as the domination of the two-stroke bikes was spoiling racing for some of the spectators. A national championship was started by Kennings, a tyre company, with rounds at National motorcycle meetings, usually at the end of the day after the main race, but we were hobnobbing with top riders.

I was organising the Vintage parade at Staverton, and decided to ring up Geoff Duke, to me still the best motorcycle racer. I must admit I was in awe just speaking to a demigod, "Mr Duke, we're running a vintage parade at the Staverton Road Race meeting in Gloucestershire. I understand you used to do a lot of trials riding in Gloucestershire in the 1950's, would you be guest of honour?" He was very friendly and helpful, "it's a little difficult for me at the moment, there's a lot going on in the Isle of Man, why don't you ask Bob Foster, he was a Gloucester man and was World Champion in 1949?" I contacted Bob who said he'd be pleased to be guest of honour.

RUSSELL WEBB, JOHN DALY, JOHN GOODALL, ME, UNKNOWN, TONY RUSSELL
SNETTERTON PADDOCK

At a Kennings round at Snetterton I was going well when Ken Inwood overtook me on his Norton, cutting in front, causing me to brake hard, the front wheel locked solid and I was sliding down the track damaging the fairing so couldn't continue. I bought a new fairing off Ken, who did me a special price as he'd caused the problem, but again reminded me that I'd run over him at Staverton! After fitting the fairing, I checked the bike over but couldn't see why the front wheel had locked up.

I'd started asking friends to bring their classic and vintage bikes to Staverton for the parade when a problem occurred. I rang Tony Powell, "Tony can I come and ask your VMCC members to bring their bikes to the May Staverton race for the vintage parade?" I was surprised at his response "no, the VMCC will run the parade and in August." It was left that I would speak to the CMC committee on Wednesday night! I explained to the full motorcycle committee, the work I'd done and that Bob Foster had agreed to come. It was confirmed that I would run the event in May. Again, I asked Tony "can I come to your vintage club meeting?" He reluctantly agreed, so I was a little nervous, expecting some of the members to say "get stuffed" but when I explained "I want you to ride your bikes in a parade, I'm hoping this will bring some status to the race meeting" they were all very enthusiastic. I asked if anyone had a 125cc BSA Bantam that my mother could ride, as she used to ride one, one member agreed to bring one. When I told mum she was riding a Bantam in the parade her face lit up, bringing a tear to my eye. Biting the bullet, I rang Tony Powell again "Tony would you judge the vintage parade and what classes and sort of prizes do you think we should we have?" I was relieved when he agreed and suggested; best vintage, best classic, best racer, best in show with three rosettes for each class. So, that was sorted, now more advertising to get good coverage.

My next race meeting was Cadwell Park. In the one race I got a bit grumpy, there was a pileup at the hairpin with waved yellow flags, which means danger, no overtaking, but one chap overtook several riders including me. I did report it to a marshal, but nothing happened.

At a national meeting at Donington Park, I was working on the bike when I heard on the Tannoy "will all the classic 4 stroke riders attend the race office". An ACU (motorcycle sport's governing body) official, Ernie Woods, gave us a lecture on how noisy our bikes were, the ACU had, a couple of years ago, introduced a decibel limit of 110. He told us we were all breaking the db limit, then went on to tell us how to silence the bikes, which I thought was very fair. Modern bikes had silencers, two stroke manufactures, like Yamaha, had designed an expansion chamber with silencers, but the bikes we were racing were designed in the 40's, 50's and 60's, with an open megaphone, so we were all struggling. I did at one MGP try to silence my bike by wrapping some old fire hose around the megaphone hoping to muffle the sound, but after 1 lap of practice it had burnt away, did I get some stick!

The weather was overcast, drizzling and cold. Practice had gone okay, but during our race it started to drizzle again. I was circulating mid field when Alistair Frame, riding a BeeBee Brothers Manx Norton, went flying by to lap me. The next bend, there were yellow flags out as two riders had slid off, Alistair rode round three slower riders!! In the chicane, a rider moved over causing me to brake, the front wheel locked up again. Although I was going much slower than I'd been going at Snetterton, as well as my pride, I injured my shoulder, and feeling knocked about, was taken to the first aid centre. After being checked over, as I felt woozy, I slept for a little while in my van.

Feeling better, I went to watch some of the racing, seeing the ACU official that had given us the noise lecture, I asked him what he thought about overtaking on yellow flags, "I don't like it, if I saw somebody do it, they'd be in trouble." I told him about Cadwell and today, and asked him to have a word with Alistair Frame. I was surprised to hear him say "you'll have to make an official complaint." I didn't really want to do all that, I just wanted him to have a word, but he insisted.

I was mumbling profanities on the way to the race office, I'd changed from Mr Nice to Mr Nasty. In the race office, I said "I saw Alistair Frame overtaking on a yellow flag." They gave me a pad and pen and told me to write out the details. With my sore arm I was struggling to write the complaint, and I had to pay £10. The group of race officials, including Bill Smith and Ernie Woods, went in to a huddle. "Sorry, we can't do anything as it's over two hours since the incident." "But I fell off in the race, I was in the first aid centre for ages, then went for a sleep as I still felt poorly." Their response was "sorry, can't do anything it's too late." In a bad mood, I said "from now on only show me two flags, the start and a finish flag if you're not going reprimand riders for disregarding flag signals when reported. You're a load of wankers and you've pissed me off." I think they were somewhat taken aback by my outburst and weren't smiling when they went back into a huddle. They gave me my £10 back and said "the ruling is two hours but we will have a word with Alistair Frame." A call was put out on the Tannoy "Alistair Frame to report to the race office." I waited for a while but he didn't turn up, so I left it that they would have a word with him. As I was leaving the circuit, I saw the man from BeeBee Brothers, I told him that I didn't think much of his rider overtaking on yellow flags and asked where Alistair was, "he's changing, I'll tell him what you said." On the way out of the circuit I saw a phone box, and rang the circuit to speak to an ACU official, "George Ridgeon, I just made a complaint, Alistair Frame is still there."

Following the brake locking up again, I got an engineer friend to strip it down, he found that when the wheel was rebuilt, one brake drum had been pulled out of true, I got it skimmed.

With my sore shoulder I couldn't ride, so had more time to sort out the vintage/classic parade. Like most people with an arm in a sling I wasn't supposed to drive but everybody does. I had Pat to help me with the paperwork and although I couldn't knock stakes in I was at Staverton on Saturday helping where I could, and asking officials to make an area for the classic bike display. Arriving early on Sunday, I was relieved when the first few bikes arrived and got the riders to sign on. I had a list of who had entered and had arranged for the first parade to be just before the start of racing so that marshals could have their lunch break. Bob Foster, now 68 was not well, he'd suffered lifelong with asthma, which stopped when the bike started in the race, and started again after the race finished, perhaps it was something to do with adrenaline. We had Ron Langston's ex works Manx Norton racer, Ron Roebury was on an ex-works Honda 125cc and many riders from the world of vintage racing in the parade, many different makes of bike, a 1904 sidecar outfit which Bob Foster had a ride in, and the 1912 Triumph that was in "Wings" the TV series about First World War Flyers.

A REALLY HAPPY DAY FOR MUM

The tannoy sounded "will all marshals please return to their posts, vintage and classic riders please get ready." Mother was there, brought to the circuit by Tony Price, wearing her suede coat, blue stripe trousers and black corker helmet, she'd even found the old leather handbag, on a long strap, that she used to hang over her shoulder, but the man with the Bantam hadn't turned up. Mother was looking very sad when a gentleman with a BSA Bantam asked if she'd like to ride his Bantam, mother's eyes lit up. The bikes were all on the circuit when John Husband, a mechanic at Malcolm Davies Motorcycles, turned up on a 500 Thruxton Velo "am I too late George?" Although he hadn't signed the disclaimer, waving my good arm, I told him to get out there quick, and take it steady. As the bikes were circulating, the commentator mentioned the star names and pointed out the many makes of bike. I was pleased to see the spectators showed great interest. It was quite comical with some of the older vintage bikes and mother going steadily and racers revving their machines to 14,000 rpm! One entrant, Curley Rogers, a motorcycle dealer from Redditch, had a 1947 plunger Goldstar, as I was feeling left out, I waved Curley down and got on the back for a lap, with no helmet and my arm in a sling.

I got back in time to watch the bikes come in, mother rode in with a big smile "I wasn't half going George, but I went onto the grass at the hairpin." "Don't worry mother, we've all been on the grass at the hairpin." There was so much interest that a second parade was hurriedly fixed up. The man who'd promised a Bantam for mum, did turn up eventually, but mother didn't want to go out again, well, she was 75 and hadn't ridden for 15 years. The bikes and their rosettes were put on display. We got a good write up in the local paper, with a photo of Bob Foster showing a pretty lady a Manx Norton. The headline was; This is the machine Geoff Duke rode when he took my world title in 1950.

My shoulder got better in time for the long drive to Scarborough, for the next Kennings 4 stroke race. As usual I arrived just in time for Scrutineering, but noticing that the clutch lever was loose, I left the bike in the Scrutineering Bay. I went to the nearest van, BeeBee Brothers, and asked if they could lend me screwdriver. He looked me straight in the face, and said "I haven't got a screwdriver in the van." I thought *you lying git*! It was payback as I'd complained about his rider. Practice went okay, and I finished midfield in the race but, I scared myself coming down the hill to the start/finish. The G50 was quicker than the Greeves.

After buying what some would call junk, from the auction at Stonehouse, I had to find ways of selling it to make some money and clear some space. I took some items to race meetings like cable ties and bike covers, making a few pounds each meeting. The city council ran a Saturday stall market on the Cattle Market car park. Although it was £3 to have a pitch, I thought I'd see how it went. The first week I made £7, I sold the oil to a bus company, and the radio style boxes, cheap to an electric shop but it was money and space. The bike covers, well machine covers, I sold for a £1 each, and gave some to Jim Curry and Dave Parry, on a sale or return basis. I got a call from Jim asking how many covers I'd got, a motorcycle spares business man, wanted to buy them for 75p each. I had over 400, so for £34 outlay I made £300.

Every Saturday, except when I was racing or working, I was at the cattle market selling cable ties. I had bought 300+ small Phillips screwdrivers, which I sold to another dealer cheap. I must admit I was enjoying it, chatting to all the ladies, especially when the sun was shining. I ended up doing some exchanges; somebody offered me a push bike for an old-fashioned mowing machine. I started going to local house auctions and an MOD sale to see some welding gear. The welding gear was no good, but I stayed, and sat next to a chap who wanted to buy the 56lb iron weights for scrap but was moaning the sale was going on a long time. I offered to bid for him and took his details. My ears pricked up when I heard lot 130 mentioned, which I got for the price he wanted, but then the auctioneer said "now the 56lb weights," *what the hell have I bought?* The weights went for much more than the £20 that I had paid for the lot before, I'd ended up with 20 portable clothes ringers aka mangles, they had trestles.

The lot also included various metal fire guards and some other items. The trouble was, modern washing machines with a spin dryer were becoming more popular, and fire guards for coal fires were on the way out, with central heating and night storage heaters!! I saw 500 ammunition boxes 19" x 16" x 6", *they would make good toolboxes*. I was amazed when the bidding struggled at £1, I got them for £5. Unfortunately, they were in Haverford West, at least the fire guards and mangles were local! Luckily Ernie, a retained fireman, was a driver for a haulage company, and fixed it for me to hire a lorry. He told me, once I'd gone 50 miles, to disconnect the speedometer cable drive off the gearbox to save me the mileage charge, but not to forget to reconnect it. Haverford West is near the Welsh West Coast. I found the army camp but unfortunately not only were the boxes wooden not metal but they were also 19" x 16" x 16" not 6." I completely filled the lorry having to leave more than half behind, I wouldn't be going back. When I got home, Tony Price came to help me unload, mother was nearly in tears, but Tony said some soothing words to her. Once I'd returned the lorry, I had to take the boxes, three at a time, in a wheelbarrow to the top of the garden, over 80 trips!

Aunty Wynn's house, well mine now, was let, and money was coming in. The first tenant, Ian Bailey, a news reporter with Glos Independent News, was okay, but he moved on. It's difficult to remember everyone I rented to but, the three girls were good, they kept it clean. I used to pop in when passing, to see if everything was all right, fixing the odd dripping tap or toilet not flushing. Sadly they gave a month's notice after 3 months. They said, "When we lived at home we didn't pay much and went out regularly. Now we're living together we've less money so we can't afford to go out." They were the only ones to leave the house as clean, if not cleaner, than when they moved in.

I was inspired by Nigel Kirby, someone I worked with at Cheltenham. He'd bought a house after leaving the Army, got married and paid off his mortgage by doing extra jobs. He then bought the cottage next door and had an old lady in paying rent. I kept an eye on the local paper, and seeing a house for £3800 had a look round the three storey end terrace in Worcester Street. It had 3 bedrooms, a small courtyard and an outside toilet. I offered £2500, got a quick no so offered £3000 which they accepted! *Oh my God, what have I done? I've bought another house*! I went back to the bank, "I'll need to spend another £6000 on renovations, for a bathroom and kitchen, to get the council improvement grant." The bank agreed to let me have the money at 3 % above base rate.

I saw a 1960, R60 600cc BMW for sale, £100. Although it had bent front forks due to front-end crash, I bought it. It looked and sounded lovely, when Jim Curry heard I had it he offered me £200 but at that time I had plans for it.

One Saturday at the weekly market, a lady bought a fireguard, they had four sides which touched the ground if it was laid down flat. I asked her what she wanted it for, "to keep my rabbit in when it's on the lawn" she said, so I started selling them for rabbits. A trader bought all the trestles from the washing mangles to make trestle tables. I sold the G clamps which held the mangle for 50p, I did sell the odd mangle as you could still clamp them to a table. I had a few ammo boxes on sale, they were good for storing items in for sale and carrying more items! From the auction I had some coal effect fire fronts, somebody bought one for a model railway. I found that the flexible tubes fitted a VW beetle which gave me a few more ideas for selling. I went to an MOD sale at RAF Quedgeley which brought back memories, I needed to keep taking new items to sell at the Saturday market, so people had something different to look at. At RAF Quedgeley, inspecting what was for sale, I saw some large wood boxes that were used to carry helicopter blades, there was still some parts from helicopters in them. I got these cheap but it was so much work pulling them apart left most of them there, I didn't really have the time to break them all up into planks. It was good-quality wood, I should have contacted the builder who reclaimed building materials, having previously bought a lot of wood and other materials from him for Barnwood Road and now Worcester Street.

There'd been a change to the MGP regulations, 500cc bikes were now allowed in the Jnr race, as the Snr had been increased to 750cc. I contacted the organisers to see if I entered my G50 in the Jnr which was on Tuesday, would they let me enter the 250cc race on Thursday, it was allowed. Mick Dunn would enter me on his Greeves and concentrate on his Yamaha. Mick still rode it on short circuits and in the S100, trying to get the British 250cc award. I mentioned about being sponsored on it by an old rival, in the blurb for the MGP commentator.

I was following the TT reports on the BBC radio news, there'd been a tragedy, Snuffy Davies, who'd won the 1977 Snr MGP had been killed.

I spent £1000 at an auction, buying 250,000 cable ties, several packets of 1000 shorter ties, more electric motors and too much other stuff to list. As usual I got carried away, but with the sort of stuff I was buying I was doing a lot of bartering, like swapping the push bike for a coffee table with ceramic tiles. A man offered me £9 for the table. I said, "not a penny below £10." I saw a friend looking at it and asked him if he'd like it for £10. He said "yes," the man said "I wanted that," I said, "too late."

The joint councils who ran Staverton Airport told CMC that the August meeting would be the last. We started a petition, Save Staverton Races, and tried to find other ways we could fight this. The Club entered a float in Cheltenham Carnival and had forms printed for folk to send to their councillor or MP if they wanted to support us. The CMC and NGMCC were now on friendly terms, Brian Smith, NGMCC commentator, who worked for British Sugar, arranged for us to borrow one of their flatbed lorries, which he'd drive. We organised solos for the flatbed and for Keith Sylvester to be towed behind on his sidecar outfit. I borrowed a recording of 'Come along and see me riding at the TT races' by George Formby.

On the day of the Carnival, we had flags flying from the lorry and used a Tannoy system to play the record and make speeches. The parade moved slowly, with walkers each side handing out the leaflets. Keith, being towed behind, dropped the clutch on his outfit and revved it up a few times which made everybody jump.

We were lucky enough to stop opposite the podium where all the mayoral guests, the Cheltenham MP and dignitaries sat. I shouted "ladies and gentlemen, these are the people that are stopping the road racing at Staverton Airport. Thousands of Gloucestershire people go three times a year to watch motorcycle racing, contact your MP and councillor, get them to change their mind. The Cheltenham Motor Club are putting this on for you, with members giving up their time for nothing. As well as giving an income to the airport it brings in money to the local economy" I was very pleased to get a cheer and round of applause, even if those on the podium looked embarrassed!

We had "Save Staverton Races" strips, for cars and vans and T-shirts. I contacted the Gloucester Citizen newspaper and asked "if I get five pretty girls wearing 'Save Staverton Races' T-shirts and my Greeves to the Citizen

Newspaper office will you take and publish a photo?" It appeared in the paper so thank you; Jeanie Price and Rose Little, both from Ash Lane, Dexter Price's latest girlfriend, Bruce Bray's teenage daughter and a young lady Pat worked with. A similar photo appeared in the Cheltenham Echo. I contacted John Watkinson labour MP for West Glos, he showed interest in our fight and asked to be kept informed. I was pleased he beat Paul Marland in the 1974 election as Marland didn't like motorcycles.

The enforced rest because of my shoulder, not only gave me time to organise the May Staverton vintage parade, it also helped with applying to the City Council for an improvement grant for a new toilet, bathroom and kitchen. These improvement grants had been around for some time to help update pre-war property, but there were many forms to fill in, which for me was a bit of a struggle. They gave me a list of improvements to carry out to get the grant, 500 new roof tiles and relevant work, a new damp proof course and new window frames, all at my expense. Before fitting the tiles, I had to cover the roof with roofing felt, fixing it to the roof joists. This only took a few hours and at least it would stop any rain damaging the property. The roofer I was recommended, delivered the tiles, he was a foot shorter than me, more like a whippet and a few years older, but he could carry 6 of these 9" x 12" concrete tiles at a time. I tried 6 first, then 4, it was only 10' from the lorry into the house!

Gordon Bircher had just sold his butchers shop; it was a compulsory purchase as British Telecom wanted the land for a switching station. He got a good price, but felt lost and needed something to do, so my house came along just at the right time. With Gordon helping, we had a good time talking about the old days butchering, and our motorcycles, I also asking various firemen to help me otherwise it would have never got finished. I contacted John Stevens to do some brickwork, he found a transport cafe around the corner which did full breakfast 75p including tea.

I bought a 250cc MZ off Mike Compton's son, Les, who joined Cheltenham just before I left. I suppose you could say it was not a pretty looking bike with a large valanced front mudguard and a lot of panelling but today, in that condition, it would be classed as a classic. Like the Bantam Racing Club, there was an MZ formula racing club, there were many made, making it a cheap racer, easy to tune up and plenty of spares. This model had a long exhaust, with a stud sticking out the back, I took it to work. Mum had asked "George is that another motorcycle up the garden?" "No mum, I just rearranged them a little!" After fire drills, a lecture then dinner, I went to get the bike out of the van using the plank I used for my racing bikes, but the plank slipped, me and the bike landed in a heap on the floor. As it was only a 2' drop, there was no major damage to the bike but the stud had gashed my leg badly, with help I loaded the bike back in. As I had to go to hospital, I told work, I'd gashed my leg falling into the pit. It needed many stitches, I whimpered.

After 2 weeks on the sick I went to see my new Doctor, Dr. Mackay who asked when I was next on duty, "if you give me 4 more days that will take me into my next 4 days off." "I don't think I can do that" he said and signing me fit for work. As it turned out I had a week's holiday booked. I went racing, a meeting I'd entered earlier, unfortunately I slid off with no injury, but it started my leg bleeding. The next week, on my last day off, a few of us were helping Len Griffin of Chequers Chippy, who'd given us fish & chips for the 9 weeks of the strike, we'd volunteered to do some concreting for him. Pete Davies was there and as he'd been in the medical corps, I asked him to have a look at my leg as my doctor had said I was fit for work.

Peter suggested that I ring the medical officer of health for Gloucestershire. I rang and explained the situation, and was told to get to the Shire Hall now. I showed him the wound, he looked thoughtful, and said he'd ring my Doctor. As he rang, I asked if he'd like me to leave, "no that is alright, just sit there." He explained to Dr Mackay that fireman have to do a strenuous job, and cannot work with an open wound. Then he said he'd send me back to him. I was sat in a nurse's room when Dr Mackay poked his head around the door, we both looked a little embarrassed. He apologised, and said he wasn't familiar with the work a fireman does. I got another week on the sick, luckily it healed up not long after. Dr Drake had retired a few months earlier, at his last surgery in the village, many villagers turned up to wish him all the best, he was amazed at how many came.

At the S100, we camped in the field close to where everything went on, which made life a lot easier, again Ray was holding my hand. I got two finishes this year, perhaps because there was no party to organise. In the campaign for the Mularney Trophy, Mick Dunn won in 22nd place, I was only 30 seconds behind him in 23rd. Mick and I were pleased as we'd had a good scratch with a Yamaha rider. His fairing had 'Poco Homes' on it, and we assumed it was his sponsor. He had 15bhp more than us, but we kept catching him up on the corners. Mick found a good photo of the 3 of us at Church Bends in the Manx newspaper. This year there was a young scruffy Irishman, who make me look smart, riding a Rea Yamaha, Joey Dunlop, I wonder if he ever became famous!

In the solo support race I was 27^{th,} it wasn't a particularly good ride. The first three were Joey Dunlop, Graham Young and George Fogarty. The sidecar races as usual were exciting, Alan Steele from Chester winning one and John Watson from Leeds the other. We had another good presentation evening in Castletown to finish off race week, with me blowing the railway horn and Mick Dunn blowing it when I went on the stage waving my union flag. On the way out of the campsite to catch the early boat, feeling mischievous, I went to a tent I thought was Chris East's from the Worcester Auto Club gang, and blew my horn, it wasn't his tent. At least I had a double entry in the MGP.

Back at work, I had what I thought was a private talk with ADO Gough, basically I told him I didn't feel I was coping very well as a leading fireman. This ended up getting all around the fire station, if anything it made the situation worse, in relation to my giving orders, it seemed to me you have to be a bit of a bastard if you're in charge. I was finding the same with tenants, you let your property, and unless you kept a tight rein they didn't care, it's your property, not theirs!

We had a call to a row of terraced houses in Tredworth. When we got there, a man was collapsed outside the house on fire. Frank sent in two with BA plus hose reel, then gave mouth-to-mouth while I was doing heart compressions, sadly the man died. It turned out that he was nothing to do with the fire, but had been trying to raise the alarm. The fire was arson, the woman who started it was found with her wrist slashed in the back. It was believed she'd tried to take her own life, very unpleasant, but was not uncommon.

Mother, born 1903, was pretty fit for her age, but started picking at her food, not eating properly and getting constipated. She liked jam tarts and cake, but roast beef and three vegetables was too much trouble living on her own. I bought some bran, like you give to rabbits, big chunky stuff, not like it is today, and got her to mix it with her cereal. "George I don't like it." "Mother you've got to eat it, it's good for you." "I saw Mrs White yesterday, she said, what a nice boy your George is Mrs Ridgeon, she doesn't know you shout at your mother." "I'm only doing it for your own good, eat it"!

I'd bought a cheap .22 air rifle, when feeling a bit fed up with the job, I used to shoot targets in Pat's back garden to relieve some tension. She had a garden gnome, and when I was feeling really grumpy, I shot at that. It all helped me forget the aggro of the fire station.

The MGP started on Bank Holiday Monday, first Practice was at 6am, but this was maybe the last Staverton race meeting. A meeting had been arranged for late September with the airport committee, the local MP and CMC members. Manx regulations stated that the latest you could start practice, was Tuesday evening, so I decided to race at Staverton, and leave immediately afterwards to catch the midnight ferry. I slept like a baby on the night sailing, pitched my tent in Noble's Park at 6am, and managed to get a few more hours sleep before signing on.

The G50 was ready, and Mick Dunn would have his 250cc Greeves ready for me at practice. Practice went well, but it was hectic with two bikes, at least Mick's dad was doing the work on the 250cc, Mick was racing his 350cc Yamaha. We both had a fairly trouble-free week, attended the MGP Supporters club dinner and MGP Riders Association AGM on Sunday morning.

The Newcomers race on Tuesday morning was held-up due to bad weather then reduced to 3 laps. It was raining hard as the race finished; the Jnr was postponed to Friday as Wednesday's weather was forecasted to be as bad. At least the riders evening cheered everybody up. My next ride was on Mick's 250cc Greeves on Thursday morning. On the parade from *Mylchreests* garage to the start the weather was still bad and our race was reduced to three laps. I was 54th averaging 76 mph, Gordon Morss 57th and Rupert Murden 60th. With our start numbers being close together, we had a good scratch over the mountain. The race was won by Cliff Patterson at 96 mph from old friend Richard Swallow. It was an exciting senior race with just 8 seconds between the winner George Linder, on a Suzuki at 102 mph from 2nd place man Steve Ward, I was shouting for Gloucestershire rider, Dave Pither, who was 3rd. The presentation took place Thursday evening but with no Jnr awards as that was being run on Friday.

MICK REPOSESSES HIS GREEVES AFTER THE RACE

The bikes were scrutineered in the paddock on race day for the Jnr instead of the night before at Mylchreests. I'd entered a CMC team with myself, Tony Russell and John Stone from Birmingham. We were waiting on the start line, but the weather was still bad so the race was delayed. When we eventually got going, we were told it was wet all around the circuit and raining in places. I saw Roger Cope sat on his backside with his Yamaha by his side at 13th Milestone, at least a 4 stroke was more tractable in the wet. I was the last rider to complete 6 laps, the race had been stopped early due to bad weather, those still on the course could not win a silver replica. All following riders were counted as 5 lap and one 4 lap finisher. There was no presentation. I saw in the results that Cheltenham Motor Club had won the club team trophy, Stroud rider, Tony Russell, starting number 108 on his Yamaha, was the first 5 lap finisher at 86 mph and 31st, John Stone on his Yam was 40th at 81 mph, I averaged 81 mph for 6 laps.

After the MGP, I had 3 weeks before my Junior Officer course or, how to be a leading fireman! Chris Witts was on his course returning on the 22nd, mine was starting on Monday 25th September.

At the crunch meeting with the airport authorities, John Watkins MP, made an impassioned speech, asking why the Joint Airport Council were stopping motorcycle racing, when it was bringing not only entertainment, but much-needed trade to Gloucestershire businesses. Their response was that all the people leaving the airport was causing traffic congestion and there was too much noise from the bikes. We pointed out that 10,000 people worked at Dowty Rotol based at Staverton, commuting every day. The races were three times a year at the weekend, there were roughly 5000 spectators, many sharing cars, so that couldn't really be used as an argument, as for noise, the aircraft made much more noise and flew most days. The races gave a lot of pleasure to thousands, not just a few. One eagle eyed counsellor, picked up that there were signatures on our petition from the Isle of Man, and asked us to explain how. I addressed the meeting, "I've just returned from the Isle of Man Southern 100 and Manx Grand Prix races, when Manx riders heard Staverton circuit was closing, they were concerned. Many riders from the IOM, and across the UK have competed there over the last 9 years. Staverton races have become well-known and respected amongst the riders as a good and friendly circuit." Sadly, despite the MP fighting our cause, and our arguments, we lost the battle. The chairman of the CMC, who worked at Cheltenham Borough Council, was threatened with the sack if he pursued the fight!

We had a call to a lorry fire. It turned out to be the brakes overheating, quite a common call with drum brakes. Whether it was the driver using his brakes too much, or bad maintenance by the lorry firm, it caused a lot of smoke, and several road users had called warning about the lorry. This lorry belonged to a local firm. Seeing Nicholas Nickleby on the door, I asked the driver why, "the owner likes Charles Dickens, each tractor unit has the name of a Dickens character, he thinks it gives the driver pride in their tractor unit".

I was now a leading fireman when riding in charge. If the driver was one who'd just passed his class III test, he had to have his first 10 drives to an incident on blue lights signed off with comments saying how he did on the drive to the emergency. My mouth gets me in trouble with senior officers, I used to write the truth, usually I just put "satisfactory or good" if it was a reasonable drive, but if they didn't do well, such as "not keeping both hands on the wheel or crossing them over doing a manoeuvre" I put it on the form which usually got me a black look from the driver, I did sometimes put "very good drive!"

The night of the charity dance I was on shift. I was I/C, and after detailing who was riding which fire appliance, I added "after you've checked your appliances, have a cuppa," then detailed various people jobs. I asked

Richard if he'd like to do a job getting ready for the dance. He refused. I was surprised at his attitude as he had been a 2nd Lt. in the commando Regiment, "alright then, I order you to do it." I carried on, "a group of you get the decorations up and the tables out." Stuart chipped in "it's a dance night, you don't give orders out." I was starting to get fed up with this attitude and snapped, "it's a charity dance, you either get the dance ready or go out and do some drill."

The appliance room was slowly coming together, when people started turning up I was pleased there was a little more urgency in the lads. The evening was going well, I was jiving with a lady when the bells went down, so one minute she had a partner, seconds later she didn't!

Two pumps were dispatched to National Carriers Ltd, Great Western Road. We could see nothing out of place until we turned into the huge industrial estate, part of British Rail, where we saw about eight lorries on fire. The reason smoke wasn't evident was, the vehicles were parked under a huge shed style structure, which also covered the railway lines where the trains used to arrive and unload onto the lorries, the roof had a drop down of 6' made from corrugated iron, the smoke was being held in the roof cavity. As we arrived, one of the lorry's fuel tanks exploded, I can still visualise this as if it was yesterday. It was like something from a James Bond movie, a huge fireball. The 200+ gallons of very hot diesel, released when the fuel tank split and exposed to the fire, mushroomed into a fireball. We'd had lectures on LPG tankers, if one of these tankers ruptured, and the escaping gas caught fire it's called a "BLEVE, boiling liquid expanding vapour explosion." In 1972 a tanker in Spain crashed catching fire, as it rolled across a campsite it killed 200 people. The next lorry fuel tank exploded, then the next, about four had exploded before I urgently radioed back for two more pumps, my driver, Arthur Williams, suggested we get the hydraulic pump. We had two lines of fire hose out, about 50' from the fire, when the whole roof section fell in engulfing both appliances in smoke and flames. I was near one of the pumps, after disconnecting the fire hose, I jumped in and started reversing. We couldn't see more than 10' away. Trying to reverse using the reversing mirrors was very difficult, the pump escape in front of me was also reversing. As I couldn't see a thing, I slowed, when the wheels of the escape ladder crashed through the front window! To say it made me jump is an understatement, luckily I wasn't injured and got 2 firemen to back both pumps out safely.

315

By the time we'd got two lines of hose going again, and two firemen looking for fire hydrants the retained pump and hydraulic platform had arrived with ADO John Gough who took over, after receiving my report, and seeing the situation. He radioed for two more pumps. The final tally was eight fire pumps, a hydraulic platform and the canteen/control unit. After about two hours, I found two minutes to gulp a cuppa and devour a sandwich before starting again.

We were lucky nobody was seriously injured, there was a large number of cylinders that were exploding and a trailer carrying compressed air cylinders caught fire, due to the heat from the main fire. As these cylinders are designed to hold air at up to 3000 PSI, it was lucky that all the safety plugs were working. This reminded me of fire when I was still a gofer with Sub O Lawson in Cheltenham. We attended a fire in a large shed that stored ex-army gear, I was stood with the Sub O when an explosion nearly knocked the pair of us off our feet, the full force of the blast missing us by inches. It was a 5 gallon Gerry can which, although empty, was sealed, the air in it expanded until the can split open. Goodness knows what could have happened if those compressed air cylinders had exploded. As things started to die down. I had time to look at my watch. It was now 06:00, I'd left the dance at 23:00 hours, 7 hours without stopping, except for, snatching a cuppa and sandwich. I wanted to go back to station but they wouldn't let me, not for another hour. I got back at 07:30, helped wash the truck off and check inventory.

Sunday, I was racing at RAF Keevil in Wiltshire with the NGMCC. During practice, I had a minor problem with the gearbox on the G50 and spent some time trying to fix it. I was feeling knackered, and just finished in time for the first race, but I was riding round to make the numbers up. It was the same on the Greeves, my eyes felt like p*** holes in the snow.

Calling back at the fire station on the way home I picked up all my fire kit, including my still damp fire jacket out of the drying room, and put it in the kit bag that I first used when I went to Reigate back in 1969. The Junior Officer course was at Moreton in Marsh. After having a bath and some food at Pat's I was on my way. I got to the main gates at 22:00. I reported in, name, brigade and which course I was on, they let me in telling me to call in at reception. I found the divisional officer and booking in, he suggested that I go to the bar, there was just 20 minutes left. I chatted to the other students there, before leaving at just after 23:00, to find my room. I carried as much kit as I could, dropping it on the floor to open my door. The doors either side opened, I said to the two heads that had popped out "hello, I'm George, you'll be looking after me for the next six weeks." One of them was Ian Sabiston from London Fire Brigade, who lived in Aldershot. He'd come up with Ron Stemp, a leading fireman in Aldershot. My head hit the pillow, I'd been awake for 36 hours, morning coming too quickly.

The first day was quite easy, each squad had a Divisional Officer, Assistant Divisional Officer and Stn O. The first hour was in a lecture theatre, "proper job" as one of my racing friends from Burford used to say. These were tiered lecture areas, the instructor at the bottom and screens that could be seen from all angles with no one's head in the way. We were given timetables for the week, what lessons, where and when they were held, and some dos and don'ts. The officers then took us around the site in vans, showing us the drill areas, which included concrete buildings, even a concrete ship, The Sir Henry, a DC 10 aircraft fuselage and gas and oil installations. We were later to find out they set fire to it all, well not the DC 10 fuselage, which was used for aircraft crash scenarios. The last visit was to the leisure centre area, which was used by local people at the weekends, as well as those students who stayed over. The swimming instructor told us that if anybody wanted to learn to swim go and see him. When I had a moment I told him I was interested in learning to swim better. Mealtimes were breakfast 06:30 – 08:00, dinner 12:45 – 13:45, and tea, as I call it being common, at 17:45 – 18:30. This gave you time to get a shower then some studying done, or in my case, writing down anything I wasn't too sure of, if I left too long, I couldn't understand my own writing, before meeting in the bar for an hour. Our JO course was a good bunch, I teamed up with Ian, who was also a biker, and Ron. When my head hit the pillow I thought *that's the first day of the 6 weeks done!*

Next day, learning started in earnest. The first two hours were lectures, after tea break, we had a fire drill. It was never more than two hours study without something physical in between, it helped with the concentration. Even in the two hours, I found I was nodding off, especially if the lecture or the lecturer was not that inspiring! We were given reams of paperwork to study in the evenings. The meals were good, in fact too good, I started to put weight on. It was probably being a war baby and mother telling me not to waste any food. It didn't help in the morning and afternoon lectures when my eyes started to close.

At breakfast Tuesday morning, I was trying not to eat too much, *I must try to keep fit*. I collected a cereal or grapefruit, then scrambled egg not fried, bacon and sausage, I have no will power where food is involved, especially when it's free. Luckily, I had fixed up swimming lessons on Tuesdays and Thursdays.

For the first swimming lesson, I tried not to eat too much at the evening meal. The coach after watching me suggested I go for the Bronze Lifesavers medal, he said, "you may not be lovely to watch but you can swim very well and you'll get better during the course." One part of the Bronze, was to swim 4 lengths of the 25 yard pool, using breaststroke without diving in, in 3 minutes or less. My first effort was over 4 minutes.

There were a few of us doing the Bronze Lifesavers, there were about 400 firemen and firewomen on site as there were other courses going on at the same time. Another thing we had to do for the medal, was dive into to the deep end of the pool to collect something of the bottom. I found this easier, my big brother had taught me to swim underwater after we saw the film The Silent Enemy about Lionel "Buster" Crabbe in WW2. We also had to swim a quarter of a mile, and tread water for 5 minutes. I found rescuing somebody while swimming backwards quite difficult, having to learn the frog kick with the legs and using one arm, while holding the person under the chin with the other. We were shown how, if the person started to struggle, to squeeze their nose and hold their mouth closed so they couldn't breathe, they'd then stop struggling. The instructor pointed out "it's no good you drowning as well as them." After the swimming lesson I went to the bar for an hour before catching up with my notes. The rooms were small but compact, small sink and mirror, shaver point, single bed and a small table/desk for studying.

I practiced doing the 4 lengths. There was just time after drying off, to go for the evening meal, followed by an hour's studying, before a pint with the lads to discuss the day.

We'd been shown a film, which they hoped would help us be junior officers and give orders. The film was 12 o'clock High, which I'd seen when I was much younger, being a war film, I liked it. One US squadron was having a lot of bad luck, the officer was a nice guy and didn't want to upset anybody. Gregory Peck was put in charge and was much stricter, they all wanted to leave and transfer, he held up their transfer applications, until he had them working as a team. As I was to find out, this was easy in the film, much harder in real life, especially if you don't get any help from above, and I'm not referring to God!

Thursday night, there was a dance at the Rugby Club, as I liked dancing, I walked down with a few others from our squad. We found out why it was called The Ugly Bugs Ball, the evening was free for the ladies, but some were past their sell by date, but as I liked dancing, it didn't bother me. The Rugby Club put this dance on weekly, with 400 captive students it helped keep the club going, many of the local pubs were also doing well. There was a varying ages of ladies, from teenagers to those in their 60's, I was virtually dancing every dance which helped keep me in shape.

Most students went home at the weekends, but there were some from Scotland, Yorkshire and Northern Ireland as well as those from abroad. Travel costs were usually covered by the brigade. As I only lived 25 miles away, it was no problem for me. One weekend, there was a NGMCC race meeting, I wasn't racing so offered my services. I ended up running the assembly area, finding out how difficult it is to be an official! In the first 500cc heat, I was checking the bikes in on my tick sheet, which would then go to the commentator, when I saw one bike had white back plates with black numbers, which indicated the unlimited class. I asked him why he hadn't got yellow side plates on. He said "it's my first meeting, I didn't know." He reminded me of me when I was 20, so I told him to read the ACU handbook, let him out into the race, and told him to get it changed before the next meeting.

The CMC was now looking for a new circuit. As I was unable to attend any Wednesday night meetings, I called round to see some of the committee at the weekend, it looked like we were going to use an old airfield circuit near Stratford upon Avon that was already being used for sprinting, Long Marston.

Back at Morton in Marsh there were some sports I'd never done before. I always thought badminton was a sissy game, but after 10 minutes playing, I was sweating. Most sports were in the sports hall, 5-a-side football and volleyball which was played at the stations, it was supposed to keep you fit, although I think there were more injuries at volleyball than at fires. The College had various sports challenges between the courses, volleyball being one, I was not selected as I was useless. Once every 6 weeks, there was a run of about 3 miles, around the old airfield perimeter. I was last away and going slowly, everybody else had rushed off, but after a while I started passing people as they slowed up or stopped and quietly died on the floor, I wasn't last.

One course challenge was a comic swim night, where we had to dress up. I'd borrowed Pat's swimming costume and a wig, and had a sash with Miss Ugly Bug on. At Ian's retirement 20 years later, I put on a lady's wig and in a squeaky voice said "Ian you promised to marry me." In his speech, Ian said he'd always believed it was down to me dressing up as a woman at the comic swim night that it was renamed "The Miss Intercourse Competition." As I wasn't in the volleyball team, I borrowed a dress from Pat, her wig, stuffed my roll neck jumper with paper for boobs, and went along to support our team, shouting in a squeaky voice "come on JO2." I wonder why the other firemen moved away?

During the last week, as well as lots of exams I had to pass my swimming exam. There were 6 taking it, so there were several officials as well as the main examiner. First I was asked some life-saving questions, next was diving to the bottom of the pool. The dreaded 4 lengths breaststroke, I'd got down to 3 minutes 15 seconds in practice, I felt as nervous as I did at the start of a race. I held onto the side bar so that I could push away when they said "go." Swimming as fast as I could I finished the 4 lengths and got the thumbs up from our instructor, I'd done it in 2 minutes 45 seconds.

Ian, myself and a couple of others, organised a stripper and a blue comedian for the end of the course. There was some panic on the night, when the coach was late, but we got to the show. I still remember one of the blue jokes, which I can't repeat in the book, or can I? A cowboy goes into a town "Howdy stranger what are you drinking?" "Give me a beer, and where is the gents?" "Go out the door, you'll find a big pile of S**t, climb to the top and add to it." The cowboy was sat there, when he sees another big pile in the distance with a silhouette of someone wearing a Stetson on the top. A voice booms out "howdy stranger", he replies "how do you know I am a stranger?" "You're sat in the ladies!" We had a good boozy evening with the comedian and two ladies taking their clothes off.

I was pleased I'd passed all the exams, we had a group photo taken before we left and a talk from the Commandant wishing us luck in our career. I kept in touch with Ian as he was a biker.

It was halfway through November when I got back on the job, just before the anniversary of the strike. Our watch was on nights on the 14th and it was decided we'd have a slap up meal. I suggested that if I could get it at the right price, we have sirloin steak. I went to Weddle's, an offshoot of British Beef Co, luckily some of them knew me. We had sirloin steak with vegetables, the whole meal worked out at less than £2 each. After checking the appliances at 18:00 it was all hands to the pumps in the kitchen, I don't think anybody did much more that evening.

December brought the usual round of dinners and awards nights!

CHAPTER 16   1979-Same pit lane as Mike the bike

CMC members were shown around Long Marston circuit by the farmer. As it was only 30 years after the War, the main runway was in reasonable condition, it just needed some patching, sweeping and grass removal to satisfy the ACU. Where the runways crossed with the new drag strip, the farmer had fenced the grassed area, but across the tarmac, he'd put the remains of wartime landing craft, to stop the animals getting onto the drag strip. It was agreed we could move these, but we had to supply something mobile for him to use in their place. Keith Sylvester, a scaffolder and sidecar racer, designed something using short sections of scaffolding in a crisscross with barbed wire, it reminded me of the obstacles to stop the D Day invasion. As it was in short sections it could be removed and put back after the race meeting quite easily.

We had many working parties there during January, February and March, getting it ready for the end of March meeting. Geoff Garbutt was again secretary of the meeting, he'd been doing a good job since the 70's. The farmer also had a Sunday car boot sale, we had to drive through this on the way to the race paddock, but it probably brought in a few extra spectators as they were there already.

As officer in charge, I was in the duty office of the fire station one night when the Bon Marche rang, their fire alarm kept going off, I told him we'd attend. I wrote a note for the leading fireman telling him to investigate a fire alarm sounding at Bon Marche. Then I contacted fire control and told them I'd dispatched a pump to investigate. I was surprised to be told off, "you should have called us first", "but I had a call to a fire alarm and dispatched one pump as it's a suspected faulty alarm, I'm telling you immediately." Despite moaning at me, they left it at one pump to investigate.

On my next shift, I was called in to see divisional officer Nash, who also told me off and that I mustn't do the fire control's job. I tried to defend myself, but was told not to argue, so I just left it. By chance, Brigade orders had been updated and the old ones were cut in half for notepads, I used to read what was on the other side. On one sheet I found "brigade order 19 running calls (where a member of the public contacts a fire station to report an incident) (iii) if you receive a running call to the station you dispatch one pump and inform control." Next time I saw divisional officer

Nash I quoted the brigade order, he snapped, "don't be impertinent." What are you supposed to do to please people?

Another time I was in trouble was when I was trying to save money for the brigade. They had updated BA sets with new ultra-lightweight aluminium cylinders at 3000 PSI, the paint on the cylinder, was an integral part of their protection. They also had a nylon cover which came up around the neck of the bottle leaving the steel air outlet on/off control knob exposed. The trouble was that two spare cylinders were carried in the fire appliance and stored with no covers, although they were in a wooden rack with a compartment each, the paint would rub off. There wasn't a problem with the earlier sets which were made of steel, but the new ones rattled around, which wore the paint off and could even damage the cylinder. I had an idea for covers on all cylinders.

The CB Gorman covers cost £8 each. The main problem was on the fire ground, if you had to change the cylinder and go back in the fire, it would take five minutes or more, as the covers were very tight! One fire, two firemen wearing BA, had to fit new cylinders, as there was some urgency, they fitted the cylinder without the cover, both got reprimanded. I felt a cover on the spare cylinders on the pump would stop the paint rubbing off and make them quicker to change, so I went to Higgs and Wise, well-known tent makers and repairers, who also repaired my leather racing suit when I fell off. I told them that there could be a possibility of selling the brigade 80 covers if they could make one to demonstrate. They quoted £3 each and made one which I submitted with a FS15 form to the chief fire officer, 'Sir I submit this cover which is £5 cheaper than the CB Gorman cover and will save many hours of fireman's time rubbing down and painting cylinders which are being damaged in the rear of fire appliances. It would also speed up the changeover of cylinders on the fire ground' (well, along those lines). I was surprised to have Sub.Officer Bob Warnett, BA officer, contact me and tell me to stop interfering in his job, he also made an official complaint. I am pleased I didn't get into trouble and the brigade bought 80 covers.

We had a call to the High Street, Tredworth. The fire was upstairs in a 1880's house, and when clearing up afterwards, we threw the burnt items out onto the large front garden. I got my leg pulled when a photo of this appeared in the local paper.

As well as drilling at the station, we used some of the unused warehouses at Gloucester Docks, which were classed as Elizabethan docks, and used in period TV dramas, such as the Onedin Line. The docks became more important in the 1800s when the Berkeley Sharpness Canal opened in 1827; 16 miles and 16 bridges. Huge grain mills were built and large warehouses for woollen produce, flour and the storage of many other goods, not forgetting Moorland's Match Factory which used a lot of timber, when going along the Bristol Road there was half a mile of tree trunks stored along the canal bank. We did pumping drills, pitching ladders to these derelict warehouses, practised rescuing people from the boats and canal barges docked. One warehouse we used, became Gloucester City Council Offices.

At the first Long Marston meeting, the G50 went well in practice, but the Greeves for some reason, decided to seize up solid. I didn't operate the clutch in time, so the back wheel locked and yours truly and the bike went down the road. I was walking wounded, so went steady on the 500cc for the rest of the day. Considering it was out in the wilds, there was a reasonable turnout of spectators. The May meeting was a lot better supported, following positive reports from riders and spectators. The August meeting again clashed with the Manx so I couldn't go.

The 1979 TT was approaching. I saw Mike Hailwood was racing again, having made his return to the Island the year before winning the production race. There was this big magnet pulling me to the Isle of Man, I had to see 'Mike the Bike' race in the Isle of Man. I rode the 500cc Triumph Tiger 100 that I'd bought off Pete Allen, a.k.a. Mexican Pete. Knowing I was a biker, Pete offered me the T100 as he was getting a car. Now as many of you reading this will know, I was never one for cleaning bikes, Triumphs were renowned for leaking oil, and this original 500cc was now a faded maroon colour. It didn't look pristine which didn't worry me, as long as it was safe to ride, and kept going.

When I arrived in Douglas, Friday of practice week, it was already packed, I eventually found a space on the promenade in between a 750cc Honda and a 900cc BMW. I walked up and down for 10 minutes looking at the array of brand-new and exotic bikes, when I got back, I found a dozen people all looking at my genuine 500cc Triumph. The place was heaving, luckily I'd fixed up to stop with Fred and Joc Peck in Peel, but went to watch Friday evening practice at Rhencullen. Straining over the hedge, I heard the recognisable noise of a Ducati approaching, I gasped, *I saw him, Mike Hailwood on the 900cc Ducati,* now I could die happy, as I told Fred when I got to Peel.

Calling in at the TT race office on Saturday morning, I saw Colin and Marie Arms who used to run meetings at Snetterton. Colin was now a top ACU official and gave me a programme, after I'd had a cuddle from Marie. As I left, I asked where Les Cousins was stopping. I'd made friends with Les at the S100 races, he was as big a loony as I was; we sat around talking about John Cleese and Monty Python's Flying Circus, one sketch in particular, "spot the loony Nana Nan Na". I was asking round the paddock for Les Cousins when a reply came "no George, Boyo," a Welsh accent! It was Chris Bond from Newport. Chris was a regular at the MGP but had moved up to the TT. I asked if there was anything I could do to help. "Yes George, push my bike through scrutineering please." He was riding a 350cc Yamaha. When I got back from scrutineering I asked him who was helping him, "no one, I'm on my own." "I am over for 4 days do you want some help?" I rolled up my sleeves and helped get his spare bike ready. I saw Chris off in the last practice session on Saturday, he was entered in the Snr TT on Monday.

Chris was overdue, so I asked the organisers if they had any news. Chris had crashed at Windy Corner, rider okay, Chris and the bike would be bought back by the pickup lorry. The bike wasn't too bad, but Chris was limping. I drove him to Nobles hospital in his van. I told the doctor that Chris was a TT rider who needed to get fit quickly so we needed to see a physiotherapist. The Doctor told Chris to walk up and down in the sea, exercising in the cool water.

After getting Chris back to his tent I told him "I'll be back early in the morning to take you to the sea for exercise. I'd better stop here Sunday night as I expect we'll be working late on the bike for Monday." Sunday was a sunny day, so I'm lying on the beach watching Chris, shouting "keep it going Chris, up and down again." As we had a bike to prepare, we got back to the paddock for a quick snack, and spent the rest of the day building his Yamaha, Chris as Foreman, with his leg up giving me directions. I checked the clutch plates, tyre pressures, ignition timing, gear oil level, and hoped nobody was watching me working on a Japanese motorcycle!! I fitted a new fairing and numbers and gave the bike a clean, yes you did hear right!

Once the bike had passed scrutiny, with the Australian lad I'd met on Sunday, I pushed it in to parc ferme. I asked the Aussie if he'd like to work in the pit. "You bet ya cobber" he replied, nearly taking my arm off. We loaded the pit with tools, I left the Aussie in the pit with Chris and rushed off to Dunlop, cadging some hats, as we were pitting for number 81, Chris Bond. We stood around in our posh hats until Chris had to put his crash helmet on. As the 30 minute klaxon sounded, Chris said "my leg is hurting a bit. I'll start, but only do two laps to get my start money." Luckily it was a clutch start, they'd come in some years before and the bike went off well. Shell used to give both the TT and MGP riders the fuel for free. It was a 6 lap race, the Yamaha would need to stop twice, 14 gallons of fuel would be needed plus 2 more to give some head for filling the tank. As a fireman I thought 114 pits, all with over 12 gallons of fuel in, plus all the bikes, was some fire risk! The bike was already filled with 6 gallons of fuel, and John, the Aussie lad, filled the pit quick filler for the fuel stops.

Watching the refuelling of the star riders, the 23 minutes soon passed, and Chris's light came on to say he was at Signpost. Mike Hailwood was No: 8, and had refuelled some 10 minutes earlier.

326

Chris pulled in and said "I think I'll stop now." We shouted at him "no you are not, you're averaging over 90 mph." Chris was surprised. We filled him to the brim with fuel and cleaned his visor. Although he was still protesting, he put his bike into 1st gear and we started to push him, you were now allowed two pushers, he dropped the clutch, and off he went! With his bad leg, we were surprised when just over 40 minutes later, his light came on for his last pit stop. Chris said "I'm getting tired I'll stop." We wouldn't let him, "Oh no you are not, you're still averaging over 90mph, get back out there." I made sure he was full, as my mind wandered back to the early 70's MGP, when Don Padgett ran out of petrol on his last lap, a mile from home on a Yamaha.

All the mechanics were stood on the pit wall watching the bikes go by, Mick Grant had slowed as had Alex George. There was a big cheer every time Mike Hailwood, No: 8 riding a 500cc Suzuki, went through. I hadn't been in the pits at the TT before, many times at the MGP, but to be in the same Pit Lane as 'Mike the Bike,' wow!! I watched Mike come in for his second pit stop, he was slowing down from 160 mph, the bike nearly standing on the front wheel. He was going faster slowing down, than I'd ever gone in a straight line anywhere on the mountain circuit! You could hear the screeching of his brakes, and the revs as he blipped the throttle to change down the gears, to help the RG 500cc 4 cylinder two-stroke Suzuki slowdown, the engine made a strange roaring sound. With riders coming into the pit lane and others leaving having filled up it was like Paddington Station on a busy day. When Mike stopped, although it was 100 yards away, I could see his rear wheel momentarily leave the ground.

We were all waiting for Mike Hailwood's light to come on for the final time. Commentator Peter Kneale shouted "his light is on", a huge cheer went up from the grandstand. As Mike approached, the crowd in the grandstand stood up. I had a large 6' by 3' union flag up my sweatshirt, 'just in case,' and pulled it out, waving wildly as Mike crossed the line, I heard Manx radio's Peter Kneale say "I see George Ridgeon is waving one of is blooming union flags while standing on the pit wall." The roar of the crowd, nearly drowned out the sound of the four-cylinder Suzuki. Not long after, Chris went through to start his last lap, we had 24 minutes to wait and were now redundant as mechanics. After seeing first, second and third get their awards, we drained off the fuel filler and removed the tools. We got back in time to see Chris's clock move to Ramsay and looked at each other at least he was past halfway. We were not alone, there were a few other dedicated pit crews waiting for their riders. The TT grandstand and scoreboards hadn't changed since the 1920's. Each rider had a small clock below their race number and a pad with NS, non-starter, the lap numbers, and F for finish or R if retired. The hand on the clock is moved as the rider passes various points on the course, 12 o'clock is start and finish, 3 o'clock Ballacraine, 6 o'clock Ramsay, 9 o'clock the Bungalow, before the light above comes on at Signpost. As each lap was completed, a Boy Scout would rip a sheet off the pad. We saw Chris's arrow move to 9, so now he was only 6 miles out, which at 90mph should take less than 4 minutes, seemed more like an hour, when his light came on John and I were jumping up and down like schoolchildren. As Chris crossed the line, we jumped up and down as if he'd won the race rushing down to congratulate him, I was thinking *had I really built a machine that averaged over 90 mph in the TT and lasted 6 laps?*

The excitement of being in the pit lane, watching the rocket ships of Mike Hailwood, Mick Grant, Alex George and the like, thundering down the Glencrutchery Road past the start and finish averaging over 110 mph with Chris averaging 90 mph starting his second lap, was something special.
As soon as we'd had a celebratory drink, I had to pack up my bag, and say goodbye to Aussie John, and Fred and Joc, who'd come up to watch. I rushed to the boat and rode through the night, to make it to work on Tuesday morning at 9 o'clock, I was knackered! I'd be back in 4 weeks' time for the S100 silver jubilee races.

A new filing system had been brought in at work, trying to make the drill records more efficient. The drill sheet had the names of all the firemen in your group on it, and across the top, all the drills that had to be done, such as hose running, pump operating and ladder drills. Rescues from car accidents, using jacking equipment, first aid, knots and lines, topography and knowledge of your station ground were also on the sheet. I used to spend ages filling in this sheet, when you did the drill you had to tick who was there and the date, if someone was missing you ticked when he eventually did the drill. I gather most JO's ticked everybody all the time, I was pleased to get a commendation from assistant divisional officer John Gough and divisional officer Joe Nash, I had to go and sit down!

An air of panic arose around the station as we were going to get an annual HMI fire drill. This was when the Home Office fire chief would check the brigade, the records, and do inspections. We had a call for two pumps to Fielding and Platt, for a brigade exercise. This was a large engineering firm in Gloucester. I was in charge on the Wrl, following the PE with Chris Witts in charge. Suddenly, my driver said "what the hell is the PE doing?" It went around the roundabout, and headed back to the fire station. I radioed control, and asked for permission to talk to the PE direct. I was trying to watch my language on the air while trying to find out why he was heading back to the station. We went as slow as reasonably possible, but still got to Fielding and Platt first, a senior officer told us "there's a fire in the chemical plant, get your men in BA." It was supposed to be a chemical spillage, so basically a breathing apparatus exercise, we set up BA procedure. Chris arrived not long after, with pumps arriving thick and fast as the incident had been made 8 pumps. Cheltenham pump arrived with Dick Parker who'd grown a beard, on board. As Dick was putting on his BA set, the HMI shouted "that man cannot wear breathing apparatus, no one with facial hair can wear BA." The masks were now positive pressure sets, if there was an air leak around the face mask, air would leak out rather than smoke leak in as happened to me in 1973 at Stoke Orchard I'm not too sure what happened to Dick, but an order came round that no beards to be worn if you had a BA qualification. Luckily nobody discovered why the PE was late, Chris told me he'd left his fire kit at the station!

I was in trouble again after a call to the Royal British Legion Club in Brockworth, a half-moon building which was an old wartime Nissen hut. Somehow a fire had occurred in the roof section with lots of smoke, I was wearing BA. The first thing that pissed me off was, I was wearing full fire kit and BA when divisional officer Nash was wearing undress uniform and cap, what we wore for everyday use. A firemen's full uniform was firefighting kit, unfortunately he heard me comment "of course officers can eat smoke and do not have to wear BA." He gave me a black look. In 1974 the fireman's axe was withdrawn from use and only 2 axes were kept on each appliance. I was one of a few keen fireman who would fit one at an incident. Although it wasn't a major fire our retained pump had been ordered. A retained fireman seeing me wearing the axe, asked if he could borrow it, I took the belt and axe off, gave it to him saying "it's your responsibility to return this to the pump." I got another axe when I was outside. When another retained fireman asked if he could borrow my axe I replied "you've got one on your pump go and get it." Back at the station I was called into the office again, with officers and union representatives present, and asked why I'd refused to give my axe to a retained fireman. This gave me the opportunity to air my views, "I was not being unpleasant to a retained fireman, I'd already given one axe to another. The fire service should place 4 axes on each pump, and make an order that on arrival at the fire ground an axe is worn, or are you expecting junior officers to go around carrying axes for every fireman too lazy to get one?" I wonder why I didn't get on in the brigade, could it be they didn't like being told the truth?

I'd fixed up to go to the S100 with John Daly, we were sharing the travel costs, as the boat fare was getting more expensive every year, and riders had to stop hiding people in the back of the van. At the Manx Grand Prix the year before, someone had a Yamaha engine stolen, so police and boat officials started searching the vehicles on the way back. John arrived in a large, hired transit van, the evening before we were due to sail. Next day, we unloaded his 750 Norton Commando to sort the van out, he was as untidy as me! When mother saw it, not missing the opportunity she asked if she could sit on it, mother was still a biker at heart, being a young 76 years old. Once loaded, we shared the drive to Heysham and sailed on the new Geoff Duke owned Manx Viking, called a "Ro, Ro" so named as it was Roll on and Roll off. After a quick look round, they even had a gambling room, we found somewhere to lie down for the 6 hours of the midnight crossing.

Camped in the field opposite where the bikes were scrutineered, we found there was a new hut, where the tea ladies could make refreshments, signing on was done and there was even a committee meeting room with a flush toilet, rather than the old earth bucket! As it was the 25th S100, two of the S100 committee asked me to run a party like I did for the Queen's Silver Jubilee, they'd provide prizes. I contacting Manx Radio and told them "there'll be a S100 Jubilee party for riders, mechanics, and all S100 supporters are welcome, but bring your own food and beer." 1979 was millennium year in the Isle of Man, so there were many celebrations around the island, including an Irish Pipe Band who, agreed to turn up at 1pm on Wednesday afternoon at the S100 campsite! The word spread to all the riders, that there was going to be a party, similar to that in 1977, with loads of prizes, as the club had asked local shops to donate. We had biscuits, fruit, hairspray, body lotion and much more, everyone was looking forward to it.

Tuesday morning we were woken at 5am by the karts, luckily they were camped somewhere else, but as we were near the wall, we were close to the stepladder everyone went over for water and now a decent toilet. After practice, although there was now a good toilet, we made the trip down to the pub for ablutions, and a pint! When we got back, seeing a committee member, I asked "could we have at least 4 space hoppers, and some posters, and a prize for the best silly hat parade?"

As there were no major problems in practice, I got the bikes ready for the evening race before getting back to organising the party. I was feeling cheeky so I spoke to someone at Castletown Ales, the man gave us four crates of beer just asking for the empties back, so I invited him to the party.

When we got back, the Irish pipe band was marching up and down the middle of the campsite, which had stopped everybody working on their bikes as they came to watch, so the party started there and then. There was a big round of applause when they finished, and I dished the beer out, which they appreciated. First, we had the wheelbarrow races, then space hoppers, which had everyone in fits of laughter. Again we borrowed lengths of rope, used for tying the bikes in the van, for the tugs of war. There were running races for men, ladies and children, the first three had prizes from the donated items. Again we had the 5 legged race! As the evening was approaching, we finished off with a lovely legs competition for the ladies. Lads held blankets to cover their identity, then a knobbly knees competition combined with a silly hat parade for the men, some of the ladies picked the winner.

Mick Dunn again won the Mularney Trophy, a Worcester man, Phil Hallet was second British bike on a Cotton Rotax. I finished 31st and could just see them ahead of me. There was a panic when Ex-Greeves rider, Ron Leighton, was checking the spark on his Yamaha. When pushing his bike to clear the excess fuel, he left the plugs in their caps and a spark caught the bike on fire. Luckily there was a fire extinguisher near.

As it was S100 Silver Jubilee and IOM Millennium year there were extra races, one was a solo support race which was first race on Thursday. I was 25th with John Daly 24th on his 750cc Norton, that made my bike look tidy, sorry John, but could he make it fly. At a national race at Cadwell Park I watched John finish in the top six of a national race after leading it for a while. In the championship race, George Fogarty just pipped Joey Dunlop to the win.

S100 PRESENTATION, MICK DUNN WAVING MY FLAG

More trouble at mill, well the fire station! Chris Witts and I were called into a meeting by Sub Officer Joe Bartlett, "I have just been reprimanded and lectured by Divisional officer Joe Nash about the slackness in this station, firemen lounging around using phones when they want, without asking permission and the untidiness." As Joe was bollocking us, I was wondering, if I'd been backed by senior officers dealing with the many problems I'd had as leading fireman, would things have been different. Joe continued, "You make sure they sort themselves out." Looking at each other, after Joe walked out, we mumbled "some hopes."

One shift, I was in the duty office when Mike Cox came in. Mike had been in the Parachute regiment, he was a hard-working fireman and became Benevolent Fund rep. He came in without speaking and picked up the phone to make a call. When he finished the call, I said "Mike in future if you want to make a call you must ask a junior officer," "I am Benevolent Fund rep, I can make calls when I want." "Mike, Chris and I have just had our balls chewed off by Joe Bartlett, you, in fact everyone, has to ask permission from now on." Mike stormed out of the office saying he would go and see divisional officer Nash. I carried on working, 10 minutes later Mike came into the office and apologised, I thought to myself *My God some support at last.*

Mick Dunn, again agreed to lend me his 250cc Greeves for the Manx, as he was concentrating on racing his Yamaha. Pat and I were putting the tent up in the paddock campsite when Rupert Murden, and his brother-in-law John Daly, came over "we are stopping near Dave Montgomery, 50 yards away" so the four of us manhandled the tent, walking it closer to the gang with other riders laughing at us. The lovely Ann had help this year from Pat with the cooking! The Daly family, always made you welcome, so when I had two days off in the summer, I turned up at the large house in Gravesend, where Mr. and Mrs. Daly Snr, John, Rupert, Ann and the children lived. I rang the doorbell then put my sleeping bag completely over myself with only my feet showing. I heard the door open and Ann's voice saying "George what are you doing here?" Ann didn't need to see me, she knew the stupid things I did. It was an easy couple of days, sat in the kitchen drinking tea, as John and Rupert's mates came round talking bikes.

As it was millennium year, the Prince Michael of Kent and the Princess, were due to be guests of honour at the Manx, but there was some doubt whether the Royal couple would attend after the news that Lord Louis Mountbatten had been murdered in Ireland by an IRA bomb.

After signing on, we attended the MGP safety lecture which included the warning that overtaking when a yellow flag was displayed could get you sent home. It was confirmed that the Royal couple would be attending.

Sunday, we took Mick's Greeves to Jurby airfield but it holed the piston even there, Mick's dad couldn't understand it. We couldn't do anything there so Mr Dunn took the bike away. After going up and down the runway on the G50, I did a plug chop, everything seemed okay. After Jurby I went to Douglas, Mick was running a motorcycle shop "Trail and Trial," probably over-looked by dad, sorry Mick! It had a large workshop where he was letting me, Ron Roebury and Steve Gibbs work on our bikes. Mr Dunn wanted to fit a new piston in the Greeves, as practice was early in the morning, and there wasn't enough time to get back to Jurby, we left the gearing but jetted up massively and decided to take it steady. I did one lap before holing a piston. I should've only done one lap as the bike was under geared, but I'd left my brain in the toolbox.

The beauty of entering two bikes is that you still only have to do five laps to qualify, with a minimum of two laps on each machine, one of which has to be within qualifying speed. The G50 practice was going reasonably well until Wednesday morning, when I retired due to a minor problem. I was sat leaning against the wall when a motorcycle turned up, when the rider lifted his goggles I could see it was Malcolm Davis from Gloucester, top scrambles and trials rider, with his new, pregnant wife on the back. I did get another two laps in on the G50, making it three, so I concentrated on the Greeves. We managed to qualify with another lap but we had at least two more pistons fail so I would have to do some more testing at Jurby before the race. In one of the many retirements at 7 o'clock in the morning, I was with Phil Mellor, an up-and-coming rider, who gave me a lift back, he flashed headlights at Mick, who had come to pick me up, so he turned around to follow us. I left off working on the Greeves, to finish off the G50 with new chains before taking it down to the 'Weigh in.'

The Jnr race started well, I filled up on the third lap but on the fifth lap the bike was over revving but stopped driving. I pulled in near Ballaugh Bridge and saw the primary chain had jumped off. I ran to a farmhouse close by to borrow tools, in theory, not allowed as it was getting outside assistance! The oil drip feed had broken off causing the primary chain to stretch and come off. It took ages, the gearbox was back as far as possible, but the chain was still slack, so I had to adjust the rear wheel. After taking the tools back and getting going again, I limped back with the chain jumping off once more. Pulling into the pits, I told the lads what the problem was and we started to fit the chain I'd replaced for the race, but this was taking some time even though we had the proper tools and more hands. I saw two other bikes being worked on. Jackie Wood, the secretary of the meeting, came up "George how long are you going to be, we have to open the roads?" I replied somewhat frustrated "How the hell do I know, I'm working as fast as I can," I was feeling stressed. I was about to restart the race when they all jumped on me from a great height "sorry George, the

Roads Open car has left, your race is over." They didn't even let me start the bike to ride it out of Pit Lane, didn't they trust me?

Luckily the Manx organisers had decided to change the rule on people in the Pit Lane who had not taken the flag but had not broken down so I was classed as five lap finisher, sadly Alec Swallow having major engine problems had retired in the pit area, the other rider, Ian Parkinson on a Yamaha was classed as a finisher. Whilst it wasn't good at least I would get a finishers award from Princess Michael of Kent. Prince Michael was giving the Snr awards and the Mayor of Douglas, the Ltw and NCs awards. At least the Rider's Night in the evening, at the Douglas Head Hotel, cheered me up a little. After a lie-in on Wednesday to recover, I got back to working on the Greeves problems.

We fitted a new piston, and jetted higher again. I mentioned that the gearing was too low, the bike was over revving, but Mr Dunn said "it'll be all right." We all went to Jurby for another test session but it holed the piston again. We took the plug out, it was covered with aluminium again, but as there was some compression, it may not mean a complete strip down if there was no aluminium in the crank case. I got permission from the organisers to miss the 'Weigh in' but I had to declare my gearing so that I couldn't take advantage of any weather change. The trouble was, I didn't know what gearing we were using so I guessed 19 gearbox and 44 rear wheel sprocket, similar to what I'd used on my 250cc. The piston wasn't holed and there were no nasty bits in the crankcase, so we rubbed the barrel down. Everyone else was watching the bikes at the 'Weigh In' then off to the pub, I was all on my own, yes get the violin out!! I checked the ignition timing before fitting a new crank seal, as a worn oil seal was a major cause of holing pistons. I did find the ignition timing was 6 mm before top dead centre, when it should be 3.5 mm! The bike was also on short circuit gearing, which was why it was over revving. When I got to scrutineering next morning I'd forgotten what I'd put down for the gearing, but I'd put 6 teeth less on the back wheel and hoped the scrutineers wouldn't check to closely.

The race was delayed due to very bad weather, we were told that the race would definitely be reduced to three laps, and would be reduced to two if there were any more delays, as the Snr race is the most important. Eventually we got the go-ahead for three laps. The bike started well, and kept going for a lap, although it still felt under geared. We'd decided to fill up at the end of the first lap, as that would give me a flying last lap, if all went well. Starting the last lap, I hoped I'd fixed the problem, but I hoped too soon, approaching the Crosby Hotel the engine cut out. I coasted to a stop and checked the spark plug, it was covered in aluminium, so another piston problem. I watched the rest of the last lap, Richard Swallow was flying and finished 4th.

On presentation night, I wore the union flag waistcoat again, that mother had made. I was unrecognisable wearing a suit, and looking smart with my starter's ladder hanging down my lapel, was I brave enough to flash the union flag waistcoat? HRH Princess Michael of Kent, was introduced to a round of applause, cheers and a few wolf whistles, which brought a smile to her face. Peter Kneale called out "finishers up to 80 mph, Ian Parkinson, George Ridgeon." I walked onto the stage as Ian was leaving. I opened my jacket, flashing the waistcoat to the Princess, then to the crowd, she burst out laughing, as did Prince Michael and most of the top table, there were cheers and shouting from the audience. I momentarily stood to attention, gave a small bow and while accepting my award and shaking her hand asked "may I kiss your hand?" I bent to kiss it, she gave me a big smile, there was more laughter and cheering and I wondered whether I would be shot or locked in the tower!! The other riders were accepting their awards wearing a variety of clothing, some just jeans and T-shirt, others suits, some a mixture of both, Alan (Budd) Jackson, was wearing his old trilby or was it a Fedora, with his long hair.

The Royal couple appeared to enjoy themselves with the relaxed atmosphere of the Manx, the riders treated them as they did everyone they met. There was a pleasant surprise when Prince Michael rode a motorcycle around on closed roads with a travelling marshal and Geoff Duke. Another Manx was over.

When I got back from the Island, I was on a BA instructor's course, I liked BA so was looking forward to the week. The first day in the lecture room I was told to stand up and tell the others how to tie a knot without using my hands. I made a complete mess of it but hadn't done anything wrong. The instructor pointed out "you must have aids to help instruction, to make it simple for those trying to learn, visual is as important as oral, a picture is worth 1000 words." There were several films, one was an old Army training film that asked the question "what's your audience thinking of, girls, football, food or nothing?" The point the film made was that you must make the lecture interesting. Then we had a more detailed session on the sets. Although we already knew how to strip them, we learnt every nut, bolt, washer and seal. To be honest I enjoyed having to put the set back together from a box of bits, it was a challenge! It was surprising how much there was to learn, but it was a good course, we all passed.

One of the morning routines was in the BA room checking the compressor oil level and the spare BA sets which were mainly used for training and were left without a charged cylinder fitted. After the course I started fitting cylinders on the spare sets, leaving them ready for use. This turned out to be a good thing. One night we had a fire call that needed 2 BA, when we got back, as I was servicing the sets, there was another call for two pumps, persons reported in the building. We needed another 10 minutes at least, to finish our sets, so we grabbed the training sets and left the station only 30 seconds later. So I filled in another FS15 to the chief fire Officer "I submit training sets are left with charged cylinders on."

83 Worcester Street was coming together. I contacted my electrician John Stanley, the plumbing was finished and I was now busy painting and fitting carpets. I did however drop a bit of bollock by buying a lot of MOD furniture too early, so had to keep moving it from room to room as I was decorating. Although it was quite plain it was solid oak furniture. I also fell in love with a mahogany writing desk and a chest of drawers made for officers; I kept it at mother's. Goodness knows why I bought a mahogany card table!! My winter nights were spent working on the house or on a bike in the fire station workshops.

Pat had a sister living in Teignmouth, so we fixed up to go down there for few days. Her sister had champion King Charles spaniels so we went to a dog show which I found interesting. We also took her dog to mate a female. I must admit, other than seeing two dogs knotted together in Berkeley in 1965, I'd never seen how they got into the mating position. I also found out dogs don't worry about humans watching, he went straight to work on the female as soon as he saw her, but I was surprised to find he had to be helped to turn around, then they were left back-to-back for several minutes!

With my dress suit, and dicky bow, I had the usual round of motorcycle functions at the end of the year, at which, since the film Saturday Night Fever had been released, everyone was dancing with their hand in the air, John Travolta style.

I was on duty when we had a call to the Star Public House on Christmas Day. Luckily for them, it turned out to be a chimney fire, so after cleaning up we had a cup of tea and a hot sausage roll. We radioed back that we were available on fire ground, we were chatting to the customers, not to mention the pretty bar maid.

CHAPTER 17 1980-I shot KH not JR!

During 1979 there was an exciting drama on TV, Roots, by American author Alex Haley. The story is set in 1750 - 1822 about a slave called Kunta Kinte, being taken as a boy to America. The slave was Alex Haley's 7th generation grandfather. Patricia suggested going on holiday to the Gambia, to visit Kunta Kinte's village. There were some nasty injections involved but the holiday was booked for the end of March/beginning of April. I had the smallpox injection at the Hospital. The doctor came in and explained "the injection is cultured on eggs, if you are allergic to eggs please say so because I can assure you it will cause a violent reaction." It went quiet with everybody looking at one another, until I went "cluck, cluck, cluck" like a chicken, the doctor who didn't have a sense of humour gave me a black look and a "huff".

Patricia started packing for the trip. She bought me a '6 Million Dollar Man' suit, a TV series about a bionic man that was all the rage. I made her take it back, she reluctantly agreed, if I didn't take my sawn off jeans, a pair of old jeans that had numerous acid holes from bikes that would be fashionable today. They'd got so tatty, I cut them off and used them as shorts, not being hemmed, the strands of cotton were hanging down. Pat was trying to get me smart, a useless effort, but she'd taken a pair of good jeans, cut them off and hemmed them properly, wearing them made me feel like a Ponce! I don't know why, but I felt happier looking scruffy, and when she wasn't looking I put my shorts back in the case. This was one of the first charter trips to the Gambia, we flew from Gatwick.

The 737 was full, Pat and I were sat next to an American couple, and while chatting asked them why they hadn't flown from America to the Gambia. Apparently, it was much cheaper to fly Laker Airways to London and catch this charter flight! Arriving at Banjul airport, it was a little like a Carry On film, we had to carry our own cases across the tarmac to a small terminal building that looked the same size as at our local airport. I left the plane, saying to Pat "the heat is lovely" but that only lasted for an hour, it was 35°C all the time, compared with 7°C in England! As we walked into the airport to show our passports, the American couple were met by a black girl who gave them hugs. She was their daughter, and had been there for many months with the Peace Corps, and had a very dark suntan.

The next shock, was a bus that looked like the single decker I used to catch to school in the 50's. After leaving the tarmac road for hardened earth, everyone was hanging on for grim death. At first sight The Hotel Atlantic looked great, it was only 100 yards from the Atlantic Ocean and we could see straw covered huts. Once booked in, we found the straw was just for show and covered the corrugated tin roof of the bedrooms! After settling in, we walked on the beach, paddled in the sea, and got to know everyone. When we went to bed, once the light was put on in our room, there were red and black cockroaches running in all directions. I spent 30 minutes trying to catch them in the waste bin before evicting them. Mr nice guy didn't last past the first night, there were more of the horrible creatures the next night, so with a shoe, I flattened them. By the end of the holiday, I would go into the room in the dark, then Pat would turn on the light so that I could kill more, I felt like 'The Exterminator'

The food seemed OK until we all went down with 'Gambian Gut,' like 'Spanish Tummy' but much worse. Sadly, on the day of the trip to Kunta Kinte's village, Patricia had a bad bout of 'Gambian Gut' and was scared to leave the bedroom.

We had a trip to see a dance demonstration which started with a boat trip up the River Gambi. The boat did not look safe, I'm sure I saw some duct tape covering holes! I was disappointed with one couple, the day before the trip, the guide had asked the ladies not to wear any expensive jewellery because the people were so poor, and it would make the natives feel very inferior, but this one lady was wearing rings, earrings, gold watch, you name it she had it on. The average daily wage was 4 Dalasi, the exchange rate was 52 = £1, this lady was wearing around £1000 in jewels!

We arrived at a ropey looking jetty, I was thinking, *I'm glad I can swim*! We sat on the floor watching 40 ladies from 8 to 80 banging two sticks or bits of metal together, and a man with a drum between his legs. After a while, one of the ladies went into the middle, then walked back after wiggling her bottom. After a few of them had done this, one started to jump up and down while the rest banged their sticks much faster. I was tapping my foot, when this wrinkled old lady grabbed my hand dragging me in to the middle to do the tribal dance, all the Brits cheered. Once I'd made a fool of myself, a few more of our group got up. I asked this pretty black lady in full African traditional dress, if I could have this dance. My jumping up and down caused much laughter amongst her friends. Pat and I started doing 'Hands Knees & Bumps a Daisy,' many of the ladies covered their eyes! A London couple took Cine Film of all this!

We had a trip to a nature reserve, but only saw a few monkeys and vultures, after an hour, we gave up waiting to see the crocodiles! There was a bit of panic when we got lost, it was a bit like one of those mazes you see in comedy films, we followed the arrows, but we kept ending up at the same place. After the third time of going wrong, we walked back to the entrance, then half a mile along the road, nearly missing the bus back.

There was a visit to a school where the chairs and desks only had three legs. This was the serious side of the trip, showing the poverty in the country. The small village had just one well, they lived in a mud huts with chickens and other animals wandering around their homes. After seeing a youth on crutches, with his leg just hanging down all withered away, I asked why his leg hadn't been fixed, and was told there was only one hospital in the Country, in the capital Banjul. There was only basic Red Cross in the villages, so a broken leg meant a lifetime on crutches, if they cut it off, there was a risk of infection!

Walking down a street in Banjul, I saw a British Bedford fire engine and called in to see the fire officer. I told him I was a British fireman, he replied smiling "I've been to Moreton in Marsh Fire College," "me too, I spent 18 weeks there." After a chat, he called his firemen and introduced me to them, I ended up giving them a talk, and having a photo taken with them! A large open sewer ran down the middle of the main street of Banjul, which nearly made Pat sick, it didn't do a great deal for me either!

We did see a large palace type building, but all the shops looked like Britain in the 1940's, and very dilapidated. As a Tommy Cooper fan, I bought a genuine fez, and asked about the rest of the native dress. On instructions from the shop owner, a young black boy, who'd attached himself to us, led us to a market stall that sold caftans. In the market, meat was on open display in temperatures of 35°C with flies everywhere. I told Pat to have something heavy in her hand, and if anybody tried to grab anything, hit them hard and run!! Luckily we weren't accosted. I bought a caftan and proper pair of sandals, but they were the most uncomfortable things I'd ever worn. It was a very memorable trip, when I hear American Pie by Don McLean, it reminds me of the American couple we met and Wimoweh (or The Lion Sleeps Tonight) reminds me of the holiday.

I finish this part of the story, hoping it has brought a smile, with an appeal. I'm still trying to find the couple, who names and contact details I've lost, that took a cine film of me tribal dancing, in a dusty village, on the edge of a Forest, after teaching the natives 'Hands Knees and Bumps a Daisy,' with a few other nutty Brits doing the Conga!! I rang the couple up, not long after returning from the holiday, but you couldn't copy cine film in those days. I lost contact with this now mystery couple. If you know this couple, are relations of, or were on the holiday, please say hello if you remember a nutty Gloucestershire Fireman who raced British motorcycles, and who did a tribal dance. If the couple and the film can be found, I'll pay to have it put on DVD and will give a large donation to any charity named by the

person who finds the film. My contact details are
georgeridgeon@btinternet.com or **01452 857160**

My first shift back, Dave Hamilton and Dave Hawkins were both having a
bank holiday off, so I was in charge. I'd taken my fez and caftan in to show
the lads, but as I was getting ready, thought *why not wear the fez and
caftan to take parade?* The lads fell about laughing, then some of the more
boisterous tried to throw me in the water tank, which was very stupid as
not only did I have my wallet and watch on, but dropping me damaging
my leg. It was hurting like hell and started swelling, luckily Neil MacDonald,
a sportsman, had some ice packs at home and took a truck to get them. As
luck would have it, we had a fire call, nothing serious, but I put in the injury
book that I'd tripped over going up the stairs. As the leg was still hurting I
booked off sick and went to A&E. The doctor said "if you don't rest your
leg you may lose it." I had to have a week off, and miss a race meeting the
next weekend due to their idiotic behaviour, but it wouldn't have
happened if I hadn't worn the fez. I was just trying to spread a little
happiness, where have I heard that before?

I'd repaired the side wall of 83 Worcester Street with sand and cement
and applied to the council for permission to paint a mural advertising
Gloucester Leisure Centre on it. I'd asked the manager of the Leisure
Centre, Dave Rolley, for free swimming in exchange. The council threw
their hands up in horror and said it had to be done professionally. As this
would take some time, I asked if I could paint a swimmer or perhaps a
sport for all sign, and was told that'd be OK as long as it wasn't an advert.
When I got home I found mother in a panic! We now had a phone and
mother said in a worried voice "the council have rang several times asking
for you to ring them urgently, what have you done wrong now George?"
The planners were panicking, I mustn't paint a sport for all sign, it's a
recognised symbol, but a swimmer was okay. I did complain that they
hadn't left a message as they upset my elderly mother!

Using white Sandtex masonry paint I painted a swimmer, a Speedo clock,
a man starting a race with a gun and another swimmer diving in. A fireman
I worked with, asked if it was to do with the Moscow Olympics, which
annoyed me, so I contacted the scaffolding man, and added a weightlifter,
bowls and squash player. As there was so much interest in the mural, I got
the scaffolding free as he had a big company sign on the scaffolding.

I got a call from the local paper asking what the painting was about. I explained that I wanted to get an advert on there for the Leisure Centre, but it had to be done by experts, so I'd painted a swimmer just to fill the space. It all escalated when the Western Daily Press wanted to cover the story, I even got a call from Midlands Today who wanted to do an interview outside the house on the Friday of TT week. Listening to the TT reports at work, I heard that Roger Corbett from Bishops Cleeve had been killed. Roger was a local racer who helped many start racing, I helped him out driving in the hot summer of 1976. I was feeling devastated, and not much like doing an interview. I found out the press can be bar stewards! The reporter doing the interview, with the house in the background said "but it's so horrible, why did you do it?" "My painting wasn't up to the standard needed for an advert, which would have to be done professionally." He kept asking stupid questions, trying to wind me up, in the end I said "sorry I've got to go, a friend has been killed" and I walked off.

I rang Roger's number, but it was out of order so I rang a friend in Bishops Cleeve and asked if he'd go round and offer my services if they were needed. I was disappointed at his reply, "oh George, leave her alone" and replied sharply "I run over Tim Miles in 1970, nobody went to see his wife for 3 weeks, I'm never going to leave anybody alone in their hour of need again." I drove over. Joan had friends with her, I asked if there anything she needed, or if she wanted to go to Liverpool? She said she was all right, but she knew where I was if she needed anything.

I went to see various businesses, artists, and paint shops, trying to find somebody to do the advert. The last business I went to suggested I try my old school. I went to Longlevens School and met the art master, explained who I was and my problem. He explained that they sent all their promising students to Glos Cat Technical College where a Mr Wilson was in charge. Mr Wilson showed great interest in the project and called Mr Rendell, their design tutor. Mr Rendell drew up a design based on my ideas. The advert, various swimming activities with Gloucester Leisure Centre underneath, was to go on the top half of the wall, the bottom half the wall blank. Mr Wilson said he may be able to get all the materials free, so I put in the planning application.

I had a call from the council, "English Heritage feel it would be a good idea to hold a competition through the Citizen newspaper for a design." I replied rather grumpily "I certainly won't be happy if you do that and I lose the people who are prepared to do it as I've had no help at all from you,

only severe hindrance." I went to see Mr Wilson "I'm not happy about this, if you wish to refuse to do someone else's design I will resubmit the application," however, Mr Wilson was now keen to get his students to do any design so it was only Mr Rendell and I who were put out. I apologised to Mr Rendell but I didn't want the council to turn down the application. The mural was a big story in the Gloucester and Cheltenham papers as well as on the new local radio station, Severn Sound.

I contacted someone who could draw to put a design in for me, but after all the fuss and palaver, there were only three entries. This friend had done a design over the whole wall, including the small kitchen extension. Another wasn't very good, I could have done better, the last one filled the side wall and was very good! The design was of 6 rooms each with an activity in, or the Orange Man, the symbol of the leisure centre at that time, diving, playing squash and singing, a roller skate, beer glass and a football, in 3-D style which I thought very imaginative, the design even used the pitch of the roof with a tennis racket and hockey stick and in a very small room, a tennis ball. The only change on the design, which won the competition, was to move the football and beer glass to the bottom so if there was any graffiti it would be more in keeping with the football and beer mug! The words, The Gloucester Leisure Centre ran down the whole side of the building, I had a smug feeling as it ended up with the advert on the whole wall.

Dave Rolley manager of the Leisure Centre, was over the moon and so pleased he gave all the students a free swim. I again got the scaffolding free and Mr Wilson the materials free. There was an official launch of the wall early in 1981, staff of the Leisure Centre, Mr Wilson, Mr Rendell and the students were all there, it had good press coverage. Dave Rolley said "George you can have a swim or Turkish bath any time" I was pleased I had a mural.

I was called in to the station office and was wondering what I'd done wrong, "Ridgeon, you will be going on an Advanced Junior Officer course at Moreton in Marsh fire College." The course was in July, which meant missing the S100 and gifting the Mularney trophy to Mick Dunn. I found the list of names and alternative course dates, but the only one who was willing to swap was Eric Dewhurst, who'd refused his date to attend due to family commitments, but his 6 weeks was across the Manx Grand Prix, what a dilemma. I felt better about it, when I found out the S100 organisers had changed the fastest British bike to cover the whole meeting!

I got to know a motorcycling character, Frank Hill, a likeable senior citizen in his 70's. Frank rode a 1930's big port AJS grass track, he was always saying "call round for a cup of tea." He lived in a first-floor maisonette, as I was going up the stairs I saw on the landing a piece of TT history, a Honda 50cc CR110 racer. Although only 50cc, it was double overhead camshaft, 8 speed gearbox, and had a top speed of 103 mph at 14,000 rpm. I asked him what he was doing with the bike. "I'm selling it, been offered £850." When he added that he hadn't yet accepted the offer. I asked "what if I give you £850 in 4 cheques, £250 now and 3 post-dated cheques for £200, you keep the bike until all cheques cashed." I left the bike there for ages as it was in the dry.

Andy Eames, who had helped me at the MGP and racing in general, used to race a Honda CR110 in the 60's, he suggested I bring it to the Long Marston meeting, and he'd check it over. I took my Greeves and G50 through scrutineering leaving Andy servicing the little Honda. I told him Frank had recently taxed the bike and ridden it on the road, after making a silencer, so it should be ok. We started it up, what a lovely noise, I don't think the organisers worried about the decibel reading, as we were in the middle of nowhere. I asked Jeff Garbutt if I could go in the 50cc race, on a 1960's bike! What a machine, once push started in first gear, no need to slip the clutch again, although I must admit I wasn't used to revving a bike to 13,000 (max 14,000)

At breakfast, on the first morning of the course at the Fire College, I discovered I was the only leading fireman, half were Sub Officers, the rest, Stn Officers and an assistant divisional officer. We went to the lecture theatre where there was a synopsis of the course, we were told that this was the first of two 6 week courses, the second one would be in 6 months' time. As with the Junior Officer course there were many lectures and practical firefighting, each of us would take charge in turn. There was sport several times a week and the swimming instructor suggesting I go for the silver lifesavers.

On the first Thursday, at the Ugly Bugs Ball, all the girls had several chaps around them, seeing a mumsie type lady, I asked her for a dance, a quickstep then a waltz. Considering the rest of my course were Sub O and above, they behaved more like school kids, they said "Cor you can dance" but in a mickey taking way! The comment gave me an idea. There were 30 female control officers on another course, I asked if I could use the lecture theatre to give ballroom dancing lessons, charging for them to raise money for the Benevolent Fund. Unfortunately the powers that be took 3 weeks to say yes, by then the control room course was over which left only the office ladies and only one of them keen to have a go. I put up a notice advertising dancing lessons, sadly apathy ruled as only two from my course, were interested. In the end I didn't charge, we just had a pleasant hour. One night three more from our course turned up, I asked if they wanted to learn to dance, they said no, but that they'd pay to watch, "I'm not putting on a sideshow, either learn to dance or leave".

I realised I was on a hiding to nothing as the only leading fireman, but took part in all the sports, and went to the bar after doing some studying, well trying to read my writing, I sat with some of my course. As usual they were being horrible about someone, this particular night, someone started it with "he'd peed in the sink in his room." I was getting a bit fed up, so I said "for goodness sake everybody pees in the sink at some time or other," before going back to my room. At the breakfast table next morning, someone said "they've brought forward the maths exam," I passed the info down the table, but it was a hoax.

At a lecture with our assistant divisional officer, he said they'd heard people had been urinating in the sinks and that there would be random tests around all the accommodation. In the general chitchat someone said "if you flush the sink with water it will wash it away"! Although you could say I was an exhibitionist in some aspects, I was quite shy. One evening after study as I was about to go to bed, I had the urge to have a run out. It may have been because I was in my underpants and vest or because I was too lazy to walk to the toilet, but I used the sink. Following advice, I flushed the sink several times.

Ridgeon Rides Again

A few days later, a group of us were told to go a lecture room, I jokingly said "perhaps someone's sink has proved positive." Once assembled, the assistant divisional officer held up a bottle, "this is a sample that has proved positive, who is in room D28?" *My God, it's me*, "Come on gentleman, I can look it up D28, please come forward." I pulled my key out carefully to double-check but of course I knew it was mine, I stood up. Those sitting close to me made school boy noises, "Urrrrrggg peeing in the sink, get away from me." The ADO told me to report to the Commandant, Monday morning. The only good thing was, it was Friday afternoon.

I took the bottle home, and with some embarrassment, to the chemist on Saturday morning. I explained what had happed and asked if he could do a test. He told me that urine, once mixed with water, would only contain salt and to just deny I did it, maybe I'd left the bedroom door open. Still reeling from this incident and feeling very pissed off, perhaps not a good choice of words, I went racing with the NGMCC on Sunday. I felt like screwing the ass off my bike, a non-technical term, to go as fast as I could, if I fell off so be it. At the meeting, after talking to bikers, and a good thrash round, I felt better.

As there was no time to go home to unload, I returned to the fire college for a shower and some studying before bed. At breakfast, some of them were still making silly remarks, which I ignored. When Charlie, a tubby Sub Officer from Preston, said "George, I've been caught as well" I replied "no problem Charlie, there's no way they can prove it so don't worry" I later found out it was all a gigantic hoax, I was disappointed the students I thought I'd made friends with went along with the hoax, unless they didn't know!

From then on I associated as little as possible with the others, although I still took part in all the sports. I tried to find other things to do in the evening, usually seeing local motorcycle friends. One evening I went to see Jean Price, sorry Helen, as she liked to be called. Helen was now teaching, and was working in Cricklade, not far from the Fire College. She told me about her job and asked how my course was going, I skirted around the problems. She told me she'd met a nice fellow called Alan and was getting married next year. We laughed about how, on my 21st birthday, Mum and Dad had bought me a tape recorder, and were recording birthday wishes, one of which was in a squeaky 9-year-old voice, "This is Jeannie Price George, wishing you happy birthday."

I was working hard on my silver lifesavers, every day before the evening meal, I swam lengths, increasing the number by 5 each session, I had to do 70 in the exam, 1 mile. I practiced 5 minutes treading water with hands above my head and getting my pyjama bottoms wet and using them to make an airbag for the neck.

Bill Davis lived a few miles away from the course, now in his 80's, he was a top grass track racer in the 30's, 40's and 50's. Little Frank Hill had asked me to go to see him as they used to race together. I'd seen Bill when he gave a talk to the Glos and District Speedway Supporters Club at the King's Head pub. I took the Liverpool and Southampton Stn Officers with me and Bill showed us his vintage cars and bikes, I think, like me, Bill liked talking about bikes, well, anything mechanical. When we were leaving, Bill asked us to give his regards to the bikers at the pub we were on our way to, run by the parents of one of the firemen on my watch, Paul Sumner. I said "Bill Davis sends his regards to all bikers," which started everyone talking about Geoff Duke and motorcycles in general. A voice chirped up "I wouldn't let my boy ride a motorcycle." I saw a lady sat at the bar, a drink in one hand, a cigarette in the other and replied "how old is he and why not?" "He's 23, and they're dangerous," "you're smoking a cigarette, 300 people died today from smoking, they're dangerous." The two Stn officers were trying to ignore this verbal punch-up! As we left, I said "I hope I didn't upset anyone," "no, we enjoyed it."

With the course coming to an end the usual strip show had been arranged. I did seriously consider not attending, as the CMC clubhouse steward was retiring, and both events were the same night, but decided to go to the show. Watching ladies take their clothes off is normally pleasant but I was with people, most of whom I didn't get on with. There was further embarrassment, they were giving out various awards, when "sportsman of the course George Ridgeon" was announced, I reluctantly went to collect the award, nodded thank you, then put it on the table and left it there. Someone gave it me the next day with a caustic remark, but the course was over and I was pleased to get back to work, trouble was I had to go back in 6 months' time!

I was riding in charge on a call to 92 Barton Street, we knew this was derelict as we'd been called there many times. As some smoke was wafting out, I detailed 2 BA to take a hose reel. On entering, we found two tramps talking "what are we going to do Bert they've set our house on fire." Leading them out I said, "don't worry lads, we will sort it out for you,

349

anyone else using the house?" "No, we are the only ones." The driver looking after them, I put the small fire out and sent the 2 BA men searching the rest of the building. I told control that two people had been rescued and we were returning to the station. When we got back, I got hauled into the office, "why didn't you radio back, persons reported?" Trying to dig myself out of another hole I said "we'd already rescued them and it was only a small fire." I still got chewed out, I should have got the driver to radio that message back, especially after the incident with Chris Witts and our first fire in Southgate Street!

59 Barnwood Road was now let to black DJ, Major Anderson, his stage name, a nice enough chap who kept the house clean and tidy, shame he never paid the £50 a month rent! After 6 months had passed I said "if you don't pay £300 this month you're out, I'll throw you and all your clothes on to the street, I'll keep all your records and DJ kit to cover the bill, I'm past caring about publicity or the law." He whimpered "would you buy my 1975 Toyota Carina car, it's worth £850." Brother David said it was a good car and to give him £600. When I offered him £600, he turned it down, so I told him "you sell it for £850 and give me the £300 you owe me." Next time I saw him he said "give me £650 and it's a deal" I thought *it's better to pay £50 more, if he goes without paying I am out £300*! "Alright, here's a cheque for £350 move out at the end of the month." I collected the car with David lecturing me "now clean it as you never cleaned anything before."

I put an advert in the local paper, "Toyota Carina ready for the road, will sell for £850 or PX cheap car or motorcycle." A chap from the Forest of Dean with a 1978 250cc Yamaha four stroke twin rang, he was keen, but would need a finance agreement. Dave's partner, Dennis Coombes, had a sister who worked at Bowmaker, a credit/finance company in the motor trade. Bowmaker agreed, subject to references, to draw up an agreement.

I rang him, "I've fixed up credit for you on the Toyota," when I heard "I don't need it" my heart sank, until he said "I got cash," *cash, what a lovely word*! I drove the Toyota to the Forest of Dean and got £500 cash, I'd allowed him £350 for his bike. We exchanged documents, but when I showed him the car controls, my heart stopped, when the internal light went dim. I explained that perhaps the bulb was on its way out, got on the bike and rode home PDQ!

I hadn't looked that closely at the bike. There was dry rust on the forks, a few oil leaks and it was dirty, *perhaps he was like me, didn't like cleaning things*. I only needed to sell the bike for £150 to break even. The bike had self-cancelling indicators which stopped after five flashes and left-hand gear change, but as I was riding it in a more upright position and not racing, it didn't feel as dangerous as when I fell off on a left hand change racing bike!

After the DJ moved out, I had to get the house clean and ready for tenants to view. Although I'd gone in to see him to sort the money out, I hadn't taking much notice of the decor, but in daylight, to my horror I found the hall, front room and dining room, all painted chocolate brown! It took three coats of Magnolia to get it all looking liveable again, the house was tidy, but the small garden was a mess, he'd done nothing.

While preparing my G50 for a meeting, I'd found I should have been fitting small spacers at the bottom of one of the engine plates to the gearbox, without these the plate had been under tension and could have caused it to fracture. I couldn't find any suitable washers, only some 3/16" plywood, just the right thickness! Yes, I did drill it and fit it and yes, under tension the wood crushed a little and worked loose in the race. I did finish the race, but noticed it was all loose! Regrettably, I mentioned it Dave Brown, an MGP, TT rider, and was teased about 'wooden washers' for a long time!

I bought 10, G50 small valve pistons from Newcastle on Tyne. On the 260 mile trip home with Pat in her mini, I put the headlights on, as it got dark and the engine cut out, when I turned them off the engine started! I had to drive the last 100 miles home on sidelights, the ammeter was showing no charge. When we stopped at the service station, the fan belt wasn't broken and all leads were connected, so I assumed the dynamo was knackered, even an RAC man could do nothing! As the battery was flat, I had push the car so Pat could bump start it, which neither of us was happy about. Driving on sidelights was safe enough on the motorway, until it started drizzling, I had to turn the lights off to use the wipers, it was a terrible journey.

I'd found a small valve G50 Matchless cylinder head in MCN, I was told it had been modified from a 7R AJS head used by Ray Cowles, the Welsh wizard engine builder, to fit a G50. I decided to use a new small valve piston for the next meeting at Snetterton to which Gordon Bircher had agreed to come. In practice the new head started blowing, luckily I was the sort of person who took everything, including the kitchen sink, so I'd brought the G50 big valve head. The G50 engine was an integral part of the Seeley frame, so we had to take the engine out. I took the 27 screws out of the cam timing side, and got the piston to top dead centre with both valves closed. We were taking a chance that we could get the valve timing spot on, as there was no time to keep checking. With the engine back in and fingers crossed we fired it up, it sounding okay, so we fitted the fairing, just making the race. At the end of the day, Gordon looked knackered, but I was pleased. The bike went very well considering it was fairly low compression, it appeared to have more low-down torque!

83 Worcester Street was finished, after a lot of work including: roof repairs, cleaning gutters, a new bathroom, new windows, repairing floorboards and redecorating all the rooms. I drew a contract up with three lads, that only they could live there, they couldn't sublet it to anyone else without permission of the landlord. I'd also rented out number 59 again.

The first Classic Racing Motorcycle Club (CRMC) meeting at Snetterton was on the 17 August. The Club catered for all classes of classic bikes, four strokes up to 1972 and two strokes up to 1967 with certain exceptions, including the 1968 Greeves Oulton and Bultaco two strokes.

ME, JOHN SENIOR, GORDON MORSS

The first meeting was a learning curve, there were races for pre-1960's, up to 1972, 2 stroke only races, singles and twins. There were parades for people with classic bikes who didn't want to race, or more importantly didn't want to chuck them up the road and damage their pride and joy. Sadly I didn't figure in the results with the G50, even after a good start, but I did get 3rd in class on the trusty Greeves, with Gordon Morss just pipping me and John Senior, on a Ducati, in first place. The three of us were waved in by officials to have a photo taken, we wondered who had won the race as there was a 350cc class in the same race.

1ST CMCRC MEETING, HARRY LONG ON BSA

Just before leaving for the Manx Grand Prix, I advertised the 1978 Yamaha for PX. A man from Tewkesbury offered me a clean Honda RD175 twin, I got £200 and still had a motorcycle.

I'd entered the Jnr MGP on a 350cc AJS and the Snr on the 750cc Triumph Trident that I'd bought from Tony Tadgell. Tony had bought the bike from Roger Corbett when Roger was racing a Triumph for Bennett's, a Triumph dealer. In 1976 Roger had asked me if I'd partner him in the production TT on a Bennett's Trident. I told him that I'd love to but was two points short of an International Licence. Roger told me he'd sort it out, he could charm the birds out of a tree. I was excited when he told me he'd sorted it out with the ACU, just Bennett's to go. He asked how fast I'd lapped "91.5 mph on the G50, and 84 mph on the Greeves." Roger replied "I'll tell them 95mph." Sadly they wanted a better known rider, so that was the end of my chance to ride in the TT and still ride in the Manx. The production TT was not a world championship, you couldn't race in the MGP if you'd raced in a world championship race.

The Trident wasn't ready, and I still needed to borrow a 7R engine, but I could use my 250cc Greeves as one engine was 256 cc and ride the G50 in Snr. I put an advert in MCN "wanted 350cc for Jnr Manx GP." I got a pleasant surprise, when Richard Swallow rang me up to say his brother-in-law had just died from natural causes and left him his 350cc Greeves, all standard except for Norton forks and a disc front brake, I could borrow it.

I loaded the van with the G50, a spare frame and engine, the 250cc Greeves and spares, plus a tent and supplies, before calling in at Golcar, Huddersfield to pick up Richard's 350cc Greeves, don't ask how I got it all in! Arriving at Heysham, I caught the Geoff Duke Ferry, he'd started it last year, to challenge the Isle of Man Steam Packet Company's monopoly. I was camping close to Rupert and Ann Murden, Dave Montgomery and his nutty as me mechanic, Derek (Dogger) Cross, once my tent was pitched, along with John Daly, we all booked in at the race office. When my turn came, I was asked "name please," "George Ridgeon." "Are you riding a Triumph Trident?" "No, a 500cc G50." "Are you riding a 350 AJS?" "No a 350cc Greeves." I was told to put the changes in writing by the end of the week. Before I left, Maureen Beaumont, the lady I was dealing with, said "sign this please George," she had her hand over the photo, "what is it?" "I'll tell you after you've signed it." It was a surprise to find it was a photo of me, holding the hand of Princess Michael of Kent, about to kiss it. I asked Maureen where I could get a copy of it from.

Monday morning, after scrutineering, I pushed Richard's 350cc Greeves, out on to a dark road. The tannoy sounded, "Clerk of the Course here, weather is good, some damp patches under the trees. Please remember this is your first practice and take it steady, we will start at 06:15." I took it steady, I had no spares for the engine, had it geared lower than my 250cc and kept the revs below 7000 rpm. I did two laps, and after a cuppa with the morning tea ladies, found I'd qualified on speed, which meant I could leave the bike until race day.

As the G50 was ready for evening practice I stripped the Greeves head off to check the carburation, the piston was a nice light brownish colour, indicating it was running okay. Next I checked the primary chain for broken rollers. The engine was running well and no more practice was needed, well, not on this bike. I decided to fit a new duplex primary chain and oil seals before the race. The gearing was okay and the tyres were in good condition, so I left the bike to have some food and an afternoon nap before evening practice. I took the G50 through scrutineering, weather was still good and I did two laps. 4 laps down and 5 days to go.

Tuesday morning I pushed my 250cc Greeves through scrutineering. Scotty, the scrutineer, said "different bike this morning George?" "It's the spare one Scotty." Ken Harding, chief scrutineer and scourge of the scrutineering tent, pricked his ears up, and looking at his list said "you're down to ride a 350cc AJS," "I told them when I signed on that I was riding the 350cc Greeves, the AJS isn't ready." Ken boomed out "have you put that in writing?" "Not yet, they said do it before the end of the week." Ken snapped back "if you want to go out this morning you'll have to put it in writing." I ran up 6 flights of stairs to the commentary box in the grandstand. As I was writing out "I ask permission to change my machine...." Ken, who had chased me up said "that bike is a 250cc." I looked surprised, "no, it's an over-bored 250cc." "Why have you got green side plates on it?" I thought *you prat, why didn't you take the green side plates off.* Thinking quick, I said "I'm using my 250cc rolling chassis, but didn't get time to change the side plates." "If you go out I'll measure you," he meant the engine size, not me! As the barrel on it was 246cc having had a new liner fitted, I thought up my next lie "you've upset me now, I'm not going out as you shouldn't go out upset, I'll go back to bed!" After a snooze, I stripped down the 250cc and fitted my 256cc barrel. The regulations for the race said 310cc - 350cc to stop the over bored 251cc Yamahas, but at least it was bigger than 250cc!

Tuesday evening came, I'd checked the G50 over but on starting it died, I tried again, dead as a dodo. I put it on a rear stand, took the plug out and got another rider to spin the wheel for me, no spark, even on a fresh plug. After scratching my head there was only one option, to swap to the spare engine I'd bought off Barry Needle. I spent practice working on the bike, next practice on the G50 was Wednesday evening.

The 256cc Greeves was ready, so I took the magneto from the G50 down to the Lucas shop on Douglas Quay, but they couldn't repair it which meant a trip to Lucas Birmingham when I got back, I did cadge a new plug cap while I was there! After a cuppa, I carried on fitting the other engine, once it was up and running, I moved on to the 350cc Greeves. When I removed the primary chain engine sprocket and clutch, I found Richard's brother-in-law had made a special bearing and seal system using what appeared to be, Honda 50cc piston rings running on a hardened steel front sprocket. When I tried to refit it, I broke the rings, *Oh dash and bother*, or something like that! There was just time to get to the firm selling oil seals and tell them my problem, as there was no seal to do the job they suggested I got a special aluminium ring made to fit inside the crankcase so they could supply a seal that would fit, but it wouldn't be ready until Thursday.

I was pushing my 256cc Greeves in for scrutineering, having replaced the green side plates with blue, when I heard "Uncle Ken is looking for you George" and saw David Harding, Ken's nephew, checking bikes. "Are you refusing to check my bike David?" he did it reluctantly and I pushed it into the assembly area. I was sat astride the bike when I saw Ken bearing down on me, in policeman style, he put his hand on the front brake so I couldn't ride off, not that I had anywhere to go! "This is a 250cc", "no, it is not, it's over-bored," this was beginning to sound like a pantomime, "they don't do over-bored pistons," "they do, I'm sat on one." "If you go out George, I'll measure the engine." I replied in a calm voice, "you are quite entitled to do that Ken, I knew you'd try to upset me as you did Tuesday morning, but I don't want to go out upset." Ken asked, "where do you want it measured, here or my house" again in a calm voice I relied "I shall return here and give it to you to measure." I did one lap, then rode it up to the hut where Ken stood glowering at me. I leant the bike on the hut "here's my bike, I'm going for a cup of tea." Ken shouted "are you prepared to have this bike measured?" "Yes, you've got the bike, I'll have a cuppa then bring some tools back, unless you want to strip it yourself." Ken in a grumpy voice said "take the bike away." At least now I'd qualified with both bikes having done 5 laps.

The G50 was ready for Thursday afternoon practice so I had time to collect the items for the new seal set up, which I could fit on Friday. The G50 was ready for scrutineering, but being the pain in the ass that I've often been told I am, I had a very mischievous idea! I saw Ron Roebury with his wife Viv with their young son Dominic in the paddock, Dominic had a little Honda 50cc monkey bike. I told Ron about my problems with Ken and my 350cc and asked to borrow the monkey bike to take to scrutineering. With young Janet, Ann Murden's 14 year old daughter, I approached scrutineering, everyone was looking at me including Ken Harding as I shouted "honest, it is a 350cc Greeves." Ken gave me a black look, turned and walked away. I took the monkey bike back to Ron, and we all had a laugh.

The scrutineer checked my G50 as never before, every nut and bolt. I got dirty looks from some of the scrutineers, but others like Scotty, gave me a sly smile when nobody was looking! I took the first lap steady as the bike had new rings in. The second lap, coming onto the Sulby Straight, I lost the clutch so pulled in at Sulby Crossroads, by the pub. After borrowing some tools, I took the gearbox cover off, to find the clutch operating arm retaining ring had come loose allowing the arm to turn. I reported to the marshal that I was making adjustments and would ride back to the pits.

A kindly spectator gave me a cup of tea and I had a run out in the pub before re-starting. The lap took 1 hour 54 minutes, I wonder if it was a record? After practice and food, a gang of us went into Douglas, in the promenade was a shop that advertised making up T-shirts to order. Looking through their list of available designs, I saw "I'm a little devil" with a Red Devil holding a Trident in one hand and a bomb in the other. I asked if they could cut out the words "I'm a little devil!" and substitute "I shot KH", Dallas was a popular TV show at the time and everyone was asking who shot JR. They did it there and then for £4.

Richard Swallow's 350cc Greeves was ready, I'd fitted the new timing side oil seal and retimed it. It started okay, so other than mixing petrol and oil, one bike was completely ready for the race. Friday, Pat arrived, so I now had a cook and bottle washer! Sunday was the MGP Riders Association meeting in the Woodbourne Hotel, then back to the paddock for a cook up.

Taking the Greeves to the 'weigh in' at Mylchreest Garage, I wore my new 'I shot KH' T-shirt and had some friendly banter with Ken Harding, who spent a very long time checking the Greeves, luckily nothing was wrong with it. After that we went to the Woodbourne Hotel, Janet and little Johnny aged 13, sat quietly, but later in the evening the landlady came over "this girl shouldn't be in here," "I apologise, it's my fault, she's my 16 year old niece." Luckily she was only drinking squash. "Alright this time, if she comes again she can watch television upstairs." Good job she didn't see little John.

Race day Tuesday, I got a lift to Mylchreest, and paraded the Greeves to the pit where Fred Peck, Steve, Barry and Ray had sorted my pit out. Clutch starts had been introduced, much to my disgust. In 1971, I found out by accident that the 250cc Greeves would do 2 laps and 9 miles on a tank of fuel, this meant refilling the 5 gallon tank at the end of the 2nd and 4th laps.

I got a good start and was going well, stopped for the first fuel stop, pushed off again, and was going well until "Waaaaa!!" I took the plug out, it was burnt away. I fitted another plug hoping the piston hadn't been damaged, it started and sounding okay, I was lucky it was on the flat part of the course. It happened again, another plug change, it was certainly a good job I had my plug bag with several plugs in. When I refuelled, I exchanging the burnt out plugs. On the 5th lap approaching Ramsey Hairpin, it happened again. The plug change was okay, but how was I to start the Greeves on a short section of tarmac, it was just an area for parking, so no room to bump start? I couldn't have a pusher as it was classed as outside assistance. The marshals were displaying a stationary yellow flag to warn riders of the possible danger, me!! I used the downhill section to start the bike, having to do a U-turn but they turned a blind eye, and when nothing was coming, waved me off. As I approached to start my 6th lap the chequered flag was out, they'd finished the race early, I was lucky to have a five lap finish.

The riders' party had moved to the Palace Lido, which allowed more people to attend and take part in the usual foolish games, they'd started putting large sheets down so that the beer spilt would be absorbed. These evenings had become very popular because riders, mechanics, wives and girlfriends could relax for a few hours, although Pat kept telling me to behave myself. Dogger had brought Carol, who we'd all been chatting up the first week of practice, she was the daughter of Fred Hanks who published the TT Special. John Daly had brought a young lady called Pat over with him and with Rupert and Ann plus, Dave Montgomery, we had a good gang.

The 250cc race was first and I saw Rupert off on his Aermacchi. As the 250cc race was nearing the end I got down to the garage for my parade. I have to admit I was a little annoyed at myself, perhaps even ashamed, on the start line, the rider next to me said "I'm willing to push start if you will." I declined as we'd lose too much time, but in my heart I knew neither of us could win and only had a slim chance of a silver replica!

I was pleased I got to Bray Hill first, and felt I was going well, until the end of the 3rd lap. When I slowed for the pit stop, where Ray was waving the union flag, as I flipped my quick release fuel cap, it fell to bits. A number of mistakes were then made; covering it up so that the scrutineers didn't see it, not taking the nut off the other tank to put back together properly, or not swapping the large tank for the small one. The small tank would have meant stopping each lap to refuel, but would have been safer, as I was to find out!! Trying to close the fuel cap as best I could, I re-joined the race, but going down Bray Hill, I had fuel pouring out the tank. I was lucky the bike didn't catch fire with the fuel pouring on the hot engine, and I wasn't black flagged for losing fuel. I must have left my brain in toolbox. I sat up for the entire lap, I couldn't see through the screen, it was filled with fuel spray. The last lap and a half were a little better as I could get behind the screen, what a relief, as my arms were aching. In the twisty Glen Helen section, for some reason I changed back up to 4th gear, realising too late that I should've gone back to 2$^{nd.}$ I braked hard, but couldn't get round the tight right-hander, I went over the white line and stopped a foot from the brick wall, *you Pratt* I called myself. Luckily I'd kept the engine running, got it into 1st gear and back in the race after the nod from the marshal. As I was going past the The Black Dub I apologised to 'Snuffy' Davies and Roger 'Sooty' Corbett who'd died there in 1978 and 1980, for messing the bend. The winner was Geoff Johnson on a Yamaha at 103 mph. It was all 2 strokes down to 19th place.

Presentation night, I collected my finishers award for the Jnr race wearing my "I shot KH" T-shirt. I got many black looks from the committee and could feel Ken's eyes burning into my back. I changed into a shirt, tie and jacket with my finisher's ladder on the lapel to collect my Snr award. I was disappointed with 56th at 80 mph, but with the problem of the fuel..........

Friday was our last night, we were catching the Saturday evening ferry, and the gang went to the Crosby for our usual singalong. Carol Hanks wanted to stay an extra day with Dave Montgomery's mechanic Dogger, her father, Fred Hanks was not all that happy about it but relented and left without her on Thursday as I'd agreed to drop her off at 3 o'clock Sunday morning at the Birmingham Motorway Services. As we pulled into the Services a car flashed its headlights, I walked Carol over, the window opened and a voice shouted "get in," the car drove off, nearly running over my foot. Dogger and Carol eventually got married!

There was some sad news in October, Malcolm Davies who was the same age as me, died during a motorcycle trial in Devon, he was a top motocross and trials rider. I got to know him when I started motorcycle racing, especially after buying the Greeves, as they were Greeves agents. Malcolm was killed while waiting at the side of a country lane for petrol, he was sitting stationary on the bike, when he was hit from behind by a drunk driver who was fined £500 and banned for 18 months. I saw him at the 1979 MGP, when I broke down during early-morning practice he pulled up to say hello. He had his pregnant wife on the back of his bike, she had a little girl. RIP Malcolm.

Our watch was on day duty for the children's Christmas party. Freddy Star was flavour of the month on TV, so I decided to dress up like his Adolf Hitler character, it was the easiest to do for the children. I wore a pair of white tennis shorts and welly boots, with swastikas on the shorts and sleeves of the officer's jacket I'd borrowed from divisional officer Joe Nash. I had my fire service cap and a small black moustache. I was disappointed that the other chaps didn't dress up for the kids, but they all helped with the party, serving the food and packing up afterwards. Stuart did very good impressions of Benny Hill saluting, with old-fashioned spectacles and a black beret, and John Thomas could do either Elvis Presley or the Incredible Hulk, but for the Hulk would have to be painted green!

The children had their meal while waiting patiently for Santa Claus, in my best German accent, I said "ve vill make you enjoy yourself today," when the fire Bell sounded, I shouted to the children," "to zee fire to zee fire" all the children were laughing. The driver of the control unit said "I'll jump for you George." I went back to the party "yoz cannot get rid of me zat easy." Eddie Willey appeared with a plate of foam so with help from some children, he started spreading foam on my face. I was putting some on Eddie's face when his eight year old daughter kicked my ankle "leave my dad alone," "what about me, and Santa Claus never brought me a present!!"

CHAPTER 18   1981-My last Manx and a message

1981 started badly for the Gloucestershire fire service, Stroud was to lose one of its 2 whole-time pumps. This became a national FBU campaign, because if you take a pump from a fire station, you lose 5 men per shift, there were 3 shifts, 15 men in total, if a fireman was made redundant it would trigger a national strike. There was a march from Gloucester fire station to the Shire Hall in Westgate Street that was addressed by union officials from FBU HQ. It was a really good turnout with hundreds of firemen from across the country. The headline in the local paper, complete with photo, was 'The long crocodile of Firemen.'

On the bright side, my youngest niece Sally was having her 18th birthday party on January 10th. My old friend Ivor, worked at Vibixa in Cheltenham, and gave me some pieces of white cardboard 2 ft^2 to make a special card from. I spent hours painting a Union Flag card, doing it on mother's kitchen table, which was company for mum and she didn't moan about the mess I made as much as Pat! When we got to Twyning Village Hall for the party, I asked mother and Pat to tell everyone I'd be in shortly. I'd arrived in a suit, but changed in the toilet into mothers Union Flag waistcoat and put on a red, white and blue cardboard top hat, using mother's feather duster as a tickling stick, and armed with the card, I entered the hall of 50+ people shouting "how tickled I am," *apologies to Ken Dodd*! Sally ran behind big brother David shouting "dad, dad save me," "Oh dear isn't it a fancy dress party?" I asked. Most people laughed but I got some looks of shock horror. I apologised to Sally and her guests for being a horrid Uncle George, and gave her the card and a specially made silver brooch, by Ginger Blaney, a bike racing friend who ran Aardvark Jewellery in Cheltenham. The party went well, mother fell over doing the conga but not to worry, she was only 78!!

Saturday February 14th was another special day, the wedding of Jean (Helen) Price to Alan Hams, I took mother and Pat. As I'd been a pain at Sally's 18th party I thought I'd carry on and think up horrible things for the wedding. I copied to small Dictaphone, Jeanie wishing me happy 21st birthday when she was 9, I made the obligatory 'just married' card in the shape of a heart and after explaining why, asked the catering staff if they had any kippers, only having frozen mackerel, they gave me two, one went in the engine, the other in the boot. Jean looked lovely, even Tony, her dad, looked smart. Tony was always pulling my leg, "I must find you a round spanner for that round nut" and gave me a lot of grief about my mechanical ability or lack of it! Alice and Tony told me Jean found the fish in the engine but the one in the boot took some months!

In the six month break between the JOA courses we had to read about a leader: government, army, religious, whatever, but it had to be somebody who organised other peoples' lives! One of Pat's colleagues was a songstress with the Salvation Army, which gave me the idea of going to the library for a book on General Booth, who started the Salvation Army. I couldn't find one, but saw a book on Dr Barnardo, so took that. Although I struggled reading the book on Dr Barnardo, I did find what he had done quite interesting, and wrote a short synopsis of the book, which I thought I had to present when I returned to college.

Arriving at the fire training college, I felt the same strained relationship was still there, it was the same students and I was still the only leading fireman. One particular station officer, I'd describe as a ferret type personality with a real mean streak. When he made a caustic comment I said "get stuffed," or something like that, he threatened to spread the word about the practical joke they'd played on me, I replied "you do what you want, you're a nasty enough bastard," I'd gone past caring. I wondered how people could be so nasty, especially a fireman trained to save people's lives, protect property and render humanitarian services but, it takes all sorts to make a world!

Academically, it was an easy first day, I listened while they explained what we would be covering, only to find out we had to read up on Captain Scott of the Antarctic, so the book I'd read was a waste of time, in relation to the course, but I did learn about a leader. We were split into two groups, one arguing for Scott, the other group against. I was defending Scott, but the only book I could get from the college library was his diary, a very dry read that I didn't get through. I read the last chapter on the last weekend before the debate and had a tear in my eye when I got to the passage "I know I am going to die, I hope my country will look after my wife and child." I can't remember which side won the debate.

Ship fires were interesting; one lecture explained how to get into the hold of a ship that was on fire, the heat and humidity would be very bad as there was no ventilation. For the exercise we had a special Turkish bath type, piped steam room and were in full fire gear. We had our pulse, heart rate and temperature, checked and logged before going in. Wearing breathing apparatus, we went into the steam room which was 130°+

Fahrenheit. There was a platform with three steps up and three steps down, we had to carry two 5 gallon plastic drums of water weighing about 50 lbs. We had to go up and down the steps several times, run on the spot and touch our toes, I'm sure we lost a few pounds in weight. At the end of the exercise, our pulse, heart rate and temperature were checked. The reason for this, we were told, was that when fighting a fire in a hold of a ship there would be no ventilation, the heat would build up and you would use more air. Another lecture explained how unstable a ship could become if too much water was used when fire-fighting, it could capsize, also how to gain access to the ship other than going down the stairwells which could be full of smoke and heat. Large ships have a special area that you can go down, to gain access to the propeller shaft as well as access for other reasons.

Sir Henry was a concrete ship, built along a jetty, so that you had a realistic place for fire appliances to gain access, the other side of the concrete ship was for fire boat fire-fighting. The college had a rubber dinghy that could be used depending on what scenario was being re-enacted, even dockside, there was a 2' gap with water in it to make it more realistic. This exercise is where the ferret type Stn Officer had his comeuppance. We were all detailed to do various jobs, he was part of the crew gaining access into the ship to fight the fire. Although the Sir Henry is made from concrete all the hatches were steel, fires were in braziers so there was heat and smoke, he burnt his hands going through the heat barrier and had to have medical assistance, I'm not saying anything!!

Although I'd somehow passed my Stn Officers exam, most of the others had a grammar school education and were better on science and maths, I am sure Pythagoras hadn't been born when I was at school! Although I struggled, I did find it interesting, even when we were covering electricity, although I did prefer working with a motorcycle engine that went "clang, bang, knock" than with electricity you couldn't see but if you touched a wrong wire, you could get a nasty shock!

At a lecture on the elements, I just couldn't understand the fact water was two parts hydrogen and one part oxygen, hydrogen is highly inflammable and oxygen helps a fire burn, yet joined together they put a fire out!

Thank goodness for sports time, when in the swimming pool, the lifeguard suggested I go for the personal swimming award. There were many tests to do, the main ones were; swim a mile, dive down and swim through a loop under the water, and tread water for 5 minutes. I'm pleased to say I passed, mainly because I had time to practice. With my ballroom dancing skills, I was down the Ugly Bug Ball every week. At the end of the course, there was the obligatory photo with the other course members and tutors; sadly I cannot say it was one of the most enjoyable times in my life.

Having passed my BA instructors course, I fixed up a drill for searching a large open area. The week before the drill, I gave a lecture using two of my lead soldiers with string tied between them as a personal line and a length of string with a knot every inch indicating a guideline with tabs every 8', which the lads found amusing but it worked very well for showing how to search. I'd learnt on the BA course, always leave them with a taster, so said "the next shift we do a drill on searching a large open area!"

I contacted the new owners of the old Morelands Match Factory as I'd found out the upper part was still empty, the ground floor had been let to small engineering firms. The match factory had closed some years before.

I explained the drill. They would be blindfolded, each team was to have a safety officer, guidelines would be used as it was a large open area. Following further deaths of fireman using breathing apparatus all BA sets had been fitted with a pouch with a personal line attached to the belt, this had a 4' section, which could be extended to 20' when searching off a guideline. In a two-man BA team they would be attached to each other. I was acting as the foreman, and told them that a man was working on the ceiling lights and had not come out, that there may be a fire as the building was smoke logged. I put a fireman on the BA board and sent in two BA teams, after showing them a rough diagram of the supposed incident and where the missing man may be. At a real incident the OIC would ascertain all the information before entering the building.

Both teams were carrying a guideline; one team was sent straight on, the other to the right, following the wall. In the team going straight on, the No. 2 hadn't clipped his personal guideline to the team leader and started wandering off to the one side. When working with BA, the leader shouts "No. 1" and No. 2 shouts back. Although it was only a drill you could feel an air of tension when they realised they were nowhere near each other. They eventually got back together clipping on this time. The other team searching to the right had clipped on. I was observing both teams, and as the drill was supposed to be at a fire, I observed the man doing the BA board, taking the tally off each set and filling in the board correctly. As the drill was nearing the end, I detailed a fireman to take over, as I donned a BA set and teamed up with the fireman on the BA board. We were both blindfolded, and followed the guideline to the right with the drop. Although I knew the layout of the building, it's totally different when you can't see anything. At the debriefing, most comments were positive; I picked up on how the clipping on and tying off had gone.

HMI Winning did the annual County inspection, after a few days it became known that Stroud was to lose one pump. The Brigade was 8 undermanned, so with losing 15 jobs from Stroud, the extra would be spread amongst 3 whole time and Day Manning stations. It was agreed like this so there would be no redundancies, with retirements and natural wastage the Brigade wouldn't be overmanned too long, it avoided a national strike.

A few days later, Chief Fire Officer Wilson came in with another high-ranking officer and asked "May we join you for a cup of tea?" We felt like telling them to push off, but of course agreed. "This is HMI Winning, he sanctioned the reduction of the pump at Stroud would anyone like to ask any questions?" I said, "yes Sir, can you explain your reasoning behind the reduction of one pump at Stroud, because I believe you were told to do this by the government to make cuts." He explained his reasons and said he felt he'd done the right thing. I replied "I'm sorry Sir, I believe you were told to make savings, perhaps Stroud has fewer calls but with the risks in Stroud area and the difficult roads and valleys, specialist knowledge is needed" however, that's how it was left.

I was sent over to Cheltenham in the water tender to join the closing ceremony at which HMI Winning gave out long service awards at the end of his tour of inspection. He did an inspection of those on duty, stopping when he got to me, to say he felt he'd done the right thing about the Stroud pump. I replied "Sorry Sir, I can't agree with you."

83 Worcester Street was now let to three lads with an agreement that it was for three male tenants sharing, but one tenant, Ian White, had moved his girlfriend in, and not told anyone she was pregnant. 59 Barnwood Road was also let, so I had money coming in.

The RAF Wroughton course had been shortened to 1.9 miles, which was still a good length. Gordon Morss was having problems with the barrel on his Greeves so I suggested I try it on my bike, where it went well. Gordon then had a problem with his other barrel, so I lent him one of mine! We were racing one another, Gordon with my barrel as I had his. We were neck and neck, actually touching fairings going through the slow corners and chicane. We shook hands after the race. On the G50, I was sat on the grid next to Malcolm Wheeler on his G50 Seeley, I looked down and saw I had no front bolts clamping my forks, they couldn't really go anywhere but it was a clamp. As the saying goes 'I left my brain in the toolbox' and I raced with those bolts missing!

JOHN GOODALL, ANDY ALEXANDER, ME

After the start in the four stroke race, John Goodall, Andy Alexander and I pulled away from the 30 strong grid. John never seemed to be trying very hard, but Andy riding his quick 500cc Triumph squeezed by before John re-passed him. I was only feet behind both riders as we came down the straight after the start, on the last lap. As I approached the right-hand bend with white painted lines, like a zebra crossing, but for aircraft, I slammed the brakes on trying to outbrake the pair of them, but my wheel lifted off the ground, when it came down it locked solid and I slid off. It was easy to pick the bike up, I was full of adrenaline, into first gear, the marshals were running towards me but the bike started. I heard one shout "hey, where you going?" too late, I'd gone, so had John and Andy but nobody had passed me. At the next bend I had no front brake, which made me break into a sweat, the lever had moved around the clip-on. I found it in time to avoid the grass, and finished third, if the brake lever had broken off......................

The watch decided to raise £1000 for the children's ward at Gloucester Royal Hospital. After much deliberation, we agreed to row up the Berkeley Sharpness Canal, dressed as Vikings! Mike Cox, the fire service Benevolent Fund rep, was 5'8" and a ball of fire chasing the watch around to do this and that. Those of the watch that had experience of building and carpentry were making the boat/raft, the rest of us fetching and carrying. Using 6 x 45 gallon plastic drums, a frame was built using materials from Millington and Ramsted, a local builder's merchant. With my butchery connections it should be easy to find some horns to make a Viking helmet. I called into the knackers yard at Longford Lane, where we'd had many fires over the years. At one such fire, Stn Officer Corbett came as officer in charge. When he saw a long piece of dried skin he said "Oh look, a dried snake." I told him "no Sir, that is a bull's penis, it's been stretched with a weight and left to dry in the sun," he looked disgusted! They gave me a pair of huge horns, possibly from a Scottish Longhorn that I mounted on wood, they ended up on top of raft as they were so big.

Neville, the manager at British Beef Slaughterhouse found a small pair of horns floating around. While there, I saw some pig plucks one with the liver, heart, lungs. I found some caul membrane to wrap around the faggots I'd make. I took the pigs pluck, stale bread and onions to Morris Longley Butchers in Barton Street to use his mincing machine. I put the 80 odd faggots I'd made in Pat's freezer after they were cooked.

I made my Viking helmet using the smaller horns I'd acquired, made a jacket and covered up my shorts with sheepskin I'd acquired from the bone and skin yard in Cheltenham. Mick Bowen was dressed as the head Viking, with a big shield and axe made from plywood. We had one fireman steering and six rowing. On a day off, we had a test run from Tewkesbury to Gloucester on the River Severn, stopping at the odd pub on the way down, okay every pub. We sold 'Guess the time it will take us' tickets, many and various prizes had been donated.

During the early part of the year, Severn Sound, an independent radio station had started. The first day on air was CB Gorman's birthday, his name was Dennis, but as Siebe Gorman made breathing apparatus, Dennis was always called CB! Even though CB was a pain in the backside, I rang the radio station, told them it was his birthday and that he was retiring soon. We were in the kitchen at the Station, washing-up after breakfast, when we heard CB's name mentioned, the radio station even had CB on as a guest, which I think they regretted as he caused chaos on air!

I had several incidents with CB over the years, the worst was when he swore at me on the fire ground in front of a policeman, when I told him to put on BA and go into the fire with fireman McDonald. When we got back to the station we were called in the office, CB was only told not to do it again. I wish I'd had the courage to take off my epaulets and say if you're not giving me any backing, I'll go back to being a fireman.

May 31st was the date for the raft row, the 'Guess the time' tickets had raised £1000 for the children's ward at the Hospital. We took the raft to Sharpness on a large trailer, we'd been lent a motor boat which Phil Dyer was driving or is it piloting, with two more Firemen in case of accidents. Local TV, radio and reporters, together with a large crowd, were there to see us off. Wherever there were people watching the crew would shout "hear the mighty Vikings roar!" Dave Hawkins had first go at steering, he shouted "in, out, in, out," trying to get us in time, and shouted again if we got out of sequence, which was quite

often! The canal is approximately 16 miles long with 16 bridges, every mile, we would swap the man steering and the head Viking. On every bridge, a crowd of people were watching. We got to Gloucester docks in 8 hours 30 minutes 53 seconds! Many of the firemen's families were there, seeing John Thomas's 17-year-old daughter, I threw her over my shoulder, Viking style!

I decided to go to the Isle of Man TT for a few days, and contacted Liverpool fire station for permission to leave my Honda 175cc at the station. On the trip up, the RD175 Honda was going well, as I got close to the turning off the M6 onto the M62 for Liverpool I saw a motorcycle on the hard shoulder, pulling over, I asked "are you okay?" The rider was from Sweden "Ock yes, if you cee any other riders please say Odin is okay," excuse my Swedish Chef from the Muppet show accent. Three miles further along the motorway I saw a group of motorcyclists, "do you know Odin?" "Ya Vee do", "he's okay and will be with you soon, he's putting some oil in." I'd just pulled onto the M62 when the Honda stopped, I'd ran out of fuel *what an idiot*. I'd started pushing the bike up the hard shoulder when the Swedish riders arrived. I hung onto the carrier of one of the Swedes bikes, getting up to 30 mph. We'd just passed the 1 mile sign for the services and as my arm aching, I let go at the half mile sign thinking I could coast the rest of the way. I'd slowed to about 20 mph but then the speed went up, 30, 40 then 50 mph. I looked behind and one of the Swedish lads had locked his foot on to my rear foot rest, I got somewhat concerned when we were doing 70 mph. After filling up, they asked if I'd lead them through Liverpool. I smiled to myself, I had to find the fire station, and got lost at the best of times, but said "okay".

I found the fire station, left my bike there, and got on the back of one of the British bikes, the Swedish lads were riding. The thing to remember about finding Princes Dock, is that it's downhill from the centre, the lads caught the vehicle ferry and I caught the midnight boat for foot passengers only. It was the "King Orry" named after the Viking King who was credited with the introduction of the island's legal system and whose arrival on the island is seen as the starting point of Manx history as we know it. I got what sleep I could on the packed ferry, and at 6 am walked to the grandstand.

I was rooting through my army backpack filled with food and clothes, when I heard "what are you doing with rhubarb sticking out of your bag?" "This is good Gloucestershire rhubarb," "I come from Gloucestershire," "where from?" "Chipping Camden" "Do you know Rusty Hart?" "Yes, my brother is Geoff Hands" "Geoff, I raced against Geoff in the Manx," "you're not George Ridgeon are you?" "Only believe the bad bits", "yes I've heard there are plenty" we laughed! He said he was off to Peel so I got a lift to Fred and Jocelyn Peck's place, where I was staying!

I was sat on Fred's doorstep at 6:45 as I didn't want to wake them up early, I was having a chat with a lady scrubbing her step, when the front door opened. Fred was laughing as he asked "how the hell can I sleep with your voice carrying 100 miles?" A cup of tea with sausage, eggs and bacon was very welcome. I gave them half the rhubarb and apples I'd brought with me. Fred showed me the Triumph he had in the back yard, looking all sad and covered over "I must do that one day" he said, *where have I heard that before, oh yeah me and dad!* Joc lent me her 125cc Honda, then off they went to work at Manx Hauliers, a firm Fred and Jocelyn had set up delivering food, and other items around the Isle of Man as well as 'the other island.' You're not allowed to say the mainland when referring to the UK. I rode to Douglas to see Doris Jackson, giving her the rest of the apples and rhubarb before going to the paddock area and race office, where I cadged a programme. I started a lap, and called in the Crosby for food, they had 100's of photos on the walls and a pre-war Norton racer in a glass case, at the entrance to the bar.

Saturday evening, I watched practice before calling in the Ship Inn to see S100 friends. Sunday I did the rounds and ended up sleeping on the floor at Mick Dunn's home in Colby. I got up early Monday morning and went for a ride across some mountains and followed the coast, the views were beautiful, and as it was early there was lots of wildlife. Coming out at Kirk Michael on the TT course I decided to finish the lap, the 125cc Honda would do over 100 mpg if you rode steady. After filling up in Douglas, I watched the morning race from the grandstand, moving to Quarter Bridge for the Jnr race in the afternoon. At Fred's, we spent a quiet night in listening to a recording of the Goons. The Goon Show was a radio programme that had starting in the 1950s, the first comedy programme of its kind, with Harry Secombe, Peter Sellers, Spike Milligan and Michael Bentine. We were all laughing at the sketches, one, when the Captain of a pirate ship said "standby to repel boarders" then Eccles said "tell the landlady not to change the bed sheets" I was crying with laughter!!!! Next day Fred ran me to Douglas, to catch the 8am boat back to Liverpool. At the fire station, I collected my bike, making sure to fill it up before heading home.

At long last I started to get the 750cc Trident together, other than to give it a service, there wasn't a great deal to do to the rolling chassis, the motor was the problem, it'd dropped an exhaust valve. I went into Dean Motorcycles and explained that I needed a little help with technical expertise, and asked if I could use their parts washer. The mechanic, a German called Reiner, helped with the engine after I'd stripped it down. It only needed new shells, with Reiner's help the crank was built-up. Next the crank cases, we made sure all the oil ways were flushed through using the parts washer, before rebuilding them with a lot of advice from Reiner. I'd bought a new Trident head without valve guides, but time was limited, and following advice from Mr Baker, who ran an engineering business in Churchdown, I asked him to clean up the old head. Mr. Baker was a competitor, in car and motorcycle events before WW2 and offered good prices for a fellow competitor.

The engine was in the frame with the S100 a week away, not enough time to fit a fairing, just oval number plates, front and each side. I was catching the 1am boat on Sunday morning, so I got up early Saturday to collect parts from Dean Motorcycles, but on the way home, as I was waiting in traffic to turn right by the Cattle Market, I heard a crunching noise and had no drive, the gearbox had gone bang. I asked each motorist behind me if they could tow me home, eventually a driver who had a tow bar agreed. Leaving the van at Ash Lane, he drove me to Pat's in Longlevens. He showed interest in the fact that I was going racing, and was happy with the gallon of petrol I gave him for his trouble. I rang Gordon Morss at his garage, but there was no answer as it was after midday when the garage closed, he was probably working on his racing bikes or his own car. Driving over, I found he was there, so explained the problem. He took me over to a van centre where he knew the salesmen, they had a Ford Transit van I would've bought if it had an MOT, the sales lady said "my husband has a van for sale, taxed and tested." We rushed around to Gloucester Road, it was a Bedford Dormobile with side windows, it had a 4-speed gearbox, with the gear-lever coming from the back, having been converted from the column change. He was asking £225, after Gordon gave it his seal of approval, I tried haggling, but paid the £225 as I was over a barrel and it would cost as much to hire a van. Gordon drove the van home then I ran him back.

Back at Ash Lane, I fitted the cable I'd gone to get in the first place and the new 12v battery to the Triumph Trident. Gordon came to assist, which was good as it was 6 pm and I still had to load the van. We agreed that if the bike didn't start after two tries I'd take the G50 and Greeves, if it did go I'd take it and the G50! First push it went bang on one cylinder, on a twin it's easy to swap the plug leads over, but with a triple you have three to play with! We swapped two over and pushed again, the bike fired up and sounded as sweet as a nut. I rode it up and down as did Gordon, we agreed it was okay so loaded up. I had the G50, if the Triumph wasn't that good, I could ride it in both races. As Gordon was wishing me luck, he saw the Bessicar caravan I'd bought cheap and pointed out that the van had a tow bar and electrics, I'd try it when I got back.

We were camped again in the Paulson Park. Practice on the G50 went well, I knew the gearing to use, the Trident was a different kettle of fish. I hadn't had the bike out of 1st gear yet. I was hoping it was a lot more powerful than my 500cc, but it weighed a lot more, it had a single disc front brake which was more powerful than the drum brakes I was used to. I took it steady but on the third lap, as I shut down for Ballabeg Hairpin the revs stayed at 4000, beads of sweat immediately appeared on my forehead, I braked very hard and changing down, which meant some clunking of gears! Luckily I got it into 1st just before the hairpin *but how was I to get around it*? Brakes, hard on and clutch only half in, I could feel the resistance that was keeping the revs down so the engine didn't go bang. I was lucky this had happened after couple of laps, if I could finish this lap I would qualify. I used the same procedure at Cross Four Ways and Town Corner, having extra torque saved a gear change on many of the corners. Even more hairy was trying to get into the pit area, avoiding machines, people wandering around and working out how to stop the bike. I flicked my visor up and tried to shout above all the noise to those helping me. I put the front wheel up against the wall with the bike in gear and put the back brake on hard hoping it would stall the engine while shouting "put your hands over the carburettor to choke it!" As I was relating my heroic ride, describing how I got round the hairpin, they all just laughed.

The problem appeared to be the throttle cables were too long, although they were the ones Tony Tadgell had used. The gear pedal was also fractured and needed repairing. I went to a scrap dealer at Ballasalla, Mr Hogg, whose son Phil raced, he had some Triumph parts which he let me have, on a sale or return basis, Manx people are like that. I took the gear pedal to the garage in Castletown, and was waiting behind Andrea Williams, Peter Williams sister, well now Mrs Tom Heron, although Tom died in 1979 Andrea still liked helping at meetings. I asked the mechanic to weld the gear pedal, he told me "there's the bottles do it yourself," "sorry I can't weld." He wasn't impressed, "b***** riders who can't weld" but he did it. I was chatting to a rider on a Trident before one of the practices, when I was riding my G50. Afterwards, he took his throttle cables off for me to try as he'd already qualified, these were the right length, and I had a much better practice. As my race was first, he told me to keep them on, now *that* is sportsmanship!

I was waiting on the start line, close to my friend John Daly who was also on a Trident, having bought a Rob North replica complete with full fairing. I was even more nervous than usual as the first race was on the Trident, I looked at the rider next to me on a 4 cylinder 1000cc Suzuki, he had his chin on his hands and looked pensive. I shouted to him "do you know the worst thing that can happen to you today?" he looked at me with dread in his eyes "no, what's that?" "You could finish the race!" It made him smile, then I shouted very loud "all Japanese bike riders are sissies." There was a great roar from the grandstand full of spectators as the flag dropped and we were away.

I got away in front of John but he passed me at Church Bends. I was pleased I finished, but I only did 10 laps, the leaders did 12, so I was lapped twice. Although there was no problem with the revs sticking or clutch problems, the single disc, which I thought was going to be the bees knees, was going back to the bar by halfway through the race, so something would have to be done for the MGP! While the 750cc Trident was much more powerful than the G50, but the G50 was a much easier ride! I was 25th, not bad for the first ride on the bike and with no fairing. First job after the race was to take the cables off and return them to the Triumph rider, with thanks.

SHOWING JOHN DALY ROUND CHURCH BENDS, BUT NOT FOR LONG

I was ready to go with the G50, being tall I could always start well and was in the front half of the field rushing down to the first corner before we starting to string out, the quick having disappeared through Cow Shit Corner, as it was nicknamed. There were four of us having a battle: a big BMW, Grant Sellers on his Norton and a very fast British twin. For half of the race, the four of us were swapping places, the leaders lapped us, but it was all quite exciting. We were approaching The Black Hole and saw what looked like a bad crash involving Pete Swallow, we were still together when we got back to the same place on the next lap, and all looked up to catch the marshal giving a thumbs up. We started scratching seriously again until Grant's Norton expired, then there were three, that was until the big BMW started losing a spray of oil and slowed. Then there were 'two green bottles.' The British twin was indecently fast, it didn't appear to be a Triumph, but I didn't really have time to worry what it was, I was just trying to keep up. We were virtually touching at Town Corner, the last bend before the long start and finish straight. I could see the last lap flag was out, as we crossed the line so did the winner! As the other bike didn't slow up neither did I, we raced past the pit area having overtaken the winner as he slowed, I don't think I'd tried as hard before, I was certainly enjoying myself. Our machines had the same top speed, I couldn't pass him on the straight, my last chance would be the Black Hole. As we approached he slowed, *how did I miss him?* I momentarily looked back at

Cross Four Ways but could see no machine, I had a lonely lap being the last man to finish.

After parking up, I made my way to the tea girls where I found out that the big BMW rider was Dave Croft, he finished 8 laps. I asked at the medical tent how Pete Swallow was, injured, but recovering.

I walked to the presentation to get my finishers awards. On the G50 I was 26th on 9 laps, the other locals, Neil Cudworth from Bidford on Avon was 14th after winning a good scrap with Rick Andrews from the Forest of Dean who was 15th. I started to feel ill and told friends I was going back to the tent, but after lying down I had to get up to be sick, I think I had sun or heat stroke! There was a sting in the tail, on calling into the MGP race office, I learnt I'd been rejected for the Jnr race, I suppose I was lucky to be accepted on the Trident in the Snr with all the aggro I gave Ken Harding last MGP with the "I shot KH" T shirt!

It cheered me up when I got back to find the tow bar and electrics fitted to the Dormobile all worked. I used the caravan for the next four meetings, talk about luxury, arriving at the meeting without having to unload, and having somewhere to sleep. I felt like Barry Sheene, except his camper was better, the disadvantages were it took longer to get there and the MPG was lower!

Ash Lane residents decided to hold a party for Prince Charles's wedding on the 29th July with the usual food, music and dancing. Many people dressed up, I wore my Viking outfit. Newly married Jeanie, sorry Helen, Hams and her husband Alan came, so I chased her around in my Viking outfit.

One of the watch found out there was a charity raft row at Ironbridge with prize-money. As I'd already done one, I and a couple of others stood down to allow others have a go. I drove

Pat up in her mini to support the lads, taking my Viking outfit with me. I helped load the raft into the water then, dressed as a Viking, watched all the rafts away from the start. I drove a few miles downriver looking for a viewing area, cheered as the rafts went by before I moved on. At the next viewing area, there were a few fishermen who looked at me rather strangely, when I asked if they'd seen a Viking raft, they must have thought I'd escaped from somewhere. After the lads came by, I moved to the finish. We were pleased our raft won a £50 prize for the best dressed raft and crew which helped with our petrol home.

We got back to Pat's, me, still in my Viking outfit. Her unfriendly neighbour, Eileen, was sat on the couch in her front room reading the paper, her daughter was sat in another chair. Stepping over the dividing wall I shouted "hello Eileen." I could see she heard me, but she started staring at the paper harder. I banged on the window, but she still didn't look up, so I took my helmet off and banged the horn the window, "I got the horn Eileen." Her daughter was in fits, but Pat was pleading with me "leave her alone, she'll give me grief." Eileen had her head in the paper as if I didn't exist, *wishful thinking on her part.*

Eddie Willey was Sub Officer of green watch, but everybody called it black watch, his watch was short of a Leading Fireman, he just had Dave Baker, who I'd joined the fire service with. I had a quiet word with Eddie and Dave and said that I was willing to come across, after explaining the lack of discipline on my watch. I applied for and was granted the post with my 2 weeks holiday for the MGP confirmed.

I started on black watch, just weeks before my trip to the Manx, Eddie told me what he wanted, he ran a different regime to Dave Hamilton. All firemen were involved in doing group work, even making the duty roster out, so if somebody had a complaint about who was riding what appliance, they could complain to the person who made the rota out, although junior officers were in charge and made final decisions, they also had to do their share of the menial work, mopping the appliance room floor, cleaning the drill yard and duties in the kitchen, which I enjoyed.

I arrived at the 1981 MGP with two main improvements to my Trident, a full fairing, and I'd converted the single disc front brake to double discs. I could have spent a fortune on this with new front forks and twin discs, but found out that when they raced Slippery Sam, as the Trident production racer had been called, all parts used had to be a production parts so they

377

used another road single disc and slider, turning it round the other way so you had one leading and one trailing disc. I'd been told it wasn't quite as efficient as a twin leading shoe brake, but on testing it in Ash Lane, it felt much better. I went over to the Island on my own. I camped opposite Rupert and Ann, with little Janet and Johnny. Janet was now 15 and had brought her school friend, Siobhan over. Ann was kindly keeping an eye on me, cooking me a nice meal every so often, which was very much appreciated.

I signed on and attended the safety lecture, I confirmed I'd brought the Trident, and decided not to say anything about being turned down for the Jnr until after the race, as I'd brought my Seeley G50 matchless in case I had any problems. As well as the tent for living in, I'd acquired an Army flysheet, which I used for storing the bikes and working under if it was raining. Jonathan Parkes, at the S100 races, had recommended Gulf 40 oil, which he used in his Trident. I'd acquired a gallon which was in the bike, assuming I could get more in the island! I'd also set up an oil pressure gauge, something else to watch on my first lap, as it was recommended not to let it fall below 75 psi. Thinking of Jonathan reminds me of a race I had with Jon at the S100, I was committed going into Cow Shit Corner, the left-hander at Ballanorris Farm, when Jonathan came underneath me, we were two abreast when another rider went inside Jon, with me on the outside, we were three abreast! They were going quicker than me, so I backed off and was ready to go through the open gate, Jon was heading for the brick wall, luckily he only rattled the straw bale, I rode through a hail of straw. I can still feel the sweat inside my helmet when I think about it!

At 6.15am it was just light enough, as Bill Boak tapped me on the shoulder to go. I was in 5th gear as I crossed St Ninian's, but went down Bray Hill on half throttle to let the tyres warm up, at Ago's leap the bike went light, I also went slow, well 80 mph towards Quarter Bridge, taking the revs to 6800. Once round Braddon Bridge, it was Union Mills then four miles in top gear. With the large tank that Roger Corbett had made, before he sold the bike to Tony Tadgell, the flat-out position felt comfortable. I said a special hello to Roger Corbett as I went past the Black Dub in the Glen Helen section not forgetting Snuffy Davies. Everything seemed to be going well, I took Ballaugh Bridge gingerly, gave a high girl's wave to Gwen then approaching Ramsey, changing down to first for Parliament Square. I started the climb up May Hill past Stella Maris, again thinking of Roger, as he fell off there in his first MGP and named his house after it. Around

378

Ramsey Hairpin, which wasn't as bad as I thought it might be with a much heavier machine. There weren't any problems, but I wasn't as fast as I would like, but as a few good rides had told me over the years "you can lose a lot of time on a slow corner if you try and rush it," and it was only my first lap. It pulled much easier up mountain, but was quite difficult at Governors Bridge and The Dip, being 200 pounds heavier than the G50.

I started a second lap, getting into top gear at the top of St Ninian's thinking *here we go* as I rushed down Bray Hill, but hitting the bottom of Bray I thought I was off, the bike was shaking its head and bouncing all over the road, if I'd been a smaller rider I'm sure I would have be off. I was fighting with it for what seemed like ages, wondering *how did I miss the wall on the left hand side*? As they say in cowboy films when riding a Bronco, I let it have its head! By the time I got control, I was past Ago's Leap, so was even steadier round Quarter Bridge than on the first lap. I was struggling to concentrate on where I was going, as I was concerned about what the problem was, the bike seemed to handle in a straight line and around fast bends, but obviously didn't like to change direction at the bottom of Bray Hill!!

After practice, and asking the world and his wife for advice, we ended up putting thicker oil in the forks and buying a set of shock absorbers off Roger Sutcliffe that he'd used on a 1000cc Kawasaki at the TT. Someone suggested moving the forks through the yokes an inch to lower the front-end. With Rupert's help, I got the bike ready for Monday night practice and just did one lap.

Tuesday night practice I again took it steady for the first lap, as I crossed the start/finish line I put it in top gear, just before St Ninian's crossroads I thought *here we go again*, as I hit the bottom it was all over the road again, I was fighting a lock to lock wobble. Perhaps this is how all top riders ride their bikes, you just have to have the nerve and do it, but somehow I don't think I had the guts they appeared to have. The rest of the lap was okay although I was nervous through the bottom of Barregarrow, it was only flat out for me on the 250cc Greeves! The double disc brakes were working well, especially on the drop-down from Kate's Cottage to Creg Na Baa, I'd done five laps now.

After checking the bike from front wheel to back I decided to put some even heavier oil in the forks, it was now up to 30 grade, and dropped the forks through the yokes another inch. I double checked to see if there was any play in the steering head or swinging arm which could affect handling. The rear chain tension was okay, I took the primary chain outer cover off, to check triplex primary chain, overall, everything was good. I had no more Gulf 40 oil, and after asking all the traders in the paddock, couldn't find a supplier in the Isle of Man, but the oil level hadn't dropped and it didn't appear dirty. The bike seemed perfect, but why was it all over the place at the bottom of Bray Hill? Of course I only had a road frame, but so did Slippery Sam and it had won the production race, five years running.

Wednesday was another hot day, practise was due to start at 6 pm. At about 5pm I was still fiddling with the bike when Ann shouted "George, dinner ready," "busy for a few minutes Ann," "your dinner's ready now, have it while it hot." I replied "I'm not here to eat, I'm here to race." I'm reminded of this many times when we're talking about the old days! I got the tap on the shoulder and went down Bray Hill in fifth gear, slowly, having twice lost control of the bike. I started the second lap and although in fifth gear, I'd chickened out again, of going flat out down Bray Hill in top gear! Pulling up the mountain, the bike was still going very well, however the oil pressure had dropped to below 75 psi. I backed-off to finish the lap, which wasn't a major problem as I'd now qualified. The oil problem could be discussed at the MGP supporter's club dinner on Wednesday night.

Gwen Crellin, a.k.a. the lady in white, was the first lady Marshal and although in her 60's, a ball of fire. Gwen had started the Manx GP helicopter fund and was Madam Chairman of the MGP Supporters Club (MGPSC) After the meal, speeches, awards and auction, as I was chatting to the Bishop and Lt. Governor of the Isle of Man, the representative of the Queen, I noticed a pretty girl sat at the top table, she was the daughter of Gwen's friend. We danced all night and fixed up a date for Thursday evening. She lived near Gwen in Ballaugh.

As we couldn't get any Gulf 40 oil and I wanted to get some practice, I applied to ride my G50 with your friend and mine, Chief Scrutineer Ken Harding, who said "you have to do 5 laps on this machine if you want to ride it in the race and you've only got three days left." I thanked him for the information trying, with great difficulty, to be pleasant, I didn't want to get banned from my only race! I was certainly hoping to go back to the Trident, but there was only three days to sort the oil problem, and the battery kept running down. The bike was using standard points and coil with a total loss battery system. There wasn't time to fix up electronic ignition. In practice I'd only been doing two laps at a time. I'd gone to the Douglas Motorcycle Centre, a new dealer on the Island, and asked if they'd lend me a battery for the race so I could change it on the third lap. They said for my cheek, they'd lend me one if I bought one, which solved my problem, as it wouldn't do 6 laps on one battery and mine was suspect. For the race, I painted Douglas Motorcycle Centre on the fairing. Thursday afternoon practice on the G50 single went well, it was really enjoyable after the large lump of Trident, a bit like riding my Greeves after the G50. I didn't break any world records but was in the high 80's. I didn't intend going out Friday morning at 6 am as I had a date with the young lady that evening.

I couldn't find my date's house, so went to Gwen's for a cuppa and a piece cake, which was always on offer. Gwen phoned her friend then passed me the phone. I was shocked to hear my date had gone out. I don't know if Gwen knew, but I later found out that the mother had stopped her daughter from going out with me by telling a downright lie, it seemed she didn't trust this upstanding fireman to take her daughter out!!

I got back to the paddock about 9 pm, feeling fed up, I decided to go out for practice in the morning, the only trouble was, I had to check the bike over. No need to worry about tappet clearance, plug colour was okay, but when I took the oil drain plug out, it had some metal on it, it looked like a steel shim was breaking up. Dropping the primary cover off and holding the engine sprocket, I pulled it sideways, it moved in and out. As the main bearing on the timing side governs the end float, this meant I had to take the timing side off, those 27 screws!! I'd hoped that the large nut holding the gear drive on the main shaft was loose allowing the end float, but it was tight, so there was nothing I could do but put it all back together, fairing on and bed just before 2 am.

Somehow I fought my way out of the sleeping bag at 5.30 am, the bikes starting up provided a free alarm clock. The clerk of the course announced the conditions as good although there was mist around the course and damp under the trees. I did one lap as I was worried about the steel shim, but the bike seemed to handle so well it was a shame there was mist at Hillberry and Bedstead, I would've liked to see a dry lap time. Although I hadn't considered riding the bike in the race as I still needed two more laps on it to qualify, the shim problem made the decision final!

I had all day Friday to sort out the Triumph but there was no Gulf 40 engine oil on the Island, the consensus of opinion from other riders, and the Merlin of the paddock, Ken Inwood, was to use the best quality 20/50 oil I could find. I don't know why I ended up going to the local car spares shop who suggested ELF 20/50. I was working on the bike when Ann shouted "I know you're not here to eat George but your dinner is ready," "alright mother I'm coming," Ann called me a cheeky bugger!! This was one of the good things about the Manx, the banter between riders and pulling each other's legs. Dave "the Mont" Montgomery and his mechanic Derek "Dogger" Cross said "we're not here to eat we are here to race" whenever dinner was mentioned. Having finished the meal I must have pulled Janet's leg about something as she, and her friend Siobhan started beating me up and jumping on top of me. I was thinking, *I must try to not enjoy this too much,* luckily they did have trousers on but their tight jumpers were doing me no good at all. I shouted for Ann to come and rescue me, Rupert and Ann just laughed then shouted "Janet put that man down, you don't know where he's been."

Just before the last practice I saw Phil Landeg, one of the Welsh racers who knew Ray Cowles, "the Welsh Wizard". I asked him what grade of oil Ray used in the front forks of his Triumph 750cc Trident, "George Boyo, he uses straight 50." There wasn't time to change the fork oil before the last practice, the main test was to see if the Elf oil was okay. I was pleased the oil pressure stayed above 75 PSI even when I took the revs higher. I talked to other Trident riders who told me that 60 even 50 psi was okay.

After the MGPRA meeting Sunday morning, and a nice meal in the paddock, our group were sat around when Alex George stopped by. We all sat in the sun talking about bikes. I was trying to find out how Alex went so fast on a Trident, but I think it was just me being slow!! It was a nice easy couple of hours before we all got back to working on our bikes, the 50 grade oil was now in the forks. It had been the best practice week weather wise I could remember, we only had rain one afternoon.

The rider's night party was again at the Palace Lido, our gang sat together. I with the Mont, Dogger and John Daly, we'd just finished a tug-of-war, but as we were going back to our table Ken Harding, with his party hat on came up to us, "you three come with me" John Daly scurried away. We went behind the stage where Ken told us to roll up our trouser legs, "what for?" "Don't argue do it." Then he told us to take our shirts and vests off. Ken had a commanding sort of voice, assuming it was for some sort of entertainment, we did it. Our faces dropped when he gave each of us a grass skirt and coconuts attached with string that looked like a ladies bra. We were asking each other if we were really going to do this when we heard Ken announce "ladies and gentlemen, please give a warm welcome to the beautiful Hawaiian dancers from the Palace Lido Hotel." The band played some Hawaiian music, there was applause and cheering from the assembled riders, mechanics and Manx enthusiasts, but when the three of us walked out, the place fell about laughing. Rupert later told me he was crying with laughter. We were doing our best at Hawaiian style dancing and I'm told I did some very suggestive movements, anyway it was the end to a good night out.

Wednesday was final preparation for the "weigh in." I had two batteries, and had bought 2 two prong electrical plugs, like on mowers that clipped together quickly and couldn't be connected the wrong way round! The changing of the batteries would be coming at the end of the third lap, at the same time as refuelling. Steve, Barry and Andy Eames, who'd come over with his wife Barbara, were helping in the pit, even Ray Whitefield had come for a few days. We did practice battery changes several times, I rode around the paddock, pulled up, stopped, they changed the battery then push started me away. Janet and little John timed us until after many goes we were all satisfied.

Wednesday night, because of the battery troubles, we took the Trident down to Mylchreests Garage for the "weigh in" in the van. I pushed the Triumph into the garage covered with a large union flag, well duvet cover material that I'd got at the Saturday market in Gloucester! Ken Harding said "oh no, I knew you would mess me about changing the bike back to the Triumph."

Thursday morning it was the Ltw race so I helped Rupert Murden in his pit. I saw the Lt. Gov. arrive, and, with a large group of Manx officials walk down the Pit Lane. When I shouted "it can't be!" Rupert looked at me, I stood frozen as the group got closer. Rupert asked "what's the matter George?" Stuttering, I replied "Is it, it can't be" then "Yes it is, Norman Wisdom." Norman had made me laugh, at the age of nine, with his antics in "Trouble in Store," a 1953 film. I rushed up to shake his hand, "Norman Wisdom how are you," "Who are you" he said looking up at me. "I'm George Ridgeon, riding in the Snr," "are you, on what bike?" "A 750cc Triumph Trident all British and this is Rupert who's riding now and his wife Ann, she also races." Norman's eyes lit up at seeing a pretty lady. At this point one of the Manx officials grabbed him "Mr Wisdom we have to carry on with the inspection." It made my day! The Ltw race was won by Graham Cannel, I was pleased as he was riding a Cotton Rotax, Stroud rider Tony Russell had a creditable 13th at 96 mph, sadly it was a DNF for Cheltenham rider Bob Eva and Rupert.

I went with John Daly to collect our bikes, he'd been having trouble in practice with his cam followers. We went onto the start line and queued up, I was No: 83, and chatting to No: 84 when the Clerk of the Course gave his report "fine, all the way round, you may start your machines."

We reached the cones and paddled the bike forward, I still thought it should be a push start, for tradition and to save the bike overheating. Whenever you started to think about something else, the roar of the bikes pulling off the start line every 10 seconds brought you back to reality. As the two bikes in front started, I looked at No 84 on my right, stretched across with my left hand, as the bike was still in neutral, to shake of his hand shouting for him to have a good ride, pulled in the clutch, into 1st gear and we were off. I was soon up to 7000 rpm, into 2nd, 3rd but stayed in 4th down Bray Hill as I was close to another rider and I just missed the wall at Braddon Church. The bike was going well as I went through Ballacraine, Cronk-y-Voddy Straight didn't seem so bumpy, perhaps because of the weight of the bike, which I was still getting used to and the 50 grade oil in the forks, *stop thinking, start concentrating* I shouted at myself. At the 11th milestone, I always thought of Dave Williams crashing there in 1976, breaking his back. I always thought to myself as if speaking to God *Please don't let me get injured like that racing*. Rattling through Kirk Michael, the 3 into 1 megaphone, with the engine revving at 7000 rpm, must have sounded lovely, but the street seemed very narrow at 130 mph. I got to the right then left close to the White House at Rhencullen then the rise just afterwards where the front wheel left the ground, even this lump of a machine! Bishops Court, although flat out on the Greeves, I eased a little, was I being sensible on the Trident? All of a sudden I was at Parliament Square climbing towards Ramsay Hairpin and the mountain.

I found the mountain section went quickly, and took a wide sweep at Governors Bridge, the bike was going well. At the end of the third lap I slowed to a stop for fuel. My friends in the pits had union flag hats on, one changed the battery, one refuelled me and another wiped my visor, it was covered in flies. Thank goodness they now allowed a pusher, as the Trident was much heavier than I was used to. There was a throaty roar from the open megaphone as the bike fired up, I chickened out again and kept it in 4th for Bray, *will I be brave enough to go down in fifth gear before the end of the race?* The bike was 200 pounds in weight heavier than the G50, I was still on a learning curve.

Despite having the heavier 50 grade oil in, and the bike handling well around the course, having lost control of the Trident twice, I just didn't the nerve to do Bray flat in top gear. I knew it could be done, but I just wasn't man enough, unlike Malcolm Uphill, Mick Grant, Ray Pickerel, Tony Jefferies, Alex George and Percy Tate on the road going 750cc Trident. It could have been a set up problem somewhere, who said it could be me being a wimp?

I gave a last wave to Gwen Crellin, then climbed the mountain in the sunshine. Approaching Bungalow Bridge there was a funny shaped building which I found out was to do with Manx telecom, I changed back to 5th gear before slowing for the Bungalow, changing down to 4th I went into neutral, I changed down again but on letting the clutch out, the bike lurched when the back wheel locked, my heart stopped for split-second. I'd gone from fifth to third gear, "you prat" I shouted at myself. I wobbled around the left-hand bend at the Bungalow and across the railway lines that take the electric trams up to the top of Snaefell Mountain, back into 4th then 5th gear for the last uphill rise to the 32nd and the highest part of the course. I'd gone round it in fifth gear on the Greeves, but that was 1971, 10 years ago, which felt like a lifetime. This short straight had given me time to settle back down around the 3 left-handers, the bike having much more pulling power and torque was easier to ride around Windy Corner, I was looking at the car park where I'd stopped with a young lady one night! "Your mind is wondering again George" I shouted at myself.

Apart from the scare at Bungalow I felt quite fresh as I approached Kate's Cottage, I braked hard and went into second gear for the Creg, I was pleased the twin discs were still working well even after 6 laps. Close to the bank on the left-hand side a group of people were waving union flags, I gave them a wave back. I was now approaching Governors, although it was two-way when roads are open, it didn't look much wider than 16' and was quite bumpy. As it was sort of downhill with an adverse camber, I tried to work my way over to the left to negotiate the tight right-hand hairpin then a sharp left, a strange sort of road, I never found out why it was designed that way.

Coming onto the start/finish straight I saw the chequered flag being waved but thought it must be for somebody else and wanted to go on because I felt so fresh. The nice lady was there waving a red flag indicating the finish of the race, I was now several hundred yards past the end of pit Lane. Flicking my visor up I shouted "I have another lap to do," "you've finished George, you've done six laps" "have I really?" "Yes, and the roads open car has left, get off the track" she gave me a smile. As I was pulling through the gate I saw her little girl with her granny "hello, do you want a ride?" "Yes please" so granny lifted her up onto the tank, I rode steadily up to where we were parking the bikes and gave her back to granny. I lent the bike against the fence and flopped onto the floor, although I'd wanted to go on a few minutes ago, the 6 laps, 226 miles started to take their toll and I just felt knackered. I was sat daydreaming when I heard "Can I sit with you?" I was awoken from my trance looking up at Norman Wisdom. "You finished then?" he enquired "yes thank you, but not very fast." I was surprised when he asked me for my advice "I want to buy a bike, what sort do you think I should get?" "Well Mr Wisdom, I don't want to be rude, but you're not very big, they don't make the Tiger Cub anymore which would be British, but Honda make a nice 125 cc possibly 250cc." I found out afterwards he'd bought a 900 BMW!

At the presentation, I collected my finishers award, I'd averaged 89 mph, my fastest ever race average for 6 laps, but my fastest lap at just over 90 mph was in 1976 on my 500cc G50. I was thinking *if I could have gone down Bray Hill in fifth*………but it was all history now, and I was pleased with myself. As I left the stage a group of young Manx lads asked if they could have my autograph, so I signed their piece of paper and drew a union flag.

As the landlord had asked me a few days before if we were coming in, and said he'd have some pies for us, Friday night, we went down to the Crosby.

I was sat in the bar with John and his dad's Gibson guitar. John had the ability to accompany what ditty we made up, this year it was entitled "In the Mist." "Ridgeon finished on his Triumph in the mist", "Ridgeon finished on his Triumph in the mist", "Ridgeon finished on his Triumph, Ridgeon finished on his Triumph, Ridgeon finished on his Triumph in the mist," emphasising 'in the mist' the last time. We were trying to think of another verse when we saw Grant Sellers and Peter Swallow at the next table, they'd both ridden Manx Norton's in the Snr race. We went with "Sellers beat Swallow in the mist", "Sellers beat Swallow in the mist" etc. The pub had several bars, and when the landlord, Bob Grimshaw, came into the bar we all stood up, pointed at him and sang "Grimshaw lost the pies in the mist," etc. Bob did a 'James Cagney' against the bar with his arms outstretched (a film actor in a 1940's gangster movie when the prison spotlight gets him) minutes later, out came a tray of pies for all the riders! So another Manx was over. It'd been the driest Manx ever, only half a day's rain in 2 weeks, unlike some years in the early 70's when we were nearly washed out. I remember saying goodbye to Bill Swallow and his girlfriend, who were in swimming costumes packing up what was left of their tent!

I was trying to get used to everyone's name on the new watch, there was a new member, Dave Flello, who'd transferred from Birmingham City, that I got on with quite well. We'd done a ladder drill, where we rescue a body, well the dummy, by throwing the rescue line over the round, after dropping a fireman into the floor where the body was, then extending the 45' ladder to the floor above and lowering the dummy down. Dave said that the West Midlands Fire Brigade had made a steel adapter to go over the round for the line to run through. The adapter was to save damaging the line, as the round had small ridges on to stop your foot slipping, Dave gave me a diagram. Following the Southern 100 races and being embarrassed by the welder in the garage's comment about "B***** riders who can't weld," I'd started a nine week welding course at night school. By the second week, I could weld steel fairly well and asked the tutor if I could have a go at making an adapter.

October was the first meeting with NGMCC at Castle Combe. I took all three bikes, but couldn't get anyone to come to help me, all my friends now had families and with so many things going on I forgot to put the word out that I needed help at the CMC weekly meetings. I must admit it was a bit hectic getting all the bikes through scrutineering, pushing the first bike up, leaving it on the stand and explaining that I had to get another two bikes up. Luckily, the Hewlett twins from Worcester said "don't worry

George, we'll keep an eye on them until you get back." When I got back with the last bike I found that the first two bikes had been scrutineered. Unlike the Manx, and some other meetings, the NGMCC were still doing push starts. The Greeves and G50 were easy enough, the Trident was heavier, but it started okay and I had three finishes.

Down Hatherley village fete was on Saturday the 30th September, luckily I wasn't working or racing. I decided to run two stalls. One stall was using the air rifle, I called it "Deadeye Dick's." We put it against the hedge on the side of the field, so that any stray pellets wouldn't injure anyone. For the second stall, I used a pair of my fire rubber boots that had passed their 'sell by date' for use in the fire service, for "welly wanging," it was all the rage. After setting up my stalls early, I was asked, as I knew Cheltenham, to collect the clairvoyant, or was it Gypsy Rose Lee, to tell fortunes. I'd wanted to have my fortune told but even with Pat's help, running two stalls didn't leave me enough time. I had a couple of goes on the skittles, but as it was on grass, I was useless, also on a few of the other stalls like throwing balls and darts. We had a bit of a laugh on the "welly wanging" as the Lady Mayor of Tewkesbury, wearing her large chain of office had a go, swinging her arm round, the Wellington boot went backwards and everybody scattered.

On the way to Snetterton for the last CRMC meeting of the year, I felt tired just over halfway, pulled into a lay-by and got my head down for a couple of hours in the caravan, *this is the life*! I saw Alan Adcock at the meeting, he was also a fireman, well, Divisional officer in the West Midlands, so I parked near him. During practice, Alan asked me for advice on his carburettor as he thought his bike didn't accelerate very well. I rode his 500cc Velocette to an area of the paddock where I could open it up. The carburettor seemed to be working okay, but the clutch was slipping as I pulled away. I told Alan but he didn't agree. His lovely wife Elaine was there with their two boys, so at least Pat had someone to talk to. We were both in the same race, but when I got back to the paddock, Alan was already back having a cuppa. He said his clutch was slipping, with a smile on my face, I said "I don't want to say I told you so, but...." When we meet I don't let him forget it, he gets me back with grief about my bike preparation!

Pat and I went to a silly hat party in Birmingham, it was for Mike and Hillary Oldfield, who were waiting for a Visa to move to the USA, as soon as it came they would be off. Mike and Hillary were as daft as me, Hillary made green bread and pink rice for an impromptu BBQ at a S100 party, at which I met a young and fast, Dave Madsen Mygdal. I wore my Viking helmet, but was amazed, as there were some brilliant hat designs! One was an Australian hat with Corks hanging down, there was a hat with a mini rotating fan on and a school hat with a plywood axe sewn in. There were lots of racers there and it was a good night.

The houses were ticking over, Ian White's girlfriend, had her baby and it was just them living in number 83 Worcester Street, his so-called friends had moved out. White had also taken me to the Rent Officer to try and get the rent reduced, so I asked Gordon Bircher to come to the tribunal for moral support. After the Chairman's opening remarks, Ian White started to put his case, he complained about many minor items. One was that the skirting boards had square edges, and collected dust as they had no nosing, slight round edge. I'd picked up some 4" x ½" planks cheap, yes, I have been called cheapskate but I told the Commissioner, that we'd fitted this as a design feature. Another complaint was that the house was near the Gloucester City Rugby Football Club, so he had the noise of people leaving. I asked if he did any sporting activity, "yes", "what sport do you play?" "Rugby." "So you moved into the house knowing the rugby ground was there. If it's that noisy why don't you move?" The Chairman dismissed all of his claims.

I'd seen an auction sign on the house opposite No: 3, contacting the auctioneers, I found there were several properties for sale on the same day. The house opposite, was three floors, a flat on each floor. Although it was a middle terrace house, it was very large, each flat had two 10' x 15' rooms, a kitchen and bathroom. However only the top floor flat was self-contained, the middle and ground floor flats could be made self-contained, but it would need an external stairwell of some sort putting in. Another point in its favour was that it had a rear entrance with a large garden, so easy parking when working on the house. The guide price was £6-£10,000. Another property being auctioned was near the railway crossing by the old cinema which is now the Elim Pentecostal Church. It was a middle terrace in very bad condition with holes in the roof. It was also rented to an old man, who was paying 25p a week, yes 25p, 5/- in old money!

I went to see the bank manager and told him about the property for sale opposite no 3, I was thinking of offering Ian White the bottom flat on a short hold tenancy, which was now in statute. The bank agreed I could go up to £10,000, 12k at a push. I mentioned the other property, the manager said that I wasn't much of a risk, if the other house was the right money to go for it.

October was getting busy, the forthcoming auction, my last meeting of the season at Brands Hatch, and Pat had decided to have Halloween party. After the success of Mick and Hillary's party, we made it a "silly hat" party, no dressing up, just a silly hat! This was to be held at Down Hatherley Village Hall on Halloween. It was lucky I went to inspect the hall, I ended up redecorating the toilets because they were scruffy and the graffiti was obscene in the men's, even worse in the ladies! I ended up giving the hall, a general once over with a lick of paint, in the kitchen as well. They gave me a reduction in the hire fee.

Every Thursday was the welding course. Wednesday night was CMC, Tuesday was the Woodpeckers shooting club at RAF Quedgeley, and then there was the weekly skittles that had been started. It was made up of members from Down Hatherley and Longford, our home alley was at the Kings Head, Norton, on Monday nights, but could change, depending on the away team's night, so I had a stand in at fire station if needed. This was just a fun night, although I am competitive and tried not to miss the wooden skittles. If I missed with the first ball, I would roll one trouser leg up, if I missed a second time, I would roll the other trouser leg up. If you didn't knock any down, you had to pay a fine, which went towards the party at the end of the season. It was also a tradition, certainly when dad alive, that everyone sang "why was he born so beautiful, why was he born at all."

I found some help for Brands, a CMC biker's 17-year-old son agreed to come. I was only taking the Greeves, and had fixed up to go the night before, stopping at Gravesend with the Daly household. It was sort of organised chaos, but always great fun. The Daly home, was called the Ace Cafe of Gravesend, as the world and his wife seemed to drop in! I picked the young man up, and as we approached Northleach, I pointed out the lay-by that police had made me pull into when I had no lights or number plate and was speeding. Moments later I saw a blue light and pulled over. I got out to meet what turned out to be a pretty police lady, kissing her hand I asked "is there something wrong officer?" "We're just checking suspicious vehicles." I relaxed a little as we actually hadn't done anything wrong, putting on a sad face, I asked "do I look suspicious, does that mean you don't like me?" The police lady tried to be professional, "stop messing about and give me my hand back, I may be trying to arrest you." I carried on messing about "that doesn't stop me being nice to you." I then tried a bit of namedropping, "why weren't you at the Joe Brown 999 do at The Roundabout, a couple weeks ago?" "I was" she replied. "Were you one of those three young girls in short skirts, on the front row?" "Yes I was." I told her that it was a shame I'd had a lady with me! We were chatting about the evening, when her male colleague in the car gave the thumbs up, meaning that my registration number had checked out okay, so I carried on.

This was not long after another incident with two police ladies. We were leaving Pat's house in Longlevens to attend the 999 swim night at Gloucester Leisure Centre that Frank Prentice, a keen swimmer had started up, it was open to the police, ambulance and fire service. Going down Orchard Road there were cars along my side of the road. There was a car with its headlights on facing me so I waited a few minutes, as it did not move, I started to drive down the road, it then started moving towards me. As the pavements were 6' wide, to save reversing in the dark, I drove onto the pavement at a dropped kerb, and went past the car. Unfortunately it was a police car, pulling back onto the road I stopped, but he didn't put his blue light on, so I carried on to the swim night. Next day, Pat contacted me to say that the police had called around wanting to see me about driving on the pavement and would come back tomorrow at 11.00. Luckily this gave me time to check the car over, and fix a broken brake light. Two nice police ladies arrived, after they introduced themselves, I kissed their hands, again they said "Sir, we may be arresting you," "surely that doesn't stop me being nice to you" I replied making them smile. After checking my documents they gave me a caution about driving on the pavement, informing me I would be contacted by a senior officer. I talked to Alice Price whose cousin was a senior police officer and who suggested I write along lines of "any resulting bad publicity between the Police and Fire Service etc may be detrimental to both services also that I was very sorry, I'd only done it to avoid an accident knowing the pavement to be very wide. I was attending the 999 swim night which fire, police and ambulance personnel attend as I was lifeguard that night," yes, grovelling again!

When Frank found out I had passed my lifesavers, he'd asked me if I'd be lifeguard once a month. It meant you had to sit on the side of the pool with the whistle, when anybody was running or messing about, you blew it and pointed at them, which I used to enjoy. Most important was keeping an eye on the swimmers, being ready to dive in and save anybody if they were in trouble, which luckily didn't happen.

One evening when I was in the pool, an ambulance lady was hanging onto the side. I asked her why she was clinging to the side, "I can't swim, I just like being in the water." I told her to come into the middle with me, knowing I was a lifeguard gave her some confidence. After a few minutes I had her swimming on her back, "that's right you're swimming" she started to lift her head "don't lift your head up or your feet will go down." I then spent a little time doing the breaststroke with her, I felt very pleased that I had taught her to swim a few strokes.

After swimming a few lengths I noticed a young lad possibly 8 or 9, he'd swum at least 10 widths, I asked him why he didn't swim a length. He told me he was in the pool on his own, his mum was upstairs watching and wouldn't let him. After checking it was alright with his mum, we started at the shallow end, he was obviously going slowly so I just did the lifesavers kick. We did three lengths, keeping my head turned towards him, I shouted encouragement every so often. As we approached the shallow end, on the fourth length, I was sunk, when about four or five other 8 to 10-year-olds jumped on me.

We were made welcome at Gravesend. After talking about the Manx and other projects, I checked my leathers, they needed emergency duct tape repairs. When John Jnr saw the duct tape he asked to borrow some, repaired whatever it was then, when some of his friends came in, he offered it to them to use. I spluttering out "don't mind giving all my duct tape away John!!" Ann said "that's my little brother for you." We had an early start in the morning. This was a two-day International meeting, the classic race was the last race on Sunday. Saturday was practice in the morning, which didn't go very well for me, it was damp and cold. With the young lad and John helping, I had my electrics apart, I don't know how many times, due to the lack of a good spark. I did get three laps in, so just qualified. As Rupert wasn't racing, he and Ann had gone home early as it was so cold, and so that Ann could have a warm meal ready when we got back. Little Janet was getting on with the young man very well, when I mentioned the silly hat party they decided to come, so I fixed up for them to stop with Tony Evans, our skittles captain, in the Ash Lane.

Up early Sunday morning, and back to Brands Hatch for an emergency practice session. The electrics were still playing up, it was still cold and damp, but at least I'd qualified. I don't know how many times we took the Steffa unit off to try and sort it out, I tested and retested many times, as it brightened up, so did my electrics, and the bike was now ready for the race. I hoped the gearing was right, I'd only done three laps on the full course, I was more used to the short-circuit. I jetted up as it was cold, and made sure the tank was full.

The clocks had gone back Saturday night, but as there was TV coverage of the big race, The Race of the South, which was just before ours, the start of the race had to fit in with the TV scheduling, which meant the light was starting to go by the time we got to the line for the start, at just after 4 o'clock. Vehicles were leaving the circuit with their headlights on! Our race, was a round of the Classic Bike Magazine Championship which had been held over 10 rounds. I hadn't figured in any of the points, probably as I couldn't get to all the rounds, and I was riding whichever of my bikes was going at the time, the G50 or Greeves. On this occasion, not having had a chance to check the G50 after the MGP, and knowing there was movement on the crank, I was on the Greeves, no way was I going to ride the Trident around Brands Hatch. Our race was a mixture of 500, 350 and 250 machines, I made a reasonable start and was in a pack of riders. It started to drizzle, practice was bad enough on the full circuit in the daylight, but now I was racing in the dusk and drizzle, I asked myself *why is my bottom lip going up and down? I must be off my trolley racing in the rain and dark!* Around Clearways and I was back on the part of the course I knew, you could see the camera flashes going off in the Grandstand. I settled in, there was a group of us, including an Aermacchi, so at least I had a good scratch.

Five laps of the 10 lap race had gone, I couldn't see any riders in front of us and we'd lost most of the other bikes around us, there was just a Goldstar a few yards behind, and I was riding as close as I felt safe, in the conditions, to the back wheel of an Aermacchi. As we went past the start and finish a yellow flag with a black cross was being displayed indicating last lap. Keeping with the Aermacchi all the way round I managed to cut underneath it at Clearways just beating him to the flag. I put my hand out in a gesture of friendship but sadly he didn't feel like reciprocating, his attitude was unusual! I found out later that Bob Moore almost took me out when he tried to go inside me at Hawthornes, but hit the curb in the bad light when his front wheel was level with my back!

The young man, John and I loaded up, said goodbye to everybody and got off straightaway because I wanted to get back for 8 o'clock as the last part of 'Churchill the Wilderness Years,' a good TV drama leading up to WW2, was on. I dropped the lad off and made it home just in time.

The house auction was just before the Silly Hats party. There were two properties I was interested in, luckily the house I wanted was first. It started off at £2000 rising quickly to £5000 then going up by £500 a bid to £7500. I bid £8000, it went quiet for what seemed like an age, *for God's sake put hammer down* "bang," I'd bought another house. The next property was the one being rented out at 25p a week when petrol was £1.60 a gallon. It started off in the hundreds, slowly going up to £2000. I bid £2100. There was only me, and one other chap bidding, when he bid £3400, I chickened out. I'm sure the Bank Manager wouldn't have minded if I'd gone higher, as it was a house for £3500, but I had enough work with one.

Janet and John the 3rd had come with Ann and Rupert for the Silly Hats party as Janet was smitten with the young lad. His dad brought him over and I let him wear my Viking helmet, whoever was judging gave him 1st prize. I wore my cardboard, red white and blue top hat that I'd made for the S100. Many of Mum's Ash Lane neighbours came, including Dennis and Mary Limerick, with their daughter Sally and her boyfriend. The boyfriend worked at the MEB with Dennis, who had his hard hat from work on under a bobble hat, with a teddy bear sewn on the front. Brother Dave had a Robin Hood hat on, Sue Julie and Sally were all dressed up with silly hats on, as was mother and the Price family. It was a good party, Dave commented that you had to smile as you were talking to somebody in a suit who had a silly hat on! I had a supply of comic hats, for those who turned up thinking they were going to get away without looking silly!!

The weekend before bonfire night, a football match had been fixed up with Frank's watch and our watch, I volunteered to go in goal, as I felt running around for 90 minutes, was a long time. The morning of the football match was not only freezing but very foggy. I took the ex-army long combs, that I'd bought for 25p for winter riding, with me. When I got to the Civil Service Club, there was still frost on the ground, so I put the long combs on under my football shorts. The shorts were the ones I wore at school, nearly down to my knee, but I was pleased they still fitted. I did get lots of comical/rude comments from the lads! By the time the game started, it was so foggy I couldn't see the goal at the other end. The trouble with being a goalie was that, either there was nothing to do, or you're working your bollocks off trying to stop people getting the ball past you! Near the end of the first half, Dennis Stevens hurt his ankle, so at half-time he went in goal, and I was running around the field like a loony. *Bloody hell the ball is coming close to me, I suppose I had better try and kick it.* My foot and an opposition player's foot, hit the ball together, an electric shock wave went up my leg and I fell to the ground. On getting up I fell down again, my leg felt dead, it didn't want to move. After a couple of lads rubbed my leg for a few minutes, some life came back into it, but I kept well away from the ball for the rest of the game.

Thursday November 5th was bonfire night, although my village, Down Hatherley, was having one on Saturday, sadly I was working. Thursday was our day shift, for some reason I used Pat's bicycle to get to work. As I sat down for dinner, Pete Davies said "the Rotary Club are having a firework night at Westgate Bridge this evening at 7pm and need help letting the fireworks off." Although very keen on my welding course, I did like fireworks, and as I was working Saturday night and would miss the village bonfire I volunteered. Cycling from the fire station to Frank Prentice's mum's, I popped in to say hello and had a cup of tea. She was sewing something for The Children's Supplies Shop, that she'd run since the war, I explained that I was helping at the bonfire, and asked if she minded if I went and bought some chips as there was a good chippy over the road from her. After sausage and chips, a cuppa and a chat to Mrs P I cycled the mile and a half to Westgate Bridge. The fire was lit and we starting letting off the fireworks at 7 pm. As it was all finished by 7.30, I cycled to the college to do an hour of the welding course, telling the tutor that I'd been helping at a charity bonfire.

I started on the new house I'd bought, removing weeds from, and fixing the guttering and downpipe and clearing the back garden so that I could park my van in it as it had access to a small lane. I felt the house had a lot of potential. I spent Saturday 14th at mother's, putting the bikes down for hibernation for the winter, before leaving for work, passing the bonfire I would have been at if not working.

After the MGP I'd part exchanged the 175cc Honda for a Honda 90 step through, plus some cash. It was a bit tatty, but with a clean, a second-hand top box and mudguards from Tredworth breakers, it looked okay. I'd ridden the Honda 90 to Lucas in Birmingham to collect a magneto I'd had serviced, it went well, flat-out was 50 mph, not too bad for 90 cc with 14 stone on it. One of Pat's new neighbours saw me scooting around on it and asked if he could buy it for work, I made another £10 profit. As I now didn't have a bike taxed for the road, I was looking to see what I could get going. The selling of the Honda 90 was the end of the money owed to me in rent, I made a lot more than the £300 owed, when I bought the Toyota Carina for £650.

On Sunday 15th November 1981, I arrived at Gloucester City Fire Station, 20 minutes early, to start the 15 hour night shift at 18:00. Sub O Eddie Willey took the roll call and detailed jobs, I was No 1 on the water tender. An old car had been brought over from the local car breakers George Onions, brother of Patrick Onions, of Gloucester Cotton Motorcycle Company and NGMCC fame. They were always having small fires so it was a bit of "you scratch our back and we'll scratch yours." They'd come and collect the parts left over after we'd completed our cutting them up drills and after we'd taken such things as light bulbs and door handles, if they fitted our cars! Eddie set the drill as a person trapped in a car following a road accident, and told us to get to work. We carried out the drill as if we were on the fire ground. We rescued the dummy using cutting and jacking gear, as it was dark, we used the search light and some halogen lights working off the portable generator. We wrapped it up at 19:55 and after Sub O had praised us for what we'd done right, he pointed out where we went wrong. Then we went to the lecture room to do topography (learning the station ground) up to 21:30, then supper time.

Most chaps, after washing up went to watch the box, but I wanted to write a letter to the Fire Chief of Daytona Fire Dept. as I was considering entering my G50 in the Daytona Classic Race, "Dear Sir, I am a British fireman, I hope to enter my motorcycle at Daytona, can you please put me up?" was the gist of the letter.

I'd contacted the USAF Base at Fairford. We'd had a risk visit there the month before, they flew Boeing KC-135 Stratotankers for mid-air refuelling, which carried 6,875 US gallons, plus extra fuel for refuelling, so quite a risk. Their fire dept. demonstrated a special foam tanker, delivering light water now, with a large delivery outlet at each end, a bit like a "push me pull you" if you have seen the Dr Doolittle film. This fire appliance could deliver 5000 gallons of light water, in 2½ minutes. Seeing the demonstration, hearing the lecture and seeing some gruesome photos, we were reminded of the consequences, if you don't get the fire out in 2 ½ minutes, it was some sort of machine. After being shown over a

Stratotanker, I even got a chance of lying in the position that an airman would be in if they were refuelling another aircraft, I felt quite privileged. When I rang up, I'd spoken to a senior officer, explained about Daytona, and asked if they could fly my bike and me over on one of their regular runs to the States. The Officer didn't sound too hopeful but said that he would make enquiries, I'm still awaiting the decision!

I finished the letter at 23:25 and went to have a cuppa and chat with the lads in the kitchen before going up to my bunk, we were allowed to rest between 23:00 – 06:00 subject to calls, I must have dropped off straight away!

The alarm sounded at 00.30, I'd only laid my head down at 23.55!
The Tannoy announced one pump required and gave a garbled address. I turned on the radio of the Water tender and asked Control to confirm the address, it was a chimney fire at 92 London Road, Gloucester.

As we came over a rise known as Wotton Pitch, I could see flames and smoke all over the road, I thought *if that's a chimney fire I want more help!* I radioed for another pump.

I jumped out the water tender, and before my feet had touched the ground, I heard a panicked shout. "There are people trapped inside." I radioed in again, with more urgency, persons reported, this triggers ambulance, senior officers, police etc. Little did I know that this was to be my last ever message!

The driver, still in overalls, was getting the pump ready, Firemen Smith & Flello were slipping on their BA sets as lives were in danger. I saw flames and smoke engulfing the front room, spreading across the ground floor hallway and rushing up the stairwell.

"Run a jet out," I yelled, we were doing this, when there was another shout from somewhere, "There's someone at the top window," this was the second floor, so over 20 feet up. Dropping the hose we slipped the 35' ladder, we had to do a confined pitch as the pavement was only 7' wide and cars were parked close to the kerb. We jammed the ladder against a car body and the kerb, what are a few scratches when life is at risk?

PHOTO BY KIND PERMISSION OF CORONOR'S OFFICE
ROOM OF ORIGIN, GROUND FLOOR

As the lads had BA on, I ran up the ladder to tell the person inside to hang on, that another fire engine was on the way. The window was a 4' sash window, typical for the servant's rooms 90 years earlier, so it was only a 2' opening! My face was just 12" from his, a frail-looking man, choking and dying in front of my eyes, as smoke was pouring out of the window. I was coughing, but this poor chap had suffered this for 10 minutes or more already! We'd trained to do carry downs, although under safety rules, when we carried another fireman, even then, they had an Everest safety device on. Eventually, this was deemed dangerous, so we trained carrying a dummy, which wasn't as good or realistic, but even this practice was in dispute. I thought *I can, and I have to do this.* I started to pull the man out onto my shoulder but he was struggling, no wonder, he was choking to death with all that smoke from the ground floor. I had half of him on my shoulder, his feet were nearly out of the window, I was saying "Relax don't struggle!" I saw his foot go against the wall, he pushed hard, I thought *My God we are going to fall*, I'd had many dreams about falling.

PHOTO BY KIND PERMISSION OF THE CORONOR'S OFFICE.
HEAD OF LADDER IN ORIGINAL POSITION, HEEL DRAWN OUT INTO GUTTER

**PHOTO BY KIND PERMISSION OF CORONOR'S OFFICE SHOWING
HEEL OF LADDER ON PAVEMENT WHERE ORIGINALLY PITCHED, CAR
MOVED FORWARD FROM DIRECTLY OPPOSITE HEEL**

I looked up and saw a pretty face looking down at me "am I in heaven, are you are an angel?" I was surprised when the vision answered "no, not an angel, a nurse you're in Gloucester Royal Hospital Ward 16." "What happened?" "You had an accident at work, some of your colleagues and family are here." I tried to look around but couldn't move anything except my eyes. I looked down, I could see my arms, but they wouldn't move. My head wanted to move a little, but there appeared to be something stopping me. Moving my eyes to the left and right I saw and spoke to brother David "hello Dave" then seeing mother "hello Mum", "what have you been doing George?" mother asked. I then saw the Mr Wilson, Chief Fire Officer, in his uniform. Mother squeezed my hand, although I felt it, it was a strange sensation! Dave said "are you in trouble again little brother?" I saw Patricia in the background, but I was still in a sort of daze.

Mr Wilson explained that the rescue had gone wrong, we'd both fallen 20', sadly the man I was rescuing had died. I asked the older nurse, who I later learnt was Sister Newman, how long I'd be like this. She told me 7 weeks, so I asked Dave and Pat to get the letter posted to Daytona Fire Department as the race wasn't until March. Mr Wilson was being pleasant to me, I asked "am I dying Mr. Wilson?" "No George, of course not." Me and my sense of humour, I then asked him "why are you being so nice to me, normally you shout at me." I saw my brother Dave smiling, you can see why I never got on the fire service. The visitors had to leave because the nurses had to turn me, I remember Sister Newman saying in a very stern voice "I'm not going to have any patients of mine with pressure sores." I used to say "good morning Dragon" to her, even when ill, I was still a pain in the backside. Sister Newman was a lovely lady really, but very strict, when she told someone to do something, they did it.

Other visitors popped in to see me all day and had many messages from others who couldn't visit. Flowers were arriving all the time, even some from America. The flowers had come from the volunteer fire department that had come over a few months ago. Their visit had been arranged by an ex-Gloucester resident, now living in America, who was a USA volunteer fireman. I'd met them at socials at the station, I remember a skittles match where I put my arm around one of the pretty volunteer fire ladies showing her how to play. I asked "how the heck did they find out about it?" A fireman replied "bad news travels fast George, but they're thinking of you." I didn't realise, well not at first that the flowers had come from a local florist, they just ordered them.

Thinking I was going to be better in 7 weeks, I was quite cheerful, talking to anybody I could see. I couldn't move my head easily as I was on traction, but as it didn't hurt, I didn't mind too much, the main problem was they couldn't fit the headphones on, for me to listen to the radio when I had no visitors. If I couldn't see anyone, I would shout to other patients asking who they were. When it was a little quieter the nursing staff told me that because I had neck injury, I had to have traction with a weight on to restrict movement, allowing the injury to get better slowly.

The last visitors left at 8pm, I can't remember who fed me during the day but the nursing staff often persuaded visitors to. As I was lying flat on my back with only my eyes that moved, I was being fed with a small spoon, "open wide George," I also learnt to drink from a cup with a bendy straw, it was something I had to get used to. I had my last drink before going to sleep, well trying to, as I'd nodded off during the day. I must have got some sleep, but I kept waking up hearing coughing, snoring and farting. It was the worst night's sleep I'd ever had, I could do nothing, not even pull the bedclothes over my head, if I did nod off, they woke me every two hours to turn me.

They woke me up at 6am to wash me, ignoring all pleas to leave me alone. Hooray, breakfast and a cup of tea, with a pretty nurse to feed me. I asked a lot of questions. I found out a lady in the ladies ward had been injured when a lorry crashed through the fence coming down the hill into Nailsworth. This crash was the week before my accident, it had been attended by Stroud with Nailsworth retained station first on the scene, with the rescue appliance from Cheltenham sent on. Sadly the ladies husband had been killed. It had been headlines in the local Citizen Newspaper and made the national news. I asked the nurse the ladies Christian name and shouted "is that Mary from Nailsworth?" "Yes, who's shouting at me?" "George, I was injured in a fire yesterday," "I heard about you," she replied "I read about you last week, Mary." We had a conversation that lasted some minutes, probably annoying the other patients, if not the staff, Mary was in a ward at least 30' away.

Big brother David visited me early, on his way to work. After "how are you little brov?" I gave him a list of jobs. The highest on the list was a radio with an earpiece, so I could at least listen to something during the night, I explained that the hospital head phones wouldn't fit. "Good morning Herr General" I greeted Sister Newman, she used to give me some cheek back, "I'll give you it for calling me Herr General, I'll have you standing to attention when you're better!" I did enjoy chatting up all the nurses, *why do I always fall in love with them?* I shouted to the lady in the next ward "how are you today Mary?" "Alright thank you George." With the many family and friends visiting during the day, the doctor's visits, and being turned every 2 hours, the day passed quickly. At least that night was better, listening to my radio instead of all the snoring!!

As days passed, I was still getting many visitors and with so many things going on, I felt quite relaxed as long as I was talking to someone. Of course each day at certain times, the curtains were drawn around the bed. When this happened, visitors were asked to leave, so that the nursing staff or doctors could do a check-up, if the nurse was pretty, I used to say "ignore all the screams!"

I was informed that I'd be going to Stoke Mandeville Hospital on the 26th November for specialist treatment. The day before I was due to leave two ambulance men came in, I knew them, one was Hobby, Derek Hobbs, son of the caretaker at Twigworth School in the early 50's. They'd come to work out how to transport me with my traction, I enjoyed talking to them, and making suggestions.

The day of the move came, what a palaver, I was transferred into the ambulance, with numerous reporters, cameramen and Leslie Leach from the BBC and Mike Charity from the ITV. These lads used to come in to Gloucester and Cheltenham fire stations when the bars were open, to get information on fires, buying a round if they got a story aired. Mike gave me a photo of myself rescuing a heifer in calf with two other firemen, Andrew Finch and Graham Leighton. Les gave me one of my house, 83 Worcester Street, when the Leisure Centre mural was officially launched! I had someone sitting with me all the way, my arms were strapped across my body because once they moved, I couldn't move them back. I quipped, "looks like you're getting me ready for a coffin," the reply was "with bad jokes like that, I'll gag your mouth next" then I was given a drink with the dreaded straw. It was a 70 mile trip and took roughly 4 hours, the person sitting with me described Stoke Mandeville to me as we arrived, as lots of army style huts with corroders going in all directions. My stretcher was transferred onto a trolley, then wheeled along many long corridors before arriving at Ward 2.

"I'm Sister Rose in charge of Ward 2," I thought *dragon number 2*. There were 2 ward orderlies, big Dave, as I called him, was 6'6" and looked like a wrestler, and Pepe who was Spanish, the orderlies, nurses and care staff were an International bunch. The orderlies along with two nurses transferred me to bed. I asked a pretty nurse why she had a red belt on, "I'm a qualified nurse, but on six months training for spinal injuries."

There was so much happening, visits from nurses, doctors and physiotherapists. The physios I saw several times a day, their job was making sure my hands, feet and legs were moved regularly, this went on for six weeks. It was the same for all new spinal injury patients, with

Paraplegics, it was only in their feet and legs that didn't move, they had full hand and arm movement, but the damage was in my neck! I was classed as a Tetraplegic, or Quadriplegic, all four limbs were affected.

Ward 2 was run with a rod of iron by Sister Rose, she was a lot like Sister Newman, although only 5' 2" what she said was done with no questions or arguments, as I was to find out. Even big hairy Dave replied "yes Sister Rose" but when the other sister was on, it was "Oh yes sister, I'll do that sometime!"

A huge black man came up to me in a white jacket and trousers so I assumed he was nursing staff of some sort. He reminded me of Louis Armstrong, Satchmo from satchel mouth, from blowing his trumpet, he had a big wide smile, and said "hello my name is Angelo, I'm the Catheter King." The smiling Angelo explained that he oversaw catheter insertion, water retention, how much water was being passed and kept records. After pulling out the catheter, he would lean on your stomach to see if you passed any water. Although I had touch sensation, I couldn't actually feel anything properly, I knew, and could see him, leaning on my stomach with 17 stone behind his fist, but I had no feeling of pain, it was ever so unnerving! The ability to pass urine was one of the major problems for Para and Tetraplegics, one of many problems, as I was to find out. If you're unable to pass urine the bladder could rupture causing blood poisoning, eventually death. With the damage to the spinal cord you can't give any messages to open and close the sphincter muscle in the bladder or any bodily function systems, in my case everything below the chest.

When it was quiet, I said "who's next to me?" Eventually a foreign voice answered "my name is Andreas Nikolaos." He was a Greek Cypriot. He worked for a large British insurance firm in Nicosia, and had fallen off the roof, working on the water tank. Andreas explained that the water tanks are on the roof in Cyprus as they have very little rain. We struggled a little with conversation as my Greek was non-existent, and his English was very broken. On my other side was Richard Kember. The Duke of Edinburgh had visited the day before I arrived, to lay a foundation stone for the new spinal unit being built. Being a royalist, I was disappointed I'd missed him, perhaps they'd made sure he visited before I arrived, *I wonder why?*

In came someone who shouted out "how do you tell a Scotsman's clan by lifting up his kilt? If he has 2 quarter pounders he's a McDonald!" This was Jimmy Savile, who was a well-known TV presenter on Top of the Pops and

405

the very popular TV show, Jim'll Fix It. I was to get on very well with Jimmy as we had the same sense of humour and were both noisy people. Jimmy was always telling jokes and keeping our spirits up, he certainly did mine.

My watch had done a "raft row" while I was racing in the 1981 Manx Grand Prix, giving the money raised to the Stoke Mandeville fund that Jimmy had started, it was the year of the disabled. During the raft row which was on the river Severn, Bob Alison a new fireman to the watch, had fallen in, got caught on the raft, and had to be rescued! The hospital had been due for closure, it was opened in 1944 and many buildings were coming to the end of their days due to lack of maintenance. In the late 70's a large rally, with hundreds of previous patients who had survived spinal injuries, turned up making national news. Jimmy Savile, who'd broken his back in a mining accident in Yorkshire, luckily recovering, took up the battle against its closure.

Mealtimes were a bit of a problem as there were far more patients than staff, the paraplegics could feed themselves, but with a neck injury you couldn't move your arms, so had to wait for someone to feed you. There were volunteers that came in to help as well as people visiting. Two chaps in uniform came in, "Hello George, we're Aylesbury fireman, Ron Rymer and Ken Parkin." Ken knew me from motorcycle racing, he was a friend of Robin Spring from Wendover, who I used to race against, in fact, I saw him at Aberdare Park in July 1981 and at my last race meeting at Brands, he had a nice sister called Iris. Ken remembered me racing at RAF Little Rissington, I thought, *he must be older than he looks*. They ended up feeding me, and we talked about the fire service and the accident.

In the evening, after the physio had worked my hands and feet again, she put something into my palm, wrapped my hand around it, then bandaged it very tight, it looked like I was going boxing. At first it wasn't too bad but after a while there was some discomfort, I was told it was to keep my hands in good condition.

Night came and the radio came into its own, as it had in Gloucester Royal Hospital. I had to get a nurse or ward orderly to put the earplug in, and getting the volume of the radio just right was a bit of a problem, with me saying "up a bit" or "down a bit," it reminded me of the 1960's radio programme, The Navy Lark, with the saying "left hand down a bit!" I heard every news report, midnight, 1 o'clock, 2 o'clock, I must have nodded off at times but at least when awake, I had something to listen to! It was like

Gloucester Royal, just as I was getting to sleep they would wake me up every 2 hours to turn me, just like when mother made to go to bed when I was wide awake, and got me up when I was half asleep! As Stoke Mandeville was a specialist hospital, the bed I was in was made up of three sections lengthways, with electric motors. This meant the bed could be flat, or if an outside section was up, you were leaning to the left or right. When on my back, I was just staring at the ceiling, but when I was turned right or left I could see that the ward was a long army style hut, like my brother was in when I went to see him in 1953 at RAF Melksham. There were also a lot of pillows involved as the feet were jammed up with pillows to keep tension on the ankles.

I was woken up Saturday morning with only a quick wash and brush up. Then it was breakfast, but as there were no volunteers at 8am you had to wait for a nurse or ward orderly. For some reason I preferred a nurse, rather than big hairy Dave or a Teddy Boy type, who was a mate of Dave's, I think they used to go out beating people up at night, only joking. The physio came and took the bandages off my hands, what a relief that was, then she wiggled everything again. Not realising what was wrong with me, I used to enjoy all these pretty girls playing with various parts of my body, you have to make the best of a bad job, or is it be thankful for small mercies!

As it was the weekend, there wasn't a great deal going on, there were still some doctor's rounds but I didn't meet Mr Frankel, the Dr looking after me, until later. Mr Frankel had been a young doctor under Ludwig Goodman, who'd started Stoke Mandeville on 1st of February 1944. Ludwig Goodman was a German Jew, who escaped from Germany just before the war started, with his wife and two children. Years later, I found out that when he was 15, and working as a hospital orderly, he saw a miner who'd broken his back, take 5 weeks to die. He started studying to be a doctor, specialising in neurosurgery. He devised a method of keeping paralysed people alive, started the paraplegic games in 1948 and was knighted for his work with spinal injuries. He died in 1980.

At dinner time a fireman from Gloucester visited, bringing Pat with him, so I had someone to feed me. I was to find that every day, a fireman from Gloucester fire service would come to see me, if there were enough on duty. It's difficult to remember exactly who came to see me that first weekend, I was lucky and very appreciative to have so many firemen, old friends, motorcycle racing friends and family visiting me. If I had more than two or three visitors, they would go and talk to, or help feed someone else, as did the other patients visitors, if anyone was short of help. As all visitors started drifting away, I'd get the last person to plug my radio in. The days were interrupted by being turned every two hours as well as visits from doctors and the physiotherapist working my hands and feet. The drugs round was about one hour after teatime. I was now on Warfarin which is rat poison, no comments please, one large pill that I couldn't swallow so they had to break it into 4 which made them very grumpy, this was in addition to all the other pills I had to take, one at a time! Every second evening they gave me some Senokot, I was told that this was to help me go to toilet, I remember mother putting hot water on senna pods to have the same effect, then the physio bandaged my hands, radio in and try to sleep.

Although I'd been turned every two hours, on this morning, I was turned onto my left side, legs bent and padded with pillows and a pillow in my back. They inserted two suppositories, this was not the most pleasant of feelings. The only other times I'd had suppositories was when I was constipated. I was lying on my side for what seemed like ages, then I got a strange feeling in my stomach, a movement happened with much passing of wind, alright farting! I suppose you could say I liked doing what I wanted, when I wanted and how I wanted, and helping other people, this was an extremely humbling, if not embarrassing situation, which I didn't like at all, but there was nothing I could do about it! Each bed had a curtain all the way round it, mine was drawn, although I was laying on my side, I couldn't see out, but I didn't mind on this occasion, as no one could see in!! In came an orderly, there were special paper towels which absorbed the motion, but then the orderly, wearing a plastic glove, put his finger up my backside to see if there was any more toilet to come out. This was a worse sensation than the suppositories, but as with bladder problems, lack of going to toilet also killed a lot of disabled people in the early days, not a pleasant death! This procedure took the staff some time, as there were 20 beds in the ward, and each person would go to toilet usually every two days. Caring for the disabled takes a lot of manpower, womanpower as well. After going to toilet, you had to be washed all over. Being on traction, you had to have at least 4 to lift you, one at your head to make sure the tension was kept steady. When completely in the air, your back, legs and nether regions would be washed with soapy water and dried off. Clean sheets were put on the bed, then you were laid back down. This was quite a risky operation, as any head movement could make the injury worse.

Sunday I was pleased to get more visitors, an Aylesbury fireman and one from Gloucester, so I had somebody to talk to, or if it was mealtime, to feed me. I'd lie staring at the ceiling, and listening to the radio when on my own. Patients were always moving up and down the ward, new patients, and those with any problems, like myself, would be near the nursing station and ward sister's office. There was some movement in the bay next to me, Richard Kember had been moved up the ward, and Paul Beauchamp was moved next to me. He was training to be a fireman, but had been knocked off his motorcycle while going to work, breaking his neck. He'd been in about a month, but had a setback, and moved back down the ward. Paul was about 10 years younger than me but as bikers and firemen, we got on well and shared visitors. As he was young, many of my younger lady visitors would go and see him!

Monday morning already, and Sister Rose was on shift. After breakfast the physio arrived, took the bandages off and manipulated my hands first, then moved on to my feet then legs. The physio was bending my knee, and bending my leg up towards my chest. I was trying to get my brain to move the leg, or at least I thought I was helping it move! Various doctors came around at different times, specialists in their own particular field. I met Dr Frankel, my consultant, several other doctors and specialists like Dr Raba Sandra and Dr El Masri. Sometimes they all came together, sometimes separately. One of them stuck pins in my feet, asking me if it was a pin or a pencil, this was done daily.

I had a visit from an occupational therapist who explained "I'll be training you to do things, eating, making things, in fact living in general." As I was under the mistaken impression that I was going to get better in 7 weeks, I thought, *I have to practice*. I had no hand movement, but my biceps had started working. They were only affected by the initial injury, so after the first few weeks of total paralysis, I could bring my arm up, but as my triceps didn't work, I couldn't move it back down again. The occupational therapist had brought a small leather pouch, in several pieces, all with little holes in them already, like the moccasins you could get to make yourself. Some black plastic thread was attached to my hand, then threaded through two holes, I had to pull the thread in a large circular movement. The occupational therapist had to help a lot, like with the physio, I thought I was moving something, but she was moving my arm. I was getting some discomfort in my left shoulder when moving it in a circular motion, probably from where I'd hit the ground.

During the day, I'd accidentally move my arm, after a while it started to become uncomfortable so I'd shout "nurse," they'd come and put my arm straight, but moments later I'd accidentally move it again, they must have the patience of saints putting up with everything I inflicted on them without cursing me, although, some did get pissed off, snapping "George stop moving your arm you're a pain!"

Jimmy Savile popped by all times of the day, if I had visitors, they were pleased to see him, he always had a nice word for everybody and made them feel special.

I started getting used to the routine, every second day the suppository treatment, after Senokot the night before. This one time, after being turned on my side, I'd gone to toilet but just been left lying there for 30 or more minutes, and was in a lot of pain in my left shoulder. Laying on it was really hurting, so I shouted for a nurse, as nothing happened after five minutes, I shouted again. I'm not sure how many times I shouted, but after one shout, a nurse put her head inside the curtain and said "George, somebody is dying next door, be quiet." I felt ashamed of myself, all I was suffering was some pain, and somebody else was dying, so I said the Lord's Prayer, then asked God for forgiveness for being so selfish. I'm really pleased to say they managed to save the person.

They changed the small calliper, Gloucester Royal Hospital had fitted to my head, to a large U, well scissors type, a bit like a pair of tongs that went either side of my head and had side brackets so that the cable and the weights could be fitted. The nurse said "I am going to give you an injection." I went into a panic, shouting for mother. She explained "we'll screw the calliper into your head to secure it, the screws will be just in front of your ears by your temples." Luckily with the injection, which did hurt, I didn't feel any pain, just a very strange sensation as the screws went into the side of my head! The device meant that the orderlies could now catch hold of me more easily.

Early on, in my first week there, the Almoner came to see me. She explained that she would help me sort out my pensions, disability benefits and any other paperwork I had, if I had any non-medical problem she'd help with those as well if she could. She was a lovely lady, with a nice smile, she reminded me of the dinner ladies at primary school. Although I didn't say anything, strange for me, I was wondering why I was having a pension if I was getting better.

Another lady came to see me, "I'm your librarian," "but I don't like reading, and I can't hold a book" I replied. "Give me chance" she said "we also do talking books for patients like yourself." She read out titles and explained what the stories were about. When she got to A Child of the Forest by Winifred Foley, a story of growing up in the Forest of Dean in the 1920's. I shouted "I'll have that one please as I'm from Gloucester." I also asked if she had an English to Greek phrase book, she said she'd have a look. Later on she brought a twin real tape recorder. She put the tape on and the earphones on me, luckily missing the new headgear that had just been fitted, and started it, as there were no visitors, physio or occupational therapist around at the time. She'd also found a Greek phrase book which I had to get visitors to read to me. I really enjoyed A Child of the Forest, listening to tales of the author growing up like when she was six, and went on stage to read a poem but her knickers kept falling down. Someone shouted "take them off or do something with them" so she took them off! Her poem or recital was so good that the audience as well as clapping threw farthings halfpennies even the odd penny onto the stage. She shouted out "mum you won't have to hide when the grocer knocks on the door for the bill now." I was crying with laughter, a nurse asked me if there was anything wrong, "No nurse, I'm laughing."

Later that day I got a phone call, phone calls caused a lot of aggro as there was only one phone on wheels for 20 beds and for Tetraplegics, someone had to hold the phone to the ear. It was Mike Pye from Malcolm Davies Motorcycles, he asked how I was etc. During the conversation I asked him how the pretty little girl behind the counter was. When I went in to get motorcycle spares I was usually served by Mike, he had this pretty assistant, she was a real cracker. Mike said he'd hand me over to Mr Davies. I carried on chatting, "Hello Mr Davies, how's the little girl?" "She's not here today George, sadly her husband died last night while working under his van on the exhaust, he got carbon monoxide poisoning." I burst into tears thinking *why am I alive like this when that girl's husband died whilst working on a van?* Later in the day, when it went all quiet again, I asked a nurse to put my ear phones on and turn the story back on, the happy bits made me smile, but when somebody died in the story I burst into tears again!

I was lying on my own listening to something, when another angel flew down from heaven. Well it was a pretty nurse with dark hair and large eyes. She was in full uniform with the cape with the red straps on. "Hello, are you George Ridgeon?" With a lecherous look on my face, I answered "yes I am, what can I do for you?" "Would you like the local Triumph Owners Club to come and see you?" "I would indeed, but how do they know I'm in here?" "We were watching you in the Isle of Man as you were on a Triumph," "that would be lovely, I hope you'll come along with them." She smiled, "I'll come over as much as I can."

Visiting time was a very relaxed atmosphere, as we were in for a longer time than in a normal hospital, visitors weren't in and out like in an ordinary NHS hospital, it was more of a family affair. The next evening a group of bikers came in. I introduced them to Paul, telling them that he was a biker too. It cheered me up talking about motorcycles, they told me that they'd seen me ride and cheered for me in what turned out to be my last MGP. From time to time just one or another would pop in on their way home from work, it all helped the days go by.

I got on very well with Jimmy Savile, I asked him why he brought so many of his guests over to me, not that I minded. He told me it was because I was cheerful and his guests were donating money for the new hospital. We were still in the wooden huts, ward 2 being one of them. One day he brought a pretty young lady over "George this is Samantha" "hello Samantha" "hello George" "Samantha is a stripper," "is she Jim?" It turned out she was a reporter, we all had a laugh about it.

On one of the doctor's visits, and strangely it wasn't Dr Frankel who was supposed to be my consultant, but Dr Raba Chandra, the one who used to stick pins in my feet, said "George I'm sorry to say you'll never walk again." I thought *why has this large black cloud appeared over my bed*? I asked if there was any hope but was told none, they'd done the tests and unless there was a miracle, I was confined to a wheelchair for the rest of my life.

I believe I wasn't my usual jovial self for some days if not longer. Visitors asked "what's up George?" When I told them, they were as dumbfounded as I was. Things did start to get a better slowly, I still had the physios doing my hands, feet and legs, and the occupational therapist continued with my sewing class, working on the small bag. I had lots of visitors, so didn't have much time to stay miserable really, thank you everybody.

One Triumph owner came in after he finished work, so he got saddled with feeding me, when finished, he said "I am off now, anything I can do before I go?" I asked him to mix me a weak squash and strained my head over as much as possible, and moved my eyes to watch him. When I tasted it "Ugg, that is too strong, more water please." As he put more water in, he commented "this is a bit of a weak mixture, we don't want you to seize up." This comment started me laughing as it was so funny, my body started shaking, my mouth was open but no noise came out. "What's wrong George?" I couldn't speak and had tears in my eyes, he shouted "nurse, there was something wrong with George." A nurse came over "what's the matter George?" I still couldn't speak, the nurse called a more senior nurse, I ended up with a group of people around me all looking concerned. Eventually, with my mouth open, I had a sharp intake of breath with a resulting loud noise which a few people make when laughing but with me it sounded a little like a donkey braying. After several minutes I started to calm down, and although I was still laughing, I blurted out "nothing wrong, I'm laughing." Although relieved, I was asked not to scare them like that again!

As Christmas was approaching, the Prices from Ash Lane, who helped me start racing, their daughter Jean and her husband Alan, called in to see me. Jean started filling me in with what was happening in the world outside, then told me about her goldfish. "George, my goldfish wasn't very well, lying on its side and unable to feed" I said "is this story on the level?" making Alan smile! Jean continued "I took it to the vet" which made me smile more, "he suggested I ask at the pet shop as he had no expertise in fish" I chirped in "is this a shaggy dog or shaggy goldfish story?" Jean tried to ignore me and carried on "the man at the pet shop suggested putting the fish in a shallow tray so it can feed." Jean explained "I only had a meat tray to put it in." With tears in my eyes I said "you can't afford a turkey for Christmas?" Poor Jean was looking for sympathy, she was really concerned about the goldfish, but Alan and I were crying with laughter!!

Also in late December, Rupert, Ann, Janet and Johnnie visited. Janet brought me a large poster of a Gorilla, which was put on the wall behind my bed. When Sister Rose or a physio came to see me I would ask them if it was relation of theirs, it usually got me a black look. Although lying down, I could just see another patient who had broken his neck but was getting better, he was now walking, well hobbling, on crutches. He later walked with two sticks, when he was feeling brave, he would do a Charlie Chaplin, and swing one stick around in the air like in the silent movies!

During the build-up to Christmas week, I heard some singing, so took a look the best I could. I saw a lady in a uniform, with some Brownies. They were going from bed to bed singing carols to the patients, which I thought was very nice. When they came to my bed, the lady asked if I'd like the local group of Brownies to sing me a Carol. I said that I'd like it very much, but that I'd like to know who was singing to me, and asked if they could jump up one at a time so I could see them, and call out their names. The first one jumps up, "Mary", then "Jane", then "Emma" etc, then they sang Good King Wenceslas. When they finished they said "cheerio," I shouted "Hi di hi" they replied "Ho di ho".

The dreaded Christmas was approaching, but at least I didn't have to write any cards, *bah humbug*. Big Gordon and Mary Bircher came in, with Charles and Katherine, Mary always made me a cake. Fred and Linda Pettit with new baby Vincent, named after the Vincent motorcycle, Brother Dave and Sue with Julie and Sally all came in to see me although Julie and Sally immediately went to see either Paul or a new Turkish croupier, who looked like a young Anthony Quinn or was it Omar Sharif? Christmas morning, after ablutions and breakfast, the physio did hands, feet and bumps a daisy, *sorry, being silly there!* By this time my hands were always aching in the morning, due to the tight bandages. With limited triceps movement coming back, I could bring my hand to my mouth, and using my teeth on the bandage, pull it out where it was tucked in. After ablutions and breakfast I had plenty of time before anybody came to see me, once the end of the bandage was out, I would struggle and unwrap them. The first few times, the physio would arrive by the time I got half of one undone. As the days went by, I could get them both off, and start trying roll them up. The physio had to undo them before rolling them up again, but at least I had done it, I was quite pleased with myself!

The staff gave each of us a present, mine was a 4"x 5"x 8" package, we were supposed to open them ourselves. This of course took a long time, nearly an hour, but when I eventually opened it they'd given me an audio storage box which wouldn't break if it fell on the floor, I still have it.

About 12 o'clock I saw Mick Gough, a Gloucester fireman who'd brought Patricia up for Christmas Day. The dinner was special, and there were some visitors with more presents. This actually made me feel quite sad. As I was a bachelor with no family of my own, I used to go to midnight mass to celebrate the birth of Jesus, then to Mrs P's, but being paralysed was a strange feeling, I was unable to help myself, let alone other people. This Christmas, I couldn't buy any presents or send any cards, it made me feel very inadequate. As a fireman for the last 13 years I was always helping people, now I found it difficult to accept that I had to have help, not a nice feeling for someone like me!

I also had two new neighbours as Andreas and Paul had moved up the Ward, Len was from Windsor and married to Betty, my other new neighbour was Derek Doe, both had broken backs and were paraplegics. They didn't stay next to me very long, as both were much fitter. I'd moved up the ward, but been brought back when I had a flare-up, a water infection which makes you quite poorly, you had to have your curtain around the bed, lay naked with two fans blowing cold air over you as well as being rubbed down with wet flannels.

Christmas Day was moving along, the doctors and consultants came around wishing everybody Merry Christmas, so did the nurses, occupation therapists and physios. The effervescent Jimmy Savile cheered everyone up, and made the visitors very welcome. The time was going by, Patricia and Mick were still there, I'd had other visitors, but teatime came and they had to make their way home. Luckily an Aylesbury fireman came in to help me, as it was another large meal.

I was quite satisfied with hospital food but was being fed rich Christmassy food, there was so much of it around. Then it happened, I felt uncomfortable, *Oh no* I thought, I could feel my stomach grumbling. People were beginning to drift away, as my visitors left, the ladies gave me a peck on the cheek, the fellas patted my hand, I was hoping nothing would happen. I hoped in vain, and soon had 'an accident,' it turned out to be a very messy motion! Everybody was saying goodbye to everybody else, although my visitors had gone, many others were coming over to say goodbye, I was hoping the smell wouldn't drift upwards, when someone commented "you're quiet George," I relied "yes, I must be feeling tired with all the excitement!!"

After all the visitors had gone I told a nurse that I'd had 'an accident.' Depending on who you were telling, and what mood they were in, they may reply "have you crashed a car George?" or "blooming heck George, have you?" It wasn't a good end to Christmas Day 1981, having to be lifted by 4 people, one on my head calliper and another washing all my parts because it was everywhere, a bicycle clips job, if you have heard the old joke, *when did you first notice you had diarrhoea? When I took my bicycle clips off!!!!*

415

On Boxing Day, Gordon and Mary Bircher with their children Charles and Katherine came to see me, they met some of the Aylesbury fireman. While Mary and the kids were away from my bed I told Gordon and the fireman about my accident on Christmas Day. They were in fits of laughter, Gordon said "you're always in the sh*t George, it's just the level that varies." Near the end of the day I had a surprise visitor, it was the Red Cross lady who was also a Brown Owl and who'd brought the Brownies to sing carols. She asked me if I was keen on motorcycles, the array of motorcycle posters and get well cards with bikes on might have given her a clue. She explained "I have a friend, a young 18-year-old girl in the Ladies Ward with a badly broken neck, she's has a tracheotomy and is quite poorly. She's a Barry Sheene fan, do you think you could get an autograph or something to cheer her up?" I told her I'd do what I could and while she was there, I asked if she could clean my teeth, which was another problem with being a Tetraplegic, trying to find somebody to clean your teeth for you. She started to pop in after work, so I got my teeth cleaned more often, there were never enough nurses and orderlies. I used to suck a sugar free Polo mint to make my mouth feel fresher as well as chew Orbit sugar free gum.

I got a visitor to help me ring Jim Curry next day, Jim was a top class continental circus racer who was always telling dirty Barry Sheene jokes. "Jim, George here" "hello George, how are you?" "I've still got a broken neck, but can you get Barry Sheene's autograph?" I explained about the young girl "she may die any minute," getting my violin out, "a card, letter or photo from Barry will really cheer her up." Jim said he'd leave a message on Barry's answer machine, as he never picks the phone up. Early in the New Year a letter came addressed to Beverley, c/o George Ridgeon, Ward 2, Stoke Mandeville Hospital. I got one of my visitors to take it unopened to Beverley. When the Red Cross lady came to see me she said Beverley was over the moon, she'd got a signed photo of Barry Sheene. I got a message to Jim asking him to thank Barry very much. Really it was all holiday between Christmas and the New Year, the physios and I believe the occupation therapists were working a few days, the doctors did limited rounds. Where possible the hospital got as many patients home, at least for the holiday, I said goodbye to the Charlie Chaplin man, his bed became available and was soon filled up.

For a short time, I had a special mirror mounted on a monkey pole, that I could turn to any angle and see people in the other beds. I noticed a black man, who I found out, had hurt himself on a trampoline, I think he'd injured his neck but he had some movement coming back. Being Christmas time, his wife and two sisters came in, so I and my big mouth shouted "its Diana Ross and the Supremes" which made them and everyone else smile, the ladies came over to say hello.

New Year's Eve came, I was remembering what I'd been told in Gloucester when I asked how long will I'd be like this. Well the 7 weeks were up, the Dr in Gloucester was talking about the traction being on for 7 weeks, not as I thought, that I'd be better. Under doctors' orders, the nurses took the weights off my traction, which did give me some relief. There'd been many visitors during the day but they were now drifting away as the night staff, the orderlies and nurses who'd drawn the short straw, were arriving to be on duty. For the pill round, most staff were in fancy dress, or at least a silly hat, some of the off duty staff also came in, there was a jovial atmosphere as there was a party in the gym, where patients do various exercises and sport.

When one of the nice physios came in dressed as a bunny girl I could see her ears and Basque type corset just to the start of her waist. I asked "have you got fishnet stockings on?" "Yes George" "could you stand on a chair please as I haven't seen a real pair of legs for 7 weeks," "No I'm not" "Oh go on be a sport" "no" "please" I begged and I pleaded then begged and pleaded some more, who said I was a little pleader? Sadly she didn't stand on the chair, so I had to be satisfied with watching television to see a pair of legs! Midnight came, we sang Auld Lang Syne then in with my earpiece the last thing I heard was "Here is the 1 o'clock news" I woke up to a New Year, 1982!

CHAPTER 19   1982-My second home

I'd become used to the routine at Stoke Mandeville, 5 weeks had passed in my new home, how time flies when you're enjoying yourself! I'd started to take the bandages off my hands before the physio came to give me the once over, but all this would be coming to an end soon as they only did it for the first 6 weeks of paralysis.

I'd finished listening to the audio book, A Child of the Forest, and was now on a wartime story, The Shetland Bus, which was nothing to do with buses. It was about Norwegian fishermen who'd escaped German occupation and were helping British spies, going back to the fjords, under the guise of fishing. Being a war baby I enjoyed this book, although some of the stories were quite harrowing. My next audio book was about the Napoleonic wars, but I fell asleep through Napoleon's retreat from Moscow!!!

I could hear a dull drone, when I asked what the noise was I was told that it was air being pumped into a special air bed for an 18 year old who'd been injured and was quite poorly; if you wanted to be at peace, you had to ignore such noises. I'd been having problems hearing the radio, having to ask for it to be turned up much louder, so I asked a visitor to investigate. They found the small hole in the earplugs blocked with earwax, I had to ask them to do the unpleasant job of clearing it, luckily it only took a pin. This was the sort of situation where I felt very inadequate, simple things so easily done, but now I was so reliant on other people, I hated myself!

There was some confusion which caused a lot of amusement; we thought that a Roman Catholic priest had been brought in with his wife and children! However, it was the driver of a coach trip of priests going to a Christian festival, the coach had crashed, the driver breaking his back. His wife and children had come with him from another hospital, but it gave us a chuckle and something to pull his leg over when he was a little better.

When normal routines started again after the Christmas break, two staff told me they were going to take my calliper off. I'd reported a dull aching sensation on the left side of my jaw, near where the screw was. I asked if they were going to give me an injection to unscrew the screws, "No need, it won't hurt" they said, I screamed the hospital down!! When they took the left side out, it hurt like hell, but once the pain had stopped, it was heaven.

Next day I was told I was going to have a shower. I must admit, I was wondering how I could have a shower lying on a bed, I got my answer when I saw what looked like a trolley. It was all plastic with 6" sides, when I was being lifted in, I could see a drain plug to get rid of the water. As I went past Sister Rose, she said in a stern voice "as you've been so much trouble we're going to give you an ice cold shower" so I started singing "it's a long way to Tipperary, it's a long way to go," she gave me a huff! I was pleased the water going over my chest and head was warm, but I could feel no heat sensation any lower, just something touching my stomach and legs. I did enjoy that shower, but with 20 patients this was a once a month luxury.

Although I could now move my head a little, I still had the adjustable mirror which made me feel like a budgerigar. When lying on my back I could see the Ward, and the reaction when I spoke to someone. It showed how poor the hospital was that they only had one of these mirrors per ward, it was taken away from me a few days later!

Watching television had its difficulties. One problem was there was only one TV which was about 7' up on the wall, by the nurses' station. For us Tetraplegics, they had some special glasses, a bit like something they used in the trenches to see over the top, so that we could see straight ahead. The nurses had to move the beds to face the TV, it was very time-consuming.

There was a new comedy show on TV, Last of the Summer Wine, I personally enjoyed old cowboy and war films. Saturday afternoon was sport, which I didn't usually watch as it was all football, but I remember a rugby match at Twickenham as a young lady streaked across the ground topless. It was shown on the news many times, we all watched. I had the bed turned to watch TV but somebody in my line of sight had to have their curtains drawn just when there was an exciting part in the film Capricorn One, "Grrr" or worse!

I heard a lot of kerfuffle and strained to see what was going on, it was Jimmy Savile and a pretty lady going to each bed in turn. When she got to my bed, she shook my hand, I asked if she could keep hold of it so that I could kiss her hand. I lifted my arm as my bicep was a lot stronger, she thanked me and asked me about myself. As this pretty and voluptuous lady was going, I said in my lecherous voice "I hope to see more of you sometime" she replied "you cheeky boy and winked." When they told me it was Erica Rowe, I said "she was very nice, has she done anything special" in a disbelieving voice someone answered "she's the one that ran topless across Twickenham," "Oh, I thought that was Nora Batty." "You daft bugger," came the reply "Nora Batty is the one with wrinkly stockings in The Last of the Summer Wine." I admit I got it wrong, okay I'm daft!

My niece Sally's 19th birthday had been and gone on January 10th but February 3rd was approaching and Julie would be 21. My biceps worked better now and there was no calliper on my head, but there seemed little improvement anywhere else. I started wondering if there was a way I could get taken down on a stretcher to Julie's 21st birthday party, but it wasn't very practical to have a bed in wherever the party was!

I'd been transferred to a new bed, this one had a back that came up so they could sit me up. I could see more of the Ward and who was floating about, but having been laid down for 8 weeks I was only sat up for about 15 minutes before I was asking to be put down again as I felt giddy, but each day I was able to sit up for longer. The Lion Sleeps Tonight by Tight Fit, which reminded me of my tribal dancing in the Gambia and Oh Julie by Shakin' Stevens were in the charts, I wondered how I could get Shaky to sign a birthday card for Julie! It was good timing to get a visit from big Frank and family, I told him what I was thinking and asked him if he could go to Julie's party dressed up as something stupid to represent me and take a card, he said he'd think of something.

I was talking to a nurse about Shakin' Stevens, luckily she read the New Musical Express and told me his fan club address was in it. When she was off duty, we drafted a letter to the Fan Club asking them to ask Shaky if he could sign a card I'd made, 'to Julie, number 1 at 21' as I was seriously ill in hospital. I enclosed two stamped envelopes, one to Shaky the other addressed to Julie, we crossed our fingers. I told Dave just in case the card did arrive, unlikely as it was!

With the back support on the bed, I was staying up longer and not feeling too bad so they suggested lifting me into a wheelchair but after 10 minutes I was asking to get back into bed. Again, this got easier and better each time we did it. The Occupational Therapist tortured me by making me sew my bag, my left shoulder was still hurting, but any movement was causing pain, because my muscles hadn't worked for such a long time. When the bag was finished it went on the arm of my wheelchair for carrying small change and my leather hand strap to hold a spoon or a fork.

One day, *Eureka, my big toe moved*, "nurse, nurse" I shouted in a panicked voice "what's the matter George?" "My toe moved." "Blooming heck George, we thought it something serious, don't shout like that again." In trouble again! When I told a doctor he said, "sorry George, we don't think that there'll be any major recovery for you, the good news is you're classed as incomplete." That made me think I had something missing, no comments please. It means that the spinal cord is not completely broken, a little like the electrical wires in the wiring harness of a vehicle, some wires may still be attached but not enough, it gave me touch, but no pain sensation, to use an Irish joke "Be thankful for small Murphy's!" Then my thumb started to move a little, as did my little finger, but hardly anything.

Sitting up in bed and in the wheelchair, I got to talk to more of other people's visitors, and the nurses, one of them, told me that PC Philip Olds had been on ward 2. I remembered him being on the TV news, he'd been shot in the back while on duty in 1980, injured on duty as I was.

The local press were reporting on my progress so I asked them if they could get a national newspaper to do a story about trying to find the London couple who'd taken cine film of me tribal dancing in the Gambia in March 1980, Patricia couldn't find the piece of paper with their name and phone number on. They got a reporter to come and take photos. The photographer was stood on a chair, about to take a photo, when a voice boomed "Stop all that." A lady came over, "I'm the secretary here, you have to have permission to take photos." After explaining, he went off to sign a form before coming back to finish off the photos. The reporter left after taking notes on the names, dates and other info about the fire and the trip to the Gambia.

The stern lady was Janet and I became friends with her, along with Sylvia, another secretary for the spinal unit who when off duty would help raise money for the hospital. I looked in the papers for a couple of weeks but nothing, it appears something else happened in the world and the story was scrapped, *bugger*.

I was surprised when a Stroud fireman came to see me, I knew him, but not well. He told me that he'd called in on his way up to London. We had a chat for about 30 minutes, he filled me in with what was happening in the Stroud area. Don Morgan was a biker and now a Senior Officer. I'd met him at a dance at Cirencester in the 1970's when he was a Sub Officer. When Don came to see me he told me that a fireman had mentioned that he was going past Stoke Mandeville, wanted to call in but didn't know what to say to me. Don told him "don't worry, just say hello George, he'll start talking and asking questions." When the fireman got back to the station, he gave Don a general update on my health and then said "you were right Don, after saying hello, I only had to answer George's questions which I quite enjoyed!"

Fred and Linda Pettit brought in their new baby Vincent to see me, he was getting bigger every time. For you heathens who don't know, Vincent's was a British motorcycle manufacturer between 1938 and 1955, they built a 1000cc V twin beast that would do 125 mph, I'd met Fred and John Daly at the 1975 MGP.

We had a New Zealand nurse called Hanora, very pretty and a good laugh, but she was caught in bed with the Turkish patient when he was in the side ward. As she was one of the red band nurses on a six-month course, she was sent back to her hospital. As an ex-union rep I was thinking of holding some sort of protest but I quickly ruled out going on hunger strike and as we couldn't withdraw our labour we sadly lost a jolly nurse.

There were many lovely nurses at Stoke Mandeville including a Maltese called Dala and a night nurse called Mad Shirley. I got along well with Mad Shirley, we seem to gel and she told me all her work and home problems which I tried to solve. Shirley was living on a long boat with a petrol generator outside, she complained she had to go out in the cold and damp before going to bed to turn it off!! After thinking about the problem, I asked her if she'd ever had a mower that had a little metal device on the top of the spark plug, which when pushed downward stopped the engine by shorting the spark out, then suggested she connect two wires one from the spark plug and one from an earth off the engine to a switch by her bed. I'm not sure if she ever did!

I was staying up a little longer in the wheelchair and, with pushing gloves on to protect my hands, pushed around very slowly, talking to people in the other beds. The occupational therapist had made a plastic rubber extension to my toothbrush, bedtime was approaching so I decided to have a go at cleaning my teeth myself. I was making my way to the bathroom when I came to an abrupt halt, well the wheelchair did, I was at the hallway leading to the nurses' office, storerooms, side bedroom and bath/washroom. There wasn't really a change in floor level just a small piece of wood separating the two linoleum style floor coverings. It was a very slight height difference, about 1/16" (less than 2 mm) but I didn't have the strength to push over it. After struggling for a while, I was about to give up, when I saw staff nurse Jenny, I asked her if she'd push me over the piece of wood. "No I won't, do it yourself" she said, I must admit I thought *miserable cow*. After trying a few more times, I was making my way back to my bed when I saw a relation of one of the other patients and asked them to give me a push over the piece of wood. I took some time to clean teeth and wash my face, I enjoyed doing it, it gave me a bit of pride. For some reason the strip of wood seemed flatter on the way back to bed!! To be fair to Jenny, she may have been following the teachings of Sir Ludwig Guttmann whose theory was: If they can't get help they will have to do it or die. If you keep helping people they won't get any better. I heard some spine chilling tales about him such as if Ludwig Guttmann saw a relation pushing a patient in their wheelchair he would shout at them "do you want them to get better or to be a baby for the rest of their life." The BBC did a programme called The Best of Men, before the 2012 Paralympic games, about how Stoke Mandeville started in February 1944, it was very good.

Mealtimes provided plenty of scope for a good laugh. Tetraplegics like Paul and I, whose hands didn't work very well, used straps on our hands to which the Occupational Therapist fitted a fork or spoon. We'd laugh at each other chasing our food around the plate. The plate had a plastic lip to stop the food coming off, our other hand rested on the side of the plate so that it didn't move around the table too much. It was quite hard to eat as we were all laughing at each other's efforts, until the inevitable crash happened when someone's plate ended up on the floor. It was a bit like school dinnertime with huge cheers and comments like "the food's not that bad "and "take it out of his wages!"

Frank turned up unannounced to Julie's 21st party dressed as Santa Claus. On seeing him, Julie shouted "this has got to be something to do with U.G. (uncle George)" He had a good time, and at least I was there in spirit, *thanks Frank*. Dave visited me later in February, he told me about Frank turning up and that a card had arrived with an unreadable signature on it. Julie had asked him "dad what's all this, a card with 'Oh Julie, number 1 at 21' written on it, but I can't read the signature." Dave told me he made some silly suggestions, then said "do you think it might be Barry Sheene?" Julie asked if I'd had anything to do with it. Dave said he replied "Oh Julie, I've heard that, it's a song isn't it?" Julie got excited, "is it Shakin Stevens? Wow!!!!"

Now I was up a lot longer, I started attending occupational therapy lessons. It was a bit like going back to school, I was learning to eat, cook, even to use a typewriter. I found after many failures that by using the slight thumb movement I had, if I trapped it against my index finger, I could type, using a plonker on my left hand. It was like the one I used for eating, except it had a steel shaft with the rubber off a pencil on the end, I could type with two hands, but very slowly.

At least occupational therapy was easier than the physio classes that I'd started attending, where I was linked up to some type of torture chamber. It was a huge framework that I reversed into with my arms outstretched. On each hand, I had a rope which went through a pulley with a weight on it. The idea was to move my arms down using my biceps, with the weight taking the arm back up, a bit like a bird flapping its wings. This was to get strength and movement back into my shoulders which were very weak as they hadn't been used for three months. As the days went by, the weight got heavier as I got stronger. I could now push over the piece of wood to clean my teeth.

Another form of torture, we were lifted out of the wheelchair onto a foam floor mat so we didn't hurt ourselves, and taught to try and turn ourselves, as if we were in bed, using the weight of an arm, by throwing it over and going with it. After some weeks, I could roll to the left easier as my right side seemed to have more movement. I tried not to enjoy rolling about when the lady physio and nurses were manhandling, or was it woman handling, me all over the place too much!

Those of us in a wheelchair were now wearing a leg bag, attached to the catheter tube going to the bladder. The bag was attached to the leg with a soft rubber strap above the knee and another around the calf. This Stoke Mandeville designed leg bag was called a kipper bag, as it looked like a large flat kipper. I didn't know if it was too tight as I couldn't feel any pain, and with my limited hand movement I couldn't yet turn the tap on and off to empty it, I had to get somebody else to do it for me before the rolling about on the mat, we didn't want any accidents!

I started swimming in a small hydrotherapy pool, about 5 x 3 m of warm water. The good part of this was the physio had to be in the water with you, it was a bonus looking at a pretty lady in a swimming costume. They were helping me do the backstroke, explaining that it allowed me to move my arms, so getting exercise with no pain, they called it passive movement. They then tried to stand me up which was quite scary at first. To do this, the lady physio stood on your feet so they wouldn't move, facing you in the water. You would have your arms around their neck and their arms would be around your waist, then they would throw themselves backwards. My legs had a slight spasm, which helped me to stand, it felt good standing up. One physiotherapist was little Scots Susie, she was about 5'3" against my 6'3", we had to be near the shallow end of the pool, we fell over a few times, but as it was in water it was OK, and we used to laugh a lot.

I began to realise I was relatively lucky with my lot, a lady learning to swim with me also had broken neck, but she was classed as complete. This meant her break, although the same as mine, cervical 5, she could feel nothing below her middle chest, not even the physio holding her, at least I did have touch sensation. She kept asking if they were holding her, *my God what must that be like?* She'd slipped over in the bath, as the saying goes "you have to play the cards you've been dealt."

The early part of 1982 was very cold with heavy snow, some said it was as bad as the 1962/63 winter. I remember a story Gordon Bircher who lived in Cranham, a pretty but remote Cotswold village 7 miles from Gloucester told me. He'd had a phone call saying a local farmer needed help rescuing his sheep. A gang of them made their way to the farm, he said "the snow was so deep we had to walk on the top of Cotswold stone walls." Gordon had me in tears as he kept telling me anecdotes!

Gordon Morss brought Pat up to see me and told me that the weather was bad. On his next visit a few weeks later he told me that the Cirencester road had been closed on his way back so he went via Stroud, as the Stroud road was closed as well he had to take detours, what was usually a 1½ hour journey took over 4 hours, thank you Gordon and all the other friends that visited me!

March had arrived, and my birthday was approaching on the 31st so as well as get well cards, 38th birthday cards started arriving, *boo hiss*. Gordon and Mary, who'd made me a 38th birthday cake, just to rub it in, visited along with Charles and Catherine, Dave and Sue with Julie and Sally, Tony Price, whose birthday was on the same day with Alice, Dexter and Robert, and Norman who was a year younger than me on the 30th. Mother came too, fussing around everything. I was really lucky to have so many visitors, it was a crowded birthday.

425

For staff and patients in hospital the news from the Falklands was required listening, so every day there was an update on the British Task Force that had been hurriedly assembled, along with Prince Andrew sailing on the aircraft carrier Ark Royal. We listened to the reports between work sessions, not that we got paid, with the physio, occupational therapist and swimming, as well as chasing our dinner around the table. Patients were coming and going, like new patient Martin Godfrey. Martin was 19 years old, although there was 19 years difference in age, he appeared to have the same sense of humour as me. He was at college studying for engineering degree, and was based at Rolls-Royce in Derby. Another thing I liked about Martin, he had a nice mum who used to clean my teeth for me before she left at 8/9 pm, if I'd had a day in bed.

I made friends with another new patient, Victor, who'd been working under a car when the jack failed, he broke his back! This reminds me of a joke, A vicar walking along a road heard a voice shout "bloody hell." Speaking to the man under the car, who apologised for his rude words, the vicar said "why don't you say God help me instead of swearing?" The man said he'd try it, and carried on working. When the jack failed and started unscrewing, just as it was about to squash him he said "oh God help me," the jack stopped and went back up, the vicar who'd been watching said "bloody hell, I've never seen that before!!!"

When wheeling about I met another biker, Roscoe Shepherd nicknamed Dr Roscoe, a top scrambler from Somerset. I was over the moon when after getting to know him, he sent Badger Goss and Lew Coffin over to say hello, when they came to visit him. Badger used to ride the works Cottons in the 1960's and Lew was a top grass and speedway rider who I'd seen race at Gloucester.

I was now getting stronger and a little braver, in the breaks and at weekends I escaped to the other wards to see who was about and visited the lady from Gloucestershire, who broke her back at Nettleton Bottom, so the ambulance men told me. I also visited the young girl called Beverley who'd wanted the Barry Sheene autograph.

It was a treat for us, when some of the off-duty nurses took a group of us more jolly ones, okay the noisy ones, down to the indoor Bowls Club which had a licensed bar. There was a club for hospital staff at Stoke Mandeville, but there was more room for wheelchairs at the Bowls Club as it was designed for wheelchair sport, the able-bodied from Aylesbury also used

426

the facilities midweek. Harry, senior physio and keen sportsman, told me it was used a lot during the wheelchair national games and for sports training weekends, by one wheelchair sport or another, most weekends.

These trips were somewhat hilarious if not dangerous, as there were only three or four members of staff with possibly 8 wheelchairs, we had to act like a train, hanging on the one in front, with a nurse pushing at the back and the other nurses halfway down and at the front, to guide and pull. The wheelchair at the front would usually be screaming in terror. We got there eventually, just about in one piece, and had a very good time.

I had a good laugh when Paul told the joke, "What goes, tut, tut fissssh, tut, tut fissssh?" "Someone in a wheelchair going down a steep hill, spitting on their hands, then putting them on the wheels to slow down! After we were chucked out of the pub, the trip back was uphill, so a lot harder.

PAUL AND I ENJOY THE COMPANY OF THE NURSES AT THE BOWLS CLUB

Another treat was when three of the nurses, Janet, Wendy and Welsh nurse Janice, took us back to their nurses' accommodation and cooked us chips. I never thought anything could taste so nice, salt and vinegar and bread-and-butter blooming lovely!

I started helping Jimmy Savile with his weekend collections of money from various groups. Jimmy had several members of staff, including Janet and Sylvia who, as well as working for the hospital, worked as Jim's secretaries for his charity work. Many of those helping Jimmy also gave their time to help spinally injured patients at the sports stadium at weekends and the national wheelchair games in June.

The people giving money towards the new spiral unit assembled in the Sports Hall. They turned up in groups, in total there could be over 100 waiting. I'd talk to the groups, answering what questions I could about spinal injuries. It gave me something to do and certainly helped the weekend go by when there were no activities for those of us who couldn't go home.

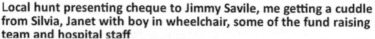

Local hunt presenting cheque to Jimmy Savile, me getting a cuddle from Silvia, Janet with boy in wheelchair, some of the fund raising team and hospital staff

Jimmy also introduced me to a 19-year-old nurse called Georgia who liked to be called Georgie. Georgie was on sick leave due to depression, she'd been involved in a fatal road accident and killed somebody. Jimmy asked me to look after her and give her some confidence again. This worked very well, we made a good team, she pushed me around the hospital, visiting various people, and down to the Bowls Club. As there was only me in a wheelchair, I could put my brakes on if I went too fast, which worked on a flat surface okay but not so well going down the steep and narrow path to

428

the Bowls Club. There were some hair-raising moments which usually ended up with me screaming "heeeeelp" as I went down it. I'm pleased my jokes, and helping me get around the hospital, helped cheer Georgie up and return to work, even more pleased, she kept coming see me in the evenings or when not on duty.

As well as physio, swimming and occupational therapy training, we were now being introduced to sport by Harry. Harry was the senior physio, he went around in shorts, was really jolly, enthusiastic, always on the go and bubbling over with enthusiasm. The sports hall had a variety of uses, sports, rolling on the floor during physio and lectures, in the evening, the general public and hospital staff could hold meetings, parties and booze ups which a lot of the patients were invited to. It was also used for church services, which patients would be pushed to in their beds, if not in their wheelchairs.

I was lying in the ward when two people came up and asked me if I'd like to come to the Christian service. Thinking about Auntie Winifred and the fact that one of the two inviting me was a pretty lady, I said "yes please." It was an ordinary type of service, held in the gym, with patients in wheelchairs or beds and any visiting relatives. There was a sermon, a few prayers, then those assembled were asked if there were any hymns they would like sung, I always shouted "Onward Christian Soldiers." I attended several of these services as it was a nice change and I liked singing. I was told that I had a good pub singing voice, as long as there was 30 more, drowning me out!!!

The first session with Harry was archery. As a Tetraplegic, I had to have my left arm strengthened with a piece of board, foam was needed under the board, then some stretch bandage used. The bow was a plastic re-curve type, my hand was wrapped around it with more foam, then more stretch bandages. On my right hand, I had a leather style glove, with a piece of metal with a hook on it, which went round the bowstring. After pulling the bowstring to the tip of my lips I released it by twisting my hand and wrist. We were also strapped in the chair so we wouldn't fall out.

Harry had us in fits of laughter with various ditties he sang as he loaded the arrow. We used a pin as a sight, Harry told us to aim the pin at the middle of the gold. The first few arrows didn't reach the target and went sliding on the floor, that was when we noticed Harry had put cardboard rabbits on the floor under the targets, which attracted various comments like "rabbit for tea" and "you're under arrest, poaching rabbits is illegal!!" We eventually hit the target by adjusting the pin height. I enjoyed archery as it was sport, and a little like rifle shooting, at least it was at a target.

Harry was very sports minded, he told us about the sports that were available and about the National Paraplegic Games that would be held at the stadium in the first two weeks of June, and the various training weekends in some of the huts.

One weekend, I was down the tea and snack bar with Ian Sabiston, the London fireman I was on the Junior Officer course with in 1978, and his wife and children when I said "Ian, get me back to the ward quick, I've had an accident." Ian's wife asked me what sort of accident, "you don't want to know Vivian" I told her "I do want to know" she insisted, "I shit myself" with a smile, I told her "I did warn you!!" It was a particularly nasty accident and ended their visit, as I had to wait by the bed with the curtains closed until the nurses and orderlies could put me to bed and wash me. Regrettably, this was not an uncommon occurrence, especially when visitors brought in rich food and homemade cakes!

John Biscoe offered to fly me to the TT races in the Isle of Man. John, as a businessman, saw the opportunity for some free publicity. He ran a TV repair shop in the Lower High Street in Cheltenham. I got to know him in the 70's when I was doing part-time butchery for Jack Council Butchers opposite his shop. John was also a Cheltenham councillor and had been a main mover in starting racing at Staverton Airport. As well as being on the Airport committee, he had a half share in a Piper Comanche. John offered me a free flight to the Isle of Man, with carers. At the time of the offer there was some doubt whether I would be fit for the TT but that was the least of my worries.

The FA Cup was between Tottenham Hotspur and Queens Park Rangers. Derek Doe's wife had brought in a portable television just in case they couldn't watch the TV on the wall. There was a group of us watching. Although I wasn't taking a great deal of interest, I tried to get in the spirit of it by borrowing one of the Derek's boys football scarves and waving it above my head while singing 'You'll Never Walk Alone.' Those of you who know me, know my singing is not very good, so everybody was laughing and joking while shouting at the television. Staff nurse Jenny stormed towards us, *Oh my God, what have I done now*, I was thinking. She went straight past me thank God, but she threw open the two narrow wartime galvanised patio doors, turned sharply, looked at me and said, "if you're going to make a terrible noise like that, get outside or if you're going to act like a child, get up the children's ward!!" I replied with a pouting bottom lip "I'm only trying to be happy Jenny."

Everyone was glued to a TV or radio when the government daily Falklands report was on. April turned into May and the Minister for Defence started reporting the death of soldiers. Then there was the shock news that a warship had been destroyed by an Exocet missile supplied by the French. There were some heated debates around the dinner table, we all had our own point of view on how the war should go. Even when having physio, occupational therapy or the nurses taking us down the Bowls Club in the evenings, the war was the main topic of conversation, everyone was eager for news.

There were two main torture chambers, sorry I mean physio areas, the furthest was down a very long corridor with four downhill sections and four flat rest areas. When being taken by some of the orderlies to this physio area they would stand on the tilt bar on the wheelchair, we'd get up quite a speed which had me shouting "help, stop, help," the other patients and visitors laughed. It reminded me of the time I passengered a racing sidecar outfit at Mallory Park, I had no control.

My physio, a tall slim lady, used to tell me to start pushing back to the ward and she'd catch me up. The first few times I hadn't got very far by the time she finished her paperwork and caught me up. After walking with me for a while and giving me encouragement, she pushed me the rest of the way. Then came the time I'd started pushing back but she didn't catch me up. I rested at every flat section and when people offered to push me, I thanked them but refused, explaining that I had to do it on my own. It took me 45 minutes to push perhaps 200 yards uphill, but I was proud of the achievement.

My physio decided to move to Oswestry Spinal Unit as did Mr. El Masri, one of the top spinal Doctors. I don't know whether it was a promotion or if she was fed up of my bad jokes, but I invited her out for a meal as a thank you for having helped me through the first four months of my new life. The night I took her out for a meal, she picked me up in her car. To get me in she did a standing transfer, which she'd shown to my friends and family. The meal was going well at the wheelchair accessible restaurant in Aylesbury, when the evening had to be cut short due to an accident, and I don't mean I dropped my plate on the floor!! Luckily she had medical pads in the car for these types of accidents to protect the car seat. She took me back to the hospital, turned on my radio and left me by the bed until staff came to sort me out. Although these were regular occurrences for everyone, I wasn't really getting used to them, when you can do nothing about it, it's very humbling! A lot depended who was with me when an accident happened, if it was firemen or bikers who had a strong stomach, there was usually a sarcastic comment making light of the situation, which made me feel easier, such as "I hope you've got your bicycle clips on George" or "baked beans for dinner again?" My new physio, another pretty lady, was Kate Moore.

June arrived, I was still making slow progress so no TT trip. I received a TT Special at the end of practice week and then after every race day. The TT special was a newspaper printed at the end of practice week and each race day, it was out by 9pm, a remarkable feat. It was started in the 1920's by Mr Davidson and carried on by Fred Hanks for every TT and Manx Grand Prix, but sadly no longer, it finished in 1986.

By the end of May into June, the war in the Falklands had got rather nasty, there'd been many deaths on both sides and a number of support ships and cruisers lost. We had at least one casualty from the war in the hospital. Argentina surrendered on the 14th of June. Sadly, many soldiers lost their lives on both sides 649 Argentine, 255 British and 3 Falkland Islanders. There were several get-togethers to celebrate the victory and I was pleased to be invited with a few others to a party. It was surprising how patriotic we were, playing Land of Hope and Glory, God Save the Queen, We'll Meet Again, and many more morale boosting songs, by the end of the night I was hoarse.

We'd all been looking forward to the National Wheelchair Games. Harry organised trips to see the various sports, on what would have been our exercise days. Having done rifle shooting before my injury, I was interested in the 10m air rifle and pistol, and getting down to the bar in the evening, although you had a job to find a space with 500 athletes and helpers on the site. We also watched weightlifting, table tennis and swimming, sadly I didn't see the archery as it was held away from the track and field events for safety. My visitors were as amazed as I was with the level of competition.

A group of us were down watching the table tennis in the main sports hall, it was packed. As they were calling competitors to their event they went up in their wheelchairs, until one man walked up, well limped really, but he completed from a wheelchair. In a break I asked why he completed in the wheelchair when he could walk. He explained that he had Spina Bifida, liked the sport, but couldn't compete on equal terms against able-bodied people, certainly not with a chance of winning. You'll gather from this, I didn't like being in a wheelchair and was struggling to understand somebody wanting to compete from a wheelchair when they could walk, however badly. I was not coming to terms with disability very well!

My right hand had some movement, and both my wrist flexors were quite strong. A flexor is a muscle that when contracted bends a limb, my wrist extensors, which when contracted straighten a limb, were virtually non-existent. This caused problems with my right hand, whilst I could hold things I couldn't let them go! My left hand had no movement at all but using my flexor, I could hold something, it also allowed me to hold onto the chair with my left arm and wrist to steady myself. I was trying the discus and club, an Indian style club like a small rounders bat, as I couldn't throw a javelin. As I could hold some things, table tennis looked promising, I could hold the bat so it didn't need bandaging on like the archery hook. By the time the games had finished a lot of us were enthusiastic about sport.

Every so often a member staff left, married or had a baby, well any excuse for a party. At a fancy dress party, the American physio turned up as the Statue of Liberty, at occupational therapy I made a coon skin cap, like Davy Crockett used to wear, and wore my check shirt, singing I'm a Lumberjack and I'm Okay, from Monty Python's Flying Circus, I knew the song was strange, but it was all the rage at the time and made people laugh. There was a young girl in her bed, decorated up with glitter, as I was talking to her, some rock 'n' roll was playing so I danced with her, no I didn't get into bed with her, we both waved our arms around in the air! There was another new pretty physio named Dorothy, she sat on my lap for one of the slow dances, not that I wheeled very far!!

I spoke with the doctors about the possibility of going to the Isle of Man for the S100, and was told that I'd have to have at least two carers, they would have to be taught how to do manual evacuation for toileting and how to fit my Conveen, a sheath worn over the penis connected to a bag worn on the leg, it replaced the catheter.

I asked Big Frank, who said he was up for it and volunteered Pete Davies. There was a long-standing joke about when Frank was a young fireman in 1967, Pete Davies had roped him in to go down to Cornwall for two weeks, at the time of the Torrey Canyon tanker disaster!! Pete was now asking if this was payback.

How do I explain what is like having two friends stick their fingers up your backside? You could never really say I was dignified, I was a scruffy bastard really who never worried what I looked like, but this was on a different level. One thing that did help was that we joked about it, which helped everyone deal with the embarrassment!

I'd only been back home once since the accident, to Charlie Moons retirement party, one of the original Gloucester City Fire Brigade firemen. That time, I stayed one night in the Leonard Cheshire home in Cheltenham. I didn't stay too long at the party because it was Charlie's night but everybody was coming up to see me, many that never gave me the time of day normally, I must admit, I felt like a bit of a sideshow. The stay at the home was an experience, but the lady carers and nurses were pleased to see me as most residents were very old. Leonard Cheshire was the youngest group captain in the RAF and one of the most highly decorated pilots of the war. After the war he founded a hospice that grew into the charity, Leonard Cheshire Disability.

When I was leaving Cheshire Home with my pile of medical gear on my lap, I had to go past an old lady. She was looking sad so I said "give us a smile." She grumpily replied "what have I got to smile about, I haven't got any presents like you have" looking at the box on my lap. I told her she could have some of my night bags and suppositories if she wanted, which made the staff and other residents smile.

Plans were made for the 3 day trip, to see the Isle of Man Southern 100 motorcycle races. I was kept informed of developments on the trip, the IOM fire service had arranged accommodation. John Biscoe, part owner of the plane, came to see me in hospital asking why I didn't want to go to the TT, I replied "I wasn't fit enough when the TT races were on and I never raced at the TT, only the S100 and MGP." John said he was sorry but he'd be away the day we wanted to fly but the co-owner of the plane would take us.

434

Tuesday morning of race week, in fire station transport, Frank collected me, taking me to Ash Lane, Down Hatherley first, there were many tears when I saw mother and all the neighbours. We went on to Pat's house in Lavington Drive, Longlevens, Frank had fixed up for Steve Bailey to make two ramps, one for mother's bungalow, the other for Pat's house, it made life a lot easier. David brought Sue, the girls and mum around for the evening but it was early to bed as we had an early start in the morning. A bed had been put in the living room for me, Frank and Pete had to turn me a couple of times during the night. I'd had ablutions at the hospital the day before, so on Wednesday, after a wash and brush up, Pat made breakfast before the Three Musketeers set off on a new adventure!!

We arrived at Staverton airport to a battery of cameras, a single engine aircraft, one fire appliance and crew and some senior officers, it was all a bit of a daze really. When Frank, Pete and I initially saw the aircraft, we wondered how the hell I was going to get in it, glancing at the fireman, I think they were thinking the same! After the obligatory photos, an interview with the press and radio station Severn Sound, I said my goodbyes to mum and Pat.

With two firemen standing on the wing of the plane, I was lifted out of the wheelchair in a standing transfer position with my arms around Frank's neck as he stood in front of me. The firemen on the wing got their arms around me and lifted. I let go of Frank's neck as he slid his hands down to my legs, the other fireman helped Pete make sure my backside didn't catch the wing and damage my skin, this had been drummed into them at Stoke Mandeville during their training. Once on the wing we all had a rest, getting into the cabin was even more precarious. I commented that I hoped this would be put onto their drill record at the fire station, which at least brought a few smiles.

The Piper Comanche was a 4 seater aircraft but there were three of us sat in the back with me in the middle wearing my protective neck brace. One pilot got in and introduced himself as the co-owner of the plane explaining that as he didn't have a full licence to fly over water, an experienced pilot would be flying the plane. The more experienced pilot got in and introduced himself. Looking at the controls, he pointed to a switch and asked "is this where you start the aircraft, the brake, the wing flaps and the radio?" Pete and Frank looked at me and as much as I could, I looked left and right at them, we were thinking *let's get out of here quick*! The pilot then turned around and explained that this check was standard practice if you were flying somebody else's aircraft, which put us at ease a little.

The flight went well, having never flown in a light aircraft before seeing the land below us was quite exhilarating even more so when we left the land flying over the sea, I added some adrenaline to the experience with comments like, how far can you swim? We arrived at Ronaldsway airport in the south of the island, close to Castletown the old capital of the Isle of Man, in less than 2 hours.

The Manx fire service were waiting for us. Godfrey Cain, the station officer of Douglas fire station, introduced fireman Roy Cain, no relation, who was to look after us, saying "any problems, give me a shout." They had a forklift truck with a large flat platform, onto which they put my wheelchair. Once out of the cockpit, I got into the wheelchair on the platform, it made getting out a lot easier than getting in. After more photos, Roy Cain, driving a hire car, took us to Douglas fire station HQ to talk about what had been set up.

On arrival first order of the day was a cup of tea, but not before some more photos and an interview with Manx radio. After having tea, we were taken to the accommodation which was a Rent a Chalet. These were really small bungalows, with two separate bedrooms, one main bedroom with a double bed, the other with bunk beds. There was a large lounge which could sleep extra people, it was ideal with the wheelchair as there was lots of space.

The fire service had fixed up the hire car which Roy Cain drove, if he wasn't available Frank and Pete were insured to drive. We'd missed Tuesday and Wednesday morning practice, so after some food we went down to Castletown, I directed them to the campsite. Everyone was in tears including myself, the last time they'd seen me, was last July when I was racing my Trident. All the tea girls plus wives of riders were giving me cuddles and kisses, which I tried not to enjoy too much! We watched the racing from behind the fence after I had supervised scrutineering, explaining to Frank and Pete the procedures. After the races we went to the pub, which Frank certainly enjoyed. Frank had been racing with me, so he knew a little of the scene but Pete admitted afterwards he was amazed at the racing and the number of people I knew.

Thursday morning and the dreaded moment had arrived for us all. I'd had my " Senokot, move it pills," as I called them the night before, they helped you go to toilet by moving the food through the digestive system as nothing works properly below the break. Frank and Pete got their idiot sheet out: 1, Lay George in the recovery position 2, make sure paper towels are on the bed, 3, insert suppositories with gloves on 4, leave for at least half an hour 5, after the movement insert finger after putting glove on and wiggle it around (not nice for anybody). The boys got full marks, plus a star for not making a mistake!

I was dressed and we were ready for another day. There was no practice today, just the finals of the heats we'd watched yesterday. After breakfast we went straight to Castletown, with a little more time we showed Pete the docks and Frank and Pete took photos of the Castle, which is impressive but ghostly looking. Arriving at the paddock I chatted to the riders I knew, especially the ones from Gloucestershire.

In the evening, it was the presentations, so we had a meal in the George Hotel, I twisted Frank's arm into have a drink! I saw friends like Mick Dunn, who was racing, Fred and Jocelyn Peck, who'd helped me with my bikes since 1974, and too many others to mention. We watched the presentation before Peter drove us back to the chalet to get ready to go home, Frank was a little legless like me.

Friday morning, as there were no ablutions, after breakfast we did a lap of the TT course, calling in at Gwen Crellin's tea and cake cafe, as she called it. Pete was amazed at the hundreds of signed photos on her wall, from Giacomo Agostini, Mike Hailwood and dozens of top riders as well as Norman Wisdom and especially the signed photos of the Red Arrows as his daughter wanted to join the Royal Air Force.

 After finishing the lap we called in to see my first landlady, Doris Jackson, before going to Douglas fire station. Roy Cain took us back to the airport and the fireman loaded me in the aircraft. John Biscoe flew us back to Staverton Airport. After collecting the things that had been left at Pat's, I said goodbye to mother and it was back to the hospital.

On Monday, Dr Frankel, who was always asking me if I was ever going to stop talking, scared me to death when he said "well you managed alright in the Isle of Man, you might as well go home now." "But, but, but," I sounded like a BSA Bantam on tick over, "what about becoming a father, how will I manage, where will I stay?" Stoke Mandeville had become my home, I had a job well, physio, occupational therapy, swimming and sport, I'd made friends, and helped Jimmy with his charity work. I think I said "I don't want to go home!"

I had a test for being a father but wasn't successful. I started to learn to get in and out of a car drivers seat, even had a driving lesson, well sat in the car driving along the back road at the hospital a few hundred yards, but I was still very weak, so I started concentrating on physio more. I started to pray to God on my own in bed as well as at the special services when they were on, asking God what I should do. Try and imagine it, I'd been in hospital for 9 months, my brain had stopped working, it took me ages to decide which meal choice to tick, now I had to make a decision on where to move to.

Ermine House was the front runner as it had physio and an occupational therapy room, I asked Frank and the lads to have a look. It was in Horton Road, where Dave used to take me when he was working on the railway 30 years before.

A physio from Ermine House called Carol, had visited me a couple of months ago, bringing Harry and Mike, two Tetraplegics from Gloucester. They told me about the Young Disabled Unit. I mentioned the Cheshire Homes, Mike said that he'd stopped there for some time. Mike was stronger than me and could get up and put himself to bed. Like me he had a broken neck, he was a C6, I was C5/6 with my right hand starting to move a little, Harry was a C5 but neither of his hands worked as well as my right hand, Mike had some movement in both hands. Rachel, an 11 year old Gloucester girl, who'd broken her back some time ago and lived at home, came in with her mother, Susan, for a check-up. She gave me some useful info. Ermine house was part of the NHS and in Gloucester, so it was closer for friends and Brother Dave who worked in Gloucester. To be honest, I was bloody scared whatever decision I made. As well as leaving the comfort zone of Stoke Mandeville, I'd have to start learning all over again.

It was now the beginning of August, I was working hard to make sure I knew everything I had to do to look after myself. The nice lady almoner made sure all my pensions were in place. I'd also applied to the DVLA for a new licence, the doctors ticked all the boxes on the form. When the licence came back, it said that the vehicle must be capable of being driven with weak arms and no leg movement, so no test *Whoopee*!

438

On one of my last weekends at Stoke Mandeville there was an air weapons training session in one of the huts. I headed off in my Everest and Jennings NHS wheelchair to the shooting hall. Luckily it was flat or downhill towards the Guttmann Stadium, it took me about 30 minutes to get the 500 yards to the shooting hall. I was made welcome by Ron Nicholls who was in charge and was chairman of the British Paraplegic Shooting Association. They showed me rifles and pistols and let me have a go, which I liked, and they encouraged me by saying that I was quite good. As dinner time was approaching and realising there was no way I could get back on my own I asked if somebody could assist me, but let me push as much as I could.

After discussion with close friends about where to stop I decided to go to Ermine House, what would life bring now? Another chapter in my life was about to start!

August 12th, just one month after coming back from the Southern 100 races, was my last day at Stoke Mandeville. Paul had a T-shirt printed with "Sister Rose Fan Club" on it, she called us the terrible twins, she couldn't decide which one of us was the worst! I said goodbye to everyone on the ward, the ladies on the other wards and all the nurses, before asking Sister Rose for a kiss!!!!

As Frank drove into Ermine House, we were *greeted* by a battery of cameras and reporters. After the initial fuss, I met the staff and other residents before being helped to settle into a six bedded bay with three other residents. Jim was perhaps a few years younger than me, Richard and John were older. Jim and Richard suffered from multiple sclerosis, John had Huntington Chorea, a neurodegenerative disease. The day drifted by, Norman and John visited in the early evening, which cheered me up before being put to bed with my radio.

FIREMEN AND STAFF WELCOME ME TO ERMINE HOUSE

WELCOME BACK GEORGE!

Saturday, I waited for staff to get me up after they'd given me breakfast in the bay, I learnt some more about John's illness. He'd already asked Jim and Richard what they had for breakfast, and would they mind him feeding Fred the rabbit, a pet rabbit for residents to look at. John then spoke to me, "I had cornflakes which were very nice, what did you have and did you enjoy it?" After I answered "Bran flakes and yes okay", he asked if I minded him feeding Fred the rabbit. During the day many people popped in including Pete Davies who brought a large wall calendar so that we could mark down appointments. At dinner time I found out more about the other residents. I also spent half an hour in the physio room which Carol had shown me. On Sunday, Dave picked me up for a meal in Tewkesbury, we collected Patricia and mother on the way. It was a nice afternoon but it was then back to Ermine House.

I was in a bit of a trance, my brain wasn't really working and I couldn't seem to comprehend anything. There was a VHS machine in the main room, a member of staff tried to explain how to operate it, but I couldn't remember what buttons to push. I kept running away, or wheeling away, from difficult things so people started organising my life.

During the first week three ladies came to see me, this was the start of the long path to shaping my life. The first was a pretty nurse who ran an archery club at Gloucester Leisure Centre, she'd seen in the notes that I'd done archery at Stoke Mandeville, and asked if I'd like to join, she'd collect me Monday. The other ladies were Edna Jones and Catherine Thornwill, they explained that they ran an evening swim class for elderly and disabled people. Catherine was the nurse at the Chamwell School for Disabled Children, which had its own heated swimming pool. Gloucester firemen had agreed to help, and Catherine would pick me up at 16:45, I readily agreed as I liked swimming.

Sharon was the Occupational Therapist based at Ermine House, she told me that I could make or adapt things myself using the occupational therapy room when I wanted. Carol came in three times a week, she had me working in the physio room, just like at Stoke Mandeville. I'm sure she had a big whip to crack while shouting orders, only joking Carol! She also gave me exercises I could do when on my own. One was using a pillow case, putting my right arm in the open end, lifting it up and dropping it on the other side of the wheelchair, then using my left arm picking it up and dropping in on the right-hand side of the chair. I started with 5 the first day and increased it each day until I was doing 30. It was a little boring but if I wanted to get stronger................

Harry, who Carol had brought up to Stoke Mandeville to meet me, regularly gave me a game of table tennis. Although we had lots of table tennis balls to start with, once we lost them, we spent what seemed like ages trying to pick them up, but it was all good exercise I suppose. Eventually we had to ask staff to get our balls, nothing rude, before losing them again!

Archery was held in the projectile area at the Leisure Centre, which I must admit I hadn't known much about. The archery club was organised by Marnie Bannister who was an occupational therapist with the NHS. I used a re-curve fibreglass bow and found some bandages and braces for my arm. Harry was there in his wheelchair, there was someone who sat on a chair to shoot, but it was mainly able-bodied archers. I enjoyed the archery before going to the bar where I saw a few more old faces, then back to Ermine House.

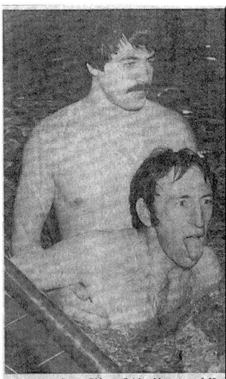

A breathless George Ridgeon finishes his sponsored 20 length swim of Charnwell School pool last night. The swim was organised in aid of the cardiac unit at the Bristol Royal Infirmary. George is an ex-Gloucester fireman injured in a fall and among the helpers was former colleague fireman Dick Oakey.

Tuesday 16:45, Catherine came to pick me up for swimming. When we got to the school, there were more cameras, but firemen Peter and Frank, whispered to me that it was also helping the school, so I didn't mind too much. As a fireman, we'd had a risk visit around the school, all the students had some form of disability. There was another school next door for students with learning disabilities, all the students used the swimming pool during school time. Edna was in overall charge, and like Catherine, was about 10 years older than me, but Edna's grandchildren called her super Gran, she was full of energy. Edna was the secretary at the school, a keen swimmer and a qualified swimming instructor. With helpers, she'd started an evening swim class for people with disabilities, problems such as arthritis, and elderly people who didn't like swimming in a pool 2 or 3°C cooler than this one.

Frank and Pete were helping me again, I think to stop me misbehaving. We'd been allotted a room, the boys lifted me onto a padded table to get me into my swimming costume, then wheeled me down to the pool. There was a special hoist that had been designed by Dowty apprentices which used a Dowty hydraulic pit prop. I was quite interested in it as dad had worked at Dowty Rotol during the war. The apprentices had reversed it, and fitted a 6' x 3' platform so that disabled people could be hoisted into the water. The swimming pool was 11 by 6 yards, built inside a ginormous conservatory type building, with large double glazed windows, so that anyone using it could look at the fields and flower gardens.

Peter and Frank were in the water with me, Edna, put a large float underneath my back and arm bands on me, although it was very restrictive, I enjoyed splashing around for 20 minutes. Over a cup of tea, I met all the other swimmers. There was one over 90-year-old gentleman, who used to cycle there as he lived close by, he could tell some stories and always had a smile on his face. Helping Edna was Phil Parker, as well as collecting money he helped Edna on the edge of the pool side. Phil used to work at the old school when it was called Oak Bank School on the Stroud Road in Gloucester. I always wondered what it was when I went past it in the early 1960's.

I told Carol one day that I thought I remembered her from somewhere, Carol said "I met you outside 83 Worcester Street, I was looking at the house next door and recommended two weeks rest when you pulled a muscle painting 3 ceilings in one day." "I remember now, I went to the Gambia doing nothing but relaxing in the sun for 2 weeks, it cured my shoulder!" Carol quipped "good, I'm glad your shoulder's better, here's some more work for you, I've fixed you up with physio twice a week at the hospital." Carol had me down the physio room on Friday afternoons, this was when Gillian and Allison, two young schoolgirls, the daughters of the Champion family, used to call in on the way home from school. They watched as I was exercising. Brother Rob was in our skittles team, it was impromptu visits like this that were making life more bearable.

What with friends visiting, physio, archery and swimming, life was going by quickly. Every Sunday I was collected by a fireman and spent the day with Pat, her neighbours came in to see me, even the dreaded Eileen from next door. Chris Witts who lived close by took me back every Sunday night, I used to ask him not to take me back, with his dry sense of humour, he'd reply "where do you want me to take you George?" "I really don't know Chris!!"

The nurse who usually took me to archery had told me that she was on duty the next week, as I enjoyed the archery I was feeling disappointed, but that changed when school and biking friend John Meadows called in on his way home from work. After making a cuppa, he asked the usual question "how are things going?" which gave me the opportunity to ask him if he'd take me to archery on Monday night. John drove a Saab 99 which was quite easy to get into as the door had a cutaway allowing the wheelchair to get closer, making it easier for me to transfer using the sliding board I'd helped to make at Stoke Mandeville. What made the evening even better, was John enjoyed the pint and chat in the bar after the archery.

I was learning more about Ermine House every day, each group sleeping bay and single room had a TV, there was also one in the lounge which doubled up as a dining area and general functions room. The kitchen, where you could go to make yourself a cuppa, was off the lounge, Ermine House was classed as our home. The staff, although registered nurses or care assistants, wore general clothes to stop you thinking you were in hospital. I was a bit worried after the first week, the staff wanted to get me to use a catheter instead of the conveen that Stoke Mandeville had advised so I refused. They also didn't like doing the suppositories then waiting for something to happen, they suggested being flushed out with an enema, but I resisted that as well. I did agree to being transferred onto a commode wheelchair after the suppositories, then being left by the bed with the curtain drawn while I had my breakfast. Although there were more staff in the daytime, I was still stuck there for some time so, after I'd finished my cereal, I started to throw one leg then the other out in front of me, using the spasm to move forward, I started to make my way to the bathroom, staff grumbled at me for being a pain in the ass, a really enjoyable place to live!

When it wasn't a commode morning, I started trying to dress myself in the mornings, using the monkey pole, until I fell out of bed! This got me in trouble again, for trying to live! They started putting up the bed sides so I would not fall out again, but this helped me to dress as I could lock my hands and arm in the sides, I could move, wriggle and lift easier. I was trying to remember what Stoke Mandeville had recommended me to do. I'd joined the Spinal Injuries Association (SIA) when in hospital, which gave advice to those with spinal cord injuries as well as their families. The SIA had a useful monthly newsletter, I bought one of their suppositories inserters, and after weeks of trying I could insert the suppositories by myself. It was a clever device with a chrome steel handle type gun and plastic parts to hold a suppository, you inserted it yourself. Everything I did was a struggle but getting better as time went by.

There was more press coverage every time I did anything out of the ordinary. I'd asked the fire service if I could visit the control room to see if I could do anything. Cameras and press were there, so I had the obligatory photo with the duty crew, although I'd moved to Gloucester in 1977 there were still a lot of them I knew. I did enjoy the day there, manning the radio and trying to write down messages, it started me wondering if I could do it for a job.

As arranged by Carol, transport came to take me to the hospital for physio. It was in an old wooden WW 2 hut which reminded me of Ward 2. I was stood up in a wooden standing frame for a while, as I had been at Stoke, then given various tasks to do. They had a large wheel which you could put a brake on if you wanted to make it harder, they had some hope. I'd turn with one hand, obviously easy with my right as I had some grip, then turning around used my left, now I know what a hamster feels like running round in his wheel!!

This didn't stop Carol giving me extra physio to do and the task of wheeling from Ermine House to the front gate and back, just over 100 yards. Although it was quite flat, it took quite a long time, so I started trying to time myself. I failed, if it was a nice day, I would wait by the road and talk to any passers-by who would stop for a chinwag or, if I was lucky, watch any young ladies walking by. I was told when I left Stoke Mandeville, "be careful and look after yourself, make sure you don't get pressure sores and don't do anything that may make you ill." One day, I had just started the morning push, when a dark cloud came over and a spot of rain fell, so I scurried back in, *what a wimp I've turned into.*

Unless something special was organised, like a quiz or party, staff and residents would play scrabble, which I was useless at. When I played against Dave Baker, during stand down period at the fire station, he wouldn't let me use bike, he said that it was abbreviation of bicycle. I had a word I thought would use all my letters and asked Dave how it was spelt. Another lesson learnt, don't trust anybody, all's fair in love, war and now scrabble it seems. Dave, pointing with his finger on the board said "yes, it's a 7 letter word, put it there." Before I could have my go, the others all put 2 and 3 letters words where he'd pointed, stopping me winning, and I thought he was a friend of mine!!

One event I did enjoy, was when we all trooped over to the hospital club, to play skittles. For the ones who had no hand movement at all Sharon, the OT, had made a gulley type trough to roll the balls down, she would ask them if they wanted it left a bit or right a bit, to make them feel as if they were actually taking part. Both myself and Harry as Tetraplegics couldn't open our hands but Harry showed me how he balanced the skittle ball on his closed hand and threw the ball up the alley. I did fairly well after a few failed attempts, getting better with the technique each week until, one time, I was about to bowl when the ball fell off my fist onto the floor with a loud and unexpected bang making everybody jump. Without thinking I went to pick it up, as I put my hand downwards for the ball my hand opened up, I just looked at it for a moment. When someone shouted "get on with it George," I brought my hand back up, it closed again. Once the ball was picked up and put on my lap, after wetting my fingers, I forced my hand around the ball, after a couple of goes I was bowling fairly normally. Skittles had become even more enjoyable.

Brother David was coming in regularly and taking me for rides in various cars he had for sale and thought I might like to see. The wall calendar showed I'd been doing something every day for the last three months. After a few weeks of swimming, I was becoming stronger and Edna suggested I get a face mask and snorkel. This enabled me to do the breaststroke on my own, I could see where I was going and keep in a straight line as I could follow the black line on the bottom and, I could keep out of the way of other swimmers! I kept up the swimming for many years, with a variety of firemen helping me. They'd made up a shift pattern which is still relevant today, you can wear one carer/helper/friend out very quickly!

A gentleman called Ron Farley visited a resident in Ermine House, he used to do air pistol shooting. I was interested, I'd always liked shooting since big brother had taken me to the fairground when I was little. Ron brought his air pistol in, it was an Italian FAS. After the initial panic by some staff on seeing a gun, we got permission to shoot it inside using cleaning buds which were made of hard packed cotton wool. As I wasn't too bad at it, Ron brought down a special pellet catching target holder, I shot outside with real .177 pellets when the weather was good, very enjoyable, especially when I hit the target! As weeks turned into months, the novelty of my new home wore off a little. I was still in a routine with hospital visits for physio, archery, swimming and pistol shooting with Ron Farley. I discovered there was an air pistol and rifle club in Tewkesbury, which met on Wednesday nights in an old school, these trips helped to break the monotony of living in Ermine House.

It was all a bit much, having to relearn how to do everything again, but during the nine months lying in hospital, I slowly started realising I was going to have to learn how again, as I did when a child! The only trouble was you didn't realise you were learning when you were growing up, it was something you just did. Now at 38 years old, I knew I had to learn how to live again, and I hated it. This didn't help my general frame of mind and I started to get depressed.

I started seeing a psychiatric nurse of some sort. I told her I didn't want to live anymore, her reply was "why don't you kill yourself then?" This started me contemplating suicide, but how to do it, there's the rub! I started taking my knife to bed, leaving it by my radio. I'd bought the knife on a shopping trip, the Occupational Therapist had put a large plastic handle on it which made it much easier to hold, it became a general cutting tool for many jobs such as opening letters etc. I was surprised none of the staff asked me why the knife was by my bedside, I had my answer ready "it's my knife and I may need it for something." I was trying to convince myself that I should plunge the knife into my heart as I wouldn't feel anything, but there seemed to be two people in my head arguing, was it an angel and the devil? The angel side of me thought *what about letting my family and friends down and it'd get the night staff into trouble.* The devil side thought, *if I had to choose anybody to get into trouble I could think of one night staff nurse who deserved it!* When she came to turn me I asked her if I could try to turn myself, she replied "we don't have time to mess about with that." I started struggling, banging the nurse on the head with the monkey pole, "you selfish bugger" she shouted. I realised being called selfish means you're doing what you want and not doing what they want! The argument continued in my head, *God says it is wrong to commit suicide, what if I don't go to heaven, the other place may be worse than this, if that's possible.* I even asked myself if I was already dead and this was hell!! I was too scared to do it, but every night when I went to sleep, I was hoping I wouldn't wake up, but I did, with John asking "can I feed Fred the rabbit?"

I tried to think about the other residents, a lady who could only move her head used to talk to herself, she would just chunter away for hours, and several others who were severely disabled, much worse than me, one of whom was Malcolm. I think he must have been a saint. Although he could only move his head, Malcolm liked talking to people. Sharon had fixed up a special cigarette smoking device for him, he would call out "would someone light my cigarette please" but if the staff were playing Scrabble they'd reply "oh wait a minute Malcolm" and it would never happen. I tried to light it for him once and nearly set the place on fire when I dropped a lighted match on the carpet, they came and lit his cigarette then, I was in trouble again!!

447

I knew I was getting more miserable, but seemed unable to do anything about it. Thanks to all my friends taking me out, I did momentarily manage to forget I was disabled. What added to the depression was the dreaded Christmas approaching. Everything took me more than 10 times longer to do than an able-bodied person, I was worried about cards and wrapping presents. I had physio and other things that were scheduled, along with my swimming, archery and pistol shooting, but always I had to return to Ermine House.

Norman asked me if I'd I like to spend Christmas Eve with him, Tina and the children, I took him up on the offer which eased me into the festive season. Christmas Eve was quite special to me, we'd started going to this Mrs Prentice's in 1962, I gave big Frank a miniature bottle to give his mum for Christmas as I'd given her every year.

Whilst Norman had seen me in Ermine House and in hospital he hadn't picked me up before. When helping me out of the car into a wheelchair I tried to get my leg to move, Norman said "are you getting better George, how did you move your leg?" "It's called a trick movement Norm, I think about moving a muscle and it makes the rest of the leg spasm." Once inside Norman astounded me by saying that he and Frank had made a pact, if this happened to either of them, the other would finish them off, I asked why they hadn't done that for me then!! He took me back about midnight, as we entered the staff said "why did you bring him back?" He told me later that he could not believe people could be so cruel and nasty.

Dave picked me up for Christmas dinner but when we got to his place I was left to wait 10 minutes or more in the car as it was absolutely persisting down with rain! It was a good day with a lovely meal. I carefully opened my money pouch, took out a silvery 5p piece and put it in the Christmas pudding as I used to when I was able-bodied. My brother gave me a present, after struggling to take the wrapping paper off, a tin of peanuts, great!!! "Come on George, good exercise, open it up" he said. I was struggling and asked if they could do it, "no, remember what you were told at Stoke Mandeville, you must try." After much struggling I did open it and this snake popped out, making me jump, it was a spring with some snake type material on, we all burst out laughing. The day was spoilt by going back to Ermine House.

The rest of Christmas is a little bit of a blur, but I remember pushing to the front gate for my exercise, on Boxing Day. Two young men came walking up to the front gate as I was sat there resting getting ready for my return trip. "Hello George," I replied "hello, I seem to know your faces, but…….." "I'm Andy Cole from Derby, I won the Manx GP this year and I am stopping with my friend in Hereford a few days." I felt very appreciative that they should travel so far to see me. I offered my hand and said "well done Andy, tell me about it. I had a TT special delivered every day, which if anything, made me more miserable as I'd have liked to have been there, but I did get to the Southern 100". I thanked them for coming and asked if they'd like a cup of tea and a biscuit. Pushing back to Ermine House, we took the refreshments to a quiet area and had an enjoyable few hours talking about bikes. I was pleased friends and family popped in over the few days up to the New Year, looking at many of the other residents I thought *will I end up like them*? One of the residents, Richard, his brother came to see him once a year, at Christmas!!

New Year Eve I went to a friend of Pat's home, there was music, drinks and light snacks before the evening was spoilt by going back to Ermine House, goodbye 1982!

CHAPTER 20   1983-The ride of my life

I read in the MCN, that the Manx Motorcycle Club were putting on a parade for old Manx riders and machines at the Diamond Jubilee, the first Manx GP was in 1923! My old watch had invited me round for their evening shift, sat around the dining table after the evening meal, I told them about the Manx parade and said "I wonder if I could sit on the back of a bike." Paul Sumner had ridden his motorcycle to work so someone suggested trying to get me on the back of it. Before I could utter the words "yea or nay" this somewhat unnerving exercise started with firemen pulling, pushing and shoving me in all different directions while others steadied the bike which was rocking from side to side on the centre stand! They finally got me on and Paul slid on the bike in front of me, my arms were wrapped tightly around Paul's waist, more like a bear hug. The large Suzuki four-cylinder was then rolled off its stand. Paul revved the bike and slipping the clutch, we started to move, with me hanging on for grim death! Luckily the drill yard was empty, we rode round and round in circles. This seemed to go on for an age, but was probably not much more than a minute, if that. We came to a stop with cheers, applause and much jollification, it could be done. It was suggested we needed a chopper rack of some sort, like on a Harley-Davidson.

Plans were started to see if the MGP ride could be organised, at last I wanted to do something!

I didn't feel I could hang on to a rider around a lap of the TT course, as I found our 1 minute test ride at 5 mph difficult enough so everyone was looking for chopper racks as I would need to be strapped to the bike.

The regime at Ermine House had told me I had to move out. Tewkesbury Borough Council (TBC) had been contacted about accommodation and I started to look at buying a bungalow. Janet Henderson, from Stoke Mandeville, had taken the post as assistant head nurse in Ermine House, adding to the few I could trust to give me honest advice. I had several meetings with TBC officials who had told me that they were building some bungalows for the elderly, one and half bed, as I called them after seeing the plans, the second bedroom was very small. They were being built next to RAF Innsworth so not far from mother.

The Ermine House hierarchy kept pushing me to move, which depressed me even more. Can you imagine, nearly a year lying on my back staring at the ceiling having to make decisions when I couldn't carry any of them out myself, I couldn't even set the video machine!! I felt this was the darkest period in my life, for five months, every morning I'd been asked "can I feed Fred the rabbit and what were your cornflakes like?" There was the lady who just muttered to herself all the time and so many other residents with terrible diseases or disabilities, most were getting worse but all I felt was sorry for me, even the psychiatric nurse was suggesting I commit suicide!!

The depression, if possible, got worse after another incident that happened on my Sunday trip to spend the day with Pat. I couldn't do much other than watch TV unless someone came round for a chat, until a kind bunch of CB radio enthusiasts from the Forest of Dean bought and fitted a CB radio in Pat's kitchen. This did take my mind off the depression as it was a bit like being in the fire appliance, "QF 105 in attendance" except this was "breaker 19 anyone want to copy Stagecoach." Stagecoach was my handle for two reasons, I was in a wheelchair and I'd been in love with Doris Day from 1953, one of my favourite songs being The Deadwood Stage is coming over the plain. This particular Sunday Pat was washing up and rather than just sit there and watch I was trying to dry the smaller items, I dropped a China mug which smashed. Pat shouted "why can't you sit there and do nothing?" "I would rather be dead than do nothing" I replied. I was just so unhappy, I was upsetting friends but I just didn't want to live the life that had been handed out to me.

Most times Chris Witts, who I'd been a leading fireman with, would take me back to Ermine House from Pat's, as he lived few hundred yards away. Every time we had the same conversation, "Chris please don't take me back to Ermine House," "where do you want me to take you then George?" "That's the trouble Chris I don't know, I just hate going there." Chris would try to make light of the situation, saying such things as "You could be stuck with my Mrs" but every time I told him "I hate waking up every morning."

I was trying to understand how Malcolm, one of the patients/residents, could be so calm, he could only move his head, he used his chin to drive his electric wheelchair. He was the most pleasant of all the residents and so easy to hold a conversation with. I discovered he had a passion for the police, he had many badges and other memorabilia. Without letting him know what I was planning, I asked if he'd been around a police station or in a police car, "no George, that's just a dream" I then changed the subject. I contacted Brian Bailey who was a police sergeant on motorcycles. He fixed up for Malcolm to have a ride in a police car, I was told Malcolm really enjoyed it.

The staff kept trying to change the way I did things from the way I was trained to do them at Stoke Mandeville, to suit them rather than me. This was getting me down, and not helping with my depression. I felt like the shot down Spitfire pilot in a 50's war film, trapped, out of control, and there was nothing I could do! Having a fairly religious upbringing, especially with Aunty Win being a missionary and mother taking me to church on Sundays, where I'd play trains with the prayer books until I got smacked, I believed in God. I started to believe I was actually dead and in hell, being punished for all the wicked things I'd done over the years.

I was ordered into the head nurse's office, okay asked. All the staff, GP doctor, head nurse, physio, occupational therapist, social worker, even Janet who was in a difficult position, were lined up on one side of the desk with myself on the other. It was like a courtroom scene from a movie but I had no defence counsel! "George we've decided you have to leave, the ambulance lady you've been telling your problems to, has agreed to put you up, we've checked the room and facilities and feel it's best for you to move." "But, but, but" yes, the BSA Bantam was trying to start again, "the TBC bungalow will be ready soon, why can't I stay here until then?" "No, you must go, it's best for you." I assume they didn't know that I was contemplating suicide, or did they? I was taken to the house in the Oval, a nice area of Gloucester. It was agreed I would stay there one night to see how I got on. I'd been crying on everyone's shoulders, including the ambulance lady who used to take me to physiotherapy. I'd told her I had to leave. She had a spare room and it would bring her some extra money.

The house had a large lounge/dining room with a TV, there was a telephone in the hallway I could *use*. The NHS provided an antique *wooden* commode in case it was needed, there was a downstairs toilet but it *could* only be used to empty my leg bag. I could do this on my own now, although difficult, it was getting easier each time. The lady of the house was young and pretty, so that was one positive thing, and I *would be* out of Ermine House. The evening went okay, I talked with her 19-year-old son and eight-year-old daughter, and after being helped into bed, I slept okay.

I was still pleading to stay at Ermine House, yes I can be a little pleader. Although I hated the place, I didn't want to start learning a new routine, but it looked as if my exit was going ahead, whether I wanted it or not. I just wasn't man enough to stand up to them or was it, sit up?

I arranged to see how another disabled person lived so I went to see Rachel, the 11-year-old I'd met in Stoke Mandeville when she was having treatment. Frank took me as he knew Sue, her mother, they'd both worked at the Bon Marche in the early 60's. Sue and her husband showed me around their home. In the shower room, I saw a commode chair with a good padded seat that I found I could transfer to fairly easily, it was sold by Oxford Products who were 5 miles from Oxford, just off the A40.

As the date for the move, well eviction as I thought of it, from Ermine House approached, Dave Flello one of the crew on my last night shift, offered to take me in his estate car, to buy a commode chair. I'd found out that Dave, even with a BA set on, had come up the ladder to help me and was only 5' from me when I fell. We found Oxford Products and bought a commode the same as Rachel's, many hospital commodes just had a flat plastic seat which was okay if you had feeling, but when you can't, you don't know if you're injuring yourself. The move to my new home took place in late February. Firemen had made a ramp so I could get into the house and a slight ramp for the 3" door threshold inside, it was a bit of a struggle at first, but got easier each time.

A new routine had to be set up with the family or I would be stuck in the house. When the lady went to work, her son Brian was there, he was one of Mrs Thatcher's children who never worked, so someone was there if I had a problem. In my five months at Ermine House, with help and advice from the Occupational Therapist, I'd started to get dressed and get out of bed into the wheelchair. At first when getting into bed, as the monkey pole was very basic and not fixed to the bed, it would rock. I exchanged the grab handle for a strong leather belt that my arm would go through, as my hand was not strong enough to hold the grab handle.

Getting up in the morning was a much longer job, it took 2 hours or more to dress myself, not that I had anything else to do! Every other morning was commode morning and washing after breakfast, it all made the day go by. Monday nights, John picked me up for archery, Tuesday, Catherine took me for swimming, I had air pistol shooting with Ron on Wednesday and Jenny, the solicitor's secretary, offered to the take me for a ride in her car, which was a very pleasant way to spend an evening.

453

There were always stories in the news that somebody had taken an overdose with paracetamol. I thought I'd get some in case I ever got brave enough to try, I kept chickening out with the knife! The only trouble with this was that I didn't like taking pills, and I had to drink a lot of alcohol with them. The only alcohol I liked was cider, even then only in a shandy! I was wondering what my answer would be if the chemist asked me what I wanted the pills for, but in the early 1980's they didn't seem to give a damn, handing over the bottle of 100. Perhaps they knew I was the wicked George Ridgeon and didn't care if I committed suicide, I was feeling sorry for myself. I stored the pills and a bottle of wine in a box under my bed!

I'd been taken to several Mobility Roadshows by various friends and firemen, twice with Tony Evans, captain of our skittles team in his 2 ltr Ford Cortina which fitted me quite well, but pressure was building as people were pushing me to get a car. The Fire Service Benevolent Fund said that they would pay for it. It was virtually decided that I'd get a front wheel drive Ford Escort with hand controls, special power steering fitted as an extra, plus a Chair Up hoist for the roof, which was £750 in 1983, the car and all fittings was over £6,000.

Now try to get inside my head, I was a war baby brought up with nothing, "make do and mend" was one of mother's sayings. I'd never spent more than £300 on any vehicle, so to spend £6000 plus of someone else's money, with no guarantee I would be able to drive it very well, if at all, was against my nature. I eventually made a decision and contacted the person I'd met at one of the Mobility Roadshows and told him I wanted a Ford Escort with the extras, his reply was that there was a three month waiting list. I was frustrated and told him that having made the decision I wanted it now, not in three months. He told me that even three months was pushing it. This put me back into depression. I sat in the house alone contemplating *how do I jump off the Westgate* Bridge*, there's no ramp for a disabled person to commit suicide*?

I was flicking through the local paper and saw an advert for a Granada Automatic for £450. When I was at the Disability Motor Show, Alfred Bekker, one of the exhibitors who sold hand controls, kept saying in broken English with a Dutch accent, "get a Granada, it's an automatic so there's no engine or gear box abuse, power steering, plenty of spares and easy to maintain. It's a rich man's car, so not wanted after 10 years, the only negative is not many MPG." Using any excuse not to do anything, I asked him "what if I can't drive it?" "You'll only spend about £500, if you can't drive it you haven't wasted a lot of money, just the £100 on the controls."

I rang the number in the advert and the man brought round a gold coloured 1975 Mk1 Granada Saloon, like the Sweeney in the TV detective series used, with only 60,000 miles on the clock. There was a hole in the offside wing you could put a flower pot in and a few oil leaks from the engine, but oil and me go together! I found it easy to get in as it had a slightly wider door than a Ford Cortina, the owner sat beside me. My right hand was just strong enough to turn the ignition key, it sounded nice. There was no traffic parked anywhere near, so I asked "could you put it into gear and I'll try and steer it on tick over. You can grab the hand brake if there's a problem." The car crept forward a few feet, with both hands resting on the steering wheel, I wasn't steering, just keeping it straight, but everything went well, so we tried the same in reverse. It felt quite comfortable with plenty of room for my legs.

Although my brain had stopped working after months in hospital, I hadn't lost my wheeler dealer instinct and offered him £250, which he turned down. I told him I'd think about it, but I was still scared and not wanting to do anything, so I never contacted him. However, I did contact a man called Roger Tonks who was a driving instructor I'd been recommended to. Roger gave lessons to Ullenwood Star Centre students, a university for the disabled, just outside Cheltenham. I suggested to Roger that perhaps I could drive on an old airfield first as I was a little nervous, however on the first lesson Roger told me to get in the driving seat. He used a Mini, which even with the seat right back, my knees were by my ear 'oles, but having driven Patricia's mini in the 70's it wasn't a problem.

Roger said "Let's go" which gave me a surge of confidence, there was a spoke, a Bakelite bar about .75" dia. 3" long, for my hand, clamped on the steering wheel, whilst not ideal we managed. As my left hand had no grip, I managed the best I could with Roger steadying the wheel a few times. After an hour of driving around the city with Roger giving me tips, he thought I was driving well and we could start lessons when I got a car, it made me feel good.

Although I was still nervous about getting any form of car, most people when asked were saying wait for the Escort, but when I mentioned it to Edna and Kath at swimming, they told me to go for it, and when Catherine's son John was taking me home after a fete at Chamwell School he said he thought the Granada was a great idea. I had a phone call at my digs, the Granada man was willing to accept £350. Despite John, Edna and Kath's advice, I still wanted to stick my head in the sand, hoping the world would go away, so I told him it was £250 take it or leave it. To my surprise, he rang back 10 minutes later and agreed, *oh dear I've bought a car!*

The car was taxed and tested for a month, so I started to sort out insurance. When I contacted my old insurance broker, Brunsdons, he gave me a quote which I thought was expensive. I had some bumf from the Motor Shows, I rang one that advertised "good rates for disabled drivers," and got a good price which Brunsdons couldn't match, so insurance was arranged.

I was living on the phone and agreed to pay the entire phone bill, including the standing rental charge, except for £8 which was their average usage. Arranging hand controls was the next job so I contacted Alfred Bekker. I told him that I'd bought a Granada and wanted the push pull hand controls as they were best and simplest, he recommended Alan, a disabled man from Birmingham to fit them, we agreed they'd be fitted before Easter.

When things settled down a bit I contacted the Fire Service Benevolent Fund saying "as the Ford Escort will take 3 months to be ready with all the extra fittings, I've bought a cheap Granada for £250 to learn to drive better." I was somewhat disappointed when they said "as you have a car, you don't need us to buy you one, goodbye."

Easter was approaching, the car was at Down Hatherley with the Price family. Young Robert was now in his twenties and an apprentice mechanic with the Gloucestershire fire service, Dexter and father Tony were also good mechanics, they were making sure my car was "A OK." I rang up the hand control man to confirm he'd have the hand controls fitted by Easter. "Not guaranteed" he said so, I hope in a firm but friendly voice, I said "If you can't guarantee it, post them down and I'll get the fire service to fit them." He said that he'd get them fitted before Easter.

Easter Saturday arrived, I got a lift to Ash Lane and went straight to the Price family, where I saw a man working on my car. Alan Thompson was a paraplegic, Tony, Dexter and Robert were watching him work open-mouthed, they were amazed what he could do. I'd been out of hospital six months, but watching Alan made me feel even more useless. Trying to console myself I thought, *well he is a paraplegic, so not as disabled as me*.

This was when life started to get better. Tony and Alice asked me if I was looking to buy a house. "Yes that's the plan, living in a room at somebody else's house isn't good and I don't know when and if TBC will have a bungalow available." Sylvia and Vince Jones were selling their wooden Bungalow in Ash Lane, which had been condemned as not fit to live in.

The sale had fallen through, so Robert and Dexter pushed me down to see them, with me screaming "slow down." They were winding me up, "try that hole there Dexter." Alice had told me the price was £20,000, it was based only on the land value as the structure had to be demolished when vacant. I told Sylvie "I'll give you £18,000 if you want to shake hands on it now, so no estate agents fees." She burst into tears, "What's the matter woman, what have I done now?" "Oh nothing George, you haven't done anything wrong, I've known you so long, it would be lovely if you owned it." How can you understand women? That reminds me of a story, a man found a bottle while on holiday in Cornwall, when he opened it a genie popped out, "thank you, I can grant you one wish", "I have family in America, I can't fly or sail, can you build a bridge to America?" "Be sensible man," "all right can you give me a small book on how to understand a woman?" "This bridge, you want lights, and I'm presuming some service stations?"

Getting back to the car, Alan had just finished, he'd also fitted a proper quad grip to the steering wheel. Alan took us all for a drive, I was in the passenger seat, Robert, Dexter and his latest girlfriend were in the back. This proved the controls worked and the car went well in the five minute drive, so I paid and thanked Alan. My wheelchair was lifted out of the boot, I struggled from the passenger seat and pushed around to the driver side, I found it easier getting into the driver's seat. Robert was in the front to help if needed, Dexter and his girlfriend in the back. I was little nervous as I started my test drive. The wheelchair was back in the boot, I really needed a Chair Up System ASAP. The proper quad grip was much better than the spoke as my wrist went in a U clamp and my hand on a spoke *so* I could push and pull to steer, without my wrist coming out of the clamp. Of course, having started the boys racing 7 years before, they were giving me a lot of stick and putting their hands together praying. The drive went well, and when we got back the boys said that I'd driven well.

As I was thanking the boys, I wondered who I could take for a drive now, they suggested I take Mum and Les out. Mum was now 80 and her boyfriend Les, 78. This short drive turned out to be 50 miles, we stopped at my brother's in Tewkesbury on the way home, David was out but we chatted to Sue for five minutes before it was time to get off. Then the first panic of my new driving experience happened, the car wouldn't start, I was turning the key but there was no ignition light and the engine didn't turn over. The indicators worked, the headlights came on and the horn sounded I thought *blooming heck has the battery gone flat*? Mother and Les weren't much help, them worrying was making it worse. I started reading the handbook, when I read the section 'How to start the car', I saw a bit that said "make sure the vehicle is in park or neutral," I was in drive, *you stupid boy Pike*, I'd tried starting it in gear! The car started with sighs of relief all round. Getting back to Ash Lane, I dropped Mum and Les off then went up to Cotswold, the name of Tony and Alice's bungalow.

Tony came out explaining that Dexter, who was supposed to follow me home to help with the wheelchair, was still up the pub, he could help me into his home, mother's, or I could wait for Dexter in the car. I thought for a moment then asked him if he could ring the lady at my digs and ask her if she'd get the wheelchair out of the car. I drove five miles on my own, with no way of getting out of the car if anything went wrong. The drive back was very nerve wracking but the adrenaline had kicked in, it made me feel a bit like I did at my first race, at least I was trying to live again.

I contacted the Chair Up people having seen their system at the Disability Roadshows, a marvellous design, a mechanism for lifting a wheelchair from the side of the car onto the roof. The firm were based in Wimborne Minster, Dorset. They gave me a date in 2 days' time to go and see them. I arranged help to drive the 100 miles, it wouldn't really have been sensible to do it on my own with the wheelchair in the back.

I watched the system being demonstrated again and asked "what's the best price you'll do?" They said £700 if I paid now. "Okay, you can fit it now or put it in the car and I'll get the fire service to fit it." A look of horror appeared on their faces "Oh you can't have this one, it's our demo model." In a stern voice I told them that I hadn't driven all that way just to look at it again. Surely they could make another easily enough or they could give me a £100 discount to come back again. They agreed to let me have the demo model, luckily it didn't take long to fit. The car cost me £250 and the hoist cost £700 after discount, as it was a demo model, perhaps I should have knocked them down some more.

Now I didn't have to wait for NHS transport, I was going where I wanted, when I wanted. There were still many things I couldn't do, but at least I could drive and get in and out of the car on my own.

ALL READY TO TAKE MUM OUT

The plans for me to move into my own accommodation with the TBC were coming along. One of the council bungalows being built for elderly people would be adapted for the disabled. The Occupational Therapist told me that I'd better start looking for a cooker, hob, fridge and washing machine. Even though I had a car, I was still unhappy with my lot in life, but at least I was driving as the able bodied did. I contacted Roger Tonks for some driving lessons in my own car. During the lesson I asked him if he ever got depressed, Roger was very easy to talk to and gave me confidence driving. I told him I thought life was grim and that I'd got 100 Paracetamol and a bottle of wine. Roger smiling said "you have to drink whiskey," "but I don't like whiskey," "does it matter if you want to die?" We both started laughing. After the lesson he told me that I was wasting my money paying him as my driving was very good, I thanking him saying "I'll take advice on the whiskey!"

Another thing that was helping me forget the depression was the possibility of a ride in the Manx GP Diamond Jubilee parade! I'd contacted Bowring, the insurance company that covered motorcycle racing and most motorsport, explaining the situation, they couldn't see a problem as it was only a parade.

On the local motorcycling scene, I had arranged with the Cheltenham Motor Club to commentate at Long Marston, asking two fire colleagues, Don Morgan and Dick Browning to help carry me up the CMC double-decker bus. I can still hear them grunting and swearing as they carried me up the twisty staircase. I certainly enjoyed commentating, as I knew most of the riders I told many tales.

The MGP ride looked more positive when someone had found a chopper rack it may even have been off a scooter as it looked lightweight, but after being fitted to a bike it looked okay. The S100 races were in July, I contacted the organisers about finding me accommodation as I was driving over, they fixed up for me to stop with Dougie Rose, an ex-Manx and S100 rider. Brian, the 19-year-old son, at my digs, agreed to come with me as he had no job prospects. I contacted George Short, ex-Manx, TT & S100 rider, who was now running S & S Motors in Castletown, he agreed to lend me a small bike for a test ride around the 4 1/4 mile, S100 course.

We arrived at Liverpool two hours early for the boat, so we called into Liverpool fire station for a cup of tea. Brian asked "how you can go into somewhere when you don't know anyone?" I tried to explain that the fire service was a large club, the fact that we spoke with different accents didn't mean anything, we were, or had done, the same job.

What a pleasant surprise, Dougie Rose lived in a bungalow built on the campsite I'd used in 1972. Again there was much emotion seeing everybody in the paddock before going back to the bungalow to sort ourselves out. In the evening we had a trip to the Rugby Club for the "signing on" of riders, then to the pub for a good night and seeing more old mates.

First practice at 5am provided a free alarm clock, Brian got up to watch the bikes going past the window. Unfortunately, I'd arranged for the nurse to come round to sort out my ablutions. After breakfast we went to the paddock, where I gave advice to riders who asked for some, and knowing me, to those that hadn't! In the afternoon, we went to see the 250cc Kawasaki, George Short had dropped off at the paddock. Friends fitted the chopper rack and I asked Mick (Kermit) Withers to ride me around before practice. With my NHS sheepskin on the seat and up the chopper rack to protect me, I was strapped on with belts and my feet with bungee straps.

ABOUT 20 SECS BEFORE THE FIRE!

We started from the field where the riders were camping, I felt comfortable, but approaching the gateway the bike stopped, I heard Mick say "the bike's on fire" we were trying to shout "help" but both having helmets on nobody could hear. Mick was trying to get off the bike when it fell over, I could see the headlines, "Racing fireman dies tied to motorcycle on fire in Isle of Man!!" Luckily it was only a wiring fault, many people came to the rescue and I was taken into Peter and Carol Swallow's tent to be checked over, I was okay. George laughed when I told him about his bike catching fire with me tied on it. Charming, who needs enemies with friends like that!! He did arrange to collect the burnt bike and bring another though.

5am next morning I wanted to get up to watch practice as there was no ablutions, Brian moaned that he was tired, I told him to get up, there were riders twice and three times his age who've got up both mornings and worked on their bikes all day. We arrived at the paddock, which was only pushing distance from Dougie's house, in time to see the end of practice, and chatted to riders until we went back for breakfast.

The chopper rack had been fitted to the new bike, but when I asked Mick if he'd ride me around before practice tonight, he ran away from me as fast as possible! Brian offered to ride me round. Thinking about it, I'm not sure if he had a driving licence, however I agreed that we'd do it after racing on Thursday. Watching the riders line up for the first race I noticed a rider with a "why am I doing this?" look on his face, "give us a smile," I said "hello George, okay just for you." At least I left him smiling. After racing we went to the pub, me and my wheelchair, were lifted up 13 steps to the top bar of the Ship Inn, the new HQ of the S100 MCRC. The place was heaving, we were sat with a group of riders reliving the races, when a chap said "thank you George", "who are you, what have I done?" "You said give me a smile," "oh yes, I could see you were scared, I used to be scared every race until the bike started. I used to tell silly jokes on the line to hide the fact that I was petrified." "If you hadn't spoken to me I may have gone out there and not enjoyed it, possibly not raced in the Isle of Man again, you helped me." I was speechless for a few seconds, alright you lot, I know that's hard to believe! I answered "I've been waiting nearly two years to hear that I can still help people, thank you very much."

The Dambusters took three bombs to break the first dam, getting the Granada was my first bomb, this rider saying "thank you George for helping me" was the second, but I needed one more bomb to break the dam and give me the will to live again.

Life changed when I saw Jackie Wood, a Manxman, an ex-rider and secretary of the MGP races. He was a friendly person, who put a lot back into the sport and would always help you when you were racing. "Jackie, I want to go in the diamond Jubilee parade." He said "we'll get you in the roads open car George," "but Jackie, I don't want to go in a car, I want to go on a motorcycle." With a look of horror on his face he replied "you can't," "why not?" "You might hurt yourself" "but Jackie, can't you see me in this wheelchair? I'm already hurt." "Sorry George, you can't do it, insurance problems, you can't do it!"

Those four magic words, "you can't do it." For nearly two years people had been saying "do something, write a book or try computers." I don't want to write a book and I don't want to play with computers, I want to race bikes, work on engines, go ballroom dancing, put fires out, none of which I can do, what is there to live for? Doing the lap of the TT course was my third bomb, but I only had six weeks to organize it!

On the trip home, having my little book of telephone numbers with me, I rang another pretty girl I'd known at Stoke Mandeville who was a red belt occupational therapist from Liverpool. When she answered I asked "is that Cilla Black from Stoke Mandeville occupation therapy?" "Is that you George, come round for a cup of tea." When we got there she suggested we all go down the pub and offered to let me sleep on the couch. Brian was amazed at the friendliness of Liverpool people. The pub turned out to be a good laugh, I was transferred from the chair to a bench that was out of the way, people in the pub didn't realise I was disabled. What a laugh seeing people's faces when the person sat in my wheelchair, got up to get another round of drinks! As we were leaving the pub I saw a face I thought I knew, it was Norman Overend's nephew. I met Norman on the boat to the MGP in 1969!

We went back to the house, and after bed and breakfast, had a good drive home, the perfect end to the Southern 100 races.

When I got back I rang Gloucestershire police and asked for the motoring division "I'm George Ridgeon, ex fireman do you know me?" "Yes George, what can I do for you?" "What can stop me riding on the back of a motorcycle on the road please?" I could feel his attitude change as he realised I was asking a serious question, I'm sure I heard a "click" as he switched on his police brain. "You must be sat astride the machine, you must be facing forward, you must have both feet on foot rests and you must be wearing protective clothing including a helmet." I told him that I could answer yes to all of those points, that we'd tried it and that I wanted to ride round in a parade on the TT course. The officer said "they have no reason stop you George" but his next statement made me break into a cold sweat "Oh yes there is, the machine must be ridden properly" Then I heard him chuckle, "they won't know that until after the ride will they. Good luck."

I contacted the Isle of Man fire service Chief Fire Officer Mr Hinnagan, he'd had been very supportive allowing Stn Officer Godfrey Cain all the leeway to help me last year. I asked him if he could tell the chief constable that I'd be riding round the Isle of Man on the back of a motorcycle at this year's Manx Grand Prix. After a general chinwag on what was going on, he said that he'd contact me in a week. When he got back to me he told me that the chief constable had no worries at all.

I contacted Dick Sheppard, "man of 1000 crashes" who'd been entertaining Gloucestershire with the world record for the longest Tunnel of Fire as well as crashing cars, motorcycles and lorries, he owned the land on which my brother had his garage, White Post Autos. Dick had been considering retiring when Jacquie De Creed, a young lady stunt driver asked him to team manage and promote her career. They starting "Stuntarama" with Jacquie leaping 232' 2" in a 5 Ltr Mustang, getting the car leap world record. It was agreed that I'd be tied on the back of Jacquie, it went out on Midlands and South-West TV and got a mention in Motorcycle News, which was good publicity. Talking with various people we, that's the Royal we, decided to turn it into a 'guess the time competition' with any money raised going to IOM charities so, more publicity.

Trial run for charity ride

FORMER Gloucester firemen George Ridgeon yesterday prepared for his charity ride around the Isle of Man TT course — strapped to a motorcycle behind a very fast lady.

Wheelchair-bound George was badly injured when he tried to rescue a man from a fire more than two years ago, and had to give up competing in the Isle of Man motorcycle races. But next month George hopes to raise money for charity by riding pillion around the famous course — and may get into the Guiness Book of Records as the first disabled person to do it.

Yesterday he sat behind another record-breaker — stunt motorcyclist Jacquie De Creed who earlier this year cleared 232 feet in a car leap — for a rather more sedate ride around the Bristol-rd. area.

On September 3 he will be

George about to set off on a trial run with Jacquie de Creed.

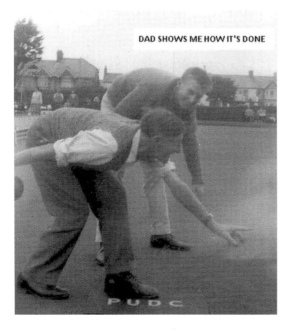

DAD SHOWS ME HOW IT'S DONE

The local Lions Club held a bowls night at Gloucester Leisure Centre for the elderly and disabled. I'd played bowls with dad on holiday in Porthcawl when 16 and had a game with mother after dad's funeral in dad's memory, but that was February 1971. I was doing unusually well, as me and ball sports never went together very well, but bowls seemed to be just right for me. I ended up going to Thornbury to play bowls regularly.

When I beat a player in a small competition he asked me how long I'd been playing, my reply of "this is my first competition" I believe, gave him the hump. I met Dr. David Peacock, who later became my mentor, and other disabled bowlers from Avon Swifts Sports Club who promoted sport for the disabled, some of them competed in the national and international wheelchair games I'd seen when in hospital. I asked Dave Rolley, manager of the Leisure Centre if he could put a hole in the wall around the bowls green and get a ramp made. He wanted to know how many disabled would use it, "I cannot really say Dave, but at the moment nobody can use it because it is not accessible." I was pleased Dave got the work done, he also fixed up some publicity by arranging for it to be officially opened by Tony Allcock, World Bowls Champion, who lived in Gloucestershire. Tony was president of the Special Olympics as his day job was looking after adults with learning difficulties in Stroud. After some trick shots he gave me a game for five ends, after which I asked him how I played. His reply of "you have got more shots in five ends, than some people I played first to 21" made me feel good. From this beginning we started Thursday night roll up's for the disabled. "Thank you, David and Tony" possibly the national wheelchair games next year............

I contacted everybody I knew for prizes for the 'guess the time competition' hoping to get 100, I was living on the phone. I asked Mick Dunn in the Isle of Man if he could arrange a British motorcycle and ride me around on it. Apart from making the phone calls in the morning, I was never at home, I was out arranging so many things.

It was agreed that Kath Thornwill's son John would look after me at the Manx, he became big John shortened to BJ and was studying to be a physical education teacher. To get more publicity Andy and Barbara Eames picked me up and took me to Snetterton for a CRMC race meeting. This is an example of what so many of my friends were doing for me, they not only came down from Burton on Trent in their van, they'd found a 3' by 6' bed which came apart and a mattress, I supplied the sheepskin and bedding. They took me the 168 miles from my home to the meeting, by the end of the weekend they would have had a 600 mile round trip.

Getting up the morning of the race I heard the announcement on the Tannoy "we need more marshals," I'd been hearing that announcement since my first race on the Bantam in 1964!! I thought *I can help,* so aided by Barbara and the children, I volunteered myself to be paddock announcer, Andy marshalled. I felt I was doing something useful, calling up riders for their practice, races and those doing parades and asking for spares when somebody had broken something, a really enjoyable day.

Les Davies, father of late Malcolm Davies and top man in the ACU governing body of motorcycle sport in the UK, had given me 2 tickets for the British Grand Prix at Silverstone. I was going with Brian, who'd come to the S100 races with me, but he backed out at the last minute, luckily after a few phone calls, Dexter Price agreed to help.

Arriving at Silverstone we went into the paddock which was a lot easier in those days. We were talking with friends and riders in the paddock when I noticed a Shell flag flying. Keith Callow was a Shell representative who went to the MGP and would give us also-rans a gallon of oil now and again. When we got to the Shell stand Mick Grant, Wayne Gardner and Steve Parrish, all top racers, were signing autographs. A Shell man told the crowd to make way for the poor disabled man and asked if I wanted their autographs. I told him I wanted to see Keith Callow, the man shouted "hey Keith, there's a bloke in a wheelchair wants to see you" Keith invited me in, pointing at Dexter I asked if I could bring my engine in. I was offered a seat next to Wayne Gardner's (world champion) mother. She was a very pleasant lady, so I asked her "do you think Wayne would give me one of his old crash helmets as a prize for the 'Guess the time' competition of my ride round the TT course at this year's MGP?" "Of course he will" she replied. We were having refreshments when I shouted at Mick Grant "hey Mick, what's this I hear about you riding in the first classic Manx?" "No George, I'm not," "I heard you were Mick." Mick is a blunt Yorkshire *man* "I've just bloody said I'm not." As we were leaving the Shell stand I asked Keith if Shell would give oil for prizes for the 'Guess the time' competition at the Honda Garage I ended up persuading them to donate a 125cc Honda as 1st prize, if this heroic ride came off!!

I contacted MCN to ask if they would do a story, I explained the 'Guess the time it takes me to get round the TT course on the back of a bike' competition with 100 prizes, 1st prize a Honda 125cc and the proceeds to Manx charities. They said they'd do a story if I had a better known rider. I rang up Mick Grant and explained the situation. After asking when the parade was he replied "I'll have finished my trial by then, yes, I'll do it." The next week MCN did a half page advert/story about me doing the ride, details of the competition and the names of the major prize sponsors. It wasn't in the MCN the next week, when I rang them they were very vague; I think they had been knobbled by the Manx authorities!

I collected John in my car which now had a new wing, doing away with the hole for a pot plant. Robert had been allowed to fit and spray the new wing at the fire station workshops. John loaded the car, my commode was taken to the Island by a local rider and would be delivered to Rent a Chalet, where I'd stopped last year. Arriving at Liverpool I saw many friends, my heart was pounding not knowing what the next two weeks would bring. As we drove off the boat, I saw the headlines on a newspaper hoarding "Manx racing fire hero to ride TT course" John and I burst out laughing, at least the publicity was working.

This was the first year of the Classic Manx which was a 3 lap race. I'd asked Robert Price to ride my Greeves. Gordon Morss, who was riding his own Greeves in the 250cc classic and a 350cc Yamaha in Jnr, had agreed to ride my Triumph Trident in the Snr race with 1976 MGP Snr winner Les Trotter, riding my G50 Matchless.

During practice week, I had to sort out any problems with doing the parade and keep an eye on 3 bikes. My only input was knowledge and enthusiasm, which I had plenty of. The Greeves, had the most problems being a two-stroke, in first practice the Woodruff key failed as had happened before. Les was looking after the G50 and Gordon was taking it steady on the Trident, if we'd had to strip the machine down it would have been a major problem!

GORDON MORSS

I was called into the race office, John accompanied me. It was a little like an a kangaroo court with Jackie Wood along with the Manx MCC chairman and Les Doherty, the Bowring insurance representative, who was also on the MMCC committee. I was asked to explain what I'd let them in for. "The Chief Constable has no problem with me riding on the back of a motorcycle, which is insured as is Mick Grant. I can start last so I don't get in the way of any other riders in the parade and if I'm caught and passed by the roads open car, we can carry on, keeping to normal road regulations, so a time can be taken, the 100 prizes that have been donated, awarded, and the money raised given to Manx charities." I was told that as the parade was on closed roads the insurance was not valid and I couldn't do it. I was surprised and asked if I could clarify, "you say there is no problem with me, the bike or the rider, it's that Bowring will not insure me to ride around the course?" "Yes that's correct." I replied quickly "so if I can get Bowring to change their mind...." Before I could finish the sentence someone said "they won't." I used president George H. Bush's words "Read my lips." Addressing them again, I said "excuse me I don't want to seem rude or dim, but you have just told me there is no problem with the bike or the rider only that Bowring will not insure me. I say again, if I can get Bowering to change their mind is everything okay?" They looked at each other and said "yes, we suppose so."

I went straight down to the fire station to see Godfrey Cain, his office became 'the war room'. I explained the problem to Godfrey who suggested we ring Bowring, we had a Manx radio reporter in the next room. The Bowring representative confirmed that they couldn't insure me to ride around the TT course. I replied "I will tell the world that you can't insure a top TT rider to ride a disabled man around in a parade!" "That's very unfair Mr Ridgeon." "It's very unfair getting a broken neck when you were trying to save a life. I haven't got much to live for, if I go down I'll take you with me. I'm looking at a Manx radio reporter who's going to interview me when I put this telephone down, do I tell him you can't insure me or that you are doing all in your power to resolve this problem?" "Please tell him we will do everything in our power to get over this problem."

Before doing the interview I told the reporter that he mustn't repeat any of what he'd heard, he agreed. I just talked about why I was doing the ride and raising money for Manx charities. Godfrey went out of the room when he heard on the Tannoy "Stn Officer Cain telephone". The Manx radio reporter had left when Godfrey came back with a big grin, "I've just had the man from Bowring on the phone, begging and pleading with me. I told him that you are a nasty bastard and would take them down with you. Apparently the Manx doctors wanted to ride on the back of the marshal's motorcycles, but there would be a claim of £1,000,000 plus if one of them was killed. The claim would be about £10 if you were killed, he said he'd do what he could."

I was in the paddock introducing John to my old racing friends, when a Manx official came up and told me that Bowring's want the officials to see me being ridden on the motorcycle to see if it was safe. I told him that Mick wasn't on the Island yet, "you can't do it then." Back to the war room. After a discussion Godfrey made a phone call, "this is the fire service, is that Mr Geoffrey Duke, would you like to help out the fire service?" After the problem was explained, he agreed to be at the grandstand at 12 noon on Thursday.

I went to the race office to tell them that Geoff Duke was coming to the paddock tomorrow 12 noon to see if I'm safe on the bike and that I hoped they'd attend. In response they looked at me and nodded. I asked for and got the okay to ring the UK. I rang Jimmy Savile, his answering machine message started with a very silly message, on hearing the beep I started to leave a message but he cut in and asked "what can I do for you George?"

470

"I'm having some problems with Manx officials, they don't want to let me ride in this parade." Jimmy told me to put one of them on the phone. I told Jackie Wood that Jimmy Savile wanted to talk to him. "Hello Mr Savile." I couldn't hear what was actually said but it sounded something like "don't you mess my mate about," "we're trying to get over the problems, can you come over?" I heard "sorry too busy raising money for charity." "Oh that's a shame" Jackie relied before handing me back the phone. "Hi Jim, what did you say?" Jimmy replied "I told them I'll bash them if they mess you about," we had a laugh then rang off.

Wednesday evening was the MGP supporters' club dinner, I saw Jackie and the other officials and got a general look of disapproval when I reminded them that Geoff Duke was coming to the grandstand tomorrow.

12 noon arrived, as did Geoff Duke, the press and the fire service who lifted me on to the bike. Mick Dunn had fixed up for me to be paraded on a Triumph Bonneville, however a MGP rider who was camping in the paddock, had an 850cc Norton twin. Various riders and friends had made the small chopper rack stronger by welding a brace on it, it was pronounced safe and secure, after being tried by various heavy riders around the paddock.

Many photos were taken by the press as I sat behind a living legend, a 'demigod', but after nearly an hour Mr Duke said "I can't wait any longer for the MMCC officials, I am sorry." Godfrey thanked him for coming and asked if he thought it was safe for me to be ridden around the course strapped to the bike. "Yes it is" he replied, "get them to contact me if they want to know any more." By this time Roger Sutcliffe had turned up, I bought a pair of rear units off him at my last MGP.

Roger got on the bike and rode it over to the race office. Jackie was stood by the door and came over to talk to us "Jackie, Geoff Duke waited for you for nearly an hour, where were you?" "I couldn't get there." Godfrey Cain had walked over as well. I told Jackie that Geoff Duke had said it was safe for me to ride round. Jackie looked at Roger Sutcliffe "Roger, would you give up your ride on the Norton to ride George around in the parade?" When Roger replied "No problem" Jackie Woods shrugged his shoulders and said "Oh." Godfrey and I looked at each other, both having the same thought, *we've done it!!*

ON THE BACK OF ROGER SUTCLIFFE

Two days later I was handed a letter that had been sent c/o the Manx Grand Prix race office, it was from Stoke Mandeville hospital "George, if we didn't have 8000 patients to look after we would all be over there with you, good luck" it was signed Jimmy Savile. It was reported on Manx Radio and printed in the TT Special Yearbook.

Last practice was delayed due to atrocious weather, Robert led the wet practice on Friday 2/9/83 for the Classic 250cc. The results posted in the race office showed, 127 R. Price 36.07.4 62.66, 2nd 121 E B Crooks 36.11.2 62.52, 3rd 106 R M Simmonds 36.53.6 61.35, we were all chuffed.

There were 3 classes in the first-ever classic Manx Grand Prix, up to 250cc Ltw, up to 350cc Jnr and up to 500cc Snr, with the 500cc bikes starting first. Although I'd caused the organizers lots of problems, as I had two bikes on the start line for this first classic race, they allowed me in the pit area so I could supervise my bikes.

ROB PRICE, RED AND BLACK LEATHERS
ARTHUR WHEELER, BLACK LEATHERS

On the 30 minute Claxton the bikes were pushed onto the start line, I shook hands with Les first as he was near the front of the 500cc class. I gave a good luck pat to all the riders I knew and had raced against, there were so many of them in the Snr class. Wheeling past the Jnr class I saw Ron Roebury, and John Stevens, both local lads. Then the Ltw class where I saw Robert with his brother Dexter and team manager mother Alice. Gordon Morss and the 1949 350cc world champion Arthur Wheeler on his Moto Guzzi were starting close together. I saw Rupert Murden, Dave Smith, and Richard Fitzsimons, who'd arranged the comical cartoon in 1975 of the noise meter tester with a megaphone on his head!

As it was a push start for the classic race, I felt Robert's engine, it was warm enough so we stopped it to allow us to put a fresh plug in that had been tested in practice. Les was long gone and the last of the 350cc class had just left the start line. Robert was now in the cone zone, we were watching from outside, the flag dropped, he bumped the bike, it started and off he went, much to the relief to us all.

Alice, Dexter and one of their friends went into the pit, John and I were watching from a safe area by the grandstand opposite Robert's pit. On the first lap, Robert was in the top six, along with Gordon Morss and Arthur Wheeler. The three of them starting close together was helping push each

473

of them on, I heard a Manx Radio report that they were vying for third place. Regrettably, on the last lap, Gordon retired with a broken primary chain, he was lucky not to come off! Before it happened, he and Robert were only 200 yards behind Arthur, Robert lost his momentum as he was on Gordon's back wheel when the chain broke and dropped to sixth place, which wasn't bad out of 21 starters and it was his first ride on the TT course. He averaged 79.78 mph and was just over a minute behind 1949 world champion Arthur Wheeler. The Lightweight Classic was won by Richard Fitzsimons. We were all very pleased but I didn't have much time to hang about, just had time to shake Robert's hand and say "well done". Les Trotter had unfortunately retired on my G50 with a magneto problem, John Goodall won the Senior.

LES TROTTER

The bike, with the chopper rack fitted, was parked in the assembly area with the allotted number 100 on it. We were awaiting the arrival of Mick Grant who was riding in the classic trial, and not as I'd accused him at Silverstone GP, the classic Manx, so I got some strong lads and using a rider's tent, I was lifted onto the grass to get my leathers and boots on, luckily they still fitted! I was wheeled back to where the bike had been, my heart stopped when I saw it was missing but Mick Grant was there asking "where's the bike George?" "It was here a minute ago Mick." My nerves were now bad for two reasons, we were about to ride around the Isle of Man TT course and where was the bike? All the other riders were now lined up on the course, we heard the beautiful noise of a Norton twin arriving, the MGP rider and owner of the machine had topped it up with fuel. They didn't tell me until later, that when they'd started it ready for the parade, it'd gone onto one cylinder and they'd had to check the plug and plug lead, luckily they'd cured the problem!

All my old mechanics and friends lifted me on the bike as I tried to direct them where to strap me to the bike, Mick Grant squeezed on in front of me. We were at the back of the bikes, which were being flagged off at 10 second intervals. Nobody was timing as it was a parade, so I arranged for somebody to time me for the 'guess the time competition.' Mick asked "are you okay?" "Yes thank you, but could you slow down at the black dub, I want to throw two roses out, one for Stuffy Davis and one for Roger Corbett." "A bit grim George," "they were good friends, in fact it helped me talking to them as the bend is dangerous." "Okay, tap me on the shoulder if I go too fast." Mick revved the bike, there was a loud clunk as it went into first gear and I had no time to reply as we headed for the start line.

See: - **http://www.youtube.com/watch?v=NR2Kitr_N0s**.

We headed across the start line, people were waving and I'm sure, although it could have been my imagination, that I heard a roar from the many people around the pit area and Grandstand over the noise of the Norton. I did the 'high girls' wave Mick Dunn had started in 1975, before locking my arms around Mick's waist. Mick accelerated hard, I was quite enjoying it as we crossed St Ninian's traffic lights, but as we were heading down Bray Hill about 100+ miles an hour, I started tapping him on the shoulder but to no avail, he didn't slow down at all. There was a huge bang and a wobble as we hit the bottom of Bray Hill and the Norton shook its head. Mick accelerated hard up towards Ago's Leap where the bike momentarily went light. I was hanging on for grim death as I thought *me and my big mouth, have I got my bicycle clips on?* We headed into the dark tree section and down to Quarter Bridge, I was again hitting hell out of Mick's back, but again it didn't seem to register with him.

As he braked hard and changed down through the gears, on the approach to Quarter Bridge, I crashed hard into his back, he cranked the bike hard right around the Quarter Bridge Hotel. On the straight road before Braddon Bridge, I decided it was pointless hitting him so I'd better just hang on. I suddenly realised the straight had passed as my body again bashed into Mick as he started braking and changing down, blipping the throttle for each gear change, then cranking hard to the left lifting up hard to the right and drifting close to the wall by Braddon Church. Everybody was waving, hundreds were still lining the circuit for this Diamond Jubilee parade so I started waving back.

Back in top gear we headed towards Union Mills, I started talking to myself, *George you want to die, yes, but what if I don't die, what if I'm only injured and in hospital for another year, it could happen, but Mick would have to fall off too.* My conversation with myself was halted as he went down three gears through Union Mills, close to the high brick wall on the right-hand side with buildings and a short brick wall on the other side with lots of sandbags but it's still not a good idea to hit it at 80 mph! Now it was the 4 mile top gear section to Greba Castle so I could start my conversation again. *He may fall off and if Mick falls off I fall off. True, but is Mick worried about falling off? Well he doesn't appear to be worried about it. If Mick isn't worried why should I be worried? Just enjoy the ride. Okay, I'll try.* All the time I was talking to myself I was waving at the people watching from the various vantage points around the 37.73 mile course, as was Mick, I thought, *Mick, keep both hands on the handlebars!!*

We were approaching the Crosby Hotel where the gang used to go singing on our last night. I could see the pub sign from a distance, a group of people were underneath the sign and one man was jumping up and down on the pavement. As we got closer everyone was pointing at the sign. This was the sign that, in 1978, Bob Grimshaw, landlord of the Crosby Hotel,

put "Good Luck Mike" on for Mike Hailwood. Both Mick and I were looking at the sign which now read "Ridgeon rides again." Mick tapped my leg twice then gave the bike another fistful with more purpose. I thought, *my mates are glad to see me back at the Manx GP,* I was crying and smiling at the same time. Mick started braking from 110 mph and changing down, the bike lurching three times as he got into second gear for Greba Castle. I was now enjoying every second of the ride, we went through the left-right hand bend then onto where, at my first Manx the sun had been shining through the trees nearly causing me to crash.

By now I didn't have a worry in the world as the sweeping bends were just passing. I was still waving at people, then Mick braked hard and cranked right for Ballacraine. The left-hand Doran's Bend, I could never get round as fast as I would like, I thought, *Grantie just went round there faster two up than I did when racing!*

Glen Helen section now, all tight and twisty bends, when I saw the white garage on the right-hand side, I reached for my two roses, the Black Dub followed, a tight left-hand bend with a white painted brick wall and a small river behind it. Mick didn't slow down as he cranked left but I didn't mind, I threw the roses for Snuffy he preferred Snuffy to Stephen, and Sooty, after Harry Corbett's glove puppet. Tears were rolling down my face, I hadn't really had a good cry before, only when I was feeling sorry for myself but here, I was crying for Snuffy and Sooty.

Although I could feel every bump on the Cronk Y Voddy Straight I didn't give a damn. We just missed the wall at Hanley's Bend. Barregarrow was similar to Bray Hill in that it was downhill with a left-hand sweep, again

Mick went through this quicker than I did racing but who cares! The three right and left-hand sweep of the 13th milestone we took at 80 mph. By the time we were in the 30 mph limit at Kirk Michael we'd passed several machines. At Ballaugh Bridge the bike went very light as we went over the humpback bridge, only half a mile to Gwen Crellin's. Gwen was now in her 60's, but acted like a 30-year-old giving a cup of tea to anyone who stopped, whether riders or marshals all were made welcome. There was Gwen, stood on the left hand pavement in her white suit, the reason Giacomo Agostini had named her 'the lady in white.' Mick was blowing kisses with his clutch hand whilst his right had the throttle wide open at 90+ mph, I was waving both arms and shouting "Gwennie."

All of a sudden we were in Ramsay, 100s of spectators were waving as he cranked into Parliament Square, at Mayhill I remembered Jonathan Parkes who's Matchless got stuffed into the wall in 1974! Past Stella Maris where I had another thought of Sooty Corbett, he'd named his bungalow after this as he crashed here in his first year, breaking his leg!

I'm not sure if I was feeling fed up with Mick going faster than me or if I was disgruntled with my riding ability when I was racing, he went round Ramsey Hairpin and again it felt quicker than I ever did. This was two up, me paralysed and having only left hospital 12 months before, but I was enjoying every minute and didn't really care.

It was a privilege to be on the back of the man who had broken Hailwood's 1967 lap record of 108 mph at 110 mph, even though it took eight years and a 750cc triple Kawasaki! We caught up more riders, as we went round the Gooseneck hairpin I looked back at Ramsey Bay, the sun was shining and the view was gorgeous. The 850cc Norton was larger capacity than most of the machines in the parade and was pulling well up the Mountain Mile, passing several riders. Around the twisty section into the Black Hut then back into top gear around the four sweeping right-hand bends of Veranda where I could see the sea to the left. Once we'd passed The Bungalow and the 32nd Milestone it was downhill to Windy Corner where I thought of the young lady who'd said no when we were in the back of my van. All of a sudden we were braking hard for Kate's Cottage, where in 1971 I ran the three quarters of a mile up, then carried the injured rider back down to Craig Na Baa on a stretcher, it seemed so long ago. Again, hundreds were waving at The Creg, we were both waving, though not when going flat out on the downhill section with the flat out right-hand sweep down to Brandish then Hillberry before braking hard for first gear,

Signpost Corner, it was very bumpy around Bedstead. As we approach Governors Bridge and the Dip I thought *how are we going to get round the tight right-hand hairpin?* Mick braked hard and went through the gears down to first, at about 5 mph he negotiated the right-hand very tight hairpin, the crowds watching in the trees and standing on the wall all waved, but I was hanging on here, Mick took it steady then gingerly around the left, especially as there were always lot of leaves in this section from the trees, but the marshals kept it clear. Accelerating hard out of Governors Dip, so-called as the Governor of the Isle of Man resided there. As we approached the start and finish line, I could see all my friends and the whole grandstand were cheering every rider as they came over the line.

We'd done the 37.73 miles lap in 36 minutes 30 seconds, an average of 62 mph! One of the old boys who had been doing a steady lap had complained to the organisers that somebody on a motorcycle with a woman on the back had overtaken him!!! I was told that he was taken aback when they informed him that it was Mick Grant with a paralysed ex-rider on the back!

The last bomb had blown the dam apart to let George Ridgeon back into society and giving me the will to want to live again, so time to celebrate. Surprisingly we all went to a pub. The major part of the work had been done although we still had Gordon Morss's ride on my Trident in the Senior.

I was pleased to be invited to many places to help raise money for Manx Charities after my lap. One memorable evening was at the Onchan Speedway Stadium where they had regular banger racing. During the break, I was taken onto the circuit and introduced to the crowd before being pushed round the circuit by friends. I nearly fell out of the wheelchair on the banked circuit, it took more to hold me in than to push my wheelchair. I felt like I was sidecar racing, I was leaning so far to the right going around the left hand banking I was knackered by the end of the quarter mile lap. The stadium had a whip round which raised more money.

I was 39 so if able-bodied, this would have been my last Manx GP, at that time once you were 40 you had to move to the TT races. Having found out that the Majestic Hotel had a large function room, I booked it and organised my 39th birthday party, advertising it on Manx Radio and in the local newspapers, with posters in the paddock and race office. Stanley Woods was one of the many guests at the Manx Diamond Jubilee celebrations doing a lap on a 1938 Mk8 Velocette. I'd previously met the legendary Stanley Woods, the first superhero of the TT, and invited him and his friend David Crawford, to come to the party. He arrived when it was in full swing, to a standing ovation which he appreciated. He gave me two pieces of leather, cut off the leather boots he'd worn to ride the Mk 8 which I think were M/X boots. In the auction the straps raised £32. David Crawford donated a pair of MV cufflinks which were bought by Pete Beale for £80. Many other items were donated so more money was made for the charities.

The week finished well. Gordon Morss had a finish at an average speed of 81+ mph on the Trident for the 226 miles. Gordon and I had a photo taken with Stanley Woods and Ernie Lyons who'd won the first Manx Grand Prix after the war in 1946 on a Triumph Grand Prix. I also met Irish racer Cromie McCandless, who I mistakenly told an Irish joke to, Cromie came back with "what's black and blue and floats up and down in the Irish Sea", "I don't know", "an English man who tells Irish jokes." "Why are Irish jokes simple?" Again I responded "I don't know," "so English men can understand them!"

So to round up the 1983 Manx GP: not only did I overcome all of the problems raised by my ride in the parade, I supervised three racing motorcycles, demonstrated the Chair Up system fitted to my car to two disabled people, held a 39th birthday party. *I even got elected on to the Manx Grand Prix Riders Association committee, which meant at least three trips a year to the Isle of Man, I saw old friends and* my old landlady, Doris Jackson. It was time to say goodbye to everybody. Although so many helped a very big thank you to Godfrey Cain, Chief Fire Officer Mr Hinnegan and all the Isle of Man Fire service who without their help I don't think the ride would have come off.

Before we left for home, I got John a small trophy with "1983 Manx Grand Prix, completed the course" engraved on it, which I presented to him at our last party when we all gathered down the pub. When I collected the cup, I was on my own so had to drive into the pedestrian area. While I was waiting outside the trophy shop a policeman said "you mustn't drive in this street," "alright officer, I'll stay here." "No Sir, you can't stay here." "But officer, you just told me I mustn't drive in the street." He started to grin "you're winding me up aren't you?" "Officer how could you accuse me of such a thing?" I returned home with memories I shall never forget.

TO BE CONTINUED........................... watch for lap 2!